AF789694

AFRICA DEVELOPMENT INDICATORS 2012/13

THE WORLD BANK

1 2 3 4 16 15 14 13

To order *Africa Development Indicators 2012/13, The Little Data Book on Africa 2012/13*, or *The Little Data Book on Gender in Africa 2012/13*, please visit http://publications.worldbank.org. For free access to *Africa Development Indicators* online, please visit http://data.worldbank.org/data-catalog.

For more information about *Africa Development Indicators* and its companion products, please visit www.worldbank.org/africa or email ADI@worldbank.org.

ISBN: 978-0-8213-9616-2
eISBN: 978-0-8213-9617-9
DOI: 10.1596/978-0-8213-9616-2
SKU: 19616

Cover design and layout: EEI Communications, Hanover, MD.

The map of Africa is provided by the Map Design Unit/World Bank.

Contents

Foreword vii

Acknowledgments ix

Indicator tables 1

Users guide 3

Part I. Basic indicators and national and fiscal accounts

1. Basic indicators
1.1 Basic indicators 7

2. National and fiscal accounts
2.1 Gross domestic product, nominal 8
2.2 Gross domestic product, nominal 9
2.3 Gross domestic product, nominal 10
2.4 Gross domestic product per capita, real 11
2.5 Gross domestic product per capita growth 12
2.6 Gross national income, nominal 13
2.7 Gross national income, *World Bank Atlas* method 14
2.8 Gross national income per capita, *World Bank Atlas* method 15
2.9 Gross domestic product deflator (U.S. dollar series) 16
2.10 Consumer price Index 17
2.11 Consumer price index, growth 18
2.12 Price indices 19
2.13 Gross domestic savings 20
2.14 Gross national savings 21
2.15 General government final consumption expenditure 22
2.16 Household final consumption expenditure 23
2.17 Final consumption expenditure plus discrepancy 24
2.18 Final consumption expenditure plus discrepancy per capita 25
2.19 Gross fixed capital formation 26
2.20 Gross general government fixed capital formation 27
2.21 Private sector fixed capital formation 28
2.22 External trade balance (exports minus imports) 29
2.23 Exports of goods and services, nominal 30
2.24 Imports of goods and services, nominal 31
2.25 Exports of goods and services as a share of GDP 32
2.26 Imports of goods and services as a share of GDP 33
2.27 Balance of payments and current account 34
2.28 Exchange rates and purchasing power parity 36
2.29 Agriculture value added 38
2.30 Industry value added 39

2.31 Services plus discrepancy value added 40
2.32 Central government finances 41
2.33 Central government expenses 43
2.34 Central government revenues 45
2.35 Structure of demand 47

Part II. Millennium Development Goals

3. Millennium Development Goals
3.1 Millennium Development Goal 1: eradicate extreme poverty and hunger 48
3.2 Millennium Development Goal 2: achieve universal primary education 51
3.3 Millennium Development Goal 3: promote gender equity and empower women 52
3.4 Millennium Development Goal 4: reduce child mortality 53
3.5 Millennium Development Goal 5: improve maternal health 54
3.6 Millennium Development Goal 6: combat HIV/AIDS, malaria, and other diseases 55
3.7 Millennium Development Goal 7: ensure environmental sustainability 57
3.8 Millennium Development Goal 8: develop a global partnership for development 59

Part III. Development outcomes

Drivers of growth
4. Private sector development
4.1 Doing Business 61
4.2 Investment climate 64
4.3 Financial sector infrastructure 66

5. Trade and regional integration
5.1 International trade and tariff barriers 68
5.2 Top three exports and share in total exports, 2010 72
5.3 Regional integration, trade blocs 74

6. Infrastructure
6.1 Water and sanitation 74
6.2 Transportation 75
6.3 Information and communication technology 77
6.4 Energy 80

Participating in growth
7. Human development
7.1 Education 84
7.2 Health 86

8. Agriculture, rural development, and environment
8.1 Rural development 90
8.2 Agriculture 92
8.3 Producer food prices 94
8.4 Environment 96
8.5 Fossil fuel emissions 98

9. Labor, migration, and population
9.1 Labor force participation 100
9.2 Labor force composition 106
9.3 Unemployment 108
9.4 Migration and population 110

10. HIV/AIDS
10.1 HIV/AIDS 112

11. Malaria
11.1 Malaria 116

12. Capable states and partnership
12.1 Aid and debt relief 117
12.2 Status of Paris Declaration indicators 120
12.3 Capable states 122
12.4 Governance and anticorruption indicators 124
12.5 Country Policy and Institutional Assessment ratings 126
12.6 Polity indicators 130

Technical notes 131

Technical notes references 190

Primary data documentation 192

Map of Africa 198

Foreword

For over a decade, Sub-Saharan Africa has been experiencing relatively rapid economic growth, averaging about 5 percent a year. Emblematic of this growth is the information and communications technology (ICT) revolution in Africa, with over 80 percent of urban Africans with access to cellphones. Thanks to economic growth, poverty has been declining, with the absolute number of people living on less than $1.25 a day falling (by about 9 million) for the first time in history. At the same time, Africa has the lowest human development indicators, with one in 16 children dying before their fifth birthday.

Striking as they are, these averages mask the great diversity of the African continent. This year's *Africa Development Indicators,* with data on 1,700 indicators stretching back to 1960, provides a detailed picture of the variety of the continent's development experience, across space and over time. For instance:

- While Africa's gross national income per capita was US$1,589 in 2010, it ranged from US$180 to US$13,720.
- Of the 89 million recorded internet users in SSA, half of them were in Nigeria. Two countries (Kenya and Nigeria) account for 62 percent of Internet users. However, Seychelles has the highest number of Internet users per 100 people.
- Although poverty is declining, Africa has the highest poverty rate in the world, with 47.5 percent of the population living on $1.25 a day. They account for 30 percent of the world's poor.
- Thirty-nine countries had child mortality reductions of over 12 percent over the last 20 years with the largest decline of over 50 percent in Malawi, Madagascar, Eritrea and Liberia.

A central question is why Africa is doing so much better today than it was, say, 20 years ago. The answer includes several factors, such as debt relief, increased aid, high commodity prices—and improved macroeconomic policies. These policies are the result of decisions by African policy makers who, in turn, are increasingly accountable to their citizens. And an informed citizenry is better able to hold its leaders to account.

On its part, the World Bank continues to make all its data freely available, resulting in continually growing use of its online resources. This volume is part of the *Africa Development Indicators* suite of products, which also includes *The Little Data Book on Africa 2012/13* and *The Little Data Book on Gender in Africa 2012/13*, the *Africa Development Indicators 2012/13* CD-ROM, and a data query and charting application for mobile services. All of these publications help to equip the public with information, so they can contribute to an evidence-based debate that will eventually lead to better public policies.

In short, *Africa Development Indicators* not only documents Africa's transformation; it supports it.

Makhtar Diop
Vice President
The World Bank Group
Africa Region

Acknowledgments

Africa Development Indicators is a product of the Africa Region of the World Bank.

This report has been prepared by a core team led by Rose Mungai comprising Francoise Genouille and Ayago Esmubancha Wambile in the production of this book and its companions—*Africa Development Indicators Online 2012/13,* and *The Little Data Book on Africa 2012/13* and *The Little Data Book on Gender in Africa 2012/13.* Yohannes Kebede coordinated the ADI Online Apps platform while Mapi Buitano coordinated the dissemination of the book and its companions. Aby Toure managed the communication aspect. Francoise Genouille coordinated all stages of production. The overall work was carried out under the guidance of Shantayanan Devarajan, Chief Economist of the Africa Region.

The technical box contributors were:

- Andrew Dabalen and Rose Mungai (Africa New Dollar Per Day [PPP] Poverty Estimates [$1.25/day] in 2008)
- DIME (What's the Coolest Region for doing Impact Evaluation? It's Africa)
- Jos Verbeek and Jose Alejandro Quijada (Africa and the MDGs: 2015 and Beyond)
- Markus Goldstein (Gender)
- Rabia Ali and Jishnu Das (Gender Differences in Risks of Death: Africa's Excess Female Mortality and Trends Over Time)
- Sumila Gulyani, Ellen Bassett and Debabrata Talukdar (A Multidimensional Portrait of Poverty and Living Conditions in Slums)
- Punam Chuhan-Pole and Vijdan Korman (CPIA results for Africa)

Azita Amjadi, Abdolreza Farivari, Shelley Lai Fu, Ugendran Machakkalai, Shanmugam Natarajan, and Malarvizhi Veerappan collaborated in the online data production. Mahyar Eshragh-Tabary, Masako Hiraga, Maurice Nsabimana, and Soong Sup Lee collaborated in the update of the live database. Software preparation and testing for mobile applications was managed by Shelley Lai Fu, with the assistance of Ramgopal Erabelly and Parastoo Oloumi. Federico Escaler and William Prince collaborated in the production of *The Little Data Book on Africa 2012/13* and *The Little Data Book on Gender in Africa 2012/13.*

Jeffrey Lecksell and Bruno Bonansea of the World Bank's Map Design Unit coordinated preparation of the maps.

Kenneth Omondi provided administrative and logistical support. The core would like to thank the many people who provided useful comments on the publication. Their feedback and suggestions helped improve this year's edition.

Staff from External Affairs oversaw printing and dissemination of the book and its companions.

Several institutions provided data to *Africa Development Indicators*. Their contribution is very much appreciated.

EEI provided design direction, editing, and layout, led by Sheila Gagen; Cindy Peters typeset the book.

Indicator tables

Part I. Basic indicators and national and fiscal accounts

1. Basic indicators

1.1 Basic indicators 7

2. National and fiscal accounts

2.1 Gross domestic product, nominal 8
2.2 Gross domestic product, nominal 9
2.3 Gross domestic product, nominal 10
2.4 Gross domestic product per capita, real 11
2.5 Gross domestic product per capita growth 12
2.6 Gross national income, nominal 13
2.7 Gross national income, *World Bank Atlas* method 14
2.8 Gross national income per capita, *World Bank Atlas* method 15
2.9 Gross domestic product deflator (U.S. dollar series) 16
2.10 Consumer price Index 17
2.11 Consumer price index, growth 18
2.12 Price indices 19
2.13 Gross domestic savings 20
2.14 Gross national savings 21
2.15 General government final consumption expenditure 22
2.16 Household final consumption expenditure 23
2.17 Final consumption expenditure plus discrepancy 24
2.18 Final consumption expenditure plus discrepancy per capita 25
2.19 Gross fixed capital formation 26
2.20 Gross general government fixed capital formation 27
2.21 Private sector fixed capital formation 28
2.22 External trade balance (exports minus imports) 29
2.23 Exports of goods and services, nominal 30
2.24 Imports of goods and services, nominal 31
2.25 Exports of goods and services as a share of GDP 32
2.26 Imports of goods and services as a share of GDP 33
2.27 Balance of payments and current account 34
2.28 Exchange rates and purchasing power parity 36
2.29 Agriculture value added 38
2.30 Industry value added 39
2.31 Services plus discrepancy value added 40
2.32 Central government finances 41
2.33 Central government expenses 43
2.34 Central government revenues 45
2.35 Structure of demand 47

Part II. Millennium Development Goals

3. Millennium Development Goals

3.1 Millennium Development Goal 1: eradicate extreme poverty and hunger 48
3.2 Millennium Development Goal 2: achieve universal primary education 51
3.3 Millennium Development Goal 3: promote gender equity and empower women 52

3.4 Millennium Development Goal 4: reduce child mortality 53
3.5 Millennium Development Goal 5: improve maternal health 54
3.6 Millennium Development Goal 6: combat HIV/AIDS, malaria, and other diseases 55
3.7 Millennium Development Goal 7: ensure environmental sustainability 57
3.8 Millennium Development Goal 8: develop a global partnership for development 59

Part III. Development outcomes

Drivers of growth
4. Private sector development
4.1 Doing Business 61
4.2 Investment climate 64
4.3 Financial sector infrastructure 66

5. Trade and regional integration
5.1 International trade and tariff barriers 68
5.2 Top three exports and share in total exports, 2010 72
5.3 Regional integration, trade blocs 74

6. Infrastructure
6.1 Water and sanitation 74
6.2 Transportation 75
6.3 Information and communication technology 77
6.4 Energy 80

Participating in growth
7. Human development
7.1 Education 84
7.2 Health 86

8. Agriculture, rural development, and environment
8.1 Rural development 90
8.2 Agriculture 92
8.3 Producer food prices 94
8.4 Environment 96
8.5 Fossil fuel emissions 98

9. Labor, migration, and population
9.1 Labor force participation 100
9.2 Labor force composition 106
9.3 Unemployment 108
9.4 Migration and population 110

10. HIV/AIDS
10.1 HIV/AIDS 112

11. Malaria
11.1 Malaria 116

12. Capable states and partnership
12.1 Aid and debt relief 117
12.2 Status of Paris Declaration indicators 120
12.3 Capable states 122
12.4 Governance and anticorruption indicators 124
12.5 Country Policy and Institutional Assessment ratings 126
12.6 Polity indicators 130

Users guide

Tables

The tables are numbered by section. Countries are listed alphabetically by subregion (Sub-Saharan Africa and North Africa). Indicators are shown for the most recent year or period for which data are available and, in most tables, for an earlier year or period (usually 1980, 1990, 1995, 2000 or 2005 in this edition). Time-series data are available on the *Africa Development Indicators*—CD-ROM and the World Bank's Open Data website (http://data.worldbank.org). The term country, used interchangeably with economy, does not imply political independence but refers to any territory for which authorities report separate social or economic statistics.

Known deviations from standard definitions or breaks in comparability over time or across countries are noted in the tables. When available data are deemed too weak to provide reliable measures of levels and trends or do not adequately adhere to international standards, the data are not shown.

Aggregate measure for region and sub-classifications

The aggregates are based on the World Bank's analytical regional classification for Sub-Saharan Africa and North Africa, which may differ from common geographic usage. Former Spanish Sahara and Mayotte are not included in any aggregates.

Statistics

Data are shown for economies as they were constituted in 2010, and historical data are revised to reflect current political arrangements. Exceptions are noted in the tables.

Additional information about the data is provided in *Primary data documentation*, which summarizes national and international efforts to improve basic data collection and gives country-level information on primary sources, census years, and other background information.

Data consistency, reliability, and comparability

Considerable effort has been made to harmonize the data, but full comparability cannot be assured, and care must be taken in interpreting indicators. Many factors affect data availability, comparability, and reliability. Statistical systems in many developing economies are still weak; statistical methods, coverage practices and definitions differ widely and cross-country and intertemporal comparisons involve complex technical and conceptual problems that cannot be resolved unequivocally. Data coverage may be incomplete because of circumstances affecting the collection and reporting of data, such as conflicts. Although drawn from sources thought to be the most authoritative, data should be construed as indicating trends and characterizing differences across economies. Discrepancies in data presented in earlier editions of *Africa Development Indicators* reflect updates from countries as well as revisions to historical series and changes in methodology. Readers are therefore advised not to compare data series between editions or across World Bank publications.

Country notes

South Sudan declared its independence on July 9, 2011. Data for Sudan include South Sudan unless otherwise noted.

Classification of economies

For operational and analytical purposes the World Bank's main criterion for classifying economies is gross national income (GNI) per capita (calculated by the *World Bank Atlas* method; box 1). Every economy is classified as low income, middle income (subdivided

Box 1 **The *World Bank Atlas* method for converting gross national income to a common denominator**

In calculating GNI and GNI per capita in U.S. dollars for certain operational purposes, the World Bank uses the *Atlas conversion factor.* The purpose of the *Atlas* conversion factor is to reduce the impact of exchange rate fluctuations in the cross-country comparison of national incomes. The *Atlas* conversion factor for any year is the average of the official exchange rate or alternative conversion factor for that year and for the two preceding years, adjusted for difference between the rate of inflation in the country and that in Japan, the United Kingdom, the United States, and the euro area. A country's inflation rate is measured by the change in its GDP deflator.

The inflation rate for Japan, the United Kingdom, the United States, and the euro area, representing international inflation, is measured by the change in the "SDR deflator." The SDR (Special drawing rights or SDRs are the International Monetary Fund's unit of account) is calculated as a weighted average of these countries GDP deflators in SDR terms, the weights being the amount of each country's currency in one SDR unit. Weights vary over time because both the composition of the SDR and the relative exchange rates for each currency change. The SDR deflator is calculated in SDR terms first and then converted to U.S. dollars using the SDR to dollar *Atlas* conversion factor. The *Atlas* conversion factor is then applied to a country's GNI. The resulting GNI in U.S. dollars is divided by the midyear population for the latest of the three years to derive GNI per capita.

When official exchange rates are deemed to be unreliable or unrepresentative of the effective exchange rate during a period, an alternative estimate of the exchange rate is used in the *Atlas* formula below.

The following formulas describe the procedures for computing the conversion factor for year *t*:

$$e_t^* = \frac{1}{3}\left[e_{t-2}\left(\frac{p_t}{p_{t-2}} / \frac{p_t^{S\$}}{p_{t-2}^{S\$}}\right) + e_{t-1}\left(\frac{p_t}{p_{t-1}} / \frac{p_t^{S\$}}{p_{t-1}^{S\$}}\right) + e_t\right]$$

and for calculating per capita GNI in U.S. dollars for year *t:*

$$Y_t^{\$} = \left(\frac{Y_t}{N_t}\right) / e_t^*$$

where e_t^* is the *Atlas* conversion factor (national currency to the U.S. dollar) for year *t*, e_t is the average annual exchange rate (national currency to the U.S. dollar) for year *t*, p_t is the GDP deflator for year *t*, $p_t^{S\$}$ is the SDR deflator in U.S. dollar terms for year *t*, $Y_t^{\$}$ is current GNI per capita in U.S. dollars in year *t*, Y_t is current GNI (local currency) for year *t*, and N_t is midyear population for year *t*.

into lower middle and upper middle), or high income (table 1). Low- and middle income economies are sometimes referred to as developing economies. The term is used for convenience; it is not intended to imply that all economies in the group are experiencing similar development or that other economies have reached a preferred or final stage of development. Classification by income does not necessarily reflect development status. Because GNI per capita changes over time, the country composition of income groups may change from one edition of *Africa Development Indicators* to the next. Once the classification is fixed for an edition, based on GNI per capita in the most recent year for which data are available (2010 in this edition), all historical data presented are based on the same country grouping.

Low-income economies are those with a GNI per capita of $1,005 or less in 2010. Middle-income economies are those with a GNI per capita of more than $1,005 but less than $12,275. Lower middle-income and upper middle-income economies are separated at a GNI per capita of $3,976. High-income economies are those with a GNI per capita of $12,276 or more.

Alternative conversion factors

The World Bank systematically assesses the appropriateness of official exchange rates as conversion factors. An alternative conversion factor is used when the official exchange rate is judged to diverge by an exceptionally large margin from the rate effectively applied to domestic transactions of foreign currencies and traded products. See *Primary data documentation* for list of countries using alternative conversion factors. Alternative conversion factors are used in the *Atlas* methodology and elsewhere in *Africa Development Indicators* as single-year conversion factors.

Symbols

..	means that data are not available or that aggregates cannot be calculated because of missing data in the years shown.
$	means current U.S. dollars unless otherwise noted.
<	means less than

Table 1	World Bank classification of economies, 2010 (GNI per capita)		
	Middle income		
Low income	Lower middle income	Upper middle income	High income
GNI per capita of $1,005 or less	GNI per capita higher than $1,006 and less than $3,975	GNI per capita of $3,976 but less than $12,275	GNI per capita of $12,276 and over
Benin	Angola	Algeria	Equatorial Guinea
Burkina Faso	Cameroon	Botswana	
Burundi	Cape Verde	Gabon	
Central Africa Republic	Congo, Rep.	Libya	
Chad	Côte d'Ivoire	Mauritius	
Comoros	Djibouti	Namibia	
Congo, Dem. Rep.	Egypt, Arab Rep.	Seychelles	
Eritrea	Ghana	South Africa	
Ethiopia	Lesotho	Tunisia	
Gambia, The	Mauritania		
Guinea	Morocco		
Guinea-Bissau	Nigeria		
Kenya	São Tomé and Príncipe		
Liberia	Senegal		
Madagascar	South Sudan		
Malawi	Sudan		
Mali	Swaziland		
Mozambique	Zambia		
Niger			
Rwanda			
Sierra Leone			
Somalia			
Tanzania			
Togo			
Uganda			
Zimbabwe			

Source: World Bank.

>	means more than
0 or 0.0	means zero or small enough that the number would round to zero at the displayed number of decimal places.
/	in dates, as in 2010/11, means that the period of time, usually covers 12 months, but straddles two calendar years and refers to a crop year, a survey year or a fiscal year.
-	in dates, as in 2010-11, means that the period of time, refers to 2010 and/or 2011

Data presentation conventions

- A blank means not applicable or, for an aggregate, not analytically meaningful.
- A billion is 1,000 million.
- A trillion is 1,000 billion.
- Growth rates are in real terms, unless otherwise specified.

The cutoff date for data for this publication is August 2012.

However, it must be noted that the database may have more recent data by the time of this publication.

Table 1.1 Basic indicators

	Population: Total (millions) 2010	Population: Growth (annual %) 2010	Land area (thousands of sq km) 2010	Population density (people per sq km) 2010	GNI per capita, *World Bank Atlas* method (current $) 2010	GDP per capita, Constant 2000 prices: $ 2010[a]	GDP per capita, Constant 2000 prices: Average annual growth (%) 2000–10	Life expectancy at birth (years) 2010	Under-five mortality rate (per 1,000) 2010	Gini index 2000–10[b]	Adult literacy rate (% ages 15 and older): Male 2009	Adult literacy rate (% ages 15 and older): Female 2009	Net official development assistance per capita (current $) 2010
SUB-SAHARAN AFRICA	**844.0**	**2.5**	**23,616**	**35.7**	**1,202**	**653**	**2.6**	**54.2**	**122**		**..**	**..**	**52.8**
Excluding South Africa	794.0	2.5	22,401	35.4	895	458	3.2	54.3	125	..	74.5	56.1	54.7
Excl. S. Africa & Nigeria	635.6	2.5	21,491	29.6	824	437	3.0	55.0	120	..	..	..	65.1
Angola	19.1	2.8	1,247	15.3	3,960	1,369	9.4	50.7	161	58.6	82.9	57.6	12.5
Benin	8.8	2.8	111	80.0	780	377	0.8	55.6	115	38.6	54.2	29.1	77.9
Botswana	2.0	1.3	567	3.5	6,750	4,190	2.7	53.1	48	..	83.8	84.4	77.8
Burkina Faso	16.5	3.0	274	60.2	550	283	2.9	54.9	176	39.8	..	..	64.5
Burundi	8.4	2.6	26	326.4	230	138	0.5	49.9	142	33.3	72.6	60.9	75.2
Cameroon	19.6	2.2	473	41.5	1,200	714	1.0	51.1	136	38.9	..	..	27.6
Cape Verde	0.5	0.9	4	123.1	3,280	1,959	5.0	73.8	36	50.5	90.1	80.3	661.1
Central African Republic	4.4	1.9	623	7.1	470	240	-0.7	47.6	159	56.3	69.1	42.1	59.3
Chad	11.2	2.6	1,259	8.9	710	300	6.1	49.2	173	39.8	44.5	23.1	43.3
Comoros	0.7	2.6	2	395.0	750	336	-0.8	60.6	86	64.3	79.7	68.7	91.5
Congo, Dem. Rep.	66.0	2.7	2,267	29.1	180	106	2.5	48.1	170	44.4	79.5	54.9	53.7
Congo, Rep.	4.0	2.5	342	11.8	2,240	1,253	1.7	57.0	93	47.3	..	..	324.6
Côte d'Ivoire	19.7	2.0	318	62.1	1,170	588	-0.6	54.7	123	41.5	64.7	45.3	42.8
Equatorial Guinea	0.7	2.8	28	25.0	13,720	8,537	12.4	50.8	121	..	97.0	89.8	121.0
Eritrea	5.3	3.0	101	52.0	340	147	-2.9	61.0	61	..	77.9	56.0	30.6
Ethiopia	82.9	2.2	1,000	83.0	390	221	6.3	58.7	106	29.8	..	..	42.5
Gabon	1.5	1.9	258	5.8	7,680	4,214	0.2	62.3	74	41.5	91.4	84.1	69.1
Gambia, The	1.7	2.7	10	172.8	610	704	1.4	58.2	98	47.3	57.6	35.8	69.5
Ghana	24.4	2.4	228	107.2	1,250	360	3.4	63.8	74	42.8	72.8	60.4	69.4
Guinea	10.0	2.2	246	40.6	390	550	5.2	53.6	130	39.4	50.8	28.1	21.8
Guinea-Bissau	1.5	2.1	28	53.9	580	161	-0.5	47.7	150	35.5	66.9	38.0	92.0
Kenya	40.5	2.6	569	71.2	810	469	1.7	56.5	85	47.7	90.5	83.5	40.2
Lesotho	2.2	1.0	30	71.5	1,100	496	2.7	47.4	85	52.5	82.9	95.3	118.0
Liberia	4.0	4.0	96	41.5	210	261	1.7	56.2	103	38.2	63.7	54.5	355.3
Madagascar	20.7	2.9	582	35.6	430	243	0.3	66.5	62	44.1	..	..	22.7
Malawi	14.9	3.1	94	158.1	330	185	2.3	53.5	92	39.0	80.6	67.0	68.6
Mali	15.4	3.0	1,220	12.6	600	273	2.0	51.0	178	33.0	..	..	70.8
Mauritania	3.5	2.4	1,031	3.4	1,000	609	3.1	58.2	111	40.5	64.5	50.3	108.2
Mauritius	1.3	0.5	2	631.0	7,780	5,181	3.1	73.0	15	..	90.6	85.3	97.8
Mozambique	23.4	2.3	786	29.7	440	384	4.9	49.7	135	45.7	70.1	41.5	83.4
Namibia	2.3	1.8	823	2.8	4,250	2,696	3.1	62.1	40	63.9	88.9	88.1	112.3
Niger	15.5	3.5	1,267	12.3	360	179	0.6	54.3	143	34.6	..	..	48.0
Nigeria	158.4	2.5	911	173.9	1,170	540	4.1	51.4	143	48.8	72.0	49.8	13.0
Rwanda	10.6	3.0	25	430.6	520	337	4.8	55.1	91	53.1	75.0	66.8	97.2
São Tomé and Príncipe	0.2	1.8	1	172.3	1,250	..	..	64.4	80	50.8	93.7	84.1	298.1
Senegal	12.4	2.7	193	64.6	1,080	562	1.5	59.0	75	39.2	61.8	38.7	74.6
Seychelles	0.1	(0.9)	0	188.1	10,460	8,788	1.8	73.0	14	65.8	..	..	647.7
Sierra Leone	5.9	2.2	72	81.9	340	268	5.0	47.4	174	42.5	52.7	30.1	79.6
Somalia	9.3	2.3	627	14.9	..	..	..	50.9	180	..	..	..	53.3
South Africa	50.0	1.4	1,214	41.2	6,090	3,753	2.7	52.1	57	63.1	..	..	20.6
Sudan	33.6	1.9	2,376	18.3	1,300	524	4.1	61.1	103	35.3	..	..	61.8
Swaziland	1.1	1.1	17	61.4	2,930	1,811	2.1	48.3	78	51.5	87.8	86.2	86.6
Tanzania	44.8	3.0	886	50.6	530	459	4.2	57.4	92	37.6	79.0	66.9	66.0
Togo	6.0	2.1	54	110.8	550	265	0.1	56.6	103	34.4	..	..	69.5
Uganda	33.4	3.2	200	167.3	500	380	4.3	53.6	99	44.3	..	..	51.6
Zambia	12.9	1.6	743	17.4	1,070	432	3.1	48.5	111	54.6	80.6	61.3	70.7
Zimbabwe	12.6	0.8	387	32.5	480	321	-6.2	49.9	80	..	94.7	89.4	58.3
NORTH AFRICA	**166.3**	**1.5**	**5,762**	**28.9**	**3,533**	**2,313**	**3.2**	**72.8**	**27**		**..**	**..**	**16.4**
Algeria	35.5	1.5	2,382	14.9	4,390	2,232	2.3	72.9	36	..	..	..	5.6
Djibouti	0.9	1.9	23	38.3	..	..	2.0	57.5	91	40.0	..	..	148.8
Egypt, Arab Rep.	81.1	1.8	995	81.5	2,420	1,976	3.2	73.0	22	30.8	..	..	7.3
Libya	6.4	1.5	1,760	3.6	..	..	3.3	74.8	17	..	95.2	82.0	1.3
Morocco	32.0	1.0	446	71.6	2,850	1,844	3.7	71.9	36	40.9	68.9	43.9	31.1
Tunisia	10.5	1.0	155	67.9	4,140	3,144	3.7	74.6	16	41.4	..	..	52.2
AFRICA	**1,010.3**	**2.3**	**29,378**	**34.4**	**1,586**	**926**	**2.6**	**57.2**	**113**	**..**	**..**	**..**	**47.3**

a. Provisional.

b. Data are for the most recent year available during the period specified.

Table 2.1 Gross domestic product, nominal

	Current prices ($ millions)									Annual average growth (%)		
	1980	1990	2004	2005	2006	2007	2008	2009	2010[a]	1980–89	1990–99	2000–10
SUB-SAHARAN AFRICA	**271,551**	**300,415**	**558,699**	**651,778**	**760,711**	**881,782**	**1,009,242**	**953,418**	**1,117,459**	**1.0**	**1.5**	**14.6**
Excluding South Africa	192,649	188,529	339,519	404,659	499,793	595,804	735,892	670,761	754,176	-0.7	1.2	15.9
Excl. S. Africa & Nigeria	124,292	160,121	251,329	291,954	352,311	429,206	527,924	501,543	556,563	3.0	0.8	15.1
Angola	..	10,260	19,775	28,234	41,789	60,449	84,178	75,492	82,471	..	-3.8	30.4
Benin	1,405	1,845	4,047	4,287	4,735	5,546	6,683	6,585	6,558	2.4	3.5	12.6
Botswana	1,061	3,792	10,049	10,255	11,256	12,379	13,443	11,537	14,905	12.6	4.7	10.3
Burkina Faso	1,929	3,101	5,109	5,463	5,845	6,756	8,351	8,348	8,825	4.8	0.0	13.9
Burundi	920	1,132	899	1,117	1,237	1,319	1,621	1,815	2,027	2.2	-3.3	10.7
Cameroon	6,741	11,152	15,775	16,588	17,957	20,684	23,736	22,182	22,480	7.4	-2.5	10.2
Cape Verde	142	307	924	972	1,108	1,331	1,562	1,601	1,659	8.7	7.0	13.3
Central African Republic	797	1,488	1,270	1,350	1,477	1,696	1,983	1,980	1,985	8.1	-4.3	8.9
Chad	1,033	1,739	4,415	5,302	6,099	7,016	8,357	7,085	8,541	5.7	-1.3	21.4
Comoros	124	250	362	387	403	465	530	535	541	8.0	-2.0	11.1
Congo, Dem. Rep.	14,395	9,350	6,512	7,191	8,824	10,014	11,675	11,204	13,110	-6.2	-7.1	12.3
Congo, Rep.	1,706	2,799	4,649	6,087	7,731	8,395	11,859	9,594	12,008	2.3	-2.4	17.7
Côte d'Ivoire	10,175	10,796	15,481	16,363	17,367	19,796	23,414	23,042	22,921	2.0	2.2	9.6
Equatorial Guinea	..	132	5,241	8,217	9,603	12,575	18,424	12,233	14,500	..	22.5	31.4
Eritrea	..	..	1,109	1,098	1,211	1,318	1,380	1,857	2,117	..	7.2	12.6
Ethiopia	..	12,083	10,054	12,307	15,164	19,553	26,642	31,963	29,684	5.9	-5.7	17.4
Gabon	4,279	5,952	7,178	8,666	9,546	11,571	14,530	10,946	13,200	-0.5	-1.7	12.5
Gambia, The	241	317	579	636	667	833	1,037	983	1,050	1.7	6.8	5.3
Ghana	4,445	5,886	8,872	10,720	20,388	24,632	28,527	25,979	32,175	3.2	2.6	23.8
Guinea	..	2,667	3,666	2,937	2,821	4,209	3,778	4,165	4,736	..	3.0	4.0
Guinea-Bissau	111	244	523	573	579	691	847	835	835	3.7	-0.6	17.4
Kenya	7,265	8,591	16,096	18,738	22,504	27,237	30,519	30,580	32,198	2.6	7.7	11.7
Lesotho	431	541	1,234	1,368	1,429	1,597	1,626	1,711	2,179	-0.8	4.1	12.6
Liberia	855	384	467	542	604	739	851	879	988	0.8	1.8	7.6
Madagascar	4,042	3,081	4,364	5,039	5,515	7,343	9,395	8,488	8,721	-5.2	3.4	9.2
Malawi	1,238	1,881	2,625	2,755	3,117	3,458	4,074	4,728	5,054	1.8	0.2	11.1
Mali	1,787	2,421	4,874	5,305	5,866	7,146	8,738	8,965	9,422	3.4	0.4	15.4
Mauritania	709	1,020	1,833	2,184	3,041	3,357	3,585	3,027	3,614	3.5	1.7	13.1
Mauritius	1,137	2,653	6,386	6,284	6,507	7,792	9,641	8,825	9,714	8.8	5.8	8.7
Mozambique	3,526	2,463	5,698	6,579	7,096	8,030	9,891	9,674	9,209	-4.7	8.3	10.7
Namibia	2,169	2,350	6,606	7,262	7,981	8,806	8,840	8,931	11,133	0.1	4.6	11.7
Niger	2,509	2,481	3,053	3,405	3,645	4,291	5,370	5,254	5,411	-0.2	-1.8	12.8
Nigeria	64,202	28,472	87,845	112,249	146,867	165,921	207,118	168,568	196,838	-12.0	3.2	18.2
Rwanda	1,163	2,584	2,089	2,581	3,111	3,738	4,712	5,253	5,624	8.6	-2.0	15.1
São Tomé and Príncipe	..	..	107	114	124	144	183	196	201	..	..	11.7
Senegal	3,503	5,717	8,030	8,714	9,378	11,320	13,386	12,769	12,855	6.2	-1.8	12.4
Seychelles	147	369	700	917	1,020	1,019	962	841	963	9.3	6.0	5.2
Sierra Leone	1,101	650	1,096	1,239	1,422	1,664	1,955	1,856	1,910	-4.3	0.6	11.9
Somalia	604	917	..	..	..	..	..	..	..	6.4	..	..
South Africa	80,710	112,014	219,093	247,064	261,007	286,172	273,870	283,012	363,523	4.2	2.1	12.0
Sudan	7,617	12,409	21,685	27,387	36,393	46,533	58,032	54,633	66,997	10.1	0.8	20.6
Swaziland	543	1,115	2,421	2,584	2,948	3,054	3,020	2,950	3,698	1.9	4.5	11.0
Tanzania	..	4,259	12,826	14,142	14,331	16,826	20,715	21,368	22,915	..	10.1	9.3
Togo	1,136	1,628	1,937	2,115	2,203	2,523	3,163	3,156	3,176	4.5	-0.1	10.7
Uganda	1,245	4,304	7,940	9,237	9,977	11,916	14,441	15,803	17,197	20.7	8.8	12.7
Zambia	3,884	3,288	5,439	7,179	10,702	11,541	14,641	12,805	16,193	-3.1	0.2	19.7
Zimbabwe	6,679	8,784	5,806	5,755	5,444	5,292	4,416	5,836	7,476	-0.1	-1.4	-1.2
NORTH AFRICA	**111,794**	**172,644**	**286,041**	**328,540**	**381,921**	**453,093**	**561,720**	**524,944**	**586,796**	**4.8**	**4.3**	**11.1**
Algeria	42,345	62,045	85,014	102,339	117,169	135,804	170,989	138,120	161,979	4.5	-1.2	13.7
Djibouti	..	452	666	709	769	848	983	1,049	..	..	1.7	7.6
Egypt, Arab Rep.	22,912	43,130	78,845	89,686	107,484	130,478	162,818	188,984	218,894	6.8	10.8	9.2
Libya	..	28,905	33,385	44,000	56,484	71,803	93,168	62,360	..	..	-0.9	15.0
Morocco	18,821	25,821	56,948	59,524	65,637	75,226	88,883	90,908	90,803	3.7	5.1	10.9
Tunisia	8,743	12,291	31,183	32,283	34,377	38,934	44,880	43,522	44,238	2.3	7.3	8.6
AFRICA	**386,370**	**472,965**	**843,939**	**979,376**	**1,141,531**	**1,333,613**	**1,569,577**	**1,477,045**	**1,704,989**	**2.2**	**2.6**	**13.2**

a. Provisional.

Table 2.2 Gross domestic product, real

	Constant prices (2000 $ millions)									Annual average growth (%)		
	1980	1990	2004	2005	2006	2007	2008	2009	2010[a]	1980–89	1990–99	2000–10
SUB-SAHARAN AFRICA	**227,134**	**273,077**	**406,992**	**431,505**	**458,686**	**488,918**	**513,732**	**524,769**	**550,762**	**1.8**	**2.4**	**5.2**
Excluding South Africa	131,834	162,145	254,784	271,274	289,484	310,343	328,716	342,653	363,414	2.1	2.7	5.9
Excl. S. Africa & Nigeria	98,923	127,126	195,946	209,263	223,630	240,245	254,412	263,133	277,664	2.6	2.8	5.7
Angola	..	8,464	12,383	14,644	17,680	21,675	24,669	25,265	26,126	..	1.0	12.9
Benin	1,084	1,412	2,650	2,727	2,839	2,970	3,121	3,240	3,337	2.7	4.7	4.0
Botswana	1,150	3,229	7,160	7,278	7,652	8,020	8,255	7,857	8,408	10.9	5.5	4.1
Burkina Faso	1,101	1,556	3,296	3,581	3,823	3,961	4,191	4,315	4,656	4.0	5.5	5.9
Burundi	659	1,019	922	930	980	1,027	1,079	1,117	1,159	4.5	-3.2	3.4
Cameroon	6,339	8,793	11,815	12,087	12,476	12,913	13,287	13,553	13,987	4.5	1.3	3.3
Cape Verde	..	280	658	701	772	838	890	923	972	6.3	5.9	6.3
Central African Republic	735	815	892	914	949	984	1,003	1,020	1,054	1.6	1.8	1.0
Chad	665	1,106	2,572	3,018	3,024	3,030	3,018	2,982	3,369	6.7	2.3	9.4
Comoros	136	181	222	232	234	236	238	242	247	2.9	1.2	1.9
Congo, Dem. Rep.	7,016	7,659	4,921	5,304	5,600	5,950	6,316	6,495	6,961	2.1	-5.0	5.5
Congo, Rep.	1,746	2,796	3,647	3,932	4,173	4,107	4,335	4,659	5,067	3.8	0.8	4.4
Côte d'Ivoire	7,727	8,298	10,287	10,417	10,488	10,668	10,916	11,331	11,603	0.7	3.5	1.1
Equatorial Guinea	..	207	3,815	4,187	4,239	5,148	5,698	6,025	5,979	..	20.7	15.7
Eritrea	..	..	782	802	794	805	726	754	771	..	7.9	0.7
Ethiopia	..	6,234	9,993	11,174	12,384	13,803	15,292	16,638	18,291	2.1	3.7	8.8
Gabon	3,594	4,298	5,361	5,523	5,588	5,899	6,036	5,951	6,344	0.5	2.9	2.2
Gambia, The	399	569	921	924	955	1,012	1,076	1,147	1,217	3.5	2.7	4.4
Ghana	2,640	3,267	6,010	6,364	6,771	7,209	7,817	8,129	8,779	2.6	4.3	5.9
Guinea	..	2,088	3,585	4,938	5,062	5,150	5,405	5,390	5,494	..	4.5	7.1
Guinea-Bissau	115	186	204	211	215	222	229	236	244	3.8	1.4	1.5
Kenya	7,078	10,544	14,327	15,173	16,134	17,262	17,526	17,990	18,988	4.1	2.2	4.4
Lesotho	377	504	838	860	898	940	991	1,019	1,076	2.4	4.0	3.7
Liberia	1,312	408	543	595	653	755	835	944	1,041	-3.3	0.2	5.2
Madagascar	3,099	3,266	4,148	4,339	4,557	4,842	5,187	4,949	5,027	0.8	1.7	3.4
Malawi	1,000	1,243	1,875	1,924	2,072	2,192	2,375	2,590	2,758	2.4	3.8	5.3
Mali	1,536	1,630	3,105	3,294	3,469	3,618	3,799	3,970	4,200	0.6	3.9	5.2
Mauritania	825	972	1,489	1,622	1,928	1,960	2,028	2,004	2,108	1.9	3.2	5.9
Mauritius	1,519	2,726	5,261	5,327	5,537	5,862	6,186	6,373	6,636	6.1	5.0	3.9
Mozambique	2,462	2,499	5,918	6,484	6,893	7,395	7,901	8,401	8,972	-0.9	6.0	7.6
Namibia	2,292	2,591	4,850	4,972	5,324	5,610	5,799	5,774	6,155	1.1	4.0	5.0
Niger	1,523	1,507	2,091	2,185	2,312	2,391	2,599	2,575	2,781	-0.4	2.4	4.2
Nigeria	31,452	34,978	58,731	61,902	65,740	69,980	74,179	79,372	85,582	0.8	2.4	6.7
Rwanda	1,368	1,673	2,293	2,507	2,737	2,888	3,211	3,343	3,584	2.5	-1.6	7.5
São Tomé and Príncipe	..	..	..	..	..	..	..	..	..	..	..	..
Senegal	2,683	3,463	5,579	5,893	6,042	6,335	6,570	6,707	6,984	2.7	2.8	4.2
Seychelles	292	395	556	598	653	716	709	713	760	3.1	4.5	2.6
Sierra Leone	929	1,014	1,125	1,206	1,294	1,377	1,454	1,500	1,574	0.5	-5.3	8.8
Somalia	..	..	..	..	..	..	..	..	..	..	..	..
South Africa	95,503	110,945	152,329	160,367	169,354	178,749	185,217	182,370	187,640	1.4	2.0	3.9
Sudan	5,525	7,062	15,088	16,043	17,855	19,669	21,014	21,847	22,819	2.4	5.4	6.7
Swaziland	470	1,139	1,651	1,692	1,748	1,809	1,852	1,874	1,912	7.4	3.3	2.5
Tanzania	..	7,547	13,335	14,318	15,282	16,375	17,593	18,652	19,966	..	2.8	7.1
Togo	939	1,043	1,352	1,368	1,423	1,456	1,491	1,539	1,596	1.5	3.6	2.3
Uganda	..	3,293	8,055	8,565	9,489	10,287	11,183	11,993	12,701	2.3	7.2	7.7
Zambia	2,730	3,028	3,886	4,093	4,348	4,617	4,880	5,192	5,587	1.0	0.3	5.6
Zimbabwe	3,654	5,622	4,834	4,558	4,400	4,239	3,490	3,699	4,032	3.3	2.9	-6.3
NORTH AFRICA	**120,356**	**180,141**	**289,670**	**304,277**	**321,442**	**338,372**	**355,930**	**369,193**	**384,775**	**4.2**	**3.2**	**4.8**
Algeria	35,291	46,367	66,190	69,565	70,956	73,085	74,839	76,635	79,164	2.9	1.7	3.9
Djibouti	..	660	619	638	669	703	744	781	..	..	-2.3	4.0
Egypt, Arab Rep.	38,506	65,579	113,666	118,749	126,876	135,869	145,592	152,415	160,259	5.5	4.3	5.1
Libya	..	..	37,771	41,511	43,960	46,598	48,368	49,384	..	..	..	5.4
Morocco	20,086	29,312	45,835	47,201	50,863	52,240	55,158	57,783	59,908	4.2	2.4	4.9
Tunisia	9,545	13,547	25,589	26,613	28,118	29,878	31,228	32,196	33,161	3.2	4.6	4.7
AFRICA	**350,017**	**454,583**	**696,649**	**735,761**	**780,101**	**827,251**	**869,622**	**893,935**	**935,730**	**2.6**	**2.7**	**5.0**

a. Provisional.

Table 2.3 Gross domestic product growth

	Annual growth (%)											
										Annual average		
	1980	1990	2004	2005	2006	2007	2008	2009	2010[a]	1980–89	1990–99	2000–10
SUB-SAHARAN AFRICA	**4.0**	**1.2**	**6.1**	**6.0**	**6.3**	**6.6**	**5.1**	**2.2**	**5.0**	**2.2**	**2.1**	**4.8**
Excluding South Africa	1.8	2.2	7.1	6.5	6.7	7.2	5.9	4.2	6.1	2.1	2.5	5.4
Excl. S. Africa & Nigeria	0.7	0.7	6.0	6.8	6.9	7.4	5.9	3.4	5.5	2.6	2.4	5.2
Angola	..	-0.3	11.2	18.3	20.7	22.6	13.8	2.4	3.4	4.2	1.0	10.6
Benin	6.8	3.2	3.1	2.9	4.1	4.6	5.1	3.8	3.0	3.1	4.5	4.2
Botswana	12.0	6.8	6.0	1.6	5.1	4.8	2.9	-4.8	7.0	11.5	5.9	4.3
Burkina Faso	0.8	-0.6	4.6	8.7	6.8	3.6	5.8	3.0	7.9	3.7	5.1	5.6
Burundi	1.0	3.5	4.8	0.9	5.4	4.8	5.1	3.5	3.8	4.3	-1.4	3.0
Cameroon	-2.0	-6.1	3.7	2.3	3.2	3.5	2.9	2.0	3.2	4.0	0.4	3.4
Cape Verde	..	0.7	4.3	6.5	10.1	8.7	6.2	3.7	5.2	6.4	5.2	7.1
Central African Republic	-4.5	-2.2	1.0	2.4	3.8	3.7	2.0	1.7	3.3	0.9	1.3	1.1
Chad	-6.1	-4.2	33.6	17.3	0.2	0.2	-0.4	-1.2	13.0	5.4	2.2	8.8
Comoros	..	5.1	-0.2	4.2	1.2	0.5	1.0	1.8	2.1	2.7	1.6	2.0
Congo, Dem. Rep.	2.2	-6.6	6.6	7.8	5.6	6.3	6.2	2.8	7.2	1.8	-5.5	3.9
Congo, Rep.	17.6	1.0	3.5	7.8	6.1	-1.6	5.6	7.5	8.8	6.8	0.8	5.0
Côte d'Ivoire	-11.0	-1.1	1.8	1.3	0.7	1.7	2.3	3.8	2.4	-0.2	2.6	0.7
Equatorial Guinea	..	3.3	38.0	9.8	1.3	21.4	10.7	5.7	-0.8	0.9	20.2	17.7
Eritrea	..	..	1.5	2.6	-1.0	1.4	-9.8	3.9	2.2	..	8.1	0.8
Ethiopia	..	2.7	13.6	11.8	10.8	11.5	10.8	8.8	9.9	2.4	2.7	8.3
Gabon	2.6	5.2	1.4	3.0	1.2	5.6	2.3	-1.4	6.6	1.9	2.5	1.9
Gambia, The	6.3	3.6	7.1	0.3	3.4	6.0	6.3	6.7	6.1	3.9	3.1	4.6
Ghana	0.5	3.3	5.6	5.9	6.4	6.5	8.4	4.0	8.0	2.0	4.3	5.7
Guinea	..	4.3	2.3	37.8	2.5	1.8	4.9	-0.3	1.9	4.5	4.3	5.9
Guinea-Bissau	-16.0	6.1	2.2	3.5	2.1	3.2	3.2	3.0	3.5	2.9	2.0	1.9
Kenya	5.6	4.2	5.1	5.9	6.3	7.0	1.5	2.6	5.6	4.2	2.2	3.8
Lesotho	-2.7	6.5	2.3	2.7	4.3	4.7	5.4	2.9	5.6	2.2	4.1	3.9
Liberia	-4.1	-51.0	-5.1	9.5	9.8	15.7	10.5	13.1	10.3	-4.5	1.2	10.1
Madagascar	0.8	3.1	5.3	4.6	5.0	6.2	7.1	-4.6	1.6	0.4	1.6	3.0
Malawi	0.4	5.7	5.5	2.6	7.7	5.8	8.3	9.0	6.5	1.7	4.1	4.5
Mali	-4.3	-1.9	2.2	6.1	5.3	4.3	5.0	4.5	5.8	0.6	3.6	5.5
Mauritania	3.4	-1.8	5.8	9.0	18.9	1.6	3.5	-1.2	5.2	2.2	2.9	4.6
Mauritius	-10.1	7.2	5.8	1.2	4.0	5.9	5.5	3.0	4.1	4.3	5.2	4.3
Mozambique	..	1.0	7.9	9.6	6.3	7.3	6.8	6.3	6.8	0.4	5.6	7.2
Namibia	..	2.5	12.3	2.5	7.1	5.4	3.4	-0.4	6.6	1.1	4.1	4.6
Niger	-2.2	-1.3	0.1	4.5	5.8	3.4	8.7	-0.9	8.0	0.0	1.9	4.0
Nigeria	4.2	8.2	10.6	5.4	6.2	6.5	6.0	7.0	7.8	0.9	3.1	6.4
Rwanda	9.0	-2.4	7.4	9.3	9.2	5.5	11.2	4.1	7.2	3.2	2.1	7.6
São Tomé and Príncipe	..	..	6.6	-1.4	6.7	6.0	9.1	4.0	4.5	..	..	5.8
Senegal	-3.3	-0.7	5.9	5.6	2.5	4.9	3.7	2.1	4.1	2.4	2.7	4.0
Seychelles	-4.3	7.0	-2.9	7.5	9.3	9.6	-1.0	0.5	6.7	2.1	4.9	2.5
Sierra Leone	4.8	3.4	7.5	7.2	7.3	6.4	5.5	3.2	5.0	1.1	-4.3	9.2
Somalia	-3.9	-1.5	..	..	..	..	..	..	..	1.7	-1.5	..
South Africa	6.6	-0.3	4.6	5.3	5.6	5.6	3.6	-1.5	2.9	2.2	1.4	3.6
Sudan	1.5	-5.5	1.8	6.3	11.3	10.2	6.8	4.0	4.5	3.4	4.4	6.5
Swaziland	12.5	21.0	2.9	2.5	3.3	3.5	2.4	1.2	2.0	8.6	4.9	2.2
Tanzania	..	7.1	7.8	7.4	6.7	7.2	7.4	6.0	7.0	3.8	3.3	6.8
Togo	14.6	-0.2	2.1	1.2	4.1	2.3	2.4	3.2	3.7	2.6	2.6	1.9
Uganda	..	6.5	6.8	6.3	10.8	8.4	8.7	7.3	5.9	3.0	6.9	7.1
Zambia	3.0	-0.5	5.4	5.3	6.2	6.2	5.7	6.4	7.6	1.4	0.4	5.4
Zimbabwe	14.4	7.0	-5.8	-5.7	-3.5	-3.7	-17.7	6.0	9.0	5.2	2.9	-4.4
NORTH AFRICA	**5.2**	**4.1**	**4.7**	**5.0**	**5.6**	**5.3**	**5.2**	**3.7**	**4.2**	**4.3**	**3.3**	**4.4**
Algeria	0.8	0.8	5.2	5.1	2.0	3.0	2.4	2.4	3.3	2.8	1.6	3.6
Djibouti	..	..	3.8	3.2	4.8	5.1	5.8	5.0	..	..	-2.0	3.6
Egypt, Arab Rep.	10.0	5.7	4.1	4.5	6.8	7.1	7.2	4.7	5.2	5.9	4.3	4.9
Libya	..	..	4.4	9.9	5.9	6.0	3.8	2.1	..	..	..	4.3
Morocco	3.6	4.0	4.8	3.0	7.8	2.7	5.6	4.8	3.7	3.9	2.8	4.6
Tunisia	7.4	8.0	6.0	4.0	5.7	6.3	4.5	3.1	3.0	3.6	5.1	4.4
AFRICA	**4.4**	**2.2**	**5.5**	**5.6**	**6.0**	**6.0**	**5.1**	**2.8**	**4.7**	**2.9**	**2.5**	**4.6**

a. Provisional.

Table 2.4 Gross domestic product per capita, real

	Constant prices (2000 $)											
										Annual average growth (%)		
	1980	1990	2004	2005	2006	2007	2008	2009	2010[a]	1980–89	1990–99	2000–10
SUB-SAHARAN AFRICA	**594**	**539**	**558**	**577**	**599**	**623**	**639**	**637**	**653**	**-0.9**	**-0.5**	**2.6**
Excluding South Africa	372	344	373	387	403	421	435	443	458	-0.8	-0.2	3.2
Excl. S. Africa & Nigeria	354	340	359	373	389	408	421	425	437	-0.2	-0.2	3.0
Angola	..	819	776	888	1,039	1,237	1,368	1,362	1,369	..	2.5	9.4
Benin	300	296	358	357	361	366	374	377	377	-0.2	1.4	0.8
Botswana	1,154	2,336	3,866	3,880	4,025	4,161	4,223	3,965	4,190	7.4	3.1	2.7
Burkina Faso	153	167	239	252	261	263	270	270	283	1.4	2.8	2.9
Burundi	160	182	131	128	131	133	136	137	138	1.4	-3.4	0.5
Cameroon	696	722	688	689	695	704	708	707	714	1.4	-1.5	1.0
Cape Verde	..	804	1,409	1,482	1,614	1,736	1,827	1,878	1,959	..	3.2	5.0
Central African Republic	323	278	226	227	232	236	237	236	240	-1.2	-0.8	-0.7
Chad	146	184	271	308	300	292	283	273	300	3.4	-0.5	6.1
Comoros	412	413	355	360	355	347	341	338	336	-0.3	-1.4	-0.8
Congo, Dem. Rep.	260	210	88	92	95	98	101	101	106	-1.2	-8.8	2.5
Congo, Rep.	971	1,170	1,058	1,113	1,150	1,101	1,130	1,182	1,253	2.3	-2.0	1.7
Côte d'Ivoire	909	663	580	578	572	572	575	586	588	-3.0	0.1	-0.6
Equatorial Guinea	..	555	6,468	6,889	6,774	7,995	8,603	8,845	8,537	..	15.3	12.4
Eritrea	..	..	181	179	171	168	147	148	147	..	..	-2.9
Ethiopia	..	129	138	150	163	178	192	205	221	..	-0.7	6.3
Gabon	5,265	4,627	3,988	4,029	4,000	4,143	4,162	4,028	4,214	-1.6	-0.9	0.2
Gambia, The	634	589	631	614	617	636	657	682	704	-0.8	0.1	1.4
Ghana	242	221	285	294	305	317	336	341	360	-1.1	1.7	3.4
Guinea	..	363	403	546	550	549	565	552	550	..	0.3	5.2
Guinea-Bissau	137	183	152	154	154	156	158	159	161	2.8	-1.2	-0.5
Kenya	435	450	413	426	442	461	456	456	469	0.3	-0.9	1.7
Lesotho	288	308	409	417	430	446	466	474	496	0.3	1.9	2.7
Liberia	682	192	176	187	197	217	228	246	261	-6.3	-2.4	1.7
Madagascar	360	289	239	243	247	255	265	246	243	-2.4	-1.7	0.3
Malawi	160	133	150	150	157	161	170	179	185	-2.3	1.9	2.3
Mali	212	188	243	250	255	258	263	266	273	-0.9	1.4	2.0
Mauritania	544	487	502	532	616	610	616	593	609	-0.7	0.4	3.1
Mauritius	1,573	2,575	4,266	4,284	4,420	4,651	4,876	4,998	5,181	4.8	3.7	3.1
Mozambique	203	184	292	312	324	339	354	368	384	-1.0	2.8	4.9
Namibia	2,263	1,831	2,373	2,391	2,513	2,599	2,636	2,575	2,696	-2.2	1.2	3.1
Niger	259	194	167	168	172	171	180	172	179	-2.8	-1.3	0.6
Nigeria	416	359	431	443	459	476	492	514	540	-2.3	0.1	4.1
Rwanda	264	235	255	272	290	297	321	324	337	-1.0	-1.2	4.8
São Tomé and Príncipe	..	..	..	..	..	..	..	..	..	..	..	..
Senegal	496	478	527	542	541	552	557	554	562	0.0	0.3	1.5
Seychelles	4,532	5,645	6,740	7,209	7,722	8,420	8,152	8,162	8,788	1.8	2.9	1.8
Sierra Leone	294	255	227	234	243	251	259	261	268	-1.8	-5.7	5.0
Somalia	..	..	..	..	..	..	..	..	..	..	..	..
South Africa	3,463	3,152	3,264	3,398	3,548	3,704	3,796	3,698	3,753	-0.8	-0.7	2.7
Sudan	275	267	402	418	454	487	507	514	524	0.5	2.8	4.1
Swaziland	779	1,320	1,625	1,663	1,716	1,773	1,795	1,796	1,811	4.1	1.3	2.1
Tanzania	..	305	363	380	394	411	429	442	459	..	-0.1	4.2
Togo	352	284	256	253	257	258	258	261	265	-2.1	-0.2	0.1
Uganda	..	186	293	301	323	339	357	371	380	..	3.5	4.3
Zambia	473	385	347	357	370	383	394	408	432	-1.9	-2.3	3.1
Zimbabwe	501	537	384	363	351	340	280	297	321	0.3	0.4	-6.2
NORTH AFRICA	**1,293**	**1,501**	**1,909**	**1,975**	**2,054**	**2,129**	**2,205**	**2,253**	**2,313**	**1.5**	**1.4**	**3.2**
Algeria	1,876	1,833	2,043	2,115	2,125	2,155	2,174	2,193	2,232	-0.1	-0.3	2.3
Djibouti	..	1,174	779	789	812	837	869	895	..	..	-4.7	2.0
Egypt, Arab Rep.	857	1,154	1,560	1,600	1,679	1,766	1,859	1,912	1,976	2.9	2.4	3.2
Libya	..	..	6,682	7,195	7,459	7,737	7,865	7,885	..	..	..	3.3
Morocco	1,019	1,172	1,503	1,531	1,632	1,659	1,734	1,797	1,844	1.3	0.9	3.7
Tunisia	1,495	1,661	2,576	2,654	2,776	2,922	3,023	3,084	3,144	0.6	3.0	3.7
AFRICA	**736**	**725**	**791**	**816**	**846**	**877**	**901**	**905**	**926**	**-0.1**	**0.0**	**2.6**

a. Provisional.

Table 2.5 Gross domestic product per capita growth

	Annual growth (%)											
										Annual average		
	1980	1990	2004	2005	2006	2007	2008	2009	2010[a]	1980–89	1990–99	2000–10
SUB-SAHARAN AFRICA	**1.1**	**-1.6**	**3.5**	**3.4**	**3.7**	**4.0**	**2.5**	**-0.3**	**2.4**	**-0.7**	**-0.6**	**2.2**
Excluding South Africa	-1.1	-0.6	4.4	3.8	4.0	4.5	3.3	1.7	3.4	-0.8	-0.2	2.8
Excl. S. Africa & Nigeria	-2.1	-2.2	3.3	4.1	4.2	4.8	3.3	0.9	2.9	-0.4	-0.4	2.5
Angola	..	-3.0	7.4	14.5	17.0	19.0	10.6	-0.4	0.6	1.5	-1.9	7.2
Benin	4.0	0.1	-0.2	-0.3	1.0	1.5	2.0	0.8	0.1	0.3	1.3	1.0
Botswana	7.9	3.6	4.7	0.4	3.7	3.4	1.5	-6.1	5.7	7.8	3.2	2.9
Burkina Faso	-1.6	-3.2	1.6	5.5	3.7	0.6	2.7	-0.1	4.7	1.1	2.3	2.6
Burundi	-1.8	1.0	1.8	-2.1	2.2	1.6	1.9	0.6	1.2	1.1	-2.8	0.3
Cameroon	-4.8	-8.8	1.4	0.0	1.0	1.2	0.7	-0.2	1.0	1.0	-2.1	1.1
Cape Verde	..	-0.9	2.8	5.2	8.9	7.6	5.3	2.8	4.3	4.8	2.9	5.7
Central African Republic	-7.0	-4.4	-0.6	0.7	2.0	1.9	0.2	-0.2	1.4	-1.7	-1.1	-0.6
Chad	-8.0	-7.1	29.1	13.6	-2.8	-2.6	-3.0	-3.8	10.1	2.6	-0.9	5.4
Comoros	..	2.6	-2.9	1.5	-1.5	-2.2	-1.7	-0.9	-0.5	-0.2	-0.9	-0.7
Congo, Dem. Rep.	-0.7	-9.9	3.5	4.7	2.6	3.3	3.3	0.1	4.3	-1.1	-8.4	1.0
Congo, Rep.	14.3	-1.7	1.1	5.1	3.4	-4.3	2.7	4.6	6.0	3.8	-1.9	2.3
Côte d'Ivoire	-14.9	-4.4	0.2	-0.4	-1.0	0.0	0.5	1.9	0.4	-4.1	-0.4	-1.1
Equatorial Guinea	..	0.1	33.8	6.5	-1.7	18.0	7.6	2.8	-3.5	-2.8	16.3	14.2
Eritrea	..	..	-2.6	-1.3	-4.4	-1.8	-12.5	0.8	-0.8	..	6.5	-2.7
Ethiopia	..	-0.6	10.8	9.2	8.3	9.0	8.4	6.5	7.6	-0.8	-0.5	5.7
Gabon	-0.3	1.9	-0.7	1.0	-0.7	3.6	0.4	-3.2	4.6	-1.2	-0.5	-0.1
Gambia, The	2.7	-0.5	3.9	-2.6	0.4	3.1	3.4	3.8	3.3	-0.4	0.0	1.6
Ghana	-1.9	0.5	3.1	3.4	3.9	3.9	5.9	1.6	5.5	-1.0	1.6	3.1
Guinea	..	-0.3	0.7	35.4	0.7	-0.1	2.9	-2.3	-0.3	1.5	0.2	4.1
Guinea-Bissau	-18.5	4.0	0.2	1.4	0.1	1.1	1.1	0.9	1.4	0.8	0.0	-0.1
Kenya	1.7	0.7	2.4	3.2	3.6	4.3	-1.0	0.0	2.8	0.4	-0.7	1.2
Lesotho	-5.3	4.5	1.4	1.8	3.3	3.7	4.3	1.8	4.5	-0.2	2.2	2.8
Liberia	-7.1	-50.3	-6.8	6.4	5.4	10.3	5.1	7.8	5.9	-5.9	-2.3	6.2
Madagascar	-1.8	0.1	2.1	1.5	1.9	3.1	4.0	-7.3	-1.3	-2.3	-1.5	0.0
Malawi	-2.6	2.0	2.7	-0.2	4.7	2.7	5.1	5.7	3.2	-2.3	2.2	1.6
Mali	-6.2	-3.7	-1.0	2.8	2.1	1.1	1.8	1.4	2.6	-1.2	1.0	2.3
Mauritania	0.4	-4.4	2.8	6.0	15.7	-1.0	0.9	-3.6	2.7	-0.6	0.0	1.8
Mauritius	-11.4	6.2	4.8	0.4	3.2	5.2	4.8	2.5	3.7	3.3	4.0	3.5
Mozambique	..	-0.3	5.1	6.8	3.7	4.7	4.3	3.9	4.4	-0.6	2.6	4.5
Namibia	..	-1.4	10.4	0.7	5.1	3.4	1.4	-2.3	4.7	-2.2	1.0	2.6
Niger	-5.0	-4.2	-3.3	0.9	2.1	-0.2	4.9	-4.4	4.2	-2.7	-1.5	0.4
Nigeria	1.3	5.5	7.9	2.8	3.6	3.8	3.4	4.4	5.2	-1.7	0.6	3.8
Rwanda	5.4	-2.2	5.6	7.0	6.4	2.6	7.9	1.0	4.0	-0.3	1.1	4.4
São Tomé and Príncipe	..	..	5.0	-2.9	5.1	4.4	7.4	2.3	2.7	..	..	4.2
Senegal	-5.7	-3.6	3.1	2.8	-0.2	2.1	1.0	-0.6	1.4	-0.5	-0.1	1.3
Seychelles	-5.5	6.1	-2.5	7.0	7.1	9.0	-3.2	0.1	7.7	1.2	3.3	1.8
Sierra Leone	2.6	2.1	2.7	3.0	3.8	3.5	3.0	0.9	2.7	-1.3	-4.5	5.5
Somalia	-9.0	-1.9	..	..	..	..	..	..	..	0.9	-1.9	..
South Africa	4.2	-2.3	3.3	4.1	4.4	4.4	2.5	-2.6	1.5	-0.3	-0.8	2.2
Sudan	-1.7	-7.7	-0.5	3.8	8.6	7.4	4.2	1.4	1.9	0.5	1.8	4.0
Swaziland	9.1	17.0	2.8	2.3	3.2	3.4	1.2	0.1	0.8	4.8	2.9	1.8
Tanzania	..	3.7	5.0	4.5	3.8	4.2	4.4	3.0	3.9	0.6	0.3	3.9
Togo	11.5	-2.7	-0.2	-1.1	1.8	0.1	0.2	1.0	1.5	-0.6	-0.1	-0.5
Uganda	..	2.8	3.4	2.9	7.2	5.0	5.2	3.8	2.6	-0.5	3.5	3.7
Zambia	-0.3	-3.2	3.0	2.9	3.6	3.5	2.9	3.5	5.9	-1.7	-2.2	3.0
Zimbabwe	10.4	3.9	-5.7	-5.5	-3.2	-3.3	-17.5	5.8	8.2	1.4	0.9	-4.6
NORTH AFRICA	**2.5**	**1.8**	**3.0**	**3.4**	**4.0**	**3.7**	**3.6**	**2.2**	**2.7**	**1.6**	**1.5**	**2.8**
Algeria	-2.5	-1.7	3.6	3.5	0.5	1.4	0.9	0.9	1.8	-0.3	-0.4	2.1
Djibouti	..	..	2.0	1.3	2.9	3.1	3.8	3.0	..	..	-4.5	1.5
Egypt, Arab Rep.	7.5	3.5	2.2	2.6	4.9	5.2	5.3	2.9	3.3	3.4	2.5	3.0
Libya	..	..	2.3	7.7	3.7	3.7	1.7	0.3	..	..	..	2.3
Morocco	1.0	2.1	3.6	1.9	6.6	1.6	4.5	3.7	2.6	1.4	1.2	3.5
Tunisia	4.6	5.4	5.0	3.0	4.6	5.3	3.5	2.0	1.9	1.0	3.3	3.4
AFRICA	**1.6**	**-0.5**	**3.1**	**3.2**	**3.6**	**3.7**	**2.8**	**0.5**	**2.3**	**0.1**	**0.0**	**2.2**

a. Provisional.

Table 2.6 Gross national income, nominal

	Current prices ($ millions)									Annual average growth (%)		
	1980	1990	2004	2005	2006	2007	2008	2009	2010[a]	1980–89	1990–99	2000–10
SUB-SAHARAN AFRICA	260,972	283,962	529,160	614,359	722,408	827,628	944,668	907,409	1,057,639	0.9	1.8	14.5
Excluding South Africa	185,402	176,347	314,219	372,086	466,485	551,236	679,974	630,840	701,347	-1.0	1.5	15.8
Excl. S. Africa & Nigeria	120,233	150,842	235,859	272,875	324,716	396,646	484,618	476,342	522,707	2.8	1.1	14.9
Angola	..	8,214	17,295	24,203	35,612	52,850	70,460	68,669	74,299	..	-2.4	31.4
Benin	1,402	1,806	4,006	4,259	4,623	5,428	6,672	6,618	6,576	2.1	3.7	12.7
Botswana	1,014	3,686	9,089	9,420	10,483	11,641	12,811	11,496	14,699	11.2	4.2	11.0
Burkina Faso	1,924	3,094	5,102	5,420	5,842	6,754	8,348	8,343	8,819	4.8	0.0	13.9
Burundi	922	1,117	919	1,135	1,246	1,325	1,625	1,821	2,033	1.9	-3.4	10.5
Cameroon	5,618	10,674	15,374	16,126	17,706	20,606	23,407	22,051	22,250	9.0	-2.5	10.8
Cape Verde	..	309	906	938	1,063	1,300	1,515	1,557	1,586	18.8	6.8	13.1
Central African Republic	800	1,465	1,268	1,348	1,473	1,686	1,961	1,974	1,981	7.8	-4.3	9.0
Chad	1,038	1,721	3,720	4,277	4,888	5,817	6,687	6,678	7,850	5.5	-1.3	20.1
Comoros	124	249	360	386	404	467	530	535	539	7.9	-2.0	11.1
Congo, Dem. Rep.	14,102	8,579	6,220	6,684	8,354	9,380	10,345	10,418	12,199	-6.9	-7.0	12.2
Congo, Rep.	1,544	2,324	3,159	4,032	5,105	5,774	8,768	6,979	9,024	1.9	-5.2	18.0
Côte d'Ivoire	9,680	9,209	14,763	15,643	16,589	18,913	22,434	22,031	21,925	1.3	3.3	9.8
Equatorial Guinea	..	124	2,312	4,173	5,223	6,678	11,471	9,085	9,338	..	16.9	33.8
Eritrea	..	..	1,094	1,089	1,202	1,311	1,368	1,839	2,097	..	7.3	12.6
Ethiopia	..	12,016	9,990	12,271	15,126	19,567	26,662	31,922	29,576	5.8	-5.8	17.5
Gabon	3,856	5,336	5,987	7,708	8,187	10,082	12,673	9,862	11,424	-0.1	-1.9	12.7
Gambia, The	237	291	544	593	619	786	991	940	1,011	1.6	7.1	5.4
Ghana	4,426	5,774	8,674	10,590	17,422	21,392	25,362	25,881	31,643	2.9	2.6	23.2
Guinea	..	2,518	3,391	2,647	2,501	3,814	3,340	3,710	4,297	..	3.3	3.0
Guinea-Bissau	105	233	512	561	573	687	833	824	834	3.4	-0.7	18.2
Kenya	7,043	8,224	15,955	18,732	22,433	27,093	30,473	30,543	32,040	2.6	8.3	11.8
Lesotho	695	902	1,544	1,870	1,872	2,025	2,156	2,259	2,711	-0.2	1.5	12.7
Liberia	930	..	308	394	452	585	691	735	809	-3.2	..	8.4
Madagascar	4,024	2,958	4,285	4,960	5,435	7,288	9,344	8,397	8,628	-6.0	3.8	9.3
Malawi	1,138	1,837	2,582	2,714	3,078	3,437	4,050	4,656	4,928	2.2	0.2	11.1
Mali	1,768	2,405	4,679	5,099	5,524	7,146	8,425	8,508	9,003	2.8	0.1	15.5
Mauritania	682	961	1,899	2,249	2,963	3,348	3,616	3,079	3,545	3.2	2.7	12.8
Mauritius	1,113	2,631	6,372	6,276	6,559	8,016	9,714	8,785	9,833	9.1	5.8	8.9
Mozambique	3,550	2,320	5,398	6,219	6,472	7,445	9,263	9,430	9,127	-5.6	8.6	11.0
Namibia	1,818	2,388	6,689	7,149	7,929	8,629	8,622	8,849	10,709	0.2	4.5	11.2
Niger	2,476	2,423	3,039	3,397	3,645	4,290	5,351	5,220	5,379	0.1	-1.7	12.9
Nigeria	61,079	25,585	78,110	98,881	141,275	154,068	194,690	154,005	178,059	-12.5	3.7	18.7
Rwanda	1,165	2,572	2,055	2,554	3,083	3,721	4,676	5,216	5,580	8.5	-2.0	15.1
São Tomé and Príncipe	..	..	..	112	127	149	185	198	203	..	..	13.9
Senegal	3,403	5,520	7,938	8,559	9,290	11,224	13,339	12,591	12,722	6.1	-1.6	12.5
Seychelles	142	355	666	877	976	955	894	795	896	8.9	5.9	5.0
Sierra Leone	1,071	580	1,034	1,176	1,364	1,629	1,916	1,856	1,910	-4.8	1.5	12.3
Somalia	603	835	..	..	..	..	..	..	..	5.5	..	..
South Africa	77,378	107,746	214,782	242,122	255,872	276,404	264,928	276,697	356,294	4.2	2.2	12.0
Sudan	7,570	11,409	19,991	26,052	34,081	42,631	53,132	50,018	60,403	9.7	1.9	20.5
Swaziland	..	1,174	2,423	2,762	2,962	3,095	3,015	2,827	3,472	..	4.6	10.2
Tanzania	..	4,072	12,775	13,836	14,154	16,666	20,481	21,186	22,772	..	10.6	9.2
Togo	1,096	1,598	1,904	2,080	2,165	2,493	3,148	3,137	3,150	4.6	-0.1	10.9
Uganda	1,237	4,227	7,818	8,966	9,728	11,687	14,160	15,517	16,865	20.7	9.1	12.6
Zambia	3,594	3,008	5,098	6,586	9,534	10,055	13,241	11,442	14,300	-4.1	0.8	18.6
Zimbabwe	6,530	8,512	5,522	5,479	5,131	4,928	4,191	5,636	7,278	-0.2	-1.7	-1.1
NORTH AFRICA	103,562	160,577	293,833	336,649	395,458	474,451	586,231	547,759	598,050	4.9	5.5	11.5
Algeria	41,147	59,955	81,414	97,259	112,669	134,004	169,689	139,577	155,538	4.5	-1.3	14.1
Djibouti	..	..	731	776	854	936	1,073	1,120	..	..	1.3	8.4
Egypt, Arab Rep.	21,453	42,025	78,638	89,432	108,015	131,655	164,178	189,146	214,530	7.5	11.2	9.0
Libya	..	..	33,139	43,719	57,559	74,070	93,533	61,985	..	..	..	22.8
Morocco	18,402	24,835	55,961	58,760	64,703	74,246	87,411	88,520	88,576	3.3	5.3	10.9
Tunisia	8,450	11,882	29,935	30,645	32,796	36,911	42,387	41,285	41,982	2.0	7.4	8.5
AFRICA	369,500	448,083	825,220	953,712	1,121,058	1,305,162	1,533,224	1,457,811	1,663,007	2.1	3.0	13.3

a. Provisional.

Table 2.7 Gross national income, *World Bank Atlas* method

	Current prices ($ millions)									Annual average growth (%)		
	1980	1990	2004	2005	2006	2007	2008	2009	2010[a]	1980–89	1990–99	2000–10
SUB-SAHARAN AFRICA	**253,599**	**299,653**	**464,248**	**582,188**	**686,195**	**782,645**	**900,718**	**952,737**	**1,014,422**	**1.0**	**1.5**	**14.4**
Excluding South Africa	188,984	180,486	295,562	353,255	424,704	504,622	615,609	670,550	710,604	-1.0	0.9	16.0
Excl. S. Africa & Nigeria	128,704	155,042	221,626	264,952	304,185	361,608	437,395	490,592	523,557	2.3	0.6	14.5
Angola	..	7,700	14,637	20,870	30,332	45,315	59,978	71,970	75,621	..	-2.3	33.2
Benin	1,433	1,723	3,708	4,316	4,605	5,091	6,063	6,729	6,918	1.1	3.2	12.8
Botswana	998	3,505	7,990	9,508	10,640	11,474	12,610	12,429	13,543	9.8	4.4	10.9
Burkina Faso	2,016	2,923	4,634	5,591	6,130	6,475	7,497	8,302	9,132	3.4	-1.1	13.7
Burundi	897	1,187	902	1,009	1,174	1,330	1,507	1,683	1,906	3.6	-4.1	9.3
Cameroon	5,432	11,128	14,183	16,295	17,781	19,486	21,733	23,168	23,429	8.5	-2.2	10.9
Cape Verde	..	303	838	982	1,091	1,240	1,419	1,562	1,627	18.0	7.3	12.4
Central African Republic	785	1,384	1,187	1,358	1,469	1,597	1,789	1,963	2,058	6.9	-4.1	8.7
Chad	1,086	1,591	3,254	4,219	4,625	5,212	5,846	7,149	7,987	4.4	-1.2	20.1
Comoros	..	234	326	390	411	435	483	531	550	10.5	-1.7	11.2
Congo, Dem. Rep.	17,085	8,370	6,344	6,851	7,835	8,799	9,849	10,871	11,907	-8.4	-6.3	12.2
Congo, Rep.	1,471	2,184	2,687	3,451	4,414	5,239	7,177	7,806	9,071	2.2	-5.8	19.0
Côte d'Ivoire	9,318	9,253	13,655	15,691	16,519	17,769	20,267	22,358	23,005	0.8	2.9	9.7
Equatorial Guinea	..	124	1,928	3,170	4,346	6,239	9,544	11,382	9,612	..	15.5	36.2
Eritrea	..	..	894	1,101	1,184	1,245	1,252	1,500	1,792	..	4.2	10.8
Ethiopia	..	12,200	9,954	12,197	14,297	17,647	22,781	28,571	32,342	8.9	-5.5	16.2
Gabon	3,337	4,577	5,357	7,009	7,663	9,209	10,876	11,259	11,567	0.3	-1.4	13.5
Gambia, The	243	292	590	585	622	723	871	991	1,057	0.7	10.8	3.5
Ghana	4,642	5,846	8,144	10,019	11,436	16,044	24,088	28,394	30,485	4.0	1.9	20.7
Guinea	..	2,588	3,423	3,828	3,130	3,085	3,347	3,750	3,900	..	4.2	1.5
Guinea-Bissau	115	219	359	563	592	645	730	824	875	3.4	-1.1	19.1
Kenya	7,445	8,848	16,077	18,609	20,944	24,678	28,331	30,890	32,736	2.4	5.7	11.3
Lesotho	594	879	1,213	1,744	1,908	2,001	2,238	2,314	2,395	0.9	2.4	11.9
Liberia	986	..	276	380	459	579	684	791	832	-3.6	..	7.5
Madagascar	4,018	2,785	5,184	5,377	5,352	6,359	7,906	8,431	8,820	-4.3	4.1	9.2
Malawi	1,169	1,723	2,813	2,828	3,093	3,382	3,907	4,466	4,872	2.0	0.7	11.7
Mali	1,752	2,270	4,365	5,195	5,546	6,534	7,457	8,413	9,207	1.3	0.7	15.3
Mauritania	730	984	1,810	2,186	2,703	3,095	3,570	3,468	3,465	3.2	3.8	12.6
Mauritius	1,203	2,579	6,157	6,658	6,935	7,630	8,658	9,257	9,960	7.7	6.3	8.9
Mozambique	..	2,338	5,185	6,152	6,590	7,383	8,566	9,772	10,212	-2.2	6.6	10.6
Namibia	..	2,429	..	6,864	7,966	8,566	8,971	9,100	9,695	1.9	4.7	11.4
Niger	2,442	2,368	2,812	3,347	3,703	4,044	4,819	5,163	5,640	-0.3	-2.4	12.8
Nigeria	55,749	25,519	73,419	87,688	119,713	142,057	177,029	178,734	185,766	-10.9	2.7	21.0
Rwanda	1,298	2,546	2,036	2,469	2,895	3,402	4,258	4,910	5,524	8.2	-3.5	12.7
São Tomé and Príncipe	..	..	..	113	127	144	167	189	207	..	..	13.4
Senegal	3,485	5,334	7,370	8,680	9,325	10,367	12,045	12,962	13,452	4.9	-1.6	12.3
Seychelles	134	351	680	814	943	1,041	983	907	905	9.5	5.9	6.3
Sierra Leone	1,243	802	1,086	1,200	1,341	1,543	1,789	1,946	2,011	-6.6	0.1	12.1
Somalia	656	959	..	..	..	..	..	..	..	5.9	..	..
South Africa	69,276	119,305	169,045	228,949	261,553	278,199	285,495	282,696	304,343	4.5	2.3	11.4
Sudan	9,123	13,641	18,105	23,263	29,761	37,359	47,056	52,137	56,656	9.8	-0.2	20.2
Swaziland	..	1,067	1,876	2,644	2,860	3,089	3,194	3,008	3,088	..	6.0	9.8
Tanzania	..	4,836	13,313	14,411	15,174	16,463	18,766	21,197	23,225	..	7.2	8.9
Togo	1,137	1,516	1,807	2,024	2,207	2,385	2,732	3,079	3,287	3.2	-0.3	10.3
Uganda	..	5,638	7,537	8,539	10,043	11,405	13,198	15,183	16,651	24.5	5.6	11.5
Zambia	3,610	3,491	4,648	5,695	7,249	9,088	12,066	12,573	13,816	-6.1	-0.2	18.4
Zimbabwe	6,692	9,014	5,417	5,523	5,349	5,090	4,293	4,964	6,082	0.1	-2.2	-1.9
NORTH AFRICA	**101,792**	**162,067**	**283,763**	**321,566**	**366,898**	**425,783**	**507,709**	**553,825**	**587,597**	**5.8**	**4.3**	**10.7**
Algeria	38,811	61,136	73,987	89,352	104,118	122,784	146,530	156,113	155,683	6.3	-2.5	14.4
Djibouti	..	..	754	803	864	925	1,029	1,105	..	..	0.6	8.5
Egypt, Arab Rep.	21,725	42,479	90,591	92,773	101,664	120,047	146,926	172,125	196,217	8.6	9.5	7.1
Libya	..	..	28,214	37,263	49,547	63,050	77,909	77,140	..	..	..	20.7
Morocco	18,733	24,776	53,196	60,348	66,313	70,674	80,889	89,096	92,583	1.9	4.7	10.6
Tunisia	8,689	11,648	29,106	32,058	34,159	36,428	40,266	42,799	43,709	2.0	7.2	8.4
AFRICA	**359,659**	**466,087**	**747,924**	**903,925**	**1,053,488**	**1,208,762**	**1,408,530**	**1,506,403**	**1,602,083**	**2.5**	**2.4**	**12.9**

a. Provisional.

Table

2.8 Gross national income per capita, *World Bank Atlas* method

	Current prices ($)									Annual average growth (%)		
	1980	1990	2004	2005	2006	2007	2008	2009	2010[a]	1980-89	1990-99	2000-10
SUB-SAHARAN AFRICA	**663**	**591**	**637**	**779**	**896**	**997**	**1,120**	**1,157**	**1,202**	**-1.9**	**-1.2**	**11.6**
Excluding South Africa	533	383	433	505	591	685	815	866	895	-3.8	-1.7	13.1
Excl. S. Africa & Nigeria	461	415	406	473	529	613	724	792	824	-0.7	-2.1	11.7
Angola	..	740	920	1,270	1,780	2,590	3,330	3,880	3,960	..	-5.1	29.2
Benin	400	360	500	570	590	630	730	780	780	-1.7	0.0	9.4
Botswana	1,000	2,540	4,310	5,070	5,600	5,950	6,450	6,270	6,750	6.3	1.8	9.4
Burkina Faso	280	310	340	390	420	430	480	520	550	0.8	-3.9	10.4
Burundi	220	210	130	140	160	170	190	210	230	0.1	-4.9	6.4
Cameroon	600	910	830	930	990	1,060	1,160	1,210	1,200	5.4	-4.6	8.5
Cape Verde	..	870	1,800	2,080	2,280	2,570	2,910	3,180	3,280	16.8	4.8	11.0
Central African Republic	350	470	300	340	360	380	420	450	470	4.1	-6.4	6.8
Chad	240	260	340	430	460	500	550	650	710	1.5	-4.3	16.5
Comoros	..	530	520	610	620	640	690	740	750	7.3	-4.0	8.3
Congo, Dem. Rep.	630	230	110	120	130	140	160	170	180	-11.0	-9.4	8.6
Congo, Rep.	820	910	780	980	1,220	1,400	1,870	1,980	2,240	-0.7	-8.3	16.0
Côte d'Ivoire	1,100	740	770	870	900	950	1,070	1,160	1,170	-3.1	0.0	7.8
Equatorial Guinea	..	330	3,270	5,220	6,940	9,690	14,410	16,710	13,720	..	11.8	32.2
Eritrea	..	..	210	250	250	260	250	290	340	..	1.8	6.6
Ethiopia	..	250	140	160	190	230	290	350	390	5.5	-8.1	13.3
Gabon	4,890	4,930	3,990	5,110	5,480	6,470	7,500	7,620	7,680	-2.7	-4.2	11.3
Gambia, The	390	300	400	390	400	450	530	590	610	-3.6	7.7	0.5
Ghana	430	400	390	460	520	710	1,040	1,190	1,250	0.7	-0.8	17.7
Guinea	..	450	390	420	340	330	350	380	390	..	0.0	-0.3
Guinea-Bissau	140	220	270	410	420	450	500	550	580	1.3	-3.4	16.6
Kenya	460	380	460	520	570	660	740	780	810	-1.3	2.8	8.4
Lesotho	450	540	590	840	910	950	1,050	1,080	1,100	-1.3	0.5	10.9
Liberia	510	..	90	120	140	170	190	210	210	-4.9	..	4.0
Madagascar	470	250	300	300	290	340	400	420	430	-6.8	1.0	6.0
Malawi	190	180	230	220	230	250	280	310	330	-2.5	-0.7	8.6
Mali	240	260	340	390	410	470	520	560	600	-0.5	-1.9	11.7
Mauritania	480	490	610	720	860	960	1,080	1,030	1,000	0.5	1.0	9.5
Mauritius	1,250	2,440	4,990	5,360	5,540	6,050	6,830	7,260	7,780	6.7	5.1	8.0
Mozambique	..	170	260	300	310	340	380	430	440	-2.7	3.5	7.8
Namibia	..	1,720	..	3,300	3,760	3,970	4,080	4,060	4,250	-1.8	1.7	9.3
Niger	420	300	220	260	280	290	330	340	360	-3.0	-5.6	8.7
Nigeria	740	260	540	630	840	970	1,170	1,160	1,170	-13.1	0.3	18.0
Rwanda	250	360	230	270	310	350	430	480	520	4.4	-3.7	9.9
São Tomé and Príncipe	..	..	..	740	820	920	1,050	1,170	1,250	..	..	11.5
Senegal	640	740	700	800	830	900	1,020	1,070	1,080	1.9	-4.3	9.3
Seychelles	2,080	5,020	8,240	9,820	11,150	12,240	11,300	10,390	10,460	8.6	4.3	5.5
Sierra Leone	390	200	220	230	250	280	320	340	340	-8.7	0.3	8.0
Somalia	100	150	..	..	..	..	..	..	..	6.0	..	..
South Africa	2,510	3,390	3,620	4,850	5,480	5,760	5,850	5,730	6,090	1.9	0.1	10.0
Sudan	450	510	480	610	760	930	1,140	1,230	1,300	6.8	-2.6	17.4
Swaziland	..	1,240	1,850	2,600	2,810	3,030	3,100	2,880	2,930	..	4.1	9.4
Tanzania	..	200	360	380	390	410	460	500	530	..	4.0	5.8
Togo	430	410	340	370	400	420	470	520	550	-0.2	-3.0	7.8
Uganda	..	320	270	300	340	380	420	470	500	19.7	2.2	8.0
Zambia	630	440	420	500	620	750	970	990	1,070	-9.0	-2.7	15.5
Zimbabwe	920	860	430	440	430	410	340	400	480	-3.6	-4.0	-1.9
NORTH AFRICA	**1,093**	**1,351**	**1,871**	**2,087**	**2,344**	**2,679**	**3,146**	**3,380**	**3,533**	**3.1**	**2.5**	**9.0**
Algeria	2,060	2,420	2,280	2,720	3,120	3,620	4,260	4,470	4,390	3.2	-4.4	12.7
Djibouti	..	..	950	990	1,050	1,100	1,200	1,270	..	..	-1.9	6.4
Egypt, Arab Rep.	480	750	1,240	1,250	1,350	1,560	1,880	2,160	2,420	6.1	7.6	5.2
Libya	..	..	4,990	6,460	8,410	10,470	12,670	12,320	..	..	..	18.2
Morocco	950	990	1,740	1,960	2,130	2,240	2,540	2,770	2,850	-0.6	3.1	9.4
Tunisia	1,360	1,430	2,930	3,200	3,370	3,560	3,900	4,100	4,140	-0.6	5.5	7.4
AFRICA	**756**	**744**	**849**	**1,003**	**1,142**	**1,281**	**1,459**	**1,525**	**1,586**	**-0.4**	**-0.1**	**10.4**

a. Provisional.

Table 2.9 Gross domestic product deflator (U.S. dollar series)

	Index (2000 = 100)									Annual average		
	1980	1990	2004	2005	2006	2007	2008	2009	2010[a]	1980–89	1990–99	2000–10
SUB-SAHARAN AFRICA	**119.6**	**110.0**	**137.3**	**151.0**	**165.8**	**180.4**	**196.5**	**181.7**	**202.9**	**105.7**	**109.0**	**147.4**
Excluding South Africa	146.1	116.3	133.3	149.2	172.6	192.0	223.9	195.8	207.5	119.2	104.7	154.1
Excl. S. Africa & Nigeria	125.6	126.0	128.3	139.5	157.5	178.7	207.5	190.6	200.4	115.8	113.2	146.9
Angola	..	121.2	159.7	192.8	236.4	278.9	341.2	298.8	315.7	95.2	91.5	204.5
Benin	129.6	130.7	152.7	157.2	166.8	186.8	214.1	203.3	196.5	103.3	115.9	157.2
Botswana	92.3	117.4	140.3	140.9	147.1	154.4	162.8	146.8	177.3	81.4	113.9	135.3
Burkina Faso	175.2	199.4	155.0	152.5	152.9	170.5	199.2	193.5	189.6	147.1	135.0	151.2
Burundi	139.6	111.1	97.5	120.1	126.2	128.4	150.2	162.6	174.9	130.1	104.5	120.9
Cameroon	106.3	126.8	133.5	137.2	143.9	160.2	178.6	163.7	160.7	102.4	125.2	135.3
Cape Verde	..	109.6	140.5	138.7	143.6	158.8	175.4	173.3	170.8	80.0	126.5	139.2
Central African Republic	108.4	182.6	142.3	147.7	155.7	172.4	197.6	194.0	188.3	117.3	142.8	148.8
Chad	155.4	157.2	171.6	175.7	201.7	231.6	276.9	237.6	253.5	120.8	129.0	183.6
Comoros	91.1	138.2	163.2	167.2	172.0	197.4	222.9	221.1	218.9	89.0	124.6	166.3
Congo, Dem. Rep.	205.2	122.1	132.3	135.6	157.6	168.3	184.8	172.5	188.3	132.9	126.4	145.5
Congo, Rep.	97.7	100.1	127.5	154.8	185.3	204.4	273.5	205.9	237.0	83.5	80.5	159.8
Côte d'Ivoire	131.7	130.1	150.5	157.1	165.6	185.6	214.5	203.4	197.5	108.1	122.6	156.7
Equatorial Guinea	..	63.7	137.4	196.3	226.5	244.3	323.3	203.0	242.5	54.3	64.8	177.6
Eritrea	..	..	141.9	137.0	152.6	163.7	190.0	246.1	274.5	..	98.6	154.0
Ethiopia	..	193.8	100.6	110.1	122.5	141.7	174.2	192.1	162.3	166.9	150.9	125.4
Gabon	119.1	138.5	133.9	156.9	170.8	196.2	240.7	183.9	208.1	96.3	104.2	153.8
Gambia, The	60.4	55.7	62.8	68.9	69.9	82.3	96.4	85.7	86.3	48.5	113.4	78.8
Ghana	168.4	180.2	147.6	168.5	301.1	341.7	365.0	319.6	366.5	176.5	165.6	223.7
Guinea	..	127.7	102.3	59.5	55.7	81.7	69.9	77.3	86.2	117.0	136.2	83.0
Guinea-Bissau	96.6	131.1	256.6	271.8	268.7	310.9	369.3	353.4	341.8	105.0	116.2	245.9
Kenya	102.7	81.5	112.3	123.5	139.5	157.8	174.1	170.0	169.6	85.9	86.2	132.2
Lesotho	114.5	107.2	147.3	159.0	159.2	169.9	164.1	167.9	202.5	95.1	120.3	141.4
Liberia	65.1	94.1	86.0	91.2	92.5	97.9	101.9	93.2	94.9	75.0	107.2	88.3
Madagascar	130.4	94.4	105.2	116.1	121.0	151.7	181.1	171.5	173.5	107.7	101.0	135.6
Malawi	123.8	151.3	140.0	143.2	150.4	157.7	171.5	182.5	183.2	118.0	132.4	147.9
Mali	116.4	148.5	157.0	161.1	169.1	197.5	230.0	225.8	224.3	108.1	131.8	165.8
Mauritania	85.9	104.8	123.2	134.7	157.7	171.3	176.8	151.1	171.5	90.7	122.8	135.9
Mauritius	74.8	97.3	121.4	118.0	117.5	132.9	155.9	138.5	146.4	71.7	106.4	121.7
Mozambique	143.2	98.6	96.3	101.5	102.9	108.6	125.2	115.2	102.6	157.3	92.8	100.4
Namibia	94.6	90.7	136.2	146.0	149.9	157.0	152.4	154.7	180.9	78.9	96.9	138.1
Niger	164.7	164.6	146.0	155.8	157.7	179.5	206.6	204.0	194.5	137.0	126.8	153.2
Nigeria	204.1	81.4	149.6	181.3	223.4	237.1	279.2	212.4	230.0	127.0	75.6	178.6
Rwanda	85.0	154.5	91.1	103.0	113.7	129.4	146.7	157.1	156.9	111.6	123.4	113.8
São Tomé and Príncipe	..	..	..	..	..	..	..	..	..	..	..	..
Senegal	130.6	165.1	143.9	147.9	155.2	178.7	203.8	190.4	184.1	119.9	135.6	149.2
Seychelles	50.5	93.3	125.8	153.4	156.1	142.3	135.8	118.1	126.7	64.8	102.7	127.2
Sierra Leone	118.5	64.0	97.4	102.8	109.9	120.8	134.5	123.8	121.3	98.2	98.6	110.0
Somalia	..	..	..	..	..	..	..	..	..	..	..	..
South Africa	84.5	101.0	143.8	154.1	154.1	160.1	147.9	155.2	193.7	88.1	115.4	135.4
Sudan	137.9	175.7	143.7	170.7	203.8	236.6	276.2	250.1	293.6	195.6	121.9	182.2
Swaziland	115.4	97.9	146.6	152.7	168.7	168.8	163.1	157.4	193.4	86.8	110.6	139.2
Tanzania	..	56.4	96.2	98.8	93.8	102.8	117.7	114.6	114.8	68.9	71.7	102.0
Togo	121.0	156.2	143.3	154.6	154.8	173.3	212.2	205.1	199.0	109.1	134.3	153.7
Uganda	..	130.7	98.6	107.8	105.1	115.8	129.1	131.8	135.4	152.8	106.6	107.7
Zambia	142.3	108.6	140.0	175.4	246.1	250.0	300.0	246.6	289.8	110.8	110.9	189.0
Zimbabwe	182.8	156.2	120.1	126.3	123.7	124.8	126.5	157.8	185.4	163.2	122.9	125.3
NORTH AFRICA	**92.9**	**95.8**	**98.7**	**108.0**	**118.8**	**133.9**	**157.8**	**142.2**	**152.5**	**90.6**	**92.3**	**116.9**
Algeria	120.0	133.8	128.4	147.1	165.1	185.8	228.5	180.2	204.6	128.0	100.6	149.4
Djibouti	..	68.5	107.7	111.1	115.0	120.6	132.1	134.4	..	..	84.7	112.9
Egypt, Arab Rep.	59.5	65.8	69.4	75.5	84.7	96.0	111.8	124.0	136.6	62.3	76.0	95.6
Libya	..	..	88.4	106.0	128.5	154.1	192.6	126.3	..	..	93.3	111.2
Morocco	93.7	88.1	124.2	126.1	129.0	144.0	161.1	157.3	151.6	72.5	98.7	127.3
Tunisia	91.6	90.7	121.9	121.3	122.3	130.3	143.7	135.2	133.4	80.1	103.5	120.1
AFRICA	**110.4**	**104.0**	**121.1**	**133.1**	**146.3**	**161.2**	**180.5**	**165.2**	**182.2**	**99.9**	**102.0**	**134.7**

a. Provisional.

Table 2.10 Consumer price Index

	Index (2005 = 100)											
										Annual average		
	1980	1990	2004	2005	2006	2007	2008	2009	2010[a]	1980–89	1990–99	2000–10
SUB-SAHARAN AFRICA	**8.9**	**35.5**	**93.5**	**100.0**	**106.5**	**113.0**	**127.1**	**135.9**	**140.7**	**19.0**	**54.1**	**104.5**
Excluding South Africa	9.3	37.8	93.3	100.0	106.6	113.8	127.3	136.9	140.8	20.0	54.2	104.3
Excl. S. Africa & Nigeria	10.0	38.1	93.5	100.0	106.5	113.0	127.2	135.9	140.7	21.0	54.9	104.5
Angola	..	0.0	81.3	100.0	113.3	127.2	143.1	162.7	186.2	..	0.2	92.6
Benin	..	..	94.9	100.0	103.8	105.1	113.5	115.9	118.6	..	68.6	101.5
Botswana	9.3	25.3	92.1	100.0	111.6	119.5	134.6	145.4	155.5	15.4	43.8	105.9
Burkina Faso	39.6	56.6	94.0	100.0	102.3	102.1	113.0	115.9	115.0	51.8	71.4	100.5
Burundi	8.3	17.1	88.1	100.0	102.8	111.4	138.2	153.4	163.2	12.0	32.0	105.1
Cameroon	25.1	54.8	98.0	100.0	105.1	106.1	111.8	115.2	116.6	41.8	71.1	103.0
Cape Verde	..	58.2	99.6	100.0	105.4	110.0	117.5	118.6	121.1	45.1	77.1	106.2
Central African Republic	45.5	61.5	97.2	100.0	106.7	107.7	117.7	121.8	123.6	58.3	74.8	104.7
Chad	..	50.8	92.7	100.0	108.0	98.3	108.5	119.3	116.8	50.5	67.3	101.8
Comoros	..	..	97.1	100.0	103.4	108.0	109.8	114.6	118.5	..	..	100.2
Congo, Dem. Rep.	0.0	0.0	82.4	100.0	113.1	132.2	155.1	..	..	0.0	0.3	88.6
Congo, Rep.	..	45.6	97.0	100.0	106.5	109.4	117.4	123.6	129.8	44.2	63.5	105.1
Côte d'Ivoire	28.8	47.5	96.3	100.0	102.5	104.4	111.0	112.1	114.0	38.5	65.7	100.1
Equatorial Guinea	..	38.4	94.7	100.0	104.4	107.3	114.4	119.7	129.1	39.6	52.0	99.6
Eritrea	..	..	..	..	..	..	..	..	..	..	..	..
Ethiopia	25.8	39.7	89.6	100.0	112.3	131.7	190.1	206.2	223.0	31.8	64.5	124.1
Gabon	41.6	73.3	96.4	100.0	98.6	103.6	109.0	111.1	112.7	59.8	78.8	100.7
Gambia, The	8.4	41.5	95.4	100.0	102.1	107.5	112.3	117.4	123.4	19.4	53.9	94.7
Ghana	0.1	4.1	86.9	100.0	110.9	122.8	143.1	170.7	188.9	1.2	14.7	104.9
Guinea	..	..	76.1	100.0	134.7	165.5	195.9	205.1	236.8	..	..	159.1
Guinea-Bissau	..	5.4	96.8	100.0	102.0	106.7	117.8	115.9	118.8	2.6	42.0	103.9
Kenya	5.0	15.6	90.7	100.0	114.5	125.6	158.6	173.2	180.1	8.7	41.0	112.6
Lesotho	10.8	37.8	96.7	100.0	106.1	114.6	126.9	135.9	140.8	20.4	58.8	103.2
Liberia	..	..	90.2	100.0	107.3	119.6	140.5	150.9	..	..	..	103.8
Madagascar	2.6	13.1	84.4	100.0	110.8	122.2	133.5	145.4	158.9	6.6	31.7	102.7
Malawi	0.7	3.3	86.7	100.0	114.0	123.0	133.8	145.0	155.8	1.5	14.4	101.7
Mali	..	61.6	94.0	100.0	101.5	103.0	112.4	114.9	116.2	61.2	75.1	101.8
Mauritania	..	39.4	89.2	100.0	106.2	114.0	122.3	125.0	132.9	31.9	53.8	99.3
Mauritius	18.6	40.9	95.3	100.0	108.9	118.5	130.1	133.4	137.2	27.1	56.5	105.7
Mozambique	..	4.4	93.3	100.0	113.2	122.5	135.1	139.5	157.3	1.7	27.6	103.3
Namibia	..	..	97.8	100.0	105.1	112.1	123.7	134.6	140.6	..	..	110.6
Niger	47.9	59.1	92.8	100.0	100.0	100.1	111.4	116.2	117.1	62.5	70.3	100.4
Nigeria	0.7	3.9	84.8	100.0	108.2	114.1	127.3	142.0	161.4	1.5	22.9	98.4
Rwanda	12.4	19.0	91.7	100.0	108.9	118.8	137.1	151.3	154.8	16.1	46.4	106.1
São Tomé and Príncipe	..	..	85.3	100.0	124.6	158.9	198.3	230.3	259.9	..	39.0	128.8
Senegal	35.2	62.1	98.3	100.0	102.1	108.1	114.3	113.1	114.5	53.3	77.4	103.2
Seychelles	51.7	69.6	99.1	100.0	99.7	105.0	143.8	189.4	184.8	61.2	74.8	117.2
Sierra Leone	..	..	..	..	100.0	111.7	128.2	140.1	163.4	..	..	128.7
Somalia	..	..	..	..	..	..	..	..	..	..	..	..
South Africa	8.5	33.2	96.7	100.0	104.6	112.1	125.0	133.9	139.6	16.8	54.3	105.3
Sudan	0.0	0.4	92.2	100.0	107.2	115.8	132.3	147.2	166.3	0.1	22.8	106.1
Swaziland	7.7	29.5	95.4	100.0	105.3	113.8	128.2	137.8	144.0	15.5	46.2	104.7
Tanzania	0.9	12.8	95.2	100.0	107.3	114.8	126.6	142.0	150.8	3.8	40.6	106.7
Togo	32.2	46.2	93.6	100.0	102.2	103.2	112.2	114.4	116.5	43.4	66.4	100.8
Uganda	0.1	32.3	92.2	100.0	107.3	113.9	127.6	144.2	150.0	4.7	59.8	106.2
Zambia	..	0.4	84.5	100.0	109.0	120.6	135.7	153.8	166.9	0.1	12.0	99.0
Zimbabwe	0.0	0.0	24.9	100.0	1,196.7	..	..	..	..	0.0	0.1	190.0
NORTH AFRICA	**31.5**	**56.6**	**97.7**	**100.0**	**103.4**	**107.9**	**116.2**	**119.8**	**123.7**	**43.3**	**72.3**	**103.2**
Algeria	7.5	19.0	98.6	100.0	102.3	106.1	111.2	117.6	122.2	11.6	54.9	101.8
Djibouti	92.3	..	97.0	100.0	103.5	108.6	121.6	123.7	128.5	102.5	..	104.6
Egypt, Arab Rep.	7.0	33.2	95.4	100.0	107.6	117.7	139.2	155.6	173.1	14.7	57.5	110.4
Libya	34.6	72.6	97.4	100.0	101.5	107.8	119.0	121.9	124.9	52.8	104.3	110.1
Morocco	31.5	63.4	99.0	100.0	103.3	105.4	109.3	110.4	111.5	47.2	80.4	101.8
Tunisia	..	56.6	98.0	100.0	104.5	108.1	113.4	117.4	122.6	43.2	72.3	102.6
AFRICA	**9.3**	**37.8**	**94.3**	**100.0**	**106.1**	**111.9**	**125.8**	**133.9**	**138.4**	**20.6**	**56.2**	**104.4**

a. Provisional.

Table 2.11 Consumer price index, growth

	Annual growth (%)									Annual average		
	1980	1990	2004	2005	2006	2007	2008	2009	2010[a]	1980–89	1990–99	2000–10
SUB-SAHARAN AFRICA	..	..	..	..	..	..	..	..	..	..	..	..
Angola	..	..	43.5	23.0	13.3	12.3	12.5	13.7	14.5	..	1,122.5	74.3
Benin	..	..	0.9	5.4	3.8	1.3	8.0	2.2	2.3	..	9.7	3.3
Botswana	13.6	11.4	7.0	8.6	11.6	7.1	12.7	8.0	7.0	10.8	10.8	8.6
Burkina Faso	12.2	-0.5	-0.4	6.4	2.3	-0.2	10.7	2.6	-0.8	5.0	4.5	2.7
Burundi	2.5	7.0	7.9	13.5	2.8	8.3	24.1	11.0	6.4	7.2	13.5	10.6
Cameroon	9.6	1.1	0.2	2.0	5.1	0.9	5.3	3.0	1.3	9.1	5.6	2.5
Cape Verde	..	10.7	-1.9	0.4	5.4	4.4	6.8	1.0	2.1	6.7	6.4	2.0
Central African Republic	..	0.0	-2.1	2.9	6.7	0.9	9.3	3.5	1.5	3.7	3.9	3.3
Chad	..	-0.7	-5.4	7.9	8.0	-9.0	10.3	10.0	-2.1	3.0	5.5	3.6
Comoros	..	..	4.5	3.0	3.4	4.5	1.7	4.4	3.4	..	..	3.8
Congo, Dem. Rep.	46.6	81.3	4.0	21.3	13.1	17.0	17.3	..	..	57.0	3,367.2	110.1
Congo, Rep.	..	2.9	2.4	3.1	6.5	2.7	7.3	5.3	5.0	1.0	8.5	3.2
Côte d'Ivoire	14.7	-0.8	1.4	3.9	2.5	1.9	6.3	1.0	1.7	6.8	6.0	2.9
Equatorial Guinea	..	0.9	4.2	5.6	4.4	2.8	6.6	4.7	7.8	-5.5	6.6	5.9
Eritrea	..	..	..	..	..	..	..	..	..	..	..	..
Ethiopia	4.5	5.2	3.3	11.6	12.3	17.2	44.4	8.5	8.1	4.6	8.0	10.7
Gabon	12.3	7.7	0.4	3.7	-1.4	5.0	5.3	1.9	1.5	6.5	3.7	1.9
Gambia, The	6.8	12.2	14.2	4.8	2.1	5.4	4.5	4.6	5.1	17.5	5.4	6.5
Ghana	50.1	37.3	12.6	15.1	10.9	10.7	16.5	19.3	10.7	48.3	27.6	17.8
Guinea	..	..	..	31.4	34.7	22.8	18.4	4.7	15.5	..	..	21.2
Guinea-Bissau	..	33.0	0.9	3.3	2.0	4.6	10.5	-1.7	2.5	70.5	37.5	3.1
Kenya	13.9	17.8	11.6	10.3	14.5	9.8	26.2	9.2	4.0	11.8	17.4	10.3
Lesotho	16.3	11.6	5.0	3.4	6.1	8.0	10.7	7.2	3.6	13.9	12.4	7.4
Liberia	..	..	7.8	10.8	7.3	11.4	17.5	7.4	..	..	..	10.9
Madagascar	18.2	11.8	13.8	18.5	10.8	10.3	9.2	9.0	9.3	18.6	17.3	10.4
Malawi	..	11.8	11.4	15.4	14.0	8.0	8.7	8.4	7.4	16.8	31.0	13.6
Mali	..	0.6	-3.1	6.4	1.5	1.4	9.2	2.2	1.1	-0.1	4.2	2.5
Mauritania	..	6.6	10.4	12.1	6.2	7.3	7.4	2.2	6.3	7.5	6.4	6.3
Mauritius	42.0	13.5	4.7	4.9	8.9	8.8	9.7	2.6	2.9	11.2	7.6	5.7
Mozambique	..	47.0	12.7	7.2	13.2	8.2	10.3	3.3	12.7	45.1	34.5	10.9
Namibia	..	..	4.2	2.3	5.1	6.7	10.4	8.8	4.5	..	..	6.1
Niger	10.3	-0.8	0.3	7.8	0.0	0.1	11.3	4.3	0.8	3.6	4.3	3.0
Nigeria	10.0	7.4	15.0	17.9	8.2	5.4	11.6	11.5	13.7	20.9	30.6	12.4
Rwanda	7.3	4.2	12.3	9.0	8.9	9.1	15.4	10.4	2.3	4.7	8.6	7.6
São Tomé and Príncipe	..	..	15.2	17.2	24.6	27.6	24.8	16.1	12.9	..	38.0	16.0
Senegal	8.7	0.3	0.5	1.7	2.1	5.9	5.8	-1.1	1.3	6.9	4.5	2.0
Seychelles	13.6	3.9	3.9	0.9	-0.4	5.3	37.0	31.8	-2.4	4.1	2.0	8.3
Sierra Leone	..	..	..	..	..	11.7	14.8	9.3	16.6	..	..	13.1
Somalia	..	..	..	..	..	..	..	..	..	..	..	..
South Africa	13.7	14.3	1.4	3.4	4.6	7.1	11.5	7.1	4.3	14.6	9.9	6.0
Sudan	25.4	65.2	8.4	8.5	7.2	8.0	14.3	11.3	13.0	36.2	80.4	9.1
Swaziland	18.7	13.1	3.5	4.8	5.3	8.1	12.7	7.5	4.5	15.0	9.5	7.6
Tanzania	30.2	35.8	4.7	5.0	7.3	7.0	10.3	12.1	6.2	30.1	23.1	6.8
Togo	12.3	1.0	0.4	6.8	2.2	1.0	8.7	2.0	1.8	5.0	7.1	2.8
Uganda	..	33.1	3.7	8.5	7.3	6.1	12.1	13.0	4.0	111.2	13.0	6.2
Zambia	..	107.0	18.0	18.3	9.0	10.7	12.5	13.4	8.5	69.3	76.2	16.5
Zimbabwe	5.4	17.4	282.4	302.1	1,096.7	..	..	..	..	12.8	28.6	340.8
NORTH AFRICA	..	..	..	..	..	..	..	..	..	..	..	..
Algeria	9.5	16.7	4.0	1.4	2.3	3.7	4.9	5.7	3.9	9.0	18.6	3.3
Djibouti	12.1	..	3.1	3.1	3.5	5.0	12.0	1.7	4.0	5.3	..	3.7
Egypt, Arab Rep.	20.8	16.8	11.3	4.9	7.6	9.3	18.3	11.8	11.3	17.4	10.5	7.9
Libya	9.7	8.5	-2.2	2.7	1.5	6.3	10.4	2.5	2.5	7.9	6.7	0.0
Morocco	9.4	6.8	1.5	1.0	3.3	2.0	3.7	1.0	1.0	7.6	4.4	1.8
Tunisia	..	6.6	3.6	2.0	4.5	3.4	4.9	3.5	4.4	7.6	4.9	3.4
AFRICA	..	..	..	..	..	..	..	..	..	..	..	..

a. Provisional.

Table 2.12 Price indices

	Inflation, GDP deflator (annual %)				Consumer price index (2005 = 100)				Exports price index (goods and services, 2000 = 100)		Imports price index (goods and services, 2000 = 100)	
	Annual %		Annual Average				Annual Average					
	2009	2010[a]	1990–99	2000–10	2009	2010[a]	1990–99	2000–10	2009	2010[a]	2009	2010[a]
SUB-SAHARAN AFRICA	**4.2**	**7.0**	**9.4**	**6.7**	**135.9**	**140.7**	**54.1**	**104.5**	**..**	**..**	**157.1**	**176.3**
Excluding South Africa	4.2	6.9	9.4	6.8	136.9	140.8	54.2	104.3	..	..	..	..
Excl. S. Africa & Nigeria	4.2	6.7	9.2	6.6	135.9	140.7	54.9	104.5	..	..	161.1	..
Angola	-7.4	22.4	1,178.8	79.9	162.7	186.2	0.2	92.6	..	..	..	..
Benin	0.1	1.4	7.4	3.2	115.9	118.6	68.6	101.5	..	..	..	..
Botswana	-5.5	14.6	9.6	8.5	145.4	155.5	43.8	105.9	143.1	161.7	168.3	185.2
Burkina Faso	2.4	2.8	3.2	2.4	115.9	115.0	71.4	100.5	..	..	..	..
Burundi	12.3	7.6	11.9	13.8	153.4	163.2	32.0	105.1	..	..	..	..
Cameroon	-3.4	3.0	5.6	2.1	115.2	116.6	71.1	103.0	271.8	300.1	258.5	247.0
Cape Verde	4.2	3.3	7.1	0.7	118.6	121.1	77.1	106.2	236.6	213.4	143.7	134.1
Central African Republic	3.5	1.8	3.8	2.8	121.8	123.6	74.8	104.7	..	..	..	..
Chad	-9.6	11.9	6.4	6.0	119.3	116.8	67.3	101.8	..	..	..	..
Comoros	4.6	3.8	3.5	4.2	114.6	118.5	..	100.2	..	..	..	..
Congo, Dem. Rep.	35.1	22.1	3,658.0	98.3	..	..	0.3	88.6	135.1	158.1	111.6	122.3
Congo, Rep.	-20.6	20.7	6.9	10.0	123.6	129.8	63.5	105.1	..	..	..	..
Côte d'Ivoire	0.0	1.9	7.5	2.9	112.1	114.0	65.7	100.1	158.6	152.7	165.0	161.2
Equatorial Guinea	-33.8	25.3	12.8	11.1	119.7	129.1	52.0	99.6	..	..	..	..
Eritrea	29.5	11.6	6.2	17.1	..	..	..	..	..	..	..	..
Ethiopia	24.2	3.9	7.2	10.1	206.2	223.0	64.5	124.1	155.4	136.3	134.8	121.6
Gabon	-19.4	18.6	6.8	6.5	111.1	112.7	78.8	100.7	204.4	260.2	152.6	166.6
Gambia, The	6.7	5.9	16.6	6.3	117.4	123.4	53.9	94.7	139.9	140.8	161.1	162.1
Ghana	16.6	16.5	25.8	26.7	170.7	188.9	14.7	104.9	..	..	..	..
Guinea	6.8	20.2	8.6	11.5	205.1	236.8	..	159.1	179.2	174.3	181.3	180.6
Guinea-Bissau	1.1	1.7	36.7	10.9	115.9	118.8	42.0	103.9	..	..	..	..
Kenya	9.2	2.2	16.1	5.9	173.2	180.1	41.0	112.6	171.7	176.9	145.3	152.4
Lesotho	5.0	4.2	10.6	7.4	135.9	140.8	58.8	103.2	91.7	109.0	98.0	113.0
Liberia	-1.2	6.4	380.9	4.2	150.9	..	..	103.8	70.0	92.8	289.3	305.7
Madagascar	8.4	8.1	18.1	10.2	145.4	158.9	31.7	102.7	135.3	..	153.3	..
Malawi	6.9	7.0	29.9	18.7	145.0	155.8	14.4	101.7	..	..	..	..
Mali	3.5	4.2	6.1	4.7	114.9	116.2	75.1	101.8	..	..	..	..
Mauritania	-5.9	19.4	11.2	7.2	125.0	132.9	53.8	99.3	275.3	361.5	127.8	137.7
Mauritius	-0.2	1.8	7.0	5.3	133.4	137.2	56.5	105.7	129.6	138.9	165.7	186.3
Mozambique	4.2	10.0	36.7	8.8	139.5	157.3	27.6	103.3	83.5	82.4	169.3	164.8
Namibia	4.2	1.0	9.4	8.6	134.6	140.6	..	110.6	183.3	350.3	132.6	276.5
Niger	4.1	0.0	4.5	3.2	116.2	117.1	70.3	100.4	..	..	..	..
Nigeria	-4.5	9.3	29.2	15.7	142.0	161.4	22.9	98.4	..	..	..	..
Rwanda	11.3	2.5	14.3	8.1	151.3	154.8	46.4	106.1	..	..	..	..
São Tomé and Príncipe	13.6	11.7	..	14.4	230.3	259.9	39.0	128.8	..	..	..	..
Senegal	-1.5	1.4	4.9	2.5	113.1	114.5	77.4	103.2	177.6	171.9	193.3	187.8
Seychelles	25.2	-4.9	1.9	10.1	189.4	184.8	74.8	117.2	73.1	..	73.1	..
Sierra Leone	5.2	14.4	46.0	8.6	140.1	163.4	..	128.7	..	..	..	..
Somalia	..	..	215.5	..	..	..	..	..	..	..	..	..
South Africa	7.7	7.9	11.0	7.6	133.9	139.6	54.3	105.3	193.3	237.0	153.0	174.7
Sudan	-0.3	17.6	73.9	10.2	147.2	166.3	22.8	106.1	..	..	..	..
Swaziland	-1.0	6.2	12.7	7.7	137.8	144.0	46.2	104.7	101.6	122.9	102.2	123.6
Tanzania	7.4	6.9	23.7	7.3	142.0	150.8	40.6	106.7	125.9	158.4	105.5	125.5
Togo	1.9	1.8	6.6	2.8	114.4	116.5	66.4	100.8	203.0	208.6	279.6	306.0
Uganda	14.6	9.5	17.8	6.8	144.2	150.0	59.8	106.2	99.5	102.6	148.0	144.1
Zambia	10.7	11.7	70.1	17.5	153.8	166.9	12.0	99.0	..	..	..	..
Zimbabwe	24.7	17.5	(3.9)	6.1	..	..	0.1	190.0	191.0	239.7	183.9	219.2
NORTH AFRICA	**1.6**	**7.4**	**6.0**	**5.1**	**119.8**	**123.7**	**72.3**	**103.2**	**..**	**..**	**140.9**	**147.2**
Algeria	-11.3	16.3	21.6	9.2	117.6	122.2	54.9	101.8	154.4	..	141.6	..
Djibouti	1.7	..	4.0	3.3	123.7	128.5	..	104.6	..	..	..	..
Egypt, Arab Rep.	11.2	10.1	10.3	8.0	155.6	173.1	57.5	110.4	94.6	96.6	105.1	103.9
Libya	-32.8	..	..	16.0	121.9	124.9	104.3	110.1	..	..	..	..
Morocco	1.5	0.7	4.6	1.6	110.4	111.5	80.4	101.8	162.1	160.1	160.1	167.4
Tunisia	3.1	4.6	5.7	3.4	117.4	122.6	72.3	102.6	174.7	183.4	172.9	190.9
AFRICA	**3.8**	**7.0**	**8.5**	**6.4**	**133.9**	**138.4**	**56.2**	**104.4**	**..**	**..**	**150.2**	**165.5**

a. Provisional.

Table

2.13 Gross domestic savings

	Share of GDP (%)											
										Annual average		
	1980	1990	2004	2005	2006	2007	2008	2009	2010[a]	1980–89	1990–99	2000–10
SUB-SAHARAN AFRICA	**25.3**	**17.2**	**15.8**	**15.8**	**15.9**	**16.6**	**16.3**	**15.1**	**16.8**	**20.1**	**15.5**	**16.1**
Excluding South Africa	11.7	11.9	14.1	14.4	14.6	15.0	13.5	11.5	..	11.9	11.9	13.7
Excl. S. Africa & Nigeria	11.7	11.9	14.1	14.4	14.6	15.0	13.5	11.5	14.4	11.9	11.9	13.8
Angola	..	29.7	25.1	41.3	56.2	43.9	41.3	14.7	32.0	24.0	22.0	32.2
Benin	-6.4	2.2	5.5	6.9	6.9	6.1	7.1	10.8	12.3	-2.4	3.8	7.1
Botswana	26.7	42.6	40.5	43.1	40.0	39.3	32.0	21.5	22.5	35.3	38.8	36.0
Burkina Faso	-7.2	5.4	1.8	4.8	2.8	..	..	..	..	-1.6	9.0	2.6
Burundi	-0.6	-5.4	-7.5	-12.1	-14.5	-17.9	-16.6	-9.3	-12.4	3.1	-5.3	-10.9
Cameroon	21.7	20.7	18.5	18.1	18.9	18.5	..	..	..	24.2	18.5	18.8
Cape Verde	..	25.3	1.9	7.2	10.5	12.0	13.2	6.8	18.3	29.8	7.0	5.6
Central African Republic	-8.9	-0.6	0.0	0.1	1.4	1.5	-1.3	2.7	..	-1.1	3.7	1.9
Chad	..	-7.7	24.5	35.1	36.4	20.5	27.4	5.7	10.7	-8.1	-0.5	13.5
Comoros	-10.1	-3.2	-8.5	-12.3	-14.8	-15.4	-20.1	-21.1	..	-4.5	-4.9	-11.1
Congo, Dem. Rep.	10.1	9.4	4.0	5.9	-0.6	8.7	8.6	15.3	..	10.9	8.8	5.9
Congo, Rep.	35.7	23.8	52.2	49.8	40.2	46.8	46.5	42.7	50.9	31.9	28.8	47.3
Côte d'Ivoire	20.4	11.3	20.0	17.2	19.6	14.6	17.9	19.4	18.9	19.6	17.8	19.3
Equatorial Guinea	..	-20.1	78.9	83.7	86.1	86.9	73.1	58.8	58.5	..	13.7	76.4
Eritrea	..	..	-35.1	-29.0	-18.2	-18.4	..	..	..	..	-29.7	-28.2
Ethiopia	..	9.7	8.8	2.6	1.5	4.2	0.4	4.1	0.4	10.5	9.7	5.3
Gabon	60.6	36.9	54.6	58.4	56.0	55.3	59.0	44.6	51.9	44.3	43.6	52.9
Gambia, The	5.8	10.7	9.7	5.1	10.7	5.7	-1.3	2.9	2.4	6.5	3.9	4.4
Ghana	4.9	5.5	7.3	3.7	6.1	3.8	2.0	9.9	15.0	4.8	7.5	6.8
Guinea	..	22.2	18.4	18.3	13.9	9.7	10.3	16.6	16.0	16.6	18.3	15.1
Guinea-Bissau	-1.0	2.8	..	..	..	..	..	..	..	-0.9	1.5	-13.2
Kenya	18.1	18.5	10.7	9.5	7.2	8.1	5.1	6.9	9.0	18.3	14.6	8.4
Lesotho	-52.0	-49.1	-46.8	-50.0	-44.9	-41.7	-36.9	-41.7	-42.1	-69.5	-36.6	-37.2
Liberia	5.0	..	-34.6	-39.1	-87.5	-61.9	-76.1	-55.8	-49.9	-8.0	..	-29.3
Madagascar	-1.4	5.6	8.5	4.9	9.3	10.6	10.0	9.0	..	2.9	4.2	9.2
Malawi	10.8	13.4	0.0	-5.5	1.2	14.4	4.5	9.0	8.2	12.7	3.4	4.1
Mali	1.1	6.4	8.6	11.0	14.8	13.0	..	..	..	-0.4	7.6	12.2
Mauritania	-3.5	4.9	6.3	9.7	25.8	18.5	12.5	13.9	15.7	3.1	10.8	10.5
Mauritius	10.4	23.0	22.1	16.5	15.3	17.6	14.1	11.9	12.5	20.3	24.1	19.3
Mozambique	-8.9	-5.8	7.7	6.5	8.8	6.3	1.6	2.2	6.0	-6.2	-2.9	6.0
Namibia	38.4	18.2	16.8	19.8	20.6	22.4	21.8	14.3	26.9	10.8	12.7	18.1
Niger	14.6	1.2	3.9	13.4	..	..	..	..	..	7.3	2.7	5.9
Nigeria	..	..	..	..	..	..	..	..	..	..	..	..
Rwanda	4.2	6.2	1.4	2.0	1.8	3.5	7.0	4.2	1.2	5.0	-5.5	2.3
São Tomé and Príncipe	..	..	..	..	..	..	..	..	..	..	..	..
Senegal	2.1	2.4	7.9	14.2	10.8	8.6	3.9	9.3	10.8	4.3	5.4	9.2
Seychelles	27.1	20.3	14.7	6.6	12.8	-1.7	5.8	14.5	..	24.1	21.7	14.0
Sierra Leone	0.9	8.7	-0.4	4.1	7.6	6.1	1.7	2.3	3.3	9.1	2.8	-1.2
Somalia	-12.9	-12.5	..	..	..	..	..	..	..	-6.3	-12.5	..
South Africa	37.9	23.2	17.8	17.5	17.2	18.3	19.1	18.7	19.1	28.5	19.4	18.6
Sudan	2.1	8.2	18.7	19.0	18.6	26.7	26.8	19.4	24.2	4.2	9.6	18.9
Swaziland	1.2	5.3	12.7	10.9	10.4	11.0	1.7	-2.0	-2.3	3.7	2.0	8.2
Tanzania	..	1.3	16.2	16.2	14.5	12.8	16.1	17.1	17.2	..	2.9	14.8
Togo	23.2	14.7	-4.8	-2.3	-1.1	-1.9	0.9	2.4	2.4	12.3	6.7	0.1
Uganda	-0.4	0.6	10.1	11.7	8.1	8.8	15.3	12.7	13.3	2.3	4.3	9.9
Zambia	19.3	16.6	19.9	21.7	31.4	30.2	24.6	25.6	31.5	14.1	9.0	19.2
Zimbabwe	13.8	17.5	-2.6	-7.4	-9.3	-1.5	-21.5	-29.8	-26.8	16.5	17.1	-6.1
NORTH AFRICA	**22.8**	**20.7**	**27.6**	**29.8**	**33.4**	**32.8**	**33.7**	**25.0**	**25.6**	**20.3**	**19.1**	**27.8**
Algeria	43.1	27.1	47.7	54.9	56.6	57.5	56.7	51.2	50.7	31.5	30.1	49.8
Djibouti	..	-10.5	4.3	8.6	12.1	17.4	..	..	..	..	-6.4	5.7
Egypt, Arab Rep.	15.2	16.2	15.6	15.7	17.1	16.3	16.8	12.6	14.1	15.5	14.2	14.8
Libya	..	27.2	42.7	48.1	66.8	63.6	67.8	..	..	..	17.6	46.6
Morocco	14.9	19.9	24.2	23.2	24.0	23.4	24.7	24.7	25.2	16.7	17.8	23.8
Tunisia	24.0	20.0	20.8	21.3	21.6	21.9	22.9	21.9	21.1	22.7	21.8	21.5
AFRICA	**24.2**	**18.8**	**21.1**	**22.1**	**23.8**	**24.0**	**24.4**	**19.3**	**20.7**	**20.2**	**17.1**	**21.3**

a. Provisional.

Table 2.14 Gross national savings

	Share of GDP (%)									Annual average		
	1980	1990	2004	2005	2006	2007	2008	2009	2010[a]	1980–89	1990–99	2000–10
SUB-SAHARAN AFRICA	**23.4**	**15.8**	**16.3**	**16.2**	**15.5**	**15.6**	**15.4**	**15.5**	**17.2**	**18.6**	**15.2**	**15.9**
Excluding South Africa	..	12.8	17.5	17.9	16.6	..	..	..	..	13.1	14.0	16.3
Excl. S. Africa & Nigeria	10.9	12.8	17.5	17.9	16.6	17.2	15.9	15.5	..	12.4	14.0	16.2
Angola	..	9.0	12.6	27.1	40.9	31.0	24.8	5.2	21.6	13.8	1.6	18.5
Benin	4.2	5.3	6.8	10.1	10.0	8.8	10.6	13.9	..	4.6	7.8	9.8
Botswana	27.4	41.7	36.2	41.5	40.9	43.3	35.0	26.4	27.7	34.3	40.5	35.8
Burkina Faso	9.3	15.9	5.4	8.3	6.9	..	..	..	..	14.6	21.5	6.7
Burundi	..	8.7	12.0	11.0	4.8	0.8	-4.8	5.2	-5.4	11.2	6.2	4.4
Cameroon	5.2	16.2	17.1	16.7	19.2	20.3	..	..	..	18.8	13.4	16.5
Cape Verde	..	53.9	25.3	32.7	32.5	32.3	30.4	23.6	34.4	59.2	34.9	27.0
Central African Republic	1.6	6.2	..	..	..	..	..	..	..	6.1	8.1	..
Chad	..	2.3	..	..	..	..	..	..	..	6.2	4.6	..
Comoros	-0.4	14.4	..	..	..	..	..	..	..	15.0	15.4	..
Congo, Dem. Rep.	..	..	..	..	..	..	..	..	..	..	..	..
Congo, Rep.	26.1	6.9	19.7	16.6	5.9	15.2	..	..	..	25.5	5.3	17.0
Côte d'Ivoire	8.6	-5.1	12.4	10.0	12.1	8.4	12.2	14.5	..	6.8	6.0	11.7
Equatorial Guinea	..	2.1	..	..	..	..	..	..	..	..	14.7	..
Eritrea	..	..	..	..	..	..	..	..	..	..	32.8	4.4
Ethiopia	..	12.8	22.1	13.7	9.7	21.6	16.6	14.8	16.6	13.4	15.5	17.5
Gabon	47.8	24.3	35.4	44.2	..	..	..	..	..	33.7	29.3	37.1
Gambia, The	16.4	21.9	15.0	9.6	16.7	10.9	2.2	12.2	9.4	16.9	8.9	10.4
Ghana	6.3	10.5	22.9	19.3	2.6	-1.1	-1.3	17.5	20.6	7.3	13.5	14.2
Guinea	..	19.2	11.4	8.0	1.8	-2.8	-0.8	6.5	7.1	12.4	18.7	8.4
Guinea-Bissau	..	14.5	..	..	..	..	..	..	..	1.8	9.0	-7.3
Kenya	17.2	18.5	16.1	16.1	14.8	15.3	12.6	14.2	15.6	18.0	21.8	14.7
Lesotho	49.6	70.5	14.0	21.2	26.5	28.6	38.4	32.6	12.7	42.0	50.6	28.9
Liberia	14.6	..	90.8	77.4	86.0	71.3	43.3	53.0	29.0	-3.9	..	64.4
Madagascar	-0.7	9.1	14.2	8.0	..	..	..	..	..	3.0	5.1	11.8
Malawi	7.9	16.4	5.1	1.6	7.6	17.2	10.6	12.8	..	12.5	8.1	8.8
Mali	8.4	15.0	8.6	11.4	14.5	18.6	..	..	..	6.1	14.7	13.1
Mauritania	5.4	7.5	..	..	..	..	..	..	..	7.2	17.3	..
Mauritius	10.4	25.8	22.6	17.4	17.1	22.1	17.2	13.9	15.6	20.2	26.5	21.2
Mozambique	-6.6	6.6	8.0	7.1	7.1	6.6	3.8	7.6	12.2	-2.3	6.0	8.1
Namibia	..	34.8	28.2	27.6	31.8	31.8	32.1	27.5	34.1	..	27.5	28.8
Niger	17.1	-0.6	6.9	18.5	..	..	..	..	..	8.8	3.7	8.6
Nigeria	..	..	..	..	..	..	..	..	..	..	..	..
Rwanda	14.0	11.3	14.8	15.1	10.4	14.1	17.2	15.0	12.2	12.0	14.2	13.3
São Tomé and Príncipe	..	..	..	..	..	..	..	..	..	..	..	..
Senegal	2.7	1.6	14.7	21.1	18.7	19.1	16.1	19.4	..	4.2	6.3	16.4
Seychelles	32.4	21.7	12.4	5.6	12.9	-6.6	2.1	14.6	..	27.3	21.5	11.1
Sierra Leone	2.9	-1.0	4.8	10.0	9.0	10.3	5.3	10.3	13.0	7.7	0.8	6.6
Somalia	20.1	..	..	..	..	..	..	..	..	19.2	..	..
South Africa	33.9	19.1	15.0	14.5	14.4	14.1	15.0	15.5	16.5	24.4	16.6	15.3
Sudan	4.5	1.2	16.1	19.4	15.5	19.2	19.0	12.8	17.5	3.7	4.0	14.1
Swaziland	..	19.7	17.2	21.6	15.4	18.7	8.5	0.4	2.4	..	16.2	15.4
Tanzania	..	10.1	20.4	17.5	17.4	15.7	18.0	19.5	20.1	..	8.7	17.4
Togo	27.2	21.0	2.2	4.9	8.2	7.9	10.6	12.4	..	16.8	10.8	6.9
Uganda	1.9	5.6	21.2	20.0	16.7	16.1	21.9	18.2	19.0	5.5	14.4	17.9
Zambia	7.8	19.6	14.1	14.9	23.9	21.9	18.9	19.0	22.5	3.2	7.1	13.6
Zimbabwe	12.0	15.6	..	..	..	..	..	..	..	14.6	15.7	..
NORTH AFRICA	**25.9**	**27.6**	**25.2**	**32.6**	**37.0**	**37.6**	**37.8**	**28.7**	**27.7**	**23.6**	**28.3**	**30.3**
Algeria	41.0	24.3	..	51.9	54.1	57.9	57.6	54.1	48.4	29.4	28.6	54.0
Djibouti	..	..	24.4	28.3	33.4	37.1	..	..	..	..	11.4	22.3
Egypt, Arab Rep.	21.0	31.1	21.1	21.8	23.0	23.6	23.6	16.9	17.8	21.8	24.7	20.1
Libya	..	..	34.4	46.0	69.8	66.5	67.1	..	..	..	..	49.7
Morocco	18.6	25.1	31.0	30.9	32.2	32.3	32.9	30.2	30.8	20.5	21.6	30.5
Tunisia	25.3	23.4	21.2	20.3	21.2	20.9	21.6	21.2	20.3	23.7	21.7	21.1
AFRICA	**24.5**	**20.8**	**19.9**	**23.8**	**25.6**	**26.0**	**26.3**	**21.4**	**22.2**	**20.8**	**18.4**	**21.6**

a. Provisional.

Table 2.15 General government final consumption expenditure

	Share of GDP (%)											
										Annual average		
	1980	1990	2004	2005	2006	2007	2008	2009	2010[a]	1980–89	1990–99	2000–10
SUB-SAHARAN AFRICA	15.1	17.5	16.5	16.7	16.4	15.9	16.2	17.5	18.2	16.5	16.7	16.4
Excluding South Africa	..	15.6	13.9	14.2	13.4	13.1	13.0	13.8	..	15.6	14.4	13.5
Excl. S. Africa & Nigeria	16.1	15.6	13.9	14.2	13.4	13.1	13.0	13.8	14.6	15.6	14.4	13.6
Angola	..	34.5	..	20.0	18.5	15.3	17.1	17.4	17.6	31.5	40.7	17.6
Benin	8.6	11.0	13.6	15.0	..	..	..	..	..	12.7	10.5	12.9
Botswana	21.3	24.1	21.1	22.4	19.0	19.4	18.9	24.3	20.9	24.4	26.7	21.3
Burkina Faso	9.2	21.1	21.6	22.2	21.7	..	..	..	..	15.6	22.5	22.2
Burundi	9.2	10.8	19.6	19.0	20.4	28.8	30.0	26.9	31.6	9.3	17.0	22.0
Cameroon	9.7	12.8	10.2	10.0	9.6	9.2	..	..	..	10.1	10.6	9.9
Cape Verde	..	16.3	28.7	28.5	25.7	25.8	25.6	25.7	26.1	14.5	17.1	26.0
Central African Republic	15.1	14.9	10.6	13.3	11.1	2.7	6.6	4.5	..	15.7	13.9	9.9
Chad	..	10.1	4.9	5.1	4.9	10.3	12.4	15.1	13.2	11.4	8.1	8.8
Comoros	30.9	24.5	14.3	13.5	14.2	14.3	15.3	15.3	..	28.6	20.3	14.7
Congo, Dem. Rep.	8.4	11.5	8.2	8.2	7.6	10.3	11.0	7.6	..	9.0	9.9	7.8
Congo, Rep.	17.6	13.9	15.0	13.0	13.9	17.0	12.0	12.2	10.4	17.7	18.1	14.1
Côte d'Ivoire	16.9	16.8	8.3	8.3	8.3	8.7	8.6	8.7	8.6	16.5	11.9	8.2
Equatorial Guinea	..	39.7	2.9	2.7	2.6	2.3	2.7	3.9	..	27.4	25.1	3.4
Eritrea	..	..	44.8	39.7	38.0	32.8	..	..	..	..	39.7	44.4
Ethiopia	..	13.2	13.1	12.3	12.1	10.4	9.7	8.2	10.2	11.2	9.8	12.4
Gabon	13.2	13.4	9.3	8.3	8.4	8.9	8.2	11.5	10.0	18.3	13.2	9.7
Gambia, The	31.2	13.8	7.1	7.7	8.0	7.9	9.6	9.3	9.6	29.1	12.2	9.1
Ghana	11.2	9.3	12.2	15.3	11.3	11.6	11.2	11.7	9.5	9.0	11.7	11.3
Guinea	..	11.0	7.0	7.0	8.1	6.8	9.3	7.9	7.5	11.6	8.2	7.6
Guinea-Bissau	27.6	10.3	..	..	..	..	..	..	..	18.9	8.4	13.1
Kenya	19.8	18.6	17.9	17.4	17.6	17.9	16.5	15.8	16.7	18.3	15.8	16.9
Lesotho	21.8	25.8	35.6	36.7	35.4	35.7	36.9	39.8	37.2	23.3	33.6	37.2
Liberia	21.3	..	11.1	11.4	9.4	13.6	18.3	20.7	18.6	24.3	..	11.4
Madagascar	12.1	8.0	6.9	9.0	8.8	12.3	11.3	11.6	..	9.8	7.9	9.5
Malawi	19.3	15.1	12.5	14.3	14.6	14.1	17.3	20.9	20.2	17.5	16.6	15.5
Mali	11.6	13.8	10.0	10.0	9.9	10.3	..	..	..	12.3	12.7	9.4
Mauritania	45.3	25.9	17.6	18.0	15.2	14.8	14.7	16.2	13.1	30.7	15.5	17.7
Mauritius	14.0	13.6	14.3	14.8	14.2	12.9	12.7	14.1	13.9	12.6	14.0	13.9
Mozambique	12.2	13.5	10.8	10.4	10.7	11.8	12.1	13.3	12.7	13.8	9.7	10.8
Namibia	17.4	30.6	20.4	19.3	19.5	20.7	20.8	25.0	24.2	27.9	31.0	21.8
Niger	10.4	15.0	12.5	11.5	..	..	..	..	..	11.9	14.6	12.2
Nigeria	..	..	..	..	..	..	..	..	..	..	..	..
Rwanda	12.5	10.1	18.4	18.2	18.2	16.5	14.7	14.5	15.5	13.0	11.5	15.0
São Tomé and Príncipe	..	..	..	..	..	..	..	..	..	..	..	..
Senegal	24.8	18.4	13.7	9.6	9.7	10.0	9.7	8.7	8.7	19.3	15.1	11.1
Seychelles	28.7	27.7	28.3	20.5	18.8	16.2	12.8	11.1	..	33.1	29.0	20.5
Sierra Leone	8.4	7.8	13.3	13.8	13.8	11.8	12.5	14.0	12.3	7.7	10.6	14.1
Somalia	15.6	..	..	..	..	..	..	..	..	17.6	..	..
South Africa	14.3	19.7	19.4	19.5	19.7	19.0	19.3	21.1	21.5	17.4	19.4	19.4
Sudan	16.0	5.8	11.8	18.2	17.3	15.5	15.8	13.9	15.2	11.1	6.1	13.2
Swaziland	27.0	14.3	15.1	15.2	13.9	14.1	13.4	14.7	26.8	21.5	17.1	16.3
Tanzania	..	17.8	16.9	17.6	17.5	19.3	17.4	17.5	18.2	..	14.8	16.0
Togo	22.4	14.2	10.3	11.5	11.4	9.2	..	..	..	16.9	12.8	10.2
Uganda	..	7.5	13.9	14.5	14.1	12.9	11.2	11.6	11.7	9.9	11.1	13.9
Zambia	25.5	19.0	18.0	9.7	10.2	10.3	8.8	13.1	13.3	23.1	17.7	11.8
Zimbabwe	18.5	19.5	21.0	15.2	5.9	3.2	2.1	13.3	19.1	20.1	17.6	14.3
NORTH AFRICA	15.9	15.2	14.3	13.8	13.2	12.9	12.5	13.7	..	16.6	15.3	13.9
Algeria	15.2	16.1	13.8	11.6	11.2	11.3	12.9	14.2	..	17.2	16.6	13.3
Djibouti	..	31.5	29.7	27.1	28.0	25.1	..	..	..	..	31.8	28.0
Egypt, Arab Rep.	15.7	11.3	12.8	12.7	12.3	11.3	10.9	11.4	11.2	16.2	10.9	11.8
Libya	..	24.4	13.1	11.8	10.7	11.6	9.3	..	..	..	24.3	14.4
Morocco	18.3	15.5	18.7	19.4	18.6	18.2	17.2	18.2	17.5	16.6	17.0	18.3
Tunisia	14.5	16.4	16.9	16.9	16.7	16.5	16.1	16.2	16.3	16.5	16.2	16.7
AFRICA	15.5	16.4	15.5	15.4	14.9	14.5	14.5	15.8	16.4	16.5	16.1	15.3

a. Provisional.

Table 2.16 Household final consumption expenditure

	Share of GDP (%)									Annual average		
	1980	1990	2004	2005	2006	2007	2008	2009	2010[a]	1980–89	1990–99	2000–10
SUB-SAHARAN AFRICA	**59.0**	**65.2**	**67.9**	**67.5**	**67.7**	**67.4**	**67.4**	**67.3**	**64.9**	**63.3**	**67.9**	**67.5**
Excluding South Africa	..	72.3	72.5	71.4	71.9	71.7	73.3	74.6	..	72.5	74.0	73.0
Excl. S. Africa & Nigeria	71.6	72.3	72.5	71.4	71.9	71.7	73.3	74.6	71.0	72.4	74.0	72.8
Angola	..	35.8	..	38.7	25.4	40.8	41.6	67.9	50.4	44.5	42.6	44.1
Benin	97.7	86.8	80.9	78.1	..	..	..	..	..	89.7	85.7	81.3
Botswana	52.0	33.2	38.4	34.5	41.0	41.4	49.2	54.2	56.6	40.4	34.5	42.7
Burkina Faso	98.0	73.5	76.6	73.0	75.5	..	..	..	..	86.0	68.5	75.2
Burundi	91.4	94.6	87.9	93.1	94.1	89.2	86.6	82.4	80.8	87.5	88.3	88.9
Cameroon	68.6	66.6	71.4	72.0	71.5	72.2	..	..	..	65.8	70.9	71.4
Cape Verde	..	58.5	69.4	64.2	63.8	62.1	61.2	67.5	55.6	55.7	75.9	68.5
Central African Republic	93.7	85.7	89.5	86.6	87.6	95.9	94.7	92.8	..	85.5	82.4	88.2
Chad	..	97.6	70.6	59.8	58.7	69.2	60.2	79.3	76.1	96.8	92.5	77.8
Comoros	79.2	78.7	94.2	98.8	100.6	101.2	104.8	105.9	..	76.0	84.6	96.4
Congo, Dem. Rep.	81.6	79.1	87.8	85.9	93.0	81.0	80.4	77.1	..	80.0	81.3	86.3
Congo, Rep.	46.8	62.4	32.8	37.2	45.9	36.2	41.6	45.0	38.6	50.3	53.1	38.6
Côte d'Ivoire	62.8	71.9	71.7	74.5	72.0	76.8	73.6	71.9	72.5	63.9	70.3	72.5
Equatorial Guinea	..	80.3	18.2	13.6	11.3	10.8	24.2	37.3	..	..	61.2	18.4
Eritrea	..	..	90.4	89.3	80.2	85.6	..	..	..	..	90.0	83.9
Ethiopia	..	77.2	78.2	85.1	86.4	85.5	89.9	87.6	89.4	78.4	80.5	82.3
Gabon	26.1	49.7	36.2	33.3	35.6	35.9	32.9	43.8	38.2	37.4	43.2	37.4
Gambia, The	63.0	75.6	83.2	87.2	81.3	86.5	91.7	87.8	88.0	64.4	84.0	86.5
Ghana	83.9	85.2	80.5	81.0	82.6	84.6	86.8	78.4	75.5	86.2	80.8	81.9
Guinea	..	66.9	74.6	74.8	78.0	83.6	80.5	75.5	76.5	71.8	73.5	77.3
Guinea-Bissau	73.3	86.9	..	..	..	..	..	..	..	82.0	90.1	100.1
Kenya	62.1	62.8	71.4	73.2	75.2	74.0	78.4	77.3	74.4	63.3	69.6	74.7
Lesotho	130.3	123.3	111.2	113.3	109.5	106.0	100.0	101.9	104.8	146.3	103.0	99.9
Liberia	73.7	..	123.6	127.8	178.2	148.3	157.8	135.1	131.3	83.7	..	118.0
Madagascar	89.3	86.4	84.5	86.2	82.0	77.1	78.8	79.4	..	87.2	87.9	81.3
Malawi	69.9	71.5	87.5	91.1	84.2	71.5	78.2	70.1	71.7	69.8	80.0	80.4
Mali	87.4	79.8	81.4	79.1	75.3	76.8	..	..	..	88.1	79.7	78.4
Mauritania	58.2	69.2	76.1	72.3	59.0	66.7	72.8	69.9	71.2	66.3	73.7	71.8
Mauritius	75.6	63.4	63.7	68.7	70.5	69.5	73.2	74.1	73.6	67.1	62.0	66.8
Mozambique	96.7	92.3	81.4	83.2	80.5	81.9	86.4	84.5	81.4	92.3	93.2	83.1
Namibia	44.2	51.2	62.8	60.9	60.0	56.9	57.5	60.6	49.0	61.3	56.3	60.2
Niger	75.1	83.8	83.6	75.1	..	..	..	..	..	80.8	82.7	81.9
Nigeria	..	..	..	..	..	..	..	..	..	..	..	..
Rwanda	83.3	83.7	80.3	79.8	80.1	80.0	78.4	81.3	83.3	82.0	94.0	82.7
São Tomé and Príncipe	..	..	..	..	..	..	..	..	..	..	..	..
Senegal	73.1	79.2	78.4	76.3	79.6	81.4	86.4	82.0	80.5	76.4	79.6	79.7
Seychelles	44.2	52.0	57.0	72.9	68.4	85.6	81.4	74.5	..	42.7	49.3	65.6
Sierra Leone	90.7	83.5	87.2	82.2	78.6	82.0	85.9	83.7	84.4	83.2	86.6	87.1
Somalia	97.3	..	..	..	..	..	..	..	..	100.6	..	..
South Africa	47.8	57.1	62.9	63.1	63.1	62.7	61.6	60.3	59.4	54.2	61.2	62.0
Sudan	81.9	86.1	69.5	62.8	64.1	57.8	57.5	66.7	60.6	84.8	84.3	67.9
Swaziland	71.8	80.5	72.2	73.9	75.7	74.9	84.9	87.3	75.5	74.7	80.9	75.5
Tanzania	..	81.0	66.9	66.3	68.0	67.9	66.4	65.5	64.7	..	82.3	69.1
Togo	54.5	71.1	94.5	90.8	89.7	92.8	..	..	..	70.8	80.5	90.4
Uganda	..	91.9	76.0	73.8	77.9	78.4	73.5	75.7	75.0	87.2	84.6	76.3
Zambia	55.2	64.4	62.1	68.6	58.4	59.5	66.5	61.3	55.2	62.9	73.3	69.0
Zimbabwe	67.7	63.1	81.6	92.2	103.5	98.3	119.4	116.4	107.7	63.4	65.3	91.7
NORTH AFRICA	**61.3**	**64.1**	**58.1**	**56.4**	**53.4**	**54.3**	**53.8**	**61.3**	**..**	**63.1**	**65.6**	**58.1**
Algeria	41.7	56.8	38.5	33.6	32.2	31.2	30.4	34.7	..	51.3	53.3	37.0
Djibouti	..	78.9	66.0	64.3	59.9	57.5	..	..	..	..	73.8	66.3
Egypt, Arab Rep.	69.2	72.6	71.7	71.6	70.6	72.4	72.3	76.1	74.7	68.3	75.0	73.4
Libya	..	48.4	44.2	40.2	22.5	24.8	22.9	..	..	..	58.1	39.0
Morocco	66.8	64.6	57.2	57.5	57.5	58.4	58.1	57.1	57.3	66.7	65.3	58.0
Tunisia	61.5	63.6	62.3	61.8	61.7	61.6	61.0	61.9	62.7	60.8	62.0	61.9
AFRICA	**60.0**	**64.7**	**63.4**	**62.5**	**61.2**	**61.4**	**61.0**	**64.7**	**66.5**	**63.2**	**66.9**	**63.7**

a. Provisional.

Table 2.17 Final consumption expenditure plus discrepancy

	Share of GDP (%)											
										Annual average		
	1980	1990	2004	2005	2006	2007	2008	2009	2010[a]	1980–89	1990–99	2000–10
SUB-SAHARAN AFRICA	**74.8**	**82.8**	**84.2**	**84.2**	**84.1**	**83.4**	**83.7**	**84.9**	**83.2**	**79.9**	**84.6**	**83.9**
Excl. South Africa	88.3	88.1	86.0	85.6	85.4	85.0	86.5	88.5	..	88.1	88.1	86.3
Excl. S. Africa & Nigeria	88.3	88.1	86.0	85.6	85.4	85.0	86.5	88.5	85.6	88.1	88.1	86.2
Angola	..	70.3	74.9	58.7	43.8	56.1	58.7	85.3	68.0	76.0	78.0	67.8
Benin	106.4	97.8	94.5	93.1	93.1	93.9	92.9	89.2	87.7	102.4	96.2	92.9
Botswana	73.3	57.4	59.5	56.9	60.0	60.7	68.0	78.5	77.5	64.7	61.2	64.0
Burkina Faso	107.2	94.6	98.2	95.2	97.2	..	..	..	..	101.6	91.0	97.4
Burundi	100.6	105.4	107.5	112.1	114.5	117.9	116.6	109.3	112.4	96.9	105.3	110.9
Cameroon	78.3	79.3	81.5	82.0	81.1	81.5	..	..	..	75.8	81.5	81.2
Cape Verde	..	74.7	98.1	92.8	89.5	88.0	86.8	93.2	81.7	70.2	93.0	94.5
Central African Republic	108.9	100.6	100.0	99.9	98.6	98.5	101.3	97.3	..	101.1	96.3	98.1
Chad	..	107.7	75.5	64.9	63.6	79.5	72.6	94.3	89.3	108.1	100.5	86.5
Comoros	110.1	103.2	108.5	112.3	114.8	115.4	120.1	121.1	..	104.5	104.9	111.1
Congo, Dem. Rep.	89.9	90.7	96.0	94.1	100.6	91.3	91.4	84.7	..	89.1	91.2	94.2
Congo, Rep.	64.4	76.2	47.8	50.2	59.8	53.2	53.6	57.3	49.1	68.1	71.2	52.7
Côte d'Ivoire	79.6	88.7	80.0	82.8	80.4	85.4	82.2	80.6	81.1	80.4	82.2	80.7
Equatorial Guinea	..	120.1	21.1	16.3	13.9	13.1	26.9	41.2	41.5	..	86.3	23.6
Eritrea	..	..	135.1	129.0	118.2	118.4	..	..	..	..	129.7	128.2
Ethiopia	..	90.4	91.2	97.4	98.5	95.8	99.6	95.9	99.6	89.5	90.3	94.7
Gabon	39.4	63.1	45.4	41.7	44.0	44.7	41.0	55.4	48.1	55.7	56.4	47.1
Gambia, The	94.2	89.3	90.3	94.9	89.3	94.4	101.3	97.1	97.6	93.5	96.1	95.6
Ghana	95.1	94.5	92.7	96.3	93.9	96.2	98.0	90.2	85.0	95.3	92.5	93.2
Guinea	..	77.8	81.6	81.8	86.1	90.3	89.7	83.4	84.0	83.4	81.7	84.9
Guinea-Bissau	101.0	97.2	..	..	..	..	..	..	..	100.9	98.5	113.2
Kenya	81.9	81.5	89.3	90.6	92.8	91.9	94.9	93.1	91.1	81.7	85.4	91.6
Lesotho	152.0	149.1	146.8	150.0	144.9	141.7	136.9	141.7	142.1	169.5	136.6	137.2
Liberia	95.0	..	134.6	139.1	187.5	161.9	176.1	155.8	149.9	108.0	..	129.3
Madagascar	101.4	94.5	91.5	95.1	90.8	89.4	90.0	91.0	..	97.1	95.8	90.8
Malawi	89.2	86.6	100.0	105.5	98.8	85.6	95.5	91.0	91.8	87.3	96.6	95.9
Mali	98.9	93.6	91.4	89.0	85.3	87.0	..	..	..	100.4	92.4	87.8
Mauritania	103.5	95.1	93.7	90.3	74.2	81.5	87.5	86.1	84.3	96.9	89.2	89.5
Mauritius	89.6	77.0	78.0	83.5	84.7	82.4	85.9	88.1	87.5	79.7	75.9	80.7
Mozambique	108.9	105.8	92.3	93.5	91.2	93.7	98.4	97.8	94.0	106.2	102.9	94.0
Namibia	61.6	81.8	83.2	80.2	79.5	77.6	78.3	85.7	73.1	89.2	87.3	82.0
Niger	85.4	98.9	96.1	86.6	..	..	..	..	..	92.7	97.3	94.1
Nigeria	..	..	..	..	..	..	..	..	..	..	..	..
Rwanda	95.8	93.8	98.6	98.0	98.2	96.5	93.1	95.8	98.8	95.0	105.5	97.7
São Tomé and Príncipe	..	..	..	..	..	..	..	..	..	..	..	..
Senegal	97.9	97.6	92.1	85.8	89.3	91.4	96.1	90.7	89.2	95.7	94.6	90.8
Seychelles	72.9	79.7	85.3	93.4	87.2	101.7	94.2	85.5	..	75.9	78.3	86.0
Sierra Leone	99.1	91.3	100.4	95.9	92.4	93.9	98.3	97.7	96.7	90.9	97.2	101.2
Somalia	112.9	112.5	..	..	..	..	..	..	..	106.3	112.5	..
South Africa	62.1	76.8	82.2	82.5	82.8	81.7	80.9	81.4	80.9	71.5	80.6	81.4
Sudan	97.9	91.9	81.3	81.0	81.4	73.3	73.2	80.6	75.8	95.8	90.4	81.1
Swaziland	98.8	94.8	87.3	89.1	89.6	89.0	98.3	102.0	102.3	96.3	98.0	91.8
Tanzania	..	98.7	83.8	83.9	85.5	87.2	83.9	83.0	82.8	..	97.1	85.2
Togo	76.8	85.3	104.8	102.3	101.1	101.9	99.1	97.6	97.7	87.7	93.3	100.0
Uganda	100.4	99.4	89.9	88.3	92.0	91.2	84.7	87.3	86.7	97.7	95.7	90.1
Zambia	80.7	83.4	80.1	78.3	68.6	69.8	75.4	74.4	68.5	86.0	91.0	80.8
Zimbabwe	86.2	82.6	102.6	107.4	109.3	101.5	121.5	129.8	126.8	83.5	82.9	106.1
NORTH AFRICA	**77.2**	**79.3**	**72.4**	**70.2**	**66.6**	**67.2**	**66.3**	**75.0**	**74.4**	**79.7**	**80.9**	**72.2**
Algeria	56.9	72.9	52.3	45.1	43.4	42.5	43.3	48.8	49.3	68.5	69.9	50.2
Djibouti	..	110.5	95.7	91.4	87.9	82.6	..	..	..	..	106.4	94.3
Egypt, Arab Rep.	84.8	83.9	84.4	84.3	82.9	83.7	83.2	87.5	85.9	84.5	85.8	85.2
Libya	..	72.8	57.3	52.0	33.2	36.4	32.2	..	..	..	82.4	53.4
Morocco	85.2	80.1	75.8	76.8	76.1	76.6	75.3	75.3	74.8	83.3	82.2	76.2
Tunisia	76.0	80.0	79.2	78.7	78.4	78.1	77.1	78.1	78.9	77.4	78.2	78.5
AFRICA	**75.8**	**81.2**	**78.9**	**77.9**	**76.2**	**76.1**	**75.6**	**80.7**	**79.3**	**79.8**	**82.9**	**78.7**

a. Provisional.

Table 2.18 Final consumption expenditure plus discrepancy per capita

	Current prices ($)											
										Annual average		
	1980	1990	2004	2005	2006	2007	2008	2009	2010[a]	1980–89	1990–99	2000–10
SUB-SAHARAN AFRICA	455	497	595	655	717	810	881	893	990	455	477	658
Excluding South Africa	367	361	371	408	468	557	675	684	698	340	312	457
Excl. S. Africa & Nigeria	382	373	380	417	479	570	691	700	714	352	321	468
Angola	..	698	928	1,005	1,077	1,934	2,739	3,470	2,938	598	484	1,483
Benin	414	378	517	523	560	642	743	683	650	330	347	530
Botswana	781	1,574	3,229	3,112	3,553	3,900	4,679	4,568	5,755	816	1,803	3,409
Burkina Faso	287	315	364	366	389	..	..	..	..	245	226	300
Burundi	224	213	137	173	189	202	238	243	272	216	173	180
Cameroon	579	726	749	774	812	918	..	..	..	663	636	682
Cape Verde	..	659	1,942	1,907	2,073	2,424	2,781	3,036	2,734	501	1,084	2,061
Central African Republic	382	510	321	336	356	402	474	446	..	359	352	338
Chad	..	311	352	352	385	538	570	611	680	224	237	400
Comoros	413	589	628	676	701	791	913	906	..	393	500	639
Congo, Dem. Rep.	479	233	112	118	150	150	171	148	..	299	158	122
Congo, Rep.	610	893	645	864	1,275	1,197	1,655	1,394	1,457	693	628	955
Côte d'Ivoire	953	765	698	752	762	907	1,013	960	941	679	642	742
Equatorial Guinea	..	424	1,877	2,208	2,128	2,562	7,478	7,406	8,587	..	418	3,210
Eritrea	..	..	347	316	308	325	..	..	..	..	239	282
Ethiopia	..	226	126	161	197	241	334	377	356	200	159	203
Gabon	2,468	4,046	2,426	2,633	3,007	3,636	4,112	4,101	4,221	2,564	2,716	2,925
Gambia, The	360	293	358	402	385	494	642	568	593	278	631	481
Ghana	387	376	389	477	864	1,043	1,202	983	1,121	353	363	655
Guinea	..	360	336	266	264	406	355	356	399	348	386	328
Guinea-Bissau	134	233	..	..	..	..	..	..	..	171	214	184
Kenya	366	299	414	476	571	668	753	721	724	299	314	530
Lesotho	501	492	885	994	993	1,075	1,046	1,129	1,426	453	557	859
Liberia	422	..	203	237	342	344	409	357	371	436	..	256
Madagascar	476	258	230	268	272	346	433	384	..	320	245	295
Malawi	177	174	211	227	233	218	278	298	311	150	183	225
Mali	244	261	349	359	368	444	..	..	..	203	237	307
Mauritania	484	486	580	647	721	852	952	772	881	451	532	666
Mauritius	1,054	1,929	4,036	4,219	4,402	5,093	6,526	6,100	6,635	1,103	2,484	4,459
Mozambique	316	192	260	296	304	345	436	414	370	275	187	297
Namibia	1,320	1,359	2,690	2,799	2,993	3,165	3,143	3,412	3,566	1,437	1,662	2,730
Niger	365	315	234	227	..	..	..	..	..	278	219	196
Nigeria	..	..	..	..	..	..	..	..	..	..	..	..
Rwanda	215	341	229	275	324	372	438	488	523	272	280	314
São Tomé and Príncipe	..	..	..	..	..	..	..	..	..	..	..	..
Senegal	633	771	699	688	749	902	1,091	957	923	574	602	728
Seychelles	1,667	4,196	7,234	10,330	10,510	12,190	10,429	8,243	..	2,170	5,142	8,404
Sierra Leone	345	149	222	231	247	285	343	316	315	255	192	253
Somalia	106	156	..	..	..	..	..	..	..	138	156	..
South Africa	1,818	2,444	3,860	4,319	4,525	4,843	4,540	4,668	5,884	2,094	2,782	3,830
Sudan	494	557	586	721	944	1,068	1,310	1,335	1,512	670	415	840
Swaziland	888	1,224	2,079	2,263	2,592	2,664	2,876	2,883	3,584	754	1,490	2,190
Tanzania	..	165	285	305	307	357	411	407	423	..	197	323
Togo	327	379	384	400	403	455	543	522	515	287	334	397
Uganda	99	242	259	287	312	358	390	426	446	231	221	307
Zambia	543	349	389	490	625	668	891	749	858	418	346	544
Zimbabwe	790	693	473	492	475	430	431	607	754	703	544	502
NORTH AFRICA	848	1,112	1,310	1,404	1,509	1,773	2,118	2,248	2,449	957	1,150	1,618
Algeria	1,281	1,788	1,373	1,404	1,523	1,701	2,149	1,930	2,250	1,697	1,216	1,509
Djibouti	..	888	803	801	820	834	..	..	..	..	830	790
Egypt, Arab Rep.	432	636	914	1,019	1,179	1,420	1,730	2,073	2,318	529	832	1,385
Libya	..	4,857	3,385	3,961	3,178	4,338	4,876	..	..	..	5,175	3,678
Morocco	819	835	1,435	1,504	1,626	1,859	2,136	2,165	2,126	641	987	1,561
Tunisia	1,041	1,205	2,487	2,534	2,662	2,973	3,350	3,258	3,310	961	1,527	2,564
AFRICA	527	610	708	772	839	959	1,076	1,107	1,217	547	597	813

a. Provisional.

Table 2.19 Gross fixed capital formation

	Share of GDP (%)											
										Annual average		
	1980	1990	2004	2005	2006	2007	2008	2009	2010[a]	1980–89	1990–99	2000–10
SUB-SAHARAN AFRICA	**22.6**	**18.3**	**17.3**	**18.2**	**19.0**	**20.3**	**21.8**	**22.1**	**20.4**	**20.1**	**17.1**	**18.7**
Excluding South Africa	..	17.5	18.5	19.5	19.5	20.5	20.9	21.6	..	16.6	17.9	19.3
Excl. S. Africa & Nigeria	18.9	17.5	18.5	19.5	19.5	20.5	20.9	21.6	21.3	17.1	17.9	19.4
Angola	..	11.1	9.1	8.9	15.4	13.5	16.2	15.2	12.6	14.2	23.2	13.2
Benin	..	13.4	17.5	18.9	18.2	21.4	20.7	25.3	26.1	14.8	15.7	20.2
Botswana	34.5	32.4	24.8	24.5	21.6	23.9	22.8	28.8	27.1	29.0	27.2	24.9
Burkina Faso	14.1	17.7	19.3	19.3	20.5	..	..	..	..	17.4	21.2	18.2
Burundi	13.9	15.2	10.3	8.7	14.2	18.2	18.7	18.8	18.0	16.1	9.0	11.7
Cameroon	20.0	17.3	18.3	17.7	16.7	17.1	..	..	..	21.1	14.5	18.0
Cape Verde	..	25.3	38.9	35.8	38.7	46.4	46.2	39.1	46.8	29.8	29.6	38.3
Central African Republic	7.0	11.4	6.2	8.9	9.2	9.0	11.6	10.8	..	10.2	11.2	8.9
Chad	..	4.8	22.7	16.7	13.2	17.0	23.9	31.6	31.8	4.5	11.0	29.3
Comoros	28.5	11.9	9.4	9.3	9.6	11.2	14.3	12.4	..	24.3	14.7	10.8
Congo, Dem. Rep.	8.8	12.8	12.8	14.0	12.6	19.5	23.8	28.7	..	11.4	8.0	14.1
Congo, Rep.	35.8	17.2	21.9	19.7	21.3	21.4	18.0	22.2	20.3	32.5	24.9	21.8
Côte d'Ivoire	24.4	8.5	9.9	9.7	9.3	8.7	10.1	11.4	13.8	15.8	11.4	10.4
Equatorial Guinea	..	17.4	40.5	37.6	31.4	33.3	28.4	60.1	..	..	59.5	43.9
Eritrea	..	..	18.9	19.7	13.3	11.0	..	..	..	..	26.1	22.3
Ethiopia	..	12.9	25.5	23.0	24.2	23.5	19.9	22.5	21.5	15.7	16.5	22.5
Gabon	26.7	21.5	24.4	21.3	25.9	25.9	24.4	27.0	26.6	33.8	25.5	24.7
Gambia, The	..	22.3	24.2	21.6	23.8	18.3	14.0	18.0	19.4	19.0	10.6	15.7
Ghana	6.1	14.4	28.4	29.0	21.6	20.1	21.5	19.7	21.8	7.9	19.7	23.1
Guinea	..	22.9	19.8	18.6	16.6	13.9	15.6	21.3	20.0	16.4	20.0	17.6
Guinea-Bissau	28.2	29.9	..	..	..	..	..	..	..	32.0	25.9	12.0
Kenya	18.3	20.7	16.3	18.7	19.1	19.4	19.4	19.1	19.9	18.8	17.6	18.2
Lesotho	35.6	57.0	26.5	21.1	21.5	22.0	28.2	28.0	28.5	40.3	65.4	29.5
Liberia	..	..	6.3	13.3	24.4	27.1	34.2	24.6	34.5	..	..	17.2
Madagascar	14.4	14.8	23.4	22.2	25.3	32.4	40.4	33.0	..	10.8	12.4	24.2
Malawi	22.2	20.1	16.2	20.2	22.7	24.0	23.3	21.8	21.7	15.8	15.2	19.0
Mali	15.5	23.0	21.0	22.7	22.9	22.4	..	..	..	17.2	22.5	23.4
Mauritania	21.4	20.0	44.4	59.0	27.4	27.6	27.3	24.6	24.5	27.1	20.2	28.1
Mauritius	23.2	30.6	21.6	21.4	24.3	25.1	24.6	26.4	24.9	21.2	26.9	23.5
Mozambique	7.6	22.1	18.7	18.7	17.7	16.1	15.7	20.7	24.7	12.2	20.7	21.4
Namibia	27.2	21.2	18.6	18.6	21.6	23.7	26.1	25.5	25.7	18.6	21.0	21.5
Niger	25.5	11.4	15.8	18.5	..	..	..	..	..	14.2	9.0	14.2
Nigeria	..	..	..	..	..	..	..	..	..	..	..	..
Rwanda	12.2	14.7	15.0	15.8	16.0	18.1	22.7	21.6	21.0	14.4	14.5	18.5
São Tomé and Príncipe	..	..	..	..	..	..	..	..	..	..	..	..
Senegal	14.6	18.0	22.7	29.6	28.2	30.9	30.2	27.9	29.0	17.4	19.9	26.3
Seychelles	36.5	23.0	12.7	23.8	24.8	29.7	24.5	22.0	..	25.6	29.2	23.9
Sierra Leone	14.9	9.6	10.5	17.0	15.2	13.2	14.7	15.4	15.8	11.4	7.2	12.7
Somalia	43.1	14.9	..	..	..	..	..	..	..	26.9	14.9	..
South Africa	25.9	19.1	16.0	16.8	18.3	20.2	22.7	22.7	19.6	23.1	16.3	17.9
Sudan	10.8	10.4	17.2	24.1	25.1	26.5	22.7	21.8	20.4	12.4	10.6	18.9
Swaziland	35.0	14.6	15.3	15.0	12.8	12.3	11.1	11.0	11.1	25.4	16.7	15.4
Tanzania	..	25.8	22.2	24.7	27.2	29.2	29.4	28.4	28.4	..	21.5	23.5
Togo	28.2	25.3	15.7	15.8	16.2	14.4	14.0	16.0	18.9	19.0	15.6	15.5
Uganda	..	12.7	19.9	22.2	20.9	21.9	22.8	23.9	23.3	9.3	15.9	21.3
Zambia	18.2	13.5	23.0	22.4	22.5	23.8	22.2	22.2	22.4	12.5	12.4	21.5
Zimbabwe	14.1	18.2	5.1	2.0	2.2	5.1	3.3	2.4	5.7	16.0	19.0	6.7
NORTH AFRICA	**26.8**	**24.5**	**19.7**	**20.3**	**21.6**	**24.3**	**25.6**	**26.2**	**..**	**27.9**	**21.3**	**21.7**
Algeria	33.8	27.0	24.1	22.3	22.9	26.0	26.4	38.3	..	31.9	26.2	25.2
Djibouti	..	14.2	21.5	19.0	29.6	37.5	..	..	..	..	11.1	18.6
Egypt, Arab Rep.	24.6	26.9	16.4	17.9	18.7	20.9	22.3	18.9	18.6	27.8	20.4	18.6
Libya	..	13.9	13.9	15.8	20.7	25.0	27.9	..	..	..	12.7	16.9
Morocco	22.2	24.0	26.3	27.5	28.1	31.3	33.0	30.9	30.7	23.1	22.2	28.1
Tunisia	28.3	24.4	22.1	21.3	22.6	23.0	23.5	24.2	24.3	27.5	25.0	23.6
AFRICA	**24.5**	**21.1**	**18.4**	**19.2**	**20.2**	**22.1**	**23.6**	**23.9**	**21.0**	**23.5**	**19.0**	**20.1**

a. Provisional.

Table 2.20 Gross general government fixed capital formation

	Share of GDP (%)											
										Annual average		
	1980	1990	2004	2005	2006	2007	2008	2009	2010[a]	1980–89	1990–99	2000–10
SUB-SAHARAN AFRICA	**6.6**	**5.6**	**5.4**	**5.2**	**5.8**	**6.5**	**7.6**	**8.6**	**7.6**	**6.1**	**4.7**	**5.9**
Excluding South Africa	..	7.2	6.3	6.1	6.5	6.8	7.2	8.0	..	6.6	6.5	6.4
Excl. S. Africa & Nigeria	..	7.2	6.3	6.1	6.5	6.8	7.2	8.0	7.5	6.3	6.5	6.5
Angola	..	..	4.9	5.5	13.0	11.5	14.1	12.4	9.7	..	7.8	8.9
Benin	..	7.4	5.4	6.7	4.6	7.5	5.8	9.7	10.0	9.1	7.5	7.1
Botswana	0.0	8.6	8.3	7.2	6.2	8.6	12.5	15.8	13.2	9.7	11.7	10.4
Burkina Faso	..	9.7	7.2	7.3	7.9	..	..	..	..	10.4	10.5	7.0
Burundi	12.8	12.5	7.6	4.7	6.2	9.2	9.4	9.1	8.0	13.8	9.3	6.4
Cameroon	4.5	5.5	2.6	2.5	2.4	2.4	..	..	..	6.9	2.9	2.3
Cape Verde	..	11.3	10.8	12.9	12.8	11.4	13.8	14.0	18.8	21.4	20.2	12.7
Central African Republic	3.7	4.7	2.0	4.0	3.7	2.7	4.5	3.8	..	5.5	6.2	3.6
Chad	..	..	7.8	7.8	8.1	7.3	7.9	10.5	9.1	3.8	7.4	9.1
Comoros	23.2	5.2	4.4	4.5	5.0	6.2	9.3	4.7	..	18.7	7.0	5.3
Congo, Dem. Rep.	5.1	4.0	2.8	3.7	3.0	8.8	12.6	22.9	..	4.4	1.7	5.8
Congo, Rep.	..	5.6	6.5	6.3	9.5	10.4	8.9	10.8	10.1	11.1	6.4	8.6
Côte d'Ivoire	11.4	3.6	2.8	2.7	3.1	2.6	3.1	3.0	4.6	7.1	5.6	3.0
Equatorial Guinea	..	10.5	13.1	10.3	15.1	16.9	16.9	43.0	..	..	6.9	14.6
Eritrea	..	..	14.4	17.9	12.2	9.8	..	..	..	..	17.6	17.1
Ethiopia	..	4.0	15.8	14.7	16.7	16.8	14.0	16.6	16.5	4.9	6.6	14.8
Gabon	5.3	3.9	4.2	4.2	4.8	4.5	4.6	6.0	9.2	6.7	6.5	4.8
Gambia, The	..	7.4	10.0	8.0	8.4	4.7	3.7	7.4	8.2	10.4	7.4	7.2
Ghana	..	7.5	12.4	12.0	8.8	8.5	9.4	5.2	3.9	6.3	11.1	9.1
Guinea	..	9.7	3.7	2.8	2.6	2.3	3.5	4.6	4.3	7.5	6.1	3.8
Guinea-Bissau	..	27.4	..	..	..	..	..	..	..	33.3	20.2	10.9
Kenya	0.0	9.7	4.3	2.5	3.1	3.9	4.4	5.3	0.0	0.8	7.1	3.7
Lesotho	9.9	26.2	7.7	4.3	5.5	4.7	9.0	11.5	12.7	17.2	18.7	8.9
Liberia	..	..	2.1	1.1	1.3	2.2	3.0	3.5	5.7	..	..	4.2
Madagascar	..	7.9	10.0	8.7	10.6	7.0	7.1	3.2	..	6.9	6.9	7.3
Malawi	17.5	7.7	9.1	7.2	7.8	14.8	9.4	6.9	10.1	9.5	9.2	8.9
Mali	..	10.5	7.5	7.7	8.6	8.4	..	..	..	10.2	10.1	7.7
Mauritania	21.4	6.2	8.9	6.8	5.9	6.7	6.5	7.1	7.9	17.6	3.4	7.3
Mauritius	8.4	11.4	6.6	6.3	7.7	5.4	4.1	6.6	6.1	7.4	9.2	6.6
Mozambique	7.6	12.0	10.7	8.6	11.8	11.7	11.5	12.9	13.6	9.5	12.1	11.5
Namibia	15.7	8.2	6.3	6.4	6.8	2.9	3.5	5.5	6.5	10.7	8.2	5.8
Niger	20.4	7.4	5.1	6.3	..	..	..	..	..	11.2	5.6	7.0
Nigeria	..	..	..	..	..	..	..	..	..	..	..	..
Rwanda	12.2	5.9	8.9	8.7	7.5	8.7	10.9	11.1	11.5	12.1	7.2	8.2
São Tomé and Príncipe	..	..	..	..	..	..	..	..	..	..	..	..
Senegal	4.7	4.1	6.7	10.0	9.7	11.2	10.0	10.1	10.8	3.7	4.5	8.2
Seychelles	..	8.2	3.1	4.4	7.7	4.5	3.2	3.0	..	12.0	9.9	7.1
Sierra Leone	5.3	3.9	4.5	5.7	5.1	3.5	6.2	7.8	7.7	4.0	3.8	5.4
Somalia	..	..	..	..	..	..	..	..	..	..	..	..
South Africa	6.4	3.9	4.3	4.3	5.0	6.1	8.0	9.2	7.7	5.7	2.8	5.3
Sudan	6.9	..	5.0	5.9	6.7	9.5	6.5	5.5	7.3	4.3	0.7	5.2
Swaziland	11.9	4.5	8.1	7.9	6.8	6.5	5.8	5.8	5.8	8.0	5.4	6.4
Tanzania	..	10.5	5.7	6.0	5.9	7.2	8.2	8.6	8.3	..	6.0	6.0
Togo	20.2	7.3	1.6	2.8	3.4	2.0	3.2	5.5	7.9	11.2	3.7	3.1
Uganda	..	6.2	4.9	5.0	4.6	4.9	4.5	6.2	5.6	4.4	5.6	5.3
Zambia	..	6.2	8.7	7.0	4.1	4.1	5.1	4.4	4.1	..	6.8	7.5
Zimbabwe	1.8	3.4	5.1	2.0	2.2	1.3	0.3	0.8	5.6	2.9	3.0	2.2
NORTH AFRICA	**..**	**10.8**	**8.4**	**8.9**	**8.9**	**10.2**	**10.6**	**11.1**	**12.0**	**13.0**	**10.4**	**9.2**
Algeria	11.0	8.2	10.6	10.8	12.0	16.5	16.1	24.0	27.7	13.8	7.2	14.1
Djibouti	..	9.1	7.7	9.3	7.5	12.2	..	..	..	..	6.1	6.6
Egypt, Arab Rep.	..	14.7	8.8	9.3	8.0	7.8	7.9	8.0	6.4	16.9	14.5	8.4
Libya	..	..	12.3	14.1	16.7	19.8	22.0	..	..	..	..	14.9
Morocco	..	4.8	3.8	3.7	3.6	3.6	4.6	6.0	5.7	7.1	4.2	4.4
Tunisia	15.0	8.7	3.5	3.0	3.1	2.9	2.8	3.5	..	14.1	9.3	3.5
AFRICA	**..**	**7.8**	**6.7**	**6.9**	**7.2**	**8.2**	**9.0**	**9.7**	**9.4**	**8.9**	**7.1**	**7.4**

a. Provisional.

Table 2.21 Private sector fixed capital formation

	Share of GDP (%)											
										Annual average		
	1980	1990	2004	2005	2006	2007	2008	2009	2010[a]	1980–89	1990–99	2000–10
SUB-SAHARAN AFRICA	**16.3**	**13.0**	**12.0**	**13.0**	**13.2**	**13.8**	**14.1**	**13.4**	**12.8**	**14.4**	**12.5**	**12.7**
Excluding South Africa	..	10.8	12.3	13.5	13.1	13.5	13.5	13.4	13.7	9.8	11.5	12.8
Excl. S. Africa & Nigeria	..	10.8	12.3	13.5	13.1	13.5	13.5	13.4	13.7	9.8	11.5	12.8
Angola	..	1.7	4.2	3.4	2.4	2.0	2.1	2.8	3.0	9.3	16.5	4.3
Benin	..	6.0	12.1	12.2	13.6	13.9	14.9	15.6	16.1	4.5	8.3	13.2
Botswana	34.5	23.8	16.5	17.3	15.4	15.3	10.3	13.1	14.0	19.4	15.5	14.5
Burkina Faso	..	8.0	..	..	..	..	..	..	..	8.8	10.8	10.4
Burundi	1.1	2.7	2.7	4.0	8.0	9.0	9.3	9.8	10.0	2.3	-0.3	5.3
Cameroon	15.6	11.9	15.7	15.2	14.3	14.7	12.5	12.4	12.6	14.2	11.7	14.8
Cape Verde	..	14.0	28.2	23.0	25.9	35.0	32.4	25.0	28.1	8.4	9.4	25.6
Central African Republic	3.2	6.7	4.1	4.9	5.6	6.3	7.1	7.0	..	4.7	5.0	5.3
Chad	..	..	14.9	8.9	5.1	9.7	16.0	21.0	22.7	0.6	4.3	20.2
Comoros	5.3	6.7	5.0	4.8	4.7	5.0	5.0	7.7	..	5.5	7.7	5.4
Congo, Dem. Rep.	3.7	8.9	10.0	10.4	9.6	10.7	11.3	5.8	..	7.1	6.3	8.3
Congo, Rep.	..	11.6	15.4	13.5	11.7	11.1	9.2	11.4	10.2	11.4	18.5	13.2
Côte d'Ivoire	13.0	4.9	7.1	7.0	6.3	6.1	7.1	8.4	9.2	8.7	6.2	7.5
Equatorial Guinea	..	6.9	27.4	27.4	16.2	16.4	11.5	17.2	..	..	52.6	29.2
Eritrea	..	..	4.5	1.9	1.2	1.3	..	..	..	..	8.6	5.1
Ethiopia	..	8.9	9.7	8.3	7.6	6.7	5.9	5.9	5.0	12.8	9.9	7.7
Gabon	21.4	17.6	20.2	17.1	21.1	21.5	19.8	21.0	17.4	27.2	18.9	19.9
Gambia, The	..	14.9	14.2	13.6	15.5	13.6	10.3	10.6	11.2	8.6	14.9	12.7
Ghana	..	6.9	16.0	17.0	12.8	11.6	12.1	14.6	17.9	3.8	8.6	14.1
Guinea	..	8.8	16.1	15.8	14.0	11.6	12.1	16.7	15.7	8.9	11.7	13.8
Guinea-Bissau	..	8.4	..	..	..	..	..	..	..	10.0	7.7	1.1
Kenya	8.2	10.9	12.0	16.2	16.0	15.5	15.0	13.8	19.9	10.7	9.8	12.6
Lesotho	25.7	30.8	18.7	16.8	16.0	17.3	19.3	16.5	15.8	23.1	46.8	20.6
Liberia	..	..	4.2	12.2	23.1	24.9	31.2	21.1	28.8	..	..	13.0
Madagascar	..	6.9	13.4	13.5	14.8	25.4	33.3	29.8	..	3.6	5.5	16.9
Malawi	4.8	12.4	7.1	13.0	15.0	9.2	13.9	14.9	16.9	6.3	6.0	10.0
Mali	..	12.4	13.5	15.0	14.3	14.0	..	..	..	9.9	12.4	15.7
Mauritania	0.0	13.8	35.5	52.1	21.4	20.8	20.8	17.5	16.6	9.5	16.8	20.8
Mauritius	14.9	19.2	15.0	15.1	16.6	19.7	20.5	19.8	18.8	13.8	17.7	16.9
Mozambique	0.0	10.1	8.0	10.1	5.8	4.4	4.1	7.8	11.0	2.7	8.6	9.9
Namibia	11.4	13.0	15.7	16.2	18.4	16.2	14.9	16.1	16.3	7.8	12.9	15.5
Niger	5.1	4.0	10.7	12.2	..	..	..	..	..	3.0	3.4	7.2
Nigeria	..	..	..	..	..	..	..	..	..	..	..	..
Rwanda	..	8.7	6.2	7.0	8.5	9.3	11.8	10.6	9.5	7.8	7.2	10.2
São Tomé and Príncipe	..	..	..	..	..	..	..	..	..	..	..	..
Senegal	9.9	13.9	16.0	19.7	18.5	19.7	20.2	17.8	18.2	13.7	15.4	18.2
Seychelles	..	14.8	9.7	19.4	17.2	25.2	21.3	19.0	..	10.1	19.3	16.8
Sierra Leone	9.5	5.7	5.9	11.3	10.1	9.7	8.6	7.6	8.0	7.3	3.3	7.3
Somalia	..	..	..	..	..	..	..	..	..	..	..	..
South Africa	19.5	15.3	11.7	12.5	13.4	14.1	14.8	13.5	11.9	17.4	13.5	12.6
Sudan	3.9	..	12.2	18.2	18.4	17.0	16.2	16.3	13.1	8.9	9.9	13.8
Swaziland	23.1	10.1	7.2	7.1	6.1	5.8	5.2	5.2	5.3	17.3	11.3	9.1
Tanzania	..	15.3	16.5	18.7	21.3	22.1	21.2	19.9	20.1	..	15.6	17.5
Togo	8.0	18.0	14.1	13.1	12.8	12.4	10.8	10.5	11.0	7.8	11.8	12.4
Uganda	..	6.5	15.0	17.2	16.3	16.9	18.3	17.7	17.7	5.4	10.3	16.0
Zambia	..	7.3	14.3	15.5	18.5	19.8	17.1	17.8	18.3	4.9	5.7	14.0
Zimbabwe	12.3	14.8	0.0	0.0	0.0	3.8	3.0	1.7	0.1	13.1	16.0	4.5
NORTH AFRICA	**..**	**15.4**	**11.3**	**11.4**	**12.7**	**14.1**	**15.0**	**..**	**..**	**12.8**	**12.2**	**12.7**
Algeria	22.8	18.8	13.6	11.5	11.0	9.5	10.2	..	..	18.1	19.0	12.3
Djibouti	..	5.1	13.8	9.7	22.0	25.2	..	..	..	..	5.8	11.9
Egypt, Arab Rep.	..	12.3	7.7	8.6	10.7	13.1	14.4	10.9	12.2	9.3	5.9	10.2
Libya	..	..	1.6	1.7	4.0	5.2	5.9	..	..	..	..	3.2
Morocco	16.7	19.2	22.4	23.8	24.5	27.6	28.4	24.9	24.9	16.1	18.0	23.7
Tunisia	13.3	15.6	18.6	18.3	19.5	20.2	20.7	20.7	..	13.5	15.7	20.0
AFRICA	**..**	**14.0**	**11.7**	**12.3**	**13.0**	**13.9**	**14.5**	**14.1**	**13.7**	**13.3**	**12.3**	**12.9**

a. Provisional.

Table 2.22 External trade balance (exports minus imports)

	Share of GDP (%)											
										Annual average		
	1980	1990	2004	2005	2006	2007	2008	2009	2010[a]	1980–89	1990–99	2000–10
SUB-SAHARAN AFRICA	**1.1**	**1.0**	**-1.3**	**-1.3**	**-1.9**	**-2.5**	**-3.7**	**-4.3**	**-2.7**	**-0.5**	**-1.5**	**-1.7**
Excluding South Africa	-4.8	-2.3	-2.0	-1.9	-1.6	-2.2	-4.2	-6.8	-4.7	-4.8	-4.5	-3.1
Excl. S. Africa & Nigeria	-8.7	-6.1	-5.4	-5.8	-5.3	-6.1	-8.1	-10.4	-7.5	-6.2	-6.5	-6.2
Angola	..	18.0	16.0	32.4	40.8	30.4	25.1	-0.5	19.4	9.1	2.2	19.1
Benin	-21.5	-12.0	-12.7	-12.7	-11.3	-15.3	-13.6	-14.5	-13.8	-17.5	-12.5	-13.3
Botswana	-13.4	5.3	7.3	16.8	16.4	12.3	3.7	-10.3	-7.0	5.3	9.8	7.5
Burkina Faso	-22.3	-13.5	-13.5	-15.5	-15.1	..	..	..	..	-19.6	-13.5	-14.2
Burundi	-14.5	-19.9	-18.0	-20.7	-28.6	-36.1	-35.3	-28.2	-30.4	-13.5	-14.4	-22.5
Cameroon	0.8	2.9	-0.4	-1.0	2.1	0.8	-3.0	-4.8	-3.1	0.4	3.7	-0.7
Cape Verde	-49.9	0.0	-37.6	-28.8	-27.6	-35.0	-33.0	-32.3	-28.5	-32.0	-22.6	-32.8
Central African Republic	-15.9	-12.9	-6.2	-8.8	-7.9	-7.5	-12.9	-8.0	..	-12.1	-7.8	-6.9
Chad	-11.9	-14.4	0.3	17.2	22.0	2.5	2.6	-27.0	-22.0	-13.5	-13.6	-17.5
Comoros	-43.2	-22.9	-17.9	-21.6	-24.4	-26.6	-34.4	-33.5	..	-33.3	-23.0	-21.8
Congo, Dem. Rep.	0.1	0.3	-8.8	-8.2	-13.2	-10.7	-15.2	-13.4	-12.9	-0.8	1.2	-8.7
Congo, Rep.	-0.1	7.9	29.7	29.7	18.5	25.0	28.2	20.2	30.4	-0.5	2.9	25.0
Côte d'Ivoire	-6.2	4.6	9.2	7.5	10.3	5.9	7.7	8.1	4.6	3.2	6.5	8.8
Equatorial Guinea	..	-37.4	35.1	43.8	53.7	51.6	47.3	12.2	..	-28.6	-45.8	33.4
Eritrea	..	..	-54.0	-48.8	-31.5	-29.4	-21.7	-15.9	..	..	-55.8	-44.2
Ethiopia	..	-3.3	-16.7	-20.4	-22.7	-19.3	-19.4	-18.3	-21.1	-5.3	-6.8	-17.2
Gabon	33.1	15.2	30.2	37.0	30.1	29.4	34.6	17.6	25.3	9.7	17.7	28.2
Gambia, The	-20.9	-11.7	-14.5	-16.5	-13.1	-12.6	-15.3	-15.1	-17.0	-13.2	-6.7	-11.3
Ghana	-0.7	-9.0	-21.1	-25.3	-15.5	-16.3	-19.5	-13.0	-11.8	-3.1	-12.4	-17.2
Guinea	..	-2.4	-2.3	-1.3	-3.3	-4.6	-5.3	-4.7	-4.4	0.3	-3.0	-3.1
Guinea-Bissau	-29.2	-27.1	..	..	..	..	..	..	..	-32.9	-24.5	-25.2
Kenya	-6.4	-5.6	-6.3	-7.5	-10.7	-10.9	-14.1	-12.5	-10.3	-4.9	-3.7	-9.4
Lesotho	-89.1	-105.2	-73.4	-72.0	-65.5	-65.9	-64.7	-69.8	-70.1	-110.0	-101.9	-66.7
Liberia	-0.1	..	-40.9	-52.4	-111.9	-89.0	-110.3	-80.4	-84.4	3.2	-39.6	-46.6
Madagascar	-16.4	-11.4	-14.9	-17.3	-16.0	-21.7	-30.4	-24.0	..	-7.7	-8.2	-15.1
Malawi	-14.0	-9.6	-18.2	-28.1	-24.5	-12.6	-21.8	-15.9	-16.6	-6.7	-14.3	-16.9
Mali	-14.4	-16.6	-12.4	-11.7	-8.1	-9.4	..	..	..	-17.6	-14.9	-11.2
Mauritania	-29.8	-15.1	-41.0	-51.8	-4.2	-18.0	-23.0	-16.7	-11.6	-24.4	-10.2	-21.6
Mauritius	-10.2	-7.2	-2.4	-6.0	-11.3	-9.3	-13.2	-9.4	-11.4	-3.3	-4.1	-4.8
Mozambique	-16.5	-27.9	-10.9	-12.2	-8.9	-9.8	-14.1	-18.5	-18.7	-18.4	-23.6	-15.4
Namibia	7.8	-15.5	-2.3	0.1	-1.7	-1.3	-6.8	-13.7	1.2	-7.6	-10.0	-4.2
Niger	-13.6	-6.9	-10.0	-9.2	..	..	..	..	..	-8.0	-6.2	-8.8
Nigeria	10.2	14.6	12.9	15.5	15.1	15.1	12.3	8.2	6.7	1.1	4.1	10.9
Rwanda	-12.0	-8.5	-13.6	-13.8	-14.2	-14.6	-15.8	-17.4	-19.8	-10.3	-19.9	-16.2
São Tomé and Príncipe	..	..	..	..	..	..	..	..	..	..	..	..
Senegal	-14.5	-6.8	-12.9	-15.6	-17.5	-22.3	-26.3	-18.6	-18.2	-12.1	-7.2	-15.7
Seychelles	-11.2	-4.3	2.0	-20.8	-17.1	-31.5	-18.7	-7.5	..	-2.3	-8.6	-10.8
Sierra Leone	-15.4	-1.3	-10.9	-12.9	-7.6	-7.0	-13.1	-13.1	-12.4	-3.1	-4.5	-13.9
Somalia	-55.3	-28.0	..	..	..	..	..	..	..	-35.1	..	..
South Africa	8.0	5.5	-0.3	-0.5	-2.5	-2.9	-3.0	-0.9	-0.2	5.1	2.8	0.3
Sudan	-12.6	-3.0	-3.8	-9.9	-10.9	-3.8	0.8	-5.8	0.9	-8.3	-6.7	-4.8
Swaziland	-39.4	-9.9	-2.5	-4.1	-2.4	-1.3	-9.3	-13.0	-13.4	-23.5	-15.2	-7.2
Tanzania	..	-24.8	-6.4	-8.9	-13.1	-16.9	-13.6	-11.9	-11.7	..	-19.0	-9.1
Togo	-5.3	-11.9	-19.3	-18.6	-17.9	-16.6	-16.4	-15.6	-16.5	-7.2	-9.6	-16.1
Uganda	-6.6	-12.1	-10.1	-10.6	-13.1	-13.3	-7.7	-11.4	-10.2	-6.2	-11.7	-11.6
Zambia	-4.0	-0.7	-4.4	-2.1	8.4	6.4	2.4	3.5	9.1	-2.1	-5.6	-3.1
Zimbabwe	-3.2	0.1	-7.1	-9.0	-10.9	-8.6	-26.6	-31.9	-29.7	-0.8	-2.4	-11.7
NORTH AFRICA	**-7.2**	**-6.0**	**5.6**	**8.1**	**10.1**	**6.5**	**5.6**	**-4.3**	**-2.3**	**-8.9**	**-3.1**	**3.6**
Algeria	4.0	-1.5	14.4	23.4	27.1	23.3	23.4	4.5	9.3	-2.5	1.6	16.7
Djibouti	..	-24.6	-17.2	-10.3	-17.4	-20.1	..	..	..	..	-17.5	-12.9
Egypt, Arab Rep.	-12.4	-12.7	-1.4	-2.3	-1.6	-4.6	-5.6	-6.6	-4.8	-13.2	-6.7	-4.1
Libya	..	8.6	31.1	38.1	45.8	38.2	39.9	..	..	..	3.6	29.1
Morocco	-9.4	-5.4	-5.0	-5.6	-5.5	-9.1	-13.4	-11.0	-9.9	-7.4	-4.9	-6.6
Tunisia	-5.4	-7.1	-2.5	-0.4	-1.9	-1.9	-3.0	-2.9	-5.3	-6.1	-4.2	-3.0
AFRICA	**-2.3**	**-2.0**	**1.6**	**2.7**	**3.2**	**1.3**	**0.3**	**-4.3**	**-2.6**	**-3.8**	**-2.2**	**0.6**

a. Provisional.

Table 2.23 Exports of goods and services, nominal

	Current prices ($ millions)											
										Annual average		
	1980	1990	2004	2005	2006	2007	2008	2009	2010[a]	1980–89	1990–99	2000–10
SUB-SAHARAN AFRICA	**82,272**	**79,567**	**185,099**	**233,717**	**278,472**	**323,452**	**397,178**	**300,792**	**374,652**	**64,895**	**87,503**	**234,335**
Excluding South Africa	53,753	52,145	127,221	166,090	200,187	233,953	299,421	223,380	275,208	38,474	55,756	168,508
Excl. S. Africa & Nigeria	33,576	40,208	88,566	113,791	137,155	165,863	213,004	161,187	200,864	30,911	43,527	119,586
Angola	..	3,993	13,780	24,286	33,346	44,707	64,243	41,451	51,400	2,613	4,265	27,851
Benin	222	264	539	577	538	900	1,019	922	937	214	327	636
Botswana	563	2,087	4,444	5,256	5,292	5,964	5,662	3,745	4,917	999	2,378	4,314
Burkina Faso	173	340	549	542	665	..	..	..	..	189	286	417
Burundi	81	89	64	92	93	93	106	98	124	111	89	78
Cameroon	1,880	2,251	3,061	3,393	4,131	4,563	7,718	5,895	6,502	2,240	2,198	4,058
Cape Verde	24	0	296	367	500	570	708	570	640	18	62	402
Central African Republic	201	220	168	170	207	254	211	290	..	181	185	197
Chad	175	234	2,252	3,234	3,852	3,845	4,413	2,879	3,331	153	254	2,292
Comoros	11	36	55	55	57	68	74	79	..	22	40	55
Congo, Dem. Rep.	2,372	2,759	1,976	2,450	2,621	2,707	2,719	1,908	3,412	2,016	1,595	2,026
Congo, Rep.	1,024	1,502	3,744	5,123	6,507	6,592	8,912	6,756	10,221	1,092	1,393	5,263
Côte d'Ivoire	3,561	3,421	7,517	8,354	9,144	9,466	10,890	9,722	9,316	3,142	4,129	7,734
Equatorial Guinea	..	42	4,724	7,183	8,332	10,298	14,520	8,549	..	32	160	6,160
Eritrea	..	..	64	68	84	86	61	84	..	..	132	77
Ethiopia	..	672	1,498	1,858	2,105	2,489	3,038	3,381	3,392	608	715	1,986
Gabon	2,770	2,740	4,465	5,610	5,912	7,203	9,675	6,143	8,094	1,964	2,728	5,398
Gambia, The	103	190	198	204	222	231	227	229	230	108	195	201
Ghana	376	993	3,487	3,907	5,136	6,041	7,140	7,609	9,461	554	1,684	4,849
Guinea	..	829	862	994	1,108	1,267	1,259	1,671	1,649	660	798	1,091
Guinea-Bissau	14	24	..	..	..	..	..	..	..	15	32	62
Kenya	2,145	2,207	4,283	5,342	6,101	7,294	8,411	7,386	8,861	1,805	2,594	5,478
Lesotho	91	98	696	669	765	832	915	784	955	67	187	645
Liberia	614	..	124	129	186	239	292	176	247	519	43	204
Madagascar	539	512	1,424	1,422	1,640	2,227	2,498	2,447	..	414	673	1,613
Malawi	307	447	655	663	705	1,033	1,206	1,240	1,547	295	465	834
Mali	263	415	1,237	1,359	1,884	1,871	..	..	..	255	514	1,262
Mauritania	261	465	470	671	1,454	1,449	2,114	1,521	2,241	387	556	1,036
Mauritius	579	1,724	3,450	3,761	4,009	4,509	5,103	4,323	5,098	807	2,257	3,845
Mozambique	383	201	1,759	2,087	2,722	2,839	3,192	2,398	2,421	215	373	1,961
Namibia	1,712	1,220	2,630	2,937	3,180	4,468	4,787	4,301	4,738	1,139	1,543	3,224
Niger	617	372	491	512	..	..	..	..	..	420	325	403
Nigeria	18,859	12,366	38,609	52,238	62,959	68,061	86,396	62,227	74,610	7,725	12,563	48,935
Rwanda	168	145	232	295	344	410	680	610	610	173	107	342
São Tomé and Príncipe	..	..	..	..	..	..	..	..	..	..	..	..
Senegal	837	1,453	2,123	2,344	2,401	2,871	3,498	3,117	3,186	989	1,347	2,327
Seychelles	100	230	685	717	860	993	1,091	912	..	123	298	750
Sierra Leone	252	146	247	292	355	346	319	296	327	187	155	256
Somalia	200	90	..	..	..	..	..	..	..	119	90	..
South Africa	28,555	27,149	57,890	67,647	78,318	89,549	98,005	77,548	99,399	26,088	31,523	65,869
Sudan	806	499	3,822	4,992	6,013	9,288	12,974	8,223	13,242	841	579	6,070
Swaziland	405	658	2,056	2,250	2,259	2,311	1,793	1,755	2,027	394	886	1,798
Tanzania	..	538	2,520	2,945	3,233	4,079	5,208	4,963	5,975	..	949	3,283
Togo	580	545	747	847	841	957	1,123	1,162	1,185	464	441	820
Uganda	242	312	1,008	1,310	1,524	1,993	3,506	3,753	4,087	371	500	1,812
Zambia	1,608	1,180	2,079	2,482	4,120	4,802	5,267	4,560	7,142	1,060	1,099	3,149
Zimbabwe	1,561	2,009	2,001	1,931	1,957	2,000	1,831	1,798	3,608	1,530	2,467	2,175
NORTH AFRICA	**37,700**	**47,088**	**107,580**	**139,233**	**167,999**	**198,536**	**254,602**	**177,527**	**197,350**	**34,578**	**49,081**	**139,197**
Algeria	14,541	14,546	34,067	48,761	56,953	63,297	79,123	40,454	49,939	12,221	12,420	41,927
Djibouti	..	244	246	288	307	484	..	..	..	..	210	276
Egypt, Arab Rep.	6,992	8,647	22,258	27,214	32,191	39,469	53,800	47,164	46,732	6,654	12,435	30,567
Libya	..	11,468	21,117	29,230	40,275	48,510	62,780	..	..	..	8,527	27,469
Morocco	3,273	6,830	16,726	19,234	22,449	26,892	33,312	26,094	29,965	3,790	8,363	20,236
Tunisia	3,518	5,353	13,166	14,505	15,823	19,883	24,966	19,606	21,569	3,312	7,126	15,249
AFRICA	**121,303**	**126,772**	**292,638**	**372,898**	**446,412**	**521,931**	**651,768**	**480,784**	**578,332**	**100,096**	**136,621**	**374,308**

a. Provisional.

Table

2.24 Imports of goods and services, nominal

	Current prices ($ millions)											
										Annual average		
	1980	1990	2004	2005	2006	2007	2008	2009	2010[a]	1980–89	1990–99	2000–10
SUB-SAHARAN AFRICA	**75,495**	**74,234**	**181,588**	**220,707**	**259,629**	**306,452**	**383,052**	**330,040**	**378,688**	**66,191**	**90,234**	**230,880**
Excluding South Africa	53,607	53,382	123,074	151,942	174,943	208,566	277,279	250,911	278,780	44,684	62,348	164,173
Excl. S. Africa & Nigeria	40,487	45,113	95,531	116,769	133,839	165,191	215,685	202,261	216,094	37,060	51,051	128,053
Angola	..	2,147	10,621	15,144	16,289	26,305	43,122	41,829	35,421	1,895	4,032	19,734
Benin	524	486	1,055	1,120	1,075	1,750	1,928	1,875	1,839	447	579	1,241
Botswana	705	1,888	3,707	3,534	3,451	4,438	5,159	4,934	5,956	842	1,916	3,688
Burkina Faso	603	758	1,240	1,390	1,547	..	..	..	..	567	640	1,016
Burundi	214	314	225	323	447	569	677	609	740	254	234	380
Cameroon	1,829	1,931	3,128	3,562	3,763	4,395	8,435	6,967	7,200	2,219	1,816	4,239
Cape Verde	95	0	643	647	805	1,035	1,224	1,087	1,113	62	175	746
Central African Republic	327	411	246	289	324	381	468	449	..	292	282	301
Chad	298	485	2,241	2,324	2,509	3,670	4,195	4,794	5,213	305	469	2,740
Comoros	64	93	120	138	156	192	256	258	..	67	93	143
Congo, Dem. Rep.	2,354	2,731	2,551	3,036	3,789	3,780	4,499	3,413	5,097	2,107	1,537	2,854
Congo, Rep.	1,026	1,282	2,363	3,318	5,073	4,493	5,574	4,816	6,568	1,093	1,309	3,581
Côte d'Ivoire	4,190	2,927	6,093	7,132	7,356	8,302	9,085	7,866	8,270	2,906	3,406	6,340
Equatorial Guinea	..	92	2,882	3,583	3,179	3,809	5,814	7,063	..	61	270	3,238
Eritrea	..	..	663	603	465	474	361	380	..	..	482	498
Ethiopia	..	1,069	3,175	4,366	5,548	6,262	8,215	9,240	9,653	1,093	1,330	4,980
Gabon	1,354	1,837	2,299	2,400	3,037	3,805	4,652	4,215	4,754	1,586	1,823	2,905
Gambia, The	153	227	282	309	309	336	385	377	409	137	242	291
Ghana	407	1,522	5,356	6,617	8,304	10,057	12,690	10,989	13,265	709	2,509	7,433
Guinea	..	892	947	1,031	1,202	1,460	1,460	1,865	1,859	658	905	1,206
Guinea-Bissau	46	90	..	..	..	..	..	..	..	67	91	114
Kenya	2,608	2,691	5,290	6,740	8,514	10,268	12,719	11,196	12,192	2,154	3,071	7,608
Lesotho	475	666	1,602	1,654	1,702	1,885	1,968	1,978	2,482	496	926	1,513
Liberia	614	..	315	413	862	897	1,230	883	1,081	491	180	572
Madagascar	1,202	864	2,072	2,296	2,525	3,823	5,357	4,484	..	668	942	2,624
Malawi	480	629	1,134	1,438	1,468	1,469	2,092	1,991	2,387	384	716	1,378
Mali	520	817	1,841	1,979	2,360	2,542	..	..	..	536	882	1,742
Mauritania	473	619	1,221	1,802	1,581	2,054	2,937	2,027	2,661	576	692	1,524
Mauritius	695	1,915	3,601	4,138	4,744	5,234	6,373	5,151	6,202	853	2,400	4,275
Mozambique	965	888	2,381	2,891	3,351	3,626	4,585	4,190	4,144	773	1,001	2,962
Namibia	1,542	1,584	2,780	2,927	3,317	4,583	5,387	5,524	4,603	1,284	1,844	3,514
Niger	957	545	795	825	..	..	..	..	..	583	448	629
Nigeria	12,324	8,203	27,282	34,849	40,726	43,039	61,006	48,373	61,486	7,362	11,214	35,781
Rwanda	307	364	517	651	787	955	1,423	1,524	1,721	354	405	850
São Tomé and Príncipe	..	..	..	..	..	..	..	..	..	..	..	..
Senegal	1,344	1,840	3,162	3,700	4,037	5,400	7,018	5,497	5,530	1,408	1,719	3,879
Seychelles	117	246	671	908	1,034	1,313	1,271	975	..	123	344	850
Sierra Leone	421	154	367	452	463	462	575	539	564	225	191	426
Somalia	534	346	..	..	..	..	..	..	..	403	346	..
South Africa	22,073	21,016	58,544	68,809	84,706	97,946	106,345	79,982	100,119	21,441	27,961	66,885
Sudan	1,763	877	4,650	7,701	9,992	11,042	12,537	11,381	12,665	1,744	1,289	7,383
Swaziland	619	768	2,117	2,356	2,329	2,350	2,074	2,140	2,522	515	1,109	1,971
Tanzania	..	1,595	3,343	4,205	5,116	6,915	8,035	7,511	8,653	..	1,986	4,804
Togo	640	738	1,121	1,241	1,236	1,375	1,643	1,656	1,709	542	586	1,178
Uganda	324	834	1,807	2,292	2,829	3,581	4,618	5,557	5,833	619	1,039	2,947
Zambia	1,764	1,203	2,319	2,631	3,221	4,068	4,909	4,118	5,672	1,148	1,283	3,022
Zimbabwe	1,771	2,002	2,413	2,446	2,551	2,455	3,005	3,662	5,831	1,598	2,644	2,854
NORTH AFRICA	**38,418**	**53,378**	**89,716**	**104,096**	**116,482**	**153,178**	**200,067**	**173,941**	**178,504**	**40,555**	**53,671**	**116,148**
Algeria	12,847	15,472	21,808	24,838	25,211	31,633	39,171	34,282	34,820	13,875	11,636	24,192
Djibouti	..	355	361	361	441	654	..	..	..	..	295	365
Egypt, Arab Rep.	9,822	14,109	23,330	29,246	33,931	45,443	62,909	59,713	57,200	10,787	16,572	36,045
Libya	..	8,996	10,723	12,452	14,383	21,074	25,589	..	..	..	7,464	12,328
Morocco	5,033	8,227	19,547	22,569	26,044	33,750	45,214	36,084	38,969	4,955	9,907	25,027
Tunisia	3,987	6,220	13,947	14,630	16,471	20,624	26,329	20,872	23,921	3,834	7,797	16,219
AFRICA	**115,086**	**127,918**	**271,113**	**324,566**	**375,813**	**459,396**	**582,915**	**503,682**	**557,929**	**107,439**	**144,006**	**346,946**

a. Provisional.

Table 2.25 Exports of goods and services as a share of GDP

	Share of GDP (%)											
										Annual average		
	1980	1990	2004	2005	2006	2007	2008	2009	2010[a]	1980–89	1990–99	2000–10
SUB-SAHARAN AFRICA	**31.9**	**26.4**	**31.1**	**32.7**	**33.4**	**33.7**	**36.1**	**29.9**	**31.2**	**26.9**	**27.2**	**32.3**
Excluding South Africa	29.0	27.9	34.5	36.5	35.8	35.5	36.4	31.8	34.3	25.4	29.9	34.4
Excl. S. Africa & Nigeria	28.9	24.4	32.4	34.2	34.3	34.2	35.1	30.6	33.4	26.4	27.1	32.6
Angola	..	38.9	69.7	86.0	79.8	74.0	76.3	54.9	62.3	34.8	63.5	73.9
Benin	15.8	14.3	13.3	13.5	11.4	16.2	15.2	14.0	14.3	16.6	16.4	14.1
Botswana	53.1	55.1	44.2	51.3	47.0	48.2	42.1	32.5	33.0	62.0	51.5	44.3
Burkina Faso	9.0	11.0	10.7	9.9	11.4	..	..	..	..	9.5	11.1	9.7
Burundi	8.8	7.9	7.1	8.2	7.5	7.0	6.5	5.4	6.1	10.4	9.0	6.5
Cameroon	27.9	20.2	19.4	20.5	23.0	22.1	32.5	26.6	28.9	25.7	20.9	23.5
Cape Verde	17.1	0.0	32.0	37.8	45.1	42.8	45.3	35.6	38.6	13.2	12.4	36.2
Central African Republic	25.2	14.8	13.2	12.6	14.0	15.0	10.7	14.7	..	20.5	16.2	14.6
Chad	16.9	13.5	51.0	61.0	63.2	54.8	52.8	40.6	39.0	14.3	16.1	39.2
Comoros	8.7	14.3	15.1	14.1	14.2	14.7	13.9	14.7	..	14.7	17.3	15.2
Congo, Dem. Rep.	16.5	29.5	30.4	34.1	29.7	27.0	23.3	17.0	26.0	21.4	23.1	25.1
Congo, Rep.	60.0	53.7	80.5	84.2	84.2	78.5	75.2	70.4	85.1	52.0	60.2	79.8
Côte d'Ivoire	35.0	31.7	48.6	51.1	52.7	47.8	46.5	42.2	40.6	37.1	36.8	46.1
Equatorial Guinea	..	32.2	90.1	87.4	86.8	81.9	78.8	69.9	..	35.9	52.9	89.1
Eritrea	..	..	5.8	6.2	6.9	6.5	4.4	4.5	..	..	22.0	8.0
Ethiopia	..	5.6	14.9	15.1	13.9	12.7	11.4	10.6	11.4	6.6	8.1	12.7
Gabon	64.7	46.0	62.2	64.7	61.9	62.3	66.6	56.1	61.3	53.3	54.0	61.1
Gambia, The	42.7	59.9	34.2	32.1	33.2	27.7	21.8	23.2	21.9	47.8	28.8	27.3
Ghana	8.5	16.9	39.3	36.5	25.2	24.5	25.0	29.3	29.4	11.2	25.2	35.1
Guinea	..	31.1	23.5	33.8	39.3	30.1	33.3	40.1	34.8	30.2	23.8	30.7
Guinea-Bissau	12.7	9.9	..	..	..	..	..	..	..	9.9	13.3	30.1
Kenya	29.5	25.7	26.6	28.5	27.1	26.8	27.6	24.2	27.5	25.7	27.6	25.6
Lesotho	21.0	18.1	56.4	48.9	53.5	52.1	56.3	45.8	43.8	16.9	25.0	50.3
Liberia	71.8	..	26.5	23.8	30.8	32.4	34.4	20.1	25.0	61.2	11.4	34.1
Madagascar	13.3	16.6	32.6	28.2	29.7	30.3	26.6	28.8	..	13.6	20.1	27.5
Malawi	24.8	23.8	25.0	24.1	22.6	29.9	29.6	26.2	30.6	23.7	25.1	26.3
Mali	14.7	17.2	25.4	25.6	32.1	26.2	..	..	..	15.8	20.8	28.5
Mauritania	36.8	45.6	25.7	30.7	47.8	43.2	59.0	50.2	62.0	47.9	41.2	38.9
Mauritius	51.0	65.0	54.0	59.9	61.6	57.9	52.9	49.0	52.5	54.4	61.5	57.8
Mozambique	10.9	8.2	30.9	31.7	38.4	35.4	32.3	24.8	26.3	6.8	12.8	28.7
Namibia	78.9	51.9	39.8	40.5	39.9	50.7	54.2	48.2	42.6	61.2	49.7	44.3
Niger	24.6	15.0	16.1	15.0	..	..	..	..	..	21.0	16.2	16.2
Nigeria	29.4	43.4	44.0	46.5	42.9	41.0	41.7	36.9	37.9	21.4	42.0	42.0
Rwanda	14.4	5.6	11.1	11.4	11.1	11.0	14.4	11.6	10.9	10.4	6.1	10.5
São Tomé and Príncipe	..	..	..	..	..	..	..	..	..	..	..	..
Senegal	23.9	25.4	26.4	26.9	25.6	25.4	26.1	24.4	24.8	27.4	26.4	26.5
Seychelles	68.0	62.5	97.8	78.2	84.3	97.4	113.3	108.4	..	62.1	59.9	91.8
Sierra Leone	22.9	22.5	22.5	23.6	24.9	20.8	16.3	16.0	17.1	19.5	19.8	19.7
Somalia	33.2	9.8	..	..	..	..	..	..	..	15.5	9.8	..
South Africa	35.4	24.2	26.4	27.4	30.0	31.3	35.8	27.4	27.3	28.8	23.5	29.5
Sudan	10.6	4.0	17.6	18.2	16.5	20.0	22.4	15.1	19.8	7.4	5.4	16.9
Swaziland	74.6	59.0	84.9	87.1	76.6	75.7	59.4	59.5	54.8	70.2	61.0	77.7
Tanzania	..	12.6	19.7	20.8	22.6	24.2	25.1	23.2	26.1	..	15.9	20.8
Togo	51.1	33.5	38.6	40.0	38.2	37.9	35.5	36.8	37.3	46.1	30.2	37.5
Uganda	19.4	7.2	12.7	14.2	15.3	16.7	24.3	23.8	23.8	11.6	9.8	16.0
Zambia	41.4	35.9	38.2	34.6	38.5	41.6	36.0	35.6	44.1	34.4	32.8	34.6
Zimbabwe	23.4	22.9	34.5	33.6	36.0	37.8	41.5	30.8	48.3	21.4	33.2	36.3
NORTH AFRICA	**30.2**	**26.5**	**36.8**	**40.4**	**41.4**	**41.4**	**43.0**	**28.7**	**28.4**	**24.1**	**25.9**	**34.4**
Algeria	34.3	23.4	40.1	47.7	48.6	46.6	46.3	29.3	30.8	23.8	25.8	40.0
Djibouti	..	53.8	37.0	40.6	39.9	57.1	..	..	..	..	43.2	40.7
Egypt, Arab Rep.	30.5	20.1	28.2	30.3	30.0	30.3	33.0	25.0	21.4	22.2	21.8	24.7
Libya	..	39.7	63.3	66.4	71.3	67.6	67.4	..	..	..	28.7	56.9
Morocco	17.4	26.5	29.4	32.3	34.2	35.8	37.5	28.7	33.0	22.2	26.0	31.6
Tunisia	40.2	43.6	42.2	44.9	46.0	51.1	55.6	45.1	48.8	36.9	41.2	45.1
AFRICA	**31.2**	**26.4**	**33.5**	**35.9**	**36.8**	**36.9**	**39.1**	**29.4**	**30.1**	**25.8**	**26.7**	**33.2**

a. Provisional.

Table 2.26 Imports of goods and services as a share of GDP

	Share of GDP (%)											
										Annual average		
	1980	1990	2004	2005	2006	2007	2008	2009	2010[a]	1980–89	1990–99	2000–10
SUB-SAHARAN AFRICA	**30.9**	**25.4**	**32.4**	**34.0**	**35.3**	**36.2**	**39.8**	**34.2**	**34.0**	**27.4**	**28.6**	**34.0**
Excluding South Africa	33.8	30.2	36.6	38.4	37.4	37.6	40.6	38.7	39.0	30.1	34.4	37.4
Excl. S. Africa & Nigeria	37.7	30.5	37.8	40.0	39.6	40.3	43.2	41.0	40.9	32.6	33.6	38.9
Angola	..	20.9	53.7	53.6	39.0	43.5	51.2	55.4	43.0	25.6	61.3	54.8
Benin	37.3	26.3	26.1	26.1	22.7	31.6	28.9	28.5	28.1	34.1	28.9	27.4
Botswana	66.4	49.8	36.9	34.5	30.7	35.9	38.4	42.8	40.0	56.7	41.7	36.9
Burkina Faso	31.3	24.5	24.3	25.5	26.5	..	..	..	..	29.2	24.6	23.9
Burundi	23.3	27.8	25.1	28.9	36.1	43.1	41.8	33.6	36.5	23.8	23.4	29.0
Cameroon	27.1	17.3	19.8	21.5	21.0	21.3	35.5	31.4	32.0	25.3	17.2	24.2
Cape Verde	67.0	0.0	69.6	66.6	72.7	77.8	78.4	67.9	67.1	45.2	35.0	69.0
Central African Republic	41.1	27.6	19.4	21.4	21.9	22.5	23.6	22.7	..	32.5	24.0	21.5
Chad	28.9	27.9	50.8	43.8	41.1	52.3	50.2	67.7	61.0	27.7	29.7	56.7
Comoros	51.9	37.2	33.0	35.8	38.6	41.3	48.3	48.2	..	47.9	40.2	37.0
Congo, Dem. Rep.	16.4	29.2	39.2	42.2	43.0	37.7	38.5	30.5	38.9	22.2	21.9	33.8
Congo, Rep.	60.1	45.8	50.8	54.5	65.6	53.5	47.0	50.2	54.7	52.6	57.3	54.9
Côte d'Ivoire	41.2	27.1	39.4	43.6	42.4	41.9	38.8	34.1	36.1	33.9	30.3	37.4
Equatorial Guinea	..	69.6	55.0	43.6	33.1	30.3	31.6	57.7	..	64.5	98.6	55.8
Eritrea	..	..	59.8	54.9	38.4	36.0	26.1	20.4	..	..	77.8	52.2
Ethiopia	..	8.9	31.6	35.5	36.6	32.0	30.8	28.9	32.5	11.9	14.9	30.0
Gabon	31.6	30.9	32.0	27.7	31.8	32.9	32.0	38.5	36.0	43.6	36.3	32.9
Gambia, The	63.6	71.6	48.8	48.6	46.4	40.3	37.1	38.3	38.9	61.0	35.5	38.6
Ghana	9.2	25.9	60.4	61.7	40.7	40.8	44.5	42.3	41.2	14.3	37.6	52.3
Guinea	..	33.4	25.8	35.1	42.6	34.7	38.6	44.8	39.3	29.9	26.9	33.8
Guinea-Bissau	41.8	37.0	..	..	..	..	..	..	..	42.8	37.8	55.3
Kenya	35.9	31.3	32.9	36.0	37.8	37.7	41.7	36.6	37.9	30.6	31.4	35.1
Lesotho	110.1	123.2	129.8	120.9	119.1	118.0	121.0	115.6	113.9	126.9	126.9	117.0
Liberia	71.8	..	67.4	76.3	142.7	121.4	144.6	100.4	109.5	58.0	51.0	80.7
Madagascar	29.7	28.0	47.5	45.6	45.8	52.1	57.0	52.8	..	21.3	28.3	42.6
Malawi	38.8	33.4	43.2	52.2	47.1	42.5	51.4	42.1	47.2	30.4	39.4	43.2
Mali	29.1	33.7	37.8	37.3	40.2	35.6	..	..	..	33.4	35.7	39.6
Mauritania	66.7	60.7	66.6	82.5	52.0	61.2	81.9	67.0	73.6	72.2	51.4	60.5
Mauritius	61.2	72.2	56.4	65.9	72.9	67.2	66.1	58.4	63.8	57.6	65.6	62.7
Mozambique	27.4	36.1	41.8	43.9	47.2	45.2	46.4	43.3	45.0	25.1	36.4	44.1
Namibia	71.1	67.4	42.1	40.3	41.6	52.0	60.9	61.9	41.3	68.7	59.7	48.4
Niger	38.1	22.0	26.0	24.2	..	..	..	..	..	29.0	22.4	25.0
Nigeria	19.2	28.8	31.1	31.1	27.7	25.9	29.5	28.7	31.2	20.3	37.8	31.1
Rwanda	26.4	14.1	24.8	25.2	25.3	25.6	30.2	29.0	30.6	20.7	26.0	26.7
São Tomé and Principe	..	..	..	..	..	..	..	..	..	..	..	..
Senegal	38.4	32.2	39.4	42.5	43.1	47.7	52.4	43.1	43.0	39.6	33.5	42.2
Seychelles	79.1	66.7	95.8	99.0	101.4	128.9	132.0	115.9	..	64.4	68.4	102.7
Sierra Leone	38.2	23.8	33.5	36.5	32.5	27.8	29.4	29.0	29.5	22.5	24.2	33.5
Somalia	88.5	37.7	..	..	..	..	..	..	..	50.6	37.7	..
South Africa	27.4	18.8	26.7	27.9	32.5	34.2	38.8	28.3	27.5	23.8	20.7	29.2
Sudan	23.2	7.1	21.5	28.1	27.5	23.7	21.6	20.8	18.9	15.7	12.1	21.7
Swaziland	114.1	68.9	87.5	91.2	79.0	77.0	68.7	72.5	68.2	93.7	76.1	84.9
Tanzania	..	37.5	26.1	29.7	35.7	41.1	38.8	35.2	37.8	..	34.9	29.9
Togo	56.4	45.3	57.9	58.7	56.1	54.5	51.9	52.5	53.8	53.3	39.8	53.6
Uganda	26.0	19.4	22.8	24.8	28.4	30.1	32.0	35.2	33.9	17.8	21.5	27.6
Zambia	45.4	36.6	42.6	36.7	30.1	35.2	33.5	32.2	35.0	36.5	38.4	37.6
Zimbabwe	26.5	22.8	41.6	42.5	46.9	46.4	68.1	62.7	78.0	22.2	35.6	48.0
NORTH AFRICA	**37.3**	**32.4**	**31.2**	**32.2**	**31.3**	**34.9**	**37.4**	**33.0**	**30.7**	**33.0**	**29.1**	**30.7**
Algeria	30.3	24.9	25.7	24.3	21.5	23.3	22.9	24.8	21.5	26.3	24.2	23.3
Djibouti	..	78.4	54.2	50.9	57.3	77.2	..	..	..	..	60.7	53.6
Egypt, Arab Rep.	42.9	32.7	29.6	32.6	31.6	34.8	38.6	31.6	26.1	35.4	28.5	28.8
Libya	..	31.1	32.1	28.3	25.5	29.4	27.5	..	..	..	25.1	27.8
Morocco	26.7	31.9	34.3	37.9	39.7	44.9	50.9	39.7	42.9	29.7	30.9	38.1
Tunisia	45.6	50.6	44.7	45.3	47.9	53.0	58.7	48.0	54.1	43.1	45.3	48.1
AFRICA	**33.5**	**28.4**	**31.9**	**33.2**	**33.6**	**35.6**	**38.8**	**33.7**	**32.7**	**29.6**	**28.8**	**32.6**

a. Provisional.

Table 2.27 Balance of payments and current account

	Exports of goods and services		Imports of goods and services		Total trade (exports and imports)	
	Current prices ($ millions)	Share of GDP (%)	Current prices ($ millions)	Share of GDP (%)	Current prices ($ millions)	Share of GDP (%)
	2010[a]	2010[a]	2010[a]	2010[a]	2010[a]	2010[a]
SUB-SAHARAN AFRICA	374,652	31.2	378,688	34.0	753,340	65.2
Excluding South Africa	275,208	34.3	278,780	39.0	553,987	73.2
Excl. S. Africa & Nigeria	200,864	33.4	216,094	40.9	416,958	74.2
Angola	51,400	62.3	35,421	43.0	86,822	105.3
Benin	937	14.3	1,839	28.1	2,776	42.3
Botswana	4,917	33.0	5,956	40.0	10,873	73.0
Burkina Faso	..	..	..	..	..	..
Burundi	124	6.1	740	36.5	864	42.7
Cameroon	6,502	28.9	7,200	32.0	13,702	61.0
Cape Verde	640	38.6	1,113	67.1	1,753	105.7
Central African Republic	..	..	..	..	..	..
Chad	3,331	39.0	5,213	61.0	8,544	100.0
Comoros	..	..	..	..	..	..
Congo, Dem. Rep.	3,412	26.0	5,096	38.9	8,508	64.9
Congo, Rep.	10,221	85.1	6,568	54.7	16,789	139.8
Côte d'Ivoire	9,316	40.6	8,270	36.1	17,586	76.7
Equatorial Guinea	..	..	..	..	..	..
Eritrea	..	..	..	..	..	..
Ethiopia	3,392	11.4	9,653	32.5	13,045	44.0
Gabon	8,094	61.3	4,754	36.0	12,848	97.3
Gambia, The	230	21.9	409	38.9	639	60.8
Ghana	9,461	29.4	13,265	41.2	22,726	70.6
Guinea	1,649	34.8	1,859	39.3	3,508	74.1
Guinea-Bissau	..	..	..	..	..	..
Kenya	8,861	27.5	12,192	37.9	21,053	65.4
Lesotho	955	43.8	2,482	113.9	3,437	157.7
Liberia	247	25.0	1,081	109.5	1,329	134.5
Madagascar	..	..	..	..	..	..
Malawi	1,547	30.6	2,387	47.2	3,934	77.8
Mali	..	..	..	..	..	..
Mauritania	2,241	62.0	2,661	73.6	4,902	135.6
Mauritius	5,098	52.5	6,202	63.8	11,300	116.3
Mozambique	2,421	26.3	4,144	45.0	6,564	71.3
Namibia	4,738	42.6	4,603	41.3	9,340	83.9
Niger	..	..	..	..	..	..
Nigeria	74,610	37.9	61,486	31.2	136,096	69.1
Rwanda	610	10.9	1,721	30.6	2,332	41.5
São Tomé and Príncipe	..	..	..	..	..	..
Senegal	3,186	24.8	5,530	43.0	8,716	67.8
Seychelles	..	..	..	..	..	..
Sierra Leone	327	17.1	564	29.5	891	46.6
Somalia	..	..	..	..	..	..
South Africa	99,399	27.3	100,119	27.5	199,518	54.9
Sudan	13,242	19.8	12,665	18.9	25,907	38.7
Swaziland	2,027	54.8	2,522	68.2	4,549	123.0
Tanzania	5,975	26.1	8,653	37.8	14,628	63.8
Togo	1,185	37.3	1,709	53.8	2,894	91.1
Uganda	4,087	23.8	5,833	33.9	9,920	57.7
Zambia	7,142	44.1	5,672	35.0	12,814	79.1
Zimbabwe	3,608	48.3	5,831	78.0	9,439	126.3
NORTH AFRICA	197,350	28.4	178,504	30.7	375,854	59.2
Algeria	49,939	30.8	34,820	21.5	84,759	52.3
Djibouti	..	..	..	..	..	..
Egypt, Arab Rep.	46,732	21.4	57,200	26.1	103,932	47.5
Libya	..	..	..	..	..	..
Morocco	29,965	33.0	38,969	42.9	68,934	75.9
Tunisia	21,569	48.8	23,921	54.1	45,490	102.8
AFRICA	578,332	30.1	557,929	32.7	1,136,260	62.8

a. Provisional.

Net income		Net current transfers		Current account balance		Total reserves including gold	
Current prices ($ millions) 2010[a]	Share of GDP (%) 2010[a]	Current prices ($ millions) 2010[a]	Share of GDP (%) 2010[a]	Current prices ($ millions) 2010[a]	Share of GDP (%) 2010[a]	Current prices ($ millions) 2010[a]	Share of GDP (%) 2010[a]
..	**..**	**..**	**..**	**-14,147**	**-1.5**	**163,563**	**14.6**
..	..	..	..	-4,029	-0.7	119,744	15.9
..	..	..	..	-6,506	-1.7	83,859	15.1
-8,172	-9.9	-438	-0.5	7,421	9.0	19,749	24.0
..	..	..	..	..	..	1,200	18.3
-243	-1.6	979	6.6	46	0.3	7,885	52.9
..	..	..	..	..	..	1,068	12.1
-11	-0.5	136	6.7	-301	-14.8	332	16.4
-239	-1.1	146	0.7	-856	-3.8	3,643	16.2
-68	-4.1	341	20.5	-184	-11.1	382	23.0
..	..	..	..	..	..	181	9.1
..	..	..	..	..	..	632	7.4
..	..	..	..	..	..	146	27.0
..	..	..	..	..	..	1,300	9.9
..	..	..	..	..	..	4,447	37.0
..	..	..	..	..	..	3,624	15.8
..	..	..	..	..	..	2,346	16.2
..	..	..	..	..	..	114	5.4
-64	-0.2	4,905	16.5	-425	-1.4	..	..
..	..	..	..	..	..	1,736	13.2
-8	-0.8	113	10.7	52	5.0	202	19.2
-535	-1.7	2,322	7.2	-2,700	-8.4	5,158	16.0
-77	-1.6	17	0.4	-327	-6.9	..	..
..	..	..	..	..	..	156	18.7
-155	-0.5	2,286	7.1	-2,512	-7.8	4,321	13.4
532	24.4	661	30.3	-421	-19.3	..	..
24	2.5	959	97.1	-415	-42.0	..	..
..	..	..	..	..	..	1,172	13.4
..	..	..	..	..	..	325	6.4
..	..	..	..	..	..	1,344	14.3
..	..	..	..	..	..	288	8.0
202	2.1	183	1.9	-800	-8.2	2,619	27.0
-85	-0.9	657	7.1	-1,113	-12.1	2,265	24.6
-564	-5.1	1,232	11.1	30	0.3	1,696	15.2
..	..	..	..	..	..	760	14.1
-18,623	-9.5	20,093	10.2	2,476	1.3	35,885	18.2
-46	-0.8	657	11.7	-421	-7.5	813	14.5
0	-0.2	3	1.3	-107	-53.4	49	24.6
..	..	..	..	..	..	2,047	15.9
-65	-6.7	25	2.6	-225	-23.4	236	24.5
-49	-2.5	185	9.7	-320	-16.8	409	21.4
..	..	..	..	..	..	..	..
-7,224	-2.0	-2,278	-0.6	-10,117	-2.8	43,820	12.1
-2,472	-3.7	2,131	3.2	157	0.2	1,036	1.6
-226	-6.1	400	10.8	-388	-10.5	756	20.5
-216	-0.9	824	3.6	-1,978	-8.6	3,905	17.0
..	..	..	..	..	..	715	22.5
-291	-1.7	1,313	7.6	-1,859	-10.8	2,706	15.7
-1,363	-8.4	432	2.7	1,144	7.1	2,094	12.9
..	..	..	..	..	..	..	..
..	**..**	**..**	**..**	**18,464**	**0.3**	**347,256**	**59.2**
-368	-0.2	2,650	1.6	12,146	7.5	170,461	105.2
17	..	95	..	50	..	249	..
-5,912	-2.7	12,439	5.7	-4,504	-2.1	37,029	16.9
-30	..	-1,828	..	16,801	..	106,144	..
-1,242	-1.4	7,270	8.0	-3,925	-4.3	23,609	26.0
-1,925	-4.4	1,935	4.4	-2,104	-4.8	9,764	22.1
..	**..**	**..**	**..**	**4,317**	**-0.9**	**510,820**	**30.0**

Table 2.28 Exchange rates and purchasing power parity

	Official exchange rate (local currency units to US$)			Purchasing power parity (PPP) conversion factor (local currency units to international $)			Ratio of PPP conversion factor to market exchange rate		
	2008	2009	2010	2008	2009	2010	2008	2009	2010
SUB-SAHARAN AFRICA									
Excluding South Africa									
Excl. S. Africa & Nigeria									
Angola	62.4	57.2	69.2	75.0	79.3	91.9	0.8	0.7	0.8
Benin	233.9	231.6	232.3	447.8	472.2	495.3	0.5	0.5	0.5
Botswana	3.4	3.2	3.7	6.8	7.2	6.8	0.5	0.5	0.5
Burkina Faso	204.5	207.2	210.5	447.8	472.2	495.3	0.5	0.4	0.4
Burundi	433.1	481.2	512.1	1,185.7	1,230.2	1,230.8	0.4	0.4	0.4
Cameroon	255.5	244.2	248.7	447.8	472.2	495.3	0.6	0.5	0.5
Cape Verde	68.6	70.7	72.2	75.3	79.4	83.3	0.9	0.9	0.9
Central African Republic	275.9	282.7	284.4	447.8	472.2	495.3	0.6	0.6	0.6
Chad	256.5	229.4	253.9	447.8	472.2	495.3	0.6	0.5	0.5
Comoros	235.8	244.1	250.5	335.9	354.1	371.5	0.7	0.7	0.7
Congo, Dem. Rep.	317.5	424.5	512.6	559.3	809.8	905.9	0.6	0.5	0.6
Congo, Rep.	371.3	291.6	348.1	447.8	472.2	495.3	0.8	0.6	0.7
Côte d'Ivoire	307.0	303.6	305.9	447.8	472.2	495.3	0.7	0.6	0.6
Equatorial Guinea	370.3	242.6	300.4	447.8	472.2	495.3	0.8	0.5	0.6
Eritrea	8.1	10.3	11.4	15.4	15.4	15.4	0.5	0.7	0.7
Ethiopia	3.5	4.4	4.5	9.6	11.8	14.4	0.4	0.4	0.4
Gabon	307.4	245.1	287.5	447.8	472.2	495.3	0.7	0.5	0.6
Gambia, The	7.6	8.0	8.4	22.2	26.6	28.0	0.3	0.3	0.3
Ghana	0.9	1.0	1.2	1.1	1.4	1.4	0.8	0.7	0.8
Guinea	1,992.2	2,105.5	2,501.9	4,601.7	4,801.1	5,726.1	0.4	0.4	0.4
Guinea-Bissau	229.8	229.9	231.2	447.8	472.2	495.3	0.5	0.5	0.5
Kenya	35.1	37.9	38.3	69.2	77.4	79.2	0.5	0.5	0.5
Lesotho	4.3	4.5	4.6	8.3	8.5	7.3	0.5	0.5	0.6
Liberia	32.1	31.3	33.0	63.2	68.3	71.4	0.5	0.5	0.5
Madagascar	796.0	854.0	912.4	1,708.4	1,956.2	2,090.0	0.5	0.4	0.4
Malawi	51.7	54.7	57.8	140.5	141.2	150.5	0.4	0.4	0.4
Mali	268.2	274.7	283.0	447.8	472.2	495.3	0.6	0.6	0.6
Mauritania	107.2	99.9	117.8	238.2	262.4	275.9	0.5	0.4	0.4
Mauritius	17.2	17.0	17.1	28.5	32.0	30.8	0.6	0.5	0.6
Mozambique	13.1	13.5	14.6	24.3	27.5	34.0	0.5	0.5	0.4
Namibia	5.3	5.5	5.5	8.3	8.5	7.3	0.6	0.7	0.8
Niger	235.1	242.2	239.4	447.8	472.2	495.3	0.5	0.5	0.5
Nigeria	77.1	72.9	78.8	118.6	148.9	150.3	0.7	0.5	0.5
Rwanda	239.5	263.8	267.3	546.9	568.3	583.1	0.4	0.5	0.5
São Tomé and Príncipe	9,313.4	10,464.1	11,559.3	14,695.2	16,208.5	18,498.6	0.6	0.7	0.6
Senegal	271.6	264.8	265.5	447.8	472.2	495.3	0.6	0.6	0.5
Seychelles	4.7	5.9	5.5	9.5	13.6	12.1	0.5	0.4	0.5
Sierra Leone	1,336.1	1,391.3	1,572.9	2,981.5	3,385.7	3,978.1	0.5	0.4	0.4
Somalia	..	..	..	..	..	..	..	..	..
South Africa	4.5	4.7	5.1	8.3	8.5	7.3	0.5	0.6	0.7
Sudan	1.4	1.4	1.6	2.1	2.3	2.3	0.7	0.6	0.7
Swaziland	4.2	4.1	4.3	8.3	8.5	7.3	0.5	0.5	0.6
Tanzania	460.4	489.1	517.1	1,196.3	1,320.3	1,409.3	0.4	0.4	0.4
Togo	258.0	260.2	261.8	447.8	472.2	495.3	0.6	0.6	0.5
Uganda	667.2	756.4	818.9	1,720.4	2,030.5	2,177.6	0.4	0.4	0.4
Zambia	3,193.3	3,498.9	3,864.3	3,745.7	5,046.1	4,797.1	0.9	0.7	0.8
Zimbabwe	..	..	..	..	..	..	..	..	..
NORTH AFRICA									
Algeria	40.1	35.2	40.5	64.6	72.7	74.4	0.6	0.5	0.5
Djibouti	92.8	93.4	..	177.7	177.7	177.7	0.5	0.5	..
Egypt, Arab Rep.	2.0	2.2	2.4	5.4	5.5	5.6	0.4	0.4	0.4
Libya	1.1	0.7	..	1.2	1.3	1.3	0.9	0.6	..
Morocco	5.0	5.0	5.0	7.8	8.1	8.4	0.7	0.6	0.6
Tunisia	0.6	0.6	0.6	1.2	1.4	1.4	0.5	0.5	0.4
AFRICA									

Real effective exchange rate (index: 2000 = 100)			Gross domestic product					
			PPP $ billions			Per capita PPP $		
2008	2009	2010	2008	2009	2010	2008	2009	2010
105.8	**107.6**	**106.1**	**1,749.2**	**1,814.6**	**1,931.6**	**2,176.0**	**2,203.2**	**2,288.7**
106.0	107.7	108.2	1,249.0	1,318.0	1,415.5	1,654.1	1,702.2	1,782.8
105.8	107.6	106.1	926.3	968.8	1,034.4	1,532.6	1,563.0	1,627.6
..	..	..	101.2	104.7	109.5	5,608.7	5,643.3	5,739.9
..	..	..	12.8	13.4	14.0	1,531.4	1,560.6	1,580.3
..	..	..	26.7	25.6	27.8	13,638.7	12,941.5	13,831.8
..	..	..	18.3	19.0	20.8	1,178.5	1,190.4	1,260.9
100.6	110.6	113.3	4.4	4.6	4.9	558.6	567.9	581.1
105.6	107.8	101.1	41.6	42.9	44.8	2,217.8	2,236.5	2,284.2
..	..	..	1.7	1.8	1.9	3,517.7	3,655.2	3,855.6
113.3	115.6	110.3	3.2	3.3	3.5	759.4	766.1	785.4
..	..	..	14.6	14.6	16.7	1,370.1	1,332.6	1,483.9
..	..	..	0.8	0.8	0.8	1,083.1	1,085.3	1,091.9
106.3	597.4	1,025.3	20.6	21.4	23.2	329.2	332.9	351.2
..	..	..	14.3	15.5	17.1	3,727.9	3,941.0	4,226.5
105.8	105.5	99.6	34.2	35.8	37.1	1,799.1	1,851.9	1,880.5
115.5	119.3	120.5	22.3	23.8	23.9	33,643.2	34,959.0	34,128.7
..	..	..	2.6	2.8	2.9	531.8	541.8	543.5
..	..	..	70.2	77.2	85.8	883.5	950.6	1,034.7
104.5	105.3	101.3	21.2	21.1	22.7	14,593.4	14,273.5	15,105.9
114.8	104.0	101.0	3.0	3.3	3.5	1,857.9	1,948.2	2,034.7
99.5	91.6	97.6	34.9	36.6	40.0	1,498.4	1,537.7	1,640.9
..	..	..	10.4	10.5	10.8	1,091.2	1,076.9	1,085.9
..	..	..	1.6	1.7	1.8	1,129.9	1,152.0	1,181.0
..	..	..	60.1	62.4	66.6	1,563.7	1,580.7	1,643.9
87.7	93.2	106.1	3.1	3.2	3.5	1,465.1	1,507.6	1,594.1
..	..	..	1.7	1.9	2.1	458.4	499.6	535.2
..	..	..	20.2	19.4	20.0	1,031.5	966.2	964.4
98.2	107.6	101.1	11.1	12.2	13.2	791.3	845.5	882.9
..	..	..	14.6	15.4	16.5	1,009.2	1,033.6	1,073.1
..	..	..	8.0	8.0	8.5	2,417.5	2,354.6	2,445.7
..	..	..	15.9	16.6	17.5	12,550.6	13,002.5	13,632.7
..	..	..	18.4	19.8	21.4	823.8	864.9	913.1
..	..	..	13.7	13.8	14.9	6,230.6	6,153.1	6,515.1
..	..	..	10.2	10.2	11.2	708.0	684.3	721.6
116.4	109.0	117.9	318.3	344.2	375.4	2,112.5	2,227.9	2,369.5
..	..	..	10.8	11.3	12.3	1,075.2	1,097.5	1,155.1
..	..	..	0.3	0.3	0.3	1,810.9	1,872.6	1,945.2
..	..	..	22.1	22.8	24.0	1,872.3	1,880.7	1,929.0
..	..	..	1.9	2.0	2.1	22,100.8	22,364.6	24,356.1
112.5	114.1	110.2	4.4	4.5	4.8	777.3	792.8	823.2
..	..	..	..	..	..	..	..	..
80.4	87.6	101.2	508.8	506.3	526.9	10,427.4	10,265.3	10,540.2
..	..	..	88.1	92.6	97.8	2,127.4	2,179.3	2,245.8
..	..	..	5.9	6.1	6.3	5,747.0	5,812.0	5,928.3
..	..	..	53.8	57.7	62.5	1,312.0	1,365.4	1,435.1
104.3	104.5	98.1	5.5	5.7	6.0	950.5	970.6	996.9
106.3	105.3	111.4	36.7	39.8	42.6	1,171.6	1,229.5	1,275.5
138.7	119.1	126.0	17.2	18.5	20.1	1,387.2	1,451.4	1,555.1
..	..	..	..	..	..	..	..	..
100.1	**102.0**	**98.0**	**1,052.1**	**1,102.7**	**1,162.2**	**6,518.3**	**6,728.9**	**6,987.3**
103.2	102.0	102.4	275.4	285.0	297.8	7,998.4	8,153.8	8,395.5
..	..	..	1.9	2.0	..	2,199.6	2,290.1	..
..	..	..	443.5	469.3	499.1	5,663.0	5,886.7	6,152.6
..	..	..	102.3	105.6	..	16,634.5	16,854.6	..
100.1	102.2	98.0	137.2	145.3	152.4	4,313.2	4,519.6	4,691.1
95.4	94.3	93.6	91.8	95.6	99.6	8,884.4	9,158.8	9,443.2
105.0	**105.4**	**101.9**	**2,798.5**	**2,914.5**	**3,091.5**	**2,899.2**	**2,951.5**	**3,060.0**

Table 2.29 Agriculture value added

	Share of GDP (%)											
										Annual average		
	1980	1990	2004	2005	2006	2007	2008	2008	2010[a]	1980–89	1990–99	2000–10
SUB-SAHARAN AFRICA	**18.5**	**18.8**	**17.1**	**16.5**	**16.0**	**15.8**	**13.0**	**13.5**	**11.2**	**18.4**	**18.2**	**15.8**
Excluding South Africa	31.5	31.4	27.2	26.6	25.7	25.1	22.9	24.2	..	31.0	30.7	26.7
Excl. S. Africa & Nigeria	31.5	31.4	25.7	25.3	24.2	23.3	22.9	24.2	21.1	31.0	30.7	25.0
Angola	..	17.9	8.6	8.5	7.7	7.9	6.6	10.2	9.8	15.2	11.3	8.1
Benin	35.4	36.1	32.1	32.2	..	..	..	..	..	33.8	36.1	33.7
Botswana	14.7	4.9	2.0	1.8	1.8	2.0	2.0	3.0	2.5	8.7	4.3	2.2
Burkina Faso	29.4	28.8	32.9	34.1	33.3	..	..	..	..	29.8	33.8	33.8
Burundi	62.3	55.9	44.6	44.5	43.7	37.8	35.4	35.2	35.2	58.1	50.8	41.3
Cameroon	31.3	24.6	20.5	19.5	19.9	19.5	..	..	..	25.7	24.3	20.9
Cape Verde	18.6	14.4	9.9	9.0	8.3	7.2	6.4	8.8	9.9	14.9	12.5	9.5
Central African Republic	40.0	47.6	55.3	54.4	55.0	53.9	52.9	56.5	..	44.3	48.4	55.0
Chad	45.1	29.3	23.5	12.3	11.7	12.5	13.6	..	..	36.9	36.7	25.6
Comoros	34.0	41.4	50.9	51.0	45.2	45.3	45.8	46.3	..	36.3	40.2	48.4
Congo, Dem. Rep.	26.8	31.0	47.3	45.5	45.7	42.5	40.2	42.9	..	30.4	47.0	47.6
Congo, Rep.	11.7	12.9	5.5	4.5	4.0	4.3	3.7	4.5	3.8	10.0	10.5	4.9
Côte d'Ivoire	25.9	32.5	23.2	22.8	22.9	23.9	25.0	24.7	22.8	27.2	27.2	24.1
Equatorial Guinea	..	61.6	4.1	2.6	2.8	2.7	2.0	3.2	..	65.9	41.5	4.6
Eritrea	..	..	11.6	24.2	26.1	25.4	17.4	14.5	..	..	22.9	18.2
Ethiopia	..	54.3	44.2	46.7	47.9	46.2	43.9	50.8	47.7	56.5	58.4	46.4
Gabon	6.8	7.3	5.6	4.9	4.9	4.9	4.1	5.4	4.1	7.7	7.7	5.3
Gambia, The	30.9	29.0	28.7	28.4	22.1	21.0	24.8	26.8	28.5	34.0	19.4	25.3
Ghana	60.1	45.1	41.6	40.9	30.4	29.1	31.0	31.8	29.9	52.5	42.6	35.7
Guinea	..	23.8	25.1	24.2	23.8	25.4	24.9	16.9	13.0	24.0	20.1	21.8
Guinea-Bissau	44.3	60.8	..	..	..	..	..	..	..	48.6	56.3	55.0
Kenya	32.6	29.5	28.0	27.2	26.8	25.0	25.8	27.2	25.2	32.4	30.8	27.9
Lesotho	24.6	25.0	9.6	9.0	7.9	7.7	8.0	7.7	8.6	24.7	19.3	9.5
Liberia	..	..	..	..	..	..	..	..	..	..	..	..
Madagascar	30.1	28.6	28.8	28.3	27.5	25.7	24.8	29.1	..	34.3	28.6	28.2
Malawi	43.7	45.0	34.6	32.6	31.2	30.3	30.1	30.5	..	44.2	37.3	34.0
Mali	48.3	45.5	36.4	36.6	36.9	36.5	..	..	..	44.4	46.7	37.5
Mauritania	30.4	29.6	35.5	30.5	22.9	25.6	18.9	20.2	17.2	30.4	35.6	28.7
Mauritius	13.1	12.9	6.5	6.0	5.6	4.5	4.1	3.9	3.7	14.9	10.2	5.6
Mozambique	37.1	37.1	27.4	27.0	27.9	27.7	30.5	31.5	31.9	39.7	34.7	27.8
Namibia	11.2	11.7	9.7	11.3	10.5	9.4	9.3	9.4	7.5	11.2	11.3	10.1
Niger	43.1	35.3	..	..	..	..	..	..	..	38.7	39.4	39.3
Nigeria	..	..	34.2	32.8	32.0	32.7	..	..	..	..	..	37.2
Rwanda	45.9	32.6	38.6	38.4	38.4	35.7	32.4	33.9	32.2	40.2	40.6	36.1
São Tomé and Príncipe	..	..	22.6	16.8	..	..	..	..	..	..	..	20.0
Senegal	20.1	19.9	15.9	16.7	14.8	13.4	15.6	17.2	17.4	22.0	19.7	16.5
Seychelles	6.8	4.8	3.0	2.4	2.3	2.1	2.0	1.8	..	6.1	3.9	2.6
Sierra Leone	33.0	46.9	44.9	51.6	51.1	49.9	50.2	52.3	49.0	40.0	47.9	49.9
Somalia	68.4	65.5	..	..	..	..	..	..	..	66.5	65.5	..
South Africa	6.2	4.6	3.1	2.7	2.9	3.4	3.2	3.0	2.5	5.5	4.1	3.2
Sudan	32.9	40.6	35.2	32.0	30.1	28.1	26.3	29.7	23.6	35.4	42.1	33.7
Swaziland	22.7	10.4	8.9	8.8	7.8	8.0	7.9	8.7	8.0	19.5	12.0	9.1
Tanzania	..	46.0	33.3	31.8	30.4	30.0	29.7	28.8	28.1	..	44.5	31.2
Togo	27.5	33.8	36.2	39.4	35.9	35.8	40.7	42.7	42.8	31.8	37.4	38.2
Uganda	72.0	56.6	22.9	26.7	25.6	23.6	22.7	24.7	24.3	57.6	47.9	25.5
Zambia	15.1	20.6	23.0	23.3	22.4	21.8	19.0	21.6	9.2	15.9	21.1	20.8
Zimbabwe	15.7	16.5	19.6	18.6	20.3	21.6	19.4	17.2	16.0	16.2	17.0	18.1
NORTH AFRICA	**15.7**	**17.0**	**12.3**	**11.3**	**11.2**	**10.7**	**10.2**	**12.0**	**11.9**	**16.4**	**15.6**	**12.2**
Algeria	8.5	11.4	10.2	8.2	8.0	8.0	6.9	6.9	6.9	9.9	11.2	8.6
Djibouti	..	3.1	3.6	3.5	3.5	3.9	..	..	..	3.3	3.4	3.6
Egypt, Arab Rep.	18.3	19.4	15.2	14.9	14.1	14.1	13.2	13.7	14.0	19.8	17.3	15.0
Libya	..	..	3.0	2.3	2.0	2.1	1.9	..	..	..	..	3.0
Morocco	18.5	18.3	16.3	14.7	16.9	13.7	14.6	16.4	15.4	16.4	17.8	15.8
Tunisia	16.3	17.7	11.0	10.1	10.2	9.4	8.5	8.9	8.0	15.8	15.2	9.8
AFRICA	**17.3**	**18.1**	**15.0**	**14.3**	**14.0**	**13.6**	**11.7**	**12.9**	**11.5**	**17.5**	**17.2**	**14.3**

a. Provisional.

Table 2.30 Industry value added

	Share of GDP (%)											
										Annual average		
	1980	1990	2004	2005	2006	2007	2008	2008	2010[a]	1980–89	1990–99	2000–10
SUB-SAHARAN AFRICA	37.8	32.2	30.9	31.6	31.8	31.8	32.0	29.7	30.4	..	34.4	29.6
Excluding South Africa	..	25.1	30.7	31.9	32.3	32.3	31.1	28.1	..	..	24.9	24.9
Excl. S. Africa & Nigeria	25.5	25.1	28.1	29.3	30.1	30.4	31.1	28.1	30.0	31.1	24.9	24.9
Angola	..	40.9	66.1	67.1	67.5	66.6	67.5	59.1	59.9	60.2	39.4	56.9
Benin	12.3	13.2	13.3	13.4	..	..	..	..	..	..	14.0	13.7
Botswana	50.7	61.0	51.0	50.2	54.0	52.6	52.6	40.1	45.0	46.8	57.5	54.9
Burkina Faso	20.5	21.0	23.2	22.7	22.4	..	..	..	..	..	21.0	21.1
Burundi	12.6	19.0	18.1	18.5	18.5	19.0	17.9	18.1	18.3	18.6	15.1	18.7
Cameroon	25.6	29.5	30.7	30.4	31.4	30.6	..	..	..	..	31.8	30.3
Cape Verde	17.0	21.4	15.0	15.7	16.0	15.7	18.5	18.3	18.0	17.8	18.0	19.2
Central African Republic	20.1	19.7	14.0	14.1	14.2	14.2	14.2	14.8	..	..	16.2	20.2
Chad	8.9	17.7	47.1	60.4	60.6	54.3	48.8	..	..	..	13.5	13.7
Comoros	13.2	8.3	12.2	11.0	11.8	11.9	12.0	12.1	..	..	12.5	11.4
Congo, Dem. Rep.	35.0	29.0	24.5	26.9	27.7	28.4	28.0	24.0	..	..	30.1	20.6
Congo, Rep.	46.6	40.6	65.9	71.9	75.5	73.2	77.4	71.1	75.4	76.8	45.1	45.4
Côte d'Ivoire	19.7	23.2	23.1	25.9	25.9	25.3	26.1	25.5	27.2	30.3	20.9	22.2
Equatorial Guinea	..	10.6	92.1	94.4	94.4	94.6	95.7	92.6	..	..	8.9	38.5
Eritrea	..	..	21.3	21.9	19.3	20.1	26.9	22.4	..	..	..	18.4
Ethiopia	..	11.1	14.1	13.0	12.7	13.3	13.0	10.8	14.3	12.6	11.6	10.2
Gabon	60.4	43.0	55.3	61.4	61.2	60.3	64.3	53.5	59.4	60.7	53.7	48.2
Gambia, The	14.9	13.1	14.5	14.7	15.5	14.9	13.7	12.4	12.3	12.0	13.7	6.2
Ghana	12.3	16.9	27.1	27.5	20.8	20.8	20.4	19.0	18.6	25.3	13.8	24.5
Guinea	..	33.3	33.7	38.9	43.4	43.4	46.7	52.1	47.2	..	33.6	30.1
Guinea-Bissau	19.7	18.6	..	..	..	..	..	..	..	..	15.7	12.5
Kenya	20.9	19.0	18.2	19.1	18.5	18.5	19.8	19.2	19.8	19.2	19.4	17.8
Lesotho	26.5	34.4	32.5	33.1	35.3	35.9	37.3	32.9	31.9	33.7	27.7	42.3
Liberia	..	..	..	..	..	..	..	..	..	..	..	..
Madagascar	16.1	12.8	16.0	15.8	16.1	16.3	16.2	16.0	..	..	13.8	12.2
Malawi	22.5	28.9	17.4	17.0	17.0	16.3	16.1	16.1	..	..	22.7	22.7
Mali	13.2	15.9	23.9	24.2	24.0	24.2	..	..	..	..	14.8	17.0
Mauritania	26.0	28.8	27.3	33.2	46.5	39.6	40.5	35.1	43.9	46.3	27.0	26.5
Mauritius	26.2	32.8	29.1	27.6	27.6	27.0	28.1	28.0	27.0	26.6	28.9	32.1
Mozambique	34.4	18.4	27.4	25.3	26.4	25.9	23.7	23.6	23.4	24.2	24.8	17.1
Namibia	55.8	38.0	29.4	29.2	34.6	35.6	37.8	32.7	19.6	19.6	44.3	30.6
Niger	22.9	16.2	..	..	..	..	..	..	..	..	19.8	17.4
Nigeria	..	..	42.1	43.5	41.9	40.7	..	..	..	..	..	..
Rwanda	21.6	24.6	13.9	14.1	13.8	14.0	14.8	14.4	15.0	..	21.0	19.5
São Tomé and Príncipe	..	..	21.1	20.5	..	..	..	..	..	..	..	..
Senegal	20.1	22.2	24.9	23.8	23.1	23.6	22.2	21.8	22.4	23.8	20.7	23.5
Seychelles	15.6	16.3	28.2	21.2	19.4	20.3	19.4	17.9	..	..	16.5	21.5
Sierra Leone	21.9	19.2	24.2	23.6	23.2	24.3	23.5	22.5	20.7	18.2	15.9	32.4
Somalia	8.0	..	..	..	..	..	..	..	..	..	8.0	..
South Africa	48.4	40.1	31.3	31.2	31.2	31.2	32.8	31.3	30.8	..	43.8	35.0
Sudan	..	15.3	25.8	28.3	29.2	31.2	34.0	26.0	33.0	39.8	15.4	13.5
Swaziland	30.2	43.2	46.4	44.7	46.7	46.5	46.4	50.6	46.5	45.9	32.3	43.4
Tanzania	..	17.7	22.4	22.7	22.9	23.3	23.1	24.3	25.5	26.5	..	16.4
Togo	24.8	22.5	17.2	17.2	18.4	18.7	18.2	16.0	15.7	16.0	22.0	21.0
Uganda	4.5	11.1	22.1	25.0	24.2	26.6	27.4	25.8	25.5	25.4	9.4	14.9
Zambia	42.1	51.3	27.9	31.6	35.3	38.5	41.4	34.1	37.2	37.7	45.5	39.2
Zimbabwe	29.0	33.1	26.4	28.7	32.3	33.1	31.1	27.8	26.8	22.9	30.2	30.5
NORTH AFRICA	40.8	34.7	43.0	44.7	46.3	45.1	46.7	41.3	41.6	..	36.8	36.1
Algeria	57.7	48.2	56.4	61.3	62.3	61.3	62.1	62.1	62.1	..	52.1	49.7
Djibouti	..	22.1	16.6	16.6	16.4	16.9	..	..	..	..	20.6	16.6
Egypt, Arab Rep.	36.8	28.7	36.5	35.9	38.4	36.3	37.5	37.3	37.5	36.7	30.6	31.8
Libya	..	..	68.6	75.5	78.5	76.4	78.2	..	..	..	..	..
Morocco	31.0	33.4	28.5	28.2	27.2	27.3	30.3	28.6	29.7	29.9	33.2	32.0
Tunisia	36.0	33.6	28.4	29.2	29.7	31.3	33.1	31.6	32.3	33.3	36.1	32.0
AFRICA	39.1	33.2	36.0	37.2	38.0	37.5	38.8	34.7	35.4	..	35.4	32.3

a. Provisional.

Table 2.31 Services plus discrepancy value added

	Share of GDP (%)											
										Annual average		
	1980	1990	2004	2005	2006	2007	2008	2008	2010[a]	1980–89	1990–99	2000–10
SUB-SAHARAN AFRICA	**44.7**	**49.2**	**52.0**	**51.9**	**52.2**	**52.5**	**55.1**	**56.8**	**58.4**	**47.5**	**52.2**	**53.6**
Excl. South Africa	43.9	43.8	42.1	41.4	42.0	42.7	46.0	47.7	..	44.4	44.4	43.6
Excl. S. Africa & Nigeria	43.9	43.8	46.2	45.5	45.7	46.5	46.0	47.7	48.9	44.4	44.4	46.3
Angola	..	41.2	25.3	24.4	24.8	25.6	25.9	30.8	30.2	45.4	31.8	25.9
Benin	52.3	50.7	54.6	54.4	..	..	..	..	..	52.2	50.2	52.6
Botswana	34.6	34.1	47.0	48.0	44.2	45.4	45.4	56.9	52.5	33.8	40.9	46.9
Burkina Faso	50.1	50.2	44.0	43.2	44.4	..	..	..	..	49.2	45.1	44.2
Burundi	25.1	25.2	37.3	37.1	37.9	43.2	46.8	46.7	46.6	26.8	30.5	40.5
Cameroon	43.1	46.0	48.9	50.1	48.8	49.9	..	..	..	42.5	45.4	47.3
Cape Verde	64.5	64.2	75.1	75.3	75.6	77.1	75.1	72.9	72.1	67.1	68.3	74.5
Central African Republic	39.9	32.7	30.7	31.4	30.7	31.9	32.9	28.7	..	39.5	31.4	30.3
Chad	46.0	53.0	29.4	27.3	27.8	33.2	37.5	..	..	49.6	49.6	37.1
Comoros	52.8	50.3	36.9	38.0	43.0	42.8	42.2	41.6	..	51.2	48.4	39.8
Congo, Dem. Rep.	38.2	40.0	28.3	27.6	26.6	29.1	31.8	33.1	..	39.6	32.4	28.1
Congo, Rep.	41.7	46.5	28.6	23.6	20.5	22.4	18.9	24.4	20.8	44.9	44.1	24.9
Côte d'Ivoire	54.4	44.3	53.8	51.3	51.2	50.9	48.9	49.9	50.0	52.0	50.6	51.1
Equatorial Guinea	..	27.8	3.8	3.0	2.9	2.8	2.3	4.2	..	25.2	20.0	3.8
Eritrea	..	..	67.1	53.9	54.6	54.5	55.8	63.0	..	..	58.7	59.7
Ethiopia	..	34.5	41.8	40.4	39.4	40.5	43.1	38.5	38.0	31.9	31.4	40.5
Gabon	32.8	49.7	39.1	33.8	33.9	34.9	31.6	41.2	36.5	38.6	44.0	37.7
Gambia, The	54.3	57.9	56.8	56.9	62.4	64.1	61.5	60.8	59.3	52.3	74.5	63.1
Ghana	27.6	38.1	31.4	31.6	48.8	50.2	48.6	49.2	51.4	33.6	32.9	40.1
Guinea	..	42.9	41.3	36.9	32.8	31.3	28.4	31.0	39.4	42.4	49.9	38.4
Guinea-Bissau	36.1	20.6	..	..	..	..	..	..	..	35.7	31.1	32.0
Kenya	46.6	51.4	53.7	53.7	54.8	56.5	54.4	53.6	55.0	48.2	51.5	53.7
Lesotho	48.9	40.7	57.9	57.9	56.8	56.4	54.7	59.4	59.5	47.6	38.4	56.6
Liberia	..	..	..	..	..	..	..	..	..	..	..	..
Madagascar	53.9	58.6	55.3	55.9	56.4	58.1	59.0	54.9	..	51.9	59.3	56.3
Malawi	33.7	26.1	47.9	50.3	51.9	53.4	53.8	53.4	..	33.1	40.1	48.8
Mali	38.5	38.6	39.8	39.3	39.1	..	..	..	..	40.8	36.4	38.1
Mauritania	43.6	41.6	37.2	36.3	30.5	34.8	40.6	44.7	38.9	42.6	37.9	37.4
Mauritius	60.7	54.4	64.4	66.4	66.9	68.6	67.8	68.1	69.4	56.2	57.7	65.6
Mozambique	28.5	44.5	45.2	47.7	45.7	46.4	45.9	44.9	44.8	35.6	48.2	47.1
Namibia	33.0	50.3	60.8	59.5	54.9	55.0	52.9	58.0	72.9	44.6	58.1	59.1
Niger	34.0	48.6	..	..	..	..	..	..	..	41.6	43.3	43.5
Nigeria	..	..	23.7	23.7	26.1	26.6	..	..	..	..	..	23.6
Rwanda	32.6	42.8	47.6	47.6	47.8	50.4	52.8	51.6	52.8	38.8	40.0	50.0
São Tomé and Príncipe	..	..	56.4	62.7	..	..	..	..	..	..	..	61.3
Senegal	59.9	57.9	59.2	59.6	62.2	63.1	62.3	61.0	60.3	57.3	56.8	59.9
Seychelles	77.5	78.9	68.8	72.9	73.2	77.5	78.6	80.3	..	77.4	74.7	72.5
Sierra Leone	45.0	33.9	30.9	24.8	25.7	25.9	26.3	25.2	30.4	44.2	19.7	26.0
Somalia	23.6	..	..	..	..	..	..	..	..	25.1	..	..
South Africa	45.4	55.3	65.6	66.2	66.0	65.4	64.0	65.7	66.7	50.8	60.9	65.2
Sudan	53.0	44.2	38.9	39.7	40.8	40.7	39.7	44.3	43.3	49.5	44.5	39.9
Swaziland	47.1	46.5	44.7	46.5	45.5	45.5	45.7	40.7	45.5	48.2	44.5	44.6
Tanzania	..	36.4	44.3	45.5	46.7	46.7	47.2	46.9	46.5	..	39.1	46.4
Togo	47.7	43.7	46.6	43.4	45.7	45.5	41.1	41.3	41.5	46.2	41.7	44.2
Uganda	23.5	32.4	55.0	48.3	50.2	49.8	49.9	49.5	50.3	33.0	37.2	49.9
Zambia	42.8	28.1	49.1	45.1	42.3	39.8	39.7	44.4	53.6	38.6	39.7	47.4
Zimbabwe	55.3	50.4	54.0	52.7	47.4	45.3	49.5	55.0	57.2	53.6	52.5	55.1
NORTH AFRICA	**43.5**	**48.3**	**44.7**	**43.9**	**42.5**	**44.2**	**43.2**	**46.7**	**46.5**	**46.8**	**48.2**	**45.3**
Algeria	33.8	40.5	33.5	30.5	29.7	30.7	31.0	31.0	31.0	38.0	39.1	32.5
Djibouti	..	74.9	79.8	79.9	80.1	79.3	..	..	..	76.1	80.0	80.2
Egypt, Arab Rep.	45.0	52.0	48.4	49.2	47.5	49.6	49.3	49.0	48.5	49.7	51.0	49.0
Libya	..	..	28.4	22.2	19.5	21.5	19.9	..	..	..	..	23.0
Morocco	50.5	48.3	55.2	57.1	56.0	59.0	55.0	55.0	55.0	50.4	50.2	55.9
Tunisia	47.7	48.7	60.6	60.7	60.1	59.3	58.4	59.5	59.7	48.2	52.8	59.8
AFRICA	**44.2**	**48.8**	**48.9**	**48.5**	**48.1**	**49.0**	**49.5**	**52.5**	**53.1**	**47.2**	**50.5**	**50.0**

a. Provisional.

Table 2.32 Central government finances

	Share of GDP (%)											
	Revenue, excluding grants				Expense				Cash surplus or deficit			
	1990	2000	2005	2010	1990	2000	2005	2010	1990	2000	2005	2010
SUB-SAHARAN AFRICA	..	..	23.3	..	..	..	22.8	..	..	..	-0.3	..
Angola	..	..	..	..	..	..	..	..	..	..	..	..
Benin[a]	..	..	16.4	18.2	..	..	13.6	15.0	..	..	-0.6	-1.0
Botswana[a]	50.8	..	..	..	26.7	26.7	..	..	19.1	19.1	..	..
Burkina Faso	..	..	12.8	15.6	..	..	11.6	12.1	..	..	-5.4	-5.7
Burundi[a]	..	..	..	..	..	..	..	..	..	..	..	..
Cameroon[a]	14.3	..	..	..	14.6	14.6	..	..	-5.6	-5.6	..	..
Cape Verde	..	..	27.6	..	..	..	30.2	..	..	..	-3.0	..
Central African Republic[a]	..	..	..	..	..	..	..	..	..	..	..	..
Chad	..	..	..	..	..	..	..	..	..	..	..	..
Comoros	..	..	..	..	..	..	..	..	..	..	..	..
Congo, Dem. Rep.[a]	10.1	3.7	14.7	23.4	16.7	16.7	22.1	13.7	-6.5	-6.5	-1.0	3.8
Congo, Rep.[a]	..	28.7	39.9	..	..	..	14.8	..	..	..	19.5	..
Côte d'Ivoire	..	..	12.1	..	..	..	16.9	..	..	..	-6.7	..
Equatorial Guinea	..	..	..	..	..	..	..	..	..	..	..	..
Eritrea	..	..	..	..	..	..	..	..	..	..	..	..
Ethiopia[a]	12.4	..	11.0	..	16.2	16.2	15.0	..	-6.6	-6.6	-4.5	..
Gabon	..	..	..	..	..	..	..	..	..	..	..	..
Gambia, The[a]	19.4	..	..	..	17.2	17.2	..	..	2.1	2.1	..	..
Ghana[a]	12.5	..	23.7	..	..	..	22.8	..	..	..	-1.4	..
Guinea[a]	..	..	..	..	..	..	..	..	..	..	..	..
Guinea-Bissau	..	..	..	..	..	..	..	..	..	..	..	..
Kenya[a]	..	19.7	20.2	20.3	..	..	18.2	22.4	..	..	1.5	-5.9
Lesotho[a]	44.9	50.7	52.1	..	33.6	33.6	41.9	..	-0.6	-0.6	4.2	..
Liberia[a]	..	..	0.3	..	..	..	0.2	..	..	..	0.0	..
Madagascar	..	11.7	11.0	..	..	..	11.0	..	..	..	-4.7	..
Malawi	..	..	..	..	..	..	..	..	..	..	..	..
Mali	..	13.4	18.0	..	..	..	15.1	..	..	..	-2.5	..
Mauritania	..	..	..	..	..	..	..	..	..	..	..	..
Mauritius	..	..	..	22.8	..	..	..	22.7	..	..	..	-2.4
Mozambique	..	..	..	..	..	..	..	..	..	..	..	..
Namibia[a]	31.3	30.1	28.2	..	..	..	25.6	..	..	..	-0.1	..
Niger	..	..	10.5	..	..	..	9.1	..	..	..	-1.9	..
Nigeria[a]	..	..	9.4	..	..	..	5.0	..	..	..	2.5	..
Rwanda[a]	10.8	..	..	..	12.7	12.7	..	..	-5.4	-5.4	..	..
São Tomé and Príncipe	..	..	..	..	..	..	..	..	..	..	..	..
Senegal[a]	..	16.9	..	..	..	..	..	..	..	..	..	..
Seychelles	..	38.7	44.8	36.4	..	..	37.7	31.7	..	..	2.5	1.5
Sierra Leone[a]	5.6	11.4	11.5	..	..	..	23.0	..	..	..	-1.7	..
Somalia	..	..	..	..	..	..	..	..	..	..	..	..
South Africa	..	26.4	30.1	..	..	..	29.9	..	..	..	-0.2	..
Sudan[a]	..	..	..	..	..	..	..	..	..	..	..	..
Swaziland[a]	..	25.6	..	..	..	..	..	..	..	..	..	..
Tanzania	..	..	..	..	..	..	..	..	..	..	..	..
Togo	..	..	14.7	17.6	..	..	16.1	14.5	..	..	-5.7	0.6
Uganda[a]	..	10.8	11.9	..	..	..	16.7	..	..	..	-0.8	..
Zambia[a]	20.4	..	17.6	17.4	..	..	22.9	17.2	..	..	-4.7	-1.5
Zimbabwe[a]	24.1	..	..	..	24.5	24.5	..	..	-2.6	-2.6	..	..
NORTH AFRICA	..	..	..	..	..	..	..	..	..	..	..	..
Algeria	..	..	..	..	..	..	..	..	..	..	..	..
Djibouti	..	..	..	..	..	..	..	..	..	..	..	..
Egypt, Arab Rep.[a]	23.0	..	24.3	24.8	24.0	24.0	27.4	28.9	-2.0	-2.0	-6.5	-7.7
Libya	..	..	..	..	..	..	..	..	..	..	..	..
Morocco[a]	..	..	30.7	31.8	..	..	30.0	30.6	..	..	-2.5	-2.6
Tunisia[a]	30.7	26.5	26.2	29.0	30.4	30.4	26.2	27.0	-3.2	-3.2	-2.8	-1.3
ALL AFRICA	..	..	24.3	..	..	..	24.7	..	..	..	-2.2	..

(continued)

Table 2.32 Central government finances (continued)

	Share of GDP (%)											
	Net incurrence of liabilities								Total debt			
	Domestic				Foreign							
	1990	2000	2005	2010	1990	2000	2005	2010	1990	2000	2005	2010
SUB-SAHARAN AFRICA	..	..	..	..	..	..	..	..	..	**3.9**	**3.1**	**1.2**
Angola	..	..	..	..	..	..	..	..	3.2	18.7	9.2	2.8
Benin[a]	..	..	..	-0.3	..	..	..	2.0	2.0	3.3	1.1	0.7
Botswana[a]	-0.8	..	..	..	0.0	..	..	..	2.8	1.2	0.5	0.5
Burkina Faso	..	..	0.4	2.6	..	..	4.8	3.5	1.1	1.8	0.8	0.6
Burundi[a]	..	..	..	..	..	..	..	..	3.8	2.6	3.5	0.2
Cameroon[a]	..	..	..	..	5.3	..	..	..	4.6	5.5	5.0	0.9
Cape Verde	..	..	4.9	..	..	..	3.0	..	1.9	3.0	3.7	2.2
Central African Republic[a]	..	..	..	..	..	..	..	..	2.0	1.5	0.5	0.1
Chad	..	..	..	..	..	..	..	..	0.7	1.8	1.0	0.9
Comoros	..	..	..	..	..	..	..	..	0.4	1.6	1.0	0.8
Congo, Dem. Rep.[a]	6.5	4.1	1.7	-4.7	..	..	-1.5	5.6	3.7	0.6	3.0	2.0
Congo, Rep.[a]	..	..	..	..	..	..	..	..	18.6	1.4	1.8	1.6
Côte d'Ivoire	..	..	-0.1	..	..	..	1.8	..	11.7	9.8	1.9	1.7
Equatorial Guinea	..	..	..	..	..	..	..	..	..	..	..	..
Eritrea	..	..	..	..	..	..	..	..	..	0.5	1.8	1.1
Ethiopia[a]	5.1	..	4.3	..	2.0	..	1.0	..	2.0	1.7	0.8	0.7
Gabon	..	..	..	..	..	..	..	..	3.0	6.9	2.2	3.4
Gambia, The[a]	..	..	..	..	..	..	..	..	11.9	2.7	4.5	1.9
Ghana[a]	..	..	-1.7	..	..	..	2.5	..	6.2	7.8	2.6	1.0
Guinea[a]	..	..	..	..	..	..	..	..	6.3	5.0	5.6	1.9
Guinea-Bissau	..	..	..	..	..	..	..	..	3.5	2.4	1.1	2.1
Kenya[a]	..	..	-0.5	4.9	..	..	..	1.9	9.2	4.7	2.9	1.2
Lesotho[a]	-7.9	..	..	..	9.1	..	..	..	4.3	8.3	5.8	1.6
Liberia[a]	..	..	0.0	..	..	..	0.0	..	0.8	0.1	0.2	0.6
Madagascar	..	1.3	1.3	..	..	1.7	3.9	..	7.2	3.0	1.6	0.6
Malawi	..	..	..	..	..	..	..	..	7.1	3.6	2.8	0.4
Mali	..	-1.0	-1.0	..	..	3.0	3.9	..	2.8	3.8	1.9	0.7
Mauritania	..	..	..	..	..	..	..	..	14.3	6.4	3.0	3.0
Mauritius	..	..	..	-0.2	..	..	..	1.8	5.7	9.9	3.6	1.4
Mozambique	..	..	..	..	..	..	..	..	3.2	2.3	1.2	1.0
Namibia[a]	..	1.0	1.5	..	..	0.7	-0.3	..	..	..	..	..
Niger	..	..	-0.6	..	..	..	2.6	..	4.0	1.5	1.2	0.5
Nigeria[a]	..	..	-0.1	..	..	..	..	..	11.7	4.0	7.9	0.2
Rwanda[a]	3.3	..	..	..	..	..	..	..	0.8	2.1	1.1	0.3
São Tomé and Príncipe	..	..	..	..	..	..	..	..	..	..	5.8	0.8
Senegal[a]	..	0.3	..	..	..	0.5	..	..	5.7	4.8	2.3	2.4
Seychelles	..	0.7	-8.1	17.0	..	13.1	2.9	-1.6	5.8	3.4	6.4	5.0
Sierra Leone[a]	..	..	..	..	..	..	..	..	3.3	7.3	1.4	0.6
Somalia	..	..	..	..	..	..	..	..	1.2	..	..	..
South Africa	..	1.6	2.5	..	..	0.3	0.1	..	..	2.9	1.3	1.4
Sudan[a]	..	..	..	..	..	..	..	..	0.4	2.0	1.5	0.7
Swaziland[a]	..	..	..	..	..	..	..	..	4.0	2.0	1.3	1.1
Tanzania	..	..	..	..	..	..	..	..	4.2	1.6	0.9	0.9
Togo	..	..	..	-2.7	..	..	..	1.9	5.3	2.3	1.0	1.1
Uganda[a]	..	0.6	1.2	..	..	2.0	0.8	..	3.4	1.2	1.9	0.4
Zambia[a]	6.8	..	..	..	1.1	..	..	..	6.1	5.7	3.9	0.9
Zimbabwe[a]	..	..	..	..	..	..	..	..	5.4	6.3	4.1	1.5
NORTH AFRICA	..	..	**-0.2**	**2.3**	..	..	**-0.3**	**0.2**	**10.5**	**5.0**	**4.6**	**1.8**
Algeria	..	..	..	..	..	..	..	..	14.2	8.2	5.8	0.4
Djibouti	..	..	..	..	..	..	..	..	2.4	2.4	2.2	..
Egypt, Arab Rep.[a]	..	..	15.4	9.2	..	..	-0.8	0.2	7.1	1.8	2.5	1.4
Libya	..	..	..	..	..	..	..	..	..	..	..	..
Morocco[a]	..	..	-0.2	2.3	..	..	-0.3	2.1	7.0	7.3	4.6	3.7
Tunisia[a]	3.6	0.5	-0.2	-0.6	1.8	-0.2	0.8	-0.4	11.7	8.9	6.3	5.3
ALL AFRICA	..	..	..	..	..	..	..	..	**7.9**	**4.4**	**3.5**	**1.4**

a. Data were reported on a cash basis and have been adjusted to the accrual framework.

Table
2.33 Central government expenses

	Share of expense (%)											
	Goods and services				Compensation of employees				Interest payments			
	1990	2000	2005	2009	1990	2000	2005	2009	1990	2000	2005	2009
SUB-SAHARAN AFRICA	..	..	..	..	..	..	..	..	..	..	..	..
Angola	..	..	..	..	..	..	..	..	..	..	..	..
Benin[a]	..	..	28.1	17.7	..	..	42.5	47.2	..	..	2.3	3.3
Botswana[a]	35.2	..	..	..	29.1	..	..	..	2.8	..	..	..
Burkina Faso	..	..	22.7	19.1	..	..	42.7	45.8	..	..	5.5	3.4
Burundi[a]	..	..	..	..	..	..	..	..	..	..	..	..
Cameroon[a]	16.7	..	..	..	55.6	..	..	..	7.8	..	..	..
Cape Verde	..	..	21.3	16.3	..	..	42.2	43.3	..	..	7.4	5.3
Central African Republic[a]	..	..	..	..	..	..	..	..	..	..	..	..
Chad	..	..	..	..	..	..	..	..	..	..	..	..
Comoros	..	..	..	..	..	..	..	..	..	..	..	..
Congo, Dem. Rep.[a]	56.3	56.1	22.0	21.0	25.4	27.1	19.7	32.1	7.4	..	13.4	3.7
Congo, Rep.[a]	..	25.6	30.0	..	..	27.8	30.0	..	..	35.2	18.2	..
Côte d'Ivoire	..	..	29.0	29.5	..	..	38.7	38.4	..	..	12.2	8.7
Equatorial Guinea	..	..	..	..	..	..	..	..	..	..	..	..
Eritrea	..	..	..	..	..	..	..	..	..	..	..	..
Ethiopia[a]	43.1	..	18.8	..	48.1	..	12.3	..	5.6	..	7.0	..
Gabon	..	..	..	..	..	..	..	..	..	..	..	..
Gambia, The[a]	28.3	..	..	..	28.7	..	..	..	21.4	..	..	..
Ghana[a]	..	..	18.2	16.5	..	..	40.1	40.0	..	..	16.0	15.7
Guinea[a]	..	..	..	..	..	..	..	..	..	..	..	..
Guinea-Bissau	..	..	..	..	..	..	..	..	..	..	..	..
Kenya[a]	..	21.3	23.4	20.2	..	55.2	59.8	37.3	..	17.8	10.4	10.3
Lesotho[a]	30.8	..	27.7	..	38.6	..	37.2	..	18.8	..	6.2	..
Liberia[a]	..	..	36.4	..	..	..	48.4	..	..	..	1.3	..
Madagascar	..	17.7	..	..	..	40.7	40.9	..	..	13.4	23.9	..
Malawi	..	..	..	..	..	..	..	..	..	..	..	..
Mali	..	37.6	33.3	30.6	..	36.5	32.6	34.4	..	8.0	4.4	2.5
Mauritania	..	..	..	..	..	..	..	..	..	..	..	..
Mauritius	..	..	..	11.3	..	..	..	35.7	..	..	..	13.2
Mozambique	..	..	..	..	..	..	..	..	..	..	..	..
Namibia[a]	..	20.8	16.3	..	..	51.2	49.8	..	..	6.6	9.8	..
Niger	..	..	29.3	..	..	..	38.5	..	..	..	6.4	..
Nigeria[a]	..	..	18.5	..	..	..	30.9	..	..	..	9.0	..
Rwanda[a]	35.3	..	..	..	43.6	..	..	..	7.9	..	..	..
São Tomé and Príncipe	..	..	..	..	..	..	..	..	..	..	..	..
Senegal[a]	..	26.0	..	..	..	41.4	..	..	..	10.7	..	..
Seychelles	..	24.6	25.3	37.2	..	36.3	37.1	26.8	..	17.4	14.2	20.1
Sierra Leone[a]	..	14.9	25.6	24.3	..	23.4	27.9	27.7	..	22.0	15.3	7.1
Somalia	..	..	..	..	..	..	..	..	..	..	..	..
South Africa	..	11.3	12.0	12.9	..	15.6	14.3	13.4	..	18.1	10.9	7.2
Sudan[a]	..	..	..	..	..	..	..	..	..	..	..	..
Swaziland[a]	..	26.1	..	..	..	44.6	..	..	..	2.4	..	..
Tanzania	..	..	..	..	..	..	..	..	..	..	..	..
Togo	..	..	48.3	24.2	..	..	30.8	40.3	..	..	6.5	5.5
Uganda[a]	..	55.1	29.2	31.2	..	12.3	13.1	14.2	..	5.2	8.9	8.6
Zambia[a]	..	..	25.5	19.5	..	..	36.4	43.8	..	..	19.4	10.1
Zimbabwe[a]	21.7	..	..	..	40.9	..	..	..	17.8	..	..	..
NORTH AFRICA	..	..	8.6	8.5	..	..	39.0	34.9	..	..	9.7	5.6
Algeria	..	..	..	11.3	..	..	..	33.7	..	..	..	1.4
Djibouti	..	..	..	..	..	..	..	..	..	..	..	..
Egypt, Arab Rep.[a]	22.4	..	8.6	8.0	26.6	..	28.5	24.6	16.3	..	20.2	14.0
Libya	..	..	..	..	..	..	..	..	..	..	..	..
Morocco[a]	..	..	15.2	9.0	..	..	47.2	47.8	..	..	7.8	3.7
Tunisia[a]	7.0	8.6	7.2	6.6	31.4	39.8	39.0	36.1	10.9	12.1	9.7	7.5
ALL AFRICA	..	..	..	..	..	..	..	..	..	..	..	..

(continued)

Central government expense (continued)

	Share of expense (%)							
	Subsidies and other transfers				Other expense			
	1990	2000	2005	2009	1990	2000	2005	2009
SUB-SAHARAN AFRICA	..	..	..	..	..	..	..	..
Angola	..	..	..	..	..	..	..	..
Benin[a]	..	..	1.3	29.7	..	..	25.9	2.1
Botswana[a]	31.8	..	..	..	1.2	..	..	..
Burkina Faso	..	..	10.0	11.1	..	..	19.1	20.7
Burundi[a]	..	..	..	..	..	..	..	..
Cameroon[a]	13.3	..	..	..	..	..	..	..
Cape Verde	..	..	23.5	30.1	..	..	5.6	5.0
Central African Republic[a]	..	..	..	..	..	..	..	..
Chad	..	..	..	..	..	..	..	..
Comoros	..	..	..	..	..	..	..	..
Congo, Dem. Rep.[a]	..	1.0	11.0	35.7	..	15.8	33.8	7.6
Congo, Rep.[a]	..	10.9	19.4	..	..	0.5	2.5	..
Côte d'Ivoire	..	..	14.9	16.3	..	..	5.3	7.1
Equatorial Guinea	..	..	..	..	..	..	..	..
Eritrea	..	..	..	..	..	..	..	..
Ethiopia[a]	11.2	..	41.8	..	0.2	..	20.1	..
Gabon	..	..	..	..	..	..	..	..
Gambia, The[a]	12.2	..	..	..	9.5	..	..	..
Ghana[a]	..	..	25.5	27.9	..	..	0.2	..
Guinea[a]	..	..	..	..	..	..	..	..
Guinea-Bissau	..	..	..	..	..	..	..	..
Kenya[a]	..	3.4	..	31.3	..	2.2	..	0.9
Lesotho[a]	8.9	..	28.9	..	2.9	..	0.0	..
Liberia[a]	..	..	13.9	..	..	..	..	..
Madagascar	..	9.7	..	..	..	18.6	8.6	..
Malawi	..	..	..	..	..	..	..	..
Mali	..	0.5	..	15.0	..	17.5	..	17.5
Mauritania	..	..	..	..	..	..	..	..
Mauritius	..	..	..	30.0	..	..	..	9.7
Mozambique	..	..	..	..	..	..	..	..
Namibia[a]	..	10.4	10.4	..	..	11.0	13.8	..
Niger	..	..	4.1	..	..	..	21.7	..
Nigeria[a]	..	..	41.7	..	..	..	..	..
Rwanda[a]	15.5	..	..	..	..	..	..	..
São Tomé and Príncipe	..	..	..	..	..	..	..	..
Senegal[a]	..	18.7	..	..	..	..	..	..
Seychelles	..	21.6	22.7	15.8	..	..	0.7	0.1
Sierra Leone[a]	..	5.5	19.1	22.6	..	34.3	12.1	18.4
Somalia	..	..	..	..	..	..	..	..
South Africa	..	52.9	57.7	62.9	..	2.2	6.1	4.4
Sudan[a]	..	..	..	..	..	..	..	..
Swaziland[a]	..	27.0	..	..	..	..	..	..
Tanzania	..	..	..	..	..	..	..	..
Togo	..	..	1.7	17.6	..	..	12.7	12.5
Uganda[a]	..	27.4	48.5	44.7	..	..	0.4	1.4
Zambia[a]	..	..	18.0	22.0	..	..	0.7	4.6
Zimbabwe[a]	..	..	..	..	..	..	..	..
NORTH AFRICA	..	..	26.7	41.0	..	..	10.5	10.7
Algeria	..	..	..	45.4	..	..	..	8.3
Djibouti	..	..	..	..	..	..	..	..
Egypt, Arab Rep.[a]	..	..	26.7	44.8	..	..	16.0	8.7
Libya	..	..	..	..	..	..	..	..
Morocco[a]	..	..	24.7	26.6	..	..	5.2	12.9
Tunisia[a]	44.9	..	33.6	37.2	5.8	..	10.5	12.7
ALL AFRICA	..	..	..	..	..	..	..	..

a. Data were reported on a cash basis and have been adjusted to the accrual framework.

Table 2.34 Central government revenues

	Share of revenues (%)											
	Interest payments				Taxes on income, profits and capital gains				Taxes on goods and services			
	1990	2000	2005	2009	1990	2000	2005	2010	1990	2000	2005	2010
SUB-SAHARAN AFRICA	..	..	..	..	..	..	..	..	..	..	..	..
Angola	..	..	..	..	..	..	..	..	..	..	..	..
Benin[a]	..	..	1.6	2.5	..	..	18.7	17.0	..	..	36.0	37.9
Botswana[a]	1.4	..	..	..	37.6	..	..	..	1.8	..	..	..
Burkina Faso	..	..	3.7	2.2	..	..	16.0	13.8	..	..	37.3	36.2
Burundi[a]	..	..	..	..	..	..	..	..	..	..	..	..
Cameroon[a]	8.0	..	..	..	18.9	..	..	..	22.2	..	..	..
Cape Verde	..	..	6.3	4.2	..	..	18.3	18.2	..	..	41.1	..
Central African Republic[a]	..	..	..	..	..	..	..	..	..	..	..	..
Chad	..	..	..	..	..	..	..	..	..	..	..	..
Comoros	..	..	..	..	..	..	..	..	..	..	..	..
Congo, Dem. Rep.[a]	10.1	..	8.8	2.0	21.9	10.2	4.8	10.5	15.1	14.2	9.4	13.9
Congo, Rep.[a]	..	24.1	6.5	..	..	..	4.9	..	..	15.5	6.4	..
Côte d'Ivoire	..	..	15.9	7.1	..	..	15.4	15.3	..	..	..	..
Equatorial Guinea	..	..	..	..	..	..	..	..	..	..	..	..
Eritrea	..	..	..	..	..	..	..	..	..	..	..	..
Ethiopia[a]	7.2	..	6.5	..	28.2	..	9.9	..	24.3	..	10.6	..
Gabon	..	..	..	..	..	..	..	..	..	..	..	..
Gambia, The[a]	14.3	..	..	..	9.7	..	..	..	28.3	..	..	..
Ghana[a]	10.2	..	12.1	15.2	20.6	..	20.8	22.6	26.8	..	35.9	..
Guinea[a]	..	..	..	..	..	..	..	..	..	..	..	..
Guinea-Bissau	..	..	..	..	..	..	..	..	..	..	..	..
Kenya[a]	..	15.2	8.9	10.4	..	28.5	33.0	40.0	..	41.4	44.2	40.1
Lesotho[a]	10.8	10.0	4.8	..	8.7	17.2	19.5	..	16.0	12.5	16.1	..
Liberia[a]	..	..	1.0	..	..	..	34.5	..	..	..	16.6	..
Madagascar	..	9.3	15.8	..	..	11.7	9.2	..	..	21.6	17.2	..
Malawi	..	..	..	..	..	..	..	..	..	..	..	..
Mali	..	5.0	3.0	1.7	..	12.5	14.5	19.5	..	41.6	38.0	..
Mauritania	..	..	..	..	..	..	..	..	..	..	..	..
Mauritius	..	..	..	11.7	..	..	..	22.2	..	..	..	49.6
Mozambique	..	..	..	..	..	..	..	..	..	..	..	..
Namibia[a]	1.3	6.2	8.9	..	32.6	31.8	35.0	..	23.9	22.7	24.5	..
Niger	..	..	3.2	..	..	..	8.9	..	..	..	13.7	..
Nigeria[a]	..	..	4.7	..	..	..	0.1	..	..	..	1.8	..
Rwanda[a]	7.3	..	..	..	14.0	..	..	..	27.1	..	..	..
São Tomé and Príncipe	..	..	..	..	..	..	..	..	..	..	..	..
Senegal[a]	..	7.4	..	..	..	21.3	..	..	..	33.7	..	..
Seychelles	..	18.6	11.7	16.4	..	17.3	12.5	19.2	..	5.1	33.7	35.8
Sierra Leone[a]	25.7	32.5	16.5	8.3	29.7	15.4	15.1	17.0	22.1	7.6	11.9	..
Somalia	..	..	..	..	..	..	..	..	..	..	..	..
South Africa	..	19.1	10.8	8.4	..	51.7	48.8	52.6	..	33.1	33.0	..
Sudan[a]	..	..	..	..	..	..	..	..	..	..	..	..
Swaziland[a]	..	2.0	..	..	..	24.1	..	..	..	13.2	..	..
Tanzania	..	..	..	..	..	..	..	..	..	..	..	..
Togo	..	..	7.1	4.0	..	..	18.9	16.7	..	..	48.3	37.4
Uganda[a]	..	4.7	7.7	7.7	..	9.9	16.6	22.0	..	29.4	37.1	..
Zambia[a]	7.1	..	17.9	8.5	39.5	..	30.1	35.5	37.4	..	29.4	32.3
Zimbabwe[a]	17.7	..	..	..	43.7	..	..	..	25.6	..	..	..
NORTH AFRICA	..	..	9.6	5.0	..	..	26.1	28.1	..	..	30.2	31.3
Algeria	..	..	..	1.0	..	..	..	59.7	..	..	..	..
Djibouti	..	..	..	..	..	..	..	..	..	..	..	..
Egypt, Arab Rep.[a]	16.0	..	22.4	15.2	18.1	..	23.8	27.8	12.8	..	23.7	22.1
Libya	..	..	..	..	..	..	..	..	..	..	..	..
Morocco[a]	..	..	7.5	3.1	..	..	26.1	28.4	..	..	30.2	36.1
Tunisia[a]	10.6	11.3	9.6	6.9	12.3	20.4	26.2	27.3	19.1	37.1	34.8	31.3
ALL AFRICA	..	..	..	..	..	..	..	..	..	..	..	..

(continued)

Central government revenues (continued)

Share of revenues (%)

	Taxes on international trade				Other taxes				Social contributions				Grants and other revenue			
	1990	2000	2005	2010	1990	2000	2005	2010	1990	2000	2005	2009	1990	2000	2005	2010
SUB-SAHARAN AFRICA	..	..	..	..	..	..	..	..	..	..	..	..	..	..	..	..
Angola	..	..	..	..	..	..	..	..	..	..	..	..	..	..	..	..
Benin[a]	..	..	21.6	22.1	..	..	6.5	5.8	..	..	..	2.4	..	..	17.2	15.5
Botswana[a]	12.9	..	..	..	0.1	..	..	..	..	..	..	..	47.6	..	..	..
Burkina Faso	..	..	12.6	11.0	..	..	2.1	1.9	..	..	..	..	..	..	32.0	35.7
Burundi[a]	..	..	..	..	..	..	..	..	..	..	..	..	..	..	..	..
Cameroon[a]	15.5	..	..	..	4.7	..	..	..	1.8	..	..	..	27.5	..	..	..
Cape Verde	..	..	0.1	..	..	..	..	..	..	..	10.2	10.1	..	..	30.3	..
Central African Republic[a]	..	..	..	..	..	..	..	..	..	..	..	..	..	..	..	..
Chad	..	..	..	..	..	..	..	..	..	..	..	..	..	..	..	..
Comoros	..	..	..	..	..	..	..	..	..	..	..	..	..	..	..	..
Congo, Dem. Rep.[a]	37.8	14.5	10.5	14.3	1.1	20.1	4.8	0.4	1.0	..	..	..	23.1	41.1	70.5	59.6
Congo, Rep.[a]	..	5.0	2.6	..	..	0.0	1.1	..	..	3.1	0.9	..	..	76.4	84.0	..
Côte d'Ivoire	..	..	57.1	..	..	..	3.1	..	..	..	10.2	6.4	..	..	14.2	..
Equatorial Guinea	..	..	..	..	..	..	..	..	..	..	..	..	..	..	..	..
Eritrea	..	..	..	..	..	..	..	..	..	..	..	..	..	..	..	..
Ethiopia[a]	14.3	..	33.9	..	2.2	..	0.5	..	2.0	..	..	..	29.1	..	45.2	..
Gabon	..	..	..	..	..	..	..	..	..	..	..	..	..	..	..	..
Gambia, The[a]	32.4	..	..	..	0.4	..	..	..	0.2	..	..	..	28.9	..	..	..
Ghana[a]	34.7	..	14.0	..	..	..	..	..	..	..	..	..	10.4	..	29.3	..
Guinea[a]	..	..	..	..	..	..	..	..	..	..	..	..	..	..	..	..
Guinea-Bissau	..	..	..	..	..	..	..	..	..	..	..	..	..	..	..	..
Kenya[a]	..	15.0	10.2	10.6	..	0.5	0.4	1.0	..	0.0	0.2	..	..	14.7	12.1	7.5
Lesotho[a]	43.7	41.4	49.5	..	0.1	..	0.1	..	..	..	..	..	31.6	28.9	14.8	..
Liberia[a]	..	..	36.6	..	..	..	0.4	..	..	..	..	..	..	..	11.9	..
Madagascar	..	39.6	29.1	..	..	1.2	5.0	..	..	..	..	..	..	26.0	39.5	..
Malawi	..	..	..	..	..	..	..	..	..	..	..	..	..	..	..	..
Mali	..	11.3	12.4	..	..	5.0	6.1	..	..	..	..	..	..	29.5	29.1	..
Mauritania	..	..	..	..	..	..	..	..	..	..	..	..	..	..	..	..
Mauritius	..	..	..	2.2	..	..	..	7.5	..	..	..	6.7	..	..	..	13.6
Mozambique	..	..	..	..	..	..	..	..	..	..	..	..	..	..	..	..
Namibia[a]	25.3	35.1	29.8	..	0.9	1.4	1.7	..	..	0.5	0.6	..	17.2	8.5	8.4	..
Niger	..	..	29.9	..	..	..	3.6	..	..	..	..	..	..	..	43.9	..
Nigeria[a]	..	..	..	..	..	..	..	..	..	..	..	..	..	..	98.1	..
Rwanda[a]	20.5	..	..	..	3.1	..	..	..	5.4	..	..	..	30.0	..	..	..
São Tomé and Príncipe	..	..	..	..	..	..	..	..	..	..	..	..	..	..	..	..
Senegal[a]	..	29.6	..	..	..	3.3	..	..	..	..	..	..	..	12.2	..	..
Seychelles	..	41.0	15.7	16.8	..	1.6	0.0	..	..	13.8	19.4	9.0	..	21.3	18.8	16.8
Sierra Leone[a]	38.1	29.4	23.5	..	0.2	..	..	..	..	..	..	..	9.9	47.7	49.5	..
Somalia	..	..	..	..	..	..	..	..	..	..	..	..	..	..	..	..
South Africa	..	3.0	3.8	..	..	2.8	3.6	..	..	2.1	2.0	2.2	..	7.4	8.8	..
Sudan[a]	..	..	..	..	..	..	..	..	..	..	..	..	..	..	..	..
Swaziland[a]	..	49.9	..	..	..	4.1	..	..	..	..	..	..	..	8.7	..	..
Tanzania	..	..	..	..	..	..	..	..	..	..	..	..	..	..	..	..
Togo	..	..	21.7	18.8	..	..	5.9	6.4	..	..	..	..	..	..	5.2	26.6
Uganda[a]	..	21.8	7.2	..	..	0.1	0.2	..	..	..	..	..	..	38.7	38.9	..
Zambia[a]	17.2	..	9.4	8.3	0.2	..	0.2	0.2	0.0	..	..	..	5.8	..	31.0	15.1
Zimbabwe[a]	17.1	..	..	..	1.1	..	..	..	3.3	..	..	..	9.2	..	..	..
NORTH AFRICA	..	..	6.7	5.6	..	..	4.1	4.2	..	..	..	..	..	..	15.7	14.1
Algeria	..	..	..	..	..	..	..	..	..	..	..	..	..	..	..	..
Djibouti	..	..	..	..	..	..	..	..	..	..	..	..	..	..	..	..
Egypt, Arab Rep.[a]	12.9	..	5.8	4.9	10.2	..	3.8	4.0	14.5	..	..	..	31.6	..	43.0	43.8
Libya	..	..	..	..	..	..	..	..	..	..	..	..	..	..	..	..
Morocco[a]	..	..	8.4	5.6	..	..	6.2	5.8	..	..	13.5	12.1	..	..	15.7	14.1
Tunisia[a]	27.5	10.7	6.7	6.2	4.8	4.4	4.1	4.2	13.0	17.0	17.5	20.2	23.4	10.5	10.8	10.0
ALL AFRICA	..	..	..	..	..	..	..	..	..	..	..	..	..	..	..	..

a. Data were reported on a cash basis and have been adjusted to the accrual framework.

Table 2.35 Structure of demand

	Share of GDP (%)																	
	Household final consumption expenditure			General government final consumption expenditure			Gross fixed capital formation			Exports of goods and services			Imports of goods and services			Gross national savings		
	1990	2000	2010[a]	1990	2000	2010[a]	1990	2000	2010[a]	1990	2000	2010[a]	1990	2000	2010[a]	1990	2000	2010[a]
SUB-SAHARAN AFRICA	**65.2**	**68.4**	**64.9**	**17.5**	**15.6**	**18.2**	**18.3**	**16.3**	**20.4**	**26.4**	**32.4**	**31.2**	**25.4**	**30.6**	**34.0**	**15.8**	**15.6**	**17.2**
Excluding South Africa	72.3	73.4	..	15.6	13.3	..	17.5	17.3	..	27.9	35.6	34.3	30.2	34.8	39.0	12.8	15.5	..
Excl. S. Africa & Nigeria	72.3	73.4	71.0	15.6	13.3	14.6	17.5	17.3	21.3	24.4	31.5	33.4	30.5	35.4	40.9	12.8	15.5	..
Angola	35.8	..	50.4	34.5	..	17.6	11.1	15.1	12.6	38.9	89.6	62.3	20.9	62.8	43.0	9.0	23.8	21.6
Benin	86.8	82.4	..	11.0	11.6	..	13.4	18.9	26.1	14.3	15.2	14.3	26.3	28.1	28.1	5.3	10.4	..
Botswana	33.2	30.8	56.6	24.1	25.4	20.9	32.4	25.8	27.1	55.1	53.3	33.0	49.8	41.2	40.0	41.7	41.4	27.7
Burkina Faso	73.5	78.5	..	21.1	20.8	..	17.7	18.7	..	11.0	9.1	..	24.5	25.2	..	15.9	5.1	..
Burundi	94.6	92.0	80.8	10.8	15.5	31.6	15.2	4.2	18.0	7.9	6.6	6.1	27.8	16.9	36.5	8.7	1.1	-5.4
Cameroon	66.6	70.2	..	12.8	9.5	..	17.3	16.0	..	20.2	23.3	28.9	17.3	19.7	32.0	16.2	15.3	..
Cape Verde	58.5	72.1	55.6	16.3	30.7	26.1	25.3	30.5	46.8	0.0	27.0	38.6	0.0	60.5	67.1	53.9	19.6	34.4
Central African Republic	85.7	80.8	..	14.9	14.0	..	11.4	9.5	..	14.8	19.8	..	27.6	24.1	..	6.2	..	..
Chad	97.6	86.8	76.1	10.1	7.7	13.2	4.8	20.9	31.8	13.5	16.9	39.0	27.9	34.7	61.0	2.3	..	..
Comoros	78.7	94.0	..	24.5	11.7	..	11.9	10.1	..	14.3	16.7	..	37.2	32.5	..	14.4	..	..
Congo, Dem. Rep.	79.1	88.0	..	11.5	7.5	..	12.8	3.5	..	29.5	22.4	26.0	29.2	21.4	38.9	..	..	..
Congo, Rep.	62.4	29.1	38.6	13.9	11.6	10.4	17.2	20.9	20.3	53.7	80.3	85.1	45.8	43.6	54.7	6.9	30.6	..
Côte d'Ivoire	71.9	74.9	72.5	16.8	7.2	8.6	8.5	11.2	13.8	31.7	40.4	40.6	27.1	33.3	36.1	-5.1	8.0	..
Equatorial Guinea	80.3	20.9	..	39.7	4.6	..	17.4	61.3	..	32.2	98.6	..	69.6	85.4	..	2.1	..	..
Eritrea	..	79.1	..	..	63.8	..	..	23.8	..	..	15.1	..	..	81.8	..	..	4.4	..
Ethiopia	77.2	73.8	89.4	13.2	17.9	10.2	12.9	20.3	21.5	5.6	12.0	11.4	8.9	24.0	32.5	12.8	15.9	16.6
Gabon	49.7	32.2	38.2	13.4	9.6	10.0	21.5	21.9	26.6	46.0	69.0	61.3	30.9	32.7	36.0	24.3	41.7	..
Gambia, The	75.6	89.0	88.0	13.8	11.2	9.6	22.3	4.6	19.4	59.9	25.8	21.9	71.6	30.6	38.9	21.9	..	9.4
Ghana	85.2	84.3	75.5	9.3	10.2	9.5	14.4	23.1	21.8	16.9	48.8	29.4	25.9	67.3	41.2	10.5	15.3	20.6
Guinea	66.9	77.8	76.5	11.0	6.8	7.5	22.9	18.9	20.0	31.1	23.6	34.8	33.4	27.9	39.3	19.2	15.4	7.1
Guinea-Bissau	86.9	94.6	..	10.3	14.0	..	29.9	11.3	..	9.9	31.8	..	37.0	51.6	..	14.5	..	..
Kenya	62.8	77.7	74.4	18.6	15.1	16.7	20.7	16.7	19.9	25.7	21.6	27.5	31.3	31.7	37.9	18.5	13.5	15.6
Lesotho	123.3	83.4	104.8	25.8	41.7	37.2	57.0	42.5	28.5	18.1	34.2	43.8	123.2	103.4	113.9	70.5	37.3	12.7
Liberia	..	85.7	131.3	..	7.5	18.6	..	7.5	34.5	..	26.1	25.0	..	26.9	109.5	..	..	29.0
Madagascar	86.4	83.2	..	8.0	9.0	..	14.8	15.0	..	16.6	30.7	..	28.0	38.0	..	9.1	8.8	..
Malawi	71.5	81.6	71.7	15.1	14.6	20.2	20.1	12.3	21.7	23.8	25.6	30.6	33.4	35.3	47.2	16.4	9.5	..
Mali	79.8	79.4	..	13.8	8.6	..	23.0	24.6	..	17.2	26.8	..	33.7	39.4	..	15.0	15.9	..
Mauritania	69.2	74.5	71.2	25.9	20.2	13.1	20.0	16.2	24.5	45.6	30.0	62.0	60.7	45.3	73.6	7.5	..	..
Mauritius	63.4	60.3	73.6	13.6	14.1	13.9	30.6	22.9	24.9	65.0	61.4	52.5	72.2	61.9	63.8	25.8	26.3	15.6
Mozambique	92.3	80.6	81.4	13.5	9.0	12.7	22.1	31.0	24.7	8.2	16.5	26.3	36.1	37.0	45.0	6.6	10.4	12.2
Namibia	51.2	63.1	49.0	30.6	23.5	24.2	21.2	16.6	25.7	51.9	40.9	42.6	67.4	44.6	41.3	34.8	25.4	34.1
Niger	83.8	83.4	..	15.0	13.0	..	11.4	11.2	..	15.0	17.8	..	22.0	25.7	..	-0.6	5.3	..
Nigeria	..	..	..	..	..	..	..	..	..	43.4	54.0	37.9	28.8	32.0	31.2	..	..	..
Rwanda	83.7	87.7	83.3	10.1	11.0	15.5	14.7	18.3	21.0	5.6	8.7	10.9	14.1	25.7	30.6	11.3	12.9	12.2
São Tomé and Principe	..	..	..	..	..	..	..	..	..	..	..	..	..	..	..	..	..	..
Senegal	79.2	76.0	80.5	18.4	12.8	8.7	18.0	22.4	29.0	25.4	27.9	24.8	32.2	37.2	43.0	1.6	13.8	..
Seychelles	52.0	53.9	..	27.7	24.2	..	23.0	25.2	..	62.5	78.2	..	66.7	81.4	..	21.7	18.5	..
Sierra Leone	83.5	100.0	84.4	7.8	14.3	12.3	9.6	6.9	15.8	22.5	18.1	17.1	23.8	39.3	29.5	-1.0	-3.7	13.0
Somalia	..	..	..	..	..	..	14.9	..	..	9.8	..	..	37.7	..	..	..	..	..
South Africa	57.1	63.0	59.4	19.7	18.2	21.5	19.1	15.1	19.6	24.2	27.9	27.3	18.8	24.9	27.5	19.1	15.8	16.5
Sudan	86.1	76.5	60.6	5.8	7.6	15.2	10.4	12.1	20.4	4.0	15.3	19.8	7.1	17.7	18.9	1.2	9.3	17.5
Swaziland	80.5	77.3	75.5	14.3	18.2	26.8	14.6	18.1	11.1	59.0	74.3	54.8	68.9	88.0	68.2	19.7	13.3	2.4
Tanzania	81.0	78.3	64.7	17.8	11.7	18.2	25.8	16.4	28.4	12.6	13.4	26.1	37.5	20.1	37.8	10.1	13.2	20.1
Togo	71.1	87.6	..	14.2	10.5	..	25.3	14.5	18.9	33.5	34.4	37.3	45.3	47.6	53.8	21.0	5.0	..
Uganda	91.9	77.5	75.0	7.5	14.5	11.7	12.7	19.2	23.3	7.2	10.7	23.8	19.4	22.1	33.9	5.6	14.4	19.0
Zambia	64.4	87.4	55.2	19.0	9.5	13.3	13.5	16.0	22.4	35.9	27.1	44.1	36.6	41.5	35.0	19.6	-1.4	22.5
Zimbabwe	63.1	59.9	107.7	19.5	24.3	19.1	18.2	11.8	5.7	22.9	38.2	48.3	22.8	35.9	78.0	15.6	..	..
NORTH AFRICA	**64.1**	**61.2**	**..**	**15.2**	**14.6**	**..**	**24.5**	**20.1**	**..**	**26.5**	**27.9**	**28.4**	**32.4**	**24.9**	**30.7**	**27.6**	**..**	**27.7**
Algeria	56.8	41.6	..	16.1	13.6	..	27.0	20.7	..	23.4	41.2	30.8	24.9	21.4	21.5	24.3	..	48.4
Djibouti	78.9	76.8	..	31.5	29.7	..	14.2	8.8	..	53.8	35.1	..	78.4	50.4	..	..	5.4	..
Egypt, Arab Rep.	72.6	75.9	74.7	11.3	11.2	11.2	26.9	18.9	18.6	20.1	16.2	21.4	32.7	22.8	26.1	31.1	18.1	17.8
Libya	48.4	45.7	..	24.4	20.8	..	13.9	13.1	..	39.7	35.6	..	31.1	15.5	..	..	..	..
Morocco	64.6	61.5	57.3	15.5	18.4	17.5	24.0	26.0	30.7	26.5	28.0	33.0	31.9	33.4	42.9	25.1	24.3	30.8
Tunisia	63.6	60.6	62.7	16.4	16.7	16.3	24.4	25.2	24.3	43.6	39.6	48.8	50.6	42.9	54.1	23.4	22.2	20.3
AFRICA	**64.7**	**65.1**	**66.5**	**16.4**	**15.1**	**16.4**	**21.1**	**18.0**	**21.0**	**26.4**	**30.5**	**30.1**	**28.4**	**28.2**	**32.7**	**20.8**	**17.2**	**22.2**

a. Provisional

Table 3.1 Millennium Development Goal 1: eradicate extreme poverty and hunger

	International poverty line[a]															
	Poverty headcount ratio at $1.25 a day (PPP) (% of population)				Poverty gap at $1.25 a day (PPP) (%)				Poverty headcount ratio at $2 a day (PPP) (% of population)				Poverty gap at $2 a day (PPP) (%)			
	Surveys 1990–99[c]		Surveys 2000–11[c]		Surveys 1990–99[c]		Surveys 2000–11[c]		Surveys 1990–99[c]		Surveys 2000–11[c]		Surveys 1990–99[c]		Surveys 2000–11[c]	
	Year	Percent	Year	Percent	Year	Percent	Year	Percent	Year	Percent	Year	Percent	Year	Percent	Year	Percent
SUB-SAHARAN AFRICA																
Angola		..	2000	54.31		..	2000	29.94		..	2000	70.21		..	2000	42.35
Benin		..	2003	47.3		..	2003	15.7		..	2003	75.3		..	2003	33.5
Botswana	1994	31.2		..	1994	11.0		..	1994	49.4		..	1994	22.3	..	..
Burkina Faso	1998	70.0	2009	44.6	1998	30.2	2009	14.7	1998	87.6	2009	72.6	1998	49.1	2009	31.7
Burundi	1998	86.4	2006	81.3	1998	47.3	2006	36.4	1998	95.4	2006	93.5	1998	64.1	2006	56.1
Cameroon	1996	24.9	2007	9.6	1996	6.3	2007	1.2	1996	51.8	2007	30.4	1996	18.4	2007	8.2
Cape Verde		..	2002	21.0		..	2002	6.1		..	2002	40.9		..	2002	15.2
Central African Republic	1992	83.2	2008	62.8	1992	57.4	2008	31.3	1992	91.0	2008	80.1	1992	68.8	2008	46.8
Chad		..	2003	61.9		..	2003	25.6		..	2003	83.3		..	2003	43.9
Comoros		..	2004	46.1		..	2004	20.8		..	2004	65.0		..	2004	34.2
Congo, Dem. Rep.		..	2006	87.7		..	2006	52.8		..	2006	95.2		..	2006	67.6
Congo, Rep.		..	2005	54.1		..	2005	22.8		..	2005	74.4		..	2005	38.8
Côte d'Ivoire	1998	24.1	2008	23.8	1998	6.7	2008	7.5	1998	49.2	2008	46.3	1998	18.2	2008	17.8
Equatorial Guinea		..		..		..		..		..		..		..	..	..
Eritrea		..		..		..		..		..		..		..	..	..
Ethiopia	1995	60.5	2005	39.0	1995	21.2	2005	9.6	1995	84.6	2005	77.6	1995	41.2	2005	28.9
Gabon	..	..	2005	4.8		..	2005	0.9		..	2005	19.6		..	2005	5.0
Gambia, The	1998	65.6	2003	33.6	1998	33.8	2003	11.7	1998	81.2	2003	55.9	1998	49.1	2003	24.4
Ghana	1998	39.1	2006	28.6	1998	14.4	2006	9.9	1998	63.3	2006	51.8	1998	28.5	2006	21.3
Guinea	1994	63.8	2007	43.3	1994	29.7	2007	15.0	1994	81.7	2007	69.6	1994	46.3	2007	31.0
Guinea-Bissau	1993	52.1	2002	48.9	1993	20.6	2002	16.6	1993	75.7	2002	78.0	1993	37.4	2002	34.9
Kenya	1997	19.6	2005	43.4	1997	4.6	2005	16.9	1997	42.7	2005	67.2	1997	14.7	2005	31.8
Lesotho	1994	46.2	2003	43.4	1994	25.6	2003	20.8	1994	59.7	2003	62.3	1994	36.1	2003	33.1
Liberia		..	2007	83.8		..	2007	40.9	..	..	2007	94.9		..	2007	59.6
Madagascar	1999	82.3	2010	81.3	1999	44.3	2010	43.3	1999	93.1	2010	92.6	1999	61.0	2010	60.1
Malawi	1998	83.1	2004	73.9	1998	46.0	2004	32.3	1998	93.5	2004	90.5	1998	62.3	2004	51.8
Mali	1994	86.1	2010	50.4	1994	53.1	2010	16.4	1994	93.9	2010	78.7	1994	67.2	2010	35.2
Mauritania	1996	23.4	2008	23.4	1996	7.1	2008	6.8	1996	48.3	2008	47.7	1996	17.8	2008	17.7
Mauritius		..		..		..		..		..		..		..		..
Mozambique	1996	80.6	2008	59.6	1996	41.2	2008	25.1	1996	92.6	2008	81.8	1996	58.7	2008	42.9
Namibia	1993	49.1	2004	31.9	1993	24.6	2004	9.5	1993	62.2	2004	51.1	1993	36.5	2004	21.8
Niger	1994	78.2	2008	43.6	1994	38.6	2008	12.4	1994	91.6	2008	75.2	1994	56.5	2008	30.8
Nigeria	1996	68.5	2010	68.0	1996	32.1	2010	33.7	1996	86.4	2010	84.5	1996	49.7	2010	50.2
Rwanda		..	2011	63.2		..	2011	26.6		..	2006	87.4		..	2006	52.2
São Tomé and Príncipe		..	2001	28.2		..	2001	7.9		..	2001	54.2		..	2001	20.6
Senegal	1994	53.6	2005	33.5	1994	19.2	2005	10.8	1994	79.1	2005	60.4	1994	37.6	2005	24.7
Seychelles		..	2007	0.3		..	2007	0.1		..	2007	1.8		..	2007	0.4
Sierra Leone	1990	62.8	2003	53.4	1990	44.8	2003	20.3	1990	75.0	2003	76.1	1990	54.0	2003	37.5
Somalia		..		..		..		..		..		..		..		..
South Africa	1995	21.4	2009	13.8	1995	5.2	2009	2.3	1995	39.9	2009	31.3	1995	15.0	2009	10.2
Sudan		..	2009	19.8		..	2009	5.5		..	2009	44.1		..	2009	15.4
South Sudan		..		..		..		..		..		..		..		..
Swaziland	1995	78.6	2010	40.6	1995	47.7	2010	16.0	1995	89.3	2010	60.4	1995	61.7	2010	29.3
Tanzania	1992	72.6	2007	67.9	1992	29.7	2007	28.1	1992	91.3	2007	87.9	1992	50.1	2007	47.5
Togo		..	2006	38.7	..	..	2006	11.4		..	2006	69.3		..	2006	27.9
Uganda	1999	60.5	2009	38.0	1999	24.5	2009	12.2	1999	82.7	2009	64.7	1999	42.9	2009	27.4
Zambia	1998	55.7	2006	68.5	1998	26.9	2006	37.0	1998	74.8	2006	82.6	1998	41.7	2006	51.8
Zimbabwe		..		..		..		..		..		..		..		..
NORTH AFRICA																
Algeria	1995	6.8		..	1995	1.4		..	1995	23.6		..	1995	6.5	..	..
Djibouti		..	2002	18.8		..	2002	5.3		..	2002	41.2		..	2002	14.6
Egypt, Arab Rep.	1996	2.5	2008	1.7	1996	0.3	2008	0.4	1996	26.3	2008	15.4	1996	5.0	2008	2.8
Libya		..		..		..		..		..		..		..		..
Morocco	1999	6.8	2007	2.5	1999	1.2	2007	0.5	1999	24.4	2007	14.0	1999	6.5	2007	3.2
Tunisia	1995	6.5	2005	1.4	1995	1.3	2005	0.3	1995	20.4	2005	8.1	1995	5.8	2005	1.8

National poverty line[a]											
Share of population below national poverty line (poverty headcount ratio)				Share of urban population below national poverty line (poverty headcount ratio)				Share of rural population below national poverty line (poverty headcount ratio)			
Surveys 1990–99[c]		Surveys 2000–11[c]		Surveys 1990–99[c]		Surveys 2000–11[c]		Surveys 1990–99[c]		Surveys 2000–11[c]	
Year	Percent	Year	Percent	Year	Percent	Year	Percent	Year	Percent	Year	Percent
	..		..		..	2000[e]	62.3		..		..
	..	2007[e]	33.3		..	2007	28.3		..	2007	36.1
1993	32.9	2003	30.6	1993	24.7	2003	19.4	1993	40.4	2003	44.8
	..	2009[e]	46.7		..	2009[e]	27.9		..	2009[e]	52.6
	..	2006[e]	66.9		..	2006[e]	34.0		..	2006[e]	68.9
	..	2007[e]	39.9		..	2007[e]	12.2		..	2007[e]	55.0
	..	2007[e]	26.6		..	2007[e]	13.2		..	2007[e]	44.3
	..	2008[e]	62.0		..	2008[e]	49.6		..	2008[e]	69.4
	..	2003[e]	55.0		..	2003[e]	24.6		..	2003[e]	58.6
	..	2004	44.8		..	2004	34.5		..	2004	48.7
	..	2006	71.3		..	2006	61.5		..	2006	75.7
	..	2005	50.1		..		..		..		..
1998	36.4[f]	2008	42.7[f]	1998	28.6[f]	2008	29.4[f]	1998	41.5[f]	2008	54.2[f]
	..	2006	76.8		..	2006	31.5		..	2006	79.9
1993	69.0		..	1993	62.0		..		..		..
1995	45.5	2011	29.6	1995	33.2	2011	25.7	1995	47.5	2011	30.4
	..	2005	32.7		..	2005	29.8		..	2005	44.6
	..	2010[e]	48.4		..	2010	32.7		..	2010	73.9
1998	39.5	2006	28.5	1998	19.4	2006	10.8	1998	49.6	2006	39.2
	..	2007[e]	53.0		..	2007[e]	30.5		..	2007[e]	63.0
	..	2002[e]	64.7		..	2002[e]	51.6		..	2002[e]	69.1
	..	2005[e]	45.9		..	2005[e]	33.7		..	2005[e]	49.1
1994	66.6[f]	2003	56.6[f]	1994	36.7[f]	2003	41.5[f]	1994	68.9[f]	2003	60.5[f]
	..	2007	63.8[f]		..	2007	55.1[f]		..	2007	67.7[f]
1999	71.3	2005	68.7	1999	52.1	2005	52.0	1999	76.7	2005	73.5
1998	65.3	2010	50.7	1998	54.9	2010	17.3	1998	66.5	2010	56.6
	..	2010[e]	43.6		..	2010[e]	18.9		..	2010[e]	50.6
	..	2008[e]	42.0		..	2008[e]	20.8		..	2008[e]	59.4
	..		..		..		..		..		..
1996	69.4	2008	54.7	1996	62.0	2008	49.6	1996	71.3	2008	56.9
	..	2004[e]	38.0		..	2004[e]	17.0		..	2004[e]	49.0
	..	2007[e]	59.5		..	2007[e]	36.7		..	2007[e]	63.9
	..	2004[e]	54.7		..	2004[e]	43.1		..	2004[e]	63.8
	..	2011[e]	44.9		..	2011[e]	22.1		..	2011[e]	48.7
	..	2009[e]	66.2		..	2001[e]	45.0		..	2001[e]	64.9
	..	2011[e]	46.7		..	2011[e]	33.1		..	2011[e]	57.1
	..	..	..		..		..		..		..
	..	2003	66.4		..	2003	47.0		..	2003	78.5
	..		..		..		..		..		..
1995	31.0	2006	23.0		..		..		..		..
	..	2009[e]	46.5		..	2009[e]	26.5		..	2009[e]	57.6
	..	2009[e]	50.6		..	2009[e]	24.2		..	2009[e]	55.4
	..	2001[e]	69.2		..	2001[e]	49.0		..	2001[e]	75.0
	..	2007[e]	33.4		..	2007[e]	21.8		..	2007[e]	37.4
	..	2011[e]	58.7		..	2011[e]	34.6		..	2011[e]	73.4
1999	33.8	2009	24.5	1999	9.6	2009	9.1	1999	37.4	2009	27.2
1998	66.8	2010	60.5	1998	39.5	2010	27.5	1998	83.0	2010	77.9
	..	2003[e]	72.0		..		...		..		..
1995	22.6		..	1995	14.7		..	1995	30.3		..
	..		..		..		..		..		..
1996	19.4	2008	22.0		..	2008	10.6		..	2008	30.0
	..		..		..		..		..		..
	..	2007	9.0		..	2007	4.8		..	2007	14.5
1995	6.2	2005	3.8		..		..		..		..

(continued)

Table 3.1 Millennium Development Goal 1: eradicate extreme poverty and hunger (continued)

	Share of poorest quintile in national consumption or income[b]				Prevalence of child malnutrition, underweight (% of children under age 5)				Population below minimum dietary energy consumption	
	Surveys 1990–99[c]		Surveys 2000–11[c]		Surveys 1990–99[c]		Surveys 2000–11[c]		Share (%)	Total (millions)
	Year	Percent	Year	Percent	Year	Percent	Year	Percent	2006–08[d]	2006–08[d]
SUB-SAHARAN AFRICA										
Angola		..	2000	2.0	1996	37	2007	15.6	41	7.2
Benin		..	2003	7.0	1996	26.8	2006	20.2	12	1.0
Botswana	1994	3.1		..	1996	15.1	2008	11.2	25	0.5
Burkina Faso		..	2009	6.7	1999	33.7	2009	26.0	8	1.2
Burundi		..	2006	9.0		..	2005	35.2	62	4.9
Cameroon		..	2007	6.7	1998	17.8	2006	16.6	22	4.2
Cape Verde		..	2002	4.5	1994	11.8		..	11	0.1
Central African Republic		..	2008	3.4	1995	23.3	2006	28.0	40	1.7
Chad		..	2003	6.3	1997	34.3	2004	33.9	39	4.1
Comoros		..	2004	2.6	1996	22.3	2000	25.0	47	0.4
Congo, Dem. Rep.		..	2006	5.5	1995	30.7	2007	28.2	..	36.7
Congo, Rep.		..	2005	5.0		..	2005	11.8	13	0.5
Côte d'Ivoire	1998	5.8	2008	5.6	1999	18.2	2007	29.4	14	2.9
Equatorial Guinea		..		..	1997	13.8	2004	10.6	..	..
Eritrea		..		..	1996	38.3	2002	34.5	65	3.1
Ethiopia	1995	7.2	2005	9.3		..	2005	34.6	41	32.6
Gabon		..	2005	6.2		..	2001	8.8	5	..
Gambia, The		..	2003	4.8	1996	23.2	2006	15.8	19	0.3
Ghana	1998	5.6	2006	5.2	1999	20.3	2008	14.3	5	1.1
Guinea		..	2007	6.4	1999	21.2	2008	20.8	16	1.6
Guinea-Bissau		..	2002	7.3		..	2008	17.2	22	0.3
Kenya		..	2005	4.8	1998	17.6	2009	16.4	33	12.4
Lesotho	1994	1.5	2003	3.0	1993	18.9	2010	13.5	14	0.3
Liberia		..	2007	6.4		..	2007	20.4	32	1.1
Madagascar	1999	5.9	2010	5.4	1997	35.5	2004	36.8	25	4.7
Malawi	1998	4.8	2004	7.0	1998	26.3	2010	13.8	27	3.9
Mali		..	2010	8.0	1996	38.2	2006	27.9	12	1.5
Mauritania		..	2008	6.0	1996	20.3	2008	15.9	8	0.2
Mauritius		..		..	1995	13.0		..	5	0.1
Mozambique	1996	5.6	2008	5.2	1997	28.1	2008	18.3	38	8.3
Namibia		..	2004	3.2	1992	21.5	2007	17.5	18	0.4
Niger		..	2008	8.1	1998	45.0	2006	39.9	16	2.3
Nigeria		..	2010	4.4	1999	27.3	2008	26.7	6	9.4
Rwanda		..	2011	5.2	1996	24.2	2005	18.0	32	3.0
São Tomé and Príncipe		..	2001	5.2		..	2009	14.4	5	0.0
Senegal		..	2005	6.2	1996	19.6	2005	14.5	19	2.3
Seychelles		..	2007	3.7		..		..	8	0.0
Sierra Leone		..	2003	6.1	1990	25.4	2008	21.3	35	1.9
Somalia		..		..		..	2006	32.8	..	..
South Africa	1995	3.6	2009	2.7	1999	10.1	2008	8.7	5	..
Sudan		..	2009	6.8	1993	31.8	2006	31.7	22	8.8
South Sudan		..	2009							
Swaziland		..	2010	4.1		..	2008	7.3	19	0.2
Tanzania		..	2007	6.8	1999	25.3	2010	16.2	34	13.9
Togo		..	2006	7.6	1998	23.2	2008	20.5	30	1.9
Uganda	1999	5.9	2009	5.8	1995	21.5	2006	16.4	22	6.7
Zambia	1998	3.4	2006	3.6	1999	19.6	2007	14.9	44	5.4
Zimbabwe		..		..	1999	11.5	2006	14.0	30	3.7
NORTH AFRICA									**5**	**0.2**
Algeria	1995	7.0		..	1995	11.3	2005	3.7	<5	1.4
Djibouti		..	2002	6.0	1996	16.0	2006	29.6	26	0.2
Egypt, Arab Rep.	1996	9.5	2008	9.2	1998	10.2	2008	6.8	<5	..
Libya		..		..	1995	4.2	2007	5.6	<5	..
Morocco		..	2007	6.5	1997	7.7	2004	9.9	<5	1.6
Tunisia	1995	5.7	2005	5.9	1997	3.3	2006	3.3	<5	..

National poverty estimates for Côte d'Ivoire, Gambia, Lesotho, Liberia, and Senegal are World Bank estimates.

a. Based on nominal per capita consumption expenditure average and distributions estimated from household survey data.

b. Expenditure shares by percentiles of population, ranked by per capita expenditure.

c. Survey year refers to the year in which the underlying household survey data were collected; in cases for which the data collection period bridged two calendar years, the year in which most of the data were collected is reported as the reference year. Data are for most recent year available during the period specified.

d. Data for a 3-year period have been used for the estimation of the prevalence of undernourishment.

e. Poverty estimates based on survey data from earlier year(s) are available, but not comparable with the most recent year reported here.

f. World Bank estimates.

Table 3.2 Millennium Development Goal 2: achieve universal primary education

	Net primary enrollment ratio (% of relevant age group)			Primary completion rate (% of relevant age group)			Share of cohort reaching grade 5 (% of grade 1 students)			Youth literacy rate (% ages 15–24)		
	1990	2000	2010	1990	2000	2010	1990	2000	2008–09[a]	1991	2000	2009
SUB-SAHARAN AFRICA												
Angola	..	..	85.7	..	..	46.6	..	..	44.8	..	..	73.1
Benin	41.2	..	93.8	19.5	39.8	..	27.3	84.2	60.4	..	..	54.3
Botswana	86.9	80.9	..	89.8	89.1	..	75.7	89.0	96.6	89.3	..	95.2
Burkina Faso	..	34.1	58.1	19.3	23.8	45.1	55.6	69.1	75.1	20.2	..	..
Burundi	..	44.7	..	40.9	26.3	56.1	57.2	58.8	62.4	53.6	73.3	76.6
Cameroon	71.1	..	92.4	54.2	51.0	78.7	66.6	..	76.3	..	83.1	..
Cape Verde	92.7	98.9	93.2	53.6	107.2	98.9	53.0	89.2	..	88.2	..	98.2
Central African Republic	57.9	..	70.5	30.4	..	41.1	42.7	..	56.3	..	58.5	64.7
Chad	..	54.5	..	16.3	22.9	34.5	35.6	54.9	36.5	..	37.6	46.3
Comoros	..	73.5	..	..	..	..	..	..	..	..	80.2	85.3
Congo, Dem. Rep.	..	..	..	..	..	58.7	..	..	60.0	..	..	67.7
Congo, Rep.	..	..	90.8	58.8	..	70.8	70.6	..	..	..	..	..
Côte d'Ivoire	..	56.0	..	40.1	42.7	..	60.8	88.0	66.1	..	60.7	66.6
Equatorial Guinea	..	72.1	56.3	..	..	52.4	..	..	69.6	..	94.9	97.9
Eritrea	..	37.7	33.5	..	36.2	39.8	..	60.5	69.0	..	..	88.7
Ethiopia	..	40.3	81.3	..	23.0	72.2	..	64.6	50.5	..	..	..
Gabon	..	..	..	..	..	..	..	..	..	..	..	97.6
Gambia, The	51.4	66.9	65.5	..	66.6	70.5	..	73.0	65.1	..	52.6	65.5
Ghana	..	64.2	..	..	71.1	..	..	66.3	78.4	..	70.7	80.1
Guinea	24.9	46.6	77.0	18.8	32.3	64.1	50.6	..	68.6	..	..	61.1
Guinea-Bissau	..	51.0	73.9	..	29.7	67.6	..	..	..	..	59.5	70.9
Kenya	..	65.1	..	..	..	..	..	..	..	..	80.3	92.7
Lesotho	70.7	76.0	73.4	58.4	59.8	69.6	66.3	67.2	80.4	..	90.9	92.0
Liberia	..	..	..	..	..	..	..	..	..	..	..	75.6
Madagascar	70.3	67.0	..	37.0	37.1	72.5	34.0	36.1	34.6	..	70.2	..
Malawi	..	..	..	28.1	65.5	66.8	32.3	..	60.9	..	..	86.5
Mali	..	..	62.0	..	29.4	54.8	..	..	84.0	..	..	..
Mauritania	..	61.1	74.0	29.1	..	74.8	63.8	..	74.3	..	61.3	67.7
Mauritius	97.2	92.5	93.4	113.7	95.6	96.0	..	98.4	98.0	91.2	94.5	96.5
Mozambique	44.0	56.0	91.9	26.5	16.2	60.6	33.8	52.5	53.7	..	..	70.9
Namibia	79.1	88.1	..	..	91.4	..	..	90.9	91.5	88.1	..	93.0
Niger	22.8	27.0	57.2	15.8	18.7	41.2	57.0	74.0	64.3	..	..	..
Nigeria	..	64.5	57.6	..	..	74.4	..	..	86.3	71.2	..	71.8
Rwanda	..	..	98.8	49.2	22.9	69.6	51.5	41.7	47.2	74.9	77.6	77.2
São Tomé and Príncipe	96.1	..	98.4	77.9	..	85.3	..	..	77.4	93.9	..	95.3
Senegal	45.1	59.6	75.5	42.0	40.3	59.2	72.8	72.3	73.7	..	..	65.0
Seychelles	..	..	..	..	106.6	133.2	..	91.0	94.9	..	..	..
Sierra Leone	..	..	..	..	..	..	..	..	..	..	..	57.6
Somalia	..	..	..	..	..	..	..	..	..	..	..	..
South Africa	..	89.7	..	..	86.4	..	..	..	..	..	..	..
Sudan	..	40.2	..	..	36.7	..	..	..	..	..	..	..
Swaziland	74.3	71.8	85.6	62.7	60.7	76.9	60.0	74.0	96.2	..	88.4	93.4
Tanzania	51.4	53.1	..	..	..	89.9	..	81.4	89.8	..	..	77.4
Togo	62.3	87.0	..	35.0	69.0	73.7	44.5	74.7	77.7	..	74.4	..
Uganda	..	..	90.9	..	..	57.2	..	57.1	57.1	69.8	..	..
Zambia	..	70.3	91.4	..	62.7	103.3	..	..	71.0	..	..	74.6
Zimbabwe	..	..	..	93.6	..	..	68.7	..	..	..	..	98.9
NORTH AFRICA												
Algeria	87.5	91.6	95.6	80.8	82.4	96.0	83.8	97.1	95.0	..	..	..
Djibouti	29.3	26.7	..	32.0	27.8	..	73.9	..	64.3	..	..	..
Egypt, Arab Rep.	..	90.4	94.4	..	94.3	101.0	..	..	97.2	..	..	..
Libya	..	..	..	..	..	..	..	..	..	..	..	99.9
Morocco	56.2	76.2	93.7	51.4	57.4	84.7	68.9	80.0	93.9	..	..	79.5
Tunisia	92.6	95.6	..	80.3	88.2	..	80.0	93.1	96.1	..	..	..

a. Data are for the most recent year available during the period specified.

Table 3.3 Millennium Development Goal 3: promote gender equity and empower women

	Ratio of girls to boys in primary and secondary school (%)			Ratio of young literate women to men (% ages 15–24)			Women in national parliament (% of total seats)			Share of women employed in the nonagricultural sector (%)		
	1990	2000	2010	1990	2000	2009	1990	2000	2010	1990	2000	2000-10[a]
SUB-SAHARAN AFRICA												
Angola	..	..	78.9	..	..	81.1	15.0	16.0	38.6	..	..	..
Benin	..	60.9	..	..	..	66.9	3.0	6.0	10.8	..	..	24.3
Botswana	108.0	101.7	..	..	..	103.2	5.0	..	7.9	33.5	42.9	45.2
Burkina Faso	..	70.2	87.7	..	..	..	..	8.0	15.3	23.0	23.2	26.5
Burundi	79.0	..	93.9	80.7	91.7	99.2	..	6.0	32.1	14.3	..	..
Cameroon	82.3	..	85.4	..	88.2	..	14.0	6.0	13.9	..	..	22.2
Cape Verde	94.0	..	104.2	96.1	..	101.7	12.0	11.0	18.1	..	38.9	38.9
Central African Republic	59.1	..	69.4	..	66.6	79.4	4.0	7.0	9.6	..	..	46.8
Chad	40.9	55.9	65.8	..	41.7	72.8	..	2.0	5.2	3.8	..	..
Comoros	..	84.2	..	..	92.4	98.7	0.0	..	3.0	..	..	..
Congo, Dem. Rep.	..	..	78.5	..	..	84.8	5.0	..	8.4	25.9	..	..
Congo, Rep.	88.5	85.8	..	..	..	..	14.0	12.0	7.3	26.1	..	..
Côte d'Ivoire	..	69.3	..	..	73.6	84.6	6.0	..	8.9	..	..	..
Equatorial Guinea	..	81.3	..	..	100.2	100.5	13.0	5.0	10.0	10.5	..	..
Eritrea	..	77.3	80.1	..	..	93.6	..	15.0	22.0	..	..	..
Ethiopia	..	65.0	88.8	..	..	..	..	2.0	27.8	..	..	47.3
Gabon	..	95.9	..	..	..	98.0	13.0	8.0	14.7	..	..	..
Gambia, The	..	..	99.4	..	64.3	84.5	8.0	2.0	7.5	..	..	..
Ghana	78.0	90.2	..	..	86.2	97.3	..	9.0	8.3	..	31.7	31.7
Guinea	44.0	..	..	..	..	79.1	..	9.0	..	..	24.2	28.5
Guinea-Bissau	..	65.4	..	..	61.4	81.3	20.0	..	10.0	10.8	..	..
Kenya	..	97.6	..	..	101.1	101.8	1.0	4.0	9.8	21.4	..	..
Lesotho	123.8	107.5	106.1	..	114.9	114.4	..	4.0	24.2	..	..	..
Liberia	..	73.3	..	..	..	114.9	..	..	12.5	..	..	11.4
Madagascar	95.6	..	..	..	93.9	..	7.0	8.0	..	..	..	37.7
Malawi	80.9	92.8	101.3	..	..	99.0	10.0	8.0	20.8	10.5	..	..
Mali	57.6	71.1	81.9	..	..	..	..	12.0	10.2	..	..	34.6
Mauritania	68.9	93.1	101.2	..	81.9	90.8	..	4.0	22.1	..	35.8	35.8
Mauritius	100.4	98.1	100.1	101.1	101.8	102.1	7.0	8.0	18.8	37.4	38.6	36.7
Mozambique	72.7	75.0	89.0	..	..	81.6	16.0	..	39.2	11.4	..	..
Namibia	110.8	103.7	..	..	..	104.2	7.0	22.0	24.4	..	42.8	41.4
Niger	53.0	65.1	78.3	..	..	..	5.0	1.0	..	..	..	36.1
Nigeria	76.5	82.0	90.1	..	..	83.6	..	..	7.0	..	18.6	21.1
Rwanda	94.8	96.6	101.9	..	97.9	100.5	17.0	17.0	56.3	..	33.0	33.0
São Tomé and Príncipe	..	..	100.4	..	..	101.0	12.0	9.0	18.2	..	..	..
Senegal	67.4	82.3	100.0	..	..	75.7	13.0	12.0	22.7	..	..	10.6
Seychelles	..	103.0	104.0	..	..	..	16.0	24.0	23.5	..	..	..
Sierra Leone	61.8	..	..	..	..	71.1	..	9.0	13.2	..	..	23.2
Somalia	..	..	..	..	..	..	4.0	..	6.8	21.7	..	..
South Africa	103.5	100.4	..	..	..	..	3.0	30.0	44.5	..	41.1	45.1
Sudan	..	..	..	..	..	..	..	..	25.6	22.2	..	..
Swaziland	..	96.1	94.0	..	103.2	103.2	4.0	3.0	13.6	..	..	..
Tanzania	97.1	..	..	..	..	97.3	..	16.0	30.7	..	..	30.5
Togo	58.1	69.1	..	..	76.0	..	5.0	..	11.1	41.0	..	..
Uganda	77.9	91.1	98.5	..	..	..	12.0	18.0	31.5	..	..	39.0
Zambia	..	..	..	97.4	..	82.3	7.0	10.0	14.0	16.6	22.0	22.0
Zimbabwe	96.4	..	..	..	..	101.1	11.0	14.0	15.0	15.4	20.4	21.9
NORTH AFRICA												
Algeria	81.6	..	..	..	..	..	2.0	3.0	7.7	..	..	15.0
Djibouti	72.3	71.0	..	..	..	..	0.0	0.0	13.8	..	..	26.7
Egypt, Arab Rep.	80.5	92.1	95.9	..	..	..	4.0	2.0	1.8	20.5	19.0	18.1
Libya	..	..	..	..	..	99.9	..	..	7.7	..	..	15.8
Morocco	68.8	82.6	..	..	..	83.2	0.0	1.0	10.5	..	..	20.8
Tunisia	84.6	97.6	..	..	..	..	4.0	12.0	27.6	..	24.3	25.0

a. Data are for the most recent year available during the period specified.

Table 3.4 Millennium Development Goal 4: reduce child mortality

	Under-five mortality rate (per 1,000)				Infant mortality rate (per 1,000 live births)				Child immunization rate, measles (% of children ages 12–23 months)			
	1990	2000	2009	2010	1990	2000	2009	2010	1990	2000	2009	2010
SUB-SAHARAN AFRICA												
Angola	243	200	164	161	144	119	100	98	38	41	77	93
Benin	178	143	118	115	107	89	75	73	79	70	72	69
Botswana	59	96	49	48	46	64	37	36	87	91	94	94
Burkina Faso	205	191	178	176	103	98	93	93	79	59	94	94
Burundi	183	164	143	142	110	100	89	88	74	76	91	92
Cameroon	137	148	138	136	85	91	85	84	56	49	74	79
Cape Verde	59	46	37	36	46	37	30	29	79	86	96	96
Central African Republic	165	176	161	159	110	115	107	106	82	36	62	62
Chad	207	190	175	173	113	105	100	99	32	28	49	46
Comoros	125	104	87	86	88	75	64	63	87	70	79	72
Congo, Dem. Rep.	181	181	172	170	117	117	113	112	38	46	67	68
Congo, Rep.	116	104	94	93	74	67	61	61	75	34	76	76
Côte d'Ivoire	151	148	125	123	105	100	87	86	56	68	67	70
Equatorial Guinea	190	152	125	121	118	98	82	81	88	51	51	51
Eritrea	141	93	63	61	87	60	44	42	..	76	95	99
Ethiopia	184	141	109	106	111	87	70	68	38	52	75	81
Gabon	93	88	75	74	68	63	55	54	76	55	55	55
Gambia, The	165	128	101	98	78	66	58	57	86	89	99	97
Ghana	122	99	77	74	77	64	51	50	61	98	93	93
Guinea	229	175	134	130	135	106	84	81	35	42	51	51
Guinea-Bissau	210	177	152	150	125	107	93	92	53	71	61	61
Kenya	99	111	87	85	64	69	56	55	78	75	88	86
Lesotho	89	127	92	85	72	88	67	65	80	74	85	85
Liberia	227	169	109	103	151	115	78	74	..	63	64	64
Madagascar	159	102	65	62	97	65	45	43	47	55	64	67
Malawi	222	167	98	92	131	99	61	58	81	73	92	93
Mali	255	213	182	178	131	113	101	99	43	55	60	63
Mauritania	124	116	112	111	80	77	75	75	38	62	59	67
Mauritius	24	19	15	15	21	16	13	13	76	84	99	99
Mozambique	219	177	140	135	146	119	95	92	59	71	67	70
Namibia	73	74	44	40	49	49	32	29	..	69	76	75
Niger	311	218	150	143	132	98	75	73	25	37	69	71
Nigeria	213	186	147	143	126	112	90	88	54	33	64	71
Rwanda	163	177	98	91	99	106	63	59	83	74	93	82
São Tomé and Príncipe	94	87	81	80	61	57	54	53	71	69	90	92
Senegal	139	119	79	75	70	63	51	50	51	48	79	60
Seychelles	17	14	14	14	14	12	12	12	86	97	97	99
Sierra Leone	276	233	180	174	162	142	117	114	..	37	78	82
Somalia	180	180	180	180	108	108	108	108	30	24	43	46
South Africa	60	78	61	57	47	54	43	41	79	72	65	65
Sudan	125	114	104	103	78	72	67	66	57	58	82	90
Swaziland	96	114	82	78	70	77	57	55	85	92	94	94
Tanzania	155	130	80	92	95	81	53	60	80	78	91	92
Togo	147	124	106	103	87	76	67	66	73	58	84	84
Uganda	175	144	103	99	106	88	65	63	52	57	63	55
Zambia	183	157	116	111	109	94	72	69	90	85	87	91
Zimbabwe	78	115	83	80	52	69	52	51	87	75	76	84
NORTH AFRICA												
Algeria	68	49	37	36	55	41	32	31	83	80	92	95
Djibouti	123	106	93	91	95	83	74	73	85	50	84	85
Egypt, Arab Rep.	94	47	24	22	68	37	20	19	86	98	95	96
Libya	45	27	18	17	33	22	14	13	89	93	98	98
Morocco	86	55	37	36	67	46	32	30	79	93	98	98
Tunisia	49	28	17	16	39	24	15	14	93	95	98	97

Table 3.5 Millennium Development Goal 5: improve maternal health

	Maternal mortality ratio (per 100,000 live births)					Births attended by skilled health staff (% of total)			
	Modeled estimate			National estimate		Surveys 1990–99[a]		Surveys 2000–10[a]	
	1990	2000	2010	1990–99[a]	2000–10[a]	Year	Percent	Year	Percent
SUB-SAHARAN AFRICA									
Angola	1,200	890	450	..	..	1996	22.5	2007	47.3
Benin	770	530	350	498	400	1996	59.8	2006	74.0
Botswana	140	350	160	326	200	1996	87	2007	94.6
Burkina Faso	700	450	300	484	310	1999	30.9	2006	53.5
Burundi	1,100	1,000	800	..	620	..	..	2010	60.3
Cameroon	670	730	690	..	670	1998	58.2	2006	63.0
Cape Verde	200	170	79	..	54	1998	88.5	2005	77.5
Central African Republic	930	1,000	890	1,100	540	1995	45.9	2009	43.7
Chad	920	1,100	1,100	830	1,100	1997	15	2010	22.7
Comoros	440	340	280	..	380	1996	51.6	2000	61.8
Congo, Dem. Rep.	930	770	540	..	550	..	..	2010	79.3
Congo, Rep.	420	540	560	..	780	..	..	2005	83.4
Côte d'Ivoire	710	590	400	600	540	1999	47.1	2006	56.8
Equatorial Guinea	1,200	450	240	..	..	1994	5	2000	64.6
Eritrea	880	390	240	998	..	1995	20.6	2002	28.3
Ethiopia	950	700	350	..	670	..	..	2005	5.7
Gabon	270	270	230	..	520	..	..	2000	85.5
Gambia, The	700	520	360	..	730	1990	44.1	2010	56.7
Ghana	580	550	350	..	450	1998	44.3	2008	57.1
Guinea	1,200	970	610	530	980	1999	34.8	2007	46.1
Guinea-Bissau	1,100	970	790	910	410	1995	25	2010	44.0
Kenya	400	490	360	..	488	1998	44.3	2009	43.8
Lesotho	520	690	620	..	1,200	1993	60.9	2009	61.5
Liberia	1,200	1,300	770	..	990	..	..	2007	46.3
Madagascar	640	400	240	..	500	1997	47.3	2009	43.9
Malawi	1,100	840	460	..	810	1992	54.8	2006	53.6
Mali	1,100	740	540	..	460	1996	40	2006	49.0
Mauritania	760	630	510	..	690	1991	40	2007	60.9
Mauritius	68	28	60	..	22	1999	98.5	2005	99.2
Mozambique	910	710	490	..	500	1997	44.2	2008	55.3
Namibia	200	280	200	..	450	1992	68.2	2007	81.4
Niger	1,200	870	590	590	650	1998	17.6	2006	17.7
Nigeria	1,100	970	630	..	550	1999	41.6	2008	38.9
Rwanda	910	840	340	..	750	1992	25.8	2010	69.0
São Tomé and Príncipe	150	110	70	..	160	..	..	2009	81.7
Senegal	670	500	370	560	400	1999	48.3	2005	51.9
Seychelles	..	..	..	..	57	..	..	..	..
Sierra Leone	1,300	1,300	890	..	860	..	..	2008	42.4
Somalia	890	1,000	1,000	1,000	1,000	1999	34.2	2006	33.0
South Africa	250	330	300	150	400	1998	84.4	2003	91.2
Sudan	1,000	870	730	..	1,100	1990	69.4	2006	49.2
Swaziland	300	360	320	229	589	1994	56	2010	82.0
Tanzania	870	730	460	..	450	1999	35.8	2010	48.9
Togo	620	440	300	478	..	1998	50.5	2010	60.1
Uganda	600	530	310	..	440	1995	37.8	2006	41.9
Zambia	470	540	440	..	590	1999	47.1	2007	46.5
Zimbabwe	450	640	570	700	730	1999	72.5	2009	60.2
NORTH AFRICA									
Algeria	220	140	97	117	..	1992	77	2006	95.2
Djibouti	290	290	200	74	550	..	..	2006	92.9
Egypt, Arab Rep.	230	100	66	..	55	1998	55.2	2008	78.9
Libya	99	67	58	77	..	1999	99	2008	99.8
Morocco	300	170	100	332	130	1995	39.6	2004	62.6
Tunisia	130	84	56	69	..	1995	80.5	2006	94.6

a. Data are for the most recent year available during the period specified.

Table

3.6 Millennium Development Goal 6: combat HIV/AIDS, malaria, and other diseases

	Prevalence of HIV (% ages 15–49)		Contraceptive use, any method (% of married women ages 15–49)				Children sleeping under insecticide-treated nets (% of children under age 5)	
			Surveys 1990–99[a]		Surveys 2000–10[a]		Surveys 2000–10[a]	
	1990	2009	Year	Percent	Year	Percent	Year	Percent
SUB-SAHARAN AFRICA								
Angola	0.5	2.0	1996	8.1	2001	6.2	2007	17.7
Benin	0.2	1.2	1996	16.4	2006	17.0	2006	20.1
Botswana	3.5	24.8	1996	41.7	2007	52.8	..	..
Burkina Faso	3.9	1.2	1999	11.9	2006	17.4	2006	9.6
Burundi	3.9	3.3	..	..	2010	21.9	2010	45.2
Cameroon	0.6	5.3	1998	19.3	2006	29.2	2006	13.1
Cape Verde	..	..	1998	52.9	2005	61.3	..	..
Central African Republic	3.1	4.7	1995	14.8	2006	19.0	2006	15.1
Chad	1.1	3.4	1997	4.1	2010	4.8	2010	9.8
Comoros	<0.1	0.1	1996	21.0	2000	25.7	2000	9.3
Congo, Dem. Rep.	..	..	1991	7.7	2010	17.3	2010	35.7
Congo, Rep.	5.2	3.4	..	..	2005	44.3	2005	6.1
Côte d'Ivoire	2.4	3.4	1999	15.0	2006	12.9	2006	3.0
Equatorial Guinea	0.1	5.0	..	..	2000	10.1	2000	0.7
Eritrea	0.3	0.8	1995	8.0	2002	8.0	2008	48.9
Ethiopia	..	..	1997	3.3	2005	14.7	2007	33.1
Gabon	0.9	5.2	..	..	2000	32.7	2008	55.1
Gambia, The	0.1	2.0	1990	11.8	2001	18.0	2006	49.0
Ghana	0.3	1.8	1999	22.0	2008	23.5	2008	28.2
Guinea	1.1	1.3	1999	6.2	2005	9.1	2008	4.5
Guinea-Bissau	0.3	2.5	..	..	2010	14.2	2010	35.5
Kenya	3.9	6.3	1998	39.0	2009	45.5	2009	46.7
Lesotho	0.8	23.6	1995	29.1	2009	47.0	..	..
Liberia	0.3	1.5	..	..	2007	11.4	2009	26.4
Madagascar	0.2	0.2	1999	25.0	2009	39.9	2009	45.8
Malawi	7.2	11.0	1996	21.9	2006	41.0	2010	56.5
Mali	0.4	1.0	1996	6.7	2006	8.2	2010	70.2
Mauritania	0.2	0.7	1992	4.1	2007	9.3	2004	2.1
Mauritius	<0.1	1.0	1991	74.6	2002	75.9	..	..
Mozambique	1.2	11.5	1997	5.6	2008	16.2	2008	22.8
Namibia	1.6	13.1	1992	28.9	2007	55.1	2009	34.0
Niger	0.1	0.8	1998	8.2	2010	18.0	2010	63.7
Nigeria	1.3	3.6	1999	15.3	2008	14.6	2010	29.1
Rwanda	5.2	2.9	1996	13.7	2010	51.6	2010	69.8
São Tomé and Príncipe	..	..	..	..	2009	38.4	2009	56.2
Senegal	0.2	0.9	1999	10.5	2005	11.8	2009	29.2
Seychelles	..	..	..	..	..	..	..	..
Sierra Leone	<0.1	1.6	1992	2.6	2008	8.2	2008	25.8
Somalia	0.1	0.7	1999	7.9	2006	14.6	2006	11.4
South Africa	0.7	17.8	1998	56.3	2004	59.9	..	..
Sudan	0.1	1.1	1999	7.0	2006	7.6	2009	25.3
Swaziland	2.3	25.9	..	..	2010	49.3	2007	0.6
Tanzania	4.8	5.6	1999	25.4	2010	34.4	2010	63.6
Togo	0.6	3.2	1998	23.5	2010	15.2	2010	56.9
Uganda	10.2	6.5	1995	14.8	2006	23.7	2009	32.8
Zambia	12.7	13.5	1999	22.0	2007	40.8	2010	49.9
Zimbabwe	10.1	14.3	1999	53.5	2009	64.9	2009	17.3
NORTH AFRICA								
Algeria	<0.1	0.1	1995	56.9	2006	61.4	..	..
Djibouti	0.9	2.5	..	..	2008	22.5	2009	19.9
Egypt, Arab Rep.	<0.1	<0.1	1998	51.7	2008	60.3	..	..
Libya	..	..	1995	45.2	..	..	..	..
Morocco	<0.1	0.1	1997	58.4	2004	63.0	..	..
Tunisia	<0.1	0.1	1995	60.0	2006	60.2	..	..

(continued)

Table 3.6 Millennium Development Goal 6: combat HIV/AIDS, malaria, and other diseases (continued)

	Incidence of tuberculosis (per 100,000 people)			Tuberculosis treatment success rate (% of registered cases)			
				Surveys 1990–99[a]		Surveys 2000–09[a]	
	1990	1999	2010	Year	Percent	Year	Percent
SUB-SAHARAN AFRICA							
Angola	205	250	304	1998	68.0	2009	72.0
Benin	77	85	94	1999	77.0	2009	90.0
Botswana	533	918	503	1999	71.0	2009	79.0
Burkina Faso	66	69	55	1999	61.0	2009	76.0
Burundi	148	178	129	1998	74.0	2009	90.0
Cameroon	81	168	177	1999	75.0	2009	78.0
Cape Verde	175	160	147	..	..	2008	74.0
Central African Republic	145	302	319	1995	37.0	2009	53.0
Chad	125	262	276	1998	64.0	2009	76.0
Comoros	85	56	37	1999	93.0	2008	90.0
Congo, Dem. Rep.	327	327	327	1999	69.0	2009	88.0
Congo, Rep.	169	353	372	1999	61.0	2009	78.0
Côte d'Ivoire	150	198	139	1999	63.0	2009	79.0
Equatorial Guinea	80	100	135	1997	82.0	2009	66.0
Eritrea	72	85	100	1999	44.0	2009	85.0
Ethiopia	173	235	261	1999	74.0	2009	84.0
Gabon	153	248	553	1998	50.0	2009	55.0
Gambia, The	185	225	273	1997	70.0	2009	89.0
Ghana	155	152	86	1999	51.0	2009	87.0
Guinea	119	200	334	1999	74.0	2009	79.0
Guinea-Bissau	158	192	233	1999	35.0	2009	67.0
Kenya	139	286	298	1999	79.0	2009	86.0
Lesotho	184	553	633	1999	69.0	2009	70.0
Liberia	199	242	293	1999	74.0	2009	83.0
Madagascar	177	217	266	1997	64.0	2009	82.0
Malawi	326	467	219	1999	71.0	2009	88.0
Mali	163	124	68	1999	69.0	2009	78.0
Mauritania	228	277	337	..	..	2009	63.0
Mauritius	28	24	22	1999	87.0	2009	88.0
Mozambique	401	513	544	1999	71.0	2009	85.0
Namibia	696	1077	603	1999	51.0	2009	85.0
Niger	125	152	185	1999	60.0	2009	79.0
Nigeria	128	172	133	1999	75.0	2009	83.0
Rwanda	405	286	106	1999	67.0	2009	85.0
São Tomé and Príncipe	135	114	96	1999	81.0	2009	98.0
Senegal	195	237	288	1999	58.0	2009	85.0
Seychelles	43	37	31	1999	91.0	2009	64.0
Sierra Leone	207	377	682	1999	75.0	2009	79.0
Somalia	285	285	286	1999	88.0	2009	85.0
South Africa	301	576	981	1999	57.0	2009	73.0
Sudan	119	119	119	1999	80.0	2009	80.0
Swaziland	267	803	1287	..	..	2009	69.0
Tanzania	226	236	177	1999	78.0	2009	88.0
Togo	308	374	455	1999	76.0	2009	81.0
Uganda	624	427	209	1999	61.0	2009	67.0
Zambia	710	713	462	1999	69.0	2009	90.0
Zimbabwe	296	726	633	1999	73.0	2009	78.0
NORTH AFRICA							
Algeria	66	87	90	1999	87.0	2009	91.0
Djibouti	619	619	620	1999	72.0	2009	79.0
Egypt, Arab Rep.	34	26	18	1999	85.0	2009	88.0
Libya	40	40	40	1999	67.0	2008	69.0
Morocco	147	109	91	1999	88.0	2009	84.0
Tunisia	29	24	25	1999	91.0	2009	83.0

a. Data are for the most recent year available during the period specified.

Table 3.7 Millennium Development Goal 7: ensure environmental sustainability

	Forest area (% of total land area)			Terrestrial protected areas (% of total land area)			GDP per unit of energy use (2005 PPP $ per kg of oil equivalent)		
	1990	2000	2010	1990	2000	2010	1990	2000	2009
SUB-SAHARAN AFRICA									
Angola	48.9	47.9	46.9	12.4	12.4	12.4	5.4	4.6	8.0
Benin	52.1	45.8	41.2	23.8	23.8	23.8	3.2	4.3	3.5
Botswana	24.2	22.1	20.0	30.3	30.9	30.9	7.6	9.1	11.4
Burkina Faso	25.0	22.8	20.7	13.7	13.9	14.2	..	..	..
Burundi	11.3	7.7	6.7	3.8	4.9	4.9	..	..	..
Cameroon	51.4	46.8	42.1	7.0	8.7	9.2	5.1	4.6	5.7
Cape Verde	14.4	20.4	21.1	2.5	2.5	2.5	17.1	..	..
Central African Republic	37.3	36.8	36.3	17.5	17.7	17.7	..	..	..
Chad	10.4	9.8	9.2	9.4	9.4	9.4	..	..	..
Comoros	6.5	4.3	1.6	0.0	0.0	..	29.6	..	..
Congo, Dem. Rep.	70.7	69.4	68.0	10.0	10.0	10.0	2.0	0.8	0.9
Congo, Rep.	66.6	66.1	65.6	..	..	..	10.7	11.5	10.1
Côte d'Ivoire	32.1	32.5	32.7	22.6	22.6	22.6	5.5	4.5	3.2
Equatorial Guinea	66.3	62.1	58.0	7.3	19.2	19.2	..	..	..
Eritrea	16.1	15.6	15.2	4.9	4.9	5.0	..	3.0	3.5
Ethiopia	13.7	13.7	12.3	..	..	..	1.8	1.9	2.2
Gabon	85.4	85.4	85.4	4.6	5.7	15.1	11.8	11.2	10.7
Gambia, The	44.2	46.1	48.0	1.5	1.5	1.5	24.0	..	..
Ghana	32.7	26.8	21.7	14.6	14.7	14.7	2.5	2.6	3.6
Guinea	29.6	28.1	26.6	6.8	6.8	6.8	..	..	..
Guinea-Bissau	78.8	75.4	71.9	7.7	16.1	16.1	16.5	..	..
Kenya	6.5	6.3	6.1	11.6	11.8	11.8	3.1	2.9	3.0
Lesotho	1.3	1.4	1.5	0.5	0.5	0.5	..	..	..
Liberia	51.2	48.1	44.9	..	..	..	..	..	..
Madagascar	23.5	22.6	21.6	2.2	3.1	3.1	..	..	..
Malawi	41.3	37.8	34.3	15.0	15.0	15.0	..	..	..
Mali	11.5	10.9	10.2	2.3	2.3	2.4	..	..	..
Mauritania	0.4	0.3	0.2	0.5	0.5	0.5	..	..	..
Mauritius	19.2	19.2	17.2	1.7	4.5	4.5	13.5	..	..
Mozambique	55.2	52.4	49.6	14.8	14.8	15.8	0.9	1.3	1.9
Namibia	10.6	9.8	8.9	14.4	14.5	14.9	..	8.4	7.3
Niger	1.5	1.1	1.0	7.1	7.1	7.1	..	..	..
Nigeria	18.9	14.4	9.9	11.6	12.8	12.8	2.0	2.0	2.9
Rwanda	12.9	13.9	17.6	9.9	9.9	10.0	..	..	..
São Tomé and Príncipe	28.1	28.1	28.1	..	..	..	..	..	..
Senegal	48.6	46.2	44.0	24.1	24.1	24.1	6.4	6.1	7.1
Seychelles	89.1	89.1	89.1	42.0	42.0	42.0	26.3	..	..
Sierra Leone	43.5	40.8	38.1	5.0	5.0	5.0	..	..	..
Somalia	13.2	12.0	10.8	..	..	..	..	..	..
South Africa	6.8	5.7	4.7	6.5	6.9	6.9	3.0	2.9	3.2
Sudan	32.2	29.7	29.4	4.2	4.2	4.2	2.6	3.5	5.3
Swaziland	27.4	30.1	32.7	3.0	3.0	3.0	10.9	..	..
Tanzania	46.8	42.3	37.7	26.5	26.9	..	2.2	2.1	2.7
Togo	12.6	8.9	5.3	11.3	11.3	11.3	2.8	2.1	2.0
Uganda	23.8	19.4	15.0	7.9	8.5	10.3	..	..	..
Zambia	71.0	68.8	66.5	36.0	36.0	36.0	1.8	1.7	2.1
Zimbabwe	57.3	48.8	40.4	18.0	18.1	28.0	..	..	..
NORTH AFRICA									
Algeria	0.7	0.7	0.6	6.3	6.3	6.3	7.1	6.9	6.5
Djibouti	0.3	0.3	0.3	0.0	0.0	..	11.8	..	..
Egypt, Arab Rep.	0.0	0.1	0.1	1.9	4.3	5.9	5.8	6.2	5.9
Libya	0.1	0.1	0.1	..	..	..	..	4.0	4.7
Morocco	11.3	11.2	11.5	1.2	1.6	1.6	9.7	8.3	8.8
Tunisia	4.1	5.4	6.5	1.3	1.3	..	7.4	8.0	9.5

(continued)

Table 3.7 Millennium Development Goal 7: ensure environmental sustainability (continued)

	Carbon dioxide emissions per capita (metric tons)			Population with sustainable access to an improved water source (%)			Population with sustainable access to improved sanitation (%)		
	1990	2000	2010	1990	2000	2010	1990	2000	2010
SUB-SAHARAN AFRICA									
Angola	0.4	0.7	1.4	42.0	46.0	51.0	29.0	42.0	58.0
Benin	0.2	0.3	0.5	57.0	66.0	75.0	5.0	9.0	13.0
Botswana	1.6	2.4	2.5	93.0	95.0	96.0	38.0	52.0	62.0
Burkina Faso	0.1	0.1	0.1	43.0	60.0	79.0	8.0	11.0	17.0
Burundi	0.1	0.1	0.0	70.0	72.0	72.0	44.0	45.0	46.0
Cameroon	0.1	0.2	0.3	49.0	64.0	77.0	48.0	49.0	49.0
Cape Verde	0.3	0.4	0.6	..	83.0	88.0	..	44.0	61.0
Central African Republic	0.1	0.1	0.1	58.0	63.0	67.0	11.0	22.0	34.0
Chad	0.0	0.0	0.1	39.0	45.0	51.0	8.0	10.0	13.0
Comoros	0.2	0.2	0.2	87.0	92.0	95.0	17.0	28.0	36.0
Congo, Dem. Rep.	0.1	0.0	0.1	45.0	44.0	45.0	9.0	16.0	24.0
Congo, Rep.	0.5	0.3	0.5	..	70.0	71.0	..	20.0	18.0
Côte d'Ivoire	0.5	0.4	0.4	76.0	77.0	80.0	20.0	22.0	24.0
Equatorial Guinea	0.3	0.9	7.3	..	51.0	..	..	89.0	..
Eritrea	..	0.2	0.1	43.0	54.0	..	9.0	11.0	..
Ethiopia	0.1	0.1	0.1	14.0	29.0	44.0	3.0	9.0	21.0
Gabon	5.2	0.9	1.7	..	85.0	87.0	..	36.0	33.0
Gambia, The	0.2	0.2	0.3	74.0	83.0	89.0	..	63.0	68.0
Ghana	0.3	0.3	0.4	53.0	71.0	86.0	7.0	10.0	14.0
Guinea	0.2	0.2	0.2	51.0	63.0	74.0	10.0	14.0	18.0
Guinea-Bissau	0.3	0.2	0.2	36.0	50.0	64.0	..	14.0	20.0
Kenya	0.3	0.3	0.3	44.0	52.0	59.0	25.0	28.0	32.0
Lesotho	..	..	..	80.0	80.0	78.0	..	25.0	26.0
Liberia	0.2	0.2	0.2	..	61.0	73.0	..	12.0	18.0
Madagascar	0.1	0.1	0.1	29.0	38.0	46.0	9.0	12.0	15.0
Malawi	0.1	0.1	0.1	41.0	62.0	83.0	39.0	46.0	51.0
Mali	0.1	0.1	0.0	28.0	46.0	64.0	15.0	18.0	22.0
Mauritania	1.3	0.5	0.6	30.0	40.0	50.0	16.0	21.0	26.0
Mauritius	1.4	2.3	3.1	99.0	99.0	99.0	89.0	89.0	89.0
Mozambique	0.1	0.1	0.1	36.0	42.0	47.0	11.0	14.0	18.0
Namibia	0.0	0.9	1.8	64.0	81.0	93.0	24.0	28.0	32.0
Niger	0.1	0.1	0.1	35.0	42.0	49.0	5.0	7.0	9.0
Nigeria	0.5	0.6	0.6	47.0	53.0	58.0	37.0	34.0	31.0
Rwanda	0.1	0.1	0.1	66.0	66.0	65.0	36.0	47.0	55.0
São Tomé and Príncipe	0.6	0.6	0.8	..	79.0	89.0	..	21.0	26.0
Senegal	0.4	0.4	0.4	61.0	66.0	72.0	38.0	45.0	52.0
Seychelles	1.6	7.0	7.8	..	..	..	..	..	..
Sierra Leone	0.1	0.2	0.2	38.0	46.0	55.0	11.0	11.0	13.0
Somalia	0.0	0.1	0.1	..	22.0	29.0	..	22.0	23.0
South Africa	9.5	8.4	8.9	83.0	86.0	91.0	71.0	75.0	79.0
Sudan	0.2	0.2	0.3	65.0	62.0	58.0	27.0	27.0	26.0
Swaziland	0.5	1.2	1.1	39.0	52.0	71.0	48.0	52.0	57.0
Tanzania	0.1	0.1	0.2	55.0	54.0	53.0	7.0	9.0	10.0
Togo	0.2	0.3	0.3	49.0	55.0	61.0	13.0	13.0	13.0
Uganda	0.1	0.1	0.1	43.0	58.0	72.0	27.0	30.0	34.0
Zambia	0.3	0.2	0.2	49.0	54.0	61.0	46.0	47.0	48.0
Zimbabwe	1.5	1.1	0.7	79.0	80.0	80.0	41.0	40.0	40.0
NORTH AFRICA									
Algeria	3.1	2.9	3.2	94.0	89.0	83.0	88.0	92.0	95.0
Djibouti	0.7	0.6	0.6	78.0	82.0	88.0	66.0	60.0	50.0
Egypt, Arab Rep.	1.3	2.1	2.7	93.0	96.0	99.0	72.0	86.0	95.0
Libya	9.3	9.5	9.5	54.0	54.0	..	97.0	97.0	97.0
Morocco	1.0	1.2	1.5	73.0	78.0	83.0	53.0	64.0	70.0
Tunisia	1.6	2.1	2.4	81.0	90.0	..	74.0	81.0	..

Table 3.8 Millennium Development Goal 8: develop a global partnership for development

	Debt sustainability					
	Heavily Indebted Poor Countries (HIPC) Debt Initiative		Debt service relief committed ($ millions)[a]	Public and publicly guaranteed debt service (% of exports, excluding workers' remittances)		
	Decision point[a]	Completion point[a]		1990	2000	2010
SUB-SAHARAN AFRICA						
Angola	..	..	..	7.1	20.4	4.4
Benin	Jul. 2000	Mar. 2003	460	8.4	10.7	..
Botswana	..	..	..	4.3	2.0	1.3
Burkina Faso	Jul. 2000	Apr. 2002	930	7.7	15.1	..
Burundi	Aug. 2005	Jan. 2009	1,366	40.7	25.1	1.8
Cameroon	Oct. 2000	Apr. 2006	4,917	12.5	13.5	2.7
Cape Verde	..	..	..	8.9	10.7	5.0
Central African Republic	Sep. 2007	Jun. 2009	804	7.5	..	..
Chad	May 2001	..	260	2.3	..	..
Comoros	Jun. 2010	..	136	2.5	..	..
Congo, Dem. Rep.	Jul. 2003	Jul. 2010	15,222	..	..	..
Congo, Rep.	Mar. 2006	Jan. 2010	1,738	30.9	0.5	..
Côte d'Ivoire	Mar. 2009	..	3,415	14.7	14.9	..
Equatorial Guinea	..	..	..	..	..	..
Eritrea	..	..	..	..	2.8	..
Ethiopia	Nov. 2001	Apr. 2004	3,275	33.2	12.2	3.9
Gabon	..	..	..	3.8	8.8	..
Gambia, The	Dec. 2000	Dec. 2007	112	17.3	..	7.0
Ghana	Feb. 2002	Jul. 2004	3,500	19.9	12.0	2.8
Guinea	Dec. 2000	..	800	17.7	17.6	4.9
Guinea-Bissau	Dec. 2000	Dec. 2010	790	22.0	..	..
Kenya	..	..	..	22.7	15.7	3.9
Lesotho	..	..	..	4.1	6.8	1.5
Liberia	Mar. 2008	Jun. 2010	4,600	..	..	1.0
Madagascar	Dec. 2000	Oct. 2004	1,900	31.9	8.4	..
Malawi	Dec. 2000	Aug. 2006	1,628	22.4	10.8	..
Mali	Sep. 2000	Mar. 2003	895	9.7	10.2	..
Mauritania	Feb. 2000	Jun. 2002	1,100	24.8	..	..
Mauritius	..	..	..	4.5	16.3	1.5
Mozambique	Apr. 2000	Sep. 2001	4,300	17.2	7.0	2.8
Namibia	..	..	..	..	..	..
Niger	Dec. 2000	Apr. 2004	1,190	3.2	6.0	..
Nigeria	..	..	..	22.3	8.2	0.4
Rwanda	Dec. 2000	Apr. 2005	1,316	9.4	15.3	2.3
São Tomé and Príncipe	Dec. 2000	Mar. 2007	263	28.6	19.9	5.6
Senegal	Jun. 2000	Apr. 2004	850	13.7	13.2	..
Seychelles	..	..	..	7.6	3.3	3.7
Sierra Leone	Mar. 2002	Dec. 2006	994	7.8	29.6	2.0
Somalia	..	..	..	..	..	..
South Africa	..	..	..	..	5.5	1.9
Sudan	..	..	..	4.5	10.1	4.1
Swaziland	..	..	..	5.3	2.1	1.8
Tanzania	Apr. 2000	Nov. 2001	3,000	25.1	10.3	1.3
Togo	Nov. 2008	Dec. 2010	360	8.6	3.2	..
Uganda	Feb. 2000	May. 2000	1,950	47.1	6.5	1.7
Zambia	Dec. 2000	Apr. 2005	3,900	12.6	17.4	0.8
Zimbabwe	..	..	..	18.2	..	..
NORTH AFRICA						
Algeria	..	..	..	63.3	..	0.6
Djibouti	..	..	..	..	4.8	6.8
Egypt, Arab Rep.	..	..	..	23.2	8.5	5.7
Libya	..	..	..	..	..	..
Morocco	..	..	..	23.1	23.0	6.8
Tunisia	..	..	..	23.0	20.0	8.5

(continued)

Table 3.8 Millennium Development Goal 8: develop a global partnership for development (continued)

	Youth unemployment rate (ages 15–24)						Information and communication					
	Total (share of total labor force)		Male (share of male labor force)		Female (share of female labor force)		Fixed-line and mobile telephone subscribers (per 100 people)			Internet users (per 100 people)		
	Year	Percent	Year	Percent	Year	Percent	1990	2000	2010	1995	2000	2010
SUB-SAHARAN AFRICA												
Angola	..	..	..	..	..	..	0.7	0.7	48.3	..	0.1	10.0
Benin	2002	0.8	2002	1.1	2002	0.6	0.3	1.6	81.5	..	0.2	3.1
Botswana	2000	13.6	2000	13.2	2000	14	1.9	20.4	124.6	0.1	2.9	6.0
Burkina Faso	2006	3.8	2006	4.6	2006	2.9	0.2	0.6	35.5	..	0.1	1.4
Burundi	..	..	..	..	..	..	0.1	0.6	14.1	0.0	0.1	2.1
Cameroon	..	..	..	..	..	..	0.3	1.3	46.8	..	0.3	4.0
Cape Verde	..	..	..	..	..	..	2.4	17.0	89.5	..	1.8	30.0
Central African Republic	..	..	..	..	..	..	0.2	0.4	22.4	..	0.1	2.3
Chad	..	..	..	..	..	..	0.1	0.2	24.3	..	0.0	1.7
Comoros	..	..	..	..	..	..	0.8	1.2	25.4	..	0.3	5.1
Congo, Dem. Rep.	..	..	..	..	..	..	0.1	0.1	18.0	..	0.0	0.7
Congo, Rep.	..	..	..	..	..	..	0.7	2.9	94.2	..	0.0	5.0
Côte d'Ivoire	..	..	..	..	..	..	0.6	4.4	77.6	0.0	0.2	2.6
Equatorial Guinea	..	..	..	..	..	..	0.4	2.1	59.0	..	0.1	6.0
Eritrea	..	..	..	..	..	..	..	0.8	4.6	0.0	0.1	5.4
Ethiopia	2006	24.9	2006	19.5	2006	29.4	0.3	0.4	9.4	0.0	0.0	0.8
Gabon	..	..	..	..	..	..	2.2	12.9	109.0	..	1.2	7.2
Gambia, The	..	..	..	..	..	..	0.6	3.0	88.3	0.0	0.9	9.2
Ghana	2000	16.6	2000	16.4	2000	16.7	0.3	1.8	72.6	0.0	0.2	9.6
Guinea	..	..	..	..	..	..	0.2	0.8	40.3	0.0	0.1	1.0
Guinea-Bissau	..	..	..	..	..	..	0.6	0.9	39.5	..	0.2	2.5
Kenya	..	..	..	..	..	..	0.8	1.3	62.6	0.0	0.3	25.9
Lesotho	2008	34.4	2008	29	2008	41.9	0.8	2.2	47.3	..	0.2	3.9
Liberia	2010	5.9	2010	3.9	2010	7.7	0.4	0.3	39.5	..	0.0	7.0
Madagascar	2005	2.3	2005	1.7	2005	2.8	0.3	0.8	37.9	..	0.2	1.7
Malawi	..	..	..	..	..	..	0.3	0.9	21.5	..	0.1	2.3
Mali	..	..	..	..	..	..	0.1	0.4	49.2	..	0.1	2.7
Mauritania	..	..	..	..	..	..	0.3	1.3	81.4	..	0.2	3.0
Mauritius	2010	23.4	2010	19.4	2010	29	5.5	38.8	123.2	..	7.3	28.7
Mozambique	..	..	..	..	..	..	0.4	0.8	31.3	..	0.1	4.2
Namibia	2004	41.7	2004	36.7	2004	47	3.8	10.1	73.9	0.0	1.6	6.5
Niger	2001	3.2	2001	4	2001	1.7	0.1	0.2	25.1	..	0.0	0.8
Nigeria	..	..	..	..	..	..	0.3	0.5	55.8	..	0.1	28.4
Rwanda	..	..	..	..	..	..	0.2	0.7	33.8	..	0.1	13.0
São Tomé and Príncipe	..	..	..	..	..	..	1.9	3.3	66.8	..	4.6	18.8
Senegal	2006	14.8	2006	11.9	2006	20.1	0.6	4.8	69.9	0.0	0.4	16.0
Seychelles	2002	20.3	..	..	..	..	12.4	57.4	160.5	..	7.2	41.0
Sierra Leone	2004	5.2	2004	7.3	2004	3.5	0.3	0.8	34.3	0.0	0.1	..
Somalia	..	..	..	..	..	..	0.2	1.4	8.0	0.0	0.0	..
South Africa	2009	48.2	2009	44.6	2009	52.5	9.4	30.2	109.2	0.7	5.4	12.3
Sudan	..	..	..	..	..	..	0.2	1.2	41.4	0.0	0.0	..
Swaziland	..	..	..	..	..	..	1.6	6.4	73.6	0.0	1.0	9.0
Tanzania	2006	8.8	2006	7.4	2006	10.1	0.3	0.8	47.2	..	0.1	11.0
Togo	..	..	..	..	..	..	0.3	1.9	44.2	0.0	1.9	5.4
Uganda	2009	5.4	..	..	..	..	0.2	0.8	39.4	0.0	0.2	12.5
Zambia	2005	23.4	2000	23.1	2000	19.5	0.8	1.8	42.8	0.0	0.2	10.1
Zimbabwe	2004	7.6	2004	7.6	2004	7.6	1.2	4.1	64.3	0.0	0.4	11.5
NORTH AFRICA												
Algeria	2006	24.3	2004	42.8	2004	46.3	3.2	6.1	100.7	0.0	0.5	12.5
Djibouti	..	..	..	..	..	..	1.0	1.4	20.7	0.0	0.2	6.5
Egypt, Arab Rep.	2007	24.8	2007	17.2	2007	47.9	2.8	10.1	99.0	0.0	0.6	26.7
Libya	..	..	..	..	..	..	5.1	12.3	190.9	..	0.2	14.0
Morocco	2009	21.9	2009	22.8	2009	19.4	1.6	13.1	111.8	0.0	0.7	49.0
Tunisia	2005	30.7	2005	31.4	2005	29.3	3.7	11.2	117.6	0.0	2.7	36.6

Note: 0.0 indicates less than 1.

a. As of end-July 2011.

b. Data are for the most recent year available during the period specified.

Table 4.1 Doing Business

	Overall ranking		Starting a business: Number of procedures		Starting a business: Time spent for each procedure (days)		Starting a business: Cost (% of GNI per capita)		Starting a business: Minimum capital (% of GNI per capita)		Registering property: Number of procedures		Registering property: Time required (days)		Registering property: Cost (% of property value)	
	2010	2011	2010	2011	2010	2011	2010	2011	2010	2011	2010	2011	2010	2011	2010	2011
SUB-SAHARAN AFRICA			**9**	**8**	**45**	**37**	**97.4**	**81.2**	**145.6**	**129.8**	**6**	**6**	**67**	**65**	**9.4**	**9.4**
Angola	171	172	8	8	68	68	163.0	118.9	28.7	25.3	7	7	184	184	11.5	3.2
Benin	173	175	7	6	31	29	154.3	149.9	285.3	280.4	4	4	120	120	11.8	11.8
Botswana	52	54	10	10	61	61	2.2	1.8	0.0	0.0	5	5	16	16	5.0	5.0
Burkina Faso	151	150	4	3	14	13	53.4	47.7	416.2	373.3	4	4	59	59	13.1	12.8
Burundi	177	169	9	9	14	14	124.3	116.8	0.0	0.0	5	5	94	94	5.8	5.6
Cameroon	165	161	6	5	19	15	51.2	45.5	191.8	182.9	5	5	93	93	19.3	19.2
Cape Verde	129	119	8	8	11	11	18.5	17.0	42.4	39.0	6	6	73	31	3.9	3.9
Central African Republic	183	182	8	7	22	21	228.4	175.5	468.6	452.9	5	5	75	75	18.5	11.0
Chad	182	183	13	11	75	66	226.9	208.5	386.7	345.0	6	6	44	44	18.2	18.1
Comoros	156	157	11	11	24	24	176.5	176.2	245.5	252.9	4	4	30	30	10.5	10.5
Congo, Dem. Rep.	176	178	10	10	84	65	735.1	551.4	0.0	0.0	6	6	54	54	7.0	6.8
Congo, Rep.	180	181	10	10	160	160	111.4	85.2	129.8	88.0	6	6	55	55	10.7	20.6
Côte d'Ivoire	170	167	10	10	40	32	133.0	132.6	202.9	200.4	6	6	62	62	13.9	13.9
Equatorial Guinea	161	155	21	21	137	137	147.9	101.4	21.3	14.6	6	6	23	23	6.3	6.2
Eritrea	178	180	13	13	84	84	69.2	62.6	268.4	243.0	11	11	78	78	9.1	9.1
Ethiopia	104	111	5	5	9	9	14.1	12.8	367.7	333.5	10	10	41	41	2.1	2.1
Gabon	160	156	9	9	58	58	21.9	17.3	32.7	26.4	7	7	39	39	10.5	10.5
Gambia, The	145	149	8	8	27	27	199.6	206.1	0.0	0.0	5	5	66	66	7.6	7.7
Ghana	60	63	7	7	12	12	11.9	17.3	6.5	5.5	5	5	34	34	0.8	0.7
Guinea	179	179	12	12	40	40	147.7	118.0	519.1	407.3	6	6	59	59	14.0	14.4
Guinea-Bissau	181	176	17	9	216	9	183.3	49.8	415.1	398.7	8	8	210	210	10.7	10.6
Kenya	106	109	11	11	33	33	38.3	37.8	0.0	0.0	8	8	64	64	4.2	4.3
Lesotho	142	143	7	7	40	40	26.0	24.9	12.0	11.2	6	6	101	101	8.0	8.0
Liberia	155	151	5	4	20	6	88.3	68.4	0.0	0.0	10	10	50	50	13.2	13.1
Madagascar	144	137	2	3	7	8	12.9	12.1	248.1	0.0	6	6	74	74	9.8	10.6
Malawi	141	145	10	10	39	39	108.4	90.9	0.0	0.0	6	6	49	69	3.2	3.2
Mali	148	146	6	4	8	8	79.7	90.5	306.8	348.3	5	5	29	29	11.9	12.1
Mauritania	162	159	9	9	19	19	56.0	48.3	412.1	334.9	4	4	49	49	5.2	4.7
Mauritius	21	23	5	5	6	6	3.8	3.6	0.0	0.0	4	4	26	22	10.6	10.6
Mozambique	132	139	9	9	13	13	13.9	11.7	0.0	0.0	8	8	42	42	9.9	8.7
Namibia	74	78	10	10	66	66	18.5	17.2	0.0	0.0	7	7	39	39	8.6	13.7
Niger	172	173	9	9	17	17	118.6	114.4	613.0	584.2	4	4	35	35	11.0	11.0
Nigeria	133	133	8	8	31	34	78.9	70.6	0.0	0.0	13	13	82	82	20.9	20.8
Rwanda	50	45	2	2	3	3	8.8	4.7	0.0	0.0	4	5	55	25	0.4	6.3
São Tomé and Príncipe	174	163	10	4	144	10	77.3	24.5	385.7	336.0	7	7	62	62	10.9	8.9
Senegal	157	154	4	3	8	5	63.1	68.0	205.1	203.0	6	6	122	122	20.6	20.3
Seychelles	109	103	10	10	39	39	17.5	16.0	0.0	0.0	4	4	33	33	7.0	7.0
Sierra Leone	150	141	6	6	12	12	110.7	93.3	0.0	0.0	7	7	86	86	12.2	11.8
Somalia	..	..	..	..	..	..	..	..	..	..	..	..	..	..	..	..
South Africa	36	35	6	5	22	19	6.0	0.3	0.0	0.0	6	6	24	23	8.8	5.6
Sudan	135	135	10	10	36	36	33.6	31.4	0.0	0.0	6	6	9	9	3.0	3.0
Swaziland	123	124	12	12	56	56	33.0	29.2	0.5	0.5	9	9	44	21	7.1	7.1
Tanzania	125	127	12	12	29	29	30.9	28.8	0.0	0.0	9	9	73	73	4.4	4.4
Togo	158	162	7	7	84	84	178.1	177.2	486.9	484.5	5	5	295	295	13.0	13.0
Uganda	119	123	18	16	25	34	94.4	84.5	0.0	0.0	13	13	77	48	3.2	2.9
Zambia	80	84	6	6	18	18	27.9	27.4	0.0	0.0	5	5	40	40	6.6	8.3
Zimbabwe	168	171	9	9	90	90	182.8	148.9	0.0	0.0	5	5	31	31	8.5	8.0
NORTH AFRICA			**9.4**	**9.4**	**18.4**	**18.4**	**42.0**	**41.5**	**95.9**	**95.1**	**7**	**7**	**55**	**55**	**6.4**	**6.4**
Algeria	143	148	14	14	25	25	12.9	12.1	34.4	30.6	10	10	48	48	7.1	7.1
Djibouti	167	170	11	11	37	37	169.9	169.8	434.1	434.0	7	7	40	40	13.0	13.0
Egypt, Arab Rep.	108	110	6	6	7	7	6.3	5.6	0.0	0.0	7	7	72	72	0.8	0.8
Libya	..	..	..	..	..	..	..	..	..	..	..	..	..	..	..	..
Morocco	115	94	6	6	12	12	15.8	15.7	11.2	10.7	8	8	75	75	4.9	4.9
Tunisia	40	46	10	10	11	11	5.0	4.2	0.0	0.0	4	4	39	39	6.1	6.1

(continued)

Table 4.1 Doing Business (continued)

	Enforcing contracts						Dealing with construction permits					
	Number of procedures		Time required (days)		Cost (% of debt)		Number of procedures		Time required (days)		Cost (% of GNI per capita)	
	2010	2011	2010	2011	2010	2011	2010	2011	2010	2011	2010	2011
SUB-SAHARAN AFRICA	**39**	**655**	**651**	**50**	**39.1**	**39.0**	**15**	**15**	**213**	**211**	**990.9**	**823.7**
Angola	46	1011	1,011	44	46.0	46.0	11	11	321	321	259.0	180.3
Benin	42	795	825	65	42.0	42.0	12	12	372	372	134.9	132.6
Botswana	29	625	625	28	29.0	28.0	22	22	145	145	245.4	203.0
Burkina Faso	37	446	446	82	37.0	37.0	12	12	98	98	524.1	345.0
Burundi	44	832	832	39	44.0	44.0	22	22	135	135	6,295.5	4,065.7
Cameroon	43	800	800	47	43.0	43.0	11	11	147	147	1,149.5	1,096.2
Cape Verde	37	425	425	20	37.0	37.0	17	17	122	122	570.0	523.8
Central African Republic	43	660	660	82	43.0	43.0	18	18	203	203	116.1	112.2
Chad	41	743	743	46	41.0	41.0	13	13	154	154	6,452.4	5,756.5
Comoros	43	506	506	89	43.0	43.0	15	15	155	155	63.0	62.8
Congo, Dem. Rep.	43	610	610	152	43.0	43.0	11	11	117	117	2,692.2	1,670.7
Congo, Rep.	44	560	560	53	44.0	44.0	14	14	186	186	232.4	157.7
Côte d'Ivoire	33	770	770	42	33.0	33.0	18	18	583	583	207.3	204.8
Equatorial Guinea	40	553	553	19	40.0	40.0	15	15	166	166	219.7	150.6
Eritrea	39	405	405	23	39.0	39.0	..	..	..	..	..	..
Ethiopia	37	620	620	15	37.0	37.0	9	9	128	128	406.9	369.1
Gabon	38	1070	1,070	34	38.0	38.0	13	13	201	201	26.6	21.5
Gambia, The	33	434	434	38	33.0	33.0	14	14	143	143	207.3	192.9
Ghana	36	487	487	23	36.0	36.0	16	16	218	218	598.7	560.3
Guinea	49	276	276	45	49.0	49.0	29	29	287	287	351.5	275.8
Guinea-Bissau	40	1715	1,715	25	40.0	40.0	12	12	170	170	1,075.0	1,032.7
Kenya	40	465	465	47	40.0	40.0	8	8	125	125	164.4	160.9
Lesotho	41	785	785	20	41.0	40.0	12	12	510	510	1,122.1	1,038.7
Liberia	41	1280	1,280	35	41.0	41.0	23	23	75	75	824.4	694.1
Madagascar	38	871	871	42	38.0	38.0	16	16	172	172	468.8	422.2
Malawi	42	312	312	94	42.0	42.0	18	18	200	200	1,304.7	1,077.5
Mali	36	620	620	52	36.0	36.0	11	11	187	179	390.0	439.3
Mauritania	46	370	370	23	46.0	46.0	22	18	168	119	61.4	49.9
Mauritius	36	645	645	17	36.0	36.0	16	16	136	136	32.3	30.6
Mozambique	30	730	730	143	30.0	30.0	13	13	370	370	146.0	123.0
Namibia	33	270	270	36	33.0	33.0	12	12	139	139	113.0	103.0
Niger	39	545	545	60	39.0	39.0	12	12	326	326	2,323.9	2,214.5
Nigeria	40	457	457	32	40.0	40.0	15	15	85	85	564.2	504.8
Rwanda	24	230	230	79	24.0	24.0	12	12	164	164	349.8	312.0
São Tomé and Príncipe	43	1185	1,185	51	43.0	43.0	13	13	211	211	565.1	536.8
Senegal	44	780	780	27	44.0	43.0	13	13	210	210	439.6	435.2
Seychelles	37	915	720	15	37.0	37.0	17	17	126	126	34.7	30.3
Sierra Leone	40	515	515	150	40.0	39.0	20	20	238	238	325.2	272.6
Somalia	..	..	..	..	..	..	..	..	..	..	..	..
South Africa	29	600	600	33	29.0	29.0	13	13	127	127	23.1	21.2
Sudan	53	810	810	20	53.0	53.0	16	16	270	270	100.1	88.0
Swaziland	40	972	972	56	40.0	40.0	13	13	95	95	130.0	115.2
Tanzania	38	462	462	14	38.0	38.0	19	19	303	303	1,255.5	1,170.1
Togo	41	588	588	48	41.0	41.0	12	12	309	309	998.4	994.0
Uganda	38	490	490	45	38.0	38.0	15	15	125	125	1,064.0	946.8
Zambia	35	471	471	39	35.0	35.0	14	14	196	196	2,410.5	2,015.2
Zimbabwe	38	410	410	113	38.0	38.0	12	12	614	614	7,553.7	6,154.3
NORTH AFRICA	**41**	**788**	**788**	**26**	**41.0**	**41.0**	**18**	**18**	**171**	**171**	**516.7**	**591.9**
Algeria	45	630	630	22	45.0	45.0	19	19	281	281	26.0	23.1
Djibouti	40	1225	1,225	34	40.0	40.0	14	15	171	172	1,828.1	2,285.7
Egypt, Arab Rep.	41	1010	1,010	26	41.0	41.0	22	22	218	218	173.8	155.3
Libya	..	..	..	..	..	..	..	..	..	..	..	..
Morocco	40	510	510	25	40.0	40.0	16	15	104	97	246.1	234.6
Tunisia	39	565	565	22	39.0	39.0	17	17	88	88	309.7	260.6

a. Average of the disclosure, director liability, and shareholder suits indexes.

Protecting investors (0 least protection to 10 most protection)								Resolving insolvency					
Disclosure index		Director liability index		Shareholder suits index		Investor protection index[a]		Time (years)		Cost (% of estate)		Recovery rate (cents on the dollar)	
2010	2011	2010	2011	2010	2011	2010	2011	2010	2011	2010	2011	2010	2011
5	**5**	**3**	**4**	**5**	**5**	**4.4**	**4.5**	**3**	**3**	**22.9**	**22.9**	**18.4**	**19.1**
5	5	6	6	6	6	5.7	5.7	6	6	22.0	22.0	8.4	6.9
6	6	1	1	3	3	3.3	3.3	4	4	22.0	22.0	20.2	20.2
7	7	8	8	3	3	6.0	6.0	2	2	15.0	15.0	63.7	64.5
6	6	1	1	4	4	3.7	3.7	4	4	9.0	9.0	26.8	27.3
4	8	1	6	5	4	3.3	6.0	..	..	..	..	0.0	0.0
6	6	1	1	6	6	4.3	4.3	3	3	34.0	34.0	13.6	13.6
1	1	5	5	6	6	4.0	4.0	..	..	..	..	0.0	0.0
6	6	1	1	5	5	4.0	4.0	5	5	76.0	76.0	0.0	0.0
6	6	1	1	3	3	3.3	3.3	4	4	60.0	60.0	0.0	0.0
6	6	1	1	5	5	4.0	4.0	..	..	..	..	0.0	0.0
3	3	3	3	4	4	3.3	3.3	5	5	29.0	29.0	1.1	1.2
6	6	1	1	3	3	3.3	3.3	3	3	25.0	25.0	17.8	17.9
6	6	1	1	3	3	3.3	3.3	2	2	18.0	18.0	32.8	37.6
6	6	1	1	4	4	3.7	3.7	..	..	..	..	0.0	0.0
4	4	5	5	5	5	4.7	4.7	..	..	..	..	0.0	0.0
4	4	4	4	5	5	4.3	4.3	3	3	15.0	15.0	31.3	31.4
6	6	1	1	3	3	3.3	3.3	5	5	15.0	15.0	15.2	15.2
2	2	1	1	5	5	2.7	2.7	3	3	15.0	15.0	19.8	19.3
7	7	5	5	6	6	6.0	6.0	2	2	22.0	22.0	23.7	26.0
6	6	1	1	1	1	2.7	2.7	4	4	8.0	8.0	19.4	19.3
6	6	1	1	5	5	4.0	4.0	..	..	..	..	0.0	0.0
3	3	2	2	10	10	5.0	5.0	5	5	22.0	22.0	29.8	30.9
2	2	1	1	8	8	3.7	3.7	3	3	8.0	8.0	36.4	37.4
4	4	1	1	6	6	3.7	3.7	3	3	43.0	43.0	8.4	8.4
5	5	6	6	6	6	5.7	5.7	2	2	30.0	30.0	14.3	13.5
4	4	7	7	5	5	5.3	5.3	3	3	25.0	25.0	17.9	18.5
6	6	1	1	4	4	3.7	3.7	4	4	18.0	18.0	24.6	24.9
5	5	3	3	3	3	3.7	3.7	8	8	9.0	9.0	10.3	10.3
6	6	8	8	9	9	7.7	7.7	2	2	15.0	15.0	35.1	35.1
5	5	4	4	9	9	6.0	6.0	5	5	9.0	9.0	17.7	15.5
5	5	5	5	6	6	5.3	5.3	2	2	15.0	15.0	41.5	41.9
6	6	1	1	3	3	3.3	3.3	5	5	18.0	18.0	16.0	21.9
5	5	7	7	5	5	5.7	5.7	2	2	22.0	22.0	26.8	28.2
7	7	9	9	3	3	6.3	6.3	3	3	50.0	50.0	3.2	3.2
3	3	1	1	6	6	3.3	3.3	6	6	22.0	22.0	4.0	7.4
6	6	1	1	2	2	3.0	3.0	3	3	7.0	7.0	32.0	32.0
4	4	8	8	5	5	5.7	5.7	..	..	..	..	0.0	0.0
6	6	7	7	6	6	6.3	6.3	3	3	42.0	42.0	8.4	9.2
..	..	..	..	..	..	..	..	..	..	..	..	..	..
8	8	8	8	8	8	8.0	8.0	2	2	18.0	18.0	34.4	35.2
0	0	6	6	4	4	3.3	3.3	2	2	20.0	20.0	32.3	33.2
2	2	5	5	6	6	4.3	4.3	2	2	15.0	15.0	37.6	38.2
3	3	4	4	8	8	5.0	5.0	3	3	22.0	22.0	21.9	22.0
6	6	1	1	4	4	3.7	3.7	3	3	15.0	15.0	30.6	30.5
2	2	5	5	5	5	4.0	4.0	2	2	30.0	30.0	39.7	40.2
3	3	6	6	7	7	5.3	5.3	3	3	9.0	9.0	27.2	29.3
8	8	1	1	4	4	4.3	4.3	3	3	22.0	22.0	0.2	10.0
6	**6**	**4**	**4**	**3**	**4**	**4.4**	**4.8**	**3**	**3**	**14.4**	**14.4**	**33.0**	**33.3**
6	6	6	6	4	4	5.3	5.3	3	3	7.0	7.0	41.7	41.7
5	5	2	2	0	0	2.3	2.3	5	5	18.0	18.0	15.6	16.5
8	8	3	3	5	5	5.3	5.3	4	4	22.0	22.0	17.4	17.7
..	..	..	..	..	..	..	..	..	..	..	..	..	..
7	7	2	2	1	6	3.3	5.0	2	2	18.0	18.0	38.4	38.3
5	5	7	7	6	6	6.0	6.0	1	1	7.0	7.0	51.7	52.2

Table 4.2 Investment climate

	Private sector fixed capital formation (% of GDP) 2010[a]	Net foreign direct investment ($ millions) 2010[a]	Domestic credit to private sector (% of GDP) 2010[a]	Enterprise Surveys									
					Viewed by firms as a major constraint (% of firms)								
				Firms that believe the court system is fair, impartial, and uncorrupt (%) 2010-11[b]	Corruption 2010-11[b]	Crime, theft, and discord 2010-11[b]	Tax rates 2010-11[b]	Finance 2010-11[b]	Electricity 2010-11[b]	Labor regulations 2010-11[b]	Labor skills 2010-11[b]	Transportation 2010-11[b]	Customs and trade regulations 2010-11[b]
SUB-SAHARAN AFRICA	**12.8**	**..**	**64.1**										
Angola	3.0	-4,567.6	20.9	23.6	75.6	1.5	26.4	38.5	35.7	26.1	25.9	25.3	35.8
Benin	16.1	..	23.3	..	..	..	..	..	..	..	..	..	..
Botswana	14.0	264.7	23.3	6.4	27.4	1.5	16.9	25.5	34.8	14.0	32.2	20.1	15.8
Burkina Faso	..	..	17.6	..	..	..	..	..	..	..	..	..	..
Burundi	10.0	0.8	18.7	..	..	..	..	..	..	..	..	..	..
Cameroon	12.6	35.3	13.2	..	..	..	..	..	..	..	..	..	..
Cape Verde	28.1	111.9	62.1	..	..	..	..	..	..	..	..	..	..
Central African Republic	..	..	8.9	8.9	41.4	25.6	31.9	46.0	76.1	..	..	33.4	31.9
Chad	22.7	..	5.1	..	..	..	..	..	..	..	..	..	..
Comoros	..	..	19.1	..	..	..	..	..	..	..	..	..	..
Congo, Dem. Rep.	..	..	6.6	33.0	72.7	1.8	39.5	73.3	51.6	20.0	65.0	38.8	54.0
Congo, Rep.	10.2	..	5.5	..	..	..	..	..	..	..	..	..	..
Côte d'Ivoire	9.2	..	18.0	..	..	..	..	..	..	..	..	..	..
Equatorial Guinea	..	..	7.5	..	..	..	..	..	..	..	..	..	..
Eritrea	..	..	16.0	..	..	..	..	..	..	..	..	..	..
Ethiopia	5.0	288.3	..	..	..	..	..	..	..	..	..	..	..
Gabon	17.4	..	8.1	..	..	..	..	..	..	..	..	..	..
Gambia, The	11.2	37.4	14.0	..	..	..	..	..	..	..	..	..	..
Ghana	17.9	2,527.4	15.3	..	..	..	..	..	..	..	..	..	..
Guinea	15.7	101.4	..	..	..	..	..	..	..	..	..	..	..
Guinea-Bissau	..	..	6.2	..	..	..	..	..	..	..	..	..	..
Kenya	19.9	184.2	33.8	..	..	..	..	..	..	..	..	..	..
Lesotho	15.8	119.3	13.8	..	..	..	..	..	..	..	..	..	..
Liberia	28.8	452.3	19.4	..	..	..	..	..	..	..	..	..	..
Madagascar	..	..	11.7	..	..	..	..	..	..	..	..	..	..
Malawi	16.9	..	16.0	..	..	..	..	..	..	..	..	..	..
Mali	..	..	18.0	15.9	24.8	0.5	26.3	48.1	33.5	6.4	12.2	21.4	16.9
Mauritania	16.6	..	27.9	..	..	..	..	..	..	..	..	..	..
Mauritius	18.8	301.7	87.9	..	..	..	..	..	..	..	..	..	..
Mozambique	11.0	789.8	26.8	..	..	..	..	..	..	..	..	..	..
Namibia	16.3	802.7	49.9	..	..	..	..	..	..	..	..	..	..
Niger	..	..	13.0	..	..	..	..	..	..	..	..	..	..
Nigeria	..	5,133.3	29.0	..	..	..	..	..	..	..	..	..	..
Rwanda	9.5	42.3	..	..	..	..	..	..	..	..	..	..	..
São Tomé and Príncipe	..	24.5	38.8	..	..	..	..	..	..	..	..	..	..
Senegal	18.2	..	25.9	..	..	..	..	..	..	..	..	..	..
Seychelles	..	161.2	28.0	..	..	..	..	..	..	..	..	..	..
Sierra Leone	8.0	86.6	10.4	..	..	..	..	..	..	..	..	..	..
Somalia	..	..	..	..	..	..	..	..	..	..	..	..	..
South Africa	11.9	1,385.6	145.6	..	..	..	..	..	..	..	..	..	..
Sudan	13.1	2,063.7	11.6	..	..	..	..	..	..	..	..	..	..
Swaziland	5.3	131.8	23.0	..	..	..	..	..	..	..	..	..	..
Tanzania	20.1	433.4	16.2	..	..	..	..	..	..	..	..	..	..
Togo	11.0	..	22.8	..	..	..	..	..	..	..	..	..	..
Uganda	17.7	547.3	15.6	..	..	..	..	..	..	..	..	..	..
Zambia	18.3	633.9	11.5	..	..	..	..	..	..	..	..	..	..
Zimbabwe	0.1	..	..	..	..	..	..	..	..	..	..	..	..
NORTH AFRICA	**..**	**8,347.7**	**36.9**										
Algeria	..	2,044.0	15.6	..	..	..	..	..	..	..	..	..	..
Djibouti	..	36.5	..	..	..	..	..	..	..	..	..	..	..
Egypt, Arab Rep.	12.2	5,210.1	33.1	..	..	..	..	..	..	..	..	..	..
Libya	..	-938.0	..	..	..	..	..	..	..	..	..	..	..
Morocco	24.9	660.6	68.7	..	..	..	..	..	..	..	..	..	..
Tunisia	..	1,334.5	68.8	..	..	..	..	..	..	..	..	..	..

a. Provisional.
b. Data are for the most recent year available during the period specified.

Number of tax payments 2011	Time to prepare, file, and pay taxes (hours) 2011	Total tax rate (% of profit) 2011	Enterprise Surveys: Regulation and tax administration – Highest marginal tax rate, corporate (%) 2009	Enterprise Surveys: Regulation and tax administration – Time dealing with officials (% of management time) 2010-11[b]	Enterprise Surveys: Average time to clear customs (days) – Direct exports 2010-11[b]	Enterprise Surveys: Average time to clear customs (days) – Imports 2010-11[b]	Interest rate spread (lending rate minus deposit rate) 2010	Listed domestic companies 2010	Market capitalization of listed companies (% of GDP) 2010[a]	Turnover ratio for traded stocks (%) 2010[a]
37	**318**	**57**	**..**				**9.7**	**950**	**148.8**	**..**
31	282	53.2	35.0	12.2	6.7	11.4	9.8	..	..	..
55	270	66.0	..	..	..	..	..	..	..	..
19	152	19.4	25.0	10.2	6.2	3.7	5.9	21	27.4	3.4
46	270	43.6	..	..	..	..	..	..	..	..
24	274	46.2	..	..	..	..	..	..	..	..
44	654	49.1	..	..	..	..	..	..	..	..
41	186	37.8	..	..	..	..	7.9	..	..	..
54	504	54.6	..	9.2	9.5	11.9	..	..	..	..
54	732	65.4	..	..	..	..	..	..	..	..
20	100	217.9	..	..	..	..	8.8	..	..	..
32	336	339.7	38.0	29.4	18.0	45.4	39.8	..	..	..
61	606	65.9	..	..	..	..	..	..	..	..
62	270	44.3	25.0	..	..	..	..	38	31.0	2.0
46	492	46.0	..	..	..	..	..	..	..	..
18	216	84.5	..	..	..	..	..	..	..	..
19	198	31.1	..	..	..	..	..	..	..	..
26	488	43.5	..	..	..	..	..	..	..	..
50	376	283.5	..	..	..	..	12.4	..	..	..
33	224	33.6	25.0	..	..	..	..	35	11.0	3.4
56	416	54.3	..	..	..	..	..	..	..	..
46	208	45.9	..	..	..	..	..	..	..	..
41	393	49.6	..	..	..	..	9.8	55	44.9	8.6
21	324	16.0	..	..	..	..	7.5	..	..	..
33	158	43.7	..	..	..	..	..	..	..	..
23	201	36.6	..	..	..	..	38.5	..	..	..
19	157	28.2	..	..	..	..	21.0	14	27.0	1.5
59	270	51.8	..	2.0	12.9	16.5	..	..	..	..
37	696	68.3	..	..	..	..	9.0	..	..	..
7	161	25.0	15.0	..	..	..	0.5	86	67.0	6.4
37	230	34.3	32.0	..	..	..	6.6	..	..	..
37	375	9.8	35.0	..	..	..	4.7	7	10.6	1.8
41	270	43.8	..	..	..	..	..	..	..	..
35	938	32.7	30.0	..	..	..	11.1	215	25.9	12.5
18	148	31.3	..	..	..	..	9.6	..	..	..
42	424	32.5	..	..	..	..	17.8	..	..	..
59	666	46.0	..	..	..	..	..	..	..	..
21	76	32.2	..	..	..	..	9.8	..	..	..
29	357	32.1	..	..	..	..	12.3	..	..	..
..	..	..	..	..	..	..	..	..	..	..
9	200	33.1	34.6	..	..	..	3.4	360	278.5	39.6
42	180	36.1	35.0	..	..	..	..	..	..	..
33	104	36.8	30.0	..	..	..	5.9	5	..	..
48	172	45.5	30.0	..	..	..	8.0	11	5.5	..
53	270	49.5	..	..	..	..	..	..	..	..
32	213	35.7	45.0	..	..	..	12.5	8	10.4	0.4
37	132	14.5	35.0	..	..	..	13.5	19	17.4	9.2
49	242	35.6	30.9	..	..	..	..	76	153.5	15.0
24	**270**	**53.4**	**..**				**5.5**	**342**	**45.9**	**32.9**
29	451	72.0	..	..	..	..	6.3	..	..	..
35	82	38.7	..	..	..	..	9.4	..	..	..
29	433	43.6	20.0	..	..	..	4.8	213	37.7	43.0
..	..	..	40.0	..	..	..	3.5	..	..	..
17	238	49.6	..	..	..	..	..	73	76.2	16.3
8	144	62.9	30.0	..	..	..	..	56	24.2	17.2

Table 4.3 Financial sector infrastructure

	Macroeconomy							
	Foreign currency sovereign ratings		Gross national savings (% of GDP)		Money and quasi money (M2) (% of GDP)		Real interest rate (%)	
	Long-term 2011–12[b]	Short-term 2011–12[b]	2009	2010[c]	2009	2010[c]	2009	2010[c]
SUB-SAHARAN AFRICA			**15.5**	**17.2**	**47.1**	**47.0**	**..**	**..**
Angola	B+	B	5.2	21.6	31.1	32.5	25.0	0.1
Benin	..	..	13.9	..	36.8	37.9	..	..
Botswana	..	..	26.4	27.7	47.2	40.3	20.4	-2.8
Burkina Faso	..	..	..	..	24.2	26.3	..	..
Burundi	..	..	5.2	-5.4	23.1	24.6	1.6	4.4
Cameroon	..	..	..	..	20.1	21.1	..	..
Cape Verde	..	..	23.6	34.4	81.5	78.3	6.5	7.5
Central African Republic	..	..	..	..	15.8	17.1	..	..
Chad	..	..	..	..	14.2	12.7	..	..
Comoros	..	..	..	..	28.6	31.4	5.7	6.4
Congo, Dem. Rep.	..	..	..	..	13.8	14.6	22.4	28.2
Congo, Rep.	..	..	..	..	22.2	20.5	..	..
Côte d'Ivoire	..	..	14.5	..	29.9	33.8	..	..
Equatorial Guinea	..	..	..	..	11.1	12.1	..	..
Eritrea	..	..	..	..	113.3	114.9	..	..
Ethiopia	..	..	14.8	16.6	..	..	..	..
Gabon	..	..	..	..	22.3	19.5	..	..
Gambia, The	..	..	12.2	9.4	39.6	41.1	19.0	20.0
Ghana	B+	B	17.5	20.6	25.5	26.0	..	..
Guinea	..	..	6.5	7.1	..	..	..	..
Guinea-Bissau	..	..	..	..	23.5	25.8	..	..
Kenya	..	..	14.2	15.6	41.0	45.5	5.2	11.9
Lesotho	BB-	B	32.6	12.7	36.7	38.6	7.7	6.8
Liberia	..	..	53.0	29.0	33.8	39.2	15.6	7.4
Madagascar	..	..	..	..	22.3	22.4	33.7	37.9
Malawi	..	..	12.8	..	23.5	24.8	17.1	16.5
Mali	..	..	..	..	25.3	26.0	..	..
Mauritania	..	..	..	..	32.7	29.7	26.9	-2.0
Mauritius	..	..	13.9	15.6	101.2	102.9	9.5	6.9
Mozambique	..	..	7.6	12.2	35.3	38.5	11.1	5.7
Namibia	BBB-	F3	27.5	34.1	51.4	62.4	6.6	8.6
Niger	..	..	..	..	17.6	19.5	..	..
Nigeria	BB-	B	..	..	38.1	36.1	23.9	7.6
Rwanda	B	B	15.0	12.2	..	..	4.3	13.8
São Tomé and Príncipe	..	..	..	..	34.2	34.3	15.5	15.3
Senegal	..	..	19.4	..	35.2	37.5	..	..
Seychelles	B	B	14.6	..	53.9	58.8	-7.8	18.5
Sierra Leone	..	..	10.3	13.0	23.7	25.8	16.1	6.0
Somalia	..	..	..	..	..	..	..	..
South Africa	BBB+	F2	15.5	16.5	80.5	75.7	3.8	1.8
Sudan	..	..	12.8	17.5	20.3	20.6	..	..
Swaziland	..	..	0.4	2.4	27.6	29.6	12.5	3.4
Tanzania	..	..	19.5	20.1	28.8	30.7	7.1	7.1
Togo	..	..	12.4	..	38.5	42.4	..	..
Uganda	..	..	18.2	19.0	20.9	23.2	5.6	9.7
Zambia	B+	B	19.0	22.5	20.6	20.4	10.2	8.2
Zimbabwe	..	..	..	..	..	..	..	..
NORTH AFRICA			**28.7**	**27.7**	**75.6**	**75.1**	**..**	**..**
Algeria	..	..	54.1	48.4	65.9	59.2	21.7	-7.1
Djibouti	..	..	..	..	83.0	..	9.3	..
Egypt, Arab Rep.	BB	B	16.9	17.8	79.5	76.3	0.7	0.8
Libya	B	B	..	..	53.7	..	57.8	..
Morocco	BBB-	F3	30.2	30.8	105.3	107.8	..	..
Tunisia	BBB-	F3	21.2	20.3	58.3	60.6	..	..

a. Data are consolidated for regional security markets where they exist.
b. Data are for the most recent year available during the period specified.
c. Provisional.

Intermediation						Capital markets[a]					
Domestic credit to private sector (% of GDP)		Interest rate spread (lending rate minus deposit rate)		Ratio of bank nonperforming loans to total gross loans (%)		Listed domestic companies		Market capitalization of listed companies (% of GDP)		Turnover ratio for traded stocks (%)	
2009	2010[c]	2009	2010[c]	2009	2010[c]	2009	2010[c]	2009	2010[c]	2009	2010[c]
62.9	**64.1**	**8.4**	**9.7**	**..**	**..**	**..**	**950**	**..**	**148.8**	**..**	**..**
21.2	20.9	8.1	9.8	..	..	..	..	..	..	..	..
22.5	23.3	..	..	..	..	..	..	..	..	..	..
25.8	23.3	6.3	5.9	..	..	20	21	37.1	27.4	2.6	3.4
17.0	17.6	..	..	..	..	..	..	..	..	..	..
15.9	18.7	..	..	..	..	..	..	..	..	..	..
12.1	13.2	..	..	..	..	..	..	..	..	..	..
62.0	62.1	8.1	7.9	..	..	..	..	..	..	..	..
6.6	8.9	..	..	..	..	..	..	..	..	..	..
5.0	5.1	..	..	..	..	..	..	..	..	..	..
16.0	19.1	8.6	8.8	..	..	..	..	..	..	..	..
7.3	6.6	49.3	39.8	..	..	..	..	..	..	..	..
4.8	5.5	..	..	..	..	..	..	..	..	..	..
17.3	18.0	..	..	..	..	38	38	26.7	31.0	2.0	2.0
7.0	7.5	..	..	..	..	..	..	..	..	..	..
16.8	16.0	..	..	..	..	..	..	..	..	..	..
..	..	..	..	..	..	..	..	..	..	..	..
10.2	8.1	..	..	7.2	9.9	..	..	..	..	..	..
13.5	14.0	11.5	12.4	..	..	..	..	..	..	..	..
15.7	15.3	..	..	16.2	17.6	35	35	9.7	11.0	2.0	3.4
..	..	..	..	..	..	..	..	..	..	..	..
5.6	6.2	..	..	..	..	..	..	..	..	..	..
30.3	33.8	8.8	9.8	7.9	6.3	55	55	35.2	44.9	4.6	8.6
12.8	13.8	8.2	7.5	3.7	3.7	..	..	..	..	..	..
16.0	19.4	10.1	..	..	..	..	..	..	..	..	..
11.6	11.7	33.5	38.5	..	..	..	..	..	..	..	..
14.2	16.0	21.8	21.0	..	..	15	14	29.3	27.0	1.3	1.5
17.5	18.0	..	..	..	..	..	..	..	..	..	..
30.4	27.9	11.5	9.0	..	..	..	..	..	..	..	..
82.8	87.9	0.8	0.5	3.3	2.8	89	86	53.7	67.0	8.1	6.4
24.8	26.8	6.2	6.6	1.8	1.9	..	..	..	..	..	..
48.4	49.9	4.9	4.7	2.7	2.0	7	7	9.5	10.6	3.0	1.8
12.5	13.0	..	..	..	..	..	..	..	..	..	..
38.6	29.0	5.1	11.1	29.1	17.2	214	215	19.8	25.9	11.0	12.5
..	..	..	9.6	13.1	10.8	..	..	..	..	..	..
33.4	38.8	19.2	17.8	..	..	..	..	..	..	..	..
24.8	25.9	..	..	18.7	20.2	..	..	..	..	..	..
22.8	28.0	5.6	9.8	3.8	5.5	..	..	..	..	..	..
9.5	10.4	13.1	12.3	10.6	15.6	..	..	..	..	..	..
..	..	..	..	..	..	..	..	..	..	..	..
147.7	145.6	3.2	3.4	5.9	5.8	363	360	249.0	278.5	57.3	39.6
12.3	11.6	..	..	..	..	..	..	..	..	..	..
25.0	23.0	6.0	5.9	8.1	8.0	5	5	..	..	..	..
15.3	16.2	7.1	8.0	..	..	15	11	..	5.5	..	..
19.8	22.8	..	..	..	..	..	..	..	..	..	..
13.3	15.6	11.2	12.5	4.2	2.1	8	8	23.7	10.4	0.3	0.4
12.0	11.5	15.0	13.5	..	..	19	19	21.9	17.4	..	9.2
..	..	..	..	..	..	76	76	65.6	153.5	..	15.0
35.1	**36.9**	**5.9**	**5.5**	**13.2**	**11.0**	**..**	**342**	**..**	**45.9**	**..**	**32.9**
16.5	15.6	6.3	6.3	..	..	..	..	..	..	..	..
29.4	..	9.7	9.4	..	..	..	..	..	..	..	..
36.1	33.1	5.5	4.8	13.4	11.0	305	213	47.6	37.7	60.1	43.0
10.9	..	3.5	3.5	..	..	..	..	..	..	..	..
64.7	68.7	..	..	5.5	4.4	78	73	69.2	76.2	45.7	16.3
62.2	68.8	..	..	13.2	12.1	52	56	21.0	24.2	16.2	17.2

Table 5.1 International trade and tariff barriers

	Trade											
								Annual average		Annual growth (%)		
	Total (% of GDP) 2010[a]	Merchandise trade (% of GDP) 2010[a]	Services trade (% of GDP) 2010[a]	Exports ($ millions) 2010[a]	Imports ($ millions) 2010[a]	Exports (% of GDP) 2010[a]	Imports (% of GDP) 2010[a]	Exports (% of GDP) 2000-10	Imports (% of GDP) 2000-10	Exports 2010[a]	Imports 2010[a]	Terms of trade index (2000 = 100) 2010[a]
SUB-SAHARAN AFRICA	**65.2**	**58.4**	**12.8**	**374,652**	**378,688**	**31.2**	**34.0**	**32.3**	**34.0**	**..**	**..**	**..**
Angola	105.3	90.9	23.8	51,400	35,421	62.3	43.0	73.9	54.8	-2.71	-20.89	..
Benin	42.3	51.8	..	937	1,839	14.3	28.1	14.1	27.4	..	..	..
Botswana	73.0	69.4	8.5	4,917	5,956	33.0	40.0	44.3	36.9	16.2	9.7	87.3
Burkina Faso	..	37.8	..	..	..	..	..	9.7	23.9	..	..	..
Burundi	42.7	30.1	12.2	124	740	6.1	36.5	6.5	29.0	57.8	59.2	..
Cameroon	61.0	39.4	12.9	6,502	7,200	28.9	32.0	23.5	24.2	-0.1	8.2	121.5
Cape Verde	105.7	47.4	49.1	640	1,113	38.6	67.1	36.2	69.0	24.5	9.7	159.1
Central African Republic	..	24.2	..	..	..	..	..	14.6	21.5	..	..	..
Chad	100.0	70.8	..	3,331	5,213	39.0	61.0	39.2	56.7	..	..	..
Comoros	..	38.4	..	..	..	..	..	15.2	37.0	..	..	..
Congo, Dem. Rep.	64.9	74.8	..	3,412	5,096	26.0	38.9	25.1	33.8	52.9	36.3	129.3
Congo, Rep.	139.8	92.4	..	10,221	6,568	85.1	54.7	79.8	54.9	..	..	..
Côte d'Ivoire	76.7	79.2	..	9,316	8,270	40.6	36.1	46.1	37.4	-0.5	7.6	94.8
Equatorial Guinea	..	111.7	..	..	..	..	..	89.1	55.8	..	..	..
Eritrea	..	33.2	..	..	..	..	..	8.0	52.2	..	..	..
Ethiopia	44.0	36.4	16.1	3,392	9,653	11.4	32.5	12.7	30.0	14.4	15.9	112.2
Gabon	97.3	93.6	..	8,094	4,754	61.3	36.0	61.1	32.9	3.5	3.3	156.1
Gambia, The	60.8	27.7	15.2	230	409	21.9	38.9	27.3	38.6	0.2	7.7	86.9
Ghana	70.6	57.8	13.9	9,461	13,265	29.4	41.2	35.1	52.3	24.6	21.0	..
Guinea	74.1	49.6	9.7	1,649	1,859	34.8	39.3	30.7	33.8	1.5	0.1	96.5
Guinea-Bissau	..	41.3	..	..	..	..	..	30.1	55.3	..	..	..
Kenya	65.4	53.6	17.7	8,861	12,192	27.5	37.9	25.6	35.1	16.5	3.8	116.1
Lesotho	157.7	138.6	25.9	955	2,482	43.8	113.9	50.3	117.0	2.4	8.9	96.5
Liberia	134.5	94.2	125.2	247	1,081	25.0	109.5	34.1	80.7	5.8	15.9	30.4
Madagascar	..	42.9	..	..	..	..	..	27.5	42.6	..	..	..
Malawi	77.8	58.7	..	1,547	2,387	30.6	47.2	26.3	43.2	..	..	..
Mali	..	55.2	..	..	..	..	..	28.5	39.6	..	..	..
Mauritania	135.6	106.7	..	2,241	2,661	62.0	73.6	38.9	60.5	12.2	21.8	262.5
Mauritius	116.3	68.4	48.2	5,098	6,202	52.5	63.8	57.8	62.7	10.0	7.1	74.6
Mozambique	71.3	83.6	19.6	2,421	4,144	26.3	45.0	28.7	44.1	2.2	1.7	50.0
Namibia	83.9	84.5	14.0	4,738	4,603	42.6	41.3	44.3	48.4	-42.4	-60.1	126.7
Niger	..	56.9	..	..	..	..	..	16.2	25.0	..	..	..
Nigeria	69.1	64.1	12.9	74,610	61,486	37.9	31.2	42.0	31.1	..	..	..
Rwanda	41.5	30.7	15.4	610	1,721	10.9	30.6	10.5	26.7	..	..	..
São Tomé and Príncipe	..	61.3	23.0	..	..	..	..	..	..	..	..	..
Senegal	67.8	54.0	..	3,186	5,530	24.8	43.0	26.5	42.2	5.6	3.5	91.6
Seychelles	..	109.1	107.3	..	..	..	..	91.8	102.7	..	..	..
Sierra Leone	46.6	58.0	10.7	327	564	17.1	29.5	19.7	33.5	..	..	..
Somalia	..	..	..	..	..	..	..	..	..	..	..	..
South Africa	54.9	48.4	8.9	99,399	100,119	27.3	27.5	29.5	29.2	4.6	9.6	135.6
Sudan	38.7	32.1	3.8	13,242	12,665	19.8	18.9	16.9	21.7	..	..	..
Swaziland	123.0	87.9	25.1	2,027	2,522	54.8	68.2	77.7	84.9	-4.6	-2.6	99.4
Tanzania	63.8	50.3	17.2	5,975	8,653	26.1	37.8	20.8	29.9	-4.3	-3.1	126.2
Togo	91.1	74.0	..	1,185	1,709	37.3	53.8	37.5	53.6	-0.7	-5.7	68.2
Uganda	57.7	35.8	18.9	4,087	5,833	23.8	33.9	16.0	27.6	5.6	7.8	71.2
Zambia	79.1	77.3	7.7	7,142	5,672	44.1	35.0	34.6	37.6	..	..	..
Zimbabwe	126.3	84.3	..	3,608	5,831	48.3	78.0	36.3	48.0	60.0	33.6	109.3
NORTH AFRICA	**59.2**	**52.0**	**16.1**	**197,350**	**178,504**	**28.4**	**30.7**	**34.4**	**30.7**	**..**	**-0.7**	**..**
Algeria	52.3	60.1	9.6	49,939	34,820	30.8	21.5	40.0	23.3	..	..	..
Djibouti	..	..	..	..	..	..	..	40.7	53.6	..	..	..
Egypt, Arab Rep.	47.5	36.3	17.6	46,732	57,200	21.4	26.1	24.7	28.8	-3.0	-3.2	93.0
Libya	..	..	..	..	..	..	..	56.9	27.8	..	..	..
Morocco	75.9	58.2	22.0	29,965	38,969	33.0	42.9	31.6	38.1	16.3	3.3	95.6
Tunisia	102.8	87.4	20.7	21,569	23,921	48.8	54.1	45.1	48.1	4.8	3.8	96.1

Structure of merchandise exports (% of total)					Structure of merchandise imports (% of total)				
Food 2009	Agricultural raw materials 2009	Fuel 2009	Ores and metals 2010	Manufactures 2010	Food 2010	Agricultural raw materials 2010	Fuel 2010	Ores and metals 2010	Manufactures 2010
13.7	**3.0**	**36.9**	**17.7**	**30.8**	**10.5**	**1.0**	**16.7**	**2.0**	**66.5**
..	..	..	..	..	..	..	..	..	..
..	..	..	..	..	..	..	..	..	..
5.2	0.2	0.3	14.5	79.5	12.4	0.8	14.7	2.0	68.5
26.8	60.5	0.0	1.7	9.1	15.1	0.7	22.0	0.9	61.0
67.5	4.8	1.9	5.2	5.9	13.7	1.4	2.1	0.7	81.6
..	..	..	3.0	7.5	17.7	1.6	27.5	0.8	52.4
72.6	0.0	..	0.9	17.5	27.8	1.3	11.9	1.1	57.8
..	..	..	..	..	..	..	..	..	..
..	..	..	..	..	..	..	..	..	..
..	..	..	..	..	..	..	..	..	..
..	..	..	..	..	..	..	..	..	..
..	..	..	..	..	..	..	..	..	..
48.2	5.7	30.0	0.3	16.2	19.2	0.9	23.7	1.2	54.6
..	..	..	..	..	..	..	..	..	..
..	..	..	..	..	..	..	..	..	..
77.5	11.9	0.0	1.1	8.9	11.0	0.5	18.6	1.2	68.7
..	..	..	..	..	..	..	..	..	..
53.0	1.0	0.0	9.7	10.4	36.1	0.9	20.4	0.9	40.9
..	..	..	11.3	20.7	15.3	1.1	1.0	1.2	81.1
..	..	..	..	..	..	..	..	..	..
..	..	..	..	..	..	..	..	..	..
44.0	13.2	4.2	2.0	34.7	12.1	1.6	22.1	1.5	62.8
..	..	..	..	..	..	..	..	..	..
..	..	..	..	..	..	..	..	..	..
28.8	5.2	4.9	9.5	48.2	13.6	1.0	15.2	0.4	69.5
86.6	3.8	0.1	11.1	9.0	13.6	1.1	10.0	1.0	74.1
..	..	..	0.7	20.2	11.6	0.5	26.0	0.6	61.2
..	..	..	30.4	0.0	19.4	0.5	26.4	0.2	52.9
32.4	0.9	0.0	0.4	60.2	21.1	2.2	19.3	1.1	56.4
23.3	3.1	17.5	54.5	2.0	11.6	1.0	19.9	0.5	49.6
..	..	..	..	..	..	..	..	..	..
..	..	..	59.6	14.1	15.1	2.1	12.5	0.9	69.4
4.5	1.1	90.4	1.1	6.7	10.3	0.8	1.4	1.1	86.5
42.3	1.7	0.1	36.9	7.6	..	..	..	..	..
92.4	0.7	0.0	0.0	4.7	29.8	0.8	16.1	1.1	52.0
29.5	1.1	24.0	3.8	40.1	22.4	1.5	29.9	1.7	44.4
..	..	..	..	..	..	..	..	..	..
..	..	..	..	..	..	..	..	..	..
..	..	..	..	..	..	..	..	..	..
10.2	1.9	11.1	32.7	46.6	5.8	0.9	19.8	1.6	65.4
5.6	1.4	92.1	..	..	..	..	..	..	..
..	..	..	..	..	..	..	..	..	..
35.5	9.8	1.0	33.7	24.1	10.0	0.9	27.6	1.1	60.4
..	..	..	5.6	74.2	15.7	1.4	13.9	1.9	67.2
..	..	..	1.9	22.9	12.4	1.1	20.0	1.3	65.1
7.5	1.4	0.9	86.0	6.3	4.7	0.6	11.6	21.0	61.6
19.4	23.1	0.9	34.9	36.4	18.8	2.6	11.2	13.8	52.2
6.3	**0.4**	**63.5**	**3.3**	**29.5**	**14.5**	**2.4**	**13.5**	**3.2**	**66.0**
0.3	0.0	97.7	0.3	1.8	16.3	1.6	2.1	1.5	78.4
0.4	0.0	6.5	..	..	..	..	..	..	..
..	..	..	6.3	43.4	19.1	3.2	13.4	4.1	60.1
..	..	..	..	..	..	..	..	..	..
22.1	1.6	2.0	11.7	66.3	11.5	2.2	23.1	3.3	58.8
9.2	0.5	13.6	1.6	76.0	9.4	2.1	12.6	3.6	72.3

(continued)

Table 5.1 International trade and tariff barriers (continued)

	Export indexes (0 low to 1 high)		Import indexes (0 low to 1 high)		Competitiveness Indicator (%)		Tariff barriers, all products (%)						
	Diversification 2010	Concentration 2010	Diversification 2010	Concentration 2010	Sectoral effect 2005–09	Global effect 2005–09	Binding coverage 2010	Simple mean bound rate 2010	Simple mean tariff 2010	Weighted mean tariff 2010	Share of lines with international peaks 2010	Share of lines with domestic peaks 2010	Share of lines with specific rates 2010
SUB-SAHARAN AFRICA	0.39	0.58	0.09	0.29			..	..	..	..	..	..	..
Angola	0.97	0.83	0.07	0.50	24.1	63.8	..	..	..	..	..	..	..
Benin	0.37	0.75	0.17	0.62	5.8	-14.6	39.5	28.7	13.3	15.4	50.2	0.0	0.0
Botswana	0.60	0.86	0.14	0.46	-16.8	-13.9	96.1	19.0	8.8	5.2	20.2	8.5	0.0
Burkina Faso	0.50	0.82	0.17	0.54	-8.2	-6.7	39.4	42.5	12.4	8.8	44.5	0.0	0.0
Burundi	0.54	0.75	0.10	0.51	8.0	-1.3	22.3	67.8	9.8	5.5	29.8	1.1	0.0
Cameroon	0.36	0.72	0.21	0.49	9.4	-10.8	..	..	..	..	..	..	..
Cape Verde	0.48	0.73	0.11	0.47	-5.1	17.7	100.0	15.8	14.7	11.6	44.3	11.9	0.0
Central African Republic	0.14	0.36	0.07	0.22	-1.2	-10.9	..	..	..	..	..	..	..
Chad	0.33	0.76	0.15	0.52	20.7	7.4	..	..	..	..	..	..	..
Comoros	0.51	0.75	0.11	0.53	-23.3	3.0	..	..	..	..	..	..	..
Congo, Dem. Rep.	0.37	0.81	0.07	0.49	3.2	31.1	..	..	..	..	..	..	..
Congo, Rep.	0.76	0.79	0.06	0.47	24.2	11.8	..	..	..	..	..	..	..
Côte d'Ivoire	0.35	0.70	0.25	0.48	2.9	-7.9	33.8	11.2	13.1	7.3	47.9	0.0	0.0
Equatorial Guinea	0.82	0.74	0.28	0.56	21.9	28.5	..	..	..	..	..	..	..
Eritrea	0.12	0.65	0.11	0.53	-6.1	19.4	..	..	..	..	..	..	..
Ethiopia	0.35	0.80	0.16	0.50	8.1	12.4	..	..	..	..	..	..	..
Gabon	0.74	0.84	0.08	0.46	22.3	-17.2	..	..	..	..	..	..	..
Gambia, The	0.32	0.69	0.15	0.58	-2.6	-5.2	..	..	..	..	..	..	..
Ghana	0.46	0.82	0.12	0.39	6.2	-2.0	..	..	..	..	..	..	..
Guinea	0.44	0.81	0.17	0.51	17.3	-16.2	..	..	..	..	..	..	..
Guinea-Bissau	0.89	0.75	0.16	0.57	8.8	-20.9	97.6	48.6	13.3	9.9	51.8	0.0	0.0
Kenya	0.19	0.64	0.13	0.38	0.4	-1.8	15.2	95.3	12.1	9.2	36.6	0.8	0.0
Lesotho	0.44	0.88	0.28	0.79	-7.0	-9.7	100.0	78.9	9.5	10.5	21.6	5.7	0.0
Liberia	0.43	0.69	0.63	0.81	-19.3	-36.2	..	..	..	..	..	..	..
Madagascar	0.18	0.69	0.11	0.49	-8.2	-9.0	..	..	..	..	..	..	..
Malawi	0.52	0.80	0.11	0.51	-3.9	-1.1	..	..	..	..	..	..	..
Mali	0.63	0.87	0.21	0.54	-13.7	-12.1	40.5	28.9	12.8	8.4	47.9	0.0	0.0
Mauritania	0.48	0.81	0.13	0.57	23.9	10.4	..	..	..	..	..	..	..
Mauritius	0.25	0.71	0.13	0.39	-5.0	-8.0	..	..	..	..	..	..	..
Mozambique	0.51	0.84	0.13	0.50	-5.8	7.2	..	..	..	..	..	..	..
Namibia	0.22	0.76	0.26	0.58	-4.4	-9.0	96.1	19.4	6.3	1.8	16.7	7.1	0.0
Niger	0.38	0.80	0.10	0.56	4.3	-30.6	96.6	44.9	13.0	9.1	48.9	0.0	0.0
Nigeria	0.77	0.80	0.07	0.42	23.5	-1.5	19.5	119.4	10.9	10.6	34.9	0.0	0.0
Rwanda	0.40	0.82	0.08	0.49	20.2	-49.5	100.0	89.3	9.9	6.0	31.4	1.0	0.0
São Tomé and Príncipe	0.44	0.63	0.15	0.49	1.7	-26.7	..	..	..	..	..	..	..
Senegal	0.27	0.75	0.18	0.45	5.9	-7.5	100.0	30.0	13.4	8.9	50.5	0.0	0.0
Seychelles	0.46	0.82	0.24	0.57	2.9	-19.7	..	..	..	..	..	..	..
Sierra Leone	0.27	0.71	0.36	0.63	-6.9	1.0	..	..	..	..	..	..	..
Somalia	0.41	0.75	0.28	0.67	-4.3	-0.7	..	..	..	..	..	..	..
South Africa	0.15	0.58	0.22	0.31	9.3	-5.8	96.1	19.4	7.6	4.4	17.9	7.5	0.0
Sudan	0.75	0.81	0.08	0.45	19.1	23.8	..	..	..	..	..	..	..
Swaziland	0.24	0.73	0.09	0.47	-4.3	-10.7	96.1	19.4	10.9	10.2	26.2	12.0	0.0
Tanzania	0.19	0.75	0.18	0.48	1.5	2.5	13.8	120.0	12.9	8.2	39.9	1.0	0.0
Togo	0.21	0.69	0.24	0.61	12.4	19.9	14.3	80.0	12.8	14.2	47.3	0.0	0.0
Uganda	0.19	0.74	0.15	0.45	-0.7	10.8	16.1	73.5	12.1	8.2	37.5	1.1	0.0
Zambia	0.69	0.86	0.14	0.49	12.4	2.1	..	..	..	..	..	..	..
Zimbabwe	0.20	0.76	0.10	0.50	2.4	-16.2	..	..	..	..	..	..	..
NORTH AFRICA							..	..	..	..	..	..	..
Algeria	0.52	0.79	0.09	0.49	21.6	-3.9	..	..	..	..	..	..	..
Djibouti	0.30	0.62	0.09	0.50			..	..	..	..	..	..	..
Egypt, Arab Rep.	0.13	0.59	0.07	0.39	8.0	14.3	..	..	..	..	..	..	..
Libya	0.79	0.81	0.09	0.44	21.7	11.2	..	..	..	..	..	..	..
Morocco	0.16	0.66	0.09	0.33	2.4	0.4	..	..	..	..	..	..	..
Tunisia	0.16	0.54	0.08	0.39	0.4	2.9	..	..	..	..	..	..	..

a. Provisional.
b. Data are for the most recent year available during the period specified.

Tariff barriers, primary products (%)		Tariff barriers, manufactured products (%)		Average cost to ship 20 ft container from port to final destination ($)		Average time to clear customs (days)	
Simple mean tariff 2010	Weighted mean tariff 2010	Simple mean tariff 2010	Weighted mean tariff 2010	Export 2010	Import 2010	Direct exports 2010-11[b]	Imports 2010–11[b]
..	**..**	**..**	**..**	**1,960**	**2,502**		
..	..	..	..	1,850	2,690	6.7	11.4
15.5	12.4	12.9	11.8	1,049	1,496	..	..
6.1	0.5	9.0	8.2	3,185	3,420	6.2	3.7
11.4	8.1	12.5	11.8	2,412	4,030	..	..
15.4	9.4	9.1	11.6	2,965	4,855	..	..
..	..	..	..	1,379	2,167	..	..
16.2	12.2	14.3	10.1	1,200	1,000	..	..
..	..	..	..	5,491	5,554	9.5	11.9
..	..	..	..	5,902	8,525	..	..
..	..	..	12.3	1,207	1,191	..	..
..	..	..	..	3,055	3,285	18.0	45.4
..	..	..	..	3,818	7,709	..	..
15.1	5.4	12.8	11.8	1,969	2,577	..	..
..	..	..	..	1,411	1,411	..	..
..	..	..	..	1,431	1,581	..	..
..	..	..	17.4	1,760	2,660	..	..
..	..	..	..	1,945	1,955	..	..
..	..	..	..	831	885	..	..
..	..	..	..	1,013	1,315	..	..
..	..	..	11.8	855	1,391	..	..
14.6	10.0	12.9	11.8	1,448	2,006	..	..
16.0	12.6	11.7	11.6	2,055	2,190	..	..
9.2	1.6	9.5	8.2	1,680	1,665	..	..
..	..	..	..	1,220	1,200	..	..
..	..	..	11.3	1,197	1,555	..	..
..	..	..	12.1	1,675	2,570	..	..
12.8	7.9	12.8	11.8	2,202	3,067	12.9	16.5
..	..	..	..	1,520	1,523	..	..
..	..	..	1.2	737	689	..	..
..	..	..	9.6	1,100	1,545	..	..
4.1	2.1	6.7	8.2	1,800	1,905	..	..
14.0	10.7	12.8	11.8	3,545	3,545	..	..
11.8	9.1	10.7	11.5	1,263	1,440	..	..
11.5	6.4	9.7	11.6	3,275	4,990	..	..
..	..	..	..	690	577	..	..
14.1	7.7	13.2	11.8	1,098	1,740	..	..
..	..	..	..	876	876	..	..
..	..	..	..	1,573	1,639	..	..
..	..	..	..	..	..	..	..
5.4	1.9	7.8	8.2	1,531	1,795	..	..
..	..	..	18.1	2,050	2,900	..	..
9.7	1.3	11.1	8.2	1,855	2,030	..	..
17.5	8.7	12.4	11.6	1,255	1,430	..	..
14.4	12.4	12.6	11.8	940	1,109	..	..
15.7	8.8	11.6	11.6	2,880	3,015	..	..
..	..	..	..	2,678	3,315	..	..
..	..	..	..	3,280	5,101	..	..
..	**..**	**..**	**..**	**809**	**958**		
..	..	..	..	1,248	1,318	..	..
..	..	..	..	836	911	..	..
..	..	..	..	613	755	..	..
..	..	..	..	..	..	..	..
..	..	..	..	577	950	..	..
..	..	..	..	773	858	..	..

Table 5.2 Top three exports and share in total exports, 2010

	First		Second	
	Product	Share of total exports (%)	Product	Share of total exports (%)
SUB-SAHARAN AFRICA				
Angola	Petroleum oils and oils obtained from bituminous minerals, crude	97.3		
Benin	Petroleum oils & oils obtained from bituminous minerals (other than crude) & preparation	35.3	Gold (incl. gold plated with platinum), in unwrought forms (excl. powder)	15.5
Botswana	Diamonds non-industrial unworked or simply sawn, cleaved or bruted	43.7	Nickel mattes	21.9
Burkina Faso	Cotton, not carded or combed	37.4	Gold (incl. gold plated with platinum), non-monetary, in semi-manufactured forms	15.8
Burundi	Coffee, not roasted, not decaffeinated	70.2	Black tea (fermented) and other partly fermented tea	13.1
Cameroon	Petroleum oils and oils obtained from bituminous minerals, crude	42.1	Cocoa beans, whole or broken, raw or roasted	15.8
Cape Verde	Yellowfin tunas (Thunnus albacares)	20.2	Fish, whole or in pieces, but not minced :-- Other	19.6
Central African Republic	Wood in the rough, other	31.0	Diamonds unsorted whether or not worked	22.3
Chad	Petroleum oils and oils obtained from bituminous minerals, crude	80.6	Petroleum oils & oils obtained from bituminous minerals (other than crude) & preparations	8.6
Comoros	Cloves (whole fruit, cloves and stems)	38.8	Vessels for the transport of goods & for the transport of both persons & goods	20.3
Congo	Petroleum oils and oils obtained from bituminous minerals, crude	85.1		
Congo, Dem. Rep.	Cathodes and sections of cathodes	24.7	Cobalt ores and concentrates	17.8
Cote d'Ivoire	Cocoa beans, whole or broken, raw or roasted	32.3	Petroleum oils and oils obtained from bituminous minerals, crude	12.5
Equatorial Guinea	Petroleum oils and oils obtained from bituminous minerals, crude	78.0	Natural gas, liquefied	14.7
Eritrea	Sheep	11.2	Cardamoms	9.2
Ethiopia	Coffee, not roasted, not decaffeinated	42.1	Sesamum seeds	22.5
Gabon	Petroleum oils and oils obtained from bituminous minerals, crude	75.8	Manganese ores and concentrates	12.3
Gambia, The	Cashew nuts, in shell	20.3	Crude oil	14.9
Ghana	Cocoa beans, whole or broken, raw or roasted	46.4	Cocoa paste, not defatted	7.2
Guinea	Aluminium ores and concentrates	31.7	Petroleum oils and oils obtained from bituminous minerals, crude	21.0
Guinea-Bissau	Cashew nuts, in shell, fresh or dried	92.9	Ferrous waste and scrap, iron or steel, nes	0.0
Kenya	Black tea (fermented) and other partly fermented tea	18.6	Cut flowers fresh	13.1
Lesotho	Diamonds non-industrial unworked or simply sawn, cleaved or bruted	37.0	Mens/boys trousers and shorts, of cotton, not knitted	15.0
Liberia	Technically specified natural rubber	19.4	Petroleum oils and oils obtained from bituminous minerals, crude	15.4
Madagascar	Shrimps and prawns	9.5	Vanilla	6.6
Malawi	Tobacco, partly or wholly stemmed/stripped	53.0	Black tea (fermented) and other partly fermented tea	6.9
Mali	Cotton, not carded or combed	35.7	Petroleum oils & oils obtained from bituminous minerals (other than crude) & preparations	29.1
Mauritania	Iron ores & concentrates, non-agglomerated	49.3	Copper ores and concentrates	13.6
Mauritius	Tunas, skipjack and bonito	11.3	T-shirts, singlets and other vests, of cotton, knitted	11.0
Mozambique	Aluminium unwrought, not alloyed	48.0	Electrical energy	7.5
Namibia	Natural uranium and its compounds	26.8	Diamonds non-industrial unworked or simply sawn, cleaved or bruted	16.1
Niger	Natural uranium and its compounds	80.6	Light oils and preparations	7.6
Nigeria	Petroleum oils and oils obtained from bituminous minerals, crude	85.9	Natural gas, liquefied	6.9
Rwanda	Coffee, not roasted, not decaffeinated	30.4	Niobium, tantalum and vanadium ores and concentrates	24.8
São Tomé and Príncipe	Cocoa beans, whole or broken, raw or roasted	36.3	Wrist-watches other than automatic winding	17.4
Senegal	Petroleum oils & oils obtained from bituminous minerals (other than crude) & preparations	26.4	Portland cement (excl. white cement, whether/not artificially coloured), whether/not coloured	10.5
Seychelles	Tunas, skipjack and bonito	49.6	Bigeye tunas (Thunnus obesus)	8.3
Sierra Leone	Diamonds non-industrial unworked or simply sawn, cleaved or bruted	26.9	Aluminium ores and concentrates	14.8
Somalia	Goats	31.3	Sheep	29.5
South Africa	Platinum unwrought or in powder form	7.6	Gold (incl. gold plated with platinum), in unwrought forms (excl. powder)	6.9
Sudan	Petroleum oils and oils obtained from bituminous minerals, crude	90.3		
Swaziland	Raw sugar, cane	16.5	Mixtures of odoriferous substances, of a kind used in the food or drink industries	15.2
Tanzania	Other Precious metal ores and concentrates, other than silver	14.5	Tobacco, partly or wholly stemmed/stripped	8.7
Togo	Cocoa beans, whole or broken, raw or roasted	26.7	Gold (incl. gold plated with platinum), in unwrought forms (excl. powder)	12.8
Uganda	Coffee, not roasted, not decaffeinated	32.9	Tobacco, partly or wholly stemmed/stripped	9.9
Zambia	Copper cathodes and sections of cathodes unwrought	48.0	Unrefined copper; copper anodes for electrolytic refining	26.7
Zimbabwe	Tobacco, partly or wholly stemmed/stripped	20.5	Ferro-chromium containing by weight more than 4% of carbon	15.3
NORTH AFRICA				
Algeria	Petroleum oils and oils obtained from bituminous minerals, crude	45.0	Natural gas, in gaseous state	20.0
Djibouti	Live animals, n.e.s.	49.7	Coffee, not roasted, not decaffeinated	12.3
Egypt, Arab Rep.	Petroleum oils and oils obtained from bituminous minerals, crude	18.3	Natural gas, liquefied	9.5
Libya	Petroleum oils and oils obtained from bituminous minerals, crude	82.1	Natural gas, in gaseous state	6.9
Morocco	Phosphoric acid and polyphosphoric acids	7.6	Ignition wiring sets and other wiring sets of a kind used in vehicles, aircraft or ships	6.5
Tunisia	Petroleum oils and oils obtained from bituminous minerals, crude	11.7	Ignition wiring sets and other wiring sets of a kind used in vehicles, aircraft or ships	6.8
Africa[a]	**Petroleum oils and oils obtained from bituminous minerals, crude**	**46.6 [46.6]**	**Natural gas, in gaseous state**	**3.2 [10.2]**

Note: Includes only products that account for more than 4 percent of total exports.
a. Values in brackets are Africa's share of total world exports for product.

Third		
Product	Share of total exports (%)	Number of exports accounting for 75 percent of total exports
		1
Light oils and preparations	9.3	6
Diamonds non-industrial nes excluding mounted or set diamonds	8.9	4
Gold (incl. gold plated with platinum), in unwrought forms (excl. powder)	10.8	5
		2
Tropical wood specified	7.2	6
Mackerel	12.0	6
Tropical wood specified	15.7	4
		1
Essential oils, nes	15.6	4
		1
Copper ores and concentrates	11.9	6
Cocoa paste, not defatted	8.8	10
		1
Men's/boys' shirts, of cotton	8.6	19
Cut flowers fresh	10.7	3
		1
Titanium ores and concentrates	11.2	9
Manganese ores and concentrates	5.7	9
Natural gas, liquefied	20.7	4
Logs, non-coniferous nes	0.0	1
Coffee, not roasted, not decaffeinated	6.1	48
Women's/girls', trousers & shorts, of cotton, not knitted	7.5	6
Vessels for the transport of goods & for the transport of both persons & goods	15.0	6
Jerseys, pullovers, cardigans, waist-coats & similar articles, knitted/crocheted, of wool	4.6	32
Natural uranium and its compounds	6.8	5
Sesamum seeds	7.8	4
Octopus, other than live/fresh/chilled	7.0	4
Cane/beet sugar & chemically pure sucrose, in solid form, not containing added flavouring/colouring matter	6.4	43
Natural gas, liquefied	5.0	8
Unwrought Zinc, containing by weight 99.99 % or more of zinc	13.4	6
		1
		1
Black tea (fermented) and other partly fermented tea	13.8	4
Articles of jewelry & parts thereof , of silver, whether/not plated/clad with other precious metal	9.7	8
Phosphoric acid and polyphosphoric acids	9.8	18
Yellowfin tunas (Thunnus albacares)	6.9	5
Cocoa beans, whole or broken, raw or roasted	11.8	11
Live bovine animals other than pure-bred breeding animals	13.1	4
		92
		1
Food preparations nes	10.7	20
Coffee, not roasted, not decaffeinated	6.4	24
Cement clinkers	10.1	8
Fish fillets and other fish meat (whether or not minced), fresh or chilled	9.3	13
		3
Nickel, not alloyed, unwrought	7.1	17
Natural gas, liquefied	8.7	4
Sheep	8.5	4
Light oils and preparations	5.5	76
Petroleum oils & oils obtained from bituminous minerals (other than crude) & preparations	4.5	1
		69
Mens/boys trousers and shorts, of cotton, not knitted	4.7	94
Natural gas, liquified	**3.1 [16.3]**	**34**

Table 5.3 Regional integration, trade blocs

	Year established	Year of entry into force of most recent agreement	Type of most recent agreement[a]	Merchandise exports within bloc ($ millions)								
				1990	1995	2000	2005	2006	2007	2008	2009	2010
Economic and Monetary Community of Central African States (CEMAC)	1994	1999	CU	138.7	119.6	96.1	201.0	247.4	305.0	354.7	300.5	383.0
Economic Community of the Great Lakes Countries (CEPGL)	1976		NNA	7.0	8.0	10.2	20.2	24.4	29.1	72.6	63.6	80.7
Common Market for Eastern and Southern Africa (COMESA)	1994	1994	FTA	1,146.0	1,366.9	1,442.6	2,694.4	2,917.3	4,021.0	6,674.7	6,140.4	8,157.8
East African Community (EAC)	1996	2000	CU	334.5	628.4	689.4	1,075.3	1,061.5	1,385.2	1,797.0	1,572.2	1,996.7
Economic Community of Central African States (ECCAS)	1983	2004[b]	NNA	159.7	157.1	181.6	254.6	312.8	385.4	449.2	378.3	482.5
Economic Community of West African States (ECOWAS)	1975	1993	PTA	1,532.3	1,874.8	2,728.2	5,546.1	5,955.4	6,802.2	9,469.9	7,319.6	8,910.7
Indian Ocean Commission (IOC)	1984	2005[b]	NNA	62.6	113.0	106.0	162.1	181.7	214.0	217.7	182.4	184.1
Southern African Development Community (SADC)	1992	2000	FTA	1,655.3	3,615.4	4,426.5	7,798.5	8,700.2	12,050.6	16,009.9	12,003.3	14,575.9
West African Economic and Monetary Union (UEMOA)	1994	2000	CU	620.8	559.7	760.4	1,412.1	1,531.7	1,779.4	2,339.1	1,937.6	2,250.3

	Year established	Year of entry into force of most recent agreement	Type of most recent agreement[a]	Merchandise exports within bloc (% of total bloc exports)								
				1990	1995	2000	2005	2006	2007	2008	2009	2010
Economic and Monetary Community of Central African States (CEMAC)	1994	1999	CU	2.3	2.1	1.0	0.9	0.9	1.1	0.8	1.2	1.2
Economic Community of the Great Lakes Countries (CEPGL)	1976		NNA	0.5	0.5	0.8	1.2	1.3	1.4	1.9	2.2	1.5
Common Market for Eastern and Southern Africa (COMESA)	1994	1994	FTA	4.7	6.1	4.6	4.6	3.9	4.5	5.4	7.1	7.7
East African Community (EAC)	1996	2000	CU	17.7	19.5	22.6	18.0	16.3	17.8	19.2	18.9	20.3
Economic Community of Central African States (ECCAS)	1983	2004[b]	NNA	1.4	1.5	1.0	0.6	0.5	0.6	0.4	0.6	0.6
Economic Community of West African States (ECOWAS)	1975	1993	PTA	8.0	9.0	7.7	9.4	7.9	7.9	8.7	9.9	8.8
Indian Ocean Commission (IOC)	1984	2005[b]	NNA	3.9	5.9	4.4	4.9	5.0	5.8	5.7	5.8	5.3
Southern African Development Community (SADC)	1992	2000	FTA	6.6	10.2	9.5	9.3	9.1	10.2	10.3	11.3	9.8
West African Economic and Monetary Union (UEMOA)	1994	2000	CU	13.0	10.3	13.5	13.7	13.3	15.4	16.4	13.2	14.6

	Year established	Year of entry into force of most recent agreement	Type of most recent agreement[a]	Merchandise exports by bloc (% of world exports) 1990	1995	2000	2005	2006	2007	2008	2009	2010
Economic and Monetary Community of Central African States (CEMAC)	1994	1999	CU	0.3	0.2	0.2	0.2	0.2	0.2	0.3	0.2	0.2
Economic Community of the Great Lakes Countries (CEPGL)	1976		NNA	0.0	0.0	0.0	0.0	0.0	0.0	0.0	0.0	0.0
Common Market for Eastern and Southern Africa (COMESA)	1994	1994	FTA	0.8	0.7	0.7	0.6	0.6	0.6	0.8	0.7	0.7
East African Community (EAC)	1996	2000	CU	0.1	0.1	0.1	0.1	0.1	0.1	0.1	0.1	0.1
Economic Community of Central African States (ECCAS)	1983	2004[b]	NNA	0.6	0.4	0.4	0.4	0.5	0.5	0.7	0.5	0.6
Economic Community of West African States (ECOWAS)	1975	1993	PTA	0.9	0.7	0.7	0.6	0.6	0.6	0.7	0.6	0.7
Indian Ocean Commission (IOC)	1984	2005[b]	NNA	0.1	0.1	0.1	0.0	0.0	0.0	0.0	0.0	0.0
Southern African Development Community (SADC)	1992	2000	FTA	1.4	1.1	1.1	0.8	0.8	0.8	1.0	0.8	1.0
West African Economic and Monetary Union (UEMOA)	1994	2000	CU	0.2	0.2	0.1	0.1	0.1	0.1	0.1	0.1	0.1

Note: Regional Bloc membership is as follows: **Economic and Monetary Community of Central Africa (CEMAC: formerly Central African Customs and Economic Union [UDEAC])**, Cameroon, the Central African Republic, Chad, the Republic of Congo, Equatorial Guinea and Gabon; **Economic Community of the Great Lakes Countries (CEPGL)**, Burundi, the Democratic Republic of Congo, and Rwanda; **Common Market for Eastern and Southern Africa (COMESA)**, Burundi, Comoros, the Democratic Republic of Congo, Djibouti, the Arab Republic of Egypt, Eritrea, Ethiopia, Kenya, Libyan Arab Republic, Madagascar, Malawi, Mauritius, Rwanda, Seychelles, Sudan, Swaziland, Uganda, Zambia, and Zimbabwe; **East African Community (EAC)**, Burundi, Kenya, Rwanda, Tanzania, and Uganda; **Economic Community of Central African States (ECCAS)**, Angola, Burundi, Cameroon, the Central African Republic, Chad, the Democratic Republic of Congo, the Republic of Congo, Equatorial Guinea, Gabon, and São Tomé and Príncipe; **Economic Community of West African States (ECOWAS)**, Benin, Burkina Faso, Cape Verde, Côte d'Ivoire, the Gambia, Ghana, Guinea, Guinea-Bissau, Liberia, Mali, Niger, Nigeria, Senegal, Sierra Leone, and Togo; Indian Ocean Commission, Comoros, Madagascar, Mauritius, Réunion, and Seychelles; **Southern African Development Community (SADC)**, Angola, Botswana, the Democratic Republic of Congo, Lesotho, Madagascar, Malawi, Mauritius, Mozambique, Namibia, Seychelles, South Africa, Swaziland, Tanzania, Zambia, and Zimbabwe; **West African Economic and Monetary Union (WAEMU** or **UEMOA)**, Benin, Burkina Faso, Côte d'Ivoire, Guinea-Bissau, Mali, Niger, Senegal, and Togo.

a. CU is customs union; EIA is economic integration agreement; FTA is free trade agreement; NNA is not notified agreement, which refers to preferential trade agreements established among member countries that are not notified to the World Trade Organization (these agreements may be functionally equivalent to any of the other agreements); and PTA is preferential trade agreement.

b. From the official website of the trade bloc.

Table 6.1 Water and sanitation

	Access, supply side	Access, demand side						Financing		
	Internal fresh water resources per capita (cubic meters)	Population with sustainable access to an improved water source			Population with sustainable access to improved sanitation			Committed nominal investment in water projects with private participation ($ millions)	ODA gross disbursements for water supply and sanitation sector ($ millions)	
		(% of total population)	(% of urban population)	(% of rural population)	(% of total population)	(% of urban population)	(% of rural population)			
	2009	2010	2010	2010	2010	2010	2010	2000-10[a]	2009	2010
SUB-SAHARAN AFRICA	**4,708**	**61**	**83**	**49**	**31**	**42**	**23**		**1,786.4**	**1,892.8**
Angola	7,976	51	60	38	58	85	19	..	15.1	8.7
Benin	1,197	75	84	68	13	25	5	..	54.1	69.1
Botswana	1,211	96	99	92	62	75	41	..	0.0	0.8
Burkina Faso	782	79	95	73	17	50	6	..	58.9	64.9
Burundi	1,231	72	83	71	46	49	46	..	19.5	31.5
Cameroon	14,237	77	95	52	49	58	36	0.0	6.5	17.7
Cape Verde	610	88	90	85	61	73	43	..	20.4	11.8
Central African Republic	32,653	67	92	51	34	43	28	..	9.4	5.4
Chad	1,371	51	70	44	13	30	6	..	28.6	34.5
Comoros	1,677	95	91	97	36	50	30	..	1.4	0.8
Congo, Dem. Rep.	14,018	45	79	27	24	24	24	..	65.2	98.6
Congo, Rep.	56,324	71	95	32	18	20	15	0.0	0.4	2.0
Côte d'Ivoire	3,971	80	91	68	24	36	11	0.0	30.7	36.2
Equatorial Guinea	38,173	..	..	..	..	..	..	..	0.0	..
Eritrea	549	..	..	..	..	..	4	..	7.4	7.3
Ethiopia	1,503	44	97	34	21	29	19	..	114.4	116.8
Gabon	110,997	87	95	41	33	33	30	..	2.1	8.7
Gambia, The	1,784	89	92	85	68	70	65	..	5.0	3.2
Ghana	1,272	86	91	80	14	19	8	0.0	56.2	89.6
Guinea	23,153	74	90	65	18	32	11	..	11.3	10.0
Guinea-Bissau	10,781	64	91	53	20	44	9	..	2.6	1.0
Kenya	525	59	82	52	32	32	32	..	94.7	143.0
Lesotho	2,433	78	91	73	26	32	24	..	23.1	36.5
Liberia	52,139	73	88	60	18	29	7	..	8.1	7.3
Madagascar	16,746	46	74	34	15	21	12	..	12.3	9.8
Malawi	1,118	83	95	80	51	49	51	..	16.1	22.2
Mali	4,024	64	87	51	22	35	14	..	69.2	49.0
Mauritania	118	50	52	48	26	51	9	..	82.7	78.7
Mauritius	2,158	99	100	99	89	91	88	0.0	1.1	0.5
Mozambique	4,388	47	77	29	18	38	5	..	94.8	94.1
Namibia	2,747	93	99	90	32	57	17	0.0	12.0	13.5
Niger	234	49	100	39	9	34	4	3.4	42.2	38.5
Nigeria	1,431	58	74	43	31	35	27	..	102.4	109.6
Rwanda	921	65	76	63	55	52	56	..	19.5	35.5
São Tomé and Príncipe	13,414	89	89	88	26	30	19	..	1.0	3.1
Senegal	2,131	72	93	56	52	70	39	0.0	58.3	48.7
Seychelles	..	..	100	..	..	98	..	..	0.6	0.6
Sierra Leone	27,878	55	87	35	13	23	6	..	9.7	10.4
Somalia	658	29	66	7	23	52	6	..	5.2	3.0
South Africa	908	91	99	79	79	86	67	0.0	60.9	48.7
Sudan	706	58	67	52	26	44	14	120.7	55.2	62.1
Swaziland	2,530	71	91	65	57	64	55	..	0.3	0.6
Tanzania	1,930	53	79	44	10	20	7	8.5	190.3	211.9
Togo	1,949	61	89	40	13	26	3	..	5.3	4.6
Uganda	1,205	72	95	68	34	34	34	0.0	105.9	61.1
Zambia	6,303	61	87	46	48	57	43	0.0	50.8	38.8
Zimbabwe	983	80	98	69	40	52	32	..	7.6	15.9
NORTH AFRICA	**288**	**92**	**95**	**88**	**90**	**94**	**84**		**370.6**	**358.9**
Algeria	322	83	85	79	95	98	88	468.0	10.9	11.0
Djibouti	344	88	99	54	50	63	10	..	6.8	8.1
Egypt, Arab Rep.	23	99	100	99	95	97	93	..	129.0	72.3
Libya	96	..	..	..	97	97	96	..	0.0	..
Morocco	917	83	98	61	70	83	52	..	122.3	145.2
Tunisia	402	..	99	..	..	96	..	..	94.3	116.6

a. Data are for the most recent year available during the period specified.

Table 6.2 Transportation

	Access, supply side			Access, demand side	
			Road density	Vehicle fleet (per 1,000 people)	
	Road network (km)	Rail lines (km)	Ratio to total land (road km/100 sq km of land area)	Commercial vehicles	Passenger vehicles
	2000–09[a]	2010	2000–09[a]	2000–09[a]	2000–09[a]
SUB-SAHARAN AFRICA		..			
Angola	51,429	..	4.0	38.0	8.0
Benin	19,000	..	17.0	22.0	18.0
Botswana	25,798	888	4.0	133.0	69.0
Burkina Faso	92,495	622	34.0	11.0	7.0
Burundi	12,322	..	44.0	6.0	2.0
Cameroon	28,857	977	11.0	14.0	10.0
Cape Verde	1,350	..	33.0	101.0	73.0
Central African Republic	24,307	..	4.0	0.3	0.3
Chad	40,000	..	3.0	6.0	2.0
Comoros	880	..	39.0	33.0	31.0
Congo, Dem. Rep.	153,497	3,641	7.0	5.0	..
Congo, Rep.	17,000	..	5.0	27.0	16.0
Côte d'Ivoire	81,996	639	25.0	20.0	16.0
Equatorial Guinea	2,880	..	10.0	..	..
Eritrea	4,010	..	3.0	11.0	6.0
Ethiopia	44,359	..	4.0	3.0	1.0
Gabon	9,170	810	3.0	..	..
Gambia, The	3,742	..	33.0	8.0	5.0
Ghana	109,515	..	24.0	30.0	18.0
Guinea	44,348	..	18.0	..	..
Guinea-Bissau	3,455	..	12.0	33.0	27.0
Kenya	61,945	..	11.0	23.0	13.0
Lesotho	5,940	..	20.0	..	..
Liberia	10,600	..	10.0	3.0	2.0
Madagascar	49,827	..	8.0	26.0	7.0
Malawi	15,451	..	13.0	8.0	4.0
Mali	22,474	..	2.0	14.0	8.0
Mauritania	11,066	728	1.0	..	..
Mauritius	2,066	..	99.0	166.0	129.0
Mozambique	30,331	3,116	4.0	12.0	9.0
Namibia	42,100	..	0.0	103.0	46.0
Niger	18,948	..	1.0	8.0	6.0
Nigeria	193,200	..	21.0	31.0	31.0
Rwanda	14,008	..	53.0	5.0	2.0
São Tomé and Príncipe	320	..	33.0	2.0	2.0
Senegal	14,825	..	8.0	22.0	16.0
Seychelles	508	..	110.0	173.0	103.0
Sierra Leone	11,300	..	..	6.0	5.0
Somalia	22,100	..	3.0	..	..
South Africa	362,099	22,051	30.0	162.0	110.0
Sudan	11,900	4,508	1.0	27.0	19.0
Swaziland	3,594	300	21.0	89.0	45.0
Tanzania	103,706	..	9.0	7.0	4.0
Togo	11,652	..	21.0	2.0	2.0
Uganda	70,746	..	29.0	8.0	3.0
Zambia	66,781	..	12.0	21.0	13.0
Zimbabwe	97,267	..	25.0	114.0	98.0
NORTH AFRICA		11,935			
Algeria	112,039	3,512	5.0	112.0	74.0
Djibouti	3,065	..	14.0	..	..
Egypt, Arab Rep.	100,472	5,195	10.0	45.0	33.0
Libya	83,200	..	5.0	290.0	225.0
Morocco	58,216	2,109	13.0	70.0	53.0
Tunisia	19,371	1,119	12.0	114.0	76.0

(continued)

Table 6.2 Transportation (continued)

	Quality	Pricing		Financing		
	Ratio of paved to total roads (%)	Price of diesel fuel ($ per liter)	Price of gasoline ($ per liter)	Committed nominal investment in transport projects with private participation ($ millions)	ODA gross disbursements for transportation and storage ($ millions)	
	2000–09[a]	2010	2010	2000–09[a]	2009	2010
SUB-SAHARAN AFRICA		**1.15**	**1.22**		**2,254.6**	**2,714.0**
Angola	10.4	0.43	0.65	53.0	8.3	25.0
Benin	9.5	1.21	1.04	..	92.1	116.6
Botswana	32.6	0.97	0.93	..	12.9	6.3
Burkina Faso	4.2	1.28	1.44	..	60.6	59.8
Burundi	10.4	1.42	1.43	..	46.0	55.7
Cameroon	17.0	1.10	1.20	0.0	92.0	94.7
Cape Verde	69.0	1.33	1.84	..	56.0	73.7
Central African Republic	..	1.69	1.71	..	17.8	27.0
Chad	0.8	1.31	1.32	..	45.3	5.0
Comoros	76.5	..	..	0.5	2.2	1.8
Congo, Dem. Rep.	1.8	1.27	1.28	..	136.6	146.1
Congo, Rep.	7.1	0.84	1.27	0.0	21.2	9.2
Côte d'Ivoire	7.9	1.30	1.68	0.0	17.6	26.8
Equatorial Guinea	..	..	..	..	..	..
Eritrea	21.8	1.07	2.54	..	2.9	3.2
Ethiopia	13.7	0.78	0.91	..	229.6	226.8
Gabon	12.0	..	..	3.9	10.3	25.5
Gambia, The	19.3	..	..	..	9.7	19.4
Ghana	12.6	0.83	0.82	0.0	105.9	136.4
Guinea	9.8	0.95	0.95	159.0	28.6	50.0
Guinea-Bissau	27.9	..	..	..	15.1	1.3
Kenya	14.3	1.27	1.33	404.0	127.3	118.7
Lesotho	18.3	1.07	0.97	..	9.2	16.7
Liberia	6.2	0.96	0.98	120.0	30.8	68.4
Madagascar	11.6	1.26	1.52	17.5	40.3	55.0
Malawi	45.0	1.54	1.71	..	22.3	24.9
Mali	24.6	1.25	1.42	55.4	28.1	65.8
Mauritania	26.9	0.99	1.16	..	27.6	21.0
Mauritius	98.0	1.23	1.55	..	..	6.5
Mozambique	20.8	0.86	1.11	0.0	103.0	109.6
Namibia	14.7	1.09	1.06	..	52.9	42.6
Niger	20.7	1.16	1.07	..	39.2	53.1
Nigeria	15.0	0.77	0.44	382.0	57.7	63.9
Rwanda	19.0	1.62	1.63	..	34.7	20.9
São Tomé and Príncipe	68.1	..	..	..	1.6	1.8
Senegal	32.0	1.34	1.57	264.0	89.7	111.8
Seychelles	96.5	..	..	..	..	0.0
Sierra Leone	8.0	0.94	0.94	130.0	34.1	43.1
Somalia	11.8	..	..	..	1.7	7.9
South Africa	17.3	1.14	1.19	3483.0	0.1	7.4
Sudan	36.3	0.43	0.62	30.0	79.6	85.9
Swaziland	30.0	1.10	1.07	..	0.4	0.8
Tanzania	6.7	1.19	1.22	134.0	145.5	271.1
Togo	21.0	1.17	1.18	..	0.2	1.5
Uganda	23.0	1.11	1.42	404.0	103.1	153.0
Zambia	22.0	1.52	1.66	15.6	35.0	32.9
Zimbabwe	19.0	1.15	1.29	..	0.0	3.9
NORTH AFRICA		**0.57**	**0.71**		**600.8**	**853.6**
Algeria	74.0	0.19	0.32	108.0	76.0	22.4
Djibouti	45.0	1.07	1.63	396.0	15.9	6.7
Egypt, Arab Rep.	89.4	0.32	0.48	640.0	111.3	198.6
Libya	57.2	0.13	0.17	..	..	..
Morocco	70.3	0.88	1.23	200.0	304.3	487.6
Tunisia	75.2	0.82	0.94	840.0	88.4	130.6

a. Data are for the most recent year available during the period specified.

Table 6.3 Information and communication technology

	Access, supply side			Access, demand side				Quality	
	Telephone subscribers (per 100 people)							Telephone faults	
	Total	Mainline telephone	Mobile telephone	Unmet demand (% of mainline telephones)	Households with own telephone (% of households)	Average delay for firm in obtaining a mainline phone connection (days)	Internet users (per 100 people)	Total (per 100 mainlines)	Cleared by next working day (%)
	2010	2010	2010	2008	2009-10[a]	2009-10[a]	2010	2010	2010
SUB-SAHARAN AFRICA	**46.4**	**1.4**	**45.0**	**..**			**11.3**	**..**	**..**
Angola	48.3	1.6	46.7	..	1.5	9.3	10.0	..	..
Benin	81.5	1.5	79.9	..	..	89.4	3.1	6.0	35.0
Botswana	124.6	6.9	117.8	..	..	17.1	6.0	..	..
Burkina Faso	35.5	0.9	34.7	..	..	19.5	1.4	..	..
Burundi	14.1	0.4	13.7	0.1	16.4	..	2.1	..	..
Cameroon	46.8	2.8	44.1	..	..	19.2	4.0	..	..
Cape Verde	89.5	14.5	75.0	0.4	..	8.2	30.0	3.0	93.0
Central African Republic	22.4	0.1	22.3	..	..	..	2.3	..	..
Chad	24.3	0.5	23.8	..	..	13.3	1.7	..	..
Comoros	25.4	2.9	22.5	22.9	..	..	5.1	..	..
Congo, Dem. Rep.	18.0	0.1	17.9	..	..	20.1	0.7	..	..
Congo, Rep.	94.2	0.2	94.0	..	1.0	25.5	5.0	..	..
Cote d'Ivoire	77.6	1.4	76.1	..	..	5.8	2.6	10.2	..
Equatorial Guinea	59.0	1.9	57.0	..	..	..	6.0	..	..
Eritrea	4.6	1.0	3.5	49.5	..	..	5.4	61.0	17.3
Ethiopia	9.4	1.1	8.3	2.1	..	..	0.8	5.9	64.3
Gabon	109.0	2.0	106.9	..	..	8.6	7.2	..	..
Gambia, The	88.3	2.8	85.5	..	..	..	9.2	..	..
Ghana	72.6	1.1	71.5	0.2	..	..	9.6	1.1	72.0
Guinea	40.3	0.2	40.1	..	..	..	1.0	..	..
Guinea-Bissau	39.5	0.3	39.2	..	..	..	2.5	..	..
Kenya	62.6	0.9	61.6	0.4	1.2	..	25.9	3.7	72.6
Lesotho	47.3	1.8	45.5	..	..	53.7	3.9	..	..
Liberia	39.5	0.2	39.3	..	..	..	7.0	..	..
Madagascar	37.9	0.7	37.2	0.1	1.0	29.9	1.7	12.4	83.5
Malawi	21.5	1.1	20.4	..	2.0	45.9	2.3	..	..
Mali	49.2	0.8	48.4	..	..	13.8	2.7	..	..
Mauritania	81.4	2.1	79.3	..	..	..	3.0	..	..
Mauritius	123.2	29.8	91.7	..	..	38.6	28.7	..	..
Mozambique	31.3	0.4	30.9	..	..	..	4.2	..	..
Namibia	73.9	6.7	67.2	..	..	..	6.5	..	..
Niger	25.1	0.5	24.5	..	..	13.9	0.8	..	..
Nigeria	55.8	0.7	55.1	..	0.9	..	28.4	..	..
Rwanda	33.8	0.4	33.4	..	0.3	..	13.0	0.0	98.0
São Tomé and Príncipe	66.8	4.6	62.0	..	..	..	18.8	..	..
Senegal	69.9	2.8	67.1	..	14.5	..	16.0	..	..
Seychelles	160.5	25.5	135.9	9.8	..	..	41.0	..	..
Sierra Leone	34.3	0.2	34.1	..	..	21.4	..	..	..
Somalia	8.0	1.1	7.0	..	..	..	..	..	..
South Africa	109.2	8.4	100.5	..	16.7	..	12.3	..	..
Sudan	41.4	0.9	40.5	0.0	..	..	..	..	..
Swaziland	73.6	3.7	61.8	0.2	..	..	9.0	..	..
Tanzania	47.2	0.4	46.8	..	..	..	11.0	..	..
Togo	44.2	3.5	40.7	..	..	51.0	5.4	..	..
Uganda	39.4	1.0	38.4	..	..	..	12.5	..	..
Zambia	42.8	0.7	41.6	..	..	..	10.1	..	..
Zimbabwe	64.3	3.0	61.3	..	4.1	..	11.5	36.0	87.0
NORTH AFRICA	**106.1**	**11.3**	**94.8**	**..**			**28.0**	**..**	**..**
Algeria	100.7	8.2	92.4	..	24.8	..	12.5	..	..
Djibouti	20.7	2.1	18.6	..	..	..	6.5	..	..
Egypt, Arab Rep.	99.0	11.9	87.1	0.3	43.9	..	26.7	0.1	97.5
Libya	190.9	19.3	171.5	..	..	..	14.0	..	..
Morocco	111.8	11.7	100.1	..	39.4	..	49.0	..	..
Tunisia	117.6	12.3	106.0	0.9	24.1	..	36.6	29.0	90.0

(continued)

Table 6.3 Information and communication technology (continued)

	Fixed broadband internet subscription ($ per month)	Pricing: Cost of 3-minute call during peak hours ($)		Cost of 3-minute call during off-peak hours ($)		Connection charge ($)				
		Fixed telephone local	Cellular local	Fixed telephone local	Cellular local	Residential telephone	Business telephone	Mobile cellular: Prepaid	Mobile cellular: Postpaid	Fixed broadband internet
	2010	2010	2009	2010	2009	2010	2010	2009–10[a]	2009–10[a]	2010
SUB-SAHARAN AFRICA	**55.6**	**0.23**	**0.63**	**0.13**	**0.65**	**37.6**	**46.5**			**61.2**
Angola	133.2	0.25	0.65	0.2	0.7	49.0	49.0	..	..	58.8
Benin	50.5	0.12	0.55	0.1	0.6	194.8	354.7	2.1	5.3	30.3
Botswana	29.3	0.23	0.75	0.2	0.8	37.9	55.6	1.5	1.4	40.5
Burkina Faso	83.2	0.30	0.95	0.2	1.0	59.6	59.6	..	6.4	..
Burundi	..	0.06	..	0.1	..	22.8	22.8	..	..	..
Cameroon	80.8	0.36	0.95	0.4	1.0	48.2	120.4	2.0	5.3	101.0
Cape Verde	31.8	0.14	0.91	0.1	0.9	36.0	..	..	..	27.6
Central African Republic	603.7	..	0.76	..	0.8	..	..	..	2.1	199.9
Chad	11.9	0.36	1.14	0.4	1.1	107.2	107.2	1.1	1.0	506.8
Comoros	390.4	0.13	0.64	0.1	0.6	109.0	109.0	..	..	161.5
Congo, Dem. Rep.	..	..	..	..	..	..	..	..	..	..
Congo, Rep.	180.1	0.61	..	0.6	..	168.1	168.1	1.3	..	108.1
Cote d'Ivoire	40.4	0.36	0.63	0.0	0.6	20.2	..	..	..	50.5
Equatorial Guinea	242.3	..	..	..	..	47.4	..	..	..	252.4
Eritrea	..	..	0.35	..	0.4	..	..	50.1	100.2	..
Ethiopia	295.7	0.01	0.21	0.0	0.2	16.8	16.8	2.7	14.4	..
Gabon	..	..	..	..	..	..	..	2.0	..	..
Gambia, The	292.9	..	0.37	..	0.4	..	..	0.3	11.3	35.7
Ghana	31.5	0.13	0.31	0.1	..	31.5	31.5	0.7	0.7	38.4
Guinea	903.5	0.03	..	0.0	..	5.2	19.0	..	..	2371.7
Guinea-Bissau	..	..	0.57	..	0.6	..	..	1.0	1.1	..
Kenya	37.9	0.23	0.31	0.2	0.3	42.9	42.9	0.6	1.3	50.5
Lesotho	50.5	0.23	0.70	0.2	0.7	46.0	..	6.8	5.9	61.5
Liberia	..	0.00	..	0.0	..	0.2	..	..	..	..
Madagascar	89.5	0.28	0.65	0.1	0.7	28.2	28.2	1.0	0.5	0.0
Malawi	562.2	0.18	0.59	0.1	0.6	13.9	..	..	2.8	702.7
Mali	50.5	0.11	0.70	0.1	0.7	78.0	78.0	0.0	2.1	98.9
Mauritania	23.6	0.37	0.63	0.3	0.6	0.0	18.1	1.8	1.9	25.3
Mauritius	16.2	0.08	0.13	0.1	0.1	37.4	74.7	3.5	3.1	37.4
Mozambique	50.1	0.27	0.72	0.1	0.7	14.3	14.3	0.7	0.7	..
Namibia	117.7	0.25	0.89	0.2	0.9	40.1	40.1	2.7	2.2	40.1
Niger	60.1	0.15	0.79	0.2	0.8	30.3	30.3	1.6	3.2	48.1
Nigeria	53.2	0.18	0.60	0.2	0.6	0.0	..	1.0	..	0.0
Rwanda	162.9	0.37	0.45	0.3	0.5	51.5	..	0.0	1.8	171.5
São Tomé and Príncipe	282.8	0.09	0.47	0.1	0.5	22.7	22.7	4.5	8.6	113.1
Senegal	36.3	0.24	0.54	0.1	0.5	46.5	46.5	4.2	4.2	50.5
Seychelles	47.2	0.06	0.92	0.1	0.9	46.2	46.2	2.0	3.7	60.9
Sierra Leone	..	0.00	..	0.0	..	0.0	0.0	..	..	..
Somalia	..	..	..	..	..	..	..	..	..	..
South Africa	27.2	0.27	0.89	0.2	0.9	67.1	67.1	..	17.6	81.7
Sudan	28.6	..	0.18	..	0.2	..	..	2.2	2.2	47.7
Swaziland	867.2	0.08	0.78	0.0	0.8	29.1	48.6	2.1	1.8	316.3
Tanzania	31.9	0.30	0.59	0.2	..	18.2	..	0.5	0.4	..
Togo	166.8	0.21	0.73	0.1	0.7	71.5	71.5	2.1	2.1	119.1
Uganda	16.2	0.21	0.50	0.1	..	67.8	67.8	..	1.5	135.5
Zambia	58.0	0.83	0.70	0.5	0.7	10.4	31.3	..	..	962.8
Zimbabwe	..	..	..	..	..	..	..	..	..	..
NORTH AFRICA	**13.3**	**0.09**	**0.41**	**0.1**	**0.4**	**14.0**	**77.1**			**0.0**
Algeria	14.8	0.15	0.33	0.2	0.3	5.4	..	5.5	6.9	..
Djibouti	60.2	0.09	0.54	0.1	0.5	56.3	56.3	60.2	28.1	60.2
Egypt, Arab Rep.	8.0	0.03	0.11	0.0	0.1	6.1	97.8	2.5	2.9	0.0
Libya	39.5	..	..	..	..	..	..	7.9	..	55.3
Morocco	11.8	0.24	1.34	0.2	1.3	71.3	142.6	2.5	14.9	0.0
Tunisia	10.5	0.02	0.49	0.0	0.5	14.0	14.0	3.6	3.7	0.0

a. Data are for the most recent year available during the period specified.

Financing					Annual revenue ($ millions)		
Annual investment ($ millions)			Committed nominal investment in telecommunication projects with private participation ($ millions)	ODA gross disbursements for communication ($ millions)			
Fixed telephone service	Mobile communication	Telecommunications			Fixed telephone service	Mobile communication	Telecommunications
2010	2010	2010	2010	2010	2010	2010	2010
140.4	**1,477.2**	**2,728.5**	**11,957.0**	**145.3**	**1,914.6**	**11,904.9**	**14,137.3**
..	..	..	534.0	2.9	..	..	..
-	93.4	93.4	394.0	2.1	21.8	339.0	360.8
..	..	..	59.0	0.4	..	..	..
..	..	..	299.0	3.1	..	..	..
..	..	..	-	1.3	..	..	..
..	..	..	233.0	1.2	138.4	712.8	851.2
..	..	..	16.0	0.2	..	..	..
0.3	26.8	27.1	10.0	0.5	2.0	54.3	57.8
..	..	..	345.0	0.2	..	221.4	228.2
..	..	..	..	0.0	..	..	..
1.3	119.5	120.9	174.0	2.0	5.7	644.3	650.0
..	..	..	77.0	0.2	..	..	..
31.4	..	..	319.0	0.7	..	..	..
..	..	..	..	..	..	..	..
2.6	..	..	-	..	28.0	38.8	67.7
..	..	..	-	6.8	175.5	313.8	489.3
..	..	..	125.0	0.0	..	..	..
..	..	..	-	0.7	..	..	..
..	752.3	766.4	290.0	7.5	102.6	1,044.0	1,171.0
..	..	..	71.0	0.2	..	..	..
..	..	..	19.0	1.0	..	..	..
..	..	..	492.0	6.8	..	..	..
..	11.2	11.2	11.0	0.0	..	..	66.2
..	..	..	15.0	0.0	..	..	..
12.6	..	..	132.0	0.3	34.7	210.3	245.0
..	..	..	116.0	1.2	..	..	..
12.2	180.8	193.0	254.0	0.3	47.7	515.5	563.3
..	..	..	133.0	0.2	..	..	..
..	..	..	26.0	0.0	44.3	154.9	234.2
..	..	..	80.0	8.6	..	..	..
..	..	..	..	(5.5)	..	..	..
..	..	..	107.0	0.9	..	..	..
..	..	740.6	3,036.0	14.9	346.9	6,323.0	6,670.0
..	..	181.5	63.0	5.6	..	..	167.1
..	..	..	..	0.1	..	..	..
48.5	278.6	327.1	236.0	1.0	583.5	698.6	1,282.0
..	..	..	..	0.0	..	..	..
..	..	..	38.0	0.6	..	..	..
..	..	..	-	..	..	..	..
..	..	..	2,101.0	21.2	..	..	..
..	..	..	478.0	1.6	..	..	..
..	..	26.9	15.0	0.0	94.0	..	..
..	..	..	625.0	6.2	..	..	..
31.5	14.6	46.1	23.0	0.0	106.4	194.5	300.9
..	..	194.3	257.0	2.5	183.1	439.6	732.6
..	..	..	453.0	1.2	..	..	..
..	..	..	301.0	0.4	..	..	..
193.1	**1,132.0**	**4,252.9**	**4,440.0**	**19.4**	**2,207.8**	**7,632.0**	**11,275.0**
..	..	..	237.0	0.4	..	..	..
..	..	..	..	9.1	..	..	..
193.1	1,132.0	3,537.0	2,113.0	1.5	956.8	4,549.0	6,974.0
..	..	..	..	0.0	..	..	..
..	..	715.9	1,124.0	2.0	1,251.0	3,083.0	4,301.0
..	..	..	966.0	5.6	..	..	..

Table 6.4 Energy

	Access, demand side							
	Energy production						Electric power consumption (kWh per capita)	GDP per unit of energy use (2005 PPP $ per kg of oil equivalent)
	Total (billion kWh)	Source[a] (% of total)						
		Hydroelectric	Coal	Natural gas	Nuclear	Oil		
	2009	2009	2009	2009	2009	2009	2009	2009
SUB-SAHARAN AFRICA	**418.4**	**18.2**	**56.6**	**4.6**	**3.1**	**4.2**	**517.4**	**3.2**
Angola	4.2	76.1	0.0	0.0	0.0	24.0	202.2	8.0
Benin	0.1	0.0	0.0	0.0	0.0	100.0	91.3	3.5
Botswana	0.4	0.0	100.0	0.0	0.0	0.0	1,503.4	11.4
Burkina Faso	..	..	..	..	..	..	..	..
Burundi	..	..	..	..	..	..	..	..
Cameroon	5.7	70.0	0.0	7.2	0.0	22.7	271.2	5.7
Cape Verde	..	..	..	..	..	..	..	..
Central African Republic	..	..	..	..	..	..	..	..
Chad	..	..	..	..	..	..	..	..
Comoros	..	..	..	..	..	..	..	..
Congo, Dem. Rep.	7.8	99.6	0.0	0.4	0.0	0.1	103.9	0.9
Congo, Rep.	0.5	64.0	0.0	36.1	0.0	0.0	146.4	10.1
Côte d'Ivoire	5.9	35.9	0.0	61.9	0.0	0.1	203.5	3.2
Equatorial Guinea	..	..	..	..	..	..	..	..
Eritrea	0.3	0.0	0.0	0.0	0.0	99.3	51.0	3.5
Ethiopia	4.1	87.3	0.0	0.0	0.0	12.4	45.8	2.2
Gabon	1.7	53.2	0.0	26.4	0.0	20.1	922.5	10.7
Gambia, The	..	..	..	..	..	..	..	..
Ghana	9.0	76.8	0.0	0.0	0.0	23.2	265.1	3.6
Guinea	..	..	..	..	..	..	..	..
Guinea-Bissau	..	..	..	..	..	..	..	..
Kenya	6.9	31.6	0.0	0.0	0.0	44.1	147.4	3.0
Lesotho	..	..	..	..	..	..	..	..
Liberia	..	..	..	..	..	..	..	..
Madagascar	..	..	..	..	..	..	..	..
Malawi	..	..	..	..	..	..	..	..
Mali	..	..	..	..	..	..	..	..
Mauritania	..	..	..	..	..	..	..	..
Mauritius	..	..	..	..	..	..	..	..
Mozambique	17.0	99.9	0.0	0.1	0.0	0.0	453.4	1.9
Namibia	1.7	82.0	17.5	0.0	0.0	0.5	1,576.2	7.3
Niger	..	..	..	..	..	..	..	..
Nigeria	19.8	22.9	0.0	64.3	0.0	12.8	120.5	2.9
Rwanda	..	..	..	..	..	..	..	..
São Tomé and Príncipe	..	..	..	..	..	..	..	..
Senegal	2.9	8.4	0.0	1.8	0.0	86.4	196.0	7.1
Seychelles	..	..	..	..	..	..	..	..
Sierra Leone	..	..	..	..	..	..	..	..
Somalia	..	..	..	..	..	..	..	..
South Africa	246.8	0.6	94.1	0.0	5.2	0.0	4,532.0	3.2
Sudan	6.8	47.8	0.0	0.0	0.0	52.2	114.3	5.3
Swaziland	..	..	..	..	..	..	..	..
Tanzania	4.6	60.2	2.7	36.2	0.0	0.9	85.7	2.7
Togo	0.1	73.8	0.0	0.0	0.0	24.6	110.8	2.0
Uganda	..	..	..	..	..	..	..	..
Zambia	10.3	99.7	0.0	0.0	0.0	0.3	635.0	2.1
Zimbabwe	7.9	53.3	46.4	0.0	0.0	0.3	1,026.2	..
NORTH AFRICA	**249.9**	**6.4**	**4.5**	**66.6**	**0.0**	**21.7**	**1,356.4**	**6.4**
Algeria	42.8	0.8	0.0	97.2	0.0	2.0	971.0	6.5
Djibouti	..	..	..	..	..	..	..	..
Egypt, Arab Rep.	139.0	9.3	0.0	68.7	0.0	21.3	1,548.6	5.9
Libya	30.4	0.0	0.0	41.0	0.0	59.0	4,170.1	4.7
Morocco	21.4	12.1	52.4	13.3	0.0	20.3	755.6	8.8
Tunisia	15.7	0.5	0.0	89.7	0.0	9.2	1,311.3	9.5

a. Shares may not sum to 100 percent because other sources of generated electricity (such as geothermal, solar, and wind) are not shown.
b. Data are for the most recent year available during the period specified.

Quality						Financing	
Firms identifying electricity as major or very severe obstacle to business operation and growth (%) 2009–10[b]	Average delay for firm in obtaining electrical connection (days) 2009–10[b]	Electric power transmission and distribution losses (% of output) 2009	Electric power outages in a typical month (number) 2009–10[b]	Firms that share or own their own generator (%) 2009–10[b]	Firms using electricity from generator (%) 2009–10[b]	Committed nominal investment in energy projects with private participation ($ millions) 2009-10[b]	ODA gross disbursements for energy ($ millions) 2010
		11.2					**1,278.1**
35.7	7.7	10.1	5.4	79.0	17.3	..	1.3
51.9	86.8	..	13.9	50.5	10.1	..	13.8
34.8	39.2	79.3	4.5	34.5	0.6	..	13.2
53.9	23.1	..	10.8	28.3	2.5	..	28.7
..	..	..	..	..	..	..	14.9
58.6	17.6	9.4	10.6	34.8	4.5	0.0	5.4
53.1	30.5	..	4.9	48.8	10.9	..	63.0
76.1	11.8	..	32.7	81.5	14.8	..	0.1
74.6	10.6	..	22.6	75.5	52.0	..	1.2
..	..	..	..	..	..	..	..
51.6	48.0	4.9	21.8	49.3	4.2	..	30.3
71.1	8.4	73.5	25.3	81.8	43.2	..	0.4
39.8	20.9	25.0	3.8	6.5	1.0	0.0	59.6
..	..	..	..	..	..	..	0.0
0.2	0.0	11.9	3.0	36.8	1.0	..	15.7
..	..	9.5	..	..	..	4.0	118.0
58.0	34.5	18.2	7.2	22.9	1.8	..	7.9
..	..	..	..	..	..	..	1.3
..	..	23.3	..	..	..	..	111.7
..	..	..	..	..	..	..	0.3
..	..	..	..	..	..	..	1.2
..	..	15.5	..	..	..	116.0	81.5
44.3	13.9	..	6.8	30.9	0.0	..	0.2
59.1	0.0	..	5.4	66.5	63.1	170.0	22.6
54.6	92.1	..	13.6	29.3	5.2	..	4.5
37.6	59.2	..	1.0	25.3	2.0	..	16.2
33.5	32.9	..	5.3	20.1	0.5	..	23.4
..	..	..	..	..	..	..	65.8
42.9	18.6	..	3.2	24.5	0.8	..	0.5
..	..	9.0	..	..	..	..	31.8
..	..	15.3	..	..	..	..	2.4
63.2	37.1	..	20.1	34.5	5.2	..	0.1
..	..	5.9	..	..	..	..	29.8
..	..	..	..	..	..	..	40.9
..	..	..	..	..	..	..	0.2
..	..	17.0	..	..	..	..	7.9
..	..	..	..	..	..	..	..
53.4	14.8	..	15.9	81.8	36.6	..	14.1
..	..	..	..	..	..	..	0.3
..	..	9.8	..	..	..	..	9.6
..	..	28.1	..	..	..	..	37.6
..	..	..	..	..	..	..	..
..	..	19.4	..	..	..	..	136.1
50.9	53.9	..	11.1	63.6	9.3	..	3.7
..	..	..	..	..	..	27.0	135.6
..	..	23.4	..	..	..	..	20.1
..	..	6.6	..	..	..	..	16.3
		12.9					**822.6**
..	..	20.6	..	..	..	..	0.9
..	..	..	..	..	..	..	16.1
..	..	10.5	..	..	..	..	397.2
..	..	14.0	..	..	..	..	27.2
..	..	11.7	..	..	..	..	108.9
..	..	13.0	..	..	..	..	260.9

Table 7.1 Education

	Literacy rate (%)						Primary education						
	Youth (ages 15–24)			Adult (ages 15 and older)			Gross enrollment ratio (% of relevant age group)			Net enrollment ratio (% of relevant age group)			Student-teacher ratio
	Total 2009	Male 2009	Female 2009	Total 2009	Male 2009	Female 2009	Total 2010	Male 2010	Female 2010	Total 2010	Male 2010	Female 2010	2010
SUB-SAHARAN AFRICA	..	..	..	..	..	..	..	103.2	95.8	..	77.4	73.1	45.7
Angola	73.1	80.8	65.5	70.0	82.9	57.6	124.5	137.3	111.6	85.7	93.1	78.2	45.8
Benin	54.3	64.9	43.4	41.7	54.2	29.1	125.9	134.6	117.1	93.8	..	..	46.4
Botswana	95.2	93.7	96.7	84.1	83.8	84.4	..	..	..	..	..	..	..
Burkina Faso	..	..	..	..	..	..	75.6	79.1	72.0	58.1	60.4	55.6	47.8
Burundi	76.6	76.9	76.3	66.6	72.6	60.9	156.3	157.3	155.3	..	..	..	50.6
Cameroon	..	..	..	..	..	..	119.8	128.6	110.9	92.4	98.7	85.9	45.5
Cape Verde	98.2	97.4	99.0	84.8	90.1	80.3	109.6	113.9	105.3	93.2	94.3	92.1	23.6
Central African Republic	64.7	72.2	57.3	55.2	69.1	42.1	93.4	109.3	77.7	70.5	80.8	60.4	84.3
Chad	46.3	53.5	39.0	33.6	44.5	23.1	92.5	107.0	78.0	..	..	..	62.2
Comoros	85.3	85.8	84.7	74.2	79.7	68.7	..	..	..	..	..	..	..
Congo, Dem. Rep.	67.7	73.3	62.1	67.0	79.5	54.9	93.7	100.4	87.0	..	..	..	37.0
Congo, Rep.	..	..	..	..	..	..	115.0	117.9	112.0	90.8	92.3	89.3	49.2
Côte d'Ivoire	66.6	72.1	61.0	55.3	64.7	45.3	..	..	..	..	..	..	..
Equatorial Guinea	97.9	97.7	98.2	93.3	97.0	89.8	86.6	87.9	85.4	56.3	56.5	56.0	27.2
Eritrea	88.7	91.6	85.8	66.6	77.9	56.0	44.6	48.5	40.6	33.5	35.8	31.0	38.0
Ethiopia	..	..	..	..	..	..	101.6	106.2	96.8	81.3	83.9	78.6	54.1
Gabon	97.6	98.6	96.6	87.7	91.4	84.1	..	..	..	..	..	..	..
Gambia, The	65.5	71.0	60.0	46.5	57.6	35.8	82.6	81.7	83.5	65.5	64.4	66.6	..
Ghana	80.1	81.2	78.9	66.6	72.8	60.4	..	..	..	..	..	..	..
Guinea	61.1	68.1	53.8	39.5	50.8	28.1	94.4	102.6	85.9	77.0	83.2	70.5	42.2
Guinea-Bissau	70.9	78.2	63.6	52.2	66.9	38.0	123.1	127.1	119.2	73.9	75.5	72.4	51.9
Kenya	92.7	91.9	93.6	87.0	90.5	83.5	..	..	..	..	..	..	..
Lesotho	92.0	85.7	98.1	89.7	82.9	95.3	103.2	104.5	102.0	73.4	72.0	74.8	33.8
Liberia	75.6	70.4	80.9	59.1	63.7	54.5	..	..	..	..	..	..	..
Madagascar	..	..	..	..	..	..	148.6	149.8	147.3	..	..	..	40.1
Malawi	86.5	86.9	86.0	73.7	80.6	67.0	135.5	133.0	138.0	..	..	..	79.3
Mali	..	..	..	..	..	..	80.4	85.9	74.7	62.0	66.3	57.4	50.4
Mauritania	67.7	70.9	64.3	57.5	64.5	50.3	102.0	99.5	104.5	74.0	72.5	75.7	37.2
Mauritius	96.5	95.5	97.6	87.9	90.6	85.3	99.4	99.1	99.7	93.4	92.4	94.5	21.5
Mozambique	70.9	78.1	63.7	55.1	70.1	41.5	115.1	121.1	109.0	91.9	94.5	89.2	58.5
Namibia	93.0	91.1	94.9	88.5	88.9	88.1	..	..	..	..	..	..	..
Niger	..	..	..	..	..	..	66.3	72.5	59.7	57.2	62.8	51.2	38.6
Nigeria	71.8	78.2	65.3	60.8	72.0	49.8	83.3	87.1	79.3	57.6	60.2	54.9	36.0
Rwanda	77.2	77.0	77.4	70.7	75.0	66.8	142.6	141.1	144.0	98.8	..	..	64.6
São Tomé and Príncipe	95.3	94.9	95.8	88.8	93.7	84.1	130.7	130.9	130.4	98.4	97.1	99.7	26.2
Senegal	65.0	74.2	56.2	49.7	61.8	38.7	86.8	84.4	89.3	75.5	73.3	77.7	33.7
Seychelles	..	..	..	..	..	..	117.2	117.3	117.2	..	..	..	12.6
Sierra Leone	57.6	67.6	48.1	40.9	52.7	30.1	..	..	..	..	..	..	..
Somalia	..	..	..	..	..	..	..	..	..	..	..	..	..
South Africa	..	..	..	..	..	..	..	..	..	..	..	..	..
Sudan	..	..	..	..	..	..	..	..	..	..	..	..	..
Swaziland	93.4	91.9	94.9	86.9	87.8	86.2	115.8	120.7	110.9	85.6	86.1	85.0	32.3
Tanzania	77.4	78.5	76.4	72.9	79.0	66.9	102.3	101.5	103.1	..	..	..	50.8
Togo	..	..	..	..	..	..	139.6	147.1	132.2	..	..	..	40.6
Uganda	..	..	..	..	..	..	121.1	120.3	122.0	90.9	89.6	92.1	48.6
Zambia	74.6	81.8	67.3	70.9	80.6	61.3	115.3	114.5	116.0	91.4	90.3	92.5	58.0
Zimbabwe	98.9	98.4	99.5	91.9	94.7	89.4	..	..	..	..	..	..	..
NORTH AFRICA	..	..	..	..	..	..	..	..	..	..	..	..	25.6
Algeria	..	..	..	..	..	..	110.2	113.4	106.8	95.6	96.6	94.6	23.3
Djibouti	..	..	..	..	..	..	..	..	..	..	..	..	..
Egypt, Arab Rep.	..	..	..	..	..	..	100.7	102.8	98.4	94.4	..	..	26.3
Libya	99.9	99.9	99.8	88.9	95.2	82.0	..	..	..	..	..	..	..
Morocco	79.5	86.7	72.2	56.1	68.9	43.9	111.4	115.0	107.6	93.7	94.5	92.8	26.2
Tunisia	..	..	..	..	..	..	..	..	..	..	..	..	..

Secondary education							Tertiary education			Public spending on education (%)	
Gross enrollment ratio (% of relevant age group)			Net enrollment ratio (% of relevant age group)			Student-teacher ratio	Gross enrollment ratio (% of relevant age group)			Share of government expenditure	Share of GDP
Total 2010	Male 2010	Female 2010	Total 2010	Male 2010	Female 2010	2010	Total 2010	Male 2010	Female 2010	2010	2010
..	**43.5**	**35.6**	**..**	**..**	**..**	**..**	**..**	**8.3**	**5.2**	**..**	**4.7**
31.3	37.2	25.5	..	..	..	38.7	3.7	4.1	3.3	8.5	3.4
..	..	..	..	..	..	..	..	..	..	..	..
..	..	..	..	..	..	..	..	..	..	..	..
20.7	23.4	17.9	15.6	17.5	13.6	30.3	3.3	4.5	2.2	20.8	4.0
24.8	28.9	20.7	16.2	17.7	14.6	29.9	3.3	4.2	2.3	25.1	9.2
42.2	46.0	38.4	..	..	..	..	11.5	12.6	10.3	17.9	3.5
87.5	79.7	95.4	65.9	61.1	70.8	17.5	17.8	15.6	20.2	14.4	5.6
12.6	16.0	9.3	..	..	..	52.3	2.6	3.9	1.3	12.0	1.2
24.6	34.6	14.6	..	..	..	32.5	2.2	3.7	0.6	10.1	2.8
..	..	..	..	..	..	..	7.9	9.1	6.7	..	..
37.7	47.8	27.6	..	..	..	16.0	..	..	..	8.9	2.5
..	..	..	..	..	..	..	5.5	..	..	..	6.2
..	..	..	..	..	..	..	..	..	..	..	..
..	..	..	..	..	..	..	..	..	..	..	..
31.9	36.3	27.6	28.6	32.4	24.9	38.7	2.0	3.0	1.0	..	..
35.7	39.3	32.1	..	..	..	43.1	5.5	8.0	2.9	25.4	4.7
..	..	..	..	..	..	..	..	..	..	..	..
54.1	55.6	52.6	..	..	..	..	..	..	..	22.8	5.0
..	..	..	..	..	..	..	..	..	..	24.4	5.5
..	..	..	..	..	..	..	..	..	..	..	..
..	..	..	..	..	..	..	..	..	..	..	..
..	..	..	..	..	..	..	..	..	..	17.2	6.7
46.4	39.0	53.9	29.9	22.8	37.0	..	..	..	..	..	..
..	..	..	..	..	..	..	..	..	..	..	..
..	..	..	..	..	..	..	3.7	3.9	3.5	..	..
32.1	33.6	30.6	27.5	27.9	27.2	..	0.7	0.9	0.6	12.1	4.6
37.7	44.3	30.9	29.5	34.8	23.9	..	5.8	8.1	3.4	22.0	4.5
24.4	26.4	22.4	..	..	..	..	4.4	6.2	2.5	15.3	4.3
89.4	89.5	89.3	..	..	..	15.9	..	..	..	..	..
25.5	28.0	22.9	16.1	17.0	15.2	35.0	..	..	..	..	..
..	..	..	..	..	..	..	..	..	..	..	8.1
13.4	16.1	10.7	..	..	..	29.6	1.5	2.2	0.8	16.9	3.9
44.1	46.8	41.2	..	..	..	33.1	..	..	..	..	..
32.2	31.9	32.4	..	..	..	..	5.5	6.2	4.8	18.2	5.0
50.9	50.2	51.7	..	..	..	..	4.5	4.5	4.4	..	..
37.4	39.9	34.9	..	..	..	32.3	7.9	9.9	5.9	..	5.6
119.3	114.4	124.7	..	..	..	12.2	..	..	..	..	..
..	..	..	..	..	..	..	..	..	..	..	..
..	..	..	..	..	..	..	..	..	..	..	..
..	..	..	..	..	..	..	..	..	..	19.2	6.0
..	..	..	..	..	..	..	..	..	..	..	..
58.1	58.1	58.1	32.8	28.7	37.0	18.2	..	..	..	16.0	7.4
..	..	..	..	..	..	..	2.1	2.3	1.9	18.3	6.2
..	..	..	..	..	..	..	..	..	..	..	4.5
28.1	30.4	25.8	..	..	..	..	..	..	..	..	..
..	..	..	..	..	..	..	..	..	..	..	..
..	..	..	..	..	..	..	6.2	6.9	5.5	8.3	2.5
..	**..**	**..**	**..**	**..**	**..**	**..**	**..**	**..**	**..**	**..**	**..**
..	..	..	..	..	..	..	30.8	25.2	36.6	..	..
..	..	..	..	..	..	..	..	..	..	..	..
72.5	73.9	71.1	70.1	71.4	68.6	13.5	32.4	34.0	30.7	..	..
..	..	..	..	..	..	..	..	..	..	..	..
..	..	..	..	..	..	..	..	..	..	..	..
..	..	..	..	..	..	..	..	..	..	..	..

Table 7.2 Health

	Mortality						Diseases			
	Life expectancy at birth (years)			Under-five mortality rate (per 1,000)	Infant mortality rate (per 1,000 live births)	Maternal mortality ratio, modeled estimate (per 100,000 live births)	Prevalence of HIV (% ages 15–49)	Incidence of tuberculosis (per 100,000 people)	Malaria	
	Total	Male	Female						Clinical cases reported[b]	Reported deaths[b]
	2010	2010	2010	2010	2010	2008	2010	2010	2010	2010
SUB-SAHARAN AFRICA	**54.2**	**53.1**	**55.3**	**122**	**77**	**505**	**5.5**	**277**	**71,412,328**	**132,524**
Angola	50.7	49.2	52.1	161	98	450	2.0	304	2,783,619	8,114
Benin	55.6	53.8	57.5	115	73	350	1.2	94	1,432,095	964
Botswana	53.1	54.0	52.2	48	36	160	24.8	503	12,196	8
Burkina Faso	54.9	54.0	56.0	176	93	300	1.2	55	5,409,156	9,024
Burundi	49.9	48.5	51.3	142	88	800	3.3	129	2,919,866	2,677
Cameroon	51.1	50.1	52.1	136	84	690	5.3	177	1,845,691	4,536
Cape Verde	73.8	70.1	77.7	36	29	79	..	147	47	1
Central African Republic	47.6	46.1	49.2	159	106	890	4.7	319	66,484	526
Chad	49.2	47.8	50.7	173	99	1,100	3.4	276	466,034	..
Comoros	60.6	59.3	62.0	86	63	280	0.1	37	47,364	53
Congo, Dem. Rep.	48.1	46.5	49.7	170	112	540	..	327	7,439,440	23,476
Congo, Rep.	57.0	55.8	58.2	93	61	560	3.4	372	0	..
Côte d'Ivoire	54.7	53.7	55.9	123	86	400	3.4	139	..	1,023
Equatorial Guinea	50.8	49.6	52.2	121	81	240	5.0	135	0	..
Eritrea	61.0	58.7	63.4	61	42	240	0.8	100	53,750	27
Ethiopia	58.7	57.2	60.3	106	68	350	..	261	4,068,764	1,581
Gabon	62.3	61.3	63.4	74	54	230	5.2	553	159,313	182
Gambia, The	58.2	57.0	59.4	98	57	360	2.0	273	116,353	151
Ghana	63.8	62.9	64.8	74	50	350	1.8	86	2,642,221	3,859
Guinea	53.6	52.1	55.3	130	81	610	1.3	334	1,092,554	735
Guinea-Bissau	47.7	46.2	49.3	150	92	790	2.5	233	0	..
Kenya	56.5	55.4	57.6	85	55	360	6.3	298	4,585,712	26,017
Lesotho	47.4	48.1	46.6	85	65	620	23.6	633	..	..
Liberia	56.2	55.2	57.2	103	74	770	1.5	293	2,263,973	1,422
Madagascar	66.5	64.9	68.1	62	43	240	0.2	266	202,450	122
Malawi	53.5	53.4	53.5	92	58	460	11.0	219	6,851,108	8,206
Mali	51.0	49.9	52.1	178	99	540	1.0	68	1,018,846	3,006
Mauritania	58.2	56.6	60.0	111	75	510	0.7	337	238,565	211
Mauritius	73.0	69.5	76.7	15	13	60	1.0	22	..	..
Mozambique	49.7	48.7	50.7	135	92	490	11.5	544	1,522,577	3,354
Namibia	62.1	61.5	62.7	40	29	200	13.1	603	25,889	63
Niger	54.3	53.8	54.7	143	73	590	0.8	185	620,058	3,929
Nigeria	51.4	50.6	52.2	143	88	630	3.6	133	3,873,463	4,238
Rwanda	55.1	53.8	56.4	91	59	340	2.9	106	638,669	670
São Tomé and Príncipe	64.4	63.0	65.8	80	53	70	..	96	2,262	14
Senegal	59.0	57.9	60.0	75	50	370	0.9	288	0	..
Seychelles	73.0	68.4	77.9	14	12	..	..	31	..	..
Sierra Leone	47.4	46.8	48.0	174	114	890	1.6	682	934,028	8,188
Somalia	50.9	49.4	52.5	180	108	1,000	0.7	286	24,553	6
South Africa	52.1	51.4	52.8	57	41	300	17.8	981	8,060	83
Sudan	61.1	59.4	62.9	103	66	730	1.1	119	1,465,496	1,023
Swaziland	48.3	48.8	47.9	78	55	320	25.9	1,287	1,722	8
Tanzania	57.4	56.5	58.3	92	60	460	5.6	177	0	..
Togo	56.6	55.1	58.1	103	66	300	3.2	455	617,101	1,507
Uganda	53.6	53.0	54.3	99	63	310	6.5	209	11,084,045	8,431
Zambia	48.5	48.0	48.9	111	69	440	13.5	462	4,229,839	4,834
Zimbabwe	49.9	50.7	49.0	80	51	570	14.3	633	648,965	255
NORTH AFRICA	**72.8**	**70.9**	**74.8**	**27**	**23**	**78**	**0.1**	**52**	**4,673**	**4**
Algeria	72.9	71.4	74.4	36	31	97	0.1	90	408	..
Djibouti	57.5	56.1	59.0	91	73	200	2.5	620	3,962	0
Egypt, Arab Rep.	73.0	71.1	75.0	22	19	66	<0.1	18	85	2
Libya	74.8	72.2	77.4	17	13	58	..	40	..	..
Morocco	71.9	69.7	74.2	36	30	100	0.1	91	218	2
Tunisia	74.6	72.6	76.7	16	14	56	<0.1	25	..	..

Prevention and treatment										
Child immunization rate (% of children ages 12–23 months)		Malnutrition (% of children under age 5)		Births attended by skilled health staff (% of total)	Contraceptive use (% of married women ages 15–49)		Children under age 5 sleeping under insecticide-treated nets (%)	Tuberculosis case detection rate (%, all forms)	Tuberculosis treatment success rate (% of registered cases)	Children under age 5 with fever receiving any antimalarial treatment same or next day (%)
Measles	DPT[c]	Stunting	Underweight		Any method	Modern method				
2010	2010	2007–10[a]	2007–10[a]	2007–10[a]	2007–10[a]	2007–10[a]	2007–10[a]	2009	2009	2007–10[a]
75	**77**					**..**	**..**	**48.0**	**79.0**	
93	91	29.2	15.6	47.3	..	..	17.7	75.0	72.0	29.3
69	83	..	..	..	..	..	..	47.0	90.0	..
94	96	31.4	11.2	94.6	52.8	51.2	..	62.0	79.0	..
94	95	35.1	26.0	..	..	..	..	14.0	76.0	..
92	96	..	..	60.3	21.9	..	45.2	25.0	90.0	17.2
79	84	..	..	..	..	..	..	70.0	78.0	..
96	99	..	..	..	..	..	..	44.0	..	..
62	54	..	..	43.7	..	..	..	60.0	53.0	..
46	59	..	..	22.7	4.8	..	9.8	26.0	76.0	35.7
72	74	..	..	..	..	..	..	46.0	..	..
68	63	45.8	28.2	79.3	17.3	5.5	35.7	46.0	88.0	39.1
76	90	..	..	..	..	..	..	69.0	78.0	..
70	85	39.0	29.4	..	..	..	..	27.0	79.0	..
51	33	..	..	..	..	..	..	89.0	66.0	..
99	99	..	..	..	..	..	48.9	58.0	85.0	13.1
81	86	..	..	..	..	..	33.1	50.0	84.0	9.5
55	45	..	..	..	..	..	55.1	42.0	55.0	..
97	98	..	..	56.7	..	..	..	47.0	89.0	..
93	94	28.6	14.3	57.1	23.5	16.6	28.2	31.0	87.0	43.0
51	57	40.0	20.8	46.1	..	..	4.5	26.0	79.0	73.9
61	76	28.1	17.2	44.0	14.2	..	35.5	59.0	67.0	51.2
86	83	35.2	16.4	43.8	45.5	38.9	46.7	85.0	86.0	23.2
85	83	39.0	13.5	61.5	47.0	45.6	..	93.0	70.0	..
64	64	39.4	20.4	46.3	11.4	10.3	26.4	52.0	83.0	67.2
67	74	49.2	..	43.9	39.9	28.2	45.8	44.0	82.0	19.7
93	93	47.8	13.8	..	..	42.2	56.5	49.0	88.0	30.9
63	76	..	..	..	..	..	70.2	16.0	78.0	..
67	64	23.0	15.9	60.9	9.3	8.0	..	24.0	63.0	20.7
99	99	..	..	..	..	..	..	41.0	88.0	..
70	74	43.7	18.3	55.3	16.2	12.2	22.8	46.0	85.0	36.7
75	83	29.6	17.5	81.4	55.1	53.5	34.0	76.0	85.0	20.3
71	70	..	..	..	18.0	..	63.7	36.0	79.0	..
71	69	41.0	26.7	38.9	14.6	8.1	29.1	19.0	83.0	49.1
82	80	..	..	69.0	51.6	26.1	69.8	19.0	85.0	10.8
92	98	31.6	14.4	81.7	38.4	33.1	56.2	49.0	98.0	8.4
60	70	..	..	..	..	..	29.2	31.0	85.0	9.1
99	99	..	..	..	..	..	..	57.0	64.0	..
82	90	37.4	21.3	42.4	8.2	6.0	25.8	31.0	79.0	30.1
46	45	..	..	..	..	..	..	42.0	85.0	..
65	63	23.9	8.7	..	..	..	..	74.0	73.0	..
90	90	..	..	..	..	..	25.3	52.0	80.0	35.8
94	89	40.4	7.3	82.0	49.3	63.0	0.6	67.0	69.0	0.6
92	91	42.5	16.2	48.9	34.4	26.1	63.6	77.0	88.0	59.1
84	92	26.9	20.5	60.1	15.2	13.2	56.9	10.0	81.0	33.8
55	60	..	..	..	..	..	32.8	44.0	67.0	59.6
91	82	45.8	14.9	46.5	40.8	26.5	49.9	80.0	90.0	34.0
84	83	..	..	60.2	64.9	..	17.3	46.0	78.0	23.6
96	**97**					**..**	**..**	**..**	**..**	
95	95	..	..	..	..	..	..	100.0	91.0	..
85	88	..	..	..	22.5	..	19.9	71.0	79.0	0.9
96	97	30.7	6.8	78.9	60.3	57.6	..	63.0	88.0	..
98	98	21.0	5.6	99.8	..	..	..	82.0	..	..
98	99	..	..	..	..	..	..	93.0	84.0	..
97	98	..	..	..	..	..	..	86.0	83.0	..

(continued)

Table 7.2 Health (continued)

	Water and sanitation						Human resources		
	Population with sustainable access to an improved water source			Population with sustainable access to improved sanitation			Health workers (per 1,000 people)		
	(% of total population) 2010	(% of urban population) 2010	(% of rural population) 2010	(% of total population) 2010	(% of urban population) 2010	(% of rural population) 2010	Physicians 2008–09[a]	Nurses and midwives 2008–09[a]	Community workers 2008–09[a]
SUB-SAHARAN AFRICA	**61**	**83**	**49**	**31**	**42**	**23**	**..**	**..**	**..**
Angola	51	60	38	58	85	19	..	..	..
Benin	75	84	68	13	25	5	0.1	0.8	..
Botswana	96	99	92	62	75	41	..	..	..
Burkina Faso	79	95	73	17	50	6	0.1	0.7	..
Burundi	72	83	71	46	49	46	..	..	..
Cameroon	77	95	52	49	58	36	..	..	..
Cape Verde	88	90	85	61	73	43	0.6	1.3	..
Central African Republic	67	92	51	34	43	28	..	..	..
Chad	51	70	44	13	30	6	..	..	..
Comoros	95	91	97	36	50	30	..	..	..
Congo, Dem. Rep.	45	79	27	24	24	24	..	..	..
Congo, Rep.	71	95	32	18	20	15	..	..	..
Côte d'Ivoire	80	91	68	24	36	11	0.1	0.5	..
Equatorial Guinea	..	..	..	..	..	..	..	..	..
Eritrea	..	..	..	..	..	4	..	..	..
Ethiopia	44	97	34	21	29	19	..	..	..
Gabon	87	95	41	33	33	30	..	..	..
Gambia, The	89	92	85	68	70	65	0.0	0.6	0.1
Ghana	86	91	80	14	19	8	0.1	1.1	0.2
Guinea	74	90	65	18	32	11	..	..	..
Guinea-Bissau	64	91	53	20	44	9	0.1	0.6	..
Kenya	59	82	52	32	32	32	..	..	..
Lesotho	78	91	73	26	32	24	..	..	..
Liberia	73	88	60	18	29	7	0.0	0.3	..
Madagascar	46	74	34	15	21	12	..	..	..
Malawi	83	95	80	51	49	51	0.0	0.3	0.7
Mali	64	87	51	22	35	14	0.1	0.3	..
Mauritania	50	52	48	26	51	9	0.1	0.7	..
Mauritius	99	100	99	89	91	88	..	..	..
Mozambique	47	77	29	18	38	5	0.0	0.3	..
Namibia	93	99	90	32	57	17	..	..	..
Niger	49	100	39	9	34	4	0.0	0.1	..
Nigeria	58	74	43	31	35	27	0.4	1.6	0.1
Rwanda	65	76	63	55	52	56	..	..	..
São Tomé and Príncipe	89	89	88	26	30	19	..	..	..
Senegal	72	93	56	52	70	39	0.1	0.4	..
Seychelles	..	100	..	..	98	..	..	..	..
Sierra Leone	55	87	35	13	23	6	0.0	0.2	0.0
Somalia	29	66	7	23	52	6	..	..	..
South Africa	91	99	79	79	86	67	..	..	..
Sudan	58	67	52	26	44	14	0.3	0.8	..
Swaziland	71	91	65	57	64	55	..	..	..
Tanzania	53	79	44	10	20	7	..	..	..
Togo	61	89	40	13	26	3	0.1	0.3	..
Uganda	72	95	68	34	34	34	..	..	..
Zambia	61	87	46	48	57	43	..	..	..
Zimbabwe	80	98	69	40	52	32	..	..	..
NORTH AFRICA	**92**	**95**	**88**	**90**	**94**	**84**	**2.1**	**3.0**	**..**
Algeria	83	85	79	95	98	88	..	..	..
Djibouti	88	99	54	50	63	10	..	0.8	..
Egypt, Arab Rep.	99	100	99	95	97	93	2.8	3.5	..
Libya	..	..	..	97	97	96	1.9	6.8	..
Morocco	83	98	61	70	83	52	0.6	0.9	..
Tunisia	..	99	..	..	96	..	1.2	3.3	..

a. Data are for the most recent year available during the period specified.
b. Data for Sudan, after 1999, only represents 15 northern states.
c. Diphtheria, pertussis, and tetanus toxoid.

Expenditure on health								
Share of GDP (%)			Share of total expenditure on health (%)			Out-of-pocket (% of private expenditure on health)	Private prepaid plans (% of private expenditure on health)	Health expenditure per capita ($)
Total 2010	Public 2009	Private 2009	Public 2010	Private 2010	External resources for health 2010	2010	2010	2010
6.5	**2.9**	**3.7**	**45.2**	**54.8**	**10.4**	**58.6**	**32.8**	**85.0**
2.9	4.1	0.5	82.5	17.5	2.9	100.0	0.0	123.2
4.1	2.3	1.9	49.5	50.5	35.9	92.7	7.3	31.1
8.3	8.2	2.1	72.5	27.5	18.3	29.5	5.6	614.6
6.7	3.9	2.4	51.0	49.0	22.9	73.8	3.7	39.8
11.6	6.0	7.1	38.2	61.8	45.8	61.4	0.2	20.7
5.1	1.6	4.0	29.6	70.4	13.2	94.5	0.0	61.3
4.1	2.9	1.0	75.0	25.0	11.9	99.7	0.3	154.6
4.0	1.7	2.6	35.4	64.6	13.4	95.0	0.0	18.2
4.5	3.9	3.1	25.0	75.0	7.9	96.7	0.2	30.6
4.5	2.1	1.3	67.2	32.8	19.2	100.0	0.0	33.2
7.9	4.9	4.7	42.5	57.5	32.7	62.5	0.2	15.8
2.5	1.6	1.4	46.7	53.3	4.1	100.0	0.0	72.3
5.3	1.0	4.1	21.6	78.4	9.8	98.8	1.2	59.8
4.5	3.4	0.5	75.9	24.1	2.0	92.1	0.0	896.2
2.7	1.0	1.2	48.2	51.8	38.0	100.0	0.0	11.9
4.9	2.0	2.2	53.5	46.5	39.4	80.1	1.5	15.7
3.5	1.7	1.9	52.9	47.1	2.4	100.0	0.0	302.1
5.7	3.0	3.0	50.9	49.2	41.2	48.4	3.1	26.1
5.2	3.1	3.8	59.5	40.5	16.9	66.4	6.2	67.0
4.9	0.9	4.9	11.3	88.7	10.8	99.4	0.0	23.0
8.5	1.6	4.5	10.0	90.0	23.3	73.8	0.0	46.9
4.8	1.5	2.9	44.3	55.7	36.1	76.7	9.3	36.9
11.1	5.6	2.6	76.2	23.8	19.5	69.0	0.0	108.9
11.9	5.3	8.0	32.5	67.5	55.1	52.2	0.0	29.2
3.8	2.8	1.4	60.3	39.7	9.0	68.3	15.2	15.9
6.6	3.6	2.6	60.2	39.8	63.8	27.9	15.8	25.6
5.0	2.7	2.9	46.6	53.4	27.4	99.5	0.5	31.7
4.4	1.6	1.0	53.1	46.9	10.1	94.5	0.6	42.7
6.0	2.1	3.6	41.7	58.3	2.0	88.8	6.3	448.9
5.2	4.1	1.5	71.7	28.3	24.2	48.3	0.0	21.3
6.8	4.0	2.0	58.4	41.6	19.0	17.9	61.2	361.3
5.2	3.5	2.6	50.9	49.1	29.4	84.1	4.4	18.3
5.1	2.1	3.7	37.9	62.1	9.2	95.3	3.1	62.8
10.5	3.9	5.1	50.1	49.9	47.0	44.4	10.2	55.5
7.2	2.9	4.2	38.3	61.7	21.0	86.7	0.0	90.0
5.7	3.1	2.5	55.5	44.5	18.5	78.5	17.9	58.5
3.4	3.1	0.9	91.9	8.1	4.2	67.7	23.0	368.5
13.1	0.9	12.2	11.3	88.7	20.6	89.5	1.0	42.5
..	..	..	..	..	..	..	..	..
8.9	3.4	5.1	44.1	55.9	2.2	29.6	66.1	648.7
6.3	2.0	5.3	29.8	70.2	3.3	95.7	1.0	83.9
6.6	4.0	2.3	63.7	36.3	17.2	42.5	19.0	203.1
6.0	3.8	1.4	67.3	32.7	48.8	41.7	10.1	30.9
7.7	1.7	4.2	44.2	55.8	15.2	84.2	4.3	40.6
9.0	1.6	6.7	21.7	78.3	25.9	63.6	0.2	46.7
5.9	2.5	2.3	60.3	39.7	39.3	66.7	3.6	72.9
..	..	..	..	..	..	..	..	..
4.7	**3.0**	**2.3**	**50.6**	**49.4**	**0.4**	**93.5**	**6.0**	**160.6**
4.2	5.0	0.8	77.9	22.1	0.0	94.7	5.1	178.3
7.2	5.4	1.6	65.3	34.7	23.9	99.1	0.9	91.7
4.7	2.1	2.9	37.4	62.6	0.6	97.7	1.7	123.2
3.9	2.6	1.3	68.8	31.2	0.6	100.0	0.0	483.7
5.2	1.9	3.6	38.0	62.0	0.4	86.3	13.7	148.0
6.2	3.4	2.9	54.3	45.7	0.3	87.0	11.2	237.8

Table 8.1 Rural development

	Rural population (%)								
	Share of total population			Annual growth			Rural population density (rural population per sq km of arable land)		
	1990	2000	2010	1990	2000	2010	1990	2000	2009
SUB-SAHARAN AFRICA	**71.9**	**67.4**	**62.7**	**2.2**	**1.9**	**1.7**	**273.2**	**342.2**	**352.4**
Angola	62.9	51.0	41.5	0.6	1.1	0.7	224.2	236.8	196.7
Benin	65.5	61.7	58.0	2.0	2.5	2.2	193.6	169.0	205.0
Botswana	58.1	46.8	38.9	-2.1	-0.1	-0.7	191.2	235.1	314.4
Burkina Faso	86.2	83.4	79.6	2.3	2.5	2.5	228.3	253.8	216.8
Burundi	93.7	91.7	89.0	2.2	1.2	2.2	564.4	608.9	810.7
Cameroon	59.3	50.1	41.6	1.4	0.5	0.2	121.6	131.8	136.4
Cape Verde	55.9	46.6	38.9	-2.8	-0.1	-1.0	474.7	463.1	324.8
Central African Republic	63.2	62.4	61.1	1.9	1.8	1.6	96.6	119.7	135.7
Chad	79.2	76.6	72.4	2.9	3.0	2.0	145.5	178.9	185.3
Comoros	72.1	71.9	71.8	1.8	2.7	2.5	404.8	505.5	642.9
Congo, Dem. Rep.	72.2	70.2	64.8	3.7	2.0	1.8	394.1	520.0	626.9
Congo, Rep.	45.7	41.7	37.9	1.8	1.7	1.5	227.9	266.9	301.8
Côte d'Ivoire	60.3	56.5	49.9	2.9	1.3	0.7	310.6	334.6	349.4
Equatorial Guinea	65.3	61.2	60.3	1.7	3.2	2.5	187.8	245.0	312.0
Eritrea	84.2	82.2	78.4	1.3	3.3	2.5	..	538.4	582.5
Ethiopia	87.4	85.1	82.4	3.1	2.4	1.8	..	558.1	481.4
Gabon	30.9	19.9	14.0	-1.0	-2.3	-1.5	97.3	75.6	65.8
Gambia, The	61.7	50.9	41.9	2.3	0.8	0.8	327.5	235.8	179.7
Ghana	63.6	56.0	48.5	1.7	1.0	0.8	348.5	271.7	266.6
Guinea	72.0	69.0	64.6	4.1	1.0	1.5	145.4	267.9	222.9
Guinea-Bissau	71.9	70.3	70.0	0.4	2.0	2.0	292.4	290.7	346.7
Kenya	81.8	80.3	77.8	3.1	2.4	2.2	384.4	513.1	570.7
Lesotho	86.0	80.0	73.1	1.3	0.8	0.0	444.7	476.1	473.6
Liberia	54.7	45.7	38.5	-3.3	3.0	2.3	332.4	342.4	375.7
Madagascar	76.4	72.9	69.8	2.2	2.8	2.4	316.9	386.2	478.5
Malawi	88.4	84.8	80.2	3.3	2.3	2.5	368.6	346.3	323.8
Mali	76.7	72.1	66.7	1.3	2.3	2.2	324.0	177.5	157.7
Mauritania	60.3	60.0	58.6	1.1	2.8	2.1	300.8	324.9	509.2
Mauritius	56.1	57.3	57.4	0.4	1.2	0.4	594.0	680.1	842.1
Mozambique	78.9	69.3	61.6	0.2	1.3	1.0	309.8	323.4	282.4
Namibia	72.3	67.6	62.0	3.5	1.6	0.9	155.0	157.1	175.4
Niger	84.6	83.8	83.3	2.8	3.4	3.5	59.7	65.5	83.6
Nigeria	64.7	57.5	50.2	1.4	1.1	1.1	213.7	237.1	231.4
Rwanda	94.6	86.2	81.1	-0.3	5.3	2.6	764.3	775.6	645.5
São Tomé and Príncipe	56.4	46.6	37.8	0.2	-0.2	-0.4	3,274.5	1,095.2	627.6
Senegal	61.0	59.4	57.1	2.5	2.3	2.2	142.9	185.1	180.4
Seychelles	50.7	49.0	44.7	0.9	0.4	-2.0	3,549.0	3,975.4	3,944.1
Sierra Leone	67.1	64.5	61.6	0.9	2.4	1.7	549.7	545.4	327.5
Somalia	70.3	66.8	62.6	0.0	2.3	1.6	453.9	473.9	574.9
South Africa	48.0	43.1	38.3	1.0	1.4	0.1	125.7	128.5	133.3
Sudan	73.4	63.9	54.8	1.9	0.7	0.3	117.3	108.5	91.1
South Sudan	..	..	..	..	..	..	..	..	..
Swaziland	77.1	76.7	74.5	3.1	0.1	0.8	369.6	435.6	445.9
Tanzania	81.1	77.7	73.6	2.7	2.0	2.4	229.6	300.5	322.3
Togo	69.9	63.5	56.6	1.7	2.0	0.9	122.0	121.3	153.7
Uganda	88.9	87.9	86.7	3.1	3.0	3.0	314.7	401.6	426.0
Zambia	60.6	65.2	64.3	2.8	3.3	1.4	164.8	236.2	244.8
Zimbabwe	71.0	66.2	61.7	1.9	0.2	0.0	257.2	231.3	185.6
NORTH AFRICA	**51.4**	**48.7**	**46.3**	**1.5**	**1.1**	**1.0**	**834.6**	**862.5**	**1,016.5**
Algeria	47.9	40.2	33.5	0.8	-0.4	-0.4	171.1	160.2	159.1
Djibouti	24.3	16.7	11.9	4.1	-1.4	-1.4	13,663.7	12,223.2	5,363.4
Egypt, Arab Rep.	56.5	57.4	57.2	2.2	1.9	1.7	1,406.2	1,386.3	1,582.2
Libya	24.3	23.6	22.1	1.8	1.5	0.7	58.4	68.0	79.7
Morocco	51.6	46.7	43.3	0.5	0.5	0.2	146.9	153.4	171.4
Tunisia	42.1	36.6	32.7	0.5	0.1	-0.2	118.0	122.2	127.7

a. Data are for the most recent year available during the period specified.
b. Poverty estimates based on survey data from earlier year(s) are available, but are not comparable with the most recent year reported here.
c. World Bank estimates.

Share of rural population below the national poverty line				Rural population poverty gap (%)				Share of rural population with sustainable access (%)					
Surveys 1990–99[a]		Surveys 2000–11[a]		Surveys 1990–99[a]		Surveys 2000–11[a]		To an improved water source			To an improved sanitation facilities		
Year	Percent	Year	Percent	Year	Percent	Year	Percent	1990	2000	2010	1990	2000	2010
								35.2	**41.6**	**48.6**	**19.3**	**20.6**	**23.4**
	..		..		..		..	40.0	40.0	38.0	6.0	11.0	19.0
	..	2007	36.1		..	2003	14.0	49.0	59.0	68.0	0.0	3.0	5.0
1993	40.4	2003	44.8		..	2003	18.4	88.0	90.0	92.0	22.0	32.0	41.0
	..	2009[b]	52.6		..	2009[b]	17.4	38.0	55.0	73.0	2.0	4.0	6.0
	..	2006[b]	68.9		..	2006[b]	24.2	68.0	70.0	71.0	44.0	45.0	46.0
	..	2007[b]	55.0		..	2007[b]	17.5	31.0	42.0	52.0	37.0	37.0	36.0
	..	2007[b]	44.3		..	2007[b]	14.3	..	81.0	85.0	..	25.0	43.0
	..	2008[b]	69.4		..	2008[b]	35.0	47.0	49.0	51.0	5.0	16.0	28.0
	..	2003[b]	58.6		..	2003[b]	23.3	37.0	41.0	44.0	4.0	5.0	6.0
	..	2004	48.7		..	2004	17.8	83.0	92.0	97.0	11.0	23.0	30.0
	..	2006	75.7		..	2006	34.9	27.0	27.0	27.0	4.0	13.0	24.0
	..		..		..	2005	20.6	..	36.0	32.0	..	18.0	15.0
1998	41.5[c]	2008	54.2[c]	1998	14.3[c]	2008	20.3[c]	67.0	67.0	68.0	8.0	10.0	11.0
	..	2006	79.9		..	2006	49.8	..	42.0	..	..	87.0	..
	..		..		..		..	39.0	50.0	..	0.0	2.0	4.0
1995	47.5	2011	30.4	1995	13.4	2005	8.5	5.0	19.0	34.0	1.0	6.0	19.0
	..	2005	44.6		..	2005	16.0	..	47.0	41.0	..	30.0	30.0
	..	2010	73.9		..	2003	30.5	67.0	77.0	85.0	..	60.0	65.0
1998	49.6	2006	39.2	1998	18.2	2006	13.5	36.0	58.0	80.0	4.0	6.0	8.0
	..	2007[b]	63.0		..	2007[b]	22.0	37.0	52.0	65.0	6.0	9.0	11.0
	..	2002[b]	69.1		..	2002[b]	27.8	32.0	43.0	53.0	4.0	5.0	9.0
	..	2005[b]	49.1		..	2005[b]	17.5	33.0	43.0	52.0	25.0	28.0	32.0
1994	68.9[c]	2003	60.5[c]	1993	26.5[c]		..[c]	78.0	76.0	73.0	..	22.0	24.0
	..	2007	67.7[c]		..	2007	26.3[c]	..	50.0	60.0	..	3.0	7.0
1999	76.7	2005	73.5	1999	21.4	2005	28.9	15.0	24.0	34.0	7.0	10.0	12.0
1998	66.5	2010	56.6	1998	23.9	2004	8.6	35.0	57.0	80.0	38.0	45.0	51.0
	..	2010[b]	50.6		..	..[b]	..	20.0	36.0	51.0	10.0	12.0	14.0
	..	2008[b]	59.4		..	2008[b]	22.3	26.0	37.0	48.0	8.0	9.0	9.0
	..		..		..		..	99.0	99.0	99.0	88.0	88.0	88.0
1996	71.3	2008	56.9	1996	29.9	2008	22.2	26.0	27.0	29.0	4.0	4.0	5.0
	..	2004[b]	49.0		..	2004[b]	16.0	51.0	72.0	90.0	9.0	13.0	17.0
	..	2007[b]	63.9		..	2007[b]	21.2	31.0	35.0	39.0	2.0	3.0	4.0
	..	2004[b]	63.8		..	2004[b]	26.6	30.0	36.0	43.0	36.0	32.0	27.0
	..	2011[b]	48.7		..	2005[b]	26.0	64.0	63.0	63.0	34.0	45.0	56.0
	..	2001[b]	64.9		..	2001[b]	24.7	..	70.0	88.0	..	15.0	19.0
	..	2011[b]	57.1		..	2011[b]	18.6	43.0	49.0	56.0	22.0	31.0	39.0
	..		..		..		..	..	..	..	..	..	..
	..	2003	78.5		..	2003	34.6	26.0	30.0	35.0	5.0	5.0	6.0
	..		..		..		..	..	15.0	7.0	..	10.0	6.0
	..		..		..		..	66.0	71.0	79.0	60.0	63.0	67.0
	..	2009[b]	57.6		..	2009[b]	21.3	58.0	55.0	52.0	18.0	16.0	14.0
	..	2009[b]	55.4		..	..[b]							
	..	2001[b]	75.0		..	2001[b]	37.0	25.0	41.0	65.0	44.0	49.0	55.0
	..	2007[b]	37.4		..	2007[b]	11.0	46.0	45.0	44.0	6.0	7.0	7.0
	..	2011[b]	73.4		..	2006[b]	29.3	36.0	38.0	40.0	8.0	5.0	3.0
1999	37.4	2009	27.2	1999	11.2	2009	7.6	39.0	54.0	68.0	26.0	30.0	34.0
1998	83.0	2010	77.9	1998	44.5	2006	38.8	23.0	36.0	46.0	37.0	40.0	43.0
	..		..		..		..	71.0	70.0	69.0	35.0	34.0	32.0
								79.9	**84.2**	**88.4**	**54.6**	**71.7**	**84.4**
1995	30.3		..	1995	4.5		..	88.0	84.0	79.0	77.0	82.0	88.0
	..		..		..		..	70.0	63.0	54.0	45.0	30.0	10.0
	..	2008	30.0		..		..	90.0	95.0	99.0	57.0	79.0	93.0
	..		..		..		..	55.0	55.0	..	96.0	96.0	96.0
	..	2007	14.5		..		..	54.0	58.0	61.0	27.0	43.0	52.0
	..		..		..		..	62.0	77.0	..	44.0	57.0	..

Table 8.2 Agriculture

	Agriculture value added (% of GDP)	Gross Production Index 2004-2006=100					Cereal (thousands of metric tons)			Trade			
										Agricultural		Food	
		Agriculture total	Crop	Livestock	Food	Cereal	Production	Exports	Imports	Exports ($ millions)	Imports ($ millions)	Exports ($ millions)	Imports ($ millions)
	2010[a]	2010	2010	2010	2010	2010	2010	2009	2009	2009	2009	2009	2009
SUB-SAHARAN AFRICA	**11.2**						**123,058**	**2,534**	**28,745**	**26,440**	**31,202**	**16,849**	**25,748**
Angola	9.8	151.2	163.2	114.3	151.8	144.4	1,136	1	700	9	2,061	8	1,555
Benin	..	116.2	117.0	106.5	122.2	149.3	1,555	4	271	432	734	321	683
Botswana	2.5	113.3	89.8	118.5	113.7	219.4	61	7	209	177	616	150	473
Burkina Faso	..	111.9	111.4	113.1	118.8	133.4	4,523	18	375	364	312	104	244
Burundi	35.1	49.9	42.9	136.9	49.8	112.7	313	0	67	60	81	6	76
Cameroon	..	123.3	123.2	123.4	125.7	146.9	2,805	0	907	970	799	749	722
Cape Verde	9.9	120.2	109.5	129.8	120.2	128.4	8	-	135	1	202	0	169
Central African Republic	..	114.4	112.9	116.0	114.3	104.9	239	-	42	19	67	17	59
Chad	..	102.0	96.8	113.1	106.5	118.6	1,912	-	195	76	148	54	120
Comoros	..	93.4	91.5	112.1	93.4	102.5	26	-	46	10	52	10	49
Congo, Dem. Rep.	..	104.2	102.6	117.2	104.1	100.4	1,528	5	479	55	859	13	756
Congo, Rep.	3.8	124.7	115.0	157.3	125.1	112.6	25	0	40	29	92	11	78
Côte d'Ivoire	22.8	105.8	104.6	120.1	105.9	100.6	1,461	127	1,665	5,101	1,342	4,272	1,157
Equatorial Guinea	..	108.2	108.3	107.6	112.1	..	..	..	25	2	84	2	51
Eritrea	..	101.3	81.4	117.7	101.2	95.6	247	1	127	15	77	15	76
Ethiopia	47.7	125.1	127.5	119.6	124.7	126.5	15,638	0	2,229	1,318	1,184	774	1,109
Gabon	4.1	110.5	109.3	113.9	109.6	120.2	41	-	133	27	412	2	332
Gambia, The	28.5	133.3	138.7	107.9	133.3	181.3	364	1	219	49	134	44	105
Ghana	29.9	125.2	124.9	128.8	125.1	156.2	2,907	0	835	1,655	1,281	1,607	1,167
Guinea	13.0	113.1	110.9	129.2	113.0	129.8	2,859	15	413	55	306	25	261
Guinea-Bissau	..	119.9	120.4	117.6	120.4	132.8	237	-	25	102	65	101	48
Kenya	25.2	123.5	112.9	136.0	124.9	115.3	4,100	19	2,711	2,479	1,618	589	1,473
Lesotho	8.6	112.2	116.7	109.3	112.8	153.3	173	0	254	1	144	1	116
Liberia	..	101.6	97.6	134.1	122.2	207.2	296	0	192	83	167	11	145
Madagascar	..	121.6	121.7	121.4	121.5	141.4	5,164	1	221	187	333	166	278
Malawi	..	165.9	166.2	162.4	164.6	209.3	4,039	15	215	1,038	281	160	209
Mali	..	147.9	152.0	140.6	161.0	201.0	6,418	4	263	203	413	127	341
Mauritania	17.2	112.8	145.0	107.1	112.8	180.3	276	..	556	24	504	18	438
Mauritius	3.7	97.1	89.1	121.2	97.1	254.6	1	42	328	307	669	261	517
Mozambique	31.9	114.9	117.8	100.7	113.4	181.2	2,506	16	804	308	663	155	582
Namibia	7.5	93.1	111.1	87.4	93.6	95.6	116	3	119	228	349	182	209
Niger	..	155.2	176.4	131.6	155.5	148.0	5,204	30	172	90	273	80	203
Nigeria	..	89.4	86.9	115.2	89.3	73.8	19,512	5	4,035	985	4,244	819	3,789
Rwanda	32.2	137.1	137.3	135.5	136.9	189.4	746	0	131	82	164	7	146
São Tomé and Príncipe	..	110.0	109.8	112.2	110.0	130.0	4	0	18	6	35	6	28
Senegal	17.4	151.8	158.6	134.7	153.6	170.7	1,768	104	1,348	303	1,190	192	1,074
Seychelles	..	76.9	70.4	81.2	79.4	..	..	0	17	5	78	1	67
Sierra Leone	49.0	113.8	112.2	127.6	116.1	116.4	1,008	-	88	26	143	23	123
Somalia	..	114.5	100.0	116.7	114.4	77.5	258	0	516	88	418	87	355
South Africa	2.5	120.4	107.0	136.2	121.1	123.2	14,733	1,824	2,153	5,458	4,362	3,852	2,742
Sudan	23.6	118.6	97.5	129.5	119.5	69.3	3,562	9	2,329	563	1,503	451	1,259
Swaziland	8.0	103.9	101.8	111.8	104.2	97.8	69	1	159	222	219	208	178
Tanzania	28.1	110.0	109.7	111.1	109.7	117.0	6,688	71	950	827	604	316	530
Togo	42.8	119.9	119.0	126.0	126.9	126.6	1,046	32	163	372	208	325	187
Uganda	24.3	108.1	107.1	112.6	108.2	123.7	2,963	105	514	774	542	208	463
Zambia	9.2	142.9	161.2	108.7	143.8	229.2	3,098	71	70	390	248	205	182
Zimbabwe	16.0	96.6	89.0	107.4	95.8	78.8	1,429	0	1,277	860	926	115	825
NORTH AFRICA	**11.9**						**33,256**	**910**	**22,860**	**7,747**	**22,012**	**6,631**	**18,236**
Algeria	6.9	123.6	131.5	110.2	123.7	120.9	4,686	6	7,910	124	6,459	98	5,470
Djibouti	..	207.5	114.4	223.1	207.5	100.0	0	-	193	63	440	62	397
Egypt, Arab Rep.	14.0	110.0	105.5	123.9	110.9	84.2	19,408	774	6,043	4,522	7,605	3,806	6,329
Libya	..	111.6	108.7	116.5	111.9	97.3	218	1	2,317	9	2,079	1	1,895
Morocco	15.4	125.7	123.0	131.9	125.9	105.1	7,834	100	4,415	1,811	3,785	1,585	2,904
Tunisia	8.0	103.1	100.8	110.0	103.2	56.1	1,109	30	1,981	1,218	1,644	1,079	1,241

a. Provisional.

b. Data are for the most recent year available during the period specified.

Share of land area (%)		Agricultural irrigated land (% of agricultural land)	Fertilizer consumption (100 grams per hectare of arable land)	Agricultural machinery (tractors per 100 sq km of arable land)	Agricultural employment (% of total employment)	Agriculture value added per worker (2000 US$)	Cereal yield (kilograms per hectare)
Permanent cropland 2008	Cereal cropland 2009	2000–08[b]	2009	2000–08[b]	2000–10[b]	2010	2010
1.0	**4.0**		**10.5**			**..**	**1,336**
0.2	1.4	..	1.1	..	..	333	644
2.7	10.0	..	..	..	42.7	..	1,402
0.0	0.2	0.0	..	134.8	29.9	534	544
0.2	15.7	..	9.1	..	84.8	..	1,054
13.6	9.1	..	0.9	..	..	84	1,346
3.0	3.5	..	7.4	..	61.3	..	1,711
0.7	8.5	..	..	11.2	..	3,335	222
0.1	0.3	..	..	..	..	..	1,466
0.0	2.0	..	..	..	..	..	775
32.3	12.0	..	..	..	..	..	1,157
0.3	0.9	..	0.5	..	..	..	772
0.2	0.1	..	1.1	..	35.4	..	785
13.5	2.7	..	15.9	32.1	..	1,056	1,717
2.5	..	..	..	..	..	..	..
0.0	4.6	..	..	8.3	..	..	536
1.0	9.3	0.5	7.9	..	79.3	226	1,674
0.6	0.1	..	6.1	..	24.2	1,825	1,782
0.5	32.3	..	6.8	..	..	440	1,127
12.3	7.0	..	11.9	4.5	57.2	..	1,814
2.8	8.3	..	0.6	25.1	..	242	1,409
8.9	5.4	..	..	..	..	..	1,555
1.1	4.5	0.1	32.5	25.2	61.1	351	1,613
0.1	6.3	..	..	..	..	215	909
2.2	2.6	..	..	..	48.9	672	1,179
1.0	3.0	2.2	2.6	1.9	80.4	..	2,987
1.3	19.5	..	26.6	..	..	169	2,206
0.1	3.3	..	3.2	2.2	66.0	..	1,615
0.0	0.3	..	..	9.8	..	813	946
2.0	0.1	21.4	209.5	..	8.7	5,692	10,000
0.3	3.2	..	..	..	80.5	234	1,006
0.0	0.4	..	1.6	..	16.3	881	373
0.1	8.4	..	0.1	..	56.9	..	490
3.3	15.2	..	2.1	6.6	44.6	..	1,413
11.4	15.7	..	1.1	0.5	78.8	..	1,930
46.9	1.3	..	..	..	27.9	..	3,000
0.3	7.7	0.7	5.0	2.1	33.7	271	1,197
4.4	..	..	36.0	..	..	..	..
1.8	9.1	..	..	..	68.5	..	1,554
0.0	1.0	..	..	12.0	..	..	432
0.8	2.9	..	49.2	43.0	5.1	3,951	4,162
0.1	3.3	1.3	7.9	13.8	..	929	452
0.9	3.3	..	..	87.1	..	1,213	1,226
1.7	5.7	..	8.7	23.3	76.5	289	1,333
3.3	16.2	..	3.3	0.6	54.1	531	1,187
11.3	9.4	..	2.1	..	65.6	200	1,608
0.1	1.6	..	27.3	..	72.2	214	2,547
0.3	4.9	..	28.0	..	64.8	161	752
0.9	**2.1**		**..**			**3,028**	**2,772**
0.4	1.3	2.1	7.8	139.6	20.7	2,254	1,568
..	0.0	..	..	60.0	..	..	1,111
0.8	3.0	..	502.8	390.6	31.6	3,265	6,541
0.2	0.2	..	40.3	218.9	..	..	662
2.2	11.3	4.4	20.8	..	40.9	3,315	1,548
14.4	4.2	4.0	42.3	142.6	..	3,050	1,702

Table 8.3 Producer food prices

	Rice, paddy (per tonne, current US$)					Maize (per tonne, current US$)				
	1991	1995	2000	2005	2009	1991	1995	2000	2005	2009
SUB-SAHARAN AFRICA										
Angola	..	..	..	..	..	..	..	..	..	..
Benin	..	..	..	..	..	..	..	..	..	..
Botswana	..	..	..	..	..	..	..	..	..	..
Burkina Faso	351.5	245.6	119.4	392.2	643.6	212.7	148.5	91.3	192.4	259.9
Burundi	220.4	272.3	277.5	609.2	841.0	270.0	208.2	253.0	314.3	336.9
Cameroon	177.2	136.2	144.6	269.1	309.7	283.6	152.3	163.7	113.2	129.1
Cape Verde	..	..	..	..	..	313.9	432.0	247.9	334.6	449.5
Central African Republic	..	..	..	..	..	..	..	..	..	..
Chad	..	..	..	..	..	..	..	..	..	..
Comoros	..	..	..	..	..	..	..	..	..	..
Congo, Dem. Rep.	..	..	..	..	..	..	..	..	..	..
Congo, Rep.	265.9	150.3	178.4	220.1	313.2	212.7	200.3	262.6	359.6	507.2
Cote d'Ivoire	212.7	220.4	154.5	222.2	586.7	159.5	162.9	119.4	233.0	331.3
Equatorial Guinea	..	..	..	..	..	..	..	..	..	..
Eritrea	..	..	..	..	..	..	295.1	354.3	347.0	573.6
Ethiopia	..	260.8	201.6	127.7	1,028.1	..	154.3	119.3	144.7	388.5
Gabon	..	..	..	..	..	..	..	..	..	..
Gambia, The	170.4	206.2	136.9	175.0	222.7	211.3	419.0	134.5	311.2	252.9
Ghana	416.9	393.3	306.6	577.8	506.8	188.9	215.1	171.7	366.5	384.8
Guinea	220.2	245.1	405.5	138.2	178.5	191.0	245.1	166.7	152.0	149.6
Guinea-Bissau	..	..	351.1	474.8	962.5	..	76.2	842.7	1,168.0	1,324.2
Kenya	72.7	107.2	299.9	378.8	749.8	104.3	155.6	190.3	201.7	309.3
Lesotho	..	..	..	..	..	..	..	..	..	..
Liberia	..	..	..	..	..	..	..	..	..	..
Madagascar	119.9	170.0	190.6	203.4	314.5	337.8	178.6	143.8	152.8	220.4
Malawi	139.1	117.8	594.4	718.5	1,293.9	96.3	47.1	111.9	184.7	365.1
Mali	223.3	236.4	154.5	269.7	316.4	134.7	166.3	107.7	197.5	176.2
Mauritania	..	..	..	..	..	..	..	..	..	..
Mauritius	..	..	..	..	..	303.5	287.6	171.4	185.9	190.6
Mozambique	181.1	135.8	90.6	163.3	322.3	132.7	92.4	51.8	154.5	298.3
Namibia	..	..	..	..	..	166.6	193.3	145.1	276.6	281.8
Niger	260.4	214.4	154.5	201.0	259.8	163.0	138.2	118.0	173.0	226.0
Nigeria	761.3	652.2	279.4	545.1	426.9	334.8	661.3	198.4	477.5	401.3
Rwanda	199.7	873.4	582.1	480.2	1,094.9	259.0	194.5	211.0	104.2	434.1
São Tomé and Príncipe	..	..	..	..	..	..	..	..	..	..
Senegal	..	..	..	..	..	..	..	..	..	..
Seychelles	..	..	..	..	..	..	..	..	..	..
Sierra Leone	..	..	..	..	..	..	..	..	..	..
Somalia	..	..	..	..	..	..	..	..	..	..
South Africa	..	..	..	..	..	129.3	159.1	78.5	99.3	156.3
Sudan	962.2	205.2	388.9	497.3	1,270.4	1,538.6	328.1	621.9	184.6	427.6
Swaziland	..	..	..	..	..	..	..	..	..	..
Tanzania	..	..	..	..	..	..	..	..	..	..
Togo	283.6	232.4	165.7	258.3	341.9	205.6	190.3	120.8	294.4	350.3
Uganda	..	..	..	..	..	..	..	..	..	..
Zambia	..	..	..	..	..	..	..	..	..	..
Zimbabwe	..	..	..	..	..	..	..	..	..	..
NORTH AFRICA										
Algeria	270.7	544.5	344.8	421.4	516.7	173.2	335.7	212.6	259.8	318.6
Djibouti	..	..	..	..	..	..	..	..	..	..
Egypt, Arab Rep.	127.5	193.4	167.9	185.0	211.0	140.5	151.5	174.8	179.3	208.0
Libya	..	..	..	..	..	..	..	..	..	..
Morocco	436.5	445.0	276.4	325.2	294.7	242.3	292.7	223.0	225.8	272.4
Tunisia	..	..	..	..	..	..	..	..	..	..

Sorghum (per tonne, current US$)					Millet (per tonne, current US$)				
1991	1995	2000	2005	2009	1991	1995	2000	2005	2009
..	..	..	..	..	..	..	..	..	..
..	..	..	..	..	..	..	..	..	..
..	..	..	..	..	..	..	..	..	..
212.7	134.4	84.3	178.7	217.8	212.7	152.9	84.3	178.7	210.9
330.6	328.3	374.7	324.2	439.5	..	..	..	..	..
177.2	160.3	313.8	217.0	247.5	..	..	..	..	..
..	..	..	..	..	..	..	..	..	..
..	..	..	..	..	..	..	..	..	..
..	..	..	..	..	..	..	..	..	..
..	..	..	..	..	..	..	..	..	..
..	..	..	..	..	..	..	..	..	..
..	..	..	..	..	..	..	..	..	..
342.4	252.2	2,103.1	336.6	293.4	460.8	391.3	245.7	415.4	307.4
..	..	..	..	..	..	..	..	..	..
..	212.4	284.7	391.7	657.5	..	337.2	434.3	645.3	1,070.2
..	193.2	142.1	188.7	487.9	..	216.0	144.8	170.0	507.9
..	..	..	..	..	..	..	..	..	..
213.6	193.3	129.0	334.3	272.8	218.8	388.9	128.2	310.1	229.9
217.5	212.9	153.1	424.4	469.5	308.6	245.0	205.9	495.3	570.0
187.0	263.8	179.4	120.7	164.1	..	..	..	..	..
..	..	351.1	854.6	1,235.1	..	..	..	..	..
207.7	194.1	204.1	331.8	472.1	256.6	361.3	311.1	485.5	672.6
..	..	..	..	..	..	..	..	..	..
..	..	..	..	..	..	..	..	..	..
..	..	..	..	..	..	..	..	..	..
176.6	72.0	500.6	514.4	753.2	133.2	65.1	518.6	642.7	1,071.8
145.3	198.3	87.4	233.6	235.7	156.0	194.3	85.1	254.5	286.6
..	..	..	..	..	..	..	..	..	..
..	..	..	..	..	..	..	..	..	..
63.9	47.9	51.8	141.3	216.4	..	..	..	..	..
147.8	182.0	157.4	263.2	262.2	147.8	209.5	157.4	263.2	262.2
140.2	96.2	77.3	117.4	153.9	150.1	96.2	108.2	135.1	175.5
368.1	847.7	190.3	509.0	290.8	339.6	413.3	184.5	493.7	323.1
234.0	450.1	211.0	138.8	434.1	..	..	..	..	..
..	..	..	..	..	..	..	..	..	..
..	..	..	..	..	..	..	..	..	..
..	..	..	..	..	..	..	..	..	..
..	..	..	..	..	..	..	..	..	..
..	..	..	..	..	..	..	..	..	..
106.8	132.9	74.9	70.9	179.0	..	..	..	..	..
943.0	92.7	165.6	335.2	312.7	1,206.4	278.6	655.1	433.6	1,065.2
..	..	..	..	..	..	..	..	..	..
..	..	..	..	..	..	..	..	..	..
237.5	246.4	140.5	364.6	378.0	265.9	238.4	122.2	305.8	361.0
..	..	..	..	..	..	..	..	..	..
..	..	..	..	..	..	..	..	..	..
..	..	..	..	..	..	..	..	..	..
152.3	207.7	131.5	160.8	197.1	..	..	..	..	..
..	..	..	..	..	..	..	..	..	..
141.2	166.9	184.0	186.7	251.4	..	..	..	..	..
..	..	..	..	..	..	..	..	..	..
218.2	402.8	218.3	292.5	370.6	..	..	..	..	..
..	..	..	..	..	..	..	..	..	..

Table 8.4 Environment

	Forest area (% of land area)		Renewable internal fresh water resources: Total (billions of cubic meters)	Renewable internal fresh water resources: Per capita (cubic meters)	Annual fresh water withdrawals (billions of cubic meters)	Water productivity (2000 $ per cubic meter of fresh water withdrawal)	Water pollution: Emissions of organic water pollutants (kilograms per day)	Energy: Energy production (kilotons of oil equivalent)		Energy: Energy use (kilotons of oil equivalent)		Energy: Combustible renewables and waste (% of total energy use)	
	1990	2010	2009	2009	2009	2009	2000–07[a]	1990	2009	1990	2009	1990	2009
SUB-SAHARAN AFRICA	**31.2**	**28.0**	**3,884**	**4,708**	**124.6**	**4.3**		**474,530**	**808,735**	**313,233**	**511,206**	**55.9**	**57.3**
Angola	48.9	46.9	148	7,976	0.6	39.5	..	28,652	100,958	5,883	11,896	73.5	60.1
Benin	52.1	41.2	10	1,197	0.1	24.9	..	1,774	1,996	1,661	3,475	94.2	57.4
Botswana	24.2	20.0	2	1,211	0.2	40.5	3,246	910	938	1,261	2,048	33.4	23.6
Burkina Faso	25.0	20.7	13	782	1.0	4.4	..	..	..	..	..	..	..
Burundi	11.3	6.7	10	1,231	0.3	3.9	..	..	..	..	..	..	..
Cameroon	51.4	42.1	273	14,237	1.0	14.1	..	10,976	8,849	4,980	6,918	76.7	64.1
Cape Verde	14.4	21.1	0	610	0.0	42.0	..	..	..	29	..	..	..
Central African Republic	37.3	36.3	141	32,653	0.1	15.3	..	..	..	..	..	..	..
Chad	10.4	9.2	15	1,371	0.4	8.1	..	..	..	..	..	..	..
Comoros	6.5	1.6	1	1,677	0.0	24.2	..	..	..	18	..	..	..
Congo, Dem. Rep.	70.7	68.0	900	14,018	0.6	10.4	..	12,019	23,346	11,798	22,921	84.7	93.7
Congo, Rep.	66.6	65.6	222	56,324	0.1	101.3	..	8,746	15,276	797	1,402	59.5	51.1
Côte d'Ivoire	32.1	32.7	77	3,971	1.4	8.0	..	3,382	11,891	4,323	10,353	73.5	75.2
Equatorial Guinea	66.3	58.0	26	38,173	0.0	346.3	..	..	..	..	..	..	..
Eritrea	16.1	15.2	3	549	0.6	1.3	2,540	..	562	..	726	..	77.4
Ethiopia	13.7	12.3	122	1,503	5.6	3.0	32,159	14,052	30,373	14,866	32,678	93.9	92.0
Gabon	85.4	85.4	164	110,997	0.1	45.8	..	14,630	13,587	1,181	1,794	62.9	61.8
Gambia, The	44.2	48.0	3	1,784	0.1	16.1	..	..	..	62	..	..	..
Ghana	32.7	21.7	30	1,272	1.0	8.3	16,048	4,392	7,047	5,291	9,240	73.7	69.8
Guinea	29.6	26.6	226	23,153	1.6	3.3	..	..	..	..	..	..	..
Guinea-Bissau	78.8	71.9	16	10,781	0.2	1.4	..	..	..	75	..	..	..
Kenya	6.5	6.1	21	525	2.7	6.6	..	9,013	15,573	10,940	18,723	77.9	76.0
Lesotho	1.3	1.5	5	2,433	0.1	20.4	5,252	..	..	..	..	..	..
Liberia	51.2	44.9	200	52,139	0.2	5.3	..	..	..	..	..	..	..
Madagascar	23.5	21.6	337	16,746	14.7	0.3	92,770	..	..	..	..	..	..
Malawi	41.3	34.3	16	1,118	1.0	2.7	32,672	..	..	..	..	..	..
Mali	11.5	10.2	60	4,024	6.6	0.6	..	..	..	..	..	..	..
Mauritania	0.4	0.2	0	118	1.6	1.3	..	..	..	..	..	..	..
Mauritius	19.2	17.2	3	2,158	0.7	8.8	15,446	..	..	480	..	..	..
Mozambique	55.2	49.6	100	4,388	0.7	11.3	..	5,608	11,918	5,922	9,766	93.9	81.8
Namibia	10.6	8.9	6	2,747	0.3	19.3	..	..	329	..	1,713	..	12.0
Niger	1.5	1.0	4	234	2.4	1.1	..	..	..	..	..	..	..
Nigeria	18.9	9.9	221	1,431	10.3	7.7	..	150,452	228,722	70,582	108,252	80.2	84.9
Rwanda	12.9	17.6	10	921	0.2	22.3	..	..	..	..	..	..	..
São Tomé and Príncipe	28.1	28.1	2	13,414	0.0	..	..	..	..	23	..	..	..
Senegal	48.6	44.0	26	2,131	2.2	3.0	6,621	964	1,256	1,686	2,939	56.7	41.1
Seychelles	89.1	89.1	..	..	0.0	52.0	..	..	..	38	..	..	..
Sierra Leone	43.5	38.1	160	27,878	0.5	3.0	..	..	..	..	..	..	..
Somalia	13.2	10.8	6	658	3.3	..	..	..	..	..	..	..	..
South Africa	6.8	4.7	45	908	12.5	14.6	229,582	114,535	160,637	93,876	144,041	11.1	9.8
Sudan	32.2	29.4	30	706	37.1	0.6	38,567	8,775	35,198	10,629	15,815	81.8	68.0
Swaziland	27.4	32.7	3	2,530	1.0	1.8	..	..	..	309	..	..	..
Tanzania	46.8	37.7	84	1,930	5.2	3.6	30,322	9,064	18,046	9,733	19,616	91.7	87.7
Togo	12.6	5.3	12	1,949	0.2	9.1	..	1,054	2,191	1,263	2,627	82.8	83.1
Uganda	23.8	15.0	39	1,205	0.3	36.4	2,105	..	..	..	..	..	..
Zambia	71.0	66.5	80	6,303	1.7	3.0	..	4,918	7,241	5,399	7,856	74.3	80.9
Zimbabwe	57.3	40.4	12	983	4.2	0.9	..	8,550	8,530	9,297	9,514	50.9	65.6
NORTH AFRICA	**1.3**	**1.4**	**47**	**288**	**94.3**	**3.9**		**235,228**	**337,026**	**77,423**	**156,831**	**2.8**	**2.3**
Algeria	0.7	0.6	11	322	6.2	12.4	..	100,114	152,292	22,192	39,758	0.1	0.1
Djibouti	0.3	0.3	0	344	0.0	41.1	..	..	..	130	..	..	..
Egypt, Arab Rep.	0.0	0.1	2	23	68.3	2.2	..	54,869	88,186	31,825	72,015	3.3	2.2
Libya	0.1	0.1	1	96	4.3	11.4	..	73,173	87,136	11,330	20,405	1.1	0.8
Morocco	11.3	11.5	29	917	12.6	4.6	73,989	773	782	6,941	15,083	4.6	3.2
Tunisia	4.1	6.5	4	402	2.9	11.3	..	5,728	7,811	4,946	9,200	12.9	14.1

a. Data are for the most recent year available during the period specified.
b. Hydrofluorocarbons, perfluorocarbons, and sulphur hexafluoride.

Carbon dioxide (thousands of metric tons)		Greenhouse gas emissions: Methane: Total (kilotons of carbon dioxide equivalent)		Methane: Agricultural (% of total)		Methane: Industrial (% of total)		Nitrous oxide: Total (metric tons of carbon dioxide equivalent)		Nitrous oxide: Agricultural (% of total)		Nitrous oxide: Industrial (% of total)		Other greenhouse gases[b] (thousands of metric tons of carbon dioxide equivalent)		ODA gross disbursements for forestry ($ millions)	ODA gross disbursements for general environment protection ($ millions)
1990	2008	1990	2005	1990	2005	1990	2005	1990	2005	1990	2005	1990	2005	1990	2005	2010	2010
462,711	**687,172**	**..**	**..**	**44.0**	**44.0**	**32.1**	**30.2**	**..**	**..**	**64.5**	**66.1**	**0.3**	**0.8**	**..**	**..**	**245.8**	**683.0**
4,430	24,371	49,530	45,409	26.4	27.9	21.6	11.6	41,667	38,881	39.2	38.4	0.0	0.0	0	20	0.5	2.6
715	4,067	4,847	4,080	36.7	47.8	16.1	8.9	3,695	2,902	50.5	61.5	0.0	0.0	0	0	0.6	20.2
2,178	4,840	5,812	4,501	90.5	84.1	7.7	17.9	5,511	3,081	90.9	92.0	..	0.0	0	0	0.1	3.9
587	1,856	..	..	..	..	..	..	..	..	..	..	..	..	..	..	3.8	13.9
304	180	..	..	..	..	..	..	..	..	..	..	..	..	..	..	0.0	5.5
1,738	5,302	13,503	18,518	55.2	42.4	20.2	17.9	10,530	9,127	68.1	75.9	0.0	0.0	932	419	12.2	20.4
88	308	..	..	..	..	..	..	..	..	..	..	..	..	..	..	0.5	9.2
198	260	..	..	..	..	..	..	..	..	..	..	..	..	..	..	1.4	0.7
147	495	..	..	..	..	..	..	..	..	..	..	..	..	..	..	0.0	6.7
77	125	..	..	..	..	..	..	..	..	..	..	..	..	..	..	0.0	1.2
4,070	2,816	96,593	56,445	25.6	23.1	47.9	49.6	87,098	54,643	37.9	31.3	0.0	0.0	0	0	15.8	35.9
1,188	1,936	6,231	5,584	37.3	31.9	10.4	7.7	4,307	3,566	48.6	51.8	0.0	0.0	0	5	0.8	11.3
5,798	7,015	11,243	10,997	18.3	17.4	18.9	11.2	7,485	7,364	22.7	29.3	0.0	0.0	0	0	17.1	4.9
121	4,815	..	..	..	..	..	..	..	..	..	..	..	..	..	..	0.1	0.3
..	414	1,884	2,467	78.7	73.2	11.0	7.5	1,028	1,189	93.0	90.9	0.0	0.0	0	0	0.8	0.7
3,018	7,107	39,325	52,243	81.6	72.5	9.3	10.0	25,545	30,510	91.9	88.8	0.0	0.0	0	10	26.1	16.9
4,844	2,472	8,103	8,218	0.9	1.2	46.5	79.9	305	482	25.6	23.3	0.0	0.0	0	9	8.0	7.6
191	411	..	..	..	..	..	..	..	..	..	..	..	..	..	..	0.1	6.3
3,931	8,592	7,238	8,990	49.0	39.5	13.8	10.7	5,187	4,899	75.5	70.5	0.0	0.0	596	15	15.6	29.1
1,056	1,393	..	..	..	..	..	..	..	..	..	..	..	..	..	..	1.1	1.3
253	282	..	..	..	..	..	..	..	..	..	..	..	..	..	..	0.1	2.0
5,823	10,392	17,952	22,130	74.3	65.5	15.7	18.0	9,222	10,542	91.9	88.8	0.0	0.0	0	0	22.0	62.0
..	..	..	..	..	..	..	..	..	..	..	..	..	..	..	..	0.1	0.8
484	609	..	..	..	..	..	..	..	..	..	..	..	..	..	..	0.2	4.9
986	1,911	..	..	..	..	..	..	..	..	..	..	..	..	..	..	1.3	12.4
612	1,228	..	..	..	..	..	..	..	..	..	..	..	..	..	..	20.7	13.7
422	594	..	..	..	..	..	..	..	..	..	..	..	..	..	..	2.2	10.7
2,666	1,999	..	..	..	..	..	..	..	..	..	..	..	..	..	..	0.0	9.0
1,463	3,953	..	..	..	..	..	..	..	..	..	..	..	..	..	..	..	37.9
1,001	2,314	10,863	12,843	66.3	44.2	17.5	16.9	10,881	9,501	82.0	71.4	0.0	0.0	0	282	13.4	16.8
7	3,968	3,435	5,057	95.8	94.9	3.7	4.7	2,580	3,797	93.2	94.3	0.0	0.0	0	0	1.0	13.6
832	851	..	..	..	..	..	..	..	..	..	..	..	..	..	..	0.1	6.4
45,375	95,756	117,467	130,317	18.5	19.8	47.3	45.5	19,153	21,565	82.1	77.3	0.0	0.0	242	669	0.5	8.0
682	704	..	..	..	..	..	..	..	..	..	..	..	..	..	..	1.4	8.7
66	128	..	..	..	..	..	..	..	..	..	..	..	..	..	..	0.0	0.2
3,183	4,976	5,277	7,129	68.8	68.3	4.5	4.7	2,976	4,083	88.1	88.5	0.0	0.0	0	0	0.3	43.8
114	682	..	..	..	..	..	..	..	..	..	..	..	..	..	..	..	0.1
389	1,335	..	..	..	..	..	..	..	..	..	..	..	..	..	..	0.0	2.6
18	649	..	..	..	..	..	..	..	..	..	..	..	..	..	..	..	0.0
333,514	435,878	51,179	63,785	37.3	31.4	52.4	54.3	21,300	24,048	63.3	59.8	3.6	7.3	1,491	2,552	8.2	27.5
5,559	14,052	43,370	67,441	87.1	85.2	21.4	21.5	36,669	49,472	92.0	92.6	0.0	0.0	0	0	4.5	10.2
425	1,093	..	..	..	..	..	..	..	..	..	..	..	..	..	..	0.0	0.3
2,373	6,465	25,817	32,024	73.9	63.2	21.3	20.3	21,468	21,647	82.8	78.8	0.0	0.0	0	0	3.5	30.1
774	1,419	2,752	2,889	52.9	39.9	18.4	14.8	2,209	1,738	74.3	67.5	0.0	0.0	0	0	0.0	9.2
818	3,748	..	..	..	..	..	..	..	..	..	..	..	..	..	..	4.8	13.9
2,446	1,889	26,944	19,294	66.1	59.3	8.2	5.7	35,669	25,068	75.2	71.7	0.0	3.7	0	0	0.5	10.3
15,504	9,076	10,112	9,539	79.1	73.3	22.2	24.8	7,284	6,114	84.2	85.2	5.9	0.0	0	0	0.0	0.9
232,367	**453,399**	**104,128**	**134,629**	**21.7**	**20.6**	**51.5**	**48.2**	**24,023**	**33,358**	**72.0**	**75.3**	**5.6**	**7.9**	**2,668**	**3,950**	**4.5**	**71.4**
78,896	111,304	40,726	54,219	9.1	8.2	61.2	66.3	3,843	4,898	64.3	58.6	4.4	7.2	326	489	0.0	4.6
400	524	..	..	..	..	..	..	..	..	..	..	..	..	..	..	0.1	0.4
75,944	210,321	27,839	46,996	38.0	31.7	33.4	31.2	11,818	18,996	71.5	80.0	8.2	11.5	2,059	3,181	0.0	12.6
40,319	58,331	22,473	14,682	4.9	5.7	79.1	77.6	1,176	1,285	67.2	51.9	0.0	0.0	282	280	..	0.0
23,542	47,906	9,132	10,573	58.8	51.8	6.2	2.6	5,180	5,814	85.1	82.6	0.0	0.0	0	0	0.3	25.5
13,267	25,013	3,958	8,160	44.9	25.5	26.2	32.1	2,006	2,366	59.0	66.4	10.6	4.2	0	0	3.4	23.1

Table 8.5 Fossil fuel emissions

	Carbon dioxide emissions						Carbon dioxide emissions from fossil fuel (thousand metric tons)					
	Total (thousand metric tons of carbon dioxide)			Per capita (metric tons)			Total			Solid fuel consumption		
	1990	2005	2008	1990	2005	2008	1990	2005	2008	1990	2005	2008
SUB-SAHARAN AFRICA	**462,711**	**647,225**	**687,172**	**0.9**	**0.9**	**0.9**	**129,277**	**180,471**	**191,223**	**110,635**	**142,854**	**149,617**
Angola	4,430	19,156	24,371	0.4	1.2	1.4	1,208	5,224	6,646	0	0	0
Benin	715	2,567	4,067	0.2	0.3	0.5	195	700	1,109	0	0	0
Botswana	2,178	4,525	4,840	1.6	2.4	2.5	594	1,234	1,320	592	702	624
Burkina Faso	587	1,126	1,856	0.1	0.1	0.1	160	307	506	0	0	0
Burundi	304	165	180	0.1	0.0	0.0	83	45	49	4	2	4
Cameroon	1,738	3,696	5,302	0.1	0.2	0.3	..	..	..	..	..	..
Cape Verde	88	293	308	0.3	0.6	0.6	24	80	84	0	0	0
Central African Republic	198	235	260	0.1	0.1	0.1	54	64	71	0	0	0
Chad	147	400	495	0.0	0.0	0.1	40	109	135	0	0	0
Comoros	77	110	125	0.2	0.2	0.2	21	30	34	0	0	0
Congo, Dem. Rep.	4,070	2,369	2,816	0.1	0.0	0.1	1,110	646	768	209	273	317
Congo, Rep.	1,188	1,606	1,936	0.5	0.5	0.5	324	438	528	0	0	0
Cote d'Ivoire	5,798	7,825	7,015	0.5	0.4	0.4	1,581	2,134	1,913	0	0	0
Equatorial Guinea	121	4,712	4,815	0.3	7.8	7.3	33	1,285	1,313	0	0	0
Eritrea	..	766	414	..	0.2	0.1	..	209	113	..	0	0
Ethiopia	3,018	5,490	7,107	0.1	0.1	0.1	823	1,497	1,938	0	0	0
Gabon	4,844	1,786	2,472	5.2	1.3	1.7	1,321	487	674	0	0	0
Gambia, The	191	323	411	0.2	0.2	0.3	52	88	112	0	0	0
Ghana	3,931	7,008	8,592	0.3	0.3	0.4	1,072	1,911	2,343	2	0	0
Guinea	1,056	1,360	1,393	0.2	0.2	0.2	288	371	380	0	0	0
Guinea-Bissau	253	264	282	0.3	0.2	0.2	69	72	77	0	0	0
Kenya	5,823	8,562	10,392	0.3	0.2	0.3	1,588	2,335	2,834	110	91	112
Lesotho	..	..	..	..	..	..	..	..	..	..	..	..
Liberia	484	741	609	0.2	0.2	0.2	132	202	166	0	0	0
Madagascar	986	1,705	1,911	0.1	0.1	0.1	269	465	521	9	12	9
Malawi	612	917	1,228	0.1	0.1	0.1	167	250	335	13	43	37
Mali	422	568	594	0.1	0.0	0.0	115	155	162	0	0	0
Mauritania	2,666	1,657	1,999	1.3	0.5	0.6	727	452	545	4	0	0
Mauritius	1,463	3,410	3,953	1.4	2.7	3.1	399	930	1,078	54	264	471
Mozambique	1,001	1,823	2,314	0.1	0.1	0.1	273	497	631	42	0	7
Namibia	7	2,659	3,968	0.0	1.3	1.8	2	725	1,082	0	14	299
Niger	832	825	851	0.1	0.1	0.1	227	225	232	88	103	104
Nigeria	45,375	104,044	95,756	0.5	0.7	0.6	12,374	28,373	26,113	35	8	8
Rwanda	682	689	704	0.1	0.1	0.1	186	188	192	0	0	0
São Tomé and Príncipe	66	128	128	0.6	0.8	0.8	18	35	35	0	0	0
Senegal	3,183	5,860	4,976	0.4	0.5	0.4	868	1,598	1,357	0	114	184
Seychelles	114	697	682	1.6	8.4	7.8	31	190	186	0	0	0
Sierra Leone	389	1,261	1,335	0.1	0.2	0.2	106	344	364	0	0	0
Somalia	18	579	649	0.0	0.1	0.1	5	158	177	0	0	0
South Africa	333,514	408,199	435,878	9.5	8.7	8.9	90,950	111,317	118,865	72,352	95,970	100,605
Sudan	5,559	11,995	14,052	0.2	0.3	0.3	1,516	3,271	3,832	0	0	0
Swaziland	425	1,019	1,093	0.5	1.0	1.1	116	278	298	116	104	112
Tanzania	2,373	5,086	6,465	0.1	0.1	0.2	647	1,387	1,763	3	54	65
Togo	774	1,338	1,419	0.2	0.3	0.3	211	365	387	0	0	0
Uganda	818	2,340	3,748	0.1	0.1	0.1	223	638	1,022	0	0	0
Zambia	2,446	2,259	1,889	0.3	0.2	0.2	667	616	515	227	85	1
Zimbabwe	15,504	10,774	9,076	1.5	0.9	0.7	4,228	2,938	2,475	3,662	2,315	1,943
NORTH AFRICA	**232,367**	**399,960**	**453,399**	**1.9**	**2.6**	**2.8**	**63,367**	**109,070**	**123,643**	**3,576**	**6,204**	**6,228**
Algeria	78,896	107,128	111,304	3.1	3.3	3.2	21,515	29,214	30,353	825	666	793
Djibouti	400	473	524	0.7	0.6	0.6	109	129	143	0	0	0
Egypt, Arab Rep.	75,944	174,641	210,321	1.3	2.4	2.7	20,710	47,625	57,355	917	837	787
Libya	40,319	52,093	58,331	9.3	9.0	9.5	10,995	14,206	15,907	4	0	0
Morocco	23,542	42,823	47,906	1.0	1.4	1.5	6,420	11,678	13,064	1,278	3,844	3,788
Tunisia	13,267	22,801	25,013	1.6	2.3	2.4	3,618	6,218	6,821	72	0	0

Note: 0 refers to a negligible value that rounds to 0.

Carbon dioxide emissions from fossil fuel (thousand metric tons)

Liquid fuel consumption			Gas fuel consumption			Gas flaring			Cement production		
1990	2005	2008	1990	2005	2008	1990	2005	2008	1990	2005	2008
41,937	46,087	50,785	..	..	..	..	..	..	2,901	4,842	6,113
489	1,292	2,476	276	341	347	409	3,412	3,633	35	179	190
154	666	891	0	0	0	0	0	0	41	34	218
2	532	696	0	0	0	0	0	0	0	0	0
160	303	502	0	0	0	0	0	0	0	4	4
79	43	45	0	0	0	0	0	0	0	0	0
..	..	..	..	..	..	..	..	..	..	..	..
24	80	84	0	0	0	0	0	0	0	0	0
54	64	71	0	0	0	0	0	0	0	0	0
40	109	135	0	0	0	0	0	0	0	0	0
21	30	34	0	0	0	0	0	0	0	0	0
838	373	447	0	0	4	0	0	0	63	0	0
265	358	444	1	12	13	46	0	0	12	69	71
1,513	1,136	995	0	910	829	0	0	0	68	88	88
33	142	166	0	605	865	0	538	283	0	0	0
..	203	107	..	0	0	..	0	0	..	6	6
777	1,284	1,690	0	0	0	0	0	0	46	213	248
244	387	539	138	65	104	924	0	0	16	35	31
52	87	111	0	1	1	0	0	0	0	0	0
978	1,653	2,085	0	0	0	0	0	0	92	258	258
288	322	331	0	0	0	0	0	0	0	49	49
69	72	77	0	0	0	0	0	0	0	0	0
1,273	1,956	2,296	0	0	0	0	0	0	205	289	426
..	..	..	..	..	..	..	..	..	..	..	..
125	182	144	0	0	0	0	0	0	7	20	22
252	433	475	0	0	0	0	0	0	8	20	37
141	184	265	0	0	0	0	0	0	13	23	33
112	155	162	0	0	0	0	0	0	3	0	0
709	411	501	0	0	0	0	0	0	14	41	44
345	666	607	0	0	0	0	0	0	0	0	0
220	392	472	0	38	53	0	0	0	11	67	99
2	711	783	0	0	0	0	0	0	0	0	0
136	115	121	0	0	0	0	0	0	3	7	7
9,823	10,616	8,695	2,041	5,307	6,718	0	12,075	10,013	476	367	680
177	173	177	0	0	0	0	0	0	8	14	14
18	35	35	0	0	0	0	0	0	0	0	0
801	1,120	733	3	7	6	0	0	0	64	357	435
31	190	186	0	0	0	0	0	0	0	0	0
106	321	332	0	0	0	0	0	0	0	23	32
0	158	177	0	0	0	0	0	0	5	0	0
16,596	11,519	13,846	940	2,269	2,601	0	0	0	1,062	1,559	1,814
1,493	3,226	3,787	0	0	0	0	0	0	23	45	45
0	173	186	0	0	0	0	0	0	0	0	0
571	962	1,192	0	185	287	0	0	0	73	186	218
157	256	278	0	0	0	0	0	0	54	109	109
219	552	934	0	0	0	0	0	0	4	86	88
381	471	419	0	0	0	0	0	0	59	59	95
471	542	478	0	0	0	0	0	0	95	82	54
34,280	51,706	61,967	17,525	39,938	40,510	..	..	..	4,177	9,075	11,173
6,835	8,413	11,299	10,619	16,706	13,295	2,373	1,688	2,600	862	1,741	2,366
109	129	143	0	0	0	0	0	0	0	0	0
14,323	24,317	29,438	3,552	18,057	21,690	0	0	0	1,918	4,414	5,440
6,058	9,347	10,217	2,599	3,010	2,806	1,969	1,357	2,068	367	492	816
4,541	6,102	7,484	30	237	296	0	0	0	571	1,496	1,496
2,414	3,398	3,386	682	1,831	2,325	1	79	82	449	910	1,028

Table 9.1 Labor force participation

	Ages 15 and older								
	Labor force								
	Total (in thousands)			Male (% of total labor force)			Female (% of total labor force)		
	2000	2005	2010	2000	2005	2010	2000	2005	2010
SUB-SAHARAN AFRICA	**255,432**	**293,820**	**337,519**	**55.0**	**54.2**	**54.3**	**45.0**	**45.8**	**45.7**
Angola	5,198	6,063	7,106	51.6	53.1	54.1	48.4	46.9	45.9
Benin	2,561	3,049	3,618	53.5	52.5	52.5	46.6	47.5	47.5
Botswana	817	924	1,037	53.1	53.3	53.7	46.9	46.7	46.3
Burkina Faso	5,502	6,433	7,544	51.8	52.2	52.4	48.2	47.8	47.6
Burundi	2,916	3,518	4,312	46.8	47.4	47.9	53.2	52.6	52.1
Cameroon	6,195	7,147	8,210	54.9	54.6	54.3	45.1	45.4	45.7
Cape Verde	163	193	225	61.9	61.7	61.6	38.2	38.3	38.4
Central African Republic	1,678	1,840	2,065	53.6	53.2	52.9	46.4	46.8	47.1
Chad	3,217	3,827	4,423	54.5	54.6	54.7	45.5	45.4	45.3
Comoros	180	210	242	72.0	70.9	69.8	28.0	29.1	30.2
Congo, Dem. Rep.	18,514	21,499	25,266	49.9	49.8	50.2	50.1	50.2	49.9
Congo, Rep.	1,250	1,441	1,693	51.9	51.2	51.5	48.1	48.8	48.6
Côte d'Ivoire	6,385	6,989	7,788	65.0	63.8	62.6	35.0	36.2	37.4
Equatorial Guinea	260	313	369	55.7	55.5	55.3	44.3	44.5	44.7
Eritrea	1,660	2,179	2,596	52.7	51.7	51.4	47.4	48.3	48.6
Ethiopia	28,965	34,881	40,781	54.8	53.1	52.8	45.2	47.0	47.2
Gabon	443	505	588	54.5	53.8	53.7	45.6	46.2	46.3
Gambia, The	544	640	751	53.0	52.5	52.1	47.0	47.6	47.9
Ghana	8,426	9,112	10,366	51.9	52.1	52.4	48.2	47.9	47.6
Guinea	3,294	3,619	4,092	55.4	55.3	54.8	44.6	44.7	45.2
Guinea-Bissau	498	568	648	54.5	53.4	52.7	45.5	46.6	47.3
Kenya	11,858	13,236	15,456	53.2	53.5	53.6	46.8	46.6	46.5
Lesotho	848	850	894	51.0	52.5	54.0	49.1	47.5	46.0
Liberia	964	1,088	1,374	51.0	51.3	52.3	49.0	48.7	47.7
Madagascar	7,300	8,584	10,148	51.3	51.1	51.1	48.7	49.0	48.9
Malawi	4,819	5,718	6,708	50.3	51.5	48.5	49.7	48.5	51.5
Mali	3,056	3,609	4,297	62.5	63.9	64.5	37.5	36.1	35.5
Mauritania	760	934	1,117	76.7	74.9	73.5	23.3	25.1	26.5
Mauritius	527	550	595	65.5	64.2	62.4	34.5	35.9	37.7
Mozambique	8,727	9,882	11,077	45.0	45.7	46.4	55.0	54.3	53.6
Namibia	638	782	929	55.6	54.2	53.7	44.4	45.9	46.3
Niger	3,528	4,284	5,114	69.1	69.1	68.8	31.0	30.9	31.2
Nigeria	39,248	43,730	50,280	59.9	56.7	57.2	40.1	43.3	42.8
Rwanda	3,798	4,497	5,228	47.7	47.8	48.2	52.3	52.2	51.8
São Tomé and Príncipe	45	52	59	64.7	63.9	62.8	35.3	36.2	37.2
Senegal	3,950	4,617	5,385	57.1	56.6	56.1	42.9	43.4	43.9
Seychelles	..	..	..	..	..	..	..	..	..
Sierra Leone	1,561	1,977	2,261	46.8	48.8	49.3	53.2	51.3	50.7
Somalia	2,347	2,639	2,924	67.2	66.9	66.4	32.8	33.1	33.6
South Africa	15,233	17,212	18,163	56.9	56.3	57.2	43.1	43.8	42.8
Sudan	8,318	9,561	10,791	72.1	71.8	71.3	27.9	28.2	28.7
Swaziland	315	333	368	59.7	60.1	60.3	40.3	39.9	39.7
Tanzania	16,702	19,283	22,138	50.3	49.9	50.2	49.7	50.1	49.8
Togo	2,151	2,536	2,939	51.0	49.5	49.5	49.0	50.5	50.5
Uganda	10,128	11,451	13,426	50.0	50.5	50.7	50.0	49.5	49.3
Zambia	4,476	4,951	5,511	52.8	53.7	53.9	47.2	46.4	46.1
Zimbabwe	5,469	6,517	6,617	53.6	51.2	50.7	46.4	48.8	49.3
NORTH AFRICA	**44,267**	**50,735**	**56,192**	**78.1**	**77.8**	**76.3**	**21.9**	**22.2**	**23.7**
Algeria	8,796	9,983	11,204	86.3	85.0	83.1	13.7	15.0	16.9
Djibouti	210	248	292	67.6	66.3	65.2	32.4	33.7	34.8
Egypt, Arab Rep.	20,077	23,941	27,104	78.5	78.6	75.8	21.5	21.4	24.2
Libya	1,801	2,127	2,379	73.9	72.1	72.0	26.1	27.9	28.0
Morocco	10,197	10,995	11,386	72.1	72.3	72.9	27.9	27.7	27.1
Tunisia	3,186	3,441	3,827	75.1	73.6	73.1	24.9	26.4	26.9

Ages 15 and older								
Participation rate								
Total (% of total population)			Male (% of male population)			Female (% of female population)		
2000	2005	2010	2000	2005	2010	2000	2005	2010
69.0	**69.2**	**69.5**	**76.9**	**76.0**	**76.1**	**61.3**	**62.7**	**63.0**
71.3	70.2	69.7	75.4	76.3	77.0	67.4	64.4	62.7
72.2	72.1	72.6	81.2	78.6	78.3	64.0	66.1	67.1
74.9	75.7	76.6	80.4	80.8	81.5	69.5	70.7	71.6
83.7	83.8	83.8	90.6	90.6	90.5	77.3	77.4	77.5
85.0	83.3	82.8	84.3	82.3	81.9	85.6	84.1	83.7
69.1	69.7	70.5	76.9	76.9	77.3	61.6	62.6	63.9
63.8	64.9	66.4	83.8	83.0	83.1	46.0	48.0	50.2
78.2	78.4	78.7	86.1	85.5	85.2	70.7	71.7	72.5
72.3	72.2	72.2	80.2	80.1	80.2	64.6	64.5	64.5
54.4	56.0	57.5	78.6	79.7	80.4	30.3	32.5	34.7
71.7	71.3	71.3	72.9	72.3	72.4	70.6	70.5	70.2
68.2	69.5	70.5	71.4	71.6	72.7	65.1	67.5	68.2
66.2	66.6	66.8	81.9	81.7	81.3	48.8	50.2	51.5
87.1	86.7	86.7	93.3	92.5	92.3	80.4	80.4	80.6
82.1	83.7	84.6	90.3	89.8	90.0	74.6	78.0	79.6
81.7	84.6	84.0	90.9	91.1	89.9	72.8	78.4	78.3
60.8	60.0	60.5	67.2	65.0	64.9	54.6	55.1	56.0
77.1	77.4	77.6	83.4	83.4	83.2	71.1	71.8	72.4
74.6	69.8	69.2	76.6	72.0	71.6	72.6	67.7	66.8
70.8	71.0	71.8	78.3	78.3	78.3	63.3	63.7	65.2
70.6	72.1	72.9	78.5	78.3	78.2	63.1	66.1	67.8
68.1	64.9	66.3	73.2	69.9	71.5	63.1	60.0	61.2
73.5	68.1	65.8	80.1	75.3	73.3	67.6	61.6	58.7
60.0	60.3	60.9	61.8	62.4	64.0	58.2	58.3	57.8
86.8	86.6	86.1	89.7	89.2	88.7	84.0	84.1	83.5
79.2	82.7	83.1	81.2	86.3	81.2	77.2	79.2	85.0
51.2	51.8	52.9	66.3	68.0	69.7	37.2	36.4	36.8
50.2	52.1	53.7	78.1	78.6	79.1	23.1	26.0	28.4
60.6	58.8	59.5	80.7	76.8	75.7	41.2	41.4	43.9
85.4	85.5	84.7	82.7	83.3	83.0	87.7	87.4	86.3
56.4	61.5	64.0	64.5	68.1	69.8	48.8	55.2	58.4
62.7	64.5	64.6	88.4	90.6	90.1	38.0	39.2	39.8
55.8	54.7	55.5	66.8	61.9	63.0	44.8	47.5	47.8
85.9	84.8	85.8	85.4	83.8	85.2	86.4	85.7	86.3
55.7	57.9	59.4	73.8	75.6	76.4	38.4	40.9	43.2
76.1	76.4	76.9	88.5	88.3	88.3	64.1	64.9	66.0
..	..	..	..	..	..	..	..	..
65.4	67.2	67.6	63.3	67.8	68.9	67.3	66.6	66.4
56.8	57.0	56.9	77.8	77.6	77.0	36.6	37.1	37.6
52.2	53.4	52.0	61.0	61.5	60.4	43.8	45.7	43.8
52.3	53.0	53.6	75.7	76.1	76.5	29.1	29.9	30.8
56.3	56.2	56.6	71.7	70.8	70.7	42.7	42.9	43.5
88.8	89.5	89.3	90.8	90.5	90.3	87.0	88.6	88.3
79.0	80.2	80.8	82.0	80.9	81.2	76.0	79.6	80.3
81.6	78.6	77.9	82.6	80.0	79.6	80.7	77.1	76.2
80.2	79.9	79.5	85.4	86.0	85.7	75.1	73.8	73.3
75.0	86.6	86.1	81.5	90.1	89.5	68.7	83.1	82.9
47.5	**47.9**	**47.8**	**74.7**	**75.0**	**73.5**	**20.7**	**21.1**	**22.5**
43.8	43.2	43.3	75.5	73.2	71.7	12.0	13.0	14.7
48.8	49.9	51.2	66.5	66.5	67.0	31.4	33.4	35.5
46.4	48.2	48.8	73.1	75.8	74.2	19.9	20.6	23.5
50.9	53.1	53.8	73.0	75.3	76.9	27.4	30.2	30.4
53.3	51.9	49.5	78.9	77.4	74.7	29.0	27.9	25.9
47.6	46.2	47.4	71.6	68.3	69.7	23.7	24.3	25.3

Table 9.1 Labor force participation (continued)

	Ages 15–64								
	Labor force								
	Total (thousands)			Male (% of total labor force)			Female (% of total labor force)		
	2000	2005	2010	2000	2005	2010	2000	2005	2010
SUB-SAHARAN AFRICA	**247,188**	**284,133**	**326,648**	**55.7**	**54.9**	**55.0**	**45.7**	**46.3**	**46.3**
Angola	5033.0	5871.0	6886.0	51.6	53.2	54.1	48.4	46.8	45.9
Benin	2446.0	2920.0	3462.0	53.6	52.6	52.5	46.4	47.4	47.5
Botswana	796.0	898.0	1004.0	53.0	53.1	53.5	47.0	46.9	46.5
Burkina Faso	5359.0	6278.0	7369.0	51.7	52.0	52.3	48.3	48.0	47.7
Burundi	2789.0	3381.0	4163.0	47.2	47.7	48.2	52.9	52.3	51.8
Cameroon	5889.0	6799.0	7831.0	54.5	54.2	54.0	45.5	45.8	46.0
Cape Verde	156.0	186.0	218.0	60.9	61.3	61.0	38.5	38.7	38.5
Central African Republic	1572.0	1723.0	1936.0	53.9	53.5	53.3	46.1	46.5	46.8
Chad	3041.0	3633.0	4214.0	54.5	54.6	54.8	45.5	45.4	45.2
Comoros	172.0	202.0	234.0	72.1	70.8	69.7	27.9	29.2	30.3
Congo, Dem. Rep.	17669.0	20536.0	24163.0	50.0	50.0	50.2	50.0	50.0	49.8
Congo, Rep.	1190.0	1373.0	1617.0	52.2	51.4	51.5	47.8	48.7	48.5
Côte d'Ivoire	6086.0	6630.0	7369.0	64.7	63.4	62.3	35.3	36.6	37.7
Equatorial Guinea	250.0	303.0	358.0	56.0	55.8	55.3	44.0	44.2	44.4
Eritrea	1619.0	2129.0	2534.0	52.5	51.5	51.4	47.5	48.5	48.7
Ethiopia	28065.0	33599.0	39262.0	54.5	52.7	52.5	45.5	47.3	47.5
Gabon	415.0	478.0	559.0	55.2	54.4	54.0	44.8	45.6	46.0
Gambia, The	521.0	616.0	724.0	52.6	52.1	51.8	47.4	47.9	48.2
Ghana	8046.0	8701.0	9885.0	51.8	52.0	52.2	48.2	48.0	47.8
Guinea	3162.0	3474.0	3930.0	55.5	55.4	54.9	44.5	44.6	45.1
Guinea-Bissau	479.0	547.0	624.0	54.5	53.4	52.7	45.5	46.6	47.3
Kenya	11286.0	12676.0	14860.0	53.3	53.5	53.7	46.7	46.5	46.4
Lesotho	797.0	802.0	850.0	51.1	52.7	54.4	48.9	47.3	45.7
Liberia	926.0	1046.0	1320.0	50.9	51.2	52.1	49.2	48.9	47.9
Madagascar	6988.0	8225.0	9739.0	51.0	50.8	50.9	49.0	49.2	49.1
Malawi	4523.0	5425.0	6290.0	50.3	51.5	48.5	49.7	48.5	51.5
Mali	2992.0	3541.0	4220.0	62.5	63.9	64.6	37.5	36.1	35.4
Mauritania	738.0	907.0	1085.0	76.7	75.0	73.6	23.2	25.0	26.5
Mauritius	525.0	550.0	595.0	65.3	64.0	62.2	34.5	36.0	37.8
Mozambique	8252.0	9324.0	10445.0	45.0	45.7	46.6	55.1	54.3	53.5
Namibia	618.0	758.0	902.0	55.7	54.2	53.9	44.3	45.8	46.2
Niger	3411.0	4152.0	4956.0	69.0	69.2	69.0	31.0	30.8	31.1
Nigeria	37176.0	41202.0	47331.0	60.1	56.8	57.2	39.9	43.2	42.8
Rwanda	3678.0	4356.0	5070.0	47.7	47.7	48.1	52.3	52.3	51.9
São Tomé and Príncipe	44.0	50.0	57.0	63.6	64.0	63.2	36.4	36.0	36.8
Senegal	3821.0	4474.0	5231.0	57.1	56.6	56.2	42.9	43.4	43.8
Seychelles	..	..	..	..	..	..	..	..	..
Sierra Leone	1527.0	1938.0	2221.0	46.4	48.4	48.9	53.6	51.7	51.1
Somalia	2298.0	2583.0	2867.0	67.1	66.7	66.3	32.9	33.3	33.7
South Africa	15334.0	17311.0	18055.0	56.9	56.3	57.2	43.2	43.8	42.8
Sudan	9888.0	11427.0	13399.0	71.6	71.2	70.7	28.4	28.8	29.3
Swaziland	321.0	350.0	401.0	59.5	60.0	60.4	40.5	40.0	39.7
Tanzania	16079.0	18501.0	21193.0	50.1	50.0	50.2	49.9	50.0	49.8
Togo	2065.0	2437.0	2823.0	50.9	49.5	49.5	49.1	50.5	50.6
Uganda	9722.0	10961.0	12866.0	49.9	50.5	50.8	50.1	49.5	49.2
Zambia	4247.0	4688.0	5284.0	53.1	53.9	54.2	46.9	46.1	45.8
Zimbabwe	5177.0	6172.0	6246.0	53.8	51.3	50.9	46.2	48.7	49.2
NORTH AFRICA	**43344.0**	**49800.0**	**55048.0**	**78.3**	**78.0**	**76.5**	**23.1**	**23.2**	**24.2**
Algeria	8732.0	9912.0	11129.0	86.3	84.9	83.1	13.7	15.1	16.9
Djibouti	207.0	245.0	289.0	67.6	66.1	65.1	32.4	33.9	35.0
Egypt, Arab Rep.	19696.0	23600.0	26643.0	78.4	78.3	75.7	21.7	21.7	24.3
Libya	1769.0	2090.0	2333.0	73.7	71.9	71.8	26.3	28.1	28.2
Morocco	9893.0	10650.0	10956.0	72.0	72.4	73.6	28.0	27.6	26.4
Tunisia	3047.0	3303.0	3698.0	74.7	73.2	72.9	25.4	26.8	27.1

Ages 15–64								
Participation rate								
Total (% of total population)			Male (% of male population)			Female (% of female population)		
2000	2005	2010	2000	2005	2010	2000	2005	2010
70.0	**70.2**	**70.5**	**77.6**	**76.6**	**76.7**	**62.5**	**63.9**	**64.3**
72.5	71.3	70.8	76.3	77.2	77.9	68.8	65.6	64.0
73.0	73.0	73.4	81.5	78.8	78.6	65.2	67.4	68.5
76.7	77.8	78.9	81.3	81.8	82.8	72.1	73.7	74.8
85.1	85.2	85.3	91.2	91.2	91.1	79.5	79.6	79.8
86.0	84.2	83.8	85.0	83.0	82.6	86.8	85.3	84.9
70.0	70.5	71.5	76.8	76.9	77.4	63.2	64.2	65.6
67.2	68.9	70.5	86.4	85.9	86.1	49.8	52.4	54.8
78.6	78.7	79.1	86.4	85.8	85.5	71.1	71.9	72.8
72.6	72.5	72.6	80.1	80.1	80.2	65.2	65.2	65.2
54.8	56.6	58.2	78.7	79.9	80.8	30.8	33.1	35.4
72.1	71.7	71.7	73.0	72.3	72.6	71.3	71.2	70.9
69.3	70.7	71.8	72.5	72.7	73.8	66.1	68.8	69.7
66.6	67.2	67.5	82.2	82.2	81.9	49.5	51.0	52.4
89.2	88.5	88.3	95.3	94.4	94.0	82.6	82.1	82.0
83.8	85.3	86.3	91.0	90.5	90.8	77.0	80.3	82.0
83.7	86.3	85.8	92.2	91.9	90.7	75.5	80.8	80.9
61.9	61.2	61.7	68.7	66.5	66.4	55.2	56.0	57.1
77.2	77.5	77.8	83.2	83.2	83.0	71.5	72.2	72.8
75.5	70.8	70.4	77.2	72.5	72.3	73.9	69.0	68.4
72.3	72.4	73.2	79.5	79.5	79.5	64.9	65.3	66.8
72.0	73.5	74.4	79.7	79.5	79.4	64.6	67.7	69.4
68.3	65.3	66.8	73.3	70.2	71.9	63.3	60.4	61.8
74.7	69.4	67.1	81.0	76.4	74.5	69.0	62.9	60.0
60.5	60.9	61.5	61.8	62.5	64.2	59.1	59.3	58.9
88.1	88.0	87.5	90.5	90.0	89.5	85.9	86.0	85.4
78.8	83.2	82.6	80.6	86.5	80.3	77.0	79.9	84.9
52.7	53.1	54.2	67.7	69.3	70.9	38.5	37.6	37.9
51.1	53.0	54.6	79.0	79.5	79.9	23.6	26.5	29.0
64.9	63.3	64.3	85.2	81.5	80.5	44.8	45.3	48.3
85.6	85.6	84.9	82.5	83.0	82.7	88.3	88.0	86.8
57.8	63.2	66.0	65.8	69.6	71.6	50.2	57.0	60.5
63.2	65.2	65.4	89.0	91.6	91.1	38.4	39.6	40.2
56.0	54.7	55.5	67.0	61.7	62.9	44.9	47.6	48.0
87.4	86.1	87.2	86.4	84.7	86.2	88.3	87.5	88.2
58.4	60.8	62.1	76.6	78.5	78.9	40.8	43.6	45.8
77.2	77.5	78.0	89.8	89.7	89.7	65.0	65.9	66.9
..	..	..	..	..	..	..	..	..
66.4	68.2	68.7	63.9	68.4	69.6	68.7	67.9	67.8
58.5	58.7	58.7	79.7	79.5	78.9	37.9	38.5	39.0
54.7	56.4	55.2	63.2	64.1	63.2	46.5	48.9	47.2
53.1	53.9	54.6	75.9	76.4	76.8	30.2	31.2	32.2
57.5	57.5	58.0	72.8	71.9	71.8	43.9	44.2	44.9
90.2	90.8	90.6	91.4	91.3	91.2	89.1	90.3	90.0
80.3	81.6	82.2	82.9	81.8	82.3	77.8	81.4	82.2
82.7	79.2	78.5	83.1	80.4	79.9	82.3	78.0	77.0
80.4	80.1	79.8	85.7	86.3	86.1	75.2	74.0	73.5
75.5	87.6	87.3	81.8	90.9	90.4	69.2	84.3	84.3
50.0	**50.6**	**50.6**	**78.0**	**78.7**	**77.3**	**22.0**	**22.6**	**23.9**
46.4	45.8	45.9	79.4	77.0	75.4	12.8	14.0	15.7
50.6	51.9	53.4	68.4	68.6	69.3	32.9	35.1	37.4
48.9	51.1	51.8	76.2	79.7	78.1	21.3	22.3	25.3
52.6	55.2	56.2	75.2	77.8	79.9	28.6	31.6	32.0
55.6	54.4	51.6	82.0	80.8	78.3	30.5	29.3	26.4
50.6	49.4	50.7	75.7	72.6	74.0	25.6	26.4	27.5

Table 9.1 Labor force participation (continued)

	Ages 15–24								
	Labor force								
	Total (thousands)			Male (% of total labor force)			Female (% of total labor force)		
	2000	2005	2010	2000	2005	2010	2000	2005	2010
SUB-SAHARAN AFRICA	**70,787**	**81,250**	**90,735**	**53.7**	**53.1**	**53.1**	**47.5**	**47.9**	**47.9**
Angola	1,450	1,704	1,994	50.5	51.8	52.7	49.5	48.2	47.3
Benin	755	861	995	51.3	49.3	49.1	48.7	50.8	51.0
Botswana	234	259	264	53.0	52.5	52.3	47.0	47.5	47.7
Burkina Faso	1,998	2,267	2,562	53.6	53.6	53.5	46.5	46.5	46.5
Burundi	903	1,106	1,239	48.0	47.7	47.2	52.1	52.4	52.8
Cameroon	1,530	1,752	1,939	54.2	54.0	53.8	45.8	46.0	46.2
Cape Verde	55	64	68	61.8	62.5	61.8	38.2	37.5	38.2
Central African Republic	467	521	571	54.4	54.3	53.9	45.6	45.7	46.1
Chad	908	1,090	1,255	50.0	50.3	50.4	50.0	49.7	49.6
Comoros	50	54	53	70.0	70.4	69.8	30.0	29.6	30.2
Congo, Dem. Rep.	4,339	5,142	6,057	45.1	44.9	46.1	54.9	55.2	53.9
Congo, Rep.	287	313	352	50.2	50.2	50.3	49.8	49.8	49.7
Côte d'Ivoire	1,739	1,879	2,047	60.7	60.5	60.4	39.3	39.5	39.6
Equatorial Guinea	57	82	103	57.9	58.5	58.3	42.1	41.5	41.8
Eritrea	684	756	818	52.6	51.6	51.8	47.4	48.4	48.2
Ethiopia	9,641	11,599	13,562	52.9	51.9	51.8	47.1	48.1	48.2
Gabon	70	70	80	54.3	54.3	53.8	45.7	45.7	46.3
Gambia, The	180	204	228	48.9	49.5	49.6	51.1	50.5	50.4
Ghana	2,097	1,831	1,879	50.6	51.0	51.2	49.4	49.0	48.8
Guinea	858	955	1,077	54.1	53.8	53.2	45.9	46.2	46.8
Guinea-Bissau	128	150	167	53.1	52.0	51.5	46.9	48.0	48.5
Kenya	3,049	3,152	3,372	53.7	55.0	55.1	46.3	45.1	44.9
Lesotho	274	249	229	55.1	57.4	58.5	44.9	42.6	41.5
Liberia	206	228	274	51.0	50.9	51.1	49.0	49.1	48.9
Madagascar	2,171	2,466	2,992	50.5	50.3	50.5	49.5	49.7	49.5
Malawi	1,305	1,799	1,812	47.7	51.1	45.4	52.3	48.9	54.6
Mali	946	1,087	1,240	62.3	62.4	62.6	37.7	37.6	37.4
Mauritania	205	240	276	76.1	74.2	72.5	23.9	25.8	27.5
Mauritius	106	86	88	64.2	60.5	59.1	35.9	39.5	40.9
Mozambique	2,579	2,742	3,045	44.0	45.2	45.7	56.0	54.8	54.3
Namibia	119	156	192	54.6	53.2	52.6	45.4	46.8	47.4
Niger	1,024	1,283	1,610	66.4	67.7	68.2	33.6	32.4	31.8
Nigeria	8,899	10,337	11,557	57.9	54.2	54.5	42.1	45.8	45.5
Rwanda	1,317	1,553	1,625	48.3	48.3	48.6	51.7	51.7	51.4
São Tomé and Príncipe	13	15	15	69.2	66.7	66.7	30.8	33.3	33.3
Senegal	1,338	1,523	1,715	60.2	60.2	60.1	39.8	39.8	39.9
Seychelles	..	..	..	..	..	..	..	..	..
Sierra Leone	340	451	503	42.4	43.2	43.9	57.7	56.8	56.1
Somalia	675	700	779	64.9	64.9	64.6	35.1	35.1	35.4
South Africa	2,623	2,902	2,667	54.8	54.9	55.3	45.2	45.1	44.7
Sudan	2,422	2,695	3,022	63.2	62.8	62.4	36.8	37.2	37.6
Swaziland	103	116	132	57.3	57.8	58.3	42.7	42.2	41.7
Tanzania	5,670	6,457	7,185	50.1	49.7	49.9	50.0	50.3	50.1
Togo	652	745	829	50.2	48.2	48.3	49.9	51.8	51.8
Uganda	3,140	3,496	4,021	48.5	50.0	50.0	51.5	50.0	50.0
Zambia	1,446	1,607	1,765	51.9	52.2	52.2	48.1	47.9	47.8
Zimbabwe	1,735	2,506	2,480	54.2	51.6	51.1	45.8	48.4	48.9
NORTH AFRICA	**11,015**	**12,306**	**10,905**	**73.2**	**73.9**	**74.2**	**28.6**	**27.8**	**27.5**
Algeria	2,553	2,422	2,048	83.1	84.6	84.5	16.9	15.4	15.5
Djibouti	67	77	84	55.2	54.6	54.8	44.8	45.5	45.2
Egypt, Arab Rep.	4,407	5,968	5,439	70.4	70.9	71.2	29.6	29.1	28.8
Libya	454	487	420	69.4	68.0	68.3	30.6	32.0	31.7
Morocco	2,822	2,676	2,256	69.4	72.1	73.6	30.6	28.0	26.4
Tunisia	712	676	658	66.2	67.5	67.5	33.9	32.5	32.5

Ages 15–24								
Participation rate								
Total (% of total population)			Male (% of male population)			Female (% of female population)		
2000	2005	2010	2000	2005	2010	2000	2005	2010
53.2	**53.3**	**52.9**	**56.3**	**55.9**	**55.4**	**50.0**	**50.7**	**50.4**
54.0	53.2	52.8	54.9	55.6	56.1	53.2	50.9	49.6
60.2	57.7	57.0	62.9	57.5	56.4	57.6	58.0	57.6
59.4	59.8	59.6	62.3	62.2	61.8	56.4	57.3	57.4
78.2	77.7	77.1	82.8	82.1	81.4	73.5	73.1	72.7
70.6	67.6	65.1	68.3	64.7	61.7	72.9	70.5	68.4
47.7	47.8	47.8	51.5	51.4	51.2	43.9	44.1	44.4
60.6	60.2	59.8	74.8	73.7	72.6	46.4	46.3	46.4
63.5	63.3	62.7	69.8	69.4	68.3	57.4	57.3	57.2
56.8	56.7	56.6	56.9	57.0	57.0	56.7	56.5	56.3
39.6	40.5	39.6	54.9	55.9	54.1	24.0	24.7	24.7
46.2	45.8	45.4	41.6	41.0	41.8	50.8	50.6	49.1
44.9	44.8	44.9	44.9	44.7	45.1	44.8	44.9	44.8
51.3	51.5	51.1	62.0	62.2	61.7	40.5	40.8	40.6
76.9	76.0	76.0	89.3	88.1	88.0	64.4	63.7	63.8
79.4	77.4	77.3	83.5	80.7	80.4	75.3	74.3	74.2
78.9	79.3	77.1	83.7	82.5	79.8	74.2	76.2	74.5
29.0	25.5	25.1	31.5	27.5	26.9	26.5	23.4	23.3
65.5	65.3	64.4	66.4	66.1	64.6	64.7	64.6	64.3
53.9	41.7	38.6	53.5	41.6	38.7	54.4	41.9	38.6
53.5	53.7	54.4	56.8	56.9	56.9	50.1	50.5	51.7
53.1	54.8	55.2	56.6	57.2	56.7	49.6	52.5	53.6
44.5	39.7	39.9	47.7	43.6	43.9	41.4	35.9	35.9
62.8	51.8	45.2	68.9	59.0	52.6	56.6	44.4	37.7
35.0	35.1	35.3	35.5	35.4	35.7	34.5	34.8	34.9
75.1	73.7	72.8	75.8	74.1	73.6	74.3	73.2	72.1
58.9	71.4	59.7	56.1	72.8	53.9	61.7	69.9	65.5
40.5	40.7	40.9	49.7	49.9	50.3	31.1	31.2	31.2
38.0	39.0	39.9	56.9	56.9	56.8	18.4	20.6	22.4
50.6	42.7	40.7	64.4	51.1	47.3	36.7	34.1	33.8
71.6	67.7	66.1	64.4	61.4	60.6	78.5	74.1	71.6
30.9	36.6	39.8	33.5	38.8	41.7	28.2	34.3	37.8
53.6	56.1	57.0	76.8	80.6	80.4	33.6	34.3	35.1
35.6	36.8	37.4	40.4	39.2	40.0	30.5	34.4	34.6
75.9	73.1	73.6	74.8	71.3	72.1	77.1	74.9	75.0
41.2	42.8	40.8	55.9	57.6	54.4	26.3	27.8	26.8
67.5	66.9	66.6	81.2	80.3	79.6	53.8	53.5	53.3
..	..	..	..	..	..	..	..	..
40.6	44.3	44.2	35.2	39.3	39.8	45.9	49.2	48.5
47.3	45.8	45.0	61.6	59.5	58.2	33.1	32.1	31.8
28.7	29.5	26.5	31.4	32.2	29.2	26.0	26.7	23.8
35.7	35.6	35.3	44.6	44.0	43.3	26.7	26.8	26.9
45.1	44.5	44.5	52.6	51.6	51.6	37.9	37.4	37.3
82.1	82.0	81.0	82.0	81.5	80.7	82.1	82.5	81.2
65.9	66.2	66.2	66.3	64.1	64.2	65.5	68.3	68.2
65.4	61.3	59.9	63.5	61.5	60.2	67.3	61.1	59.6
68.4	68.8	67.7	70.9	71.5	70.5	65.9	66.0	64.8
59.6	80.4	79.6	64.5	83.5	82.2	54.6	77.4	77.1
36.2	**37.2**	**33.2**	**52.1**	**54.0**	**48.2**	**20.0**	**20.0**	**17.7**
36.9	32.5	28.1	60.3	54.0	46.5	12.7	10.2	8.9
45.3	44.6	44.1	49.6	48.5	47.8	41.0	40.5	40.3
31.5	37.8	34.0	43.6	52.8	47.6	19.0	22.3	19.9
35.2	38.2	37.4	48.2	51.1	50.0	21.8	24.8	24.2
46.4	42.1	36.0	64.7	61.1	53.0	28.2	23.3	19.0
36.4	32.9	33.0	47.7	43.9	43.8	24.9	21.6	21.8

Table 9.2 Labor force composition

	Sector[a]					
	Agriculture		Industry		Services	
	Male (% of male employment) 2000–10[b]	Female (% of female employment) 2000–10[b]	Male (% of male employment) 2000–10[b]	Female (% of female employment) 2000–10[b]	Male (% of male employment) 2000–10[b]	Female (% of female employment) 2000–10[b]
SUB-SAHARAN AFRICA						
Angola	..	..	..	..	..	..
Benin	53.1	32.7	9.8	9.2	34.5	57.5
Botswana	35.1	24.3	19.2	10.8	45.7	64.9
Burkina Faso	82.3	87.2	3.9	2.1	13.7	10.2
Burundi	..	..	..	..	..	..
Cameroon	57.7	64.7	10.9	7.4	23.5	21.8
Cape Verde	..	..	..	..	..	..
Central African Republic	..	..	..	..	..	..
Chad	..	..	..	..	..	..
Comoros	..	..	..	..	..	..
Congo, Dem. Rep.	..	..	..	..	..	..
Congo, Rep.	31.3	39.3	20.0	21.2	45.9	38.7
Côte d'Ivoire	..	..	..	..	..	..
Equatorial Guinea	..	..	..	..	..	..
Eritrea	..	..	..	..	..	..
Ethiopia	8.7	10.3	25.4	19.5	75.6	63.9
Gabon	17.3	33.7	18.6	2.5	64.1	63.8
Gambia, The	..	..	..	..	..	..
Ghana	61.4	53.2	13.4	13.8	25.1	33.0
Guinea	..	..	..	..	..	..
Guinea-Bissau	..	..	..	..	..	..
Kenya	54.5	68.0	10.8	2.3	34.6	29.7
Lesotho	..	..	..	..	..	..
Liberia	49.5	48.3	13.5	4.8	37.0	46.8
Madagascar	79.8	81.1	5.6	1.8	14.6	17.1
Malawi	..	..	..	..	..	..
Mali	67.8	63.9	8.0	2.7	24.1	33.3
Mauritania	..	..	..	..	..	..
Mauritius	9.5	7.8	32.1	22.0	58.3	70.4
Mozambique	69.2	89.9	7.0	0.4	23.8	9.7
Namibia	22.7	8.2	24.4	9.1	52.8	82.6
Niger	64.1	37.8	8.3	18.4	26.5	43.0
Nigeria	49.1	38.7	11.8	11.2	37.0	47.9
Rwanda	..	..	..	..	..	..
São Tomé and Príncipe	30.6	22.8	26.3	5.9	42.6	70.7
Senegal	34.1	33.0	20.2	4.9	32.7	42.3
Seychelles	..	..	..	..	..	..
Sierra Leone	66.0	71.1	10.3	2.5	23.7	26.4
Somalia	..	..	..	..	..	..
South Africa	6.3	3.7	34.5	13.3	59.2	82.9
Sudan	..	..	..	..	..	..
Swaziland	..	..	..	..	..	..
Tanzania	72.7	80.0	6.6	2.1	20.7	17.9
Togo	60.5	48.2	9.5	4.4	28.6	45.7
Uganda	68.6	81.7	8.6	2.8	22.7	15.5
Zambia	65.9	78.9	10.9	3.1	23.7	17.3
Zimbabwe	58.8	71.1	14.0	4.4	17.3	13.2
NORTH AFRICA						
Algeria	20.4	22.3	25.6	28.2	53.8	49.5
Djibouti	..	..	..	..	..	..
Egypt, Arab Rep.	28.2	45.6	27.3	5.6	44.4	48.8
Libya	..	..	..	..	..	..
Morocco	34.2	59.2	24.0	15.4	41.6	25.2
Tunisia	..	..	..	..	..	..

a. Components may not sum to 100 percent because of unclassified data.
b. Data are for the most recent year available during the period specified.

Status[a]								
Wage and salaried workers			Self-employed workers			Contributing family workers		
Total (% of total employed) 2000–10[b]	Male (% of males employed) 2000–10[b]	Female (% of females employed) 2000–10[b]	Total (% of total employed) 2000–10[b]	Male (% of males employed) 2000–10[b]	Female (% of females employed) 2000–10[b]	Total (% of total employed) 2000–10[b]	Male (% of males employed) 2000–10[b]	Female (% of females employed) 2000–10[b]
..	..	..	..	..	..	..	..	..
10.1	16.3	4.2	89.9	83.7	95.8	16.1	13.9	18.2
60.5	62.2	58.6	39.5	37.8	41.4	3.2	2.1	4.4
7.1	9.7	4.0	90.4	87.8	93.5	46.0	26.5	69.2
5.2	..	..	94.7	..	..	30.8	..	..
16.0	29.3	8.7	84.0	66.5	88.9	26.8	9.5	27.2
38.9	43.8	33.0	42.1	39.1	45.7	10.3	6.5	14.8
..	..	..	..	..	..	..	..	..
..	..	..	..	..	..	..	..	..
..	..	..	..	..	..	..	..	..
..	..	..	..	..	..	..	..	..
21.7	35.5	8.6	76.2	61.7	89.9	4.0	3.3	4.7
19.6	25.4	12.2	76.3	70.1	84.3	28.2	15.8	44.2
..	..	..	..	..	..	..	..	..
..	..	..	..	..	..	..	..	..
7.9	9.3	6.2	91.8	90.3	93.5	50.3	34.6	68.5
44.8	52.2	34.5	54.0	46.4	64.6	4.1	2.3	6.7
..	..	..	..	..	..	..	..	..
19.9	29.7	10.9	79.9	70.2	89.1	20.4	11.7	28.5
..	..	..	..	..	..	..	..	..
..	..	..	..	..	..	..	..	..
..	..	..	..	..	..	..	..	..
..	..	..	..	..	..	..	..	..
18.1	27.5	8.7	81.7	72.3	91.1	16.1	12.5	19.7
13.4	16.0	10.8	86.4	83.9	89.1	52.3	32.1	73.0
..	..	..	..	..	..	..	..	..
8.0	12.4	3.6	82.9	76.5	89.0	26.4	18.5	34.1
..	..	..	..	..	..	..	..	..
80.0	77.9	83.8	20.0	22.1	16.2	2.4	1.0	4.9
8.8	15.7	3.0	91.2	84.3	97.0	36.7	12.7	56.8
72.8	76.0	68.8	26.7	23.6	30.7	4.4	3.2	5.8
5.3	5.9	3.9	85.4	83.8	89.5	3.2	3.3	2.8
..	..	..	..	..	..	..	..	..
..	..	..	..	..	..	..	..	..
..	..	..	..	..	..	..	..	..
21.6	26.1	15.1	77.7	73.2	84.1	24.0	23.5	24.7
..	..	..	..	..	..	..	..	..
7.6	11.3	3.7	92.4	88.7	96.3	18.1	14.8	21.6
..	..	..	..	..	..	..	..	..
84.6	84.3	85.1	15.4	15.8	14.9	0.9	0.4	1.4
..	..	..	..	..	..	..	..	..
..	..	..	..	..	..	..	..	..
10.5	15.3	6.1	89.5	84.7	93.9	11.4	9.7	13.0
10.9	16.6	5.7	89.1	83.4	94.3	25.9	23.1	28.4
23.6	22.2	7.5	76.4	77.8	92.5	29.2	10.3	40.5
17.0	25.7	9.0	82.0	74.3	91.0	38.0	25.4	61.8
37.7	51.0	23.1	62.3	49.0	76.9	11.9	10.4	13.6
38.2	36.0	51.1	34.4	34.4	34.0	7.2	7.2	7.3
..	..	..	..	..	..	..	..	..
58.5	61.4	47.9	41.5	38.6	52.1	14.1	8.7	33.9
..	..	..	..	..	..	..	..	..
44.4	47.5	34.0	53.3	52.4	65.9	22.9	15.0	48.6
64.3	..	..	35.6	..	..	8.7	..	..

Table 9.3 Unemployment

	Unemployment (% ages 15 and older)			Youth unemployment (% ages 15–24)		
	Total 2000–10[b]	Male 2000–10[b]	Female 2000–10[b]	Total 2000–10[b]	Male 2000–10[b]	Female 2000–10[b]
SUB-SAHARAN AFRICA						
Angola	..	..	..	..	..	..
Benin	0.7	0.9	0.4	0.8	1.1	0.6
Botswana	17.6	15.3	19.9	13.6	13.2	14.0
Burkina Faso	3.3	2.9	1.7	3.8	4.6	2.9
Burundi	..	..	..	..	..	..
Cameroon	2.9	2.5	3.3	..	..	..
Cape Verde	..	..	..	..	..	..
Central African Republic	..	..	..	..	..	..
Chad	..	..	..	..	..	..
Comoros	..	..	..	..	..	..
Congo, Dem. Rep.	..	..	..	..	..	..
Congo, Rep.	..	..	..	..	..	..
Côte d'Ivoire	..	..	..	..	..	..
Equatorial Guinea	..	..	..	..	..	..
Eritrea	..	..	..	..	..	..
Ethiopia	20.5	12.1	29.9	24.9	19.5	29.4
Gabon	..	..	..	..	..	..
Gambia, The	..	..	..	..	..	..
Ghana	3.6	3.5	3.6	16.6	16.4	16.7
Guinea	..	..	..	..	..	..
Guinea-Bissau	..	..	..	..	..	..
Kenya	..	..	..	..	..	..
Lesotho	25.3	23.0	28.0	34.4	29.0	41.9
Liberia	3.7	3.4	4.1	5.9	3.9	7.7
Madagascar	2.6	1.7	3.5	2.3	1.7	2.8
Malawi	7.8	5.4	10.0	..	..	..
Mali	8.8	7.2	10.9	..	..	..
Mauritania	33.0	8.9	41.2	..	..	..
Mauritius	7.7	4.6	12.8	23.4	19.4	29.0
Mozambique	..	..	..	..	..	..
Namibia	37.6	32.5	43.0	41.7	36.7	47.0
Niger	1.5	1.7	0.9	3.2	4.0	1.7
Nigeria	..	..	..	..	..	..
Rwanda	..	..	..	..	..	..
São Tomé and Príncipe	16.7	11.0	24.5	..	..	..
Senegal	10.0	7.9	13.6	14.8	11.9	20.1
Seychelles	5.5	6.1	4.9	20.3	..	..
Sierra Leone	3.4	4.5	2.3	5.2	7.3	3.5
Somalia	..	..	..	..	..	..
South Africa	23.8	22.0	25.9	48.2	44.6	52.5
Sudan	..	..	..	..	..	..
Swaziland	..	..	..	..	..	..
Tanzania	4.3	2.8	5.8	8.8	7.4	10.1
Togo	..	..	..	..	..	..
Uganda	4.2	3.1	5.1	5.4	..	..
Zambia	15.9	14.1	11.3	23.4	23.1	19.5
Zimbabwe	4.2	4.2	4.1	7.6	7.6	7.6
NORTH AFRICA						
Algeria	11.4	10.0	20.0	24.3	42.8	46.3
Djibouti	59.5	54.6	68.6	..	..	..
Egypt, Arab Rep.	9.4	5.2	22.9	24.8	17.2	47.9
Libya	..	..	..	..	..	..
Morocco	10.0	9.8	10.5	21.9	22.8	19.4
Tunisia	14.2	13.1	17.3	30.7	31.4	29.3

a. Components may not sum to 100 percent because of unclassified data.
b. Data are for the most recent year available during the period specified.

Unemployment by education level[a] (% of total unemployed)								
Primary			Secondary			Tertiary		
Total 2000–10[b]	Male 2000–10[b]	Female 2000–10[b]	Total 2000–10[b]	Male 2000–10[b]	Female 2000–10[b]	Total 2000–10[b]	Male 2000–10[b]	Female 2000–10[b]
..	..	..	..	..	..	..	..	..
..	..	..	..	..	..	..	..	..
61.5	60.1	62.6	24.1	22.8	25.2	28.2	26.2	29.8
47.0	44.4	58.3	19.7	16.7	33.3	6.1	5.6	8.3
..	..	..	..	..	..	..	..	..
..	..	..	..	..	..	..	..	..
..	..	..	..	..	..	..	..	..
..	..	..	..	..	..	..	..	..
..	..	..	..	..	..	..	..	..
..	..	..	..	..	..	..	..	..
..	..	..	..	..	..	..	..	..
..	..	..	..	..	..	..	..	..
..	..	..	..	..	..	..	..	..
..	..	..	..	..	..	..	..	..
..	..	..	..	..	..	..	..	..
35.9	50.6	30.8	13.3	19.0	11.3	3.2	5.7	2.3
..	..	..	..	..	..	..	..	..
..	..	..	..	..	..	..	..	..
..	..	..	..	..	..	..	..	..
..	..	..	..	..	..	..	..	..
..	..	..	..	..	..	..	..	..
..	..	..	..	..	..	..	..	..
57.2	57.9	56.5	33.5	26.4	40.4	0.4	0.4	0.4
..	..	..	..	..	..	..	..	..
43.9	42.9	44.4	23.8	25.8	22.7	9.3	14.0	6.6
..	..	..	..	..	..	..	..	..
..	..	..	..	..	..	..	..	..
..	..	..	..	..	..	..	..	..
43.5	43.4	43.6	29.6	25.2	32.2	7.9	9.6	7.0
..	..	..	..	..	..	..	..	..
..	..	..	..	..	..	..	..	..
..	..	..	..	..	..	..	..	..
..	..	..	..	..	..	..	..	..
60.7	62.8	59.4	24.1	23.0	24.9	5.9	0.5	9.4
..	..	..	..	..	..	..	..	..
40.2	42.2	37.9	6.9	7.5	6.2	2.5	2.8	2.1
..	..	..	..	..	..	..	..	..
..	..	..	..	..	..	..	..	..
..	..	..	..	..	..	..	..	..
15.4	18.6	12.5	80.7	77.0	84.0	0.8	0.9	0.7
..	..	..	..	..	..	..	..	..
..	..	..	..	..	..	..	..	..
71.6	74.6	69.3	7.2	7.8	6.7	..	..	..
..	..	..	..	..	..	..	..	..
..	..	..	..	..	..	..	..	..
..	..	..	..	..	..	..	..	..
16.2	14.3	17.2	82.0	83.6	81.0	0.3	0.7	0.1
59.3	65.2	32.5	23.0	21.4	30.4	11.4	6.6	33.0
..	..	..	..	..	..	..	..	..
..	..	..	..	..	..	..	..	..
..	..	..	..	..	..	..	..	..
51.1	57.7	36.6	22.4	21.7	23.9	21.6	16.2	33.5
41.4	46.0	31.9	37.7	37.3	38.5	13.6	9.0	23.3

Table 9.4 Migration and population

	International migration							Population				
								Population dynamics				
	Migrant stock			Worker remittances, received		Migrant remittance inflows						
	Share of population (%)	Total	Net migration	Total ($ millions)	Share of GDP (%)	Total ($ millions)	Share of GDP (%)	Total (millions)	Male (% of total)	Female (% of total)	Annual growth rate (%)	Fertility rate (births per woman)
	2010	2010	2010	2010	2010	2010	2010	2010	2010	2010	2010	2010
SUB-SAHARAN AFRICA	**2.07**	**17,645,403**	**-1,985,547**	**..**	**..**	**20,501.5**	**1.8**	**844.0**	**50.0**	**50.0**	**2.5**	**4.9**
Angola	0.34	65,387	82,005	18.0	0.0	18.0	0.0	19.1	49.5	50.5	2.8	5.4
Benin	2.62	232,036	50,000	..	..	149.9	2.3	8.8	49.3	50.7	2.8	5.3
Botswana	5.72	114,838	18,730	12.1	0.1	62.6	0.4	2.0	50.4	49.6	1.3	2.8
Burkina Faso	6.33	1,043,035	-125,000	..	..	110.6	1.3	16.5	49.6	50.4	3.0	5.9
Burundi	0.72	60,770	370,000	34.5	1.7	34.5	1.7	8.4	49.1	50.9	2.6	4.3
Cameroon	1	196,570	-19,000	93.6	0.4	114.9	0.5	19.6	49.9	50.1	2.2	4.5
Cape Verde	2.43	12,053	-17,279	130.4	7.9	132.5	8.0	0.5	49.5	50.5	0.9	2.4
Central African Republic	1.83	80,492	5,000	..	..	..	..	4.4	49.3	50.7	1.9	4.6
Chad	3.46	388,251	-75,000	..	..	..	..	11.2	49.7	50.3	2.6	6.0
Comoros	1.84	13,525	-10,000	..	..	..	..	0.7	50.4	49.7	2.6	4.9
Congo, Dem. Rep.	0.67	444,672	-23,975	..	..	..	..	66.0	49.7	50.3	2.7	5.8
Congo, Rep.	3.54	143,203	49,872	..	..	..	..	4.0	50.1	50.0	2.5	4.5
Côte d'Ivoire	12.19	2,406,713	-360,000	..	..	185.5	0.8	19.7	51.0	49.0	2.0	4.4
Equatorial Guinea	1.06	7,447	20,000	..	..	..	..	0.7	51.3	48.7	2.8	5.2
Eritrea	0.31	16,484	55,000	..	..	..	..	5.3	49.3	50.8	3.0	4.5
Ethiopia	0.66	547,984	-300,000	345.2	1.2	345.2	1.2	82.9	49.8	50.2	2.2	4.2
Gabon	18.87	284,127	5,000	..	..	..	..	1.5	50.2	49.9	1.9	3.3
Gambia, The	16.78	290,104	-13,742	107.3	10.2	115.7	11.0	1.7	49.4	50.6	2.7	4.9
Ghana	7.59	1,851,814	-51,258	135.9	0.4	135.9	0.4	24.4	50.9	49.1	2.4	4.2
Guinea	3.95	394,557	-300,000	44.8	1.0	60.4	1.3	10.0	50.5	49.5	2.2	5.3
Guinea-Bissau	1.27	19,244	-10,000	..	..	48.9	5.9	1.5	49.6	50.4	2.1	5.1
Kenya	2.02	817,747	-189,330	683.7	2.1	1,777.0	5.5	40.5	49.9	50.1	2.6	4.7
Lesotho	0.29	6,328	-19,998	7.4	0.3	745.9	34.2	2.2	49.2	50.9	1.0	3.2
Liberia	2.41	96,310	300,000	0.2	0.0	31.4	3.2	4.0	50.2	49.8	4.0	5.2
Madagascar	0.18	37,762	-5,000	..	..	..	..	20.7	49.9	50.2	2.9	4.7
Malawi	1.85	275,851	-20,000	..	..	16.7	0.3	14.9	50.0	50.0	3.1	6.0
Mali	1.06	162,677	-100,823	..	..	453.7	4.8	15.4	50.0	50.0	3.0	6.3
Mauritania	2.87	99,229	9,900	..	..	..	..	3.5	50.3	49.8	2.4	4.5
Mauritius	3.35	42,917	0	..	..	226.4	2.3	1.3	49.4	50.6	0.5	1.5
Mozambique	1.92	450,020	-20,000	33.4	0.4	131.9	1.4	23.4	48.7	51.4	2.3	4.9
Namibia	6.08	138,870	-1,494	6.0	0.1	15.9	0.1	2.3	49.7	50.3	1.8	3.2
Niger	1.3	202,163	-28,497	..	..	101.7	1.9	15.5	50.3	49.7	3.5	7.1
Nigeria	0.71	1,127,668	-300,000	19,650.7	10.0	10,045.0	5.1	158.4	50.6	49.4	2.5	5.5
Rwanda	4.38	465,480	15,109	98.2	1.8	103.1	1.8	10.6	49.1	50.9	3.0	5.4
São Tomé and Príncipe	3.18	5,253	-6,496	2.0	1.0	2.0	1.0	0.2	49.5	50.5	1.8	3.7
Senegal	1.69	210,061	-132,842	..	..	1,350.4	10.5	12.4	49.6	50.4	2.7	4.8
Seychelles	12.53	10,838	..	16.5	1.7	17.4	1.8	0.1	..	..	-0.9	2.5
Sierra Leone	1.82	106,776	60,000	41.6	2.2	57.5	3.0	5.9	48.9	51.2	2.2	5.0
Somalia	0.24	22,843	-300,000	..	..	..	..	9.3	49.6	50.4	2.3	6.3
South Africa	3.73	1,862,889	700,001	..	..	1,119.3	0.3	50.0	49.5	50.5	1.4	2.5
Sudan	1.73	753,447	135,000	1,290.9	1.9	1,419.6	2.1	33.6	50.4	49.6	1.9	4.4
Swaziland	3.83	40,418	-6,000	1.9	0.1	54.7	1.5	1.1	49.2	50.9	1.1	3.4
Tanzania	1.47	659,202	-300,000	10.9	0.1	24.8	0.1	44.8	50.0	50.1	3.0	5.5
Togo	3.08	185,402	-5,430	..	..	334.5	10.5	6.0	49.5	50.5	2.1	4.1
Uganda	1.93	646,548	-135,000	768.0	4.5	914.5	5.3	33.4	50.0	50.0	3.2	6.2
Zambia	1.8	233,140	-85,000	43.7	0.3	43.7	0.3	12.9	50.1	49.9	1.6	6.3
Zimbabwe	2.96	372,258	-900,000	..	..	..	..	12.6	49.3	50.7	0.8	3.3
NORTH AFRICA	**0.82**	**1,366,356**	**-1,202,222**	**20,673.0**	**4.0**	**23,016.0**	**3.9**	**166.3**	**50.1**	**50.0**	**1.5**	**2.5**
Algeria	0.68	242,324	-140,000	66.0	0.0	2,044.4	1.3	35.5	50.5	49.5	1.5	2.3
Djibouti	12.84	114,147	0	6.6	..	32.6	..	0.9	50.0	50.0	1.9	3.8
Egypt, Arab Rep.	0.3	244,714	-346,922	12,453.1	5.7	12,453.1	5.7	81.1	50.2	49.8	1.8	2.7
Libya	10.74	682,482	-20,300	..	..	..	..	6.4	50.7	49.3	1.5	2.6
Morocco	0.15	49,098	-675,000	6,422.5	7.1	6,422.5	7.1	32.0	49.0	51.0	1.0	2.3
Tunisia	0.32	33,591	-20,000	1,724.8	3.9	2,063.3	4.7	10.5	50.0	50.0	1.0	2.0

Population													
Age composition (% of total)									Dependency ratio (% of working-age population)	Geographic distribution (%)			
Ages 0–14			Ages 15–64			Ages 65 and older				Share of total population		Annual growth	
Total 2010	Male 2010	Female 2010	Total 2010	Male 2010	Female 2010	Total 2010	Male 2010	Female 2010	2010	Rural population 2010	Urban population 2010	Rural population 2010	Urban population 2010
42.5	**42.9**	**42.0**	**54.4**	**54.2**	**54.5**	**3.2**	**2.9**	**3.5**	**84.8**	**62.7**	**37.3**	**1.7**	**3.8**
46.6	47.2	46.0	51.0	50.6	51.3	2.5	2.2	2.7	96.3	41.5	58.5	0.7	4.4
43.7	44.5	42.9	53.3	53.0	53.5	3.0	2.5	3.6	87.7	58.0	42.0	2.2	3.8
32.6	32.6	32.6	63.5	64.1	62.8	4.0	3.3	4.7	57.6	38.9	61.1	-0.7	2.5
45.3	46.5	44.2	52.5	51.8	53.1	2.2	1.8	2.7	90.7	79.6	20.4	2.5	5.1
37.9	38.7	37.1	59.3	59.1	59.5	2.9	2.3	3.4	68.7	89.0	11.0	2.2	5.3
40.6	40.9	40.2	55.9	55.9	55.9	3.5	3.2	3.8	78.9	41.6	58.4	0.2	3.6
31.8	32.2	31.4	62.3	63.1	61.5	5.9	4.7	7.1	60.5	38.9	61.1	-1.0	2.1
40.4	40.8	40.0	55.6	55.6	55.7	4.0	3.6	4.4	79.7	61.1	38.9	1.6	2.3
45.4	45.9	45.0	51.7	51.6	51.8	2.9	2.6	3.2	93.5	72.4	27.6	2.0	4.3
42.6	43.1	42.1	54.7	54.5	54.8	2.7	2.4	3.0	82.9	71.8	28.2	2.5	2.8
46.3	46.7	45.9	51.1	51.0	51.1	2.7	2.3	3.0	95.9	64.8	35.2	1.8	4.5
40.6	40.9	40.3	55.7	55.8	55.7	3.7	3.4	4.0	79.4	37.9	62.1	1.5	3.2
40.9	40.3	41.6	55.3	55.7	54.8	3.8	4.0	3.6	80.9	49.9	50.1	0.7	3.3
39.3	38.5	40.1	57.9	58.7	56.9	2.9	2.8	3.0	72.9	60.3	39.7	2.5	3.2
41.6	42.7	40.6	55.9	55.4	56.4	2.5	1.9	3.0	78.8	78.4	21.6	2.5	5.1
41.5	41.9	41.0	55.2	55.0	55.4	3.3	3.1	3.6	81.2	82.4	17.6	1.8	3.9
35.5	35.7	35.2	60.2	60.3	60.1	4.3	4.0	4.7	66.1	14.0	86.0	-1.5	2.4
44.0	44.9	43.1	53.9	52.9	54.8	2.2	2.3	2.1	85.7	41.9	58.1	0.8	4.2
38.6	38.9	38.3	57.6	57.6	57.7	3.8	3.6	4.0	73.6	48.5	51.5	0.8	3.8
42.9	43.3	42.5	53.8	53.8	53.8	3.3	3.0	3.7	86.0	64.6	35.4	1.5	3.6
41.3	41.8	40.9	55.4	55.2	55.5	3.3	3.0	3.6	80.6	70.0	30.0	2.0	2.3
42.5	42.8	42.2	54.9	54.8	55.0	2.7	2.4	2.9	82.2	77.8	22.2	2.2	4.0
37.4	38.3	36.5	58.3	58.1	58.5	4.3	3.6	5.0	71.5	73.1	26.9	0.0	3.7
43.5	44.1	42.9	53.7	53.5	54.0	2.8	2.5	3.1	86.2	38.5	61.5	2.3	5.2
43.1	43.5	42.8	53.8	53.6	53.9	3.1	3.0	3.3	86.0	69.8	30.2	2.4	4.0
45.8	46.3	45.4	51.1	50.9	51.3	3.1	2.8	3.3	95.7	80.2	19.8	2.5	5.7
47.2	48.2	46.2	50.6	50.0	51.3	2.2	1.8	2.6	97.5	66.7	33.3	2.2	4.7
39.9	40.4	39.4	57.4	57.4	57.5	2.7	2.2	3.2	74.2	58.6	41.4	2.1	2.9
21.9	22.6	21.2	71.2	71.7	70.8	6.9	5.7	8.0	40.4	57.4	42.6	0.4	0.6
44.1	45.5	42.8	52.6	51.6	53.5	3.3	2.9	3.7	90.1	61.6	38.4	1.0	4.4
36.4	37.0	35.9	59.9	59.8	60.0	3.7	3.2	4.2	66.9	62.0	38.0	0.9	3.4
49.0	49.9	48.0	48.8	48.1	49.6	2.2	2.0	2.4	104.8	83.3	16.7	3.5	4.0
42.8	43.2	42.4	53.8	53.7	53.9	3.4	3.1	3.7	85.9	50.2	49.8	1.1	4.0
42.7	43.3	42.0	54.7	54.3	55.1	2.7	2.4	2.9	82.8	81.1	18.9	2.6	4.5
40.3	41.1	39.5	55.8	55.5	56.2	3.9	3.4	4.3	79.2	37.8	62.2	-0.4	3.1
43.7	44.5	42.8	53.9	53.2	54.6	2.4	2.3	2.5	85.5	57.1	42.9	2.2	3.3
..	..	..	..	..	..	..	..	..	..	44.7	55.3	-2.0	0.0
43.0	43.6	42.5	55.1	54.4	55.8	1.9	2.0	1.8	81.4	61.6	38.4	1.7	3.1
44.9	45.5	44.4	52.4	52.1	52.6	2.7	2.5	3.0	91.0	62.6	37.4	1.6	3.5
30.1	30.6	29.7	65.2	65.8	64.6	4.6	3.6	5.7	53.3	38.3	61.7	0.1	2.1
40.1	40.6	39.6	56.4	56.2	56.5	3.6	3.3	3.9	77.5	54.8	45.2	0.3	3.9
38.4	39.4	37.5	58.2	57.8	58.7	3.4	2.9	3.8	71.7	74.5	25.5	0.8	2.3
44.7	45.1	44.3	52.2	52.1	52.2	3.1	2.8	3.5	91.8	73.6	26.4	2.4	4.7
39.7	40.0	39.3	57.0	56.9	57.0	3.4	3.1	3.7	75.6	56.6	43.4	0.9	3.7
48.4	48.8	48.1	49.1	49.0	49.2	2.5	2.3	2.8	103.8	86.7	13.3	3.0	4.4
46.4	46.5	46.2	50.6	50.8	50.4	3.1	2.7	3.4	97.7	64.3	35.7	1.4	2.0
38.9	39.5	38.2	56.9	56.7	57.1	4.2	3.8	4.7	75.7	61.7	38.3	0.0	2.0
29.4	**30.0**	**28.7**	**65.5**	**65.4**	**65.7**	**5.1**	**4.6**	**5.6**	**52.8**	**46.3**	**53.7**	**1.0**	**2.0**
27.1	27.4	26.7	68.4	68.5	68.2	4.6	4.1	5.1	46.3	33.5	66.5	-0.4	2.4
35.8	36.1	35.5	60.9	60.9	60.9	3.3	3.0	3.7	64.2	11.9	88.1	-1.4	2.3
31.5	32.1	31.0	63.4	63.4	63.5	5.0	4.5	5.6	57.6	57.2	42.8	1.7	1.8
30.4	30.8	30.0	65.3	65.1	65.5	4.3	4.1	4.5	53.2	22.1	77.9	0.7	1.7
28.0	29.2	26.9	66.5	65.8	67.2	5.5	5.1	5.9	50.4	43.3	56.7	0.2	1.6
23.5	24.0	23.0	69.6	69.5	69.7	7.0	6.6	7.3	43.7	32.7	67.3	-0.2	1.6

Table 10.1 HIV/AIDS

	Estimated number of people living with HIV/AIDS (thousands)			Estimated prevalence rate (%) Adults (ages 15–49) Point estimate			Low estimate			High estimate		
	1990	2000	2009	1990	2000	2009	1990	2000	2009	1990	2000	2009
SUB-SAHARAN AFRICA												
Angola	28	140	200	0.5	1.9	2.0	0.2	1.4	1.6	1.4	2.4	2.4
Benin	6	49	60	0.2	1.4	1.2	<0.1	1.2	1.0	3.7	1.7	1.3
Botswana	23	260	320	3.5	26.0	24.8	2.9	25.1	23.8	4.2	27.1	25.8
Burkina Faso	160	150	110	3.9	2.3	1.2	2.6	1.9	1.0	4.8	2.7	1.5
Burundi	93	170	180	3.9	5.2	3.3	3.7	5.1	2.9	4.0	5.4	3.5
Cameroon	33	460	610	0.6	5.5	5.3	0.3	5.0	4.9	2.4	6.0	5.8
Cape Verde	..	..	..	..	..	..	..	..	..	..	..	..
Central African Republic	44	190	130	3.1	9.4	4.7	2.0	8.4	4.2	6.2	11.4	5.2
Chad	31	130	210	1.1	3.0	3.4	0.5	2.0	2.8	2.0	4.0	5.1
Comoros	<1.0	<0.1	<0.5	<0.1	<0.1	0.1	<0.1	<0.1	0.1	<0.1	<0.1	0.1
Congo, Dem. Rep.	..	..	..	..	...	..	1.2	1.1	1.2	1.6	1.5	1.6
Congo, Rep.	63	68	77	5.2	3.9	3.4	3.6	3.5	3.1	6.4	4.5	3.8
Côte d'Ivoire	140	640	450	2.4	6.9	3.4	1.3	6.2	3.1	7.2	7.6	3.9
Equatorial Guinea	<0.5	4	20	0.1	1.5	5.0	<0.1	1.0	3.5	0.2	2.5	6.6
Eritrea	5	25	25	0.3	1.2	0.8	0.1	0.9	0.6	0.9	1.6	1.0
Ethiopia	..	..	..	..	...	..	..	..	..	..	..	..
Gabon	4	34	46	0.9	5.2	5.2	0.6	4.1	4.2	1.5	6.6	6.2
Gambia, The	<1.0	4	18	0.1	0.5	2.0	0.1	0.3	1.3	1.7	1.1	2.9
Ghana	22	250	260	0.3	2.3	1.8	0.2	2.0	1.6	1.5	2.6	2.0
Guinea	34	78	79	1.1	1.7	1.3	0.5	1.1	1.1	7.6	2.7	1.6
Guinea-Bissau	1	13	22	0.3	1.8	2.5	0.1	1.5	2.0	0.4	2.2	3.0
Kenya	400	1,500	1,500	3.9	9.0	6.3	3.0	8.6	5.8	6.6	9.6	6.5
Lesotho	6	240	290	0.8	24.5	23.6	0.6	23.0	22.3	1.2	26.1	25.2
Liberia	3	52	37	0.3	3.3	1.5	0.1	2.2	1.3	0.6	4.5	1.8
Madagascar	12	17	24	0.2	0.2	0.2	0.2	0.2	0.2	0.2	0.2	0.3
Malawi	310	850	920	7.2	14.2	11.0	3.3	13.0	10.0	10.8	15.5	12.1
Mali	15	91	76	0.4	1.7	1.0	0.1	1.3	0.8	2.0	2.0	1.3
Mauritania	2	8	14	0.2	0.6	0.7	0.1	0.5	0.6	0.2	0.7	0.9
Mauritius	<0.5	3	9	<0.1	0.3	1.0	<0.1	0.2	0.7	0.2	0.4	1.3
Mozambique	76	750	1,400	1.2	8.6	11.5	0.9	7.8	10.6	1.5	9.4	12.2
Namibia	11	150	180	1.6	15.3	13.1	0.9	12.9	11.1	2.3	18.1	15.5
Niger	4	51	61	0.1	1.0	0.8	0.1	1.0	0.8	0.1	1.0	0.9
Nigeria	590	2,600	3,300	1.3	3.9	3.6	0.2	3.3	3.3	2.1	4.3	4.0
Rwanda	160	170	170	5.2	3.8	2.9	4.3	3.5	2.5	8.4	4.6	3.3
São Tomé and Príncipe	..	..	..	..	..	..	..	..	..	..	..	..
Senegal	6	30	59	0.2	0.6	0.9	0.1	0.5	0.7	0.2	0.7	1.0
Seychelles	..	..	..	..	..	..	..	..	..	..	..	..
Sierra Leone	<0.5	21	49	<0.1	0.9	1.6	<0.1	0.4	1.4	<0.1	1.6	2.1
Somalia	2	9	34	0.1	0.2	0.7	<0.1	<0.1	0.5	0.3	0.3	1.0
South Africa	140	4,200	5,600	0.7	16.1	17.8	0.6	15.7	17.2	0.9	16.6	18.3
Sudan	12	61	..	0.1	0.3	1.1	<0.1	0.1	0.9	0.4	0.5	1.4
Swaziland	9	120	180	2.3	22.3	25.9	1.8	21.0	24.9	2.7	23.6	27.0
Tanzania	600	1,400	1,400	4.8	7.3	5.6	4.3	6.9	5.3	5.3	8.0	6.1
Togo	11	99	120	0.6	3.6	3.2	0.1	2.8	2.5	1.2	4.3	3.8
Uganda	870	980	1,200	10.2	7.3	6.5	8.6	6.7	5.9	11.5	7.7	6.9
Zambia	500	810	980	12.7	14.4	13.5	3.4	13.8	12.8	26.4	15.2	14.1
Zimbabwe	510	1,700	1,200	10.1	24.8	14.3	8.7	23.8	13.4	11.7	26.1	15.4
NORTH AFRICA												
Algeria	..	6	18	<0.1	<0.1	0.1	<0.1	<0.1	0.1	<0.1	<0.1	0.1
Djibouti	3	12	14	0.9	2.9	2.5	<0.1	2.0	..	3.5	4.1	3.2
Egypt, Arab Rep.	<0.5	3	11	<0.1	<0.1	<0.1	<0.1	<0.1	<0.1	<0.1	<0.1	<0.1
Libya	..	..	..	..	..	..	..	..	..	..	..	..
Morocco	3	13	3	<0.1	0.1	0.1	<0.1	0.1	0.1	<0.1	0.1	0.2
Tunisia	<0.2	<1.0	2	<0.1	<0.1	<0.1	<0.1	<0.1	<0.1	<0.1	<0.1	0.1

Estimated HIV prevalence rate (%)					
Young men (ages 15–24)			Young women (ages 15–24)		
Point estimate 2009	Low estimate 2009	High estimate 2009	Point estimate 2009	Low estimate 2009	High estimate 2009
0.6	0.4	0.9	1.6	1.1	2.2
0.3	0.2	0.4	0.7	0.5	1.1
5.2	3.7	7.3	11.8	9.0	15.9
0.5	0.3	0.6	0.8	0.6	1.2
1.0	0.8	1.2	2.1	1.6	2.7
1.6	1.2	2.1	3.9	3.1	5.4
..	..	..	..	..	..
1.0	0.6	1.4	2.2	1.4	3.1
1.0	0.7	2.0	2.5	1.7	5.2
0.1	0.1	0.1	<0.1	<0.1	<0.1
..	0.4	0.6	..	0.9	1.5
1.2	0.9	1.6	2.6	2.1	3.6
0.7	0.5	1.1	1.5	1.1	2.3
1.9	1.0	3.2	5.0	2.7	7.9
0.2	0.1	0.3	0.4	0.2	0.7
..	..	..	..	..	..
1.4	0.8	2.0	3.5	2.1	5.2
0.9	0.5	1.6	2.4	1.4	4.0
0.5	0.4	0.7	1.3	0.9	1.8
0.4	0.3	0.6	0.9	0.6	1.3
0.8	0.5	1.1	2.0	1.5	2.9
1.8	1.3	2.4	4.1	3.0	5.4
5.4	4.1	7.4	14.2	11.2	19.2
0.3	0.1	0.5	0.7	0.2	1.2
0.1	0.1	0.4	0.1	<0.1	0.1
3.1	2.3	4.2	6.8	5.3	9.2
0.2	0.1	0.4	0.5	0.2	0.9
0.4	0.2	1.4	0.3	0.1	0.5
0.3	0.2	0.4	0.2	0.1	0.3
3.1	2.4	4.4	8.6	7.0	12.1
2.3	1.3	3.6	5.8	3.7	8.6
0.2	0.2	0.3	0.5	0.4	0.6
1.2	0.9	1.6	2.9	2.3	3.9
1.3	0.9	1.6	1.9	1.3	2.3
..	..	..	..	..	..
0.3	0.2	0.4	0.7	0.5	1.0
..	..	..	..	..	..
0.6	0.3	1.0	1.5	0.9	2.5
0.4	..	..	0.6	..	..
4.5	4.1	5.0	13.6	12.3	15.0
0.5	..	..	1.3	..	..
6.5	4.8	8.8	15.6	12.6	21.3
1.7	1.3	2.3	3.9	3.1	5.3
0.9	0.6	1.2	2.2	1.5	3.1
2.3	1.8	2.8	4.8	4.0	6.4
4.2	3.2	5.5	8.9	7.3	12.0
3.3	2.5	4.4	6.9	5.3	9.3
0.1	<0.1	0.2	<0.1	<0.1	0.1
0.8	..	..	1.9	..	..
<0.1	<0.1	<0.1	<0.1	<0.1	<0.1
..	..	..	..	..	..
0.1	<0.1	0.3	0.1	<0.1	0.1
<0.1	<0.1	0.1	<0.1	<0.1	<0.1

(continued)

Table 10.1 HIV/AIDS (continued)

	Deaths of adults and children due to HIV/AIDS (thousands)									AIDS orphans (ages 0–17, thousands)								
	Point estimate			Low estimate			High estimate			Point estimate			Low estimate			High estimate		
	1990	2000	2009	1990	2000	2009	1990	2000	2009	1990	2000	2009	1990	2000	2009	1990	2000	2009
SUB-SAHARAN AFRICA																		
Angola	<1.0	9.2	11.0	<0.5	5.6	7.7	3.2	13.0	16.0	2.1	54.0	140.0	<1.0	23.0	95.0	9.9	95.0	200.0
Benin	<0.2	3.0	2.7	<0.1	1.7	1.8	18.0	5.4	3.7	<0.5	11.0	30.0	<0.1	3.7	18.0	470.0	110.0	53.0
Botswana	<1.0	13.0	5.8	<0.5	11.0	2.3	<1.0	16.0	14.0	1.0	45.0	93.0	<1.0	36.0	71.0	1.7	59.0	120.0
Burkina Faso	6.7	15.0	7.1	4.1	11.0	4.8	11.0	19.0	9.7	13.0	130.0	140.0	5.2	96.0	100.0	71.0	180.0	170.0
Burundi	3.9	14.0	15.0	3.1	11.0	12.0	4.7	16.0	17.0	10.0	120.0	200.0	7.7	98.0	170.0	14.0	150.0	230.0
Cameroon	<1.0	27.0	37.0	<0.5	22.0	29.0	9.3	33.0	46.0	1.3	100.0	330.0	<1.0	67.0	270.0	36.0	210.0	420.0
Cape Verde	..	..	..	..	..	..	..	..	..	..	..	..	..	..	..	..	..	..
Central African Republic	1.0	14.0	11.0	<1.0	11.0	8.8	5.8	20.0	13.0	2.0	69.0	140.0	1.2	43.0	110.0	49.0	100.0	180.0
Chad	1.4	7.9	11.0	<1.0	4.7	8.1	2.9	12.0	15.0	5.1	43.0	120.0	2.1	22.0	79.0	11.0	79.0	170.0
Comoros	<0.1	<0.1	<0.1	<0.1	<0.1	<0.1	<0.1	<0.1	<0.1	..	..	<0.1	..	..	<0.1	..	..	<0.1
Congo, Dem. Rep.	..	..	..	12.0	23.0	26.0	26.0	34.0	40.0	..	..	..	46.0	270.0	350.0	210.0	430.0	510.0
Congo, Rep.	3.0	5.7	5.1	<1.0	4.8	4.1	6.2	7.1	6.4	6.9	48.0	51.0	<0.2	31.0	41.0	31.0	72.0	66.0
Côte d'Ivoire	3.9	48.0	36.0	2.1	34.0	29.0	12.0	65.0	44.0	7.3	230.0	440.0	4.0	140.0	330.0	16.0	410.0	550.0
Equatorial Guinea	<0.1	<0.2	<1.0	<0.1	<0.2	<1.0	<0.1	<0.5	1.4	<0.1	<0.5	4.1	<0.1	<0.2	2.5	<0.1	<1.0	6.4
Eritrea	<0.2	1.6	1.7	<0.1	<1.0	1.0	<1.0	2.5	2.5	<0.5	7.0	19.0	<0.1	3.2	12.0	2.6	16.0	28.0
Ethiopia	..	..	..	..	..	..	..	..	..	..	..	..	..	..	..	..	..	..
Gabon	<0.2	1.8	2.4	<0.1	1.4	1.6	<0.5	2.5	3.4	<0.2	6.0	18.0	<0.1	4.1	12.0	<0.5	9.2	25.0
Gambia, The	<0.1	<0.2	<1.0	<0.1	<0.1	<0.5	<1.0	<1.0	1.2	<0.1	<1.0	2.8	<0.1	<0.5	1.4	6.6	6.5	6.5
Ghana	<1.0	15.0	18.0	<0.5	11.0	14.0	6.9	20.0	22.0	1.3	47.0	160.0	<1.0	33.0	120.0	58.0	110.0	210.0
Guinea	1.1	6.1	4.7	<0.5	2.5	3.1	15.0	14.0	6.9	2.5	36.0	59.0	1.1	9.9	34.0	110.0	97.0	120.0
Guinea-Bissau	<0.1	<1.0	1.2	<0.1	<0.5	<1.0	<0.1	<1.0	1.6	<0.2	2.2	9.7	<0.1	1.3	7.7	<0.5	3.1	12.0
Kenya	10.0	120.0	80.0	6.7	98.0	61.0	22.0	140.0	99.0	17.0	710.0	1,200.0	10.0	550.0	980.0	40.0	960.0	1,400.0
Lesotho	..	12.0	14.0	<0.1	10.0	10.0	<0.2	15.0	18.0	<0.1	38.0	130.0	<0.1	29.0	110.0	<0.2	51.0	160.0
Liberia	<0.1	3.5	3.6	<0.1	2.0	2.8	<0.2	5.7	4.6	<0.1	15.0	52.0	<0.1	7.3	34.0	<0.5	25.0	76.0
Madagascar	<1.0	1.3	1.7	<1.0	1.0	1.4	1.4	1.5	2.0	6.6	9.4	11.0	4.0	7.3	9.3	12.0	12.0	14.0
Malawi	11.0	64.0	51.0	4.1	53.0	38.0	22.0	77.0	67.0	25.0	380.0	650.0	7.1	280.0	540.0	68.0	500.0	780.0
Mali	<0.5	6.9	4.4	<0.1	3.8	3.0	4.3	11.0	6.1	<0.5	29.0	59.0	<0.1	11.0	36.0	15.0	82.0	93.0
Mauritania	<0.1	<0.5	<1.0	<0.1	<0.5	<1.0	<0.2	<1.0	1.0	<0.5	1.3	3.6	<0.1	<1.0	2.7	<0.5	1.9	4.8
Mauritius	<0.1	<0.1	<0.5	<0.1	<0.1	<0.5	<0.2	<0.2	<1.0	<0.1	<0.2	1.0	<0.1	<0.1	<0.5	<0.5	<0.5	<1.0
Mozambique	2.2	36.0	74.0	1.5	28.0	57.0	3.3	45.0	92.0	6.6	180.0	670.0	2.1	84.0	..	5.6	150.0	..
Namibia	<0.5	6.7	6.7	<0.2	5.1	2.5	<1.0	8.8	11.0	<1.0	23.0	70.0	<0.5	17.0	50.0	1.4	33.0	96.0
Niger	<0.2	2.9	4.3	<0.1	2.3	3.3	<0.2	3.5	5.6	<0.5	13.0	57.0	<0.5	11.0	44.0	<0.5	16.0	73.0
Nigeria	10.0	200.0	220.0	<0.5	110.0	170.0	21.0	250.0	260.0	12.0	1,100.0	2,500.0	<0.5	300.0	1,800.0	94.0	1,700.0	3,100.0
Rwanda	8.4	15.0	4.1	5.6	12.0	<1.0	13.0	21.0	97.0	32.0	160.0	130.0	19.0	130.0	98.0	92.0	240.0	180.0
São Tomé and Príncipe	..	-	..	..	..	..	..	..	..	..	..	..	..	..	..	..	..	..
Senegal	<0.5	1.6	2.6	<0.2	1.3	1.9	<0.5	2.0	3.5	<1.0	7.3	19.0	<0.5	5.4	15.0	1.4	9.4	25.0
Seychelles	..	-	..	..	..	..	..	..	..	..	..	..	..	..	..	..	..	..
Sierra Leone	<0.1	<1.0	2.8	<0.1	<0.5	2.1	<0.1	1.9	3.7	<0.1	1.5	15.0	<0.1	<1.0	9.2	<0.1	5.1	26.0
Somalia	<0.2	<0.5	..	<0.1	<0.1	..	<1.0	<1.0	..	..	..	..	..	..	..	..	..	..
South Africa	2.9	170.0	310.0	2.0	140.0	260.0	4.3	210.0	390.0	4.4	430.0	1,900.0	2.3	340.0	1,600.0	7.4	550.0	2,400.0
Sudan	<1.0	3.0	..	<0.1	<0.5	..	3.5	6.5	..	..	..	..	..	..	..	..	..	..
Swaziland	<0.5	5.7	7.0	<0.2	4.7	4.6	<0.5	7.1	10.0	<1.0	23.0	69.0	<0.5	18.0	55.0	<1.0	29.0	86.0
Tanzania	21.0	110.0	86.0	16.0	90.0	69.0	27.0	130.0	110.0	53.0	750.0	1,300.0	37.0	610.0	1,100.0	75.0	940.0	1,500.0
Togo	<0.5	5.6	7.7	<0.1	3.8	5.3	2.0	7.4	10.0	<0.5	19.0	66.0	<0.1	8.5	47.0	23.0	39.0	89.0
Uganda	37.0	89.0	64.0	22.0	76.0	49.0	83.0	100.0	80.0	280.0	1,000.0	1,200.0	180.0	800.0	1,000.0	770.0	1,400.0	1,400.0
Zambia	23.0	66.0	45.0	<1.0	55.0	30.0	46.0	76.0	60.0	74.0	540.0	690.0	<0.1	340.0	570.0	210.0	740.0	810.0
Zimbabwe	14.0	130.0	83.0	9.7	110.0	70.0	19.0	150.0	97.0	29.0	670.0	1,000.0	18.0	550.0	910.0	53.0	840.0	1,200.0
NORTH AFRICA																		
Algeria	<0.1	<0.2	<1.0	<0.1	<0.1	<1.0	<0.1	<0.5	1.1	..	..	..	..	..	..	..	..	..
Djibouti	<0.1	<1.0	1.0	<0.1	<0.5	<1.0	<1.0	1.3	1.4	..	..	..	..	..	..	..	..	..
Egypt, Arab Rep.	<0.1	<0.2	<0.5	<0.1	<0.1	<0.5	<1.0	<0.5	<1.0	..	..	..	..	..	..	..	..	..
Libya	..	..	..	..	..	..	..	..	..	..	..	..	..	..	..	..	..	..
Morocco	<0.2	<1.0	1.2	<0.1	<0.5	<1.0	0.5	<1.0	1.6	..	..	..	..	..	..	..	..	..
Tunisia	<0.1	<0.1	<0.1	<0.1	<0.1	<0.1	<0.1	<0.1	<0.2	..	..	..	..	..	..	..	..	..

Note: 0 refers to a negligible value that rounds to 0.

HIV-positive pregnant women receiving antiretrovirals to reduce the risk of mother-to-child transmission				ODA gross disbursements ($ millions)			
	Share of total (WHO/UNAIDS methodology, %)			For social mitigation of HIV/AIDS		For STD control, including HIV/AIDS	
Total	Point estimate	Low estimate	High estimate				
2009	2009	2009	2009	2009	2010	2009	2010
				96.5	**77.2**	**3,791.1**	**4,372.8**
3,053	19	12	36	0.5	0.2	12.2	24.8
1,703	46	29	92	0.0	0.1	22.9	30.2
12,406	>95	74	>95	1.5	0.1	211.8	73.9
2,084	32	19	60	0.3	0.8	41.2	40.8
1,837	12	9	22	2.6	3.3	30.0	16.1
9,092	27	18	50	0.2	0.0	28.4	18.2
61	..	..	..	..	..	0.5	2.0
2,157	34	23	67	0.0	0.5	4.5	10.4
989	6	3	12	0.0	1.0	9.2	13.3
1	..	10	33	..	..	0.1	0.5
2,232	..	4	11	0.3	0.1	27.6	71.5
441	12	8	23	0.0	..	6.9	12.7
11,064	54	36	95	0.3	1.0	67.5	90.8
365	26	16	50	..	..	0.9	1.6
464	34	21	71	0.0	..	15.7	19.5
6,721	..	13	40	3.7	3.5	211.0	464.2
577	30	20	60	..	..	3.9	2.2
885	..	43	95	..	..	6.2	6.5
3,643	27	18	53	0.1	0.2	58.6	33.5
783	17	11	34	0.0	0.1	6.9	7.2
383	24	16	49	..	0.0	5.9	6.8
58,591	73	50	95	6.1	5.5	377.3	399.4
8,846	64	48	95	5.3	8.6	29.6	47.7
377	16	10	33	0.0	..	5.1	15.3
17	..	1	5	0.0	..	9.4	11.1
33,156	58	40	95	3.1	2.9	150.1	123.0
1,710	..	26	82	0.1	0.1	25.4	18.9
68	..	12	37	..	0.0	0.8	0.2
41	..	33	95	..	..	0.9	2.1
68,248	70	51	95	8.4	7.3	192.1	244.8
6,744	88	61	95	0.1	0.1	119.7	123.2
1,737	..	25	74	0.0	0.0	13.0	6.4
44,723	22	15	42	0.0	0.0	369.1	418.8
7,030	65	43	95	0.5	0.3	135.1	202.8
11	..	..	..	0.0	0.0	0.1	0.1
917	..	16	45	0.1	0.1	19.0	24.8
12	..	..	..	..	..	0.0	0.0
637	19	12	36	0.2	0.2	13.2	21.5
-	..	0	0	..	..	1.3	12.5
188,200	88	66	95	11.4	7.2	564.7	567.1
245	2	1	3	0.1	0.0	12.0	45.0
8,182	88	68	95	0.6	0.3	27.2	57.9
58,833	70	48	95	7.1	4.4	257.1	361.8
1,451	26	15	67	0.0	0.0	17.2	11.3
46,948	53	37	95	7.2	2.8	259.0	282.6
47,175	69	50	95	3.4	2.0	223.8	218.3
28,208	56	41	95	9.4	3.1	71.2	106.4
				0.0	**0.0**	**15.4**	**18.4**
65	..	14	59	..	..	1.2	1.1
63	10	6	21	0.0	0.0	0.7	1.9
11	..	3	10	0.0	0.0	4.2	3.8
..	..	..	..	..	..	0.0	..
90	..	13	49	..	..	5.7	7.2
3	..	6	25	..	..	3.0	4.1

Table 11.1 Malaria

	Population (millions)		Clinical cases of malaria reported[a]		Reported deaths due to malaria		Under-five mortality rate (per 1,000)		Children sleeping under insecticide-treated nets (% of children under age 5)	Children with fever receiving any antimalarial treatment (% of children under age 5 with fever)	Pregnant women receiving two doses of intermittent preventive treatment (%)	ODA disbursements for malaria control ($ millions)	
	2009	2010	2009	2010	2009	2010	2009	2010	2000–10[b]	2000–10[b]	2000–09[b]	2009	2010
SUB-SAHARAN AFRICA	**823.6**	**844.0**	**72,099,998**	**71,412,328**	**115,380**	**132,524**	**125**	**122**				**1,204.4**	**1,155.1**
Angola	18.6	19.1	2,221,076	2,783,619	10,530	8,114	164	161	17.7	29.3	2.5	28.6	30.3
Benin	8.6	8.8	1,256,708	1,432,095	1,375	964	118	115	20.1	54.0	3.0	15.1	31.5
Botswana	2.0	2.0	14,878	12,196	6	8	49	48	..	..	..	..	0.0
Burkina Faso	16.0	16.5	4,399,837	5,409,156	7,982	9,024	178	176	9.6	48.0	1.3	21.8	51.3
Burundi	8.2	8.4	1,764,343	2,919,866	1,183	2,677	143	142	45.2	17.2	..	7.6	22.0
Cameroon	19.2	19.6	1,883,199	1,845,691	4,943	4,536	138	136	13.1	57.8	5.8	9.6	2.1
Cape Verde	0.5	0.5	65	47	2	1	37	36	..	..	..	..	..
Central African Republic	4.3	4.4	175,210	66,484	667	526	161	159	15.1	57.0	8.7	0.0	1.5
Chad	10.9	11.2	182,415	466,034	221	..	175	173	9.8	35.7	..	0.3	22.7
Comoros	0.7	0.7	49,679	47,364	..	53	87	86	9.3	62.7	..	0.2	4.3
Congo, Dem. Rep.	64.2	66.0	6,749,112	7,439,440	21,168	23,476	172	170	35.7	39.1	5.1	87.5	70.2
Congo, Rep.	3.9	4.0	92,855	0	116	..	94	93	6.1	48.0	..	0.0	12.1
Côte d'Ivoire	19.4	19.7	1,847,367	..	18,156	1,023	125	123	3.0	36.0	8.3	16.2	58.4
Equatorial Guinea	0.7	0.7	78,983	0	23	..	125	121	0.7	48.6	..	3.4	5.4
Eritrea	5.1	5.3	21,298	53,750	23	27	63	61	48.9	13.1	..	0.6	21.6
Ethiopia	81.2	82.9	3,043,203	4,068,764	1,121	1,581	109	106	33.1	9.5	..	137.3	56.1
Gabon	1.5	1.5	112,840	159,313	197	182	75	74	55.1	..	..	3.9	0.9
Gambia, The	1.7	1.7	479,409	116,353	240	151	101	98	49.0	63.0	32.5	6.0	9.0
Ghana	23.8	24.4	1,899,544	2,642,221	3,378	3,859	77	74	28.2	43.0	43.7	43.5	71.1
Guinea	9.8	10.0	812,471	1,092,554	586	735	134	130	4.5	73.9	2.9	0.0	12.5
Guinea-Bissau	1.5	1.5	143,011	0	369	..	152	150	35.5	51.2	7.4	1.6	7.0
Kenya	39.5	40.5	8,123,689	4,585,712	..	26,017	87	85	46.7	23.2	15.0	73.5	71.8
Lesotho	2.1	2.2	..	..	..	..	92	85	..	..	..	0.0	..
Liberia	3.8	4.0	871,560	2,263,973	1,706	1,422	109	103	26.4	67.2	45.1	13.0	21.1
Madagascar	20.1	20.7	215,110	202,450	348	122	65	62	45.8	19.7	6.4	26.7	86.3
Malawi	14.4	14.9	6,183,816	6,851,108	8,915	8,206	98	92	56.5	30.9	44.5	20.4	29.4
Mali	14.9	15.4	1,633,423	1,018,846	2,331	3,006	182	178	70.2	31.7	4.0	14.7	17.6
Mauritania	3.4	3.5	167,705	238,565	91	211	112	111	2.1	20.7	..	0.0	0.5
Mauritius	1.3	1.3	..	..	..	..	15	15	..	..	..	..	..
Mozambique	22.9	23.4	4,310,086	1,522,577	3,747	3,354	140	135	22.8	36.7	43.1	26.6	47.3
Namibia	2.2	2.3	87,402	25,889	68	63	44	40	34.0	20.3	10.0	3.8	1.2
Niger	15.0	15.5	309,675	620,058	2,159	3,929	150	143	63.7	33.0	0.3	19.5	9.9
Nigeria	154.5	158.4	4,295,686	3,873,463	7,522	4,238	147	143	29.1	49.1	4.9	318.3	59.3
Rwanda	10.3	10.6	1,247,583	638,669	809	670	98	91	69.8	10.8	17.0	62.6	33.2
São Tomé and Príncipe	0.2	0.2	3,922	2,262	23	14	81	80	56.2	8.4	59.8	0.0	1.1
Senegal	12.1	12.4	222,232	0	574	..	79	75	29.2	9.1	52.2	27.1	17.5
Seychelles	0.1	0.1	..	..	..	..	14	14	..	..	..	..	..
Sierra Leone	5.7	5.9	646,808	934,028	1,734	8,188	180	174	25.8	30.1	10.3	4.9	8.5
Somalia	9.1	9.3	72,362	24,553	45	6	180	180	11.4	7.9	0.9	1.2	5.2
South Africa	49.3	50.0	6,117	8,060	45	83	61	57	..	..	..	0.0	..
Sudan	33.0	33.6	2,361,188	1,465,496	1,142	1,023	104	103	25.3	35.8	..	13.3	33.1
Swaziland	1.0	1.1	6,639	1,722	13	8	82	78	0.6	0.6	0.5	2.6	1.4
Tanzania	43.5	44.8	40	0	..	..	80	92	63.6	59.1	30.2	96.4	96.0
Togo	5.9	6.0	618,842	617,101	1,556	1,507	106	103	56.9	33.8	18.1	0.3	8.5
Uganda	32.4	33.4	9,775,318	11,084,045	6,296	8,431	103	99	32.8	59.6	16.2	54.4	54.9
Zambia	12.7	12.9	2,976,395	4,229,839	3,862	4,834	116	111	49.9	34.0	60.3	24.9	20.5
Zimbabwe	12.5	12.6	736,897	648,965	108	255	83	80	17.3	23.6	6.3	1.8	21.0
NORTH AFRICA	**163.9**	**166.3**	**3,019**	**4,673**	**3**	**4**	**29**	**27**				**0.2**	**0.1**
Algeria	35.0	35.5	94	408	..	..	37	36	..	..	..	..	..
Djibouti	0.9	0.9	2,686	3,962	0	0	93	91	19.9	0.9	..	0.2	0.1
Egypt, Arab Rep.	79.7	81.1	94	85	2	2	24	22	..	..	..	..	..
Libya	6.3	6.4	..	..	..	..	18	17	..	..	..	..	..
Morocco	31.6	32.0	145	218	1	2	37	36	..	..	..	..	..
Tunisia	10.4	10.5	..	..	..	..	17	16	..	..	..	..	..

a. Malaria cases reported before 2000 can be probable and confirmed or only confirmed, depending on the country.
b. Data are for the most recent year available during the period specified.

Table 12.1 Aid and debt relief

	Net official development assistance and official aid ($ millions)							
	From all donors		From DAC donors		From non-DAC donors		From multilateral donors	
	2009	2010	2009	2010	2009	2010	2009	2010
SUB-SAHARAN AFRICA	**44,070**	**44,589**	**22,564**	**23,912**	**191**	**248**	**16,387**	**16,376**
Angola	239	238	131	150	10	3	98	85
Benin	682	689	326	339	3	1	353	349
Botswana	279	156	223	106	0	0	56	51
Burkina Faso	1,083	1,062	453	456	2	5	628	598
Burundi	561	630	264	283	0	0	297	347
Cameroon	648	541	268	266	1	0	380	274
Cape Verde	196	328	162	248	0	-1	34	81
Central African Republic	242	261	99	113	1	1	143	148
Chad	561	486	356	285	0	-1	205	202
Comoros	50	67	28	22	1	16	21	28
Congo, Dem. Rep.	2,357	3,543	1,099	2,387	3	8	1,255	1,147
Congo, Rep.	283	1,312	226	1,215	0	1	57	96
Côte d'Ivoire	2,402	845	1,721	438	2	2	678	406
Equatorial Guinea	31	85	25	79	0	0	6	6
Eritrea	144	161	43	34	15	20	86	105
Ethiopia	3,819	3,525	1,817	1,927	20	35	1,983	1,562
Gabon	77	104	53	84	0	0	25	20
Gambia, The	127	120	22	33	1	1	105	85
Ghana	1,582	1,693	821	900	6	4	755	789
Guinea	214	218	171	92	-4	-2	47	128
Guinea-Bissau	147	139	51	54	1	1	95	85
Kenya	1,776	1,629	1,224	1,159	5	5	547	464
Lesotho	122	256	71	94	5	3	47	159
Liberia	513	1,419	341	703	1	2	171	715
Madagascar	444	470	242	214	2	9	201	246
Malawi	771	1,023	435	517	4	2	332	504
Mali	984	1,089	575	684	2	0	408	404
Mauritania	373	374	122	106	21	18	231	250
Mauritius	155	125	64	58	-2	-2	93	69
Mozambique	2,012	1,952	1,288	1,357	2	4	723	590
Namibia	326	256	247	211	1	1	78	44
Niger	469	745	255	381	2	3	212	361
Nigeria	1,657	2,062	688	849	2	3	967	1,210
Rwanda	934	1,032	520	548	3	2	411	482
São Tomé and Príncipe	31	49	20	33	0	..	11	16
Senegal	1,016	928	514	534	5	14	497	379
Seychelles	23	56	12	29	0	17	11	10
Sierra Leone	448	467	196	200	0	1	252	266
Somalia	662	498	500	308	10	8	152	181
South Africa	1,075	1,031	861	822	3	2	211	207
Sudan	2,351	2,076	1,911	1,509	61	50	379	487
Swaziland	56	91	19	31	-1	1	38	60
Tanzania	2,933	2,958	1,409	1,655	-1	5	1,526	1,298
Togo	499	419	362	253	1	1	136	165
Uganda	1,785	1,723	1,013	1,033	4	4	768	686
Zambia	1,267	914	701	593	2	0	564	321
Zimbabwe	736	732	620	521	0	-2	115	209
NORTH AFRICA	**3,159**	**2,730**	**1,965**	**1,579**	**42**	**100**	**951**	**795**
Algeria	319	198	200	143	12	-2	107	57
Djibouti	167	132	98	99	11	8	58	25
Egypt, Arab Rep.	999	592	580	366	122	79	296	148
Libya	41	9	32	17	1	1	8	-10
Morocco	930	993	705	599	-98	11	323	382
Tunisia	503	550	350	355	-6	3	159	192

(continued)

Table 12.1 Aid and debt relief (continued)

	Net ODA private aid ($ millions)						Net ODA aid					
	From all donors		From DAC donors		From non-DAC donors		Share of GDP (%)		Per capita ($)		Share of gross capital formation (%)	
	2009	2010	2009	2010	2009	2010	2009	2010	2009	2010	2009	2010
SUB-SAHARAN AFRICA	**10,992**	**19,305**	**10,980**	**19,275**	**12**	**30**	**4.6**	**4.0**	**53.51**	**52.8**	**23.6**	**20.8**
Angola	3,957	289	3,957	289	..	..	0.3	0.3	12.86	12.48	2.1	2.3
Benin	-35	24	-35	24	..	..	10.4	10.5	79.29	77.87	41.0	40.3
Botswana	96	84	96	84	..	..	2.4	1.1	140.88	77.8	7.6	3.6
Burkina Faso	2	9	2	9	..	..	13.0	12.0	67.74	64.51	..	..
Burundi	-27	64	-27	64	..	..	30.9	31.1	68.7	75.15	164.3	172.6
Cameroon	41	-340	41	-340	..	..	2.9	2.4	33.81	27.58	..	..
Cape Verde	17	-28	17	-28	..	..	12.2	19.8	397.87	661.07	31.3	42.2
Central African Republic	6	-10	6	-10	..	..	12.2	13.2	56.05	59.31	113.6	..
Chad	20	-21	20	-21	..	..	7.9	5.7	51.27	43.29	24.2	17.4
Comoros	-6	1	-6	1	..	..	9.4	12.4	70.48	91.49	76.0	..
Congo, Dem. Rep.	-29	-760	-29	-760	..	..	21.0	27.0	36.71	53.71	73.3	..
Congo, Rep.	160	-32	160	-32	..	..	3.0	10.9	71.87	324.58	13.1	53.3
Côte d'Ivoire	-1,889	-74	-1,889	-74	..	..	10.4	3.7	124.11	42.81	91.8	26.8
Equatorial Guinea	404	42	404	42	..	..	0.3	0.6	46.23	120.95	0.6	2.1
Eritrea	4	-1	4	-1	..	..	7.7	7.6	28.19	30.56	..	..
Ethiopia	241	108	240	108	1	..	12.0	11.9	47.04	42.5	53.2	55.2
Gabon	-294	457	-294	457	..	..	0.7	0.8	52.26	69.08	2.6	3.0
Gambia, The	11	-2	11	-2	..	..	13.0	11.5	75.8	69.54	72.1	59.0
Ghana	345	720	345	719	0	1	6.1	5.3	66.39	69.39	26.6	19.6
Guinea	-11	-10	-11	-10	..	..	5.2	4.6	21.96	21.81	24.2	23.0
Guinea-Bissau	-12	7	-12	7	..	..	17.6	16.7	98.75	91.95	..	..
Kenya	595	-12	595	-12	..	..	5.8	5.1	45.01	40.2	29.9	26.2
Lesotho	-3	-4	-3	-4	..	..	7.2	11.8	56.95	118.01	25.5	42.0
Liberia	915	890	915	890	..	..	58.3	143.7	133.62	355.34	237.0	416.4
Madagascar	270	104	270	104	..	..	5.2	5.4	22.06	22.69	15.9	..
Malawi	39	42	39	42	..	..	16.3	20.2	53.41	68.64	65.6	81.7
Mali	-26	-42	-27	-42	0	0	11.0	11.6	66.02	70.83	..	..
Mauritania	50	-48	50	-48	..	..	12.3	10.4	110.57	108.22	40.3	37.9
Mauritius	1,628	4,029	1,628	4,029	..	..	1.8	1.3	121.54	97.8	8.3	5.4
Mozambique	43	847	43	847	..	0	20.8	21.2	88.04	83.43	100.4	85.9
Namibia	307	-398	307	-398	..	..	3.7	2.3	145.19	112.31	13.0	9.0
Niger	17	-64	17	-64	0	..	8.9	13.8	31.34	48	..	..
Nigeria	2,299	-366	2,299	-366	..	..	1.0	1.1	10.73	13.02	..	..
Rwanda	81	-35	81	-35	..	1	17.8	18.4	90.54	97.16	82.3	87.4
São Tomé and Príncipe	3	-4	3	-4	..	..	15.5	24.5	187.74	298.07	..	..
Senegal	292	1	292	-19	0	20	8.0	7.2	83.94	74.61	28.5	24.9
Seychelles	39	124	39	124	0	..	2.7	5.8	260.72	647.67	12.3	..
Sierra Leone	12	-13	12	-13	..	..	24.2	24.5	78.1	79.56	156.8	155.1
Somalia	6	-16	6	-16	..	..	..	..	72.55	53.32	..	..
South Africa	1,247	2,237	1,247	2,229	0	8	0.4	0.3	21.79	20.61	2.0	1.5
Sudan	16	29	5	29	11	0	4.3	3.1	71.3	61.77	17.1	13.3
Swaziland	-3	-6	-3	-6	..	..	1.9	2.5	53.69	86.64	17.2	22.3
Tanzania	204	94	204	94	..	..	13.7	12.9	67.39	65.97	47.4	44.7
Togo	-86	-24	-86	-24	..	..	15.8	13.2	84.47	69.49	87.6	69.9
Uganda	98	66	98	66	..	..	11.3	10.0	55.14	51.56	46.8	42.7
Zambia	-13	45	-13	45	..	..	9.9	5.7	99.58	70.74	44.7	25.2
Zimbabwe	-95	30	-95	30	..	..	12.6	9.8	59.02	58.26	581.5	329.9
NORTH AFRICA	**10,730**	**6,727**	**10,653**	**6,685**	**78**	**42**	**0.6**	**0.5**	**19.28**	**16.41**	**1.8**	**1.5**
Algeria	2,917	530	2,915	529	2	1	0.2	0.1	9.12	5.59	0.5	0.3
Djibouti	50	-49	50	-49	..	..	15.9	..	191.16	148.8	..	..
Egypt, Arab Rep.	5,601	4,896	5,566	4,880	35	16	0.5	0.3	12.53	7.3	2.8	1.4
Libya	1,157	-437	1,119	-447	38	10	0.1	..	6.56	1.34	..	..
Morocco	792	2,167	790	2,160	2	7	1.0	1.1	29.39	31.06	2.9	3.1
Tunisia	54	-533	53	-540	1	8	1.2	1.2	48.16	52.17	4.7	4.7

a. As of end-July 2011.

Net ODA aid				Food aid shipments (thousands of tonnes)				Heavily Indebted Poor Countries (HIPC) Debt Initiative				
Share of imports of goods and services (%)		Share of central government expenditures (%)		Cereal		Non-cereal		Decision point[a]	Completion point[a]	In nominal terms		
										Debt service relief committed ($ millions)[a]	Assistance delivered under MDRI ($ millions)[a]	Total HIPC and MDRI assistance ($ millions)[a]
2009	2010	2009	2010	2009	2010	2009	2010					
11.6	**9.8**	**..**	**..**	**3,305**	**3,262**	**469**	**103**					
0.5	0.5	..	..	0	4	0	0	..	..	..	..	..
29.5	..	68.1	69.5	17	18	2	0	Jul. 2000	Mar. 2003	460	1,136	1,596
5.2	2.5	..	..	0	0	0	0	..	..	..	..	..
53.2	..	102.5	99.3	22	40	6	0	Jul. 2000	Apr. 2002	930	1,217	2,147
104.3	101.8	..	..	48	31	15	1	Aug. 2005	Jan. 2009	1,366	102	1,468
9.3	8.0	..	..	9	14	1	0	Oct. 2000	Apr. 2006	4,917	1,285	6,202
16.9	27.5	44.8	..	18	16	1	0	..	..	..	..	..
..	..	..	..	17	8	5	0	Sep. 2007	Jun. 2009	804	301	1,105
..	..	..	..	100	108	10	0	May 2001	..	260	..	260
..	..	..	..	8	0	0	0	Jun. 2010	..	136	..	136
..	..	111.8	196.3	151	165	39	1	Jul. 2003	Jul. 2010	15,222	1,051	16,273
..	..	..	..	4	7	3	0	Mar. 2006	Jan. 2010	1,738	204	1,941
24.2	..	58.5	..	30	21	4	0	Mar. 2009	..	3,415	..	3,415
..	..	..	..	0	0	0	0	..	..	..	..	..
..	..	..	..	0	0	0	0	..	..	..	..	..
42.0	35.3	..	..	1,036	1,364	85	41	Nov. 2001	Apr. 2004	3,275	3,280	6,555
..	..	..	..	0	0	0	0	..	..	..	..	..
35.2	36.4	..	..	2	18	2	5	Dec. 2000	Dec. 2007	112	383	495
13.8	11.7	33.8	..	38	7	1	0	Feb. 2002	Jul. 2004	3,500	3,868	7,368
13.6	11.5	..	..	11	4	4	0	Dec. 2000	..	800	..	800
47.9	..	..	..	2	4	0	3	Dec. 2000	Dec. 2010	790	146	790
15.4	11.8	27.8	22.6	217	240	53	1	..	..	..	..	..
5.4	9.0	..	..	6	6	1	0	..	..	..	..	..
27.7	78.6	..	..	22	25	4	3	Mar. 2008	Jun. 2010	4,600	266	4,866
..	..	..	..	21	21	2	5	Dec. 2000	Oct. 2004	1,900	2,393	4,293
34.8	..	..	..	91	35	6	3	Dec. 2000	Aug. 2006	1,628	1,577	3,205
29.6	..	74.9	..	23	19	7	6	Sep. 2000	Mar. 2003	895	1,992	2,887
..	..	..	..	28	37	2	2	Feb. 2000	Jun. 2002	1,100	883	1,983
2.8	2.0	8.1	5.7	0	0	0	0	..	..	..	..	..
40.9	39.7	..	..	166	78	3	0	Apr. 2000	Sep. 2001	4,300	2,032	6,332
5.9	4.0	..	..	0	1	0	0	..	..	..	..	..
17.7	..	..	..	41	154	7	1	Dec. 2000	Apr. 2004	1,190	1,062	2,252
2.6	2.2	..	..	0	0	0	0	..	..	..	..	..
61.0	60.8	..	..	22	7	7	0	Dec. 2000	Apr. 2005	1,316	512	1,827
29.1	36.3	..	..	5	3	0	0	Dec. 2000	Mar. 2007	263	69	333
18.1	..	..	..	14	23	5	18	Jun. 2000	Apr. 2004	850	2,470	3,320
1.9	4.5	9.1	18.9	0	0	0	0	..	..	..	..	..
65.8	49.8	104.5	..	15	22	2	1	Mar. 2002	Dec. 2006	994	665	1,659
..	..	..	..	318	71	44	1	..	..	..	..	..
1.2	0.9	1.2	..	0	0	0	0	..	..	..	..	..
18.5	15.1	..	..	433	473	79	3	..	..	..	..	..
2.0	3.0	..	..	2	17	0	0	..	..	..	..	..
37.1	31.6	..	..	24	37	5	0	Apr. 2000	Nov. 2001	3,000	3,810	6,810
28.1	..	100.5	91.6	25	2	0	0	Nov. 2008	Dec. 2010	360	713	360
31.0	25.6	86.8	..	121	77	16	1	Feb. 2000	May. 2000	1,950	3,493	5,443
27.9	13.0	56.5	32.9	12	6	4	0	Dec. 2000	Apr. 2005	3,900	2,747	6,647
..	..	..	..	185	79	44	4	..	..	..	..	..
1.7	**1.3**	**..**	**..**	**33**	**30**	**12**	**0**					
0.6	0.4	0.9	..	12	19	9	0	..	..	..	..	..
28.1	26.5	..	..	21	8	2	0	..	..	..	..	..
1.8	0.9	1.8	1.0	1	3	1	0	..	..	..	..	..
0.1	0.0	..	..	..	..	..	..	..	..	..	..	..
2.3	2.4	3.7	3.6	0	0	0	0	..	..	..	..	..
2.2	2.1	4.3	4.6	0	0	0	0	..	..	..	..	..

Table 12.2 Status of Paris Declaration indicators

	PDI-1	PDI-2		PDI-3	PDI-4	PDI-5	
	Operational national development strategies[a]	Reliable public financial management[b]	Reliable country procurement systems[c]	Government budget estimates comprehensive and realistic (%)	Technical assistance aligned and coordinated with country programs (%)	Aid for government sectors uses country public financial management systems (%)	Aid for government sectors uses of country procurement systems (%)
	2010	2010	2007	2010	2010	2010	2010
SUB-SAHARAN AFRICA							
Angola[d]	..	..	..	..	..	..	..
Benin	B	3.5	..	43	82	29	40
Botswana	B	..	..	63	65	65	53
Burkina Faso	C	4.5	..	84	49	53	60
Burundi	D	3.0	..	52	53	23	31
Cameroon	C	3.0	..	84	34	11	23
Cape Verde	D	4.0	..	51	40	29	79
Central African Republic	D	3.0	..	0	83	29	29
Chad	D	2.0	..	43	90	7	5
Comoros	D	2.0	..	97	54	15	30
Congo, Dem. Rep.	D	2.5	..	53	34	13	9
Congo, Rep.[d]	..	..	..	..	..	..	..
Côte d'Ivoire[d]	..	..	..	..	..	..	..
Equatorial Guinea[d]	..	..	..	..	..	..	..
Eritrea[d]	..	..	..	..	..	..	..
Ethiopia	B	3.5	..	48	86	69	55
Gabon	D	..	..	92	50	32	30
Gambia, The	C	3.5	..	33	68	12	33
Ghana	B	3.5	..	93	59	60	56
Guinea[d]	..	..	..	..	..	..	..
Guinea-Bissau	D	2.5	..	39	82	15	8
Kenya	B	3.5	..	72	42	58	38
Lesotho	C	3.5	..	66	96	38	42
Liberia	D	2.5	..	5	77	42	32
Madagascar	D	2.5	..	46	82	12	13
Malawi	B	3.0	..	90	66	66	62
Mali	C	3.5	..	66	62	32	36
Mauritania	C	3.0	..	..	72	31	34
Mauritius[d]	..	..	..	..	..	..	..
Mozambique	B	4.0	..	90	28	47	56
Namibia	C	..	C	43	48	9	14
Niger	C	3.5	..	85	55	29	23
Nigeria	B	3.0	..	..	80	33	36
Rwanda	A	4.0	..	71	92	50	64
São Tomé and Príncipe	D	3.0	..	91	73	7	43
Senegal	C	3.5	..	67	80	29	38
Seychelles[d]	..	..	..	..	..	..	..
Sierra Leone	C	3.5	..	52	86	37	21
Somalia[d]	..	..	..	..	..	..	..
South Africa	B	..	..	0	88	25	30
Sudan	B	2.0	..	35	78	14	8
Swaziland	D	..	..	..	83	4	12
Tanzania	A	3.5	..	92	26	79	72
Togo	B	3.0	..	89	37	54	47
Uganda	B	3.5	..	96	76	66	43
Zambia	B	3.5	..	52	79	52	54
Zimbabwe[d]	..	..	..	..	..	..	..
NORTH AFRICA							
Algeria[d]	..	..	..	..	..	..	..
Djibouti[d]	..	..	..	..	..	..	..
Egypt, Arab Rep.	B	..	..	24	78	49	56
Libya[d]	..	..	..	..	..	..	..
Morocco	..	..	..	98	81	86	71
Tunisia[d]	..	..	..	..	..	..	..

Note: See technical notes for further details. PDI is a Paris Declaration Indicator.

a. Ratings range from A to E, where A means the development strategy substantially achieves good practices; B means it is largely developed toward achieving good practices; C means it reflects action taken toward achieving good practices; D means it incorporates some elements of good practice; and E means it reflects little action toward achieving good practices.

b. Ratings range from 1 (low) to 6 (high).

c. Ratings range from A (high) to D (low). Indicator was not collected in 2005.

d. Did not take part in the Survey on Monitoring the Paris Declaration.

PDI-6	PDI-7	PDI-8	PDI-9	PDI-10		PDI-11	PDI-12
Project implementation units parallel to country structures (number)	Aid disbursements on schedule and recorded by government (%)	Bilateral aid that is untied (%)	Aid provided in the framework of program-based approaches (%)	Donor missions coordinated (%)	Country analysis coordinated (%)	Existence of a monitorable performance assessment framework[a]	Existence of a mutual accountability review
2010	2010	2010	2010	2010	2010	2010	2010
..	..	..	..	..	..	..	..
40	18	97	50	19	61	D	Yes
53	0	95	12	5	62	C	No
60	75	98	50	18	48	C	No
31	48	90	49	14	33	D	No
23	36	95	28	12	40	B	No
79	55	41	33	21	48	C	No
29	0	91	0	26	26	C	Yes
5	84	80	11	12	41	D	No
30	11	100	19	9	20	D	No
9	59	93	37	22	36	C	No
..	..	..	..	..	..	..	..
..	..	..	..	..	..	..	..
..	..	..	..	..	..	..	..
..	..	..	..	..	..	..	..
55	86	86	61	25	52	B	Yes
30	28	100	18	12	46	D	No
33	8	55	12	8	54	D	No
56	67	92	57	15	42	C	Yes
..	..	..	..	..	..	..	..
8	22	86	31	17	44	D	No
38	45	90	36	28	56	B	No
42	25	96	43	12	54	C	No
32	2	92	12	12	43	C	No
13	59	92	9	7	29	D	No
62	96	88	51	22	51	C	Yes
36	34	88	44	17	40	C	Yes
34	..	55	27	23	50	C	No
..	..	..	..	..	..	..	..
56	84	90	51	15	35	C	Yes
14	0	99	14	17	60	C	No
23	72	84	41	3	34	C	No
36	92	100	47	11	26	C	No
64	74	97	67	44	82	C	Yes
43	71	90	17	13	33	D	No
38	62	95	42	25	54	C	Yes
..	..	..	..	..	..	..	..
21	58	94	34	14	34	C	No
..	..	..	..	..	..	..	..
30	93	99	61	52	39	B	No
8	36	88	1	12	38	C	No
12	94	92	25	18	23	D	No
72	97	96	60	26	48	B	Yes
47	46	98	35	12	43	C	No
43	74	95	49	24	56	C	Yes
54	0	98	45	27	50	C	No
..	..	..	..	..	..	..	..
..	..	..	..	..	..	..	..
..	..	..	..	..	..	..	..
56	69	82	49	20	38	B	No
..	..	..	..	..	..	..	..
71	79	57	59	19	44	..	Yes
..	..	..	..	..	..	..	..

Table 12.3 Capable states

	Investment climate			Enforcing contracts		
	Firms that believe the court system is fair, impartial, and uncorrupt (%) 2009–11[b]	Viewed by firms as major or very severe constraints (% of firms): Corruption 2009–11[b]	Viewed by firms as major or very severe constraints (% of firms): Crime, theft, and disorder 2009–11[b]	Number of procedures 2011	Time required (days) 2011	Cost (% of claim) 2011
SUB-SAHARAN AFRICA				**655**	**50**	**39.0**
Angola	23.6	75.6	1.5	1,011	44	46.0
Benin	..	..	..	795	65	42.0
Botswana	6.4	27.4	1.5	625	28	28.0
Burkina Faso	..	..	..	446	82	37.0
Burundi	..	..	..	832	39	44.0
Cameroon	..	..	..	800	47	43.0
Cape Verde	..	..	..	425	20	37.0
Central African Republic	8.9	41.4	25.6	660	82	43.0
Chad	..	..	..	743	46	41.0
Comoros	..	..	..	506	89	43.0
Congo, Dem. Rep.	33.0	72.7	1.8	610	152	43.0
Congo, Rep.	..	..	..	560	53	44.0
Côte d'Ivoire	..	..	..	770	42	33.0
Equatorial Guinea	..	..	..	553	19	40.0
Eritrea	..	..	..	405	23	39.0
Ethiopia	..	..	..	620	15	37.0
Gabon	..	..	..	1,070	34	38.0
Gambia, The	..	..	..	434	38	33.0
Ghana	..	..	..	487	23	36.0
Guinea	..	..	..	276	45	49.0
Guinea-Bissau	..	..	..	1,715	25	40.0
Kenya	..	..	..	465	47	40.0
Lesotho	..	..	..	785	20	40.0
Liberia	..	..	..	1,280	35	41.0
Madagascar	..	..	..	871	42	38.0
Malawi	..	..	..	312	94	42.0
Mali	15.9	24.8	0.5	620	52	36.0
Mauritania	..	..	..	370	23	46.0
Mauritius	..	..	..	645	17	36.0
Mozambique	..	..	..	730	143	30.0
Namibia	..	..	..	270	36	33.0
Niger	..	..	..	545	60	39.0
Nigeria	..	..	..	457	32	40.0
Rwanda	..	..	..	230	79	24.0
São Tomé and Príncipe	..	..	..	1,185	51	43.0
Senegal	..	..	..	780	27	43.0
Seychelles	..	..	..	915	15	37.0
Sierra Leone	..	..	..	515	150	39.0
Somalia	..	..	..	..	..	..
South Africa	..	..	..	600	33	29.0
Sudan	..	..	..	810	20	53.0
Swaziland	..	..	..	972	56	40.0
Tanzania	..	..	..	462	14	38.0
Togo	..	..	..	588	48	41.0
Uganda	..	..	..	490	45	38.0
Zambia	..	..	..	471	39	35.0
Zimbabwe	..	..	..	410	113	38.0
NORTH AFRICA				**788**	**26**	**41.0**
Algeria	..	..	..	630	22	45.0
Djibouti	..	..	..	1,225	34	40.0
Egypt, Arab Rep.	..	..	..	1,010	26	41.0
Libya	..	..	..	..	..	..
Morocco	..	..	..	510	25	40.0
Tunisia	..	..	..	565	22	39.0

a. Average of the disclosure, director liability, and shareholder suits indexes.
b. Data are for the most recent year available during the period specified.

Protecting investors (0 least desirable to 10 most desirable)				Regulation and tax administration			
Disclosure index 2011	Director liability index 2011	Shareholder suits index 2011	Investor protection index[a] 2011	Number of tax payments 2011	Time required to prepare, file, and pay taxes (hours) 2011	Total tax rate (% of profit) 2011	Extractive Industries Transparency Initiative status 2011
5	**4**	**5**	**4.5**	**37**	**318**	**57.09**	
5	6	6	5.7	31	282	53.2	
6	1	3	3.3	55	270	66.0	
7	8	3	6.0	19	152	19.4	
6	1	4	3.7	46	270	43.6	Candidate
8	6	4	6.0	24	274	46.2	
6	1	6	4.3	44	654	49.1	Candidate
1	5	6	4.0	41	186	37.8	
6	1	5	4.0	54	504	54.6	Compliant
6	1	3	3.3	54	732	65.4	Candidate
6	1	5	4.0	20	100	217.9	
3	3	4	3.3	32	336	339.7	Candidate
6	1	3	3.3	61	606	65.9	Candidate
6	1	3	3.3	62	270	44.3	Candidate
6	1	4	3.7	46	492	46.0	
4	5	5	4.7	18	216	84.5	
4	4	5	4.3	19	198	31.1	
6	1	3	3.3	26	488	43.5	Candidate
2	1	5	2.7	50	376	283.5	
7	5	6	6.0	33	224	33.6	Compliant
6	1	1	2.7	56	416	54.3	Candidate
6	1	5	4.0	46	208	45.9	
3	2	10	5.0	41	393	49.6	
2	1	8	3.7	21	324	16.0	
4	1	6	3.7	33	158	43.7	Compliant
5	6	6	5.7	23	201	36.6	Suspended
4	7	5	5.3	19	157	28.2	
6	1	4	3.7	59	270	51.8	Compliant
5	3	3	3.7	37	696	68.3	Compliant
6	8	9	7.7	7	161	25.0	
5	4	9	6.0	37	230	34.3	Candidate
5	5	6	5.3	37	375	9.8	
6	1	3	3.3	41	270	43.8	Compliant
5	7	5	5.7	35	938	32.7	Compliant
7	9	3	6.3	18	148	31.3	
3	1	6	3.3	42	424	32.5	
6	1	2	3.0	59	666	46.0	
4	8	5	5.7	21	76	32.2	
6	7	6	6.3	29	357	32.1	Candidate
..	..	..	..	..	..	..	
8	8	8	8.0	9	200	33.1	
0	6	4	3.3	42	180	36.1	
2	5	6	4.3	33	104	36.8	
3	4	8	5.0	48	172	45.5	Candidate
6	1	4	3.7	53	270	49.5	Candidate
2	5	5	4.0	32	213	35.7	
3	6	7	5.3	37	132	14.5	Candidate
8	1	4	4.3	49	242	35.6	
6	**4**	**4**	**4.8**	**24**	**270**	**53.4**	
6	6	4	5.3	29	451	72.0	
5	2	0	2.3	35	82	38.7	
8	3	5	5.3	29	433	43.6	
..	..	..	..	..	..	..	
7	2	6	5.0	17	238	49.6	
5	7	6	6.0	8	144	62.9	

Table 12.4 Governance and anticorruption indicators

	Governance indicators[a]											
	Voice and accountability		Political stability and absence of violence		Government effectiveness		Regulatory quality		Rule of law		Control of corruption	
	1996	2010	1996	2010	1996	2010	1996	2010	1996	2010	1996	2010
SUB-SAHARAN AFRICA												
Angola	-1.6	-1.1	-2.1	-0.2	-0.8	-1.1	-1.5	-1.0	-1.6	-1.2	-1.2	-1.3
Benin	0.1	0.3	1.0	0.3	-0.4	-0.5	-0.2	-0.3	-0.1	-0.7	-0.9	-0.8
Botswana	0.9	0.4	0.9	0.9	0.5	0.5	0.7	0.5	0.5	0.7	0.6	1.0
Burkina Faso	-0.8	-0.2	-0.4	-0.1	-1.0	-0.6	-0.3	-0.1	-0.9	-0.2	0.2	-0.4
Burundi	-1.6	-0.9	-2.3	-1.5	-1.7	-1.1	-1.7	-1.1	-1.5	-1.2	-1.4	-1.1
Cameroon	-1.0	-1.1	-1.1	-0.6	-1.0	-0.9	-1.1	-0.7	-1.4	-1.0	-1.2	-1.0
Cape Verde	0.7	0.9	1.0	0.8	..	-0.1	-0.6	-0.1	0.5	0.4	..	0.8
Central African Republic	-0.9	-1.1	-1.2	-2.1	-1.5	-1.4	-0.9	-1.1	-1.5	-1.3	-1.4	-0.8
Chad	-1.0	-1.4	-1.0	-1.5	-0.7	-1.5	-1.3	-1.1	-0.9	-1.5	-0.9	-1.3
Comoros	-0.7	-0.4	0.4	-0.4	-1.7	-1.7	-1.2	-1.5	-1.1	-1.1	-0.9	-0.7
Congo, Dem. Rep.	-1.7	-1.4	-2.8	-2.2	-1.7	-1.7	-1.8	-1.6	-1.9	-1.6	-2.1	-1.4
Congo, Rep.	-1.0	-1.0	-1.3	-0.2	-1.2	-1.2	-1.3	-1.3	-1.5	-1.1	-1.1	-1.1
Côte d'Ivoire	-0.6	-1.1	-0.1	-1.6	-0.1	-1.3	-0.5	-0.9	-0.8	-1.2	0.2	-1.1
Equatorial Guinea	-1.5	-1.9	-0.3	0.2	-1.1	-1.7	-1.6	-1.4	-1.0	-1.3	-1.3	-1.5
Eritrea	-1.5	-2.2	-0.9	-0.9	-1.2	-1.4	-1.2	-2.2	-0.3	-1.3	0.4	-0.5
Ethiopia	-1.1	-1.3	-1.0	-1.7	-1.3	-0.3	-1.3	-0.9	-0.8	-0.8	-1.2	-0.7
Gabon	-0.3	-0.9	0.0	0.2	-0.3	-0.9	0.1	-0.6	-0.5	-0.5	-1.0	-0.8
Gambia, The	-1.3	-1.1	0.4	0.1	-0.6	-0.7	-0.9	-0.4	0.1	-0.5	-0.4	-0.6
Ghana	-0.4	0.5	-0.3	0.0	-0.1	0.0	-0.4	0.1	-0.3	-0.1	-0.2	0.1
Guinea	-1.4	-0.9	-1.2	-1.8	-1.2	-1.1	-0.7	-1.1	-1.5	-1.5	-0.5	-1.2
Guinea-Bissau	-1.1	-0.9	-1.6	-0.8	-1.5	-1.0	-0.8	-1.1	-2.1	-1.4	-1.1	-1.1
Kenya	-0.6	-0.2	-0.8	-1.2	-0.3	-0.5	-0.4	-0.1	-1.0	-1.0	-1.0	-0.9
Lesotho	-0.7	-0.2	0.2	0.5	-0.1	-0.4	-0.4	-0.6	0.1	-0.3	-0.5	0.2
Liberia	-1.5	-0.2	-2.6	-0.5	-1.9	-1.2	-2.0	-1.1	-2.2	-1.0	-1.7	-0.5
Madagascar	-0.3	-0.8	0.1	-1.1	-0.6	-0.8	-1.0	-0.6	-0.6	-0.8	0.2	-0.3
Malawi	-0.2	-0.2	-0.5	0.1	-0.5	-0.4	-0.3	-0.6	-0.4	-0.1	-0.2	-0.4
Mali	-0.1	0.2	0.3	-0.3	-1.2	-0.9	-0.5	-0.5	-0.5	-0.5	-0.4	-0.7
Mauritania	-0.5	-0.9	0.3	-1.3	-0.1	-0.9	-0.5	-0.8	-0.3	-0.9	0.0	-0.7
Mauritius	0.8	0.7	0.9	0.5	0.3	0.8	0.0	0.8	0.9	0.8	0.5	0.7
Mozambique	-0.3	-0.1	-0.2	0.3	-0.1	-0.5	-0.5	-0.4	-0.8	-0.5	-0.4	-0.4
Namibia	0.4	0.3	0.7	0.8	0.5	0.1	0.4	0.1	0.3	0.2	0.7	0.3
Niger	-1.7	-0.6	-0.2	-1.1	-1.2	-0.7	-1.1	-0.5	-1.0	-0.6	-1.1	-0.7
Nigeria	-1.7	-0.8	-1.2	-2.0	-1.0	-1.2	-0.8	-0.8	-1.2	-1.2	-1.2	-1.0
Rwanda	-1.5	-1.3	-2.1	-0.1	-1.2	-0.1	-1.5	-0.2	-1.5	-0.3	-0.9	0.5
São Tomé and Príncipe	0.0	0.1	1.0	0.1	-0.4	-0.7	-0.7	-0.8	0.2	-0.7	0.0	-0.4
Senegal	0.0	-0.3	-0.7	-0.4	0.0	-0.5	-0.2	-0.3	-0.2	-0.4	-0.2	-0.7
Seychelles	0.0	0.1	1.0	0.8	0.6	0.2	0.3	-0.6	1.0	0.0	0.9	0.3
Sierra Leone	-0.7	-0.2	-2.0	-0.2	-1.5	-1.2	-1.6	-0.7	-1.5	-0.9	-0.8	-0.8
Somalia	-2.1	-2.0	-2.7	-3.1	-2.1	-2.2	-2.5	-2.4	-2.3	-2.4	-1.7	-1.7
South Africa	0.8	0.5	-0.5	0.0	0.9	0.3	0.4	0.4	0.0	0.1	0.8	0.1
Sudan	-1.9	-1.7	-2.5	-2.7	-1.1	-1.4	-1.4	-1.4	-1.6	-1.3	-1.3	-1.3
Swaziland	-1.3	-1.3	-0.1	-0.1	-0.7	-0.5	-0.2	-0.6	-0.6	-0.5	0.0	-0.2
Tanzania	-0.7	-0.1	-0.7	0.0	-0.7	-0.5	-0.4	-0.4	-0.2	-0.5	-1.0	-0.5
Togo	-1.0	-1.0	-0.5	-0.2	-0.8	-1.4	-0.4	-0.9	-0.7	-0.9	-0.8	-1.0
Uganda	-0.9	-0.5	-1.6	-1.1	-0.7	-0.6	0.2	-0.1	-0.6	-0.4	-0.6	-0.9
Zambia	-0.4	-0.3	-0.2	0.5	-1.1	-0.8	-0.4	-0.5	-0.6	-0.5	-1.0	-0.6
Zimbabwe	-0.7	-1.5	-0.5	-1.2	-0.2	-1.6	-1.0	-2.0	-0.7	-1.8	-0.3	-1.4
NORTH AFRICA												
Algeria	-1.3	-1.0	-2.0	-1.3	-0.9	-0.6	-0.8	-1.1	-1.2	-0.8	-0.5	-0.5
Djibouti	-1.0	-1.1	-0.4	0.3	-0.9	-1.0	-1.0	-0.7	-0.8	-0.7	-0.5	-0.3
Egypt, Arab Rep.	-0.7	-1.2	-0.6	-0.9	-0.1	-0.4	0.0	-0.2	0.1	-0.1	-0.1	-0.6
Libya	-1.4	-1.9	-1.0	-0.1	-0.9	-1.2	-1.8	-1.2	-0.9	-1.0	-0.8	-1.3
Morocco	-0.4	-0.8	-0.3	-0.5	0.0	-0.2	-0.2	-0.1	0.3	-0.2	0.3	-0.2
Tunisia	-0.5	-1.3	0.1	0.1	0.4	0.2	0.0	0.0	-0.1	0.1	-0.2	-0.1

a. The rating scale for each criterion varies from -2.5 (weak performance) to 2.5 (very high performance).

b. A score of 81-100 indicates that a given country provides extensive information in its budget documents, a score of 61-80 indicates significant information, 41-60 indicates some information, 21-40 indicates minimal information, and zero-20 indicates scant or no information. In 2008, based on inputs received, the International Budget Partnership (IBP) made three changes in the methodology applied to its Open Budget Survey, which is the basis for the Open Budget Index (OBI).

c. Data are for the most recent year available during the period specified.

Share of firms (%)								
Expected to pay informal payment to public officials to get things done	Expected to give gifts to obtain an operating license	Expected to give gifts in meetings with tax officials	Expected to give gifts to secure a government contract	Identifying corruption as a major constraint	Mean corruption perceptions index score (0 low to 10 high)		Open Budget Index overall score[b]	
2010–11[c]	2010–11[c]	2010–11[c]	2010–11[c]	2010–11[c]	2010	2011	2008	2011
48.9	39.0	34.2	58.5	75.6	1.9	2.0	3.0	26.0
..	..	..	..	..	2.8	3.0	..	..
7.3	2.9	8.4	1.0	27.4	5.8	6.1	62.0	51.0
..	..	..	..	..	3.1	3.0	14.0	5.0
..	..	..	..	..	1.8	1.9	..	..
..	..	..	..	..	2.2	2.5	5.0	2.0
..	..	..	..	..	5.1	5.5	..	..
41.8	5.8	16.8	40.8	41.4	2.1	2.2	..	..
..	..	..	..	..	1.7	2.0	7.0	0.4
..	..	..	..	..	2.1	2.4	..	..
65.7	53.8	54.4	75.7	72.7	2.0	2.0	0.0	6.0
..	..	..	..	..	2.1	2.2	..	..
..	..	..	..	..	2.2	2.2	..	..
..	..	..	..	..	1.9	1.9	..	0.0
..	..	..	..	..	2.6	2.5	0.0	..
..	..	..	..	..	2.7	2.7	..	..
..	..	..	..	..	2.8	3.0	..	..
..	..	..	..	..	3.2	3.5	..	..
..	..	..	..	..	4.1	3.9	..	54.0
..	..	..	..	..	2.0	2.1	49.0	..
..	..	..	..	..	2.1	2.2	..	..
..	..	..	..	..	2.1	2.2	..	49.0
..	..	..	..	..	3.5	3.5	57.0	..
..	..	..	..	..	3.3	3.2	..	40.0
..	..	..	..	..	2.6	3.0	2.0	..
..	..	..	..	..	3.4	3.0	..	47.0
19.4	42.4	20.2	22.8	24.8	2.7	2.8	28.0	35.0
..	..	..	..	..	2.3	2.4	..	..
..	..	..	..	..	5.4	5.1	..	..
..	..	..	..	..	2.7	2.7	..	28.0
..	..	..	..	..	4.4	4.4	..	53.0
..	..	..	..	..	2.6	2.5	47.0	3.0
..	..	..	..	..	2.4	2.4	26.0	18.0
..	..	..	..	..	4.0	5.0	19.0	11.0
..	..	..	..	..	3.0	3.0	0.0	0.0
..	..	..	..	..	2.9	2.9	0.0	3.0
..	..	..	..	..	4.8	4.8	3.0	..
..	..	..	..	..	2.4	2.5	..	..
..	..	..	..	..	1.1	1.0	..	..
..	..	..	..	..	4.5	4.1	..	92.0
..	..	..	..	..	1.6	1.6	87.0	8.0
..	..	..	..	..	3.2	3.1	0.0	..
..	..	..	..	..	2.7	3.0	..	45.0
..	..	..	..	..	2.4	2.4	35.0	..
..	..	..	..	..	2.5	2.4	..	55.0
..	..	..	..	..	3.0	3.2	51.0	36.0
..	..	..	..	..	2.4	2.2	47.0	..
..	..	..	..	..	2.9	2.9	..	1.0
..	..	..	..	..	3.2	3.0	1.0	..
..	..	..	..	..	3.1	2.9	43.0	49.0
..	..	..	..	..	2.2	2.0	..	..
..	..	..	..	..	3.4	3.4	27.0	28.0
..	..	..	..	..	4.3	3.8	..	..

Table 12.5 Country Policy and Institutional Assessment ratings

	CPIA overall rating (IDA resource allocation index)[a]		Economic management							
			Average[b]		Macroeconomic management		Fiscal policy		Debt policy	
	2009	2011	2009	2011	2009	2011	2009	2011	2009	2011
SUB-SAHARAN AFRICA	**3.2**	**3.2**	**3.4**	**3.4**	**3.6**	**3.6**	**3.4**	**3.4**	**3.2**	**3.3**
Angola	2.8	2.7	3.0	3.0	3.0	3.0	3.0	3.0	3.0	3.0
Benin	3.5	3.5	3.7	3.5	4.0	4.0	3.5	3.0	3.5	3.5
Botswana[c]	..	..	..	..	..	..	..	..	..	..
Burkina Faso	3.8	3.8	4.3	4.2	4.5	4.5	4.5	4.0	4.0	4.0
Burundi	3.1	3.1	3.3	3.2	3.5	3.5	3.5	3.5	3.0	2.5
Cameroon	3.2	3.2	3.7	3.7	4.0	4.0	4.0	3.5	3.0	3.5
Cape Verde	4.2	4.0	4.5	3.8	4.5	4.0	4.5	4.0	4.5	3.5
Central African Republic	2.6	2.8	3.0	3.3	3.5	3.5	3.0	3.5	2.5	3.0
Chad	2.5	2.4	2.5	2.5	2.5	2.5	2.5	2.5	2.5	2.5
Comoros	2.5	2.7	2.3	2.5	3.0	3.0	2.0	2.5	2.0	2.0
Congo, Dem. Rep.	2.7	2.7	3.2	3.2	3.5	3.5	3.5	3.5	2.5	2.5
Congo, Rep.	2.8	3.0	3.0	3.5	3.5	3.5	3.0	3.5	2.5	3.5
Côte d'Ivoire	2.8	2.9	2.8	2.8	3.5	3.5	2.5	3.0	2.5	2.0
Equatorial Guinea[c]	..	..	..	..	..	..	..	..	..	..
Eritrea	2.2	2.2	1.8	1.8	2.0	2.0	2.0	2.0	1.5	1.5
Ethiopia	3.4	3.5	3.7	3.7	3.5	3.0	4.0	4.0	3.5	4.0
Gabon	..	..	..	..	..	..	..	..	..	..
Gambia, The	3.3	3.5	3.5	3.5	4.0	4.0	3.5	3.5	3.0	3.0
Ghana	3.8	3.9	3.7	3.8	3.5	4.0	3.5	3.5	4.0	4.0
Guinea	2.8	2.9	2.3	2.8	2.5	3.0	2.5	3.0	2.0	2.5
Guinea-Bissau	2.6	2.8	2.2	3.0	2.5	3.5	2.5	3.0	1.5	2.5
Kenya	3.7	3.8	4.2	4.2	4.5	4.0	4.0	4.0	4.0	4.5
Lesotho	3.5	3.4	4.0	3.7	4.0	4.0	4.0	3.0	4.0	4.0
Liberia	2.8	3.0	3.2	3.5	3.5	3.5	3.5	3.5	2.5	3.5
Madagascar	3.5	3.2	3.7	3.5	4.0	3.5	3.0	3.0	4.0	4.0
Malawi	3.4	3.3	3.2	3.2	3.0	2.5	3.5	3.5	3.0	3.5
Mali	3.7	3.6	4.3	4.2	4.5	4.5	4.0	4.0	4.5	4.0
Mauritania	3.2	3.2	3.2	3.3	3.5	3.5	2.5	3.5	3.5	3.0
Mauritius	..	..	..	..	..	..	..	..	..	..
Mozambique	3.7	3.7	4.5	4.5	4.5	4.5	4.5	4.5	4.5	4.5
Namibia[c]	..	..	..	..	..	..	..	..	..	..
Niger	3.3	3.4	3.8	3.8	4.0	4.0	3.5	3.5	4.0	4.0
Nigeria	3.5	3.4	4.3	4.0	4.0	4.0	4.5	4.0	4.5	4.0
Rwanda	3.8	3.8	3.8	3.8	4.0	4.0	4.0	4.0	3.5	3.5
São Tomé and Príncipe	2.9	3.1	2.8	2.8	3.0	3.0	3.0	3.0	2.5	2.5
Senegal	3.7	3.8	4.0	4.0	4.0	4.0	4.0	4.0	4.0	4.0
Seychelles	..	..	..	..	..	..	..	..	..	..
Sierra Leone	3.2	3.3	3.7	3.7	4.0	4.0	3.5	3.5	3.5	3.5
Somalia[d]	..	..	..	..	..	..	..	..	..	..
South Africa[c]	..	..	..	..	..	..	..	..	..	..
Sudan	2.5	2.4	2.7	2.3	3.5	3.0	3.0	2.5	1.5	1.5
Swaziland[c]	..	..	..	..	..	..	..	..	..	..
Tanzania	3.8	3.7	4.3	4.2	4.5	4.5	4.5	4.0	4.0	4.0
Togo	2.8	3.0	2.8	3.2	3.0	3.5	3.0	3.0	2.5	3.0
Uganda	3.9	3.8	4.5	4.2	4.5	4.0	4.5	4.0	4.5	4.5
Zambia	3.4	3.5	3.5	3.7	4.0	4.0	3.0	3.5	3.5	3.5
Zimbabwe	1.9	2.2	1.7	1.8	2.0	2.0	2.0	2.0	1.0	1.5
NORTH AFRICA										
Algeria[c]	..	..	..	..	..	..	..	..	..	..
Djibouti	3.2	..	3.0	..	3.5	..	3.0	..	2.5	..
Egypt, Arab Rep.[c]	..	..	..	..	..	..	..	..	..	..
Libya[c]	..	..	..	..	..	..	..	..	..	..
Morocco[c]	..	..	..	..	..	..	..	..	..	..
Tunisia[c]	..	..	..	..	..	..	..	..	..	..

Structural policies							
Average[b]		Trade		Financial sector		Business regulatory environment	
2009	2011	2009	2011	2009	2011	2009	2011
3.2	**3.2**	**3.7**	**3.6**	**3.0**	**3.0**	**3.1**	**3.0**
2.8	2.7	4.0	3.5	2.5	2.5	2.0	2.0
3.7	3.7	4.0	4.0	3.5	3.5	3.5	3.5
..	..	..	..	..	..	..	..
3.5	3.5	4.0	4.0	3.0	3.0	3.5	3.5
3.0	3.2	4.0	4.0	2.5	2.5	2.5	3.0
3.2	3.2	3.5	3.5	3.0	3.0	3.0	3.0
3.8	4.0	4.0	4.5	4.0	4.0	3.5	3.5
2.7	2.5	3.5	3.0	2.5	2.5	2.0	2.0
2.8	2.5	3.0	3.0	3.0	2.5	2.5	2.0
2.7	3.0	3.0	3.5	2.5	3.0	2.5	2.5
2.5	2.5	3.5	3.0	2.0	2.0	2.0	2.5
3.0	3.0	3.5	3.5	3.0	3.0	2.5	2.5
3.3	3.3	4.0	4.0	3.0	3.0	3.0	3.0
..	..	..	..	..	..	..	..
1.5	1.5	1.5	1.5	1.0	1.0	2.0	2.0
3.2	3.2	3.0	3.0	3.0	3.0	3.5	3.5
..	..	..	..	..	..	..	..
3.3	3.7	3.5	4.0	3.0	3.5	3.5	3.5
4.0	4.2	4.0	4.0	4.0	4.0	4.0	4.5
3.3	3.0	4.0	4.0	3.0	2.5	3.0	2.5
3.2	3.0	4.0	4.0	3.0	2.5	2.5	2.5
4.0	4.0	4.0	4.0	4.0	4.0	4.0	4.0
3.3	3.2	3.5	3.5	3.5	3.0	3.0	3.0
2.8	2.8	3.0	3.0	2.5	2.5	3.0	3.0
3.5	3.3	4.0	4.0	3.0	3.0	3.5	3.0
3.5	3.0	4.0	3.0	3.0	3.0	3.5	3.0
3.5	3.5	4.0	4.0	3.0	3.0	3.5	3.5
3.3	3.2	4.0	4.0	2.5	2.5	3.5	3.0
..	..	..	..	..	..	..	..
3.7	3.5	4.5	4.0	3.5	3.5	3.0	3.0
..	..	..	..	..	..	..	..
3.3	3.2	4.0	3.5	3.0	3.0	3.0	3.0
3.5	3.5	3.5	3.5	3.5	3.5	3.5	3.5
3.8	3.8	4.0	4.0	3.5	3.5	4.0	4.0
3.0	3.2	4.0	4.0	2.5	2.5	2.5	3.0
3.8	4.0	4.0	4.5	3.5	3.5	4.0	4.0
..	..	..	..	..	..	..	..
3.2	3.2	3.5	3.5	3.0	3.0	3.0	3.0
..	..	..	..	..	..	..	..
..	..	..	..	..	..	..	..
2.7	2.5	2.5	2.5	2.5	2.5	3.0	2.5
..	..	..	..	..	..	..	..
3.8	3.8	4.0	4.0	4.0	4.0	3.5	3.5
3.2	3.0	4.0	4.0	2.5	2.5	3.0	2.5
3.8	4.0	4.0	4.5	3.5	3.5	4.0	4.0
3.5	3.7	4.0	4.0	3.5	3.5	3.0	3.5
2.2	2.3	3.0	3.0	1.5	2.0	2.0	2.0
..	..	..	..	..	..	..	..
3.7	..	4.0	..	3.5	..	3.5	..
..	..	..	..	..	..	..	..
..	..	..	..	..	..	..	..
..	..	..	..	..	..	..	..
..	..	..	..	..	..	..	..

Table 12.5 Country Policy and Institutional Assessment ratings (continued)

	Policies for social inclusion/equity											
	Average[b]		Gender equality		Equity of public resource use		Building human resources		Social protection and labor		Policies and institutions for environmental sustainability	
	2009	2011	2009	2011	2009	2011	2009	2011	2009	2011	2009	2011
SUB-SAHARAN AFRICA	**3.1**	**3.2**	**3.2**	**3.2**	**3.2**	**3.3**	**3.3**	**3.4**	**3.0**	**3.0**	**2.9**	**3.1**
Angola	2.9	3.5	3.5	3.5	2.5	2.5	2.5	3.0	3.0	2.5	3.0	2.5
Benin	3.3	3.5	3.5	3.5	3.0	3.5	3.5	3.5	3.0	3.0	3.5	3.5
Botswana[c]	..	..	..	..	..	..	..	..	..	..	..	..
Burkina Faso	3.6	3.5	3.5	3.5	4.0	4.0	3.5	3.5	3.5	3.5	3.5	4.0
Burundi	3.3	4.0	4.0	4.0	3.5	3.5	3.0	3.5	3.0	3.0	3.0	3.0
Cameroon	3.1	3.0	3.0	3.0	3.0	3.0	3.5	3.0	3.0	3.0	3.0	3.0
Cape Verde	4.3	4.5	4.5	4.5	4.5	4.0	4.5	4.5	4.5	4.5	3.5	3.5
Central African Republic	2.5	2.5	2.5	2.5	2.5	3.0	2.5	2.5	2.0	2.0	3.0	3.0
Chad	2.4	2.5	2.5	2.5	2.5	2.5	2.5	2.5	2.5	2.5	2.0	2.5
Comoros	2.6	2.5	3.0	2.5	2.5	2.5	3.0	3.0	2.5	3.0	2.0	2.5
Congo, Dem. Rep.	2.8	2.5	2.5	2.5	3.0	3.0	3.0	3.5	3.0	2.5	2.5	2.5
Congo, Rep.	2.7	3.0	3.0	3.0	2.5	2.5	3.0	3.5	2.5	2.5	2.5	3.0
Côte d'Ivoire	2.4	2.5	2.5	2.5	2.0	2.5	2.5	3.0	2.5	2.5	2.5	2.5
Equatorial Guinea[c]	..	..	..	..	..	..	..	..	..	..	..	..
Eritrea	2.8	3.5	3.5	3.5	2.5	2.5	3.5	3.5	2.5	2.0	2.0	2.0
Ethiopia	3.6	3.0	3.0	3.0	4.5	4.0	4.0	4.5	3.5	3.5	3.0	3.5
Gabon	..	..	..	..	..	..	..	..	..	..	..	..
Gambia, The	3.3	3.5	3.5	3.5	3.5	4.0	3.5	4.0	2.5	2.5	3.5	3.5
Ghana	3.9	4.0	4.0	4.0	4.0	3.5	4.5	4.5	3.5	4.0	3.5	3.5
Guinea	3.0	3.0	3.5	3.0	3.0	3.0	3.0	3.5	3.0	3.0	2.5	2.5
Guinea-Bissau	2.5	2.5	2.5	2.5	3.0	3.0	2.0	2.5	2.5	2.5	2.5	3.0
Kenya	3.5	3.5	3.0	3.5	3.5	4.0	4.0	4.0	3.5	3.5	3.5	3.5
Lesotho	3.3	4.0	4.0	4.0	3.0	3.0	3.5	3.5	3.0	3.0	3.0	3.5
Liberia	2.5	3.0	2.5	3.0	3.0	4.0	2.5	2.5	2.5	2.5	2.0	3.0
Madagascar	3.6	3.5	3.5	3.5	4.0	4.0	3.5	3.0	3.5	2.5	3.5	3.5
Malawi	3.5	3.5	3.5	3.5	3.5	3.5	3.5	3.5	3.5	3.5	3.5	4.0
Mali	3.4	3.5	3.5	3.5	3.5	4.0	3.5	3.5	3.5	3.5	3.0	3.5
Mauritania	3.4	4.0	4.0	4.0	3.5	3.5	3.5	3.5	3.0	2.5	3.0	3.0
Mauritius	..	..	..	..	..	..	..	..	..	..	..	..
Mozambique	3.3	3.5	3.5	3.5	3.5	3.0	3.5	4.0	3.0	3.0	3.0	3.0
Namibia[c]	..	..	..	..	..	..	..	..	..	..	..	..
Niger	3.1	2.5	2.5	2.5	3.5	4.0	3.5	3.5	3.0	3.0	3.0	4.0
Nigeria	3.2	3.0	3.0	3.0	3.5	3.5	3.0	3.0	3.5	3.5	3.0	3.5
Rwanda	3.9	4.0	3.5	4.0	4.5	4.5	4.5	4.5	3.5	3.5	3.5	3.5
São Tomé and Príncipe	2.8	3.0	3.0	3.0	3.0	3.0	3.0	3.5	2.5	2.5	2.5	3.5
Senegal	3.4	3.5	3.5	3.5	3.5	3.5	3.5	4.0	3.0	3.0	3.5	3.5
Seychelles	..	..	..	..	..	..	..	..	..	..	..	..
Sierra Leone	3.1	3.0	3.0	3.0	3.0	3.5	3.5	3.5	3.5	3.5	2.5	3.0
Somalia[d]	..	..	..	..	..	..	..	..	..	..	..	..
South Africa[c]	..	..	..	..	..	..	..	..	..	..	..	..
Sudan	2.3	2.5	2.0	2.5	2.5	2.5	2.5	2.5	2.5	2.5	2.0	2.0
Swaziland[c]	..	..	..	..	..	..	..	..	..	..	..	..
Tanzania	3.7	3.5	3.5	3.5	4.0	4.0	4.0	3.5	3.5	3.5	3.5	3.0
Togo	2.7	3.0	3.0	3.0	2.0	3.0	3.0	3.5	3.0	3.0	2.5	2.5
Uganda	3.8	3.5	3.5	3.5	4.0	4.0	4.0	4.0	3.5	3.5	4.0	3.5
Zambia	3.5	3.0	3.5	3.0	3.5	3.5	4.0	4.0	3.0	3.0	3.5	3.5
Zimbabwe	1.6	3.0	2.5	3.0	1.5	2.0	1.0	2.0	1.0	2.0	2.0	3.0
NORTH AFRICA												
Algeria[c]	..	..	..	..	..	..	..	..	..	..	..	..
Djibouti	3.2	..	3.0	..	3.0	..	3.5	..	3.0	..	3.5	..
Egypt, Arab Rep.[c]	..	..	..	..	..	..	..	..	..	..	..	..
Libya[c]	..	..	..	..	..	..	..	..	..	..	..	..
Morocco[c]	..	..	..	..	..	..	..	..	..	..	..	..
Tunisia[c]	..	..	..	..	..	..	..	..	..	..	..	..

Note: The rating scale for each indicator ranges from 1 (low) to 6 (high).

a. Calculated as the average of the average ratings of each cluster.

b. All criteria are weighted equally.

c. Not an International Development Association (IDA) member.

d. Not rated in the IDA resource allocation index.

Public sector management and institutions											
Average[b]		Property rights and rule-based governance		Quality of budgetary and financial management		Efficiency of revenue mobilization		Quality of public administration		Transparency, accountability, and corruption in public sector	
2009	2011	2009	2011	2009	2011	2009	2011	2009	2011	2009	2011
3.0	**3.0**	**2.8**	**2.8**	**3.0**	**3.1**	**3.4**	**3.4**	**2.9**	**2.9**	**2.7**	**2.8**
2.4	2.3	2.0	2.0	2.5	2.5	2.5	2.5	2.5	2.0	2.5	2.5
3.3	3.3	3.0	3.0	3.5	3.5	3.5	3.5	3.0	3.0	3.5	3.5
..	..	..	..	..	..	..	..	..	..	..	..
3.7	3.7	3.5	3.5	4.5	4.5	3.5	3.5	3.5	3.5	3.5	3.5
2.6	2.7	2.5	2.5	3.0	3.0	3.0	3.5	2.5	2.5	2.0	2.0
2.9	2.9	2.5	2.5	3.0	3.0	3.5	3.5	3.0	3.0	2.5	2.5
4.0	4.0	4.0	4.0	4.0	4.0	3.5	3.5	4.0	4.0	4.5	4.5
2.4	2.6	2.0	2.0	2.5	3.0	2.5	3.0	2.5	2.5	2.5	2.5
2.2	2.2	2.0	2.0	2.0	2.0	2.5	2.5	2.5	2.5	2.0	2.0
2.4	2.4	2.5	2.5	2.0	2.0	2.5	2.5	2.5	2.5	2.5	2.5
2.2	2.2	2.0	2.0	2.5	2.5	2.5	2.5	2.0	2.0	2.0	2.0
2.6	2.6	2.5	2.5	2.5	2.5	3.0	3.0	2.5	2.5	2.5	2.5
2.6	2.7	2.0	2.0	2.5	3.0	4.0	3.5	2.0	2.5	2.5	2.5
..	..	..	..	..	..	..	..	..	..	..	..
2.7	2.6	2.5	2.5	2.5	2.0	3.5	3.5	3.0	3.0	2.0	2.0
3.2	3.3	3.0	3.0	3.5	3.5	3.5	3.5	3.5	3.5	2.5	3.0
..	..	..	..	..	..	..	..	..	..	..	..
2.9	3.2	3.0	3.0	3.0	3.5	3.5	3.5	3.0	3.5	2.0	2.5
3.8	3.7	3.5	3.5	3.5	3.5	4.5	4.0	3.5	3.5	4.0	4.0
2.6	2.6	2.0	2.0	3.0	3.0	3.0	3.0	3.0	3.0	2.0	2.0
2.6	2.6	2.5	2.5	2.5	2.5	3.0	3.0	2.5	2.5	2.5	2.5
3.3	3.3	2.5	2.5	3.5	3.5	4.0	4.0	3.5	3.5	3.0	3.0
3.4	3.5	3.5	3.5	3.0	3.5	4.0	4.0	3.0	3.0	3.5	3.5
2.8	2.8	2.5	2.5	2.5	2.5	3.5	3.5	2.5	2.5	3.0	3.0
3.3	2.8	3.5	3.0	3.0	2.5	4.0	3.5	3.5	2.5	2.5	2.5
3.4	3.3	3.5	3.5	3.0	3.0	4.0	4.0	3.5	3.0	3.0	3.0
3.4	3.3	3.5	3.0	3.5	3.5	3.5	3.5	3.0	3.0	3.5	3.5
3.0	3.0	3.0	3.0	3.0	3.0	3.5	3.5	3.0	3.0	2.5	2.5
..	..	..	..	..	..	..	..	..	..	..	..
3.4	3.4	3.0	3.0	4.0	4.0	4.0	4.0	3.0	3.0	3.0	3.0
..	..	..	..	..	..	..	..	..	..	..	..
3.1	3.2	3.0	3.0	3.5	3.5	3.5	3.5	3.0	3.0	2.5	3.0
2.9	2.9	2.5	2.5	3.0	3.0	3.0	3.0	3.0	3.0	3.0	3.0
3.5	3.6	3.0	3.5	4.0	4.0	3.5	3.5	3.5	3.5	3.5	3.5
3.1	3.1	2.5	2.5	3.0	3.0	3.5	3.5	3.0	3.0	3.5	3.5
3.4	3.6	3.5	3.5	3.0	3.5	4.0	4.0	3.5	3.5	3.0	3.5
..	..	..	..	..	..	..	..	..	..	..	..
2.9	3.1	2.5	3.0	3.5	3.5	2.5	3.0	3.0	3.0	3.0	3.0
..	..	..	..	..	..	..	..	..	..	..	..
..	..	..	..	..	..	..	..	..	..	..	..
2.2	2.2	2.0	2.0	2.0	2.5	3.0	3.0	2.5	2.0	1.5	1.5
..	..	..	..	..	..	..	..	..	..	..	..
3.5	3.3	3.5	3.5	3.5	3.0	4.0	4.0	3.5	3.0	3.0	3.0
2.4	2.8	2.5	3.0	2.5	3.0	3.0	3.0	2.0	2.5	2.0	2.5
3.3	3.2	3.5	3.5	4.0	3.5	3.5	3.5	3.0	3.0	2.5	2.5
3.2	3.1	3.0	3.0	3.5	3.5	3.5	3.5	3.0	3.0	3.0	2.5
2.0	2.2	1.5	1.5	2.0	2.5	3.5	3.5	1.5	2.0	1.5	1.5
..	..	..	..	..	..	..	..	..	..	..	..
2.8	..	2.5	..	3.0	..	3.5	..	2.5	..	2.5	..
..	..	..	..	..	..	..	..	..	..	..	..
..	..	..	..	..	..	..	..	..	..	..	..
..	..	..	..	..	..	..	..	..	..	..	..
..	..	..	..	..	..	..	..	..	..	..	..

Table 12.6 Polity indicators

	Revised combined polity score (–10 strongly autocratic to 10 strongly democratic)				Institutionalized democracy (0 low to 10 high)				Institutionalized autocracy (0 low to 10 high)			
	1995	2000	2005	2010	1995	2000	2005	2010	1995	2000	2005	2010
SUB-SAHARAN AFRICA												
Angola	-2.0	-3.0	-2.0	-2.0	..	1.0	2.0	2.0	..	4.0	4.0	4.0
Benin	6.0	6.0	6.0	7.0	6.0	6.0	6.0	7.0	0.0	0.0	0.0	0.0
Botswana	7.0	8.0	8.0	8.0	7.0	8.0	8.0	8.0	0.0	0.0	0.0	0.0
Burkina Faso	-5.0	-3.0	0.0	0.0	0.0	0.0	2.0	2.0	5.0	3.0	2.0	2.0
Burundi	0.0	-1.0	6.0	6.0	..	1.0	7.0	7.0	..	2.0	1.0	1.0
Cameroon	-4.0	-4.0	-4.0	-4.0	1.0	1.0	1.0	1.0	5.0	5.0	5.0	5.0
Cape Verde	8.0	8.0	10.0	10.0	8.0	8.0	10.0	10.0	0.0	0.0	0.0	0.0
Central African Republic	5.0	5.0	-1.0	-1.0	5.0	5.0	1.0	1.0	0.0	0.0	2.0	2.0
Chad	-4.0	-2.0	-2.0	-2.0	0.0	1.0	1.0	1.0	4.0	3.0	3.0	3.0
Comoros	0.0	-1.0	6.0	9.0	..	1.0	6.0	9.0	..	2.0	0.0	0.0
Congo, Dem. Rep.	0.0	0.0	4.0	5.0	..	..	..	6.0	..	..	..	1.0
Congo, Rep.	5.0	-6.0	-4.0	-4.0	6.0	0.0	0.0	0.0	1.0	6.0	4.0	4.0
Côte d'Ivoire	-6.0	4.0	0.0	0.0	0.0	5.0	..	..	6.0	1.0	..	..
Equatorial Guinea	-5.0	-5.0	-5.0	-5.0	0.0	0.0	0.0	0.0	5.0	5.0	5.0	5.0
Eritrea	-6.0	-6.0	-7.0	-7.0	0.0	0.0	0.0	0.0	6.0	6.0	7.0	7.0
Ethiopia	1.0	1.0	1.0	1.0	3.0	3.0	3.0	3.0	2.0	2.0	2.0	2.0
Gabon	-4.0	-4.0	-4.0	3.0	0.0	0.0	0.0	4.0	4.0	4.0	4.0	1.0
Gambia, The	-7.0	-5.0	-5.0	-5.0	0.0	0.0	0.0	0.0	7.0	5.0	5.0	5.0
Ghana	-1.0	2.0	8.0	8.0	1.0	3.0	8.0	8.0	2.0	1.0	0.0	0.0
Guinea	-1.0	-1.0	-1.0	5.0	1.0	1.0	1.0	6.0	2.0	2.0	2.0	1.0
Guinea-Bissau	5.0	5.0	6.0	6.0	5.0	5.0	6.0	7.0	0.0	0.0	0.0	1.0
Kenya	-5.0	-2.0	8.0	8.0	0.0	2.0	8.0	8.0	5.0	4.0	0.0	0.0
Lesotho	8.0	4.0	8.0	8.0	8.0	..	8.0	8.0	0.0	..	0.0	0.0
Liberia	0.0	0.0	5.0	6.0	..	3.0	..	7.0	..	3.0	..	1.0
Madagascar	9.0	7.0	7.0	0.0	9.0	7.0	7.0	3.0	0.0	0.0	0.0	3.0
Malawi	6.0	6.0	6.0	6.0	6.0	6.0	6.0	6.0	0.0	0.0	0.0	0.0
Mali	7.0	6.0	7.0	7.0	7.0	6.0	7.0	7.0	0.0	0.0	0.0	0.0
Mauritania	-6.0	-6.0	-5.0	-2.0	0.0	0.0	0.0	0.0	6.0	6.0	5.0	2.0
Mauritius	10.0	10.0	10.0	10.0	10.0	10.0	10.0	10.0	0.0	0.0	0.0	0.0
Mozambique	5.0	5.0	5.0	5.0	5.0	5.0	5.0	5.0	0.0	0.0	0.0	0.0
Namibia	6.0	6.0	6.0	6.0	6.0	6.0	6.0	6.0	0.0	0.0	0.0	0.0
Niger	8.0	5.0	6.0	3.0	8.0	6.0	7.0	4.0	0.0	1.0	1.0	1.0
Nigeria	-6.0	4.0	4.0	4.0	0.0	4.0	4.0	4.0	6.0	0.0	0.0	0.0
Rwanda	-6.0	-4.0	-3.0	-4.0	0.0	0.0	0.0	0.0	6.0	4.0	3.0	4.0
São Tomé and Príncipe	..	..	..	..	..	..	..	..	..	..	..	..
Senegal	-1.0	8.0	8.0	7.0	2.0	8.0	8.0	7.0	3.0	0.0	0.0	0.0
Seychelles	..	..	..	..	..	..	..	..	..	..	..	..
Sierra Leone	-7.0	0.0	5.0	7.0	0.0	..	5.0	8.0	7.0	..	0.0	1.0
Somalia	0.0	0.0	0.0	0.0	..	..	..	..	..	..	..	..
South Africa	9.0	9.0	9.0	9.0	9.0	9.0	9.0	9.0	0.0	0.0	0.0	0.0
Sudan	-7.0	-7.0	-4.0	-2.0	0.0	0.0	0.0	1.0	7.0	7.0	4.0	3.0
Swaziland	-9.0	-9.0	-9.0	-9.0	0.0	0.0	0.0	0.0	9.0	9.0	9.0	9.0
Tanzania	-1.0	-1.0	-1.0	-1.0	2.0	2.0	2.0	2.0	3.0	3.0	3.0	3.0
Togo	-2.0	-2.0	-4.0	-2.0	1.0	1.0	1.0	1.0	3.0	3.0	5.0	3.0
Uganda	-4.0	-4.0	-1.0	-1.0	0.0	0.0	1.0	1.0	4.0	4.0	2.0	2.0
Zambia	6.0	1.0	5.0	7.0	6.0	3.0	5.0	7.0	0.0	2.0	0.0	0.0
Zimbabwe	-6.0	-3.0	-4.0	1.0	0.0	1.0	1.0	3.0	6.0	4.0	5.0	2.0
NORTH AFRICA												
Algeria	-3.0	-3.0	2.0	2.0	1.0	1.0	3.0	3.0	4.0	4.0	1.0	1.0
Djibouti	-7.0	2.0	2.0	2.0	0.0	3.0	3.0	3.0	7.0	1.0	1.0	1.0
Egypt, Arab Rep.	-6.0	-6.0	-3.0	-3.0	0.0	0.0	1.0	1.0	6.0	6.0	4.0	4.0
Libya	-7.0	-7.0	-7.0	-7.0	0.0	0.0	0.0	0.0	7.0	7.0	7.0	7.0
Morocco	-7.0	-6.0	-6.0	-6.0	0.0	0.0	0.0	0.0	7.0	6.0	6.0	6.0
Tunisia	-3.0	-3.0	-4.0	-4.0	1.0	1.0	1.0	1.0	4.0	4.0	5.0	5.0

Technical notes

1. Basic indicators

TABLE 1.1. BASIC INDICATORS

Population is total population based on the de facto definition of population, which counts all residents regardless of legal status or citizenship—except for refugees not permanently settled in the country of asylum, who are generally considered part of the population of their country of origin. The values shown are midyear estimates.

Population growth rate for year *t* is the exponential rate of growth of midyear population from year t–1 to t, expressed as a percentage. Population is based on the de facto definition of population, which counts all residents regardless of legal status or citizenship—except for refugees not permanently settled in the country of asylum, who are generally considered part of the population of the country of origin.

Land area is the land surface area of a country, excluding area under inland waters, national claims to continental shelf, and exclusive economic zones.

Population density is midyear population divided by land area in square kilometers. Population is based on the de facto definition of population, which counts all residents regardless of legal status or citizenship—except for refugees not permanently settled in the country of asylum, who are generally considered part of the population of their country of origin. Land area is a country's total area, excluding area under inland waters, national claims to continental shelf, and exclusive economic zones. In most cases the definition of inland waters includes major rivers and lakes.

Gross national income (GNI) per capita, World Bank Atlas method, is GNI, calculated using the *World Bank Atlas* method (see box 1), divided by midyear population. It is similar in concept to GNI per capita in current prices, except that the use of three-year averages of exchange rates smooths out sharp fluctuations from year to year.

Gross domestic product (GDP) per capita is gross domestic product divided by midyear population. GDP is the sum of gross value added by all resident producers in the economy plus any product taxes and minus any subsidies not included in the value of the products. It is calculated without making deductions for depreciation of fabricated assets or for depletion and degradation of natural resources. Dollar figures for GDP are converted from domestic currencies using single-year official exchange rates. For a few countries where the official exchange rate does not reflect the rate effectively applied to actual foreign exchange transactions, an alternative conversion factor is used. Growth rates are in real terms and have been calculated by the least-squares method using constant 2000 exchange rates (box 2).

Life expectancy at birth is the number of years a newborn infant would live if prevailing patterns of mortality at the time of its birth were to remain the same throughout its life.

Under-five mortality rate is the probability that a newborn baby will die before reaching age 5, if subject to current age-specific mortality rates. The probability is expressed as a rate per 1,000.

Gini index is the most commonly used measure of inequality. The coefficient ranges from 0, which reflects complete equality, to 100, which indicates complete inequality (one person has all the income or consumption, all others have none). Graphically, the Gini index can be easily represented by the area between the Lorenz curve and the line of equality.

Box 2 **Growth rates**

Growth rates are calculated as annual averages and represented as percentages. Except where noted, growth rates of values are computed from constant price series. Rates of change from one period to the next are calculated as proportional changes from the earlier period. Least squares growth rates are used wherever there is a sufficiently long time series to permit a reliable calculation. No growth rate is calculated if more than half the observations in a period are missing. The least squares growth rate, r, is estimated by fitting a linear regression trend line to the logarithmic annual values of the variable in the relevant period. The regression equation takes the form

$$\ln X_{t = a + bt}$$

which is equivalent to the logarithmic transformation of the compound growth equation,

$$X_t = X_o(1 + r)^2$$

In this equation X is the variable, t is time, and $a = \ln X_o$ and $b = \ln(1 + r)$ are parameters to be estimated. If b^* is the least squares estimate of b, then the average annual growth rate, r, is obtained as $[\exp(b^*) - 1]$ and is multiplied by 100 for expression as a percentage. The calculated growth rate is an average rate that is representative of the available observations over the entire period. It does not necessarily match the actual growth rate between any two periods.

Adult literacy rate is the percentage of adults ages 15 and older who can, with understanding, read and write a short, simple statement on their everyday life.

Net official development assistance per capita is calculated by dividing net disbursements of loans and grants from all official sources on concessional financial terms by midyear population. This indicator shows the importance of aid flows in sustaining per capita income and consumption levels, although exchange rate fluctuations, the actual rise of aid flows, and other factors vary across countries and over time.

Regional aggregates for GNI per capita, GDP per capita, life expectancy at birth, and adult literacy rates are weighted by population.

Source: Data on population and life expectancy are from the (1) United Nations Population Division: World Population Prospects, (2) United Nations Statistical Division: *Population and Vital Statistics Report* (various years), (3) Census reports and other statistical publications from national statistical offices, (4) Eurostat: Demographic Statistics, (5) Secretariat of the Pacific Community: Statistics and Demography Programme, and (6) U.S. Census Bureau: International Database. Data on land are from Food and Agriculture Organization electronic files and website. Data on GNI per capita and GDP per capita are from World Bank national accounts data and Organisation for Economic Co-operation and Development (OECD) national accounts data files. Data on under-five mortality are from the Inter-agency Group for Child Mortality Estimation *Level & Trends in Child Mortality: Report 2010.* Data on Gini index for developing countries are from the World Bank Development Research Group and are based on primary household survey data obtained from government statistical agencies and World Bank country departments (http://iresearch.worldbank.org/PovcalNet/index.htm) and for high-income economies are from the Luxembourg Income Study database. Data on literacy are from United Nations Educational, Scientific and Cultural Organization Institute for Statistics. Data on aid flows are from the OECD *Geographic Distribution of Aid Flows to Developing Countries* (www.oecd.org/dac/stats/idsonline).

2. National and fiscal accounts

Africa Development Indicators uses the 1993 System of National Accounts (1993 SNA) to compile national accounts data since 2001 (see Primary Data Documentation for details). Although more countries are adopting the 1993 SNA, many still follow the 1968 SNA, and some low-income countries use concepts from the 1953 SNA.

Reporting periods: For most economies the fiscal year is concurrent with the calendar year. However, there are few countries whose ending date reported is for the fiscal year of the central government, though fiscal years for other government levels and reporting years for statistical surveys may differ. Reporting end dates are as follows for the following countries: Botswana (June 30), Egypt (June 30), Ethiopia (July 7), The Gambia (June 30), Kenya (June 30), Lesotho (March 31), Malawi (March 31), Namibia (March 31), Sierra Leone (June 30), South Africa (March

31), Swaziland (March 31), Uganda (June 30), and Zimbabwe (June 30). The reporting period for national accounts data is either calendar year or fiscal year. Most economies report national accounts and balance of payments data using calendar years, but some report on fiscal years. Fiscal year data are assigned to calendar year that contains the larger share of the fiscal year. If a country's fiscal year ends before June 30, data are shown in that first year of the fiscal year; if the fiscal year ends on or after June 30, data are shown in the second year if the period. Balance of payments data are reported by calendar year.

Revisions to national accounts data: National accounts data are revised by national statistical offices when methodologies change or data sources improve. This in turn means that *Africa Development Indicators* national accounts data are also revised when data sources change.

- Botswana: The Central Statistical Office has revised national accounts series for 2004 onward.
- Mauritania: Based on official government statistics, data have been revised for 1991 onward; the new base year for constant price series is 2004.
- Swaziland: The Central Statistical Office has revised national accounts series for 1990 onward.
- Tunisia: Based on data from the Central Bank and its *Statistical Bulletin*, national accounts have been revised from 1997 onward.
- Uganda: The Bureau of Statistics has revised national accounts series for 1998 onward; the new base year for constant price series is 2001/02.

National currencies: As of January 2009, multiple hard currencies such as rand, pound sterling, euro, and U.S. dollar are in use in Zimbabwe; however, data are reported in U.S. dollars, the most frequently used currency.

Table 2.1. Gross domestic product, nominal

Gross domestic product (GDP), nominal, is the sum of gross value added by all resident producers in the economy plus any product taxes and minus any subsidies not included in the value of the products. It is calculated without making deductions for depreciation of fabricated assets or for depletion and degradation of natural resources. GDP figures are shown at market prices (also known as purchaser values) and converted from domestic currencies using single-year official exchange rates. For the few countries where the official exchange rate does not reflect the rate effectively applied to actual foreign exchange transactions, an alternative conversion factor is used.

The sum of the components of GDP by industrial origin (presented here as value added) will not normally equal total GDP for several reasons. First, components of GDP by expenditure are individually rescaled and summed to provide a partially rebased series for total GDP. Second, total GDP is shown at purchaser value, while value-added components are conventionally reported at producer prices. As explained above, purchaser values exclude net indirect taxes, while producer prices include indirect taxes. Third, certain items, such as imputed bank charges, are added in total GDP.

Source: World Bank and Organisation for Economic Co-operation and Development national accounts data.

Table 2.2. Gross domestic product, real

Gross domestic product (GDP), real, is obtained by converting national currency GDP series to U.S. dollars using constant 2000 exchange rates. For countries where the official exchange rate does not effectively reflect the rate applied to actual foreign exchange transactions, an alternative currency conversion factor has been used. Growth rates are in real terms and calculated by the least-squares method using constant 2000 exchange rates (see box 2).

Source: World Bank and Organisation for Economic Co-operation and Development national accounts data.

Table 2.3. Gross domestic product growth

Gross domestic product (GDP) growth is the average annual growth rate of real GDP (table 2.2) at market prices based on constant local currency. Aggregates are based on constant 2000 U.S. dollars.

Source: World Bank and Organisation for Economic Co-operation and Development national accounts data.

Table 2.4. Gross domestic product per capita, real

Gross domestic product (GDP) per capita, real, is calculated by dividing real GDP (table 2.2) by corresponding midyear population.

Source: World Bank and Organisation for Economic Co-operation and Development national accounts data.

Table 2.5. Gross domestic product per capita growth

Gross domestic product (GDP) per capita growth is the average annual growth rate of real GDP per capita (table 2.4).

Source: World Bank and Organisation for Economic Co-operation and Development national accounts data.

Table 2.6. Gross national income, nominal

Gross national income (GNI), nominal, is the sum of value added by all resident producers plus any product taxes (less subsidies) not included in the valuation of output plus net receipts of primary income (compensation of employees and property income) from abroad. Data are converted from national currency in current prices to U.S. dollars at official annual exchange rates.

Source: World Bank and Organisation for Economic Co-operation and Development national accounts data.

Table 2.7. Gross national income, *World Bank Atlas* method

Gross national income (GNI), World Bank Atlas *method,* (formerly GNP) is the sum of value added by all resident producers plus any product taxes (less subsidies) not included in the valuation of output plus net receipts of primary income (compensation of employees and property income) from abroad. GNI, calculated in national currency, is usually converted to U.S. dollars at official exchange rates for comparisons across economies, although an alternative rate is used when the official exchange rate is judged to diverge by an exceptionally large margin from the rate actually applied in international transactions. To smooth fluctuations in prices and exchange rates, the *World Bank Atlas* method (see box 1) of conversion is used. This method applies a conversion factor that averages the exchange rate for a given year and the two preceding years, adjusted for the difference between the rate of inflation in the country and that in Japan, the United Kingdom, the United States, and the euro area. Growth rates are calculated by the least-squares method (see box 2).

Source: World Bank and Organisation for Economic Co-operation and Development national accounts data.

Table 2.8. Gross national income per capita, *World Bank Atlas* method

Gross national income (GNI) per capita, World Bank Atlas *method,* is GNI, calculated using the *World Bank Atlas* method (see box 1), divided by midyear population.

Source: World Bank and Organisation for Economic Co-operation and Development national accounts data.

Table 2.9. Gross domestic product deflator (U.S. dollar series)

Gross domestic product (GDP) deflator (U.S. dollar series) is nominal GDP in current U.S. dollars (table 2.1) divided by real GDP in constant 2000 U.S. dollars (table 2.2), expressed as an index with base year 2000. The series shows the effects of domestic price changes and exchange rate variations.

Source: World Bank and Organisation for Economic Co-operation and Development national accounts data.

Table 2.10. Consumer price index

Consumer price index reflects changes in the cost to the average consumer of acquiring a basket of goods and services that may be fixed or changed at specified intervals, such as yearly. The Laspeyres formula is generally used.

Source: International Monetary Fund, International Financial Statistics database and data files.

Table 2.11. Inflation

Inflation as measured by the consumer price index reflects the annual percentage change in the cost to the average consumer of acquiring a basket of goods and services that may be fixed or changed at specified intervals, such as yearly. The Laspeyres formula is generally used.

Source: International Monetary Fund, International Financial Statistics database and data files.

Table 2.12. Price indexes

Inflation, GDP deflator, is measured by the annual growth rate of the GDP implicit deflator and shows the rate of price change in the economy as a whole.

Consumer price index is a change in the cost to the average consumer of acquiring a basket of goods and services that may be fixed or changed at specified intervals, such as yearly. The Laspeyres formula is generally used.

Exports of goods and services price index is calculated by dividing the national accounts exports of goods and services in current U.S. dollars by exports of goods and services in constant 2000 U.S. dollars.

Imports of goods and services price index is calculated by dividing the national accounts imports of goods and services in current U.S. dollars by imports of goods and services in constant 2000 U.S. dollars.

Source: World Bank and Organisation for Economic Co-operation and Development national accounts data.

Table 2.13. Gross domestic savings

Gross domestic savings is calculated by deducting total consumption (table 2.17) from nominal gross domestic product (table 2.1). For 1994–2000, Nigeria's values were distorted because the official exchange rate used by the government for oil exports and oil value added was significantly overvalued.

Source: World Bank and Organisation for Economic Co-operation and Development national accounts data.

Table 2.14. Gross national savings

Gross national savings is the sum of gross domestic savings (table 2.13), net factor income from abroad, and net private transfers from abroad. The estimate here also includes net public transfers from abroad. For 1994–2000, Nigeria's values were distorted because the official exchange rate used by the Government for oil exports and oil value added was significantly overvalued.

Source: World Bank and Organisation for Economic Co-operation and Development national accounts data.

Table 2.15. General government final consumption expenditure

General government final consumption expenditure is all current expenditure for purchases of goods and services by all levels of government, including capital expenditure on national defense and security. Other capital expenditure by government is included in capital formation.

Source: World Bank and Organisation for Economic Co-operation and Development national accounts data.

Table 2.16. Household final consumption expenditure

Household final consumption expenditure (formerly *private consumption*) is the market value of all goods and services, including durable products (such as cars, washing machines, and home computers), purchased by households. It excludes purchases of dwellings but includes imputed rent for owner-occupied dwellings. It also includes payments and fees to governments to obtain permits and licenses. Here, household consumption expenditure includes the expenditures of nonprofit institutions serving households, even when reported separately by the country.

Source: World Bank and Organisation for Economic Co-operation and Development national accounts data.

Table 2.17. Final consumption expenditure plus discrepancy

Final consumption expenditure plus discrepancy (formerly *total consumption*) is the sum of household final consumption expenditure (table 2.16) and general government final consumption expenditure (table 2.15) shown as a share of gross domestic product. This estimate includes any statistical discrepancy in the use of resources relative to the supply of resources. Private consumption, not separately shown here, is the value of all goods and services purchased or received as income in kind by households and nonprofit institutions. It excludes purchases of dwellings, but includes imputed rent for owner-occupied dwellings. In practice, it includes any statistical discrepancy in the use of resources.

Source: World Bank and Organisation for Economic Co-operation and Development national accounts data.

TABLE 2.18. FINAL CONSUMPTION EXPENDITURE PLUS DISCREPANCY PER CAPITA

Final consumption expenditure plus discrepancy per capita is final consumption expenditure plus discrepancy in current U.S. dollars (table 2.17) divided by midyear population.

Source: World Bank and Organisation for Economic Co-operation and Development national accounts data.

TABLE 2.19. GROSS FIXED CAPITAL FORMATION

Gross fixed capital formation (formerly *gross domestic fixed investment*) includes land improvements (fences, ditches, drains, and so on); plant, machinery, and equipment purchases; and the construction of roads, railways, and the like, including schools, offices, hospitals, private residential dwellings, and commercial and industrial buildings. According to the 1993 SNA, net acquisitions of valuables are also considered capital formation. It comprises outlays by the public sector (table 2.20) and the private sector (table 2.21). Examples include improvements in land, dwellings, machinery, and other equipment. For some countries the sum of gross private investment and gross public investment does not total gross domestic investment due to statistical discrepancies.

Source: World Bank and Organisation for Economic Co-operation and Development national accounts data.

TABLE 2.20. GROSS GENERAL GOVERNMENT FIXED CAPITAL FORMATION

Gross general government fixed capital formation covers gross outlays by the public sector on additions to its fixed domestic assets.

Source: World Bank and Organisation for Economic Co-operation and Development national accounts data.

TABLE 2.21. PRIVATE SECTOR FIXED CAPITAL FORMATION

Private sector fixed capital formation covers gross outlays by the private sector (including private nonprofit agencies) on additions to its fixed domestic assets.

Source: World Bank and Organisation for Economic Co-operation and Development national accounts data.

TABLE 2.22. EXTERNAL TRADE BALANCE (EXPORTS MINUS IMPORTS)

External trade balance is the difference between free on board exports (table 2.23) and cost, insurance, and freight imports (table 2.24) of goods and services (or the difference between gross domestic savings and gross capital formation). The resource balance is shown as a share of nominal gross domestic product (table 2.1). For 1994–2000, Nigeria's values were distorted because the official exchange rate used by the government for oil exports and oil value added was significantly overvalued.

Source: World Bank and Organisation for Economic Co-operation and Development national accounts data.

TABLE 2.23. EXPORTS OF GOODS AND SERVICES, NOMINAL

Exports of goods and services, nominal, represent the value of all goods and other market services provided to the rest of the world. They include the value of merchandise, freight, insurance, transport, travel, royalties, license fees, and other services, such as communication, construction, financial, information, business, personal, and government services. They exclude labor and property income (formerly called factor services) as well as transfer payments, and are expressed in current U.S. dollars.

Source: World Bank and Organisation for Economic Co-operation and Development national accounts data.

TABLE 2.24. IMPORTS OF GOODS AND SERVICES, NOMINAL

Imports of goods and services, nominal, represent the value of all goods and other market services received from the rest of the world. They include the value of merchandise, freight, insurance, transport, travel, royalties, license fees, and other services, such as communication, construction, financial, information, business, personal, and government services. They exclude labor and property income (formerly called factor services) as well as transfer payments, and are expressed in current U.S. dollars.

Source: World Bank and Organisation for Economic Co-operation and Development national accounts data.

Table 2.25. Exports of goods and services as a share of GDP

Exports of goods and services represent the value of all goods and other market services provided to the rest of the world. They include the value of merchandise, freight, insurance, transport, travel, royalties, license fees, and other services, such as communication, construction, financial, information, business, personal, and government services. They exclude labor and property income (formerly called factor services) as well as transfer payments, and are expressed as a proportion of real GDP.

Source: World Bank and Organisation for Economic Co-operation and Development national accounts data.

Table 2.26. Imports of goods and services as a share of GDP

Imports of goods and services represent the value of all goods and other market services received from the rest of the world. They include the value of merchandise, freight, insurance, transport, travel, royalties, license fees, and other services, such as communication, construction, financial, information, business, personal, and government services. They exclude labor and property income (formerly called factor services) as well as transfer payments, and are expressed as a proportion of real GDP.

Source: World Bank and Organisation for Economic Co-operation and Development national accounts data.

Table 2.27. Balance of payments and current account

Exports of goods and services represent the value of all goods and other market services provided to the rest of the world. They include the value of merchandise, freight, insurance, transport, travel, royalties, license fees, and other services, such as communication, construction, financial, information, business, personal, and government services. They exclude labor and property income (formerly called factor services) as well as transfer payments, and are expressed in current U.S. dollars and as a proportion of real GDP.

Imports of goods and services represent the value of all goods and other market services received from the rest of the world. They include the value of merchandise, freight, insurance, transport, travel, royalties, license fees, and other services, such as communication, construction, financial, information, business, personal, and government services. They exclude labor and property income (formerly called factor services) as well as transfer payments, and are expressed in current U.S. dollars and as a proportion of real GDP.

Total trade is the sum of exports and imports of goods and services.

Net income is the receipts and payments of employee compensation paid to nonresident workers and investment income (receipts and payments on direct investment, portfolio investment, other investments, and receipts on reserve assets).

Net current transfers are recorded in the balance of payments whenever an economy provides or receives goods, services, income, or financial items without a quid pro quo.

Current account balance is the sum of net exports of goods, services, net income, and net current transfers. All transfers not considered to be capital are current.

Total reserves including gold are the holdings of monetary gold, special drawing rights, reserves of International Monetary Fund (IMF) members held by the IMF, and holdings of foreign exchange under the control of monetary authorities.

Source: Data on exports and imports of goods and services are from World Bank and Organisation for Economic Co-operation and Development national accounts data. Data on net income, net current transfers, current account balance, and total reserves are from the International Monetary Fund, *Balance of Payments Statistics Yearbook* and data files, and World Bank and OECD GDP estimates.

Table 2.28. Exchange rates and purchasing power parity

Official exchange rate is the exchange rate determined by national authorities or the rate determined in the legally sanctioned exchange market.

Purchasing power parity (PPP) conversion factor is the number of units of a country's currency required to buy the same amount of goods and services in the domestic market as a U.S. dollar would buy in the United States.

Ratio of PPP conversion factor to market exchange rate is the national price level, making it possible to compare the cost of the bundle of goods that make up gross domestic product across countries.

Real effective exchange rate is the nominal effective exchange rate (a measure of the value of a currency against a weighted average of several foreign currencies) divided by a price deflator or index of costs.

Gross domestic product (GDP), PPP, is gross domestic product converted to international dollars using purchasing power parity rates. An international dollar has the same purchasing power over GDP as the U.S. dollar has in the United States. GDP is the sum of gross value added by all resident producers in the economy plus any product taxes and minus any subsidies not included in the value of the products. It is calculated without making deductions for depreciation of fabricated assets or for depletion and degradation of natural resources.

Gross domestic product (GDP) per capita, PPP, is GDP per capita based on purchasing power parity. PPP GDP is gross domestic product converted to international dollars using purchasing power parity rates. An international dollar has the same purchasing power over GDP as the U.S. dollar has in the United States. GDP at purchaser's prices is the sum of gross value added by all resident producers in the economy plus any product taxes and minus any subsidies not included in the value of the products. It is calculated without making deductions for depreciation of fabricated assets or for depletion and degradation of natural resources.

Source: International Monetary Fund International Financial Statistics database. Data on PPP are from the World Bank's International Comparison Program database.

Table 2.29. Agriculture value added

Agriculture value added is the gross output of forestry, hunting, and fishing, as well as cultivation of crops and livestock production (International Standard Industrial Classification [ISIC] revision 3 divisions 1–5) less the value of their intermediate inputs. It is calculated without making deductions for depreciation of fabricated assets or depletion and degradation of natural resources. For countries that report national accounts data at producer prices (Angola, Benin, Cape Verde, Comoros, the Republic of Congo, Côte d'Ivoire, Gabon, Liberia, Niger, Rwanda, São Tomé and Príncipe, Seychelles, and Togo), gross value added at market prices is used as the denominator. For countries that report national accounts data at basic prices (all other countries), gross value added at factor cost is used as the denominator. Value added at basic prices excludes net taxes on products, while producer prices include net taxes on products paid by produces but exclude sales or value added taxes.

Source: World Bank and Organisation for Economic Co-operation and Development national accounts data files.

Table 2.30. Industry value added

Industry value added is the gross output of mining, manufacturing, construction, electricity, water, and gas (ISIC revision 3 divisions 10–45) less the value of their intermediate inputs. It is calculated without making deductions for depreciation of fabricated assets or depletion and degradation of natural resources. For countries that report national accounts data at producer prices (Angola, Benin, Cape Verde, Comoros, the Republic of Congo, Côte d'Ivoire, Gabon, Liberia, Niger, Rwanda, São Tomé and Príncipe, Seychelles, and Togo), gross value added at market prices is used as the denominator. For countries that report national accounts data at basic prices (all other countries), gross value added at factor cost is used as the denominator. Value added at basic prices excludes net taxes on products, while producer prices include net taxes on products paid by produces but exclude sales or value added taxes.

Source: World Bank and Organisation for Economic Co-operation and Development national accounts data files.

Table 2.31. Services plus discrepancy value added

Services plus discrepancy value added is the gross output of all other branches of economic activity, including wholesale and retail trade (including hotels and restaurants), transport, and government, financial, professional, and personal services such as education, health care, and real estate services (ISIC revision 3 divisions 50–99) less the value of their intermediate inputs. Also included are imputed bank service charges, import duties, and any statistical discrepancies noted by national compilers as well as discrepancies arising from rescaling. It is calculated without making deductions for depreciation of fabricated assets or depletion and degradation of natural resources. For countries that report national accounts data at producer prices (Angola, Benin, Cape Verde, Comoros, the Republic of Congo, Côte d'Ivoire, Gabon, Liberia, Niger, Rwanda, São Tomé and Príncipe, Seychelles, and Togo), gross value added at market prices is used as the denominator. For countries that report national accounts data at basic prices (all other countries), gross value added at factor cost is used as the denominator. Value added at basic prices exclude net taxes on products while producer prices include net taxes on products paid by produces but exclude sales or value added taxes.

Source: World Bank and Organisation for Economic Co-operation and Development national accounts data files.

Table 2.32. Central government finances

Revenue, excluding grants, is cash receipts from taxes, social contributions, and other revenues such as fines, fees, rent, and income from property or sales. Grants are also considered as revenue but are excluded here.

Expense is cash payments for operating activities of the government in providing goods and services. It includes compensation of employees (such as wages and salaries), interest and subsidies, grants, social benefits, and other expenses such as rent and dividends.

Cash surplus or deficit is revenue (including grants) minus expense, minus net acquisition of nonfinancial assets. In the 1986 *Government Finance Statistics Manual* nonfinancial assets were included under revenue and expenditure in gross terms. This cash surplus or deficit is closest to the earlier overall budget balance (still missing is lending minus repayments, which are now a financing item under net acquisition of financial assets).

Net incurrence of liabilities is domestic financing (obtained from residents) and foreign financing (obtained from nonresidents) and/or the means by which a government provides financial resources to cover a budget deficit or allocates financial resources arising from a budget surplus. The net incurrence of liabilities should be offset by the net acquisition of financial assets (a third financing item). The difference between the cash surplus or deficit and the three financing items is the net change in the stock of cash.

Total debt is the entire stock of direct government fixed-term contractual obligations to others outstanding on a particular date. It includes domestic and foreign liabilities such as currency and money deposits, securities other than shares, and loans. It is the gross amount of government liabilities reduced by the amount of equity and financial derivatives held by the government. Because debt is a stock rather than a flow, it is measured as of a given date, usually the last day of the fiscal year.

Source: International Monetary Fund, *Government Finance Statistics Yearbook* and data files, and World Bank and Organisation for Economic Co-operation and Development GDP estimates.

Table 2.33. Central government expenses

Goods and services include all government payments in exchange for goods and services used for the production of market and nonmarket goods and services. Own-account capital formation is excluded.

Compensation of employees consists of all payments in cash, as well as in kind (such as food and housing), to employees in return for services rendered, and government contributions to social insurance schemes such as social security and pensions that provide benefits to employees.

Interest payments (expense) include interest payments on government debt—including long-term bonds, long-term loans, and other debt instruments—to domestic and foreign residents, expressed as a proportion of expense.

Subsidies and other transfers include all unrequited, nonrepayable transfers on current account to private and public enterprises; grants to foreign governments, international organizations, and other government units; and social security, social assistance benefits, and employer social benefits in cash and in kind.

Other expenses are spending on dividends, rent, and other miscellaneous expenses, including provision for consumption of fixed capital.

Source: International Monetary Fund, *Government Finance Statistics Yearbook* and data files, and World Bank and Organisation for Economic Co-operation and Development GDP estimates.

Table 2.34. Central government revenues

Interest payments (revenue) include interest payments on government debt—including long-term bonds, long-term loans, and other debt instruments—to domestic and foreign residents, expressed as a proportion of revenue.

Taxes on income, profits, and capital gains are levied on the actual or presumptive net income of individuals, on the profits of corporations and enterprises, and on capital gains, whether realized or not, on land, securities, and other assets. Intragovernmental payments are eliminated in consolidation.

Taxes on goods and services include general sales and turnover or value added taxes, selective excises on goods, selective taxes on services, taxes on the use of goods or property, taxes on extraction and production of minerals, and profits of fiscal monopolies.

Taxes on international trade include import duties, export duties, profits of export or import monopolies, exchange profits, and exchange taxes.

Other taxes include employer payroll or labor taxes, taxes on property, and taxes not allocable to other categories, such as penalties for late payment or nonpayment of taxes.

Social contributions include social security contributions by employees, employers, and self-employed individuals, and other contributions whose source cannot be determined. They also include actual or imputed contributions to social insurance schemes operated by governments.

Grants and other revenue include grants from other foreign governments, international organizations, and other government units; interest; dividends; rent; requited, nonrepayable receipts for public purposes (such as fines, administrative fees, and entrepreneurial income from government ownership of property); and voluntary, unrequited, nonrepayable receipts other than grants.

Source: International Monetary Fund, *Government Finance Statistics Yearbook* and data files, and World Bank and Organisation for Economic Co-operation and Development GDP estimates.

Table 2.35. Structure of demand

Household final consumption expenditure (formerly *private consumption*) is the market value of all goods and services, including durable products (such as cars, washing machines, and home computers), purchased by households.

General government final consumption expenditure (formerly *general government consumption*) is all government current expenditures for purchases of goods and services.

Gross fixed capital formation (formerly *gross domestic investment*) consists of outlays on additions to the fixed assets of the economy plus net changes in the level of inventories.

Exports of goods and services represent the value of all goods and other market services provided to the rest of the world. They include the value of merchandise, freight, insurance, transport, travel, royalties, license fees, and other services, such as communication, construction, financial, information, business, personal, and government services. They exclude labor and property income (formerly called factor services) as well as transfer payments, and are expressed as a proportion of real GDP.

Imports of goods and services represent the value of all goods and other market services received from the rest of the world. They include the value of merchandise, freight, insurance, transport, travel, royalties, license fees, and other services, such as communication, construction, financial, information, business, personal, and government services. They exclude labor and property income (formerly called factor services) as well as transfer payments and are expressed as a proportion of real GDP.

Gross national savings is the gross national income less total consumption, plus net transfers.

Source: World Bank and Organisation for Economic Co-operation and Development national accounts data files.

3. Millennium Development Goals

Table 3.1. Millennium Development Goal 1: eradicate extreme poverty and hunger

Share of population below PPP $1.25 a day is the percentage of the population living on less than $1.25 a day at 2005 international prices. As a result of revisions in purchasing power parity (PPP) exchange rates, poverty rates in this edition cannot be compared with those in previous editions.

Poverty gap ratio at PPP $1.25 a day is the mean shortfall from the poverty line (counting the nonpoor as having zero shortfall), expressed as a percentage of the poverty line. This measure reflects the depth of poverty as well as its incidence.

Share of population below PPP $2 a day is the percentage of the population living on less than $2 a day at 2005 international prices. As a result of revisions in PPP exchange rates, poverty rates in this edition cannot be compared with those in previous editions.

Poverty gap ratio at PPP $2 a day is the mean shortfall from the poverty line (counting the nonpoor as having zero shortfall), expressed as a percentage of the poverty line. This measure reflects the depth of poverty as well as its incidence.

Share of population below national poverty line (poverty headcount ratio) is the percentage of the population living below the national poverty line. National estimates are based on population-weighted subgroup estimates from household surveys.

Share of poorest quintile in national consumption or income is the share of consumption, or in some cases income, that accrues to the poorest 20 percent of the population.

Prevalence of child malnutrition, underweight, is the percentage of children under age 5 whose weight for age is more than two standard deviations below the median for the international reference population ages 0–59 months. The reference population, adopted by the World Health Organization in 1983, is based on children from the United States, who are assumed to be well nourished.

Population below minimum dietary energy consumption (also referred to as prevalence of undernourishment) is the population whose dietary energy consumption is continuously below a minimum dietary energy requirement for maintaining a healthy life and carrying out a light physical activity with an acceptable minimum body weight for attained height.

Source: Data on poverty are from the World Bank Development Research Group. Data are based on primary household survey data obtained from government statistical agencies and World Bank country departments (http://iresearch.worldbank.org/PovcalNet/index.htm). Data on national poverty are from the Global Poverty Working Group and are based on World Bank country poverty assessments and country poverty reduction strategies. Data on child malnutrition are from the World Health Organization Global Database on Child Growth and Malnutrition. Data on population below minimum dietary energy consumption are from the Food and Agriculture Organization (http://www.fao.org/faostat/foodsecurity/index_en.htm).

Table 3.2. Millennium Development Goal 2: achieve universal primary education

Primary education provides children with basic reading, writing, and mathematics skills, along with an elementary understanding of such subjects as history, geography, natural science, social science, art, and music.

Net primary enrollment ratio is the ratio of children of official primary school age, based on the International Standard Classification of Education 1997, who are enrolled in primary school to the population of the corresponding official primary school age.

Primary completion rate is the percentage of students completing the last year of

Africa New Dollar Per Day (PPP) Poverty Estimates ($1.25/day) in 2008

Prepared by Andrew Dabalen and Rose Mungai

Why PPP poverty estimates? When it comes to poverty measurement, each country calculates its own (national) poverty line and uses it to track progress in reducing poverty and setting social policy. National poverty lines may be obtained through a combination of methods: social norms about a minimum level of welfare each citizen is entitled to, some basic nutritional need, a multidimensional index, and so on.

But if we need to obtain comparisons between countries of the world or countries in a region of the world (say, Africa), then the national poverty lines cannot be used because each country uses a different one. Therefore, the World Bank uses a common international poverty line to compare poverty across the world or in a region by collecting comparative price data and estimating purchasing power parities (PPPs) of the world economies. Using PPPs instead of country exchange rates to convert currencies allows welfare and the output of economies to be compared in real terms while controlling for differences in price levels. Traditionally, the World Bank counts the global (and/or regional) poor as the fraction of the population with incomes (or consumption) below two international poverty lines: $1.25/day and $2/day using PPP.

The 2005 PPP revisions: In 2005, the World Bank undertook a major revision of the global poverty count by using a completely new set of international prices that became available through the worldwide effort of the International Comparison Program (ICP). The 2005 ICP round is widely considered to be better than the previous round of ICP in 1993, in that it covered more countries and collected more (and better quality) price data. As a result, the 2005 estimates differed significantly from the estimates based on the 1993 ICP round, which are then extrapolated forward. In particular, the 2005 revisions showed that the cost of living—and, by consequence, poverty—was higher in the developing world than previously thought using the $1.25/day and $2/day international poverty lines.

Why a 2008 PPP estimates? Every three years, the World Bank updates the global poverty count. On February 29, 2012, the World Bank released the 2008 global poverty estimates. These estimates have been revised for the period 1981–2008 and may differ from previous estimates. To the extent possible, each global (or regional) poverty update would normally be based on the household surveys carried out in the year of the update. In practice, household surveys in many countries are not carried out every year so that the year of the update and the survey year may differ, sometimes by many years. When the survey year and the year of the update do not coincide, the international poverty line in local currency is projected backward or forward by adjusting the most recently available survey figure by the change in the CPI in the country.

Benchmarking the 1990 poverty and global poverty trends: In addition to the three-year update, the latest release also revises the 1990 poverty count. The 1990 poverty estimate for the world and each country is an important benchmark to measure progress toward Millennium Development Goal 1 (MDG-1): reducing extreme poverty by half between 1990 and 2015. The current revision uses 2005 PPPs, projected backward or forward using the CPI in the country.

Poverty in Africa is declining, but progress is slower than in other regions

The new global estimates indicate a significant reduction in the proportion of world population below the $1.25 per day per capita poverty line, from 43.1 percent in 1990 to 22.4 percent in 2008 (table 1). Particularly, the East Asia and Pacific region made huge progress where the percentage of the poor, measured at the $1.25

Table 1: Regional aggregation, $1.25/day and $2.00/day poverty line

Year	$1.25 per day per capita: All	East Asia and Pacific	Europe and Central Asia	Latin America and the Caribbean	Middle East and North Africa	South Asia	Sub-Saharan Africa	$2 per day per capita: All	East Asia and Pacific	Europe and Central Asia	Latin America and the Caribbean	Middle East and North Africa	South Asia	Sub-Saharan Africa
The proportion of population below the international poverty lines (%)														
1990	43.1	56.2	1.9	12.2	5.8	53.8	56.5	64.6	81.0	6.9	22.4	23.4	83.6	75.9
1993	41.0	50.7	2.9	11.4	4.8	51.7	59.4	63.0	75.7	9.2	21.7	22.1	82.6	78.1
1996	34.8	35.9	3.9	11.1	4.8	48.6	58.1	58.6	64.0	11.2	21.0	22.2	80.7	77.5
1999	34.1	35.6	3.8	11.9	5.0	45.1	57.9	57.4	61.7	12.1	22.0	21.9	77.8	77.4
2002	30.8	27.6	2.3	11.9	4.2	44.3	55.7	53.4	51.9	7.9	22.2	19.7	77.4	76.1
2005	25.1	17.1	1.3	8.7	3.5	39.4	52.3	46.9	39.0	4.6	16.7	17.3	73.3	74.1
2008	22.4	14.3	0.5	6.5	2.7	36.0	47.5	43.0	33.2	2.2	12.4	13.9	70.9	69.2
Population below the international poverty lines (millions)														
1990	1908.5	926.4	8.9	53.4	13.0	617.3	289.7	2863.3	1333.5	31.9	97.6	52.8	958.5	389.1
1993	1910.3	870.8	13.7	52.5	11.5	631.9	330.0	2940.5	1300.3	43.0	99.9	53.4	1010.0	433.9
1996	1703.8	639.7	18.2	53.6	12.3	630.8	349.2	2863.8	1139.5	52.7	101.7	57.0	1047.0	465.8
1999	1742.6	655.6	17.8	60.1	13.6	619.5	376.0	2936.4	1137.2	57.0	111.3	59.7	1068.5	502.7
2002	1639.2	523.1	10.6	62.7	12.0	640.5	390.2	2847.3	983.5	37.2	117.5	56.7	1119.2	533.2
2005	1389.5	332.1	6.3	47.6	10.5	598.3	394.8	2594.4	756.9	21.6	91.7	52.6	1112.6	558.9
2008	1289.0	284.4	2.2	36.9	8.6	570.9	386.0	2470.1	658.6	10.4	70.5	44.4	1124.2	562.1

Source: PovcalNet.

(continued)

Africa New Dollar Per Day (PPP) Poverty Estimates ($1.25/day) in 2008 (continued)

poverty line, declined from 56.2 percent to 14.3 percent between 1990 and 2008, while the number of poor people also declined from 926.4 million to 284.4 million for the same period.

For the first time since 1993, the proportion of the people living below the international poverty lines in Africa (Figure 1 at right) is declining, based on existing data, although progress has been slower than in other regions. In addition, about 9 million Africans moved out of extreme poverty between 2005 and 2008. However, because of rapid population growth, the number of people living below the international poverty lines is higher in 2008 than in 1990.

Where to obtain new estimates: The new poverty statistics based on international poverty lines are on the World Bank's website Povcalnet (http://go.worldbank.org/WE8P1I8250), which allows users to compute poverty rates and populations, setting the poverty line at any level and following the same methodology as the World Bank estimates at the $1.25 and $2 poverty lines. The Poverty & Equity Data portal (http://povertydata.worldbank.org/poverty/home/) uses the same data from Povcalnet and displays it in maps and charts at the regional and country levels. Both websites are updated periodically.

Figure 1

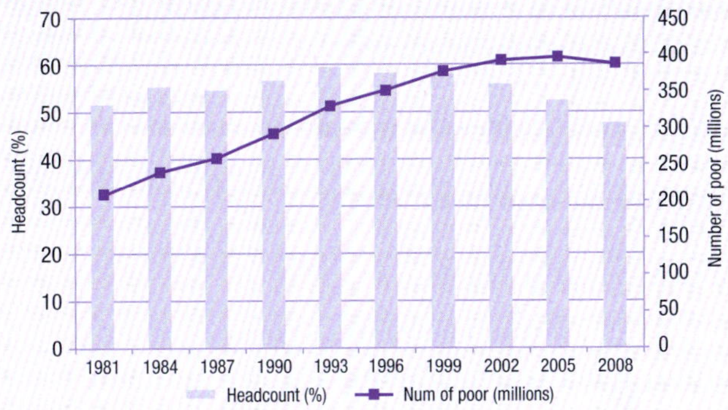

primary school. It is calculated as the total number of students in the last grade of primary school minus the number of repeaters in that grade divided by the total number of children of official graduation age.

Share of cohort reaching grade 5 is the percentage of children enrolled in grade 1 of primary school who eventually reach grade 5. The estimate is based on the reconstructed cohort method.

Youth literacy rate is the percentage of people ages 15–24 who can, with understanding, both read and write a short, simple statement about their everyday life.

Source: Data are from the United Nations Educational, Scientific and Cultural Organization Institute for Statistics. Efforts have been made to harmonize these data series with those published on the United Nations Millennium Development Goals website (http://mdgs.un.org/unsd/mdg/default.aspx), but some differences in timing, sources, and definitions remain.

Table 3.3. Millennium Development Goal 3: promote gender equality and empower women

Ratio of girls to boys in primary and secondary school is the ratio of female to male gross enrollment rate in primary and secondary school.

Ratio of literate young women to men is the ratio of the female youth literacy rate to the male youth literacy rate.

Women in national parliament are the percentage of parliamentary seats in a single or lower chamber occupied by women.

Share of women employed in the nonagricultural sector is women wage employees in the nonagricultural sector as a share of total nonagricultural employment.

Source: Data on net enrollment and literacy are from the United Nations Educational, Scientific and Cultural Organization Institute for Statistics. Data on women in national parliaments are from Inter-Parliamentary Union (IPU) (www.ipu.org). Data on women's employment are from the International Labour Organization Key Indicators of the Labour Market database.

Table 3.4. Millennium Development Goal 4: reduce child mortality

Under-five mortality rate is the probability that a newborn baby will die before reaching age 5, if subject to current age-specific mortality rates. The probability is expressed as a rate per 1,000.

Infant mortality rate is the number of infants dying before reaching 1 year of age, per 1,000 live births.

Child immunization rate, measles, is the percentage of children ages 12–23 months who

What's the coolest region for doing impact evaluation? It's Africa!

Want to do IE? Come to Africa!

The most recent count[1] of active impact evaluations (IE) within the World Bank leaves no doubts: Africa is the place to be to do IE. The region had the highest number of active IEs in 2011 and the highest ratio of active IEs to active investment loans. However, it is not only about numbers. IEs in Africa are leading the way in at least three fronts: (1) IEs have generated knowledge on the effect of development policies and programs; (2) IEs are generating cross-sector evidence to understand the underlying behavioral and delivery mechanisms that make policies work; and (3) IE products and programs have been strengthening government capacity for IE evidence-based policy making.

Impact Evaluations by Region

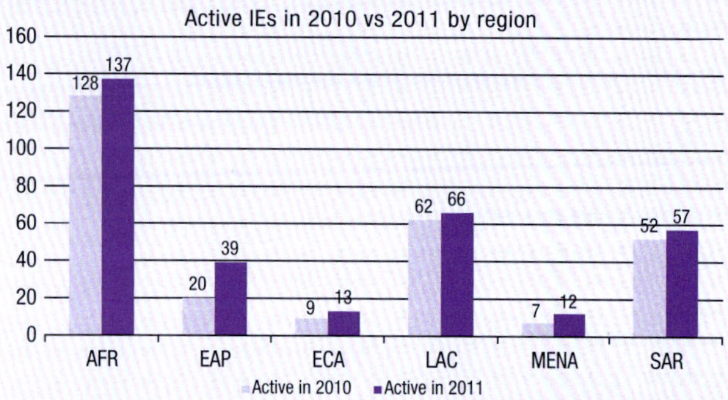

Source: DIME Progress report FY10-11; AFR=Africa, EAP=East Asia Pacific, ECA=Europe Central Asia, LAC=Latin America and Caribbean, MENA=Middle East and North Africa, SAR=South Asia

IE programs

More than half of all current IE activity within the World Bank is managed under impact evaluation programs. The programs help to maintain analytical quality of the activities they cover, take advantage of economies of scale in capacity development and dissemination of results, and use community of practice to encourage adoption and scale-up of good policies. The organization of IEs under thematic programs helps to maximize IE potential as a knowledge public good. The Development Impact Evaluation Initiative (DIME) Secretariat coordinates IE activities in 10 IE programs, 3 of which (education, HIV, and gender) are cosponsored by the Africa region, and 6 are cosponsored by networks or network units (FPD, adapt with ARD, local development and fragile states with SDV, malaria with HDNHE, and gender with PRMGE). A small program on urban and public sector governance (cosponsored by PREM and LEGJR) is also emerging in DIME. HDN coordinates IE activities in eight SIEF clusters (topics include active labor market policies, CCTs, ECD, and Result-based Financing in Health). WSS manages a program in the area of water supply and sanitation.

The impact of Impact Evaluation

The impact of IE affects the key stages of project design and implementation. First, IE researchers motivate the project team to think about the mechanisms that induce behavioral responses or address principal agent problems. By introducing variation in treatment, the project incorporates a dynamic learning agenda and the ability to steer the project mid-course on the basis of good evidence. Second, IE data requirements provide for early planning of data collection rounds that will strengthen the M&E function and reporting of key indicators. Third, when the client is an integral part of designing and implementing the IE, the impact evaluation can have important effects on counterpart practices and decision making. These often transform line ministries' ability to monitor programs, guide policy design, and encourage adoption and scale-up of successful interventions within a country and across other countries and global practices. Some examples of this follow.

Bringing the problem of the commons into the design: *Irrigation interventions hold tremendous potential to help farmers cope with increasing climate variability and to ensure food security in many poorer regions of the world. Yet improper management of irrigation schemes has led to numerous failures in this sector; empirical research in the field of water management is critical in responding to these operational challenges. DIME is taking principal agent theories to the field to support rigorous economic research on this topic in a variety of regions and contexts. By testing various institutional arrangements for water management, the IE is changing the way irrigation management will happen on the ground. In Ethiopia and Mozambique, tough questions about water management and maintenance will be tested by creating different leadership models for Water User Association groups, including one treatment arm that will reserve 30 percent of chairperson positions for women.*

Changing the way new policies are introduced: *During a December 2008 workshop in Dakar, the Senegal HIV/AIDS agency revealed its plan for rolling out its new HIV prevention strategy (peer counseling) to replace the old strategy (social mobilization). During the clinic, the government decided to randomly phase in the new policy instead. This was instrumental in enabling DIME to measure the performance of the new strategy relative to the old.*

IE data collection helps build capacity: *In the Central African Republic, as part of the community development IE, DIME is helping to build capacity in data collection and cleaning at the National Institute of Statistics. The IE data collection highlighted the institute's weaknesses, which led to the preparation of a capacity-building plan to help it perform regular data collection.*

Making decisions on the basis of evidence: *IE data and data analysis are used at various stages of the policy-making process to fine-tune interventions and to motivate adoption or scale-up. Baseline data can be used to fine-tune intervention. In The Gambia, the education IE baseline revealed pervasive school beating; this elicited a nationwide campaign against it. Later in the process, the results from experimental testing of alternative policy mechanisms led to changes in program design. In Zambia, the testing of alternative drug distribution systems led to the ongoing adaption of*

(continued)

the system that is better able to reduce drug attrition and secure effective delivery of drugs to frontline facilities. This will enable treatment of possibly hundreds of thousands of malaria cases. Finally, IE results are also used to motivate scale-up of policy at the national level. In Tanzania, the IE informed the scale-up of the CCT program as a pillar of the new safety-net strategy (0.2 percent of GDP per year) and provided guidance on the needed institutional adjustments and implementation arrangements.

Mechanisms that make policies work

A breathtaking evolution is taking place in the way impact evaluation is done. It is moving from the first-generation IE—focusing on showing whether interventions work, with less attention to the underlying channels—to **Impact Evaluation 2.0**, which focuses on generating cross-sector evidence to understand the underlying behavioral and delivery mechanisms that make policies work. Results from Africa point to the importance of mechanisms based on incentives for performance, timing, information and access, and accountability and collective action.

Inputs for agricultural technology adoption: *IDA clients are considering incentive schemes to improve the delivery of agricultural extension services at the community level. Increasing the supply of knowledge is among the main challenges, because extension workers rarely reach all villages; many countries have trained lead and peer farmers to disseminate information at the community level. Evidence from Malawi shows that incentives matter (Mobarak et al. 2012). Providing small in-kind incentives to peer and lead farmers results in a 12-percentage point increase in knowledge, which translates into a 3.6 percentage-point increase in adoption of new techniques. Furthermore, incentives have similar effects on the different types of lead/peer farmers. Incentivized women lead/peer farmers performed as well as men, fully offsetting the 11 percentage-point gender gap observed in the control group on farmers' knowledge (or a 3 percentage-point gap in adoption). Similarly, incentives fully offset the poverty gradient in the control group: poor peer farmers receiving incentives increase farmers' knowledge by 20 percentage points and adoption by 6 percentage points, while they have no significant impact in the treatment group. This evidence has motivated other countries, like Mozambique, to test similar interventions.*

Self-control and investment behavior: *Results from an impact evaluation in Ghana (Fafchamps et al. 2011) comparing cash to in-kind grants for microenterprises showed in-kind grants having larger impacts on business profits. Whereas cash could be used for household consumption, in-kind grants commit business owners to channeling their grant to investment in their business. Similarly, a recent study in Malawi (Brune et al. 2011) identified large increases in savings and agricultural investment for farmers who were offered a precommitment savings instrument. Together, the results highlight the importance of behavioral elements (such as self-control) on decision making and their potential effect on development outcomes.*

Boosting accountability in service provision: *IEs assessed different approaches to strengthening of education service-provider accountability, such as supplying information, training, and/or control over resources to local stakeholders. To date, results show that these interventions are often successful in influencing behaviors of community members and service providers. An IE testing a package of management and accountability interventions in schools in Madagascar showed significant impacts on school functioning, student attendance, and grade repetition (DIME 2010). In Kenya, IE results indicated that when an extra contract teacher was hired at a school, impacts were strongest when that teacher was accountable to a school committee that included parents (Duflo, Dupas, and Kremer 2009). An IE in The Gambia showed that management training and school grants worked much better in places where adult literacy was high—pointing to potential complements between decentralized decision making and stakeholder capacity (Blimpo and Evans 2011).*

Property rights to boost investment: *In Rwanda, improved property rights increased investment in soil and water conservation for both women and men (Ali, Deininger, and Goldstein 2011). The impact for women was double that of men (18 vs. 9 percentage-point increase in investment), proof of women's less-secure property rights and how policies to address this can have a significant economic payoff. This research has important implications for agricultural practices that have high externalities (such as erosion and water management).*

Smart ways of boosting drug treatment adherence: *The global HIV/AIDS epidemic is fueled by risky sexual behavior. Prevention programs appear to have been fairly successful in increasing awareness and knowledge, but evidence on the link to changes in sexual behavior is weak. Similarly, on the treatment side, the emphasis had been on making antiretroviral therapy (ART) available and increasing the number of HIV-infected individuals on treatment. However, ART is only beneficial when patients have very high levels of adherence to the treatment. World Bank IE work in prevention and treatment is informing the next generation of HIV/AIDS programs. In rural Tanzania (de Walque et al. 2012), providing a $20 cash transfer every four months conditional on remaining free of sexually transmitted infections (STIs) resulted in a 25 percent reduction in the incidence of STIs. In Malawi (Baird et al. 2010), schoolgirls receiving payments from a cash-transfer program engage in safer sexual behavior. Eighteen months after the program began, the HIV prevalence among schoolgirls was 60 percent lower than the control group and 75 percent lower for HSV-2 (herpes simplex virus–type 2). Attaching sexual health conditions to cash transfer programs targeting young adults may help reduce risky sexual behavior. In Kenya (Pop-Eleches et al. 2011), an IE showed that the use of mobile text reminders increases HIV drug adherence by 33 percent and reduces treatment interruptions by 10 percent. This low-cost, high-coverage solution can be scaled up to improve treatment response, especially in resource-limited but high-mobile-coverage settings such as*

(continued)

Africa. Senegal is one country moving ahead with this approach. Impact evaluations are also changing the way new policies are introduced and evaluated. On the basis of these results, Senegal has asked DIME for technical support to conduct two new IEs on text messages for ART patients and to integrate health packages. The results from these pilots will inform the scale-up of national programs.

Moving on IDA IE commitments to improve the effectiveness of the World Bank's operations

Under the IDA commitments, the World Bank committed to evaluate the impact of 51 IDA projects in the FY12–14 period and to improve selection of projects to reflect the composition of the IDA operations' portfolio. This has given the operational VPUs, especially Africa, a new mandate and responsibility that they have started to implement by selecting operations for impact evaluation strategically and by planning their approach for conducting and financing IEs. Implementation challenges include absorptive capacity building for project teams and counterparts, allocation of regional operational and analytical budgets to IE activities, and a more strategic allocation of trust fund resources across themes. These issues are especially relevant to SDN sectors, with a large list of projects lined up for impact evaluation in sectors (water, energy, and transport) not currently attended to by existing IE programs. DIME and SDN have partnered to move this forward, and they jointly organized a workshop on Innovations and Solutions in Infrastructure, Agriculture and Environment, held in Naivasha, Kenya, April 23–27, 2012. The workshop attracted 12 IDA projects from the Africa region Sustainable Development Department, six Global Agriculture and Food Security Program (GAFSP) projects, and six projects from the Alliance for a Green Revolution in Africa (AGRA). The project teams were challenged to question their project and introduce testing of critical design elements that may affect policy results in significant ways. The idea was to think about the small things that make the big and expensive investments—like roads, pipes, and poles—deliver on their promises. A couple of examples of the things questioned: On quality of infrastructure, what type of contracts and demand-side measures (like audits and social monitoring) secure accountability in procurement? On operations and maintenance (O & M), what strategies improve energy reliability? What models of road O & M and local participation are more effective? What enforcement mechanisms and repayment schemes are needed for the financial sustainability of O & M of irrigation canals?

Notes

[1] See DIME Progress Report FY10-11

References

Ali, Daniel Ayalew, Klaus Deininger, and Markus Goldstein. 2011. "Environmental and Gender Impacts of Land Tenure Regularization in Africa—Pilot Evidence from Rwanda." Policy Research Working Paper 5765, World Bank, World Bank. http://www-wds.worldbank.org/external/default/WDSContentServer/IW3P/IB/2011/08/18/000158349_20110818104704/Rendered/PDF/WPS5765.pdf

Baird, S., E. Chirwa, C. McIntosh, and B. Ozler. 2010. "The Short-Term Impacts of a Schooling Conditional Cash Transfer Program on the Sexual Behavior of Young Women." *Health Economics* 2010(19):55–68.

Blimpo, Moussa P., and David K. Evans. 2011, "School-Based Management and Educational Outcomes: Lessons from a Randomized Field Experiment," mimeo, The World Bank. http://siteresources.worldbank.org/EDUCATION/Resources/Blimpo-Evans_WSD-2012-01-12.pdf

Brune, Lasse, Xavier Giné, Jessica Goldberg, and Dean Yang. 2011. "Commitments to Save: A Field Experiment in Rural Malawi." Policy Research Working Paper 5748, World Bank, Washington, DC.

deWalque, D., W. H. Dow, R. Nathan, et al. 2012. "Incentivising Safe Sex: A Randomised Trial of Conditional Cash Transfers for HIV and Sexually Transmitted Infection Prevention in Rural Tanzania." *British Medical Journal Open* 2012(2)

DIME. 2010, "DIME BRIEF. The transformative effect of managing for results in primary education in Madagascar," mimeo, DIME. http://siteresources.worldbank.org/INTDEVIMPEVAINI/Resources/3998199-1285950237302/DIMEBRIEFMadagascarAGEMAD.pdf

Duflo, Esther, Pascaline Dupas, and Michael Kremer. 2009 "Additional Resources versus Organizational Changes in Education: Experimental Evidence from Kenya," mimeo, MIT. http://economics.mit.edu/files/4286

Fafchamps, Marcel, David McKenzie, Simon Quinn, and Christopher Woodruff. 2011. "When Is Capital Enough to Get Female Microenterprises Growing? Evidence from a Randomized Experiment in Ghana." Policy Research Working Paper 5706, World Bank, Washington, DC.

Mobarak, Mushfiq, Ariel, BenYishay, Malawi. Ministry of Food and Agriculture, 2012. Agricultural Technology Diffusion through Social Networks, mimeo, DIME.

Pop-Eleches, C., H. Thirumurthy, J. P. Habyarimana, J. G. Zivin, M. P. Goldstein, D. de Walque, L. Mackeen, J. Haberer, S. Kimaiyo, J. Sidle, D. Ngare, and D. R. Bangsberg. 2011. "Mobile Phone Technologies Improve Adherence to Antiretroviral Treatment in a Resource-Limited Setting: A Randomized Controlled Trial of Text Message Reminders." *AIDS* 25(6):825–34.

received vaccinations for measles before 12 months or at any time before the survey. A child is considered adequately immunized against measles after receiving one dose of vaccine.

Source: Data on under-five and infant mortality are from *Level & Trends in Child Mortality*. Report 2011. Estimates Developed by the UN Inter-agency Group for Child Mortality Estimation (UNICEF, WHO, World Bank, UN DESA, UNPD). Data on child immunization are from the World Health Organization and the United Nations Children's Fund (www.who.int/immunization_monitoring/routine/en/).

Table 3.5. Millennium Development Goal 5: improve maternal health

Maternal mortality ratio, modeled estimate, is the number of women who die from pregnancy-related causes during pregnancy and childbirth, per 100,000 live births. Data are estimated by a regression model using information on fertility, birth attendants, and human immunodeficiency virus (HIV) prevalence.

Maternal mortality ratio, national estimate, is the number of women who die during pregnancy and childbirth, per 100,000 live births.

Births attended by skilled health staff are the percentage of deliveries attended by personnel who are trained to give the necessary supervision, care, and advice to women during pregnancy, labor, and the postpartum period; to conduct deliveries on their own; and to care for newborns.

Source: Data on maternal mortality (modeled) are from *Trends in Maternal Mortality: 1990–2010* estimates developed by the World Health Organization (WHO), United Nations Children's Fund (UNICEF), United Nations Population Fund (UNFPA), and the World Bank. Data on maternal mortality (national) and births attended by skilled health staff are from UNICEF *State of the World's Children* and Childinfo and from Demographic and Health Surveys by Macro International.

Table 3.6. Millennium Development Goal 6: combat HIV/AIDS, malaria, and other diseases

Prevalence of HIV is the percentage of people ages 15–49 who are infected with HIV.

Contraceptive use, any method, is the percentage of women ages 15–49, married or in union, who are practicing, or whose sexual partners are practicing, any form of contraception.

Children sleeping under insecticide-treated nets is the percentage of children under age 5 with access to an insecticide-treated net to prevent malaria.

Incidence of tuberculosis is the estimated number of new tuberculosis cases (pulmonary, smear positive, and extrapulmonary), per 100,000 people.

Tuberculosis treatment success rate is the percentage of new, registered smear-positive (infectious) cases that were cured or in which a full course of treatment was completed.

Source: Data on HIV prevalence are from the Joint United Nations Programme on HIV/AIDS and the World Health Organization (WHO) *Report on the Global AIDS Epidemic.* Data on contraceptive use are from household surveys, including Demographic and Health Surveys by Macro International and Multiple Indicator Cluster Surveys, by the United Nations Children's Fund (UNICEF). Data on insecticide-treated net use are from UNICEF *State of the World's Children* and Childinfo and from Demographic and Health Surveys by Macro International. Data on tuberculosis are from the WHO *Global Tuberculosis Control Report.*

Table 3.7. Millennium Development Goal 7: ensure environment sustainability

Forest area is land under natural or planted stands of trees, whether productive or not.

Terrestrial protected areas are those officially documented by national authorities.

Gross domestic product (GDP) per unit of energy use is the GDP in purchasing power parity (PPP) U.S. dollars per kilogram of oil equivalent of energy use. PPP GDP is gross domestic product converted to 2000 constant international dollars using PPP rates. An international dollar has the same purchasing power over GDP as a U.S. dollar has in the United States.

Carbon dioxide emissions per capita are those stemming from the burning of fossil fuels and the manufacture of cement divided by midyear population. They include carbon dioxide produced during consumption of solid, liquid, and gas fuels and gas flaring.

Population with sustainable access to an improved water source is the percentage of the population with reasonable access to an adequate amount of water from an improved source, such as a household connection, public standpipe, borehole, protected well or spring, or rainwater collection. Unimproved sources include vendors, tanker trucks, and unprotected wells and springs. Reasonable access is defined as the availability of at least 20 liters a person a day from a source within 1 kilometer of the dwelling.

Population with sustainable access to improved sanitation is the percentage of the population with at least adequate access to excreta disposal facilities that can effectively prevent human, animal, and insect contact with excreta. Improved facilities range from simple but protected pit latrines to flush toilets with a sewerage connection. The excreta disposal system is considered adequate if it is private or shared (but not public) and if it hygienically separates human excreta from human contact. To be effective, facilities must be correctly constructed and properly maintained.

Source: Data on forest area are from the Food and Agricultural Organization *Global Forest Resources Assessment*. Data on nationally protected areas are from the United Nations Environment Programme and the World Conservation Monitoring Centre, as compiled by the World Resources Institute, and based on data from national authorities, national legislation, and international agreements. Data on energy use are from electronic files of the International Energy Agency. Data on carbon dioxide emissions are from the Carbon Dioxide Information Analysis Center, Environmental Sciences Division, Oak Ridge National Laboratory. Data on access to water and sanitation are from the World Health Organization and United Nations Children's Fund, Joint Measurement Programme (www.wssinfo.org).

Table 3.8. Millennium Development Goal 8: develop a global partnership for development

Heavily Indebted Poor Countries (HIPC) Debt Initiative decision point is the date at which a HIPC with an established track record of good performance under adjustment programs supported by the International Monetary Fund (IMF) and the World Bank commits to undertake additional reforms and to develop and implement a poverty reduction strategy.

HIPC Debt Initiative completion point is the date at which a country successfully completes the key structural reforms agreed on at the decision point, including developing and implementing its poverty reduction strategy. The country then receives the bulk of debt relief under the HIPC Debt Initiative without further policy conditions.

Debt service relief committed is the amount of debt service relief, calculated at the Enhanced HIPC Initiative decision point, that will allow the country to achieve debt sustainability at the completion point.

Public and publicly guaranteed debt service is the sum of principal repayments and interest actually paid in foreign currency, goods, or services on long-term obligations of public debtors and long-term private obligations guaranteed by a public entity. Exports refer to exports of goods, services, and income. Worker remittances are not included here, though they are included with income receipts in other World Bank publications, such as *Global Development Finance*.

Youth unemployment rate is the percentage of the labor force ages 15–24 without work but available for and seeking employment. Definitions of labor force and unemployment may differ by country.

Fixed-line and mobile telephone subscribers are subscribers to a fixed-line telephone service, which connects a customer's equipment to the public switched telephone network, or to a public mobile telephone service, which uses cellular technology.

Source: Data on HIPC countries are from the International Development Association and International Monetary Fund "Heavily Indebted Poor Countries (HIPC) Initiative and Multilateral Debt Relief Initiative—Status of Implementation." Data on external debt are mainly from reports to the World Bank through its debtor Reporting System from member countries that have received International Bank for Reconstruction and Development loans or International

Current MDG Developments

Sub-Saharan Africa is lagging behind other regions on most Millennium Development Goals (MDGs). However, the region has achieved more than 60 percent of the progress required to reach such goals as gender parity, primary school completion, access to safe water, and extreme poverty reduction by 2015. Progress in health-related MDGs, particularly maternal mortality, is significantly lagging with respect to the 2015 targets (figure 1).

Despite adverse initial conditions, the region is making fast progress in many areas. For instance, between 1990 and 2009, the primary school completion rate in Sub-Saharan Africa improved by more than 1.5 times that of all developing countries (from 51.2 to 66.9 in the region vs. 77.5 to 87.4 at the global level). This is also the case for MDGs related to child and maternal mortality between 1990 and 2010, where relative regional improvement was larger than in other developing countries (figure 2).

Sub-Saharan Africa is vulnerable to increases in international food prices. In most countries in this region, approximately 50 to 70 percent of household spending is devoted to food. Additionally, the region imports about 45 percent of its consumption of rice and 85 percent of its consumption of wheat. Further, high levels of malnutrition result in stunted growth for 38 percent of children. The situation is most perilous in the drought- and conflict-stricken countries of the Horn of Africa. Nevertheless, increases in cereal production, driven by higher yields since the middle of the past decade, improved the continent's ability to cope with the food price spike of 2011, compared with the experience in 2008.

In addition, nutrition has remained for decades a low government priority in the region. Nutrition in many African countries is trapped in a vicious "low priority cycle" that starts with little demand for nutrition services—followed by a weak response by governments, and ends up with ineffective implementation and poor results—which, in turn, feeds into low demand for nutrition. Senegal provides an example of a country that has made significant strides in the fight against undernutrition through its Multisectoral Forum for the Fight against Malnutrition, a National Executive Office, which ensures the day-to-day management, coordination, and monitoring of national nutrition policies. Recent estimates indicate that undernutrition reduction in Senegal is 16 times higher than the regional average.

Post-2015 Developments

Official Development Assistance (ODA) has become increasingly viewed as only one component of many international activities (such as trade and investment) that supports long-term sustainable development and poverty alleviation. Nevertheless, ODA remains a major instrument with which to engage in development cooperation. The international aid community needs to continue to improve information sharing and to facilitate the ongoing expansion of ODA agents' participation in setting the global development agenda in order to better address the needs of the poor. Also, the group of low-income countries for which the MDGs were intended is shrinking, while large contingents of poor or underserved groups live or will live in middle-income countries in the coming decade (figure 3).

Figure 1. Global and regional performances

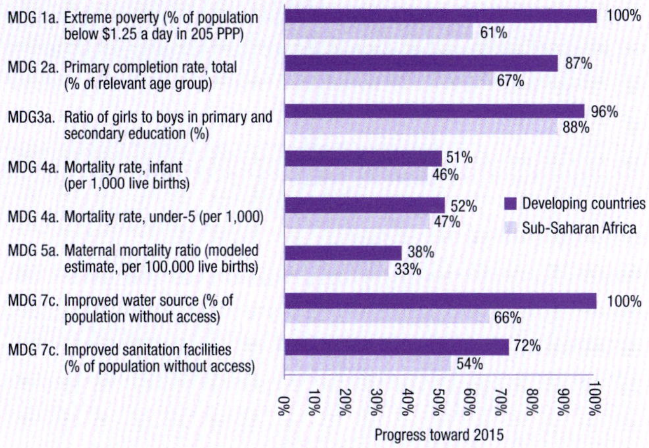

Note: A value of 100% means that respective MDG has been reached. Values denote present progress as illustrated by most recent available data: Extreme poverty—2010; Primary school completion rate—2009; Ratio of girls to boys in primary and secondary school—2009; Mortality rate, infant—2010; Mortality rate, under five—2010; Maternal mortality ratio—2008; Improved water source—2010; Improved sanitation facilities—2008.
Source: World Bank staff calculations based on data from the World Development Indicators database.

Figure 2. Improvement in MDG indicators relative to global performance

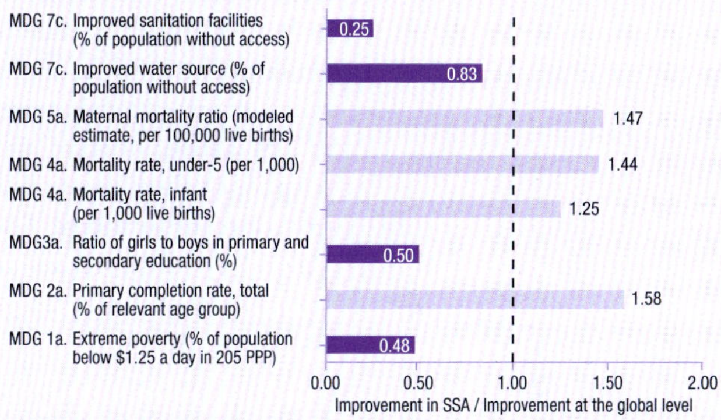

Note: Chart depicts the ratio of absolute regional improvement to global improvement by MDG. Improvement is measured as the difference between latest available value (see note, figure 1) and starting value circa 1990.
Source: World Bank staff calculations based on data from the World Development Indicators database.

Figure 3. Share of low- and middle-income countries since year 2000

Note: Chart depicts the percentage of countries in each income category per region.
Source: World Bank staff calculations based on data from the World Development Indicators database.

(continued)

Africa and the MDGs: 2015 and Beyond (continued)

There is broad agreement that the country-based development model is the most effective approach for achieving results in terms of sustained economic growth and poverty reduction in developing countries. The country-based model consists of three main strands: (1) nationally owned development strategies; (2) donor alignment around country-driven goals, with increased use of country systems wherever feasible and efforts to increase aid predictability; and (3) mechanisms of mutual accountability encompassing both donors and governments in recipient countries. Accordingly, the interplay of these three strands strengthens domestic policies and systems in recipient countries, unites donors around clear development goals, and sets out a mutual accountability framework for all stakeholders. Henceforth, moving away from global goals to country-specific ones should improve effectiveness of the development process.

Results-based monitoring and evaluation (M&E) can be a powerful public management tool if used to guide decisions on how goals can be reached most effectively and efficiently—that is, it can help ensure that countries and donors get value for money. It can be used in the context of the MDGs to help policymakers track progress and demonstrate the outcomes and impacts of a given policy, program, or project. Results-based M&E differs from traditional implementation-focused M&E in that it emphasizes inputs, activities, and outputs with a sharp focus on outcomes and impacts while identifying the critical bottlenecks to achieving those outcomes. To identify those bottlenecks, the World Bank's Country Policy and Institutional Assessment tool (CPIA) could perform a useful function in assisting countries with identifying some of those critical bottlenecks (Go and Quijada 2012).

A functioning results-based M&E system provides information that is useful both internally and externally. Country use comes about when the information from the M&E system becomes a management tool for policy makers, managing to achieve results and accomplish specified targets. Likewise, the information from a results-based M&E system is crucial to donors who expect demonstrable results from government action and aid resources.

Reference

Go and Quijada. 2012. "The Odds of Achieving the MDGs." *World Bank Research Observer* doi: 10.1093/wbro/lks005.

Development Association credits, as well as from World Bank and IMF files. Data on youth unemployment are from the International Labour Organization Key Indicators of the Labour Market database. Data on telephone subscribers and Internet users are from the International Telecommunication Union *World Telecommunication/ICT Development Report* and database, and from World Bank estimates.

4. *Private sector development*

TABLE 4.1. DOING BUSINESS INDICATORS

Number of startup procedures to start a business is the number of procedures required to start a business, including interactions to obtain necessary permits and licenses and to complete all inscriptions, verifications, and notifications to start operations.

Time required for each procedure to start a business is the number of calendar days needed to complete each procedure to legally operate a business. If a procedure can be speeded up at additional cost, the fastest procedure, independent of cost, is chosen.

Cost to start a business is normalized by presenting it as a percentage of gross national income (GNI) per capita.

Minimum capital is the paid-in minimum capital requirement, which reflects the amount that the entrepreneur needs to deposit in a bank or with a notary before registration and up to three months following incorporation. It is reported as a percentage of the country's income per capita.

Number of procedures to register property is the number of procedures required for a business to secure rights to property.

Time required to register property is the number of calendar days needed for a business to secure rights to property.

Cost to register property is the official costs required by law to register a property, including fees, transfer taxes, stamp duties, and any other payment to the property registry, notaries, public agencies, and lawyers. Other taxes, such as capital gains tax or value added tax, are excluded from the cost measure. Both costs borne by the buyer and those borne by the seller are included. If cost estimates differ among sources, the median reported value is used. It is reported as a percentage of property value, which is assumed to be equivalent to 50 times income per capita.

Number of procedures to enforce a contract is the number of independent actions, mandated by law or courts, that demand interaction between the parties of a contract or between them and the judge or court officer.

Time required to enforce a contract is the number of calendar days from the filing of the lawsuit in court until the final determination and, in appropriate cases, payment.

Cost to enforce a contract is court and attorney fees, where the use of attorneys is mandatory or common, or the cost of an administrative debt recovery procedure, expressed as a percentage of the debt value.

Number of procedures to deal with construction permits is the number of procedures required to obtain construction-related permits.

Time required to deal with construction permits is the average wait, in days, experienced to obtain a construction-related permit from the day the establishment applied for it to the day it was granted.

Cost to deal with construction permits is all the fees associated with completing the procedures to legally build a warehouse, including those associated with obtaining land use approvals and reconstruction design clearances; receiving inspections before, during, and after construction; getting utility connections; and registering the warehouse property. Nonrecurring taxes required for the completion of the warehouse project also are recorded. The building code, information from local experts, and specific regulations and fee schedules are used as sources for costs. If several local partners provide different estimates, the median reported value is used. It is reported as a percentage of the country's income per capita.

Disclosure index measures the degree to which investors are protected through disclosure of ownership and financial information. Higher values indicate more disclosure.

Director liability index measures a plaintiff's ability to hold directors of firms liable for damages to the company. Higher values indicate greater liability.

Shareholder suits index measures shareholders' ability to sue officers and directors for misconduct. Higher values indicate greater power for shareholders to challenge transactions.

Investor protection index measures the degree to which investors are protected through disclosure of ownership and financial information regulations. It is the average of the disclosure, director liability, and shareholder suits indexes. Higher values indicate better protection.

Resolving insolvency time (years) is the average time to close a business. Information is collected on the sequence of procedures and on whether any procedures can be carried out simultaneously.

Cost (% of estate) is the average cost of bankruptcy proceedings. The cost of the proceedings is recorded as a percentage of the estate's value.

Recovery rate (cents on the dollar) is the recovery rate calculated on the basis of how many cents on the dollar claimants (creditors, tax authorities, and employees) recover from an insolvent firm.

Source: Data are from the World Bank, Doing Business project (http://www.doingBusiness.org/).

Table 4.2. Investment climate

Private sector fixed capital formation is private sector fixed capital formation (table 2.21) divided by nominal gross domestic product (table 2.1).

Net foreign direct investment is net inflows of investment to acquire a lasting management interest (10 percent or more of voting stock) in an enterprise operating in an economy other than that of the investor. It is the sum of equity capital, reinvestment of earnings, other long-term capital, and short-term capital as shown in the balance of payments. This series shows net inflows (new investment inflows less disinvestment) in the reporting economy from foreign investors.

Domestic credit to private sector is financial resources provided to the private sector, such as through loans, purchases of nonequity securities, and trade credits and other accounts receivable that establish a claim for repayment. For some countries these claims include credit to public enterprises.

Firms that believe the court system is fair, impartial, and uncorrupt are the percentage of firms that believe the court system is fair, impartial, and uncorrupt.

Corruption is the percentage of firms identifying corruption as a major constraint to current operation.

Crime, theft, and disorder are the percentage of firms identifying crime, theft, and disorder as a major constraint to current operation.

Tax rates are the percentage of firms identifying tax rates as a major constraint to current operation.

Finance is the percentage of firms identifying access to finance or cost of finance as a major constraint to current operation.

Electricity is the percentage of firms identifying electricity as a major constraint to current operation.

Labor regulations are the percentage of firms identifying labor regulations as a major constraint to current operation.

Labor skills are the percentage of firms identifying skills of available workers as a major constraint to current operation.

Transportation is the percentage of firms identifying transportation as a major constraint to current operation.

Customs and trade regulations are the percentage of firms identifying customs and trade regulations as a major constraint to current operation.

Number of tax payments is the number of taxes paid by businesses, including by electronic filing. The tax is counted as paid once a year even if payments are more frequent.

Time to prepare, file, and pay taxes is the number of hours it takes to prepare, file, and pay (or withhold) three major types of taxes: the corporate income tax, the value added or sales tax, and labor taxes, including payroll taxes and social security contributions.

Total tax rate is the total amount of taxes payable by the business (except for labor taxes) after accounting for deductions and exemptions as a percentage of profit.

Highest marginal tax rate, corporate, is the highest rate shown on the schedule of tax rates applied to the taxable income of corporations.

Time dealing with officials is the average percentage of senior management's time that is spent in a typical week dealing with requirements imposed by government regulations (for example, taxes, customs, labor regulations, licensing, and registration), including dealings with officials, completing forms, and the like.

Average time to clear customs, direct exports, is the average number of days to clear direct exports through customs.

Average time to clear customs, imports, is the average number of days to clear imports through customs.

Interest rate spread is the interest rate charged by banks on loans to prime customers minus the interest rate paid by commercial or similar banks for demand, time, or savings deposits.

Listed domestic companies are domestically incorporated companies listed on a country's stock exchanges at the end of the year. They exclude investment companies, mutual funds, and other collective investment vehicles.

Market capitalization of listed companies, also known as market value, is the share price of a listed domestic company's stock times the number of shares outstanding.

Turnover ratio for traded stocks is the total value of shares traded during the period divided by the average market capitalization for the period. Average market capitalization is calculated as the average of the end-of-period values for the current period and the previous period.

Source: Data on private sector fixed capital formation are from the World Bank World Development Indicators database. Data on net foreign direct investment are from the International Monetary Fund (IMF) Balance of Payments database, supplemented by data from the United Nations Conference on Trade and Development and official national sources. Data on domestic credit to the private sector are from the IMF International Financial Statistics database and data files, World Bank and Organisation for Economic Co-operation and Development gross domestic product (GDP) estimates, and the World Bank World Development Indicators database. Data on investment climate constraints to firms, data on time dealing with officials, and average time to clear customs are based on enterprise surveys conducted by the World Bank and its partners (http://www.enterpriseSurveys). Data on regulation and tax administration and highest marginal corporate tax rates are from the World Bank Doing Business project (http://www.doingBusiness). Data on interest rate spreads are from the IMF International Financial Statistics database and data files and the World Bank World Development Indicators database. Data on listed domestic companies, turnover ratios for traded stocks, and market capitalization are from Standard & Poor's *Global Stock Markets Factbook* and supplemental Standard & Poor's data.

Table 4.3. Financial sector infrastructure

Foreign currency sovereign ratings are long- and short-term foreign currency ratings that assess a sovereign's capacity and willingness to honor in full and on time its existing and future obligations issued in foreign currencies. Short-term ratings have a time horizon of less than 13 months for most obligations, or up to 3 years for U.S. public finance, in line with industry standards, to reflect the unique risk characteristics of bond, tax, and revenue anticipation notes that are commonly issued with terms up to 3 years. Short-term ratings thus place greater emphasis on the liquidity necessary to meet financial commitments in a timely manner.

Gross national savings is the sum of gross domestic savings (table 2.13) and net factor income and net private transfers from abroad. The estimate here also includes net public transfers from abroad.

Money and quasi money (M2) are the sum of currency outside banks, demand deposits other than those of the central government, and the time, savings, and foreign currency deposits of resident sectors other than the central government. This definition of money supply is frequently called M2 and corresponds to lines 34 and 35 in the International Monetary Fund International Financial Statistics.

Real interest rate is the lending interest rate adjusted for inflation as measured by the gross domestic product deflator.

Domestic credit to private sector is financial resources provided to the private sector, such as through loans, purchases of nonequity securities, and trade credits and other accounts receivable, that establish a claim for repayment. For some countries these claims include credit to public enterprises.

Interest rate spread is the interest rate charged by banks on loans to prime customers minus the interest rate paid by commercial or similar banks for demand, time, or savings deposits.

Ratio of bank nonperforming loans to total gross loans is the value of nonperforming loans divided by the total value of the loan portfolio (including nonperforming loans before the deduction of specific loan-loss provisions). The loan amount recorded as nonperforming should be the gross value of the loan as recorded on the balance sheet, not just the amount overdue.

Listed domestic companies are domestically incorporated companies listed on a country's stock exchanges at the end of the year. They exclude investment companies, mutual funds, and other collective investment vehicles.

Market capitalization of listed companies, also known as market value, is the share price of a listed domestic company's stock times the number of shares outstanding.

Turnover ratio for traded stocks is the total value of shares traded during the period divided by the average market capitalization for the period. Average market capitalization is calculated as the average of the end-of-period values for the current period and the previous period.

Source: Data on foreign currency sovereign ratings are from Fitch Ratings (www.fitchratings.com/). Data on gross national savings are from World Bank national accounts data, and Organisation for Economic Co-operation and Development national accounts data files. Data on money and quasi money and domestic credit to the private sector are from the International Monetary Fund International Financial Statistics and data files and World Bank and OECD estimates of GDP. Data on real interest rates are from the IMF International Financial Statistics database and data files using World Bank data on the GDP deflator and the World Bank World Development Indicators database. Data on interest rate spreads are from the International Monetary Fund, International Financial Statistics and data files. Data on ratios of bank nonperforming loans to total are from the International Monetary Fund *Global Financial Stability Report*. Data on bank branches are from surveys of banking and regulatory institutions by the World Bank Research Department and Financial Sector and Operations Policy Department and the World Development Indicators database. Data on listed domestic companies and turnover ratios for traded stocks are from Standard & Poor's *Emerging Stock Markets Factbook* and supplemental data and the World Bank's World Development Indicators database. Data on market capitalization of listed companies are from Standard & Poor's *Emerging*

Stock Markets Factbook and supplemental data, World Bank and OECD estimates of GDP, and the World Bank World Development Indicators database.

5. Trade and regional integration

Table 5.1. International trade and tariff barriers

Total trade is the sum of exports and imports of goods and services measured as a share of gross domestic product.

Merchandise trade is the sum of imports and exports of merchandise divided by nominal gross domestic product.

Services trade is the sum of imports and exports of wholesale and retail trade (including hotels and restaurants), transport, and government, financial, professional, and personal services such as education, health care, and real estate (International Standard Industrial Classification revision 3 divisions 50–99) less the value of their intermediate inputs. Also included are imputed bank service charges, import duties, and any statistical discrepancies noted by national compilers or arising from rescaling. It is calculated without making deductions for depreciation of fabricated assets or depletion and degradation of natural resources. For countries that report national accounts data at producer prices (Angola, Benin, Cape Verde, Comoros, the Republic of Congo, Côte d'Ivoire, Gabon, Liberia, Niger, Rwanda, São Tomé and Príncipe, Seychelles, and Togo), gross value added at market prices is used as the denominator. For countries that report national accounts data at basic prices (all other countries), gross value added at factor cost is used as the denominator. Value added at basic prices excludes net taxes on products; value added at producer prices includes net taxes on products paid by producers but excludes sales or value added taxes.

Exports of goods and services represent the value of all goods and other market services provided to the rest of the world. They include the value of merchandise, freight, insurance, transport, travel, royalties, license fees, and other services, such as communication, construction, financial, information, business, personal, and government services. They exclude labor and property income (formerly called factor services) as well as transfer payments and are expressed in current U.S. dollars and as a proportion of nominal GDP.

Imports of goods and services represent the value of all goods and other market services received from the rest of the world. They include the value of merchandise, freight, insurance, transport, travel, royalties, license fees, and other services, such as communication, construction, financial, information, business, personal, and government services. They exclude labor and property income (formerly called factor services) as well as transfer payments and are expressed in current U.S. dollars and as a proportion of nominal GDP.

Annual growth of exports and imports is calculated using real imports and exports.

Terms of trade index measures the relative movement of export and import prices. This series is calculated as the ratio of a country's export unit values or prices to its import unit values or prices and shows changes over a base year (2000) in the level of export unit values as a percentage of import unit values.

Structure of merchandise exports and *imports* components may not sum to 100 percent because of unclassified trade.

Food comprises the commodities in Standard International Trade Classification (SITC) sections 0 (food and live animals), 1 (beverages and tobacco), and 4 (animal and vegetable oils and fats) and SITC division 22 (oil seeds, oil nuts, and oil kernels).

Agricultural raw materials comprise the commodities in SITC section 2 (crude materials except fuels), excluding divisions 22, 27 (crude fertilizers and minerals excluding coal, petroleum, and precious stones), and 28 (metalliferous ores and scrap).

Fuel comprises SITC section 3 (mineral fuels).

Ores and metals comprise the commodities in SITC sections 27, 28, and 68 (nonferrous metals).

Manufactures comprise the commodities in SITC sections 5 (chemicals), 6 (basic manufactures), 7 (machinery and transport equipment), and 8 (miscellaneous manufactured goods), excluding division 68.

Export/import diversification index measures the extent to which exports/imports are diversified. It is constructed as the inverse of a Herfindahl index, using disaggregated exports/imports at four digits (following SITC revision 3). The total number of products exported/imported includes only those whose value exceeds $100,000 or 0.3 percent of the country's total exports/imports, whichever is smaller. The maximum number of three-digit products that could be exported is 261. Ranging from 0 to 1, the index reveals the extent of the differences between the structure of trade of the country or country group and the world average. An index value closer to 1 indicates a bigger difference from the world average. A higher value indicates more export/import diversification. The index is computed by measuring absolute deviation of the country share from world structure.

Export/import concentration index, also known as the Herfindahl-Hirschmann index, is a measure of the degree of market concentration. The total number of products exported/imported includes only those whose value exceeds $100,000 or 0.3 percent of the country's total exports/imports, whichever is smaller. The maximum number of three-digit products that could be exported/imported is 261. It has been normalized to a scale of 0–1. An index value close to 1 indicates a very concentrated market (maximum concentration). Values closer to 0 reflect a more equal distribution of market shares among exporters or importers. This type of concentration indicator is vulnerable to cyclical fluctuations in relative prices, with commodity price rises making commodity exporters/importers look more concentrated.

Competitiveness indicator has two aspects: *sectoral effect* and *global effect*. To calculate both indicators, growth of exports is decomposed into three components: the growth rate of total international trade over the reference period (2005–09); the sectoral effect, which measures the contribution to a country's export growth of the dynamics of the sectoral markets where the country sells its products, assuming that sectoral market shares are constant; and the competitiveness effect, which measures the contribution of changes in sectoral market shares to a country's export growth.

Tariff barriers are a form of duty based on the value of an import.

Binding coverage is the percentage of product lines with an agreed bound rate.

Simple mean bound rate is the unweighted average of all the lines in the tariff schedule in which bound rates have been set.

Simple mean tariff is the unweighted average of effectively applied rates or most favored nation rates for all products subject to tariffs calculated for all traded goods.

Dispersion around the mean is calculated as the coefficient of variation of the applied tariff rates, including preferential rates that a country applies to its trading partners available at the six-digit product level of the Harmonized System in a country's customs schedule.

Weighted mean tariff is the average of effectively applied rates or most favored nation rates weighted by the product import shares corresponding to each partner country.

Share of lines with international peaks is the share of lines in the tariff schedule with tariff rates that exceed 15 percent.

Share of lines with domestic peaks is the share of lines in the tariff schedule with tariff rates that are more than three times the simple average tariff.

Share of lines that are bound is the share of lines in the country's tariff schedule bound subject to World Trade Organization negotiation agreements.

Share of lines with specific rates is the share of lines in the tariff schedule that are set on a per unit basis or that combine ad valorem and per unit rates.

Primary products are commodities classified in SITC revision 2 sections 0–4 plus division 68.

Manufactured products are commodities classified in SITC revision 2 sections 5–8 excluding division 68.

Average cost to ship 20 ft container from port to destination is the cost of all operations associated with moving a container from onboard a ship to the considered economic center, weighted based on container traffic for each corridor.

Average time to clear customs, direct exports, is the average number of days to clear direct exports through customs.

Average time to clear customs, imports, is the average number of days to clear imports through customs.

Source: Data on trade and services are from World Bank and Organisation for Economic Co-operation and Development national accounts data. Data on merchandise trade are from the World Trade Organization and

World Bank GDP estimates. Data on the competitiveness indicator are from the Organisation for Economic Co-operation and Development *African Economic Outlook 2011: Africa and Its Emerging Partners.* Data on the export concentration index and diversification index data are from the United Nations Conference on Trade and Development Statistical Office data files (http://unctadstat.unctad.org), with Standard International Trade Classification groups from the United Nations Statistics Division (http://unstats.un.org/unsd/cr/registry/regcst.asp?Cl=14). Data on tariffs are calculated by World Bank staff using the World Integrated Trade Solution system (http://wits.worldbank.org) and data from the United Nations Conference on Trade and Development Trade Analysis and Information System database and the World Trade Organization Integrated Data Base and Consolidated Tariff Schedules database. Data on global imports are from the United Nations Statistics Division COMTRADE database. Data on merchandise exports and imports are from World Bank country desks. Data on shipping costs are from the World Bank Sub-Saharan Africa Transport Policy Program. Data on average time to clear customs are from World Bank Enterprise Surveys (http://www.enterpriseSurveys/).

Table 5.2 Top three exports and share in total exports, 2009

Top exports and *share of total exports* are based on exports disaggregated at the four-digit level (following the Standard International Trade Classification revision 3).

Number of exports accounting for 75 percent of total exports is the number of exports in a country that account for 75 percent of the country's exports.

Source: Organisation for Economic Cooperation and Development *African Economic Outlook 2011: Africa and Its Emerging Partners.*

Table 5.3 Regional integration, trade blocs

Type of most recent agreement includes customs union, under which members substantially eliminate all tariff and nontariff barriers among themselves and establish a common external tariff for nonmembers; economic integration agreement, which liberalizes trade in services among members and covers a substantial number of sectors, affects a sufficient volume of trade, includes substantial modes of supply, and is nondiscriminatory (in the sense that similarly situated service suppliers are treated the same); free trade agreement, under which members substantially eliminate all tariff and nontariff barriers but set tariffs on imports from nonmembers; partial scope agreement, which is a preferential trade agreement notified to the World Trade Organization (WTO) that is not a free trade agreement, a customs union, or an economic integration; and not notified agreement, which is a preferential trade arrangement established among member countries that is not notified to the WTO (the agreement may be functionally equivalent to any of the other agreements).

Merchandise exports within bloc are the sum of merchandise exports by members of a trade bloc to other members of the bloc. They are shown both in U.S. dollars and as a percentage of total merchandise exports by the bloc.

Merchandise exports by bloc are the sum of merchandise exports within bloc and to the rest of the world as a share of total merchandise exports by all economies in the world.

Source: Data on merchandise trade flows are published in the International Monetary Fund (IMF) *Direction of Trade Statistics Yearbook* and *Direction of Trade Statistics Quarterly.* The data in the table were calculated using the IMF's Direction of Trade database. The information on trade bloc membership is from the World Bank Policy Research Report *Trade Blocs* (2000), the United Nations Conference on *Trade and Development Trade and Development Report 2007,* the World Trade Organization Regional Trade Agreements Information System, and the World Bank and the Center for International Business at the Tuck School of Business at Dartmouth College's Global Preferential Trade Agreements Database (http://wits.worldbank.org/gptad/).

6. Infrastructure

Table 6.1. Water and sanitation

Internal fresh water resources per capita are the sum of total renewable resources, which include internal flows of rivers and groundwater from rainfall in the country and river flows from other countries.

Population with sustainable access to an improved water source is the percentage of the population with reasonable access to an adequate amount of water from an improved source, such as a household connection, public standpipe, borehole, protected well or spring, or rainwater collection. Unimproved sources include vendors, tanker trucks, and unprotected wells and springs. Reasonable access is defined as the availability of at least 20 liters a person a day from a source within one kilometer of the user's dwelling.

Population with sustainable access to improved sanitation is the percentage of the population with at least adequate access to excreta disposal facilities that can effectively prevent human, animal, and insect contact with excreta. Improved facilities range from simple but protected pit latrines to flush toilets with a sewerage connection. The excreta disposal system is considered adequate if it is private or shared (but not public) and if it hygienically separates human excreta from human contact. To be effective, facilities must be correctly constructed and properly maintained.

Average duration of insufficient water supply is the average duration of water shortages in a typical month in the last fiscal year.

Committed nominal investment in water projects with private participation is annual committed investment in water projects with private investment, including projects for potable water generation and distribution and sewerage collection and treatment projects.

Official development assistance (ODA) gross disbursements for water supply and sanitation sector are disbursements for water supply and sanitation by bilateral, multilateral, and other donors. The release of funds to, or the purchase of goods or services for a recipient; by extension, the amount thus spent. Disbursements record the actual international transfer of financial resources or of goods or services valued at the cost of the donor.

Source: Data on freshwater resources are from the Food and Agriculture Organization AQUASTAT database. Data on access to water and sanitation are from the World Health Organization and United Nations Children's Fund, Joint Measurement Programme (www.wssinfo.org). Data on insufficient water supply are from World Bank Enterprise Surveys (http://www.enterpriseSurveys/). Data on committed nominal investment in potable water projects with private participation are from the World Bank Private Participation in Infrastructure Project Database (http://ppi.worldbank.org). Data on official development assistance disbursements are from the Development Assistance Committee of the Organisation for Economic Co-operation and Development *Geographical Distribution of Financial Flows to Developing Countries*, *Development Co-operation Report*, and International Development Statistics database (www.oecd.org/dac/stats/idsonline).

Table 6.2. Transportation

Road network is the length of motorways, highways, main or national roads, secondary or regional roads, and other roads.

Rail lines are the length of railway route available for train service, irrespective of the number of parallel tracks.

Road density, ratio to total land, is the total length of national road network per 100 square kilometers of total land area.

Vehicle fleet is the number of motor vehicles, including cars, buses, and freight vehicles but not two-wheelers.

Commercial vehicles are the number of commercial vehicles that use at least 24 liters of diesel fuel per 100 kilometers.

Passenger vehicles are road motor vehicles, other than two-wheelers, intended for the carriage of passengers and designed to seat no more than nine people (including the driver).

Road network in good or fair condition is the length of the national road network, including the interurban classified network without the urban and rural network, that is in good or fair condition, as defined by each country's road agency.

Ratio of paved to total roads is the length of paved roads—which are those surfaced with crushed stone (macadam) and hydrocarbon binder or bituminized agents, with concrete, or with cobblestones—as a percentage of all the country's roads.

Price of diesel fuel and *gasoline* is the price as posted at filling stations in a country's capital city. When several fuel prices for major cities were available, the unweighted average is used. Since super gasoline (95 octane/A95/premium) is not available everywhere, it is sometime replaced by regular gasoline (92 octane/A92), premium plus gasoline (98 octane/A98), or an average of the two.

Committed nominal investment in transport projects with private participation is annual committed investment in transport projects with private investment, including projects for airport runways and terminals, railways (including fixed assets, freight, intercity passenger, and local passenger), toll roads, bridges, and tunnels.

Official development assistance (ODA) gross disbursements for transportation and storage are disbursements for transportation and storage by bilateral, multilateral, and other donors. Disbursements record the actual international transfer of financial resources or of goods or services valued at the cost of the donor.

Source: Data on length of road network and vehicle fleet are from the International Road Federation *World Road Statistics* and electronic files, except where noted. Data on rail lines and ratio of paved to total roads are from the World Bank Transportation, Water, and Information and Communications Technologies Department, Transport Division. Data on fuel and gasoline prices are from the German Agency for Technical Cooperation. Data on committed nominal investment in transport projects with private participation are from the World Bank Private Participation in Infrastructure Project Database (http://ppi.worldbank.org). Data on official development assistance disbursements are from the Development Assistance Committee of the Organisation for Economic Co-operation and Development, Geographical Distribution of Financial Flows to Developing Countries, Development Co-operation Report, and International Development Statistics database (www.oecd.org/dac/stats/idsonline).

Table 6.3. Information and communication technology

Telephone subscribers are subscribers to a main telephone line service, which connects a customer's equipment to the public switched telephone network or to a cellular telephone service.

Unmet demand is the number of applications for connection to the public switched telephone network that have been held back because of a lack of technical facilities (equipment, lines, and the like) divided by the number of main telephone lines.

Households with own telephone are the percentage of households possessing a telephone.

Average delay for firm in obtaining a mainline phone connection is the average actual delay in days that firms experience when obtaining a telephone connection, measured from the day the establishment applied to the day it received the service or approval.

Internet users are people with access to the Internet.

Telephone faults are the total number of reported faults for the year divided by the total number of mainlines in operation multiplied by 100. The definition of fault can vary. Some countries include faulty customer equipment; others distinguish between reported and actual found faults. There is also sometimes a distinction between residential and business lines. Another consideration is the time period: some countries report this indicator on a monthly basis; in these cases data are converted to yearly estimates.

Telephone faults cleared by next working day are the percentage of faults in the public switched telephone network that have been corrected by the end of the next working day.

Fixed broadband Internet monthly subscription is the monthly subscription charge for fixed (wired) broadband Internet service. Fixed (wired) broadband is considered any dedicated connection to the Internet at downstream speeds equal to, or greater than, 256 kbit/s, using DSL. Where several offers are available, preference should be given to the 256 kbit/s connection. Taxes should be included. If not included, it should be specified in a note including the applicable tax rate.

Cost of 3-minute fixed telephone local phone call during peak hours is the cost of a three-minute local call during peak hours. Local call refers to a call within the same exchange area using the subscriber's own terminal (that is, not from a public telephone).

Cost of 3-minute cellular local call during peak hours is the cost of a three-minute cellular local call during peak hours.

Residential telephone connection charge is the initial, one-time charge involved in applying for basic telephone service. Where charges differ by exchange areas, the charge reported is for the largest urban area.

Business telephone connection charge is the one-time charge involved in applying for business basic telephone service. Where charges differ by exchange area, the charge reported is for the largest urban area.

Mobile cellular prepaid connection charge is the initial, one-time charge for a new subscription. Refundable deposits should not be counted. Although some operators waive the connection charge, this does not include the cost of the Subscriber Identity Module (SIM) card. The price of the SIM card should be included in the connection charge (for a prepaid service the cost of SIM is equivalent to connection charge). It should also be noted if free minutes or free SMS are included in the connection charge. Taxes should be included. If not included, it should be specified in a note including the applicable tax rate.

Mobile cellular postpaid connection charge is the initial, one-time charge for a new postpaid subscription. Refundable deposits should not be counted. Although some operators waive the connection charge, this does not include the cost of the SIM card. The price of the SIM card should be included in the connection charge. It should also be noted if free minutes or free SMS are included in the connection charge. Taxes should be included. If not included, it should be specified in a note including the applicable tax rate.

Fixed broadband Internet connection charge is the initial, one-time charge for a new fixed (wired) broadband Internet connection. The tariffs should represent the cheapest fixed (wired) broadband entry plan. Refundable deposits should not be counted. Taxes should be included. If not included, it should be specified in a note including the applicable tax rate.

Annual investment in fixed telephone service is the annual investment in equipment for fixed telephone service.

Annual investment in mobile communication is the annual investment on equipment for mobile communication networks.

Annual investment in telecommunications is the expenditure associated with acquiring the ownership of telecommunication equipment infrastructure (including supporting land and buildings and intellectual and nontangible property such as computer software). It includes expenditure on initial installations and on additions to existing installations.

Committed nominal investment in telecommunication projects with private participation is annual committed investment in telecommunication projects with private investment, including projects for fixed or mobile local telephony, domestic long-distance telephony, and international long-distance telephony.

Official development assistance (ODA) gross disbursements for communication are disbursements for communication by bilateral, multilateral, and other donors. Disbursements record the actual international transfer of financial resources or of goods or services valued at the cost of the donor.

Revenue from fixed telephone services is revenue received for the connection (installation) of telephone service (including charges for transferring or cancelling a service); revenue from recurring charges for subscription to telephone (and broadband and Internet access if not able to be separated from fixed telephone), including equipment rentals where relevant; and revenue from calls (local, national, and international).

Revenue from mobile networks is revenue from the provision of mobile cellular communications services, including all voice and data (narrowband and broadband) services. It refers to revenue earned by retailers, not by wholesalers.

Total revenue from all telecommunication services is the total (gross) telecommunication revenue earned from all (fixed, mobile, and data, including Internet) operators (both network and virtual) offering services within the country. It excludes revenues from nontelecommunications services as well as repayable subscribers' contributions or deposits. It refers to revenue earned by retailers and by wholesalers.

Source: Data on telephone subscribers, unmet demand, reported phone faults, cost of local and cellular calls, households with telephone, Internet users and pricing, telephone and Internet connection charges, and annual investment and revenue on telecommunications are from the International Telecommunications Union data files. Data on delays for firms in obtaining a telephone connection are from World Bank Enterprise Surveys (http://www.enterpriseSurveys/). Data on committed nominal investment are from the World Bank Private Participation in Infrastructure Project Database (http://ppi.worldbank.org). Data on official development assistance disbursements are from the Development Assistance Committee of the Organisation for Economic Co-operation and Development Geographical Distribution of Financial Flows to Developing Countries, Development Co-operation Report, and International Development Statistics database (www.oecd.org/dac/stats/idsonline).

Table 6.4. Energy

Electricity production is measured at the terminals of all alternator sets in a station. In addition to hydropower, coal, oil, gas, and nuclear power generation, it covers generation by geothermal, solar, wind, and tide and wave energy, as well as that from combustible renewable and waste. Production includes the output of electricity plants that are designed to produce electricity only as well as that of combined heat and power plants.

Hydroelectric refers to electricity produced by hydroelectric power plants.

Coal refers to all coal and brown coal, both primary (including hard coal and lignite brown coal) and derived fuels (including patent fuel, coke oven coke, gas coke, coke oven gas, and blast furnace gas). Peat is also included.

Natural gas refers to natural gas but excludes natural gas liquids.

Nuclear refers to electricity produced by nuclear power plants.

Oil refers to crude oil and petroleum products.

Electric power consumption is the production of power plants and combined heat and power plants, less distribution losses and own use by heat and power plants.

GDP per unit of energy use is nominal GDP in purchasing power parity (PPP) U.S. dollars divided by apparent consumption, which is equal to indigenous production plus imports and stock changes minus exports and fuels supplied to ships and aircraft engaged in international transport.

Firms identifying electricity as major or very severe obstacle to business operation and growth are the percentage of firms that responded "major" or "very severe" to the following question: "Please tell us if any of the following issues are a problem for the operation and growth of your business. If an issue (infrastructure, regulation, and permits) poses a problem, please judge its severity as an obstacle on a five-point scale that ranges from 0 = no obstacle to 5 = very severe obstacle."

Average delay for firm in obtaining electrical connection is the average actual delay in days that firms experience when obtaining an electrical connection, measured from the day the establishment applied to the day it received the service or approval.

Electric power transmission and distribution losses are technical and nontechnical losses, including electricity losses due to operation of the system and the delivery of electricity as well as those caused by unmetered supply. This comprises all losses due to transport and distribution of electrical energy and heat.

Electrical power outages in a typical month is the average number of electrical power outages in a typical month.

Firms that share or own their own generator are the percentage of firms that responded "Yes" to the following question: "Does your establishment own or share a generator?"

Firms using electricity from generator are the percentage of firms using electricity supplied from a generator or generators that the firm owns or shares.

Committed nominal investment in energy projects with private participation is annual committed investment in energy projects with private investment, including projects for electricity generation, transmission, and distribution as well as natural gas transmission and distribution.

Official development assistance (ODA) gross disbursements for energy are disbursements for energy by bilateral, multilateral, and other donors. Disbursements record the actual international transfer of financial resources or of goods or services valued at the cost of the donor.

Source: Data on electricity production and consumption are from the International Energy Agency (www.iea.org/stats/index.asp), *Energy Statistics of Non-OECD Countries*, *Energy Balances of Non-OECD Countries*, *Energy Statistics of OECD Countries*, and *Energy Balances of OECD Countries*. Data on PPP GDP per unit of energy use are from the International Energy Agency (www.iea.org/stats/index.asp) and World Bank PPP data. Data on solid fuels use are from household survey data, supplemented by World Bank Project Appraisal Documents. Data on firms identifying electricity as a major or very severe obstacle to business operation and growth, delays for firms in obtaining an electrical connection, electrical outages of firms, firms that share or own their own generator, and firms using electricity from generator are from World Bank Enterprise Surveys (http://www.enterpriseSurveys/). Data on transmission and distribution losses are from the International Energy Agency (www.iea.org/stats/index.asp), *Energy Statistics of Non-OECD Countries*, *Energy Balances of Non-OECD Countries*, *Energy Statistics of OECD Countries*, and *Energy Balances of OECD Countries* and the United Nations *Energy Statistics Yearbook*. Data on committed nominal investment are from the World Bank Private Participation in Infrastructure Project Database (http://ppi.worldbank.org). Data on official development assistance disbursements are from the Development Assistance Committee of the Organisation for Economic Co-operation and Development *Geographical Distribution of Financial Flows to Developing Countries*, *Development Co-operation Report*, and International Development Statistics database (www.oecd.org/dac/stats/idsonline).

7. *Human development*

Table 7.1. Education

Youth literacy rate is the percentage of people ages 15–24 who can, with understanding, both read and write a short, simple statement about their everyday life.

Adult literacy rate is the proportion of adults ages 15 and older who can, with understanding, read and write a short, simple statement on their everyday life.

Primary education provides children with basic reading, writing, and mathematics skills along with an elementary understanding of such subjects as history, geography, natural science, social science, art, and music.

Secondary education completes the provision of basic education that began at the primary level and aims to lay the foundations for lifelong learning and human development by offering more subject- or skill-oriented instruction using more specialized teachers.

Tertiary education, whether or not at an advanced research qualification, normally requires, as a minimum condition of admission, the successful completion of education at the secondary level.

Gross enrollment ratio is the ratio of total enrollment, regardless of age, to the population of the age group that officially corresponds to the level of education shown.

Net enrollment ratio is the ratio of children of official school age based on the International Standard Classification of Education 1997 who are enrolled in school to the population of the corresponding official school age.

Student-teacher ratio is the number of students enrolled in school divided by the number of teachers, regardless of their teaching assignment.

Public spending on education is current and capital public expenditure on education plus subsidies to private education at the primary, secondary, and tertiary levels by local, regional, and national government, including municipalities. It excludes household contributions.

Source: United Nations Educational, Scientific, and Cultural Organization (UNESCO) Institute for Statistics.

Table 7.2. Health

Life expectancy at birth is the number of years a newborn infant would live if prevailing patterns of mortality at the time of its birth were to remain the same throughout its life. Data are World Bank estimates based on data from the United Nations Population Division, the United Nations Statistics Division, and national statistical offices.

Under-five mortality rate is the probability that a newborn baby will die before reaching age 5, if subject to current age-specific mortality rates. The probability is expressed as a rate per 1,000.

Infant mortality rate is the number of infants dying before reaching 1 year of age, per 1,000 live births.

Maternal mortality ratio, modeled estimate, is the number of women who die from pregnancy-related causes during pregnancy and childbirth, per 100,000 live births. The data are estimated by a regression model using

Gender

Prepared by Markus Goldstein

The 2012 *World Development Report* documents four central challenges to gender equality in Africa: reducing excess female mortality, closing gaps in earnings and productivity, shrinking differences in voice in households and society, and investing in youth to break intergenerational cycles of gender inequality. While the following box discusses the issue of mortality, here we explore the other three dimensions.

Gaps in earnings and productivity

Although many more women have joined the labor force throughout the developing world in the past 25 years, access to employment has led to neither equitable opportunities nor equitable earnings between women and men. There is considerable gender segregation in accessing labor force opportunities—women are more likely to work in low-productivity sectors, less-profitable areas, wage or unpaid family employment, or the informal wage sector. In agriculture, women have less access to inputs and manage smaller plots of land, particularly in Sub-Saharan Africa.

There are three main factors that lead to gender segregation among female farmers, entrepreneurs, and wage workers: (1) gender differences in time use (primarily resulting from differences in care responsibilities); (2) gender differences in access to productive inputs (particularly land and credit); and (3) gender differences stemming from market and institutional failures.

Employment: In Sub-Saharan Africa, firms managed by women have labor productivity 6 to 8 percent lower than firms managed by men. This number prevails when compared with Europe and Central Asia, where it is 34 percent lower, and in Latin America, where value added per worker is 35 percent lower in firms managed by women. The performance lag of female-owned firms is related to market segregation, where women are often constrained to less-productive sectors. For example, industry type accounts for 9 to 14 percent of the gender differential in earnings for self-employed workers. For formal firms in urban areas of Sub-Saharan Africa, this difference in operational sector accounts for more than 20 percent of the gap, while the size of the firm accounts for another 30 percent. Women are also overrepresented among unpaid and wage workers and in the informal sector. The region has the highest rate of unpaid female family workers, at 65 percent of total employed women. Eliminating barriers that prevent women from working in certain occupations or sectors would reduce the productivity gap between male and female workers by one-third to one-half and increase output per worker by 3 to 25 percent across a range of Sub-Saharan Africa countries.

Agricultural productivity: Though 44 percent of Sub-Saharan Africa's agricultural labor force is comprised of women, female farmers in the region are less productive than male farmers, likely due to limited access to inputs including fertilizer, seed variety, as well as substantial plots of land, credit, and extension services. Productivity on farms would increase between 10 and 30 percent if women were provided with equal access to inputs. If women were granted equal access to inputs and more secure access to land, gender gaps in agricultural production would disappear and yields on women's farms would increase by 14 percent in Malawi, 17 percent in Ghana, 20 percent in Kenya, and 21 percent in Benin.

Policy case study: For female farmers in Sub-Saharan Africa, barriers to land tenure significantly limit productive potential. Rwanda's nationwide Land Tenure Regularization (LTR) program is one of a few models to address this issue at the required scale. An impact evaluation of a pilot version of this program highlights three main gender-specific effects: (1) significant and large investment impacts that are particularly pronounced for women. Households affected by LTR are almost 10 percentage points more likely to make or maintain soil conservation investments in structures such as bunds, terraces, and check dams. Women seem to benefit more in this respect; estimated effects of LTR on such investment by female-headed households is double that of men, with female-headed households exhibiting a roughly 19 percentage-point increase in the construction or maintenance of these soil conservation structures. Another main gender-specific effect is (2) improved land access for legally married women and better recording of inheritance rights. For women who are part of a union formalized through a marriage certificate, the effect of the program is overwhelmingly positive—they are 17 percentage points more likely to be regarded as joint landowners after LTR than before. The final gender-specific effect is (3) a significant increase in the probability of having documented landownership for legally married women. For women who are married but do not have a legal certificate, LTR results in a small but statistically significant reduction (by 8 percentage points) of the probability of having documented landownership. Taken together, these impacts imply that women's investments were especially hindered by a lack of tenure security, and that programs such as LTR can effectively remove this barrier.

Shrinking differences in voice in the household and society

Agency or voice is demonstrated through (1) control over resources—indicated by women's ability to earn and control income and to own, use, and dispose of material assets; (2) ability to move freely—indicated by women's freedom to decide their movements and their ability to move outside their homes; (3) decision making over family formation—measured by women's and girls' ability to decide when and whom to marry, when and how many children to have, and when to leave a marriage; (4) freedom from the risk of violence—indicated by the prevalence of domestic violence and other forms of sexual, physical, or emotional violence; and (5) the ability to have a voice in society and influence policy—indicated by participation and representation in formal politics and engagement in collective action and associations. Women's earnings opportunities and owned assets promote their bargaining power within and outside of households.

Decision making: Of the 48 countries in the region, 15 still have laws that give husbands most of the control over marital assets. Although women's control is greater in wealthier households, the region still has the lowest share of women with some control

(continued)

over decisions when it pertains to the issues of large purchases and visits to relatives. Sub-Saharan Africa also exhibits one of the highest shares of women who do not have control over decisions regarding how their own earnings are used —ranging from 34 percent of women in Malawi to 28 percent of women in the Democratic Republic of Congo. Decision-making roles outside of the household vary for women in the region and are heavily correlated with levels of education and affluence. Sub-Saharan Africa has a higher rate of female political-party membership when compared with the Middle East and North Africa, Latin America and the Caribbean, East Asia, and in OECD countries. The average rate of female parliamentarians in the region is 20 percent, and the global rate is 19 percent.

Inheritance: Thirty-four percent of daughters have unequal inheritance, and 7 percent have customary inheritance. Forty-six percent of widows have unequal inheritance, and 10 percent of widows have customary inheritance. In South Asia, this number for both daughters and widows is 50 percent; in OECD countries, Latin America and the Caribbean, and Europe and Central Asia, all daughters and widows have equal inheritance.

Gender-based violence: Violence is also a persistent issue, as, for example, 81 percent of women in Ethiopia think it is acceptable for a husband to beat his wife if the food is burned, she argues with him, or she refuses to have sex with him, and 37 percent of women in Cameroon report their first sexual intercourse as forced. Domestic violence results largely from a combination of strong social norms surrounding power within households as well as from women's limited bargaining power in their households. Additionally, lack of awareness and biased services limit women's demand for justice.

Investing in youth to break the intergenerational cycles of gender inequality

Girls' early and risky sexual activity and low education levels, along with institutionalized inequality, mutually reinforce a cycle of gender inequality.

Fertility: Currently, the fertility rate for youth between the ages of 15 and 19 in the region is 108 births per 1,000 girls, representing the highest rate of any region and nearly double the global average of 53. In East Asia, this number is 19 births per 1,000 women, and in South Asia, it is 75 births per 1,000 women. Approximately 22 percent of all women between the ages of 15 and 49 use contraception, and a little more than half of that number of girls between the ages of 15 and 24 use condoms. Young females in Sub-Saharan Africa are almost two-and-a-half times more likely to be infected with HIV than their male counterparts. For adolescents, the promotion of contraception, when combined with education interventions and skill building, and appropriately targeted to cultural and social settings, has been effective in reducing unplanned pregnancies.

Education: While the ratio of females to males in primary school in the region decreased between 1990 and 2008 (from 0.78 to 0.91), girls in areas such as Central and West Africa, where the ratio is 8 to 10, are lagging behind. Gross secondary enrollment rates for women is 32 percent, compared with 40 percent for men; and for tertiary education, it is 5 percent compared to 8 percent of men.

Policy case study: The Empowerment and Livelihood for Adolescents (ELA) program in Uganda—which includes girls' clubs, life skills, and livelihoods training—aims to reach out to youth and disrupt this cycle of gender inequality. Preliminary evidence from a randomized evaluation suggests that the program improves girls' health choices, their voice, and their economic activity. Compared with girls who did not participate in the program after two years, girls in program villages were 30 percent more likely to be working, they were 75 percent less likely to have had sex against their will, and they were 30 percent less likely to have had a child. Importantly, these improvements were achieved without increasing the school dropout rate or reducing time spent studying.

Moving forward

In all of the four priority areas, mechanisms have been identified that effectively address the existing gender disparities and thus provide potential solutions to close these gaps. Unfortunately, however, questions on how to best apply these solutions still remain unanswered. For example, we know that adequate and prompt medical attention reduces maternal mortality considerably, but we do not know how to enable mothers at risk to reach a functioning clinic in time. Programs such as ELA in Rwanda and LTR in Uganda are shedding light on what works best to address key gender inequalities in Sub-Saharan Africa, but more work needs to be done to identify innovative and effective programs.

information on fertility, birth attendants, and HIV prevalence.

Prevalence of HIV is the percentage of people ages 15–49 who are infected with HIV.

Incidence of tuberculosis is the number of tuberculosis cases (pulmonary, smear positive, and extrapulmonary) in a population at a given point in time, per 100,000 people. This indicator is sometimes referred to as "point prevalence." Estimates include cases of tuberculosis among people with HIV.

Clinical malaria cases reported are the sum of cases confirmed by slide examination or rapid diagnostic test and probable and unconfirmed cases (cases that were not tested but treated as malaria). National malaria control programs often collect data on the number of suspected cases, those tested, and those confirmed. Probable or unconfirmed cases are calculated by subtracting the number tested from the number suspected. Not all cases reported as malaria are true malaria

Gender Differences in Risks of Death: Africa's Excess Female Mortality and Trends over Time

Prepared by Rabia Ali and Jishnu Das

The facts on dying and death in low-income countries

In Iceland, 56 of every 1,000 people will die between the ages of 15 and 60; in the United States, that figure is 107. In China, that number rises to 113 and in India to 213. In Central and West Africa, these mortality rates regularly exceed 300, and in many countries it is closer to 400. And in HIV/AIDS-affected countries, the numbers rise to between 481 (Malawi) and 772 (Zimbabwe). Compare that to war-torn countries such as Iraq (285) or Afghanistan (479). Starkly put, the risk of dying for adults in many Sub-Saharan African countries is higher than being in the midst of a full-blown conflict.

In Sub-Saharan Africa, over time, trends in adult mortality have diverged sharply from those in the rest of the world. Here are the patterns:

- Infant and early childhood mortality (under-five mortality) has declined as in other parts of the world, although the rate of decline has been slower.
- In other countries, adult mortality rates have remained roughly stable over the past 25 years, but they doubled between 1980 and 2000 in Sub-Saharan Africa. A large portion of this increase is attributable to HIV/AIDS, with adult mortality rates in high-HIV-prevalence countries reaching more than half the levels seen in the years of the genocides in Rwanda and Cambodia—but on a sustained and rising basis.
- Particularly surprising is the fact that adult mortality did not decrease, and actually increased, in several countries in Sub-Saharan Africa with low HIV/AIDS prevalence, particularly those in Central and West Africa.

In 2008, the 14 countries with the highest adult mortality risk for women globally (in descending order) were Zimbabwe, Lesotho, Swaziland, Zambia, South Africa, Malawi, the Central African Republic, Mozambique, Tanzania, Chad, Uganda, Cameroon, Burundi, and Nigeria. Afghanistan comes in at number 15 and Pakistan at number 64. For child mortality (under five, per 1,000 births), the worst places for girls (in descending order) were Afghanistan, Angola, Chad, Somalia, Mali, the Democratic Republic of the Congo, Nigeria, Sierra Leone, Guinea-Bissau, the Central African Republic, Burkina Faso, Niger, Burundi, Equatorial Guinea, and Liberia.

By 2008, many African countries have become among the least hospitable places for women to live.

The sex mortality rate

Figure 1 presents the sex mortality rate (SMR), defined as the ratio of male to female mortality at every age for six African countries—South Africa and Kenya, with high HIV prevalence, Ethiopia and Eritrea with outright conflict between 1998 and 2000, and Nigeria and Burkina Faso in the western region of the continent. To interpret the SMR, it is useful to compare it to what we see in OECD countries (the thick black line in all of the figures). In OECD countries, men die at a faster rate than women throughout the life cycle (the SMR is above 1). This differential rate peaks around the early 20s, when accidents, violence, drugs, and homicides disproportionately affect men. It then declines and slowly increases again around the 60s, potentially a legacy of differential smoking rates between men and women in these countries.

South Africa looked precisely like the OECD countries in 1990, perhaps with even a higher SMR in the early 20s. By 2000, South Africa's SMR had changed completely as HIV/AIDS-related mortality sharply increased. Although both men and women were affected, the rate at which women started dying relative to men increased very rapidly, and the groups hit hardest were between the ages of 15 and 50. By 2008, things had gotten even worse. Kenya saw a similar decline in the SMR, but there is no evidence of worsening between 2000 and 2008.

Ethiopia's SMR looks very much like that in several countries around the continent: In contrast to OECD countries, in 1990, women were dying at a higher rate relative to men from the age of 5 onward, almost to age 40 (SMR <1). The SMR has increased quite dramatically since 1990, in particular for those between 15 and 25, reflecting lower mortality risks for women. Eritrea's SMR looks similar, except for the giant hump in 2000, reflecting the conflict with Ethiopia. The SMR shoots up from about 1 in the 20-to-40 age group to a peak of 10, as men died at disproportionately large numbers in the war. It comes back down by 2008, but data for 1990 and 2008 look similar.

Finally, Burkina Faso and Nigeria remain very puzzling. Like Ethiopia's SMR in 1990, their SMR drops below 1 from the age of 5 onward and never really recovers until around 40, after which it hovers just above 1. A couple of things are truly worrying: First, the SMR dips down to below 0.5 at the age of 18. Why is late adolescence such a dangerous time for women in terms of mortality risks? Second, there has been no change since 1990; if anything, the SMR between 20 and 60 appears to have constantly declined.

Excess female mortality in Sub-Saharan Africa

Given these very different patterns, figure 2 presents additional information by adding in *mortality risks*—that is, we would perhaps worry less about Nigeria and Burkina Faso if between 1990 and 2008 the mortality risk had declined, but stable mortality risks and a worsening SMR imply a more risky environment for women.

To present mortality risks in an easily comprehensible fashion, the *World Development Report 2012* (2012 *WDR*) computed two measures. Missing girls at birth were estimated through comparisons of the sex ratio at birth in countries around the world with those in comparable populations with no discrimination. The report also computed excess female (and male) mortality by comparing the mortality risks of women relative to men in every country and every age with those seen in developed economies today—the "reference population"—using methods advanced by Anderson and Ray (2010). In essence, this method weights the difference between each country SMR and the OECD SMR in 2000 by the mortality risk and the overall populations to arrive at a single number for excess female mortality at every age.

(continued)

Figure 1. Sex ratios of mortality in six African countries

Age-specific male mortality divided by female mortality

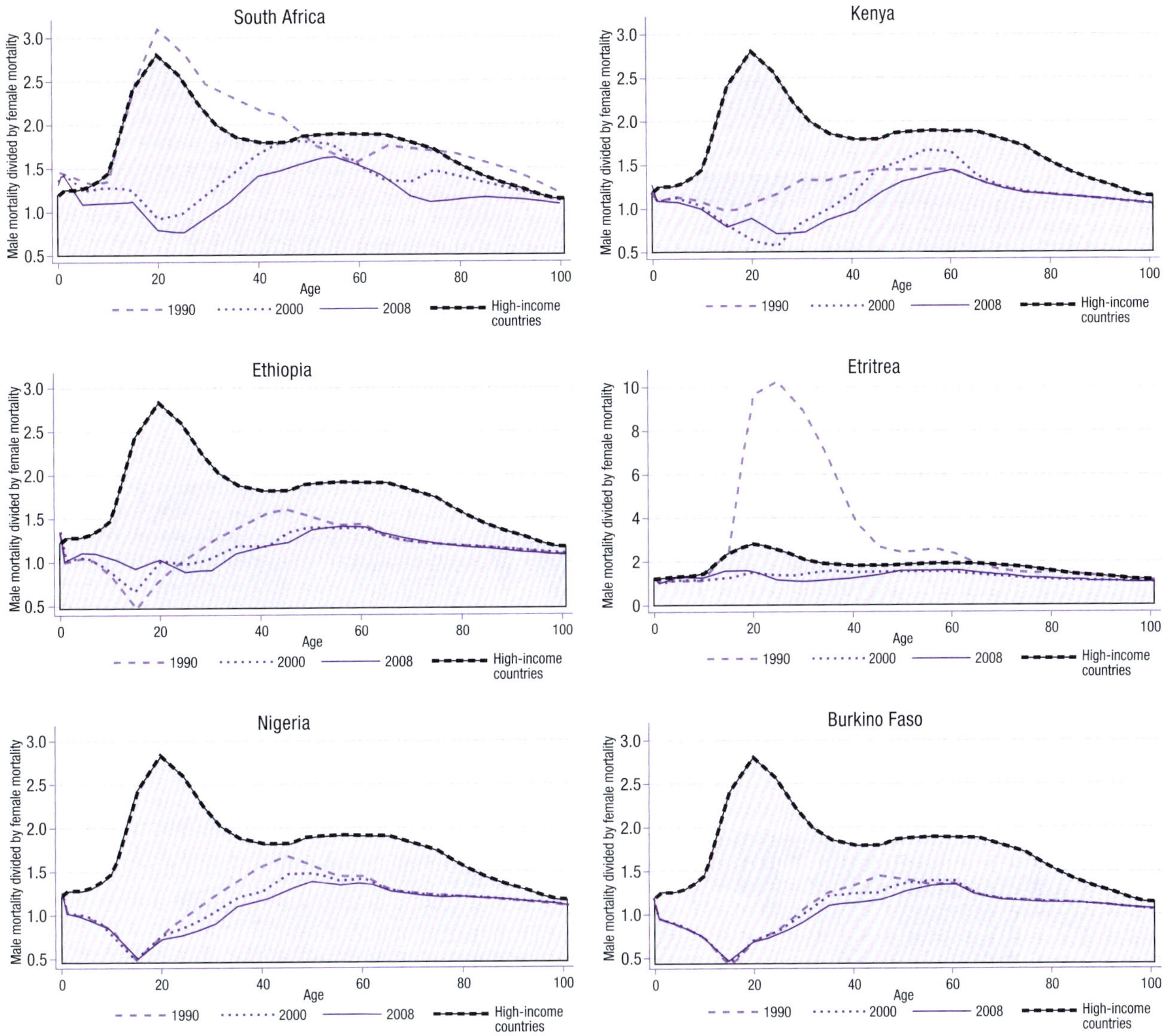

Note: A sex ratio of mortality (SRM) above the black dashed line indicates excess male mortality while an SRM below the line indicates excess female mortality.

Computations based on this excess mortality measure, conducted for all countries around the world at three points in time (1990, 2000, and 2008), suggested that missing girls at birth and excess female mortality after birth add up to more than 6 million women a year. While missing girls at birth are concentrated in India and China, excess female mortality after birth is highest in Sub-Saharan Africa, the only region where the numbers are increasing. These three population groupings—China (with a population of 1.3 billion), India (1.15 billion), and Sub-Saharan Africa (0.8 billion)—together account for 87 percent of the world's missing girls and excess female mortality.

But the age profiles of excess female mortality are very different. In Sub-Saharan Africa—a point raised by Anderson and Ray (2010) and Obermeyer and others (2010)—excess female mortality in the reproductive years accounts for 78 percent in the high-HIV/AIDS-prevalence countries and 55 percent in countries with low HIV rates. In China, by contrast, most excess female mortality is at birth, and in India, missing girls at birth and excess female mortality in early childhood and in the reproductive years each account for roughly a third. As figure 2 shows, Sub-Saharan Africa is the only region in the world where excess female mortality increased between 1990 and 2008—both absolutely (from 0.6 million a year to 1.1 million) and as a fraction of the female population. Among

(continued)

women ages 15 to 50, excess female mortality has declined in absolute numbers and as a proportion of population in every region of the world except Sub-Saharan Africa, where four distinct patterns have emerged:

HIV/AIDS-affected countries: In these countries, excess female mortality has increased even as a fraction of the female population. Examples include Botswana, Lesotho, Swaziland, South Africa, Zambia, and Zimbabwe, where about one in six to

Figure 2. Excess female mortality across the world

Excess female deaths after birth and change in excess female morality between 1990 and 2008

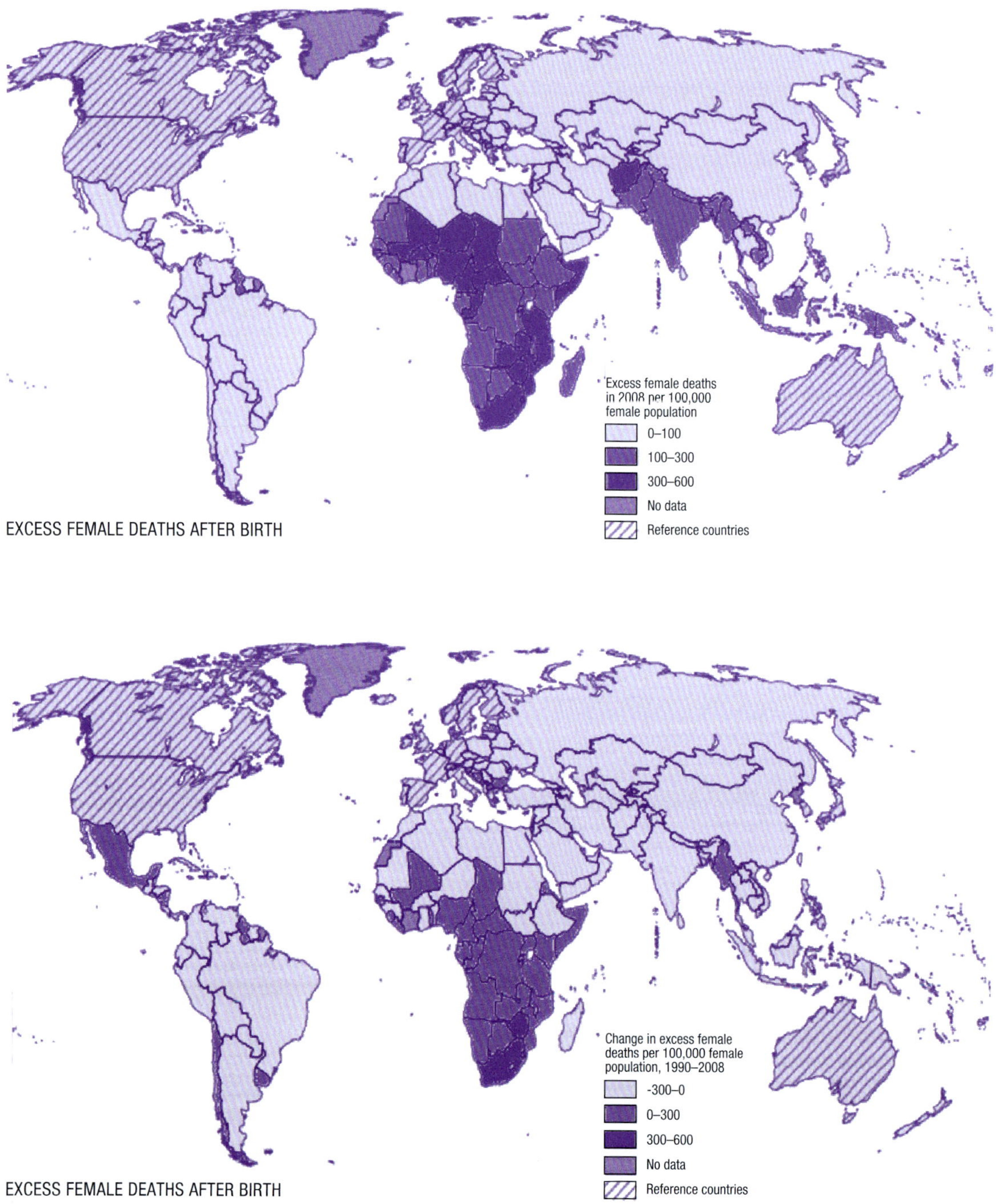

(continued)

Gender Differences in Risks of Death: Africa's Excess Female Mortality and Trends over Time (continued)

one in four adults between the ages of 15 and 49 were living with HIV/AIDS by the end of 2009. In 1990, mortality profiles for men and women in Botswana and South Africa were similar to those in high-income countries today. But by 2000, mortality risks increased in adulthood, more so for women.

Progressive Africa: In countries such as Ethiopia, Ghana, and Madagascar, which have largely escaped the HIV/AIDS epidemic, excess female mortality has been decreasing over time. Mortality rates of children under age five are about 100 per 1,000 live births (less than 76 in Ghana). Fertility rates have declined, but they remain higher than in India and Pakistan, as do under-five mortality rates.

Conflict Africa: Sub-Saharan Africa has experienced two types of conflicts over the past three decades, with different implications for mortality risks among men and women. During the 1980s and 1990s, outright war in countries like Eritrea and Liberia claimed the lives of many young men, leading to excess *male* mortality. Except for periodic flare-ups, these decreased over time. In other countries, widespread civil conflict continues to exact a heavy toll among women, leading to excess *female* mortality. One example is the Democratic Republic of Congo, where excess female mortality increased between 1980 and 2008.

Central and West Africa: The real puzzles in Sub-Saharan Africa are the Central and West African countries, including Burkina Faso, Chad, Mali, Niger, and Nigeria, among others. These countries have largely escaped the HIV/AIDS epidemic and are relatively free of conflict, but excess female mortality has increased over time, as mortality risks for women systematically increased while overall mortality risks remained unchanged or worsened. Today, Burkina Faso, the Central African Republic, Chad, Mali, Niger, and Nigeria look very much like Afghanistan in their human development outcomes, including mortality risks. Under-five mortality ranges from 170 to 220 (Afghanistan is higher, at 257), total fertility rates range from 4.5 to above 7 (Afghanistan is 6.6), and adult mortality risks are virtually the same as those in Afghanistan.

Drivers of excess female mortality in the reproductive years

Maternal mortality: Higher maternal mortality ratios are historically associated with greater excess female mortality in adulthood, as the 2012 *WDR* illustrated using excess female mortality estimates for 13 high-income countries today, in some cases going as far back in time as 1800. In 2008, there were 203,300 maternal deaths in Sub-Saharan Africa (56.7 percent of the global total). One of every 14 women in Somalia and Chad will die from causes related to childbirth. As a proportion of all births, more women die in childbirth in Liberia today than did in Sweden in the 17th century. Reducing these high maternal mortality ratios in Sub-Saharan Africa will be critical for reducing excess female mortality in adulthood.

The HIV/AIDS epidemic: In addition to maternal mortality, the HIV/AIDS epidemic is contributing to excess female mortality in Africa, where women account for 60 percent of all adult HIV infections, with the gender gap in prevalence largest for younger adults. The ratio of female-to-male prevalence for 15- to 24-year-olds is 2.4 across Sub-Saharan Africa. Not only has HIV/AIDS hit women the hardest, but coping with the crisis has had system-wide impacts on the delivery of health services. Prenatal care, care during birth, and children's vaccination rates have suffered where HIV rates are the highest in Sub-Saharan Africa. Improved access to Anti-Retroviral Therapy (ART) in Africa will reduce the number of deaths from HIV/AIDS and decrease female mortality rates in adulthood.

Further research: As seen above, the HIV/AIDS link to excess female mortality in Africa is not relevant for all countries in the region but is concentrated among the set of high-prevalence countries in southern Africa and parts of east Africa, which bear a disproportionate share of the burden of AIDS in Africa as well as globally. Central and West African countries do not belong in this category, and further research is direly needed to understand why these countries have experienced such little progress in reducing mortality risks, and why these have increased for women relative to men.

cases; most health facilities lack appropriate diagnostic services. The misdiagnosis may have led to under- or overreporting malaria cases and missing diagnosis of other treatable diseases.

Reported malaria deaths are all deaths in health facilities that are attributed to malaria, whether or not confirmed by microscopy or by rapid diagnostic test.

Child immunization rate is the percentage of children ages 12–23 months who received vaccinations before 12 months or at any time before the survey for four diseases—measles and diphtheria, pertussis (whooping cough), and tetanus (DPT). A child is considered adequately immunized against measles after receiving one dose of vaccine and against DPT after receiving three doses.

Stunting is the percentage of children under age 5 whose height for age is more than two standard deviations below the median for the international reference population ages 0–59 months. For children up to age 2 height is measured by recumbent length. For older children height is measured by stature while standing. The data are based on the WHO's new child growth standards released in 2006.

Underweight is the percentage of children under age 5 whose weight for age is more than two standard deviations below the median for the international reference population ages 0–59 months. The data are based on the WHO's new child growth standards released in 2006.

Births attended by skilled health staff are the percentage of deliveries attended by personnel trained to give the necessary supervision, care, and advice to women during pregnancy, labor, and the postpartum period; to conduct deliveries on their own; and to care for newborns.

Contraceptive use is the percentage of women ages 15–49, married or in union, who are practicing, or whose sexual partners are practicing, any form of contraception. Modern methods of contraception include female and male sterilization, oral hormonal pills, the intrauterine device, the male condom, injectables, the implant (including Norplant), vaginal barrier methods, the female condom, and emergency contraception.

Children sleeping under insecticide-treated nets are the percentage of the children under age 5 with access to an insecticide-treated net to prevent malaria.

Tuberculosis case detection rate (all forms) is the percentage of newly notified tuberculosis cases (including relapses) to estimated incident cases (case detection, all forms).

Tuberculosis treatment success rate is the percentage of new smear-positive tuberculosis cases registered under DOTS in a given year that successfully completed treatment, whether with bacteriologic evidence of success ("cured") or without ("treatment completed").

Children with fever receiving any antimalarial treatment same or next day are the percentage of children under age 5 in malaria-risk areas with fever being treated with any antimalarial drugs.

Population with sustainable access to an improved water source is the percentage of the population with reasonable access to an adequate amount of water from an improved source, such as a household connection, public standpipe, borehole, protected well or spring, or rainwater collection. Unimproved sources include vendors, tanker trucks, and unprotected wells and springs. Reasonable access is defined as the availability of at least 20 liters a person a day from a source within one kilometer of the dwelling.

Population with sustainable access to improved sanitation is the percentage of the population with at least adequate access to excreta disposal facilities that can effectively prevent human, animal, and insect contact with excreta. Improved facilities range from simple but protected pit latrines to flush toilets with a sewerage connection. The excreta disposal system is considered adequate if it is private or shared (but not public) and if it hygienically separates human excreta from human contact. To be effective, facilities must be correctly constructed and properly maintained.

Physicians are the number of physicians, including generalists and specialists.

Nurses and midwives are professional nurses, auxiliary nurses, enrolled nurses, and other nurses, such as dental nurses and primary care nurses, and professional midwives, auxiliary midwives, and enrolled midwives.

Community workers include various types of community health aides, many with country-specific occupational titles such as community health officers, community health-education workers, family health workers, lady health visitors, and health extension package workers.

Total health expenditure is the sum of public and private health expenditure. It covers the provision of health services (preventive and curative), family planning activities, nutrition activities, and emergency aid designated for health but does not include provision of water and sanitation.

Public health expenditure consists of recurrent and capital spending from government (central and local) budgets, external borrowings and grants (including donations from international agencies and nongovernmental organizations), and social (or compulsory) health insurance funds.

Private health expenditure includes direct household (out-of-pocket) spending, private insurance, charitable donations, and direct service payments by private corporations.

External resources for health are funds or services in kind that are provided by entities not part of the country in question. The resources may come from international organizations, other countries through bilateral arrangements, or foreign nongovernmental organizations. These resources are part of total health expenditure.

Out-of-pocket expenditure is any direct outlay by households, including gratuities and in-kind payments, to health practitioners and suppliers of pharmaceuticals, therapeutic appliances, and other goods and services whose primary intent is to contribute to the restoration or enhancement of the health status of individuals or population groups. It is a part of private health expenditure.

Private prepaid plans are expenditure on health by private insurance institutions. Private insurance enrollment may be contractual or voluntary, and conditions and benefits or basket of benefits are agreed on a voluntary basis between the insurance agent and the beneficiaries. They are thus not controlled by government units for the purpose of providing social benefits to members.

Health expenditure per capita is the total health expenditure. It is the sum of public and private health expenditures as a ratio of total population. It covers the provision of health services (preventive and curative), family planning activities, nutrition activities, and emergency aid designated for health but does not include provision of water and sanitation. Data are in current U.S. dollars.

Source: Data on life expectancy at birth, national maternal mortality, prevalence of HIV, incidence of tuberculosis, child immunization, malnutrition, births attended by skilled health staff, contraceptive use, children sleeping under insecticide-treated nets, and children receiving antimalarial drugs are from World Bank staff estimates based on various sources, including census reports, the United Nations Population Division's *World Population Prospects,* national statistical offices, household surveys conducted by national agencies and Macro International, the World Health Organization (WHO), and the United Nations Children's Fund. Data on under-five and infant mortality are from the *from Level & Trends in Child Mortality*. Report 2011. Estimates Developed by the UN Inter-agency Group for Child Mortality Estimation (UNICEF, WHO, World Bank, UN DESA, UNPD). Data on maternal mortality (modeled) are Trends in Maternal Mortality: 1990–2010 estimates developed by WHO, UNICEF, UNFPA, and the World Bank. Data on clinical malaria cases reported and reported malaria deaths are from WHO's *World Malaria Report 2011.* Data on physicians, nurses, and community health workers are from World Health Organization, Global Atlas of the Health Workforce. For latest updates and metadata, see http://apps.who.int/globalatlas/. Data on tuberculosis are from World Health Organization, Global Tuberculosis Control Report. Data on access to water and sanitation are from World Health Organization and United Nations Children's Fund, Joint Measurement Programme (JMP) (www.wssinfo.org/). Data on health expenditure are from the World Health Organization National Health Account database (www.who.int/nha/en) supplemented by country data.

8. Agriculture, rural development, and environment

Table 8.1. Rural development

Rural population is the difference between the total population and the urban population.

Rural population density is the rural population divided by the arable land area. Arable land includes land defined by the Food and Agriculture Organization (FAO) as land under temporary crops (double-cropped areas are counted once), temporary meadows for mowing or for pasture, land under market or kitchen gardens, and land temporarily fallow. Land abandoned as a result of shifting cultivation is excluded.

Share of rural population below the national poverty line is the percentage of the rural population living below the national poverty line.

Rural population poverty gap is the mean shortfall from the poverty line (counting the nonpoor as having zero shortfall), expressed as a percentage of the poverty line. This measure reflects the depth of poverty as well as its incidence.

Share of rural population with sustainable access to an improved water source is the percentage of the rural population with reasonable access to an adequate amount of water from an improved source, such as a household connection, public standpipe, borehole, protected well or spring, or rainwater collection. Unimproved sources include vendors, tanker trucks, and unprotected wells and springs. Reasonable access is defined as the availability of at least 20 liters a person a day from a source within 1 kilometer of the dwelling.

Share of rural population with sustainable access to improved sanitation facilities is the percentage of the rural population with at least adequate access to excreta disposal facilities that can effectively prevent human, animal, and insect contact with excreta. Improved facilities range from simple but protected pit latrines to flush toilets with a sewerage connection. The excreta disposal system is considered adequate if it is private or shared (but not public) and if it hygienically separates human excreta from human contact. To be effective, facilities must be correctly constructed and properly maintained.

Share of rural population with access to transportation is the percentage of the rural population who live within 2 kilometers of an all-season passable road as a share of the total rural population.

Source: Data on rural population are calculated from urban population shares from the United Nations Population Division's World Urbanization Prospects and from total population figures from the World Bank. Data on rural population density are from the FAO and World Bank population estimates. Data on rural population below the poverty line and rural population poverty gap are Global Poverty Working Group. Data are based on World Bank's country poverty assessments and country Poverty Reduction Strategies. Data on access to water and sanitation are from the World Health Organization and United Nations Children's Fund, Joint Measurement Programme (JMP) (www.wssinfo.org/).

Table 8.2. Agriculture

Agriculture value added is the gross output of forestry, hunting, and fishing, as well as cultivation of crops and livestock production (International Standard Industrial Classification [ISIC] revision 3 divisions 1–5) less the value of their intermediate inputs. It is calculated without making deductions for depreciation of fabricated assets or depletion and degradation of natural resources. For countries that report national accounts data at producer prices (Angola, Benin, Cape Verde, Comoros, the Republic of Congo, Côte d'Ivoire, Gabon, Liberia, Niger, Rwanda, São Tomé and Príncipe, Seychelles, and Togo), gross value added at market prices is used as the denominator. For countries that report national accounts data at basic prices (all other countries), gross value added at factor cost is used as the denominator. Value added at basic prices excludes net taxes on products, while producer prices include net taxes on products paid by producers but exclude sales or value added taxes.

Total agriculture gross production index is total agricultural production relative to the base period 1999–2001.

Crop gross production index is agricultural crop production relative to the base period 1999–2001. It includes all crops except fodder crops.

Livestock gross production index covers meat and milk from all sources, dairy products such as cheese, and eggs, honey, raw silk, wool, and hides and skins.

Food gross production index covers food crops that are considered edible and that contain nutrients. Coffee and tea are excluded because, although edible, they have no nutritive value.

Cereal gross production index covers cereals that are considered edible and that contain nutrients.

Cereal production is crops harvested for dry grain only. Cereal crops harvested for hay or harvested green for food, feed, or silage and those used for grazing are excluded.

Cereal includes wheat, rice, maize, barley, oats, rye, millet, sorghum, buckwheat, and mixed grains.

Agricultural exports and *imports* are expressed in current U.S. dollars at free on board prices. The term "agriculture" in trade refers to both food and agriculture and does not include forestry and fishery products.

Food exports and *imports* are expressed in current U.S. dollars at free on board prices for exports and cost, insurance, and freight prices for imports.

Permanent cropland is land cultivated with crops that occupy the land for long periods and need not be replanted after each harvest, such as cocoa, coffee, and rubber. It includes land under flowering shrubs, fruit trees, nut trees, and vines, but excludes land under trees grown for wood or timber.

Cereal cropland refers to harvested area, although some countries report only sown or cultivated area.

Agricultural irrigated land is areas equipped to provide water to the crops, including areas equipped for full and partial control irrigation, spate irrigation areas, and equipped wetland or inland valley bottoms.

Fertilizer consumption measures the quantity of plant nutrients used per unit of arable land. Fertilizer products cover nitrogenous, potash, and phosphate fertilizers (including ground rock phosphate). Traditional nutrients—animal and plant manures—are not included. For the purpose of data dissemination, the FAO has adopted the concept of a calendar year (January to December). Some countries compile fertilizer data on a calendar year basis, while others are on a split-year basis. Arable land includes land defined by the FAO as land under temporary crops (double-cropped areas are counted once), temporary meadows for mowing or for pasture, land under market or kitchen gardens, and land temporarily fallow. Land abandoned as a result of shifting cultivation is excluded.

Agricultural machinery refers to the number of wheel and crawler tractors (excluding garden tractors) in use in agriculture at the end of the calendar year specified or during the first quarter of the following year. Arable land includes land defined by the FAO as land under temporary crops (double-cropped areas are counted once), temporary meadows for mowing or for pasture, land under market or kitchen gardens, and land temporarily fallow. Land abandoned as a result of shifting cultivation is excluded.

Agricultural employment includes people who work for a public or private employer and who receive remuneration in wages, salary, commission, tips, piece rates, or pay in kind. Agriculture corresponds to division 1 (International Standard Industrial Classification [ISIC] revision 2) or tabulation categories A and B (ISIC revision 3) and includes hunting, forestry, and fishing.

Agriculture value added per worker is the output of the agricultural sector (ISIC divisions 1–5) less the value of intermediate inputs. Agriculture comprises value added from forestry, hunting, and fishing as well as cultivation of crops and livestock production. Data are in constant 2000 U.S. dollars.

Cereal yield, measured as kilograms per hectare of harvested land, includes wheat, rice, maize, barley, oats, rye, millet, sorghum, buckwheat, and mixed grains. Production data on cereals relate to crops harvested for dry grain only. Cereal crops harvested for hay or harvested green for food, feed, or silage and those used for grazing are excluded. The FAO allocates production data to the calendar year in which the bulk of the harvest took place. Most of a crop harvested near the end of a year will be used in the following year.

Source: Data on agriculture value added are from World Bank national accounts data, and OECD National Accounts data files. Data on crop, livestock, food, and cereal production, cereal exports and imports, agricultural exports and imports, permanent cropland, cereal cropland, agricultural machinery, cereal yield, and fertilizer consumption are from the Food and Agriculture Organization, electronic files and web site. Data on agricultural employment are from the International Labour Organization, Key Indicators of the Labour Market database.

Table 8.3. Producer food prices

Prices in U.S. dollars are equal to producer prices in local currency times the exchange rate of the selected year. The main exchange rates source used is the IMF. Where official and commercial exchange rates differ significantly, the commercial exchange rate may be applied. Producer prices are prices received by farmers for primary agricultural products as defined in the SNA 93. The producer's price is the amount receivable by the producer from the purchaser for a unit of a good or service produced as output minus any value added tax, or similar deductible tax, invoiced to the purchaser. It excludes any transport charges invoiced separately by the producer. Time series refer to the national average prices of individual commodities comprising all grades, kinds and varieties, received by farmers when they participate in their capacity as sellers of their own products at the farm gate or first-point-of-sale.

Source: Data are from the Food and Agriculture Organization, electronic files and website.

Table 8.4. Environment

Forest area is land under natural or planted stands of trees, whether productive or not.

Renewable internal fresh water resources refer to internal renewable resources (internal river flows and groundwater from rainfall) in the country.

Annual fresh water withdrawals refer to total water withdrawals, not counting evaporation losses from storage basins. Withdrawals also include water from desalination plants in countries where they are a significant source. Withdrawals can exceed 100 percent of total renewable resources where extraction from nonrenewable aquifers or desalination plants is considerable or where there is significant water reuse. Withdrawals for agriculture and industry are total withdrawals for irrigation and livestock production and for direct industrial use (including withdrawals for cooling thermoelectric plants). Withdrawals for domestic uses include drinking water, municipal use or supply, and use for public services, commercial establishments, and homes.

Water productivity is calculated as gross domestic product in constant prices divided by annual total water withdrawal.

Emissions of organic water pollutants are measured in terms of biochemical oxygen demand, which refers to the amount of oxygen that bacteria in water will consume in breaking down waste. This is a standard water-treatment test for the presence of organic pollutants.

Energy production refers to forms of primary energy—petroleum (crude oil, natural gas liquids, and oil from nonconventional sources), natural gas, solid fuels (coal, lignite, and other derived fuels), and combustible renewable and waste—and primary electricity, all converted into oil equivalents.

Energy use refers to use of primary energy before transformation to other end-use fuels, which is equal to indigenous production plus imports and stock changes, minus exports and fuels supplied to ships and aircraft engaged in international transport.

Combustible renewables and waste comprise solid biomass, liquid biomass, biogas, industrial waste, and municipal waste, measured as a percentage of total energy use.

Carbon dioxide emissions are those stemming from the burning of fossil fuels and the manufacture of cement. They include carbon dioxide produced during consumption of solid, liquid, and gas fuels and gas flaring.

Methane emissions, total, are those from human activities such as agriculture and from industrial methane production.

Methane emissions, agricultural, are those from animals, animal waste, rice production, agricultural waste burning (nonenergy, on-site), and savannah burning.

Methane emissions, industrial, are those from the handling, transmission, and combustion of fossil fuels and biofuels.

Nitrous oxide emissions, total, are those from agricultural biomass burning, industrial activities, and livestock management.

Nitrous oxide emissions, agricultural, are those produced through fertilizer use (synthetic and animal manure), animal waste management, agricultural waste burning (nonenergy, on-site), and savannah burning.

Nitrous oxide emissions, industrial, are those produced during the manufacturing of adipic acid and nitric acid.

Other greenhouse gas emissions are by-product emissions of hydrofluorocarbons, perfluorocarbons, and sulfur hexafluoride.

Official development assistance (ODA) gross disbursements for forestry are disbursements for forestry by bilateral, multilateral, and other donors. Disbursements record the actual international transfer of financial resources or of goods or services valued at the cost of the donor.

Official development assistance (ODA) gross disbursements for general environment protection are disbursements for general environment protection by bilateral, multilateral, and other donors. Disbursements record the actual international transfer of financial resources or of goods or services valued at the cost of the donor.

Source: Data on forest area and deforestation are from the Food and Agriculture Organization's (FAO) *Global Forest Resources Assessment.* Data on freshwater resources and withdrawals are from the World Resources Institute, supplemented by the FAO's AQUASTAT data. Data on emissions of organic water pollutants are from the World Bank. Data on energy production and use and combustible renewable and waste are from the International Energy Agency. Data on carbon dioxide emissions are from the Carbon Dioxide Information Analysis Center, Environmental Sciences Division, Oak Ridge National Laboratory, in the U.S. state of Tennessee. Data on methane emissions, nitrous oxide emissions, and other greenhouse gas emissions are from the International Energy Agency. Data on official development assistance disbursements are from the Development Assistance Committee of the Organisation for Economic

Co-operation and Development, Geographical Distribution of Financial Flows to Developing Countries, Development Co-operation Report, and International Development Statistics database. Data are available online at www.oecd.org/dac/stats/idsonline.

TABLE 8.5. FOSSIL FUEL EMISSIONS

Carbon dioxide emissions are those stemming from the burning of fossil fuels and the manufacture of cement. They include carbon dioxide produced during consumption of solid, liquid, and gas fuels and gas flaring.

Carbon dioxide emissions per capita are carbon dioxide emissions divided by midyear population.

Fossil fuel is any hydrocarbon deposit that can be burned for heat or power, such as petroleum, coal, and natural gas.

Total carbon dioxide emissions from fossil fuels is the sum of all fossil fuel emissions (solid fuel consumption, liquid fuel consumption, gas fuel consumption, gas flaring, and cement production).

Carbon dioxide emissions from solid fuel consumption refer mainly to emissions from use of coal as an energy source and from secondary fuels derived from hard and soft coal (such as coke-oven coke).

Carbon dioxide emissions from liquid fuel consumption refer to emissions from use of crude petroleum and natural gas liquids as an energy source, and secondary fuels derived from oil (such as jet fuel).

Carbon dioxide emissions from gas fuel consumption refer mainly to emissions from use of natural gas as an energy source and from secondary fuels derived from natural gas (such as blast furnace gas).

Carbon dioxide emissions from gas flaring refer mainly to emissions from gas flaring activities.

Carbon dioxide emissions from cement production refer mainly to emissions during cement production. Cement production is a multistep process, and carbon dioxide is actually released from clinker production during the cement production process.

Source: Data on carbon dioxide emissions are from the Carbon Dioxide Information Analysis Center, Environmental Sciences Division, Oak Ridge National Laboratory, in the U.S. state of Tennessee.

9. Labor, migration, and population

TABLE 9.1. LABOR FORCE PARTICIPATION

Labor force is people ages 15 and older who meet the International Labour Organization (ILO) definition of the economically active population. It includes both the employed and the unemployed. While national practices vary in the treatment of such groups as the armed forces and seasonal or part-time workers, the labor force generally includes the armed forces, the unemployed, and first-time job seekers, but excludes homemakers and other unpaid caregivers and workers in the informal sector.

Participation rate is the percentage of the population of the specified age group that is economically active, that is, all people who supply labor for the production of goods and services during a specified period.

Source: International Labour Organization, Key Indicators of the Labour Market database.

TABLE 9.2. LABOR FORCE COMPOSITION

Agriculture corresponds to division 1 (International Standard Industrial Classification [ISIC] revision 2) or tabulation categories A and B (ISIC revision 3) and includes hunting, forestry, and fishing.

Industry corresponds to divisions 2–5 (ISIC revision 2) or tabulation categories C–F (ISIC revision 3) and includes mining and quarrying (including oil production), manufacturing, construction, and public utilities (electricity, gas, and water).

Services correspond to divisions 6–9 (ISIC revision 2) or tabulation categories G–P (ISIC revision 3) and include wholesale and retail trade and restaurants and hotels; transport, storage, and communications; financing, insurance, real estate, and business services; and community, social, and personal services.

Wage and salaried workers are workers who hold the type of jobs defined as paid employment jobs, where incumbents hold explicit (written or oral) or implicit employment contracts that give them a basic remuneration that is not directly dependent on the revenue of the unit for which they work.

Self-employed workers are self-employed workers with employees (employers), self-employed workers without employees (own-account workers), and members of producer

A multidimensional portrait of poverty and living conditions in slums

Prepared by Sumila Gulyani, Ellen Bassett, and Debabrata Talukdar

The expansion of slums in the rapidly growing cities of the developing world is a well-known and thoroughly studied phenomenon. Studies of slums range from rich ethnographic micro-studies of specific cities, settlements, and individual residents within such settlements (for example, Peattie 1968; Perlman 1980, 2006) to macro-level analyses that present national and global urbanization trends, emphasize the inexorable increase in slum settlements, and discuss the implications of slum growth for urban service delivery and poverty (for example, UN Habitat 2003). Nevertheless, debates continue over what constitutes a slum and what policy makers should do to tackle this problem. In addition, there is a crucial gap in the literature on what might be called the "meso" level—analytical frameworks and analyses positioned between the micro-level studies that treat each neighborhood as unique and the macro-level national or global aggregations focusing on incidence of slums that lump all slums into one category.

To help fill this gap, we propose a set of three interrelated frameworks to create a multidimensional portrait of poverty and living conditions in any given neighborhood, conduct comparative analyses across neighborhoods and cities, and aggregate data at levels that can better inform policies and programs. The three frameworks—termed the Development Diamond, the Living Conditions Diamond, and the Infrastructure Polygon—present a graphical comparative picture arrayed along 16 selected dimensions. We illustrate these frameworks using empirical data from the cities of Nairobi, Kenya, and Dakar, Senegal. Specifically, we use the frameworks to present a picture of living conditions and poverty emerging from a specially commissioned survey of 3,700 slum households in the two cities.

The first framework—the Development Diamond (figure 1)—posits that poverty and development can and should be understood along at least four discrete but interrelated dimensions: monetary poverty, employment, education, and living conditions, including infrastructure access. Using this framework to analyze the situation in Nairobi and Dakar, we find that although slum residents are monetarily poor in both cities, *the nature of their poverty differs dramatically*. In Nairobi, slum residents are educated and the majority are employed, but they have appalling living conditions. In Dakar, they have fairly decent living conditions but very low levels of education and paid employment.

We next unpack living conditions through a framework termed the Living Conditions Diamond (figure 2). We posit that living conditions are themselves a composite of four dimensions: tenure, infrastructure, unit quality, and neighborhood and location. Figure 2 illustrates that, compared with Dakar, Nairobi's slums are worse off on all four dimensions. Nairobi's slums are characterized by highly mobile, tenure-insecure renters living in semi-permanent structures in poorly served neighborhoods that are widely perceived as unsafe. Dakar's slums, by contrast, are peopled primarily with owner–occupants and have low resident turnover, permanent housing structures, and superior infrastructure access.

Finally, the Infrastructure Polygon (figure 3) illustrates, in greater detail, the differences in infrastructure access and service levels across the two cities. A typical resident of Nairobi's slums has no access to electricity or organized rubbish removal. She or he purchases water from kiosks and shares a public pit latrine with an average of 57 persons. Dakar's slums are characterized by good infrastructure access, with the exception of storm-water drains.

Taken together, the frameworks demonstrate the extent of heterogeneity across slums. They graphically reveal that slums in the two cities differ dramatically from each other on nearly every indicator examined and thus contradict the notion that most African cities face similar slum problems. By extension, they also challenge the idea that one approach to—or template for—the upgrading of slums can work in all African cities. At the same time, the frameworks serve as a tool that can help practitioners and policy makers better understand local needs and priorities, and tailor their interventions to the given context.

This research also highlights the issue of living conditions. The findings from Nairobi and Dakar challenge the seemingly logical notion that education and jobs will (automatically) translate into lower poverty and improved living conditions or, conversely, the idea that poor citizens need to have education and employment before they

Figure 1

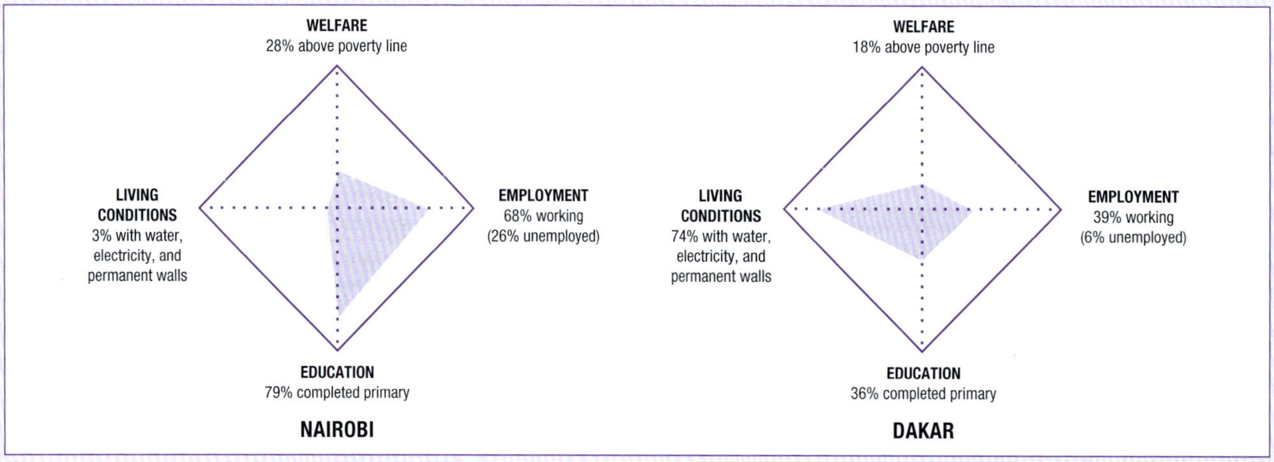

(continued)

A multidimensional portrait of poverty and living conditions in slums (continued)

Figure 2

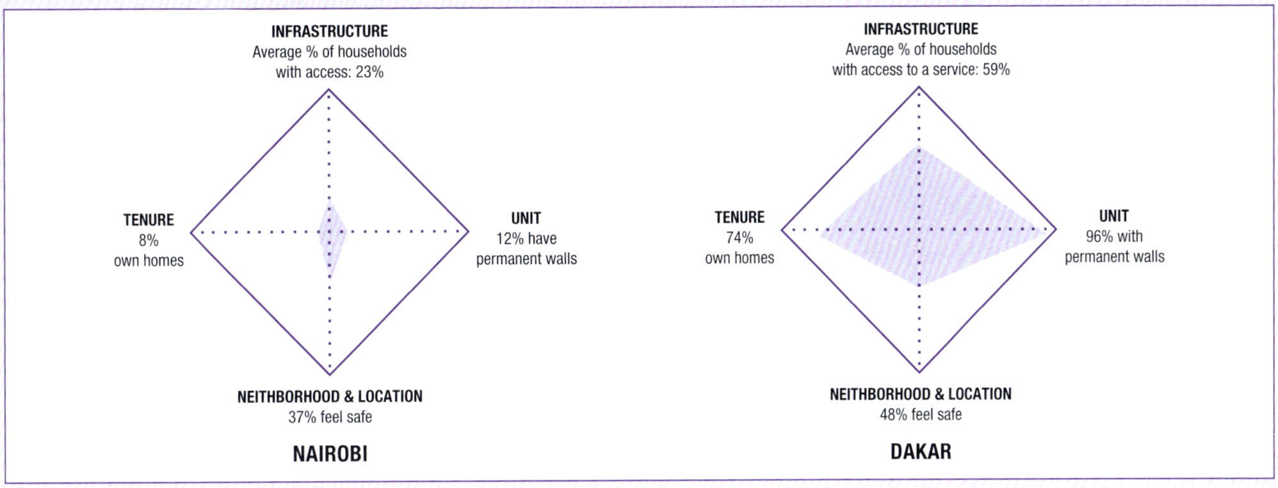

Figure 3

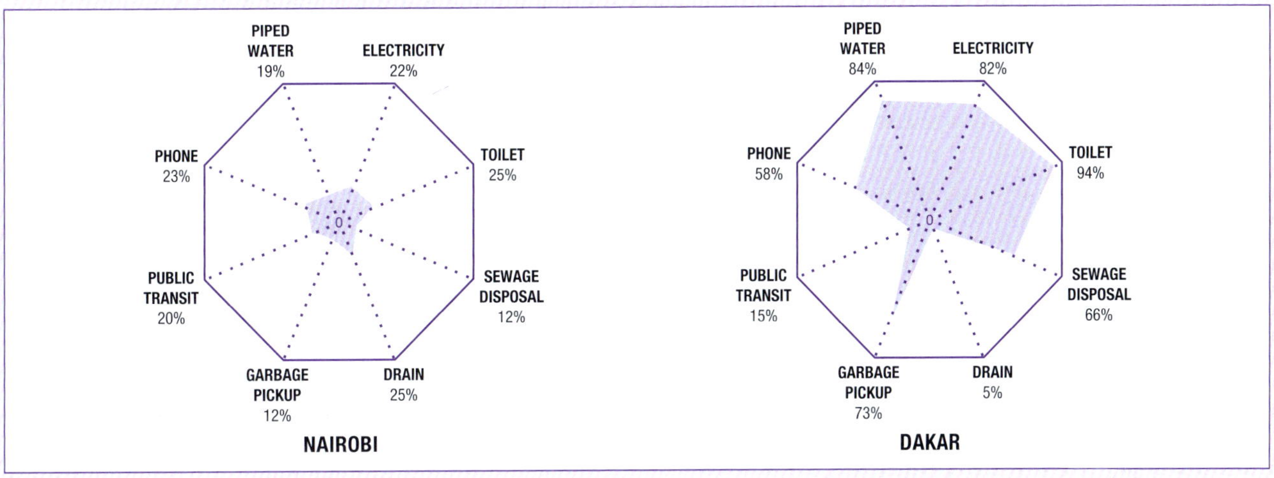

can have access to decent living conditions and basic infrastructure. At a broader level, this research leads us to the argument that living conditions are an important—but poorly analyzed and understood—dimension of poverty, one that needs to be included in the ongoing analyses of and discussions on multidimensional poverty.

References

Gulyani, S., and E. Bassett. 2010. "The Living Conditions Diamond: A Theoretical and Analytical Framework for Understanding Slums." *Environment and Planning A* 42: 2201–19.

Gulyani, S., E. Bassett, and D. Talukdar. 2012. "Living Conditions, Rents and Their Determinants in the Slums of Nairobi and Dakar." *Land Economics* 88 (2): 251–274.

——. 2011. "A Tale of Two Cities: A Multi-Dimensional Portrait of Poverty and Living Conditions in the Slums of Dakar and Nairobi."Africa Urban and Water Working Paper, Washington, DC, World Bank.

Gulyani S., and D. Talukdar. 2008. "Slum Real Estate: The Low-Quality High-Price Puzzle in Nairobi's Slums and Its Implications for Theory and Practice." *World Development* 36 (10): 1916–37.

——. 2010. "Inside Informality: The Links Between Poverty, Microenterprises and Living Conditions in Nairobi's Slums." *World Development* 38 (12): 1710–26.

Gulyani, S., D. Talukdar, and D. Jack. 2010. "Poverty, Living Conditions and Infrastructure Access: A Comparison of Slums in Dakar, Johannesburg and Nairobi." Policy Research Working Paper 5388, Washington, DC, World Bank.

Iskander, N., and S. Gulyani. 2010. "The Trouble with Silos: Water and Sanitation in the Sinking Slums of Dakar." Africa Urban and Water Working Paper, Washington, DC, World Bank.

Peattie, L. R. 1968. *The View from the Barrio.* Ann Arbor, MI: University of Michigan Press.

Perlman, J. 2006. "The Metamorphosis of Marginality: Four Generations in the Favelas of Rio de Janeiro." *Annals of the American Academy of Political and Social Science* 606: 154–77.

——. 1980. *The Myth of Marginality: Urban Poverty and Politics in Rio de Janeiro.* Berkeley, CA: University of California Press.

cooperatives. Although the contributing family workers category is technically part of the self-employed according to the classification used by the International Labour Organization (ILO), and could therefore be combined with the other self-employed categories to derive the total self-employed, they are reported here as a separate category in order to emphasize the difference between the two statuses, since the socioeconomic implications associated with each status can be significantly varied. This practice follows that of the ILO's Key Indicators of the Labour Market.

Contributing family workers (unpaid workers) are workers who hold self-employment jobs as own-account workers in a market-oriented establishment operated by a related person living in the same household.

Source: International Labour Organization, Key Indicators of the Labour Market database.

Table 9.3. Unemployment

Unemployment is the share of the labor force of the specified subgroup without work but available for and seeking employment.

Primary education provides children with basic reading, writing, and mathematics skills along with an elementary understanding of such subjects as history, geography, natural science, social science, art, and music.

Secondary education completes the provision of basic education that began at the primary level and aims to lay the foundations for lifelong learning and human development by offering more subject- or skill-oriented instruction using more specialized teachers.

Tertiary education, whether or not at an advanced research qualification, normally requires, as a minimum condition of admission, the successful completion of education at the secondary level.

Source: International Labour Organization, Key Indicators of the Labour Market database.

Table 9.4. Migration and population

Migrant stock is the number of people born in a country other than that in which they live. It includes refugees.

Net migration is the net average annual number of migrants during the period, that is, the annual number of immigrants less the annual number of emigrants, including both citizens and noncitizens. Data are five-year estimates.

Workers remittances, received, comprise current transfers by migrant workers and wages and salaries by nonresident workers.

Migrant remittance flows are the sum of worker's remittances, compensation of employees, and migrants' transfers, as recorded in the International Monetary Fund's *Balance of Payments.*

Population is total population based on the de facto definition of population, which counts all residents regardless of legal status or citizenship, except for refugees not permanently settled in the country of asylum, who are generally considered part of the population of their country of origin. The values shown are midyear estimates.

Fertility rate is the number of children that would be born to a woman if she were to live to the end of her childbearing years and bear children in accordance with current age-specific fertility rates.

Age composition refers to the percentage of the total population that is in specific age groups.

Dependency ratio is the ratio of dependents—people younger than 15 or older than 64—to the working-age population—those ages 15–64.

Rural population is calculated as the difference between the total population and the urban population.

Urban population is midyear population of areas defined as urban in each country.

Source: Data on migration are from the United Nations Population Division, Trends in Total Migrant Stock: 2008 Revision. Data on population are from (1) United Nations Population Division, World Population Prospects; (2) United Nations Statistical Division, Population and Vital Statistics Report (various years); (3) census reports and other statistical publications from national statistical offices; (4) Eurostat: Demographic Statistics; (5) Secretariat of the Pacific Community: Statistics and Demography Programme; and (6) U.S. Census Bureau: International Database. Data on dependency ratio are from World Bank staff estimates from various sources including census reports, the United Nations Population Division's World Population Prospects, national statistical offices, household surveys conducted by national agencies, and Macro International. Data on workers' remittances are from International Monetary Fund, *Balance of Payments Statistics Yearbook*, and data files, while data from migrant remittance flows are from World Bank staff estimates based on the International Monetary Fund's *Balance of Payments Statistics Yearbook 2008*.

10. HIV/AIDS

TABLE 10.1. HIV/AIDS

Estimated number of people living with HIV/AIDS is the number of people in the relevant age group living with HIV.

Estimated HIV prevalence rate is the percentage of the population of the relevant age subgroup who are infected with HIV. Depending on the reliability of the data available, there may be more or less uncertainty surrounding each estimate. Therefore, plausible bounds have been presented for each subgroup rate (low and high estimate).

Deaths of adults and children due to HIV/AIDS are the estimated number of adults and children who have died in a specific year based on the modeling of HIV surveillance data using standard and appropriate tools.

AIDS orphans are the estimated number of children who have lost their mother or both parents to AIDS before age 17 since the epidemic began in 1990. Some of the orphaned children included in this cumulative total are no longer alive; others are no longer under age 17.

HIV-positive pregnant women receiving antiretrovirals to reduce the risk of mother-to-child transmission are the number of pregnant women infected with HIV who received antiretrovirals during the last 12 months to reduce the risk of mother-to-child transmission.

Share of HIV-positive pregnant women receiving antiretrovirals, World Health Organization/Joint United Nations Programme on HIV/AIDS (WHO/UNAIDS) methodology, is the percentage of pregnant women infected with HIV who received antiretrovirals to reduce the risk of mother-to-child transmission divided by the total number of infected pregnant women infected with HIV in the last 12 months. The WHO/UNAIDS methodology may differ from country methodologies.

Official development assistance (ODA) disbursements for social mitigation of HIV/AIDS are spending on special programs to address the consequences of HIV/AIDS, such as social, legal, and economic assistance to people living with HIV/AIDS (including food security and employment); spending on support to vulnerable groups and children orphaned by HIV/AIDS; and spending on human rights advocacy for people affected by HIV/AIDS.

Official development assistance (ODA) disbursements for sexually transmitted diseases (STDs) control, including HIV/AIDS, are spending on all activities related to STDs and HIV/AIDS control, such as information, education, and communication; testing; prevention; and treatment care.

Source: Data on number of people living with HIV/AIDS, HIV prevalence rate, deaths due to HIV/AIDS, AIDS orphans, and HIV-positive pregnant women receiving antiretrovirals are from UNAIDS and WHO's *Report on the Global AIDS Epidemic.* A more detailed explanation of methods and assumptions can be found on the UNAIDS reference group on estimates, modeling, and projections website (www.unaids.org/en/KnowledgeCentre/HIVData/Epidemiology/) and in a series of papers published in *Sexually Transmitted Infections,* "Improved Methods and Tools for HIV/AIDS Estimates and Projections," 2008, 84(Suppl I), 2006, 82(Suppl III), and 2004, 80(Suppl I). Data on official development assistance disbursements are from the Development Assistance Committee of the Organisation for Economic Co-operation and Development, Geographical Distribution of Financial Flows to Developing Countries, Development Co-operation Report, and International Development Statistics database. Data are available online at www.oecd.org/dac/stats/idsonline.

11. Malaria

TABLE 11.1. MALARIA

Population is total population based on the de facto definition of population, which counts all residents regardless of legal status or citizenship, except for refugees not permanently settled in the country of asylum, who are generally considered part of the population of their country of origin. The values shown are midyear estimates.

Clinical malaria cases reported are the sum of cases confirmed by slide examination or rapid diagnostic test and probable and unconfirmed cases (cases that were not tested but treated as malaria). National malaria control programs often collect data on the number of suspected cases, those tested, and those confirmed. Probable or unconfirmed cases are calculated by subtracting the number tested from the number suspected. Not all cases reported as malaria are true malaria cases; most health facilities lack appropriate diagnostic services. The misdiagnosis may have led to under- or overreporting malaria cases and missing diagnosis of other treatable diseases.

Reported malaria deaths are all deaths in health facilities that are attributed to malaria, whether or not confirmed by microscopy or by rapid diagnostic test.

Under-five mortality rate is the probability that a newborn baby will die before reaching age 5, if subject to current age-specific mortality rates. The probability is expressed as a rate per 1,000.

Children sleeping under insecticide-treated nets is the percentage of children under age 5 with access to an insecticide-treated net to prevent malaria.

Children with fever receiving any antimalarial treatment any time are the percentage of children under age 5 in malaria-risk areas with fever being treated with any antimalarial drugs.

Pregnant women receiving two doses of intermittent preventive treatment are the number of pregnant women receiving two or more doses of sulfadoxine pyrimethamine (SP) during an antenatal care visit. In some country surveys, the site of treatment (e.g., "during the antenatal care visit") is not specified. This approach has been shown to be safe, inexpensive, and effective.

Official development assistance (ODA) disbursements for malaria control are spending on prevention and control of malaria.

Source: Data on population are from the (1) United Nations Population Division, World Population Prospects,; (2) United Nations Statistical Division, Population and Vital Statistics Report (various years); (3) census reports and other statistical publications from national statistical offices; (4) Eurostat: Demographic Statistics, (5) Secretariat of the Pacific Community: Statistics and Demography Programme; and (6) U.S. Census Bureau: International Database.. Data on clinical cases of malaria reported and reported malaria deaths are from the World Health Organization's (WHO) *World Malaria Report 2009*. Data on children with fever receiving antimalarial drugs, and pregnant women receiving two doses of intermittent preventive treatment, are from Demographic Health Surveys, Multiple Indicator Cluster Surveys, and national statistical offices. Data on deaths due to malaria are from the United Nations Statistics Division based on WHO estimates. Data on under-five mortality are harmonized estimates of the WHO, United Nations Children's Fund, and the World Bank, based mainly on household surveys, censuses, and vital registration, supplemented by World Bank estimates based on household surveys and vital registration. Data on insecticide-treated bednet use are from Demographic and Health Surveys and Multiple Indicator Cluster Surveys. Data on official development assistance disbursements are from the Development Assistance Committee of the Organisation for Economic Co-operation and Development, Geographical Distribution of Financial Flows to Developing Countries, Development Co-operation Report, and International Development Statistics database. Data are available online at www.oecd.org/dac/stats/idsonline.

12. Capable states and partnership

TABLE 12.1. AID AND DEBT RELIEF

Official development assistance is flows to developing countries and multilateral institutions provided by official agencies, including state and local governments, or by their executive agencies, that are administered with the promotion of the economic development and welfare of developing countries as their main objective and that are concessional in character and convey a grant element of at least 25 percent.

Net official development assistance (ODA) from all donors is net ODA from the Development Assistance Committee (DAC) and multilateral donors. It is consists of disbursements of loans made on concessional terms (net of repayments of principal) and grants by official agencies of the members of the DAC, by multilateral institutions, and by non-DAC countries to promote economic development and welfare in countries and territories in the DAC list of ODA recipients. It includes loans with a grant element of at least 25 percent (calculated at a rate of discount of 10 percent).

Net official development assistance (ODA) from DAC donors is net ODA from OECD's DAC donors, which include Australia, Austria, Belgium, Canada, Denmark, Finland, France, Germany, Greece, Ireland, Italy, Japan, Korea, Luxembourg, the Netherlands, New Zealand, Norway, Portugal, Spain, Sweden, Switzerland, the United Kingdom, and the United States.

Net official development assistance (ODA) from non-DAC donors is net ODA from OECD's non-DAC donors, which include the Chinese Taipei, Cyprus, Czech Republic, Estonia, Hungary, Iceland, Israel, Kuwait, Latvia, Lichtenstein, Lithuania, Malta, Poland, Romania, Russia, Saudi Arabia, the Slovak Republic, Slovenia, Thailand, Turkey, the United Arab Emirates, and other donors (includes data reported from Algeria, Iraq, Libya, and Qatar from 1970–1994).

Net official development assistance (ODA) from multilateral donors is net ODA from multilateral sources, African Development Bank (AfDB), African Development Fund (AFDF), Arab Fund, Asian Development Bank (AsDB), Caribbean Development Bank (CarDB), Arab Bank for Economic Development in Africa (BADEA), European Bank for Reconstruction and Development (EBRD), European Union (EU) Institutions, GAVI Alliance (formerly the "Global Alliance for Vaccines and Immunisation"), Global Environment Facility (GEF), Global Fund, International Atomic Energy Agency (IAEA), International Bank for Reconstruction and Development (IBRD), International Development Association (IDA), Inter-American Development Bank (IDB) Special Fund, International Fund for Agricultural Development (IFAD), International Finance Corporation (IFC), International Monetary Fund (IMF) Concessional Trust Funds, Islamic Development Bank, Montreal Protocol, Nordic Development Fund, the OPEC Fund for International Development (OFID), Organization for Security and Cooperation in Europe (OSCE), Joint United Nations Programme on HIV/AIDS (UNAIDS), United Nations Development Programme (UNDP), United Nations Economic Commission for Europe (UNECE), United Nations Population Fund (UNFPA), United Nations High Commissioner for Refugees (UNHCR), United Nations Children's Fund (UNICEF), United Nations Peace Building Fund (UNPBF), United Nations Relief and Works Agency (UNRWA), United Nations Transitional Authority (UNTA), World Food Programme (WFP), and World Health Organization (WHO).

Net private official development assistance (ODA) is private ODA transactions, which comprise direct investment, portfolio investment, and export credits (net). Private transactions are undertaken by firms and individuals resident in the reporting country. Portfolio investment corresponds to bonds and equities. Inflows into emerging countries' stock markets, are, however, heavily understated. Accordingly, the coverage of portfolio investment differs in these regards from the coverage of bank claims, which include export credit lending by banks. The bank claims data represent the net change in bank claims after adjusting for exchange rate changes and are therefore a proxy for net flow data but are not themselves a net flow figure. They differ in two further regards from other OECD data. First, they relate to loans by banks resident in countries that report quarterly to the Bank for International Settlements. Second, no adjustment has been made to exclude short-term claims.

Net official development assistance (ODA) as a share of gross domestic product (GDP) is calculated by dividing the nominal total net ODA from all donors by nominal GDP. For a given level of aid flows, devaluation of a recipient's currency may inflate the ratios shown in the table. Thus, trends for a given country and comparisons across countries that have implemented different exchange rate policies should be interpreted carefully.

Net official development assistance (ODA) per capita is calculated by dividing the nominal total net ODA (net disbursements of loans and grants from all official sources on concessional financial terms) by midyear population. These ratios offer some indication of the importance of aid flows in sustaining per capita income and consumption levels, although exchange rate fluctuations, the actual rise of aid flows, and other factors vary across countries and over time.

Net official development assistance (ODA) as a share of gross capital formation is calculated by dividing the nominal total net ODA by gross capital formation. These data highlight the relative importance of the indicated aid flows in maintaining and increasing investment in these economies. The same caveats mentioned above apply to their interpretation. Furthermore, aid flows do not exclusively finance investment (for example, food aid finances consumption), and the share of aid going to investment varies across countries.

Net official development assistance (ODA) as a share of imports of goods and services is calculated by dividing nominal total net ODA by imports of goods and services.

Net official development assistance (ODA) as a share of central government expenditure is calculated by dividing nominal total net ODA by central government expenditure.

Food aid shipments are transfers of food commodities (food aid received) from donor to recipient countries on a total-grant basis or on highly concessional terms. Processed and blended cereals are converted into their grain equivalent by applying the conversion factors included in the Rule of Procedures under the 1999 Food Aid Convention to facilitate comparisons between deliveries of different commodities. Deliveries of food aid refer to quantities of commodities that actually reached the recipient country during a given period. For cereals the period refers to July–June, beginning in the year shown.

Heavily Indebted Poor Countries (HIPC) Debt Initiative decision point is the date at which a HIPC with an established track record of good performance under adjustment programs supported by the International Monetary Fund and the World Bank commits to undertake additional reforms and to develop and implement a poverty reduction strategy.

Countries reach the decision point if they have a track record of macroeconomic stability, have prepared a Poverty Reduction Strategy through a participatory process, and have debt burden indicators above the HIPC Initiative thresholds using the most recent data for the year immediately prior to the decision point. The amount of debt relief necessary to bring countries' debt indicators to HIPC thresholds is calculated, and countries begin receiving interim debt relief on a provisional basis.

HIPC Debt Initiative completion point is the date at which the country successfully completes the key structural reforms agreed on at the decision point, including developing and implementing its poverty reduction strategy. The country then receives the bulk of debt relief under the HIPC Initiative without further policy conditions.

Burkina Faso, Mali, Mozambique, and Uganda also reached the completion point under the original HIPC Initiative, and the assistance includes original debt relief. Burkina Faso, Ethiopia, Guinea Bissau, Malawi, Niger, Rwanda, and São Tomé and Príncipe assistance includes topping up at the completion point. Liberia received Multilateral Debt Relief Initiative (MDRI)-type (beyond-HIPC) debt relief at end-June 2010, which was financed from the Liberia Administered Account.

Countries reach the completion point if they maintain macroeconomic stability under an Extended Credit Facility (ECF)-supported program, carry out key structural and social reforms, and satisfactorily implement for a minimum of one year a Poverty Reduction Strategy. Debt relief is then provided irrevocably by the country's creditors. MDRI relief is provided upon reaching the completion point.

Eritrea, Somalia, and Sudan have been assessed to meet the income and indebtedness criteria at end-2004 and end-2010 and wish to avail themselves of the HIPC Initiative.

Debt service relief committed is the amount of debt service relief, calculated at the decision point, that will allow the country to achieve debt sustainability at the completion point.

Multilateral Debt Relief Initiative is meant to provide additional support to HIPCs to reach the Millennium Development Goals while ensuring that the financing capacity of the International Financial Institutions (IFIs) is preserved. The MDRI provides a framework that commits to achieve two objectives: deepening debt relief to HIPCs while safeguarding the long-term financial capacity of IDA and the AfDF; and encouraging the best use of additional donor resources for development by allocating them to low-income countries on the basis of policy performance. Debt relief to be provided under the MDRI will be in addition to existing debt relief commitments by IDA and other creditors under the Enhanced HIPC Debt Initiative. The MDRI calls for 100 percent cancellation of IDA, AfDF, and International Monetary Fund (IMF) debt for countries that reach the HIPC completion point. The costs include principal and interest foregone for all multilaterals participating in the Initiative, except IMF, which only include principal. The estimated costs for IMF reflect the stock of debt eligible for MDRI relief, which is the debt outstanding (principal only) as of end-2004 and that has not been repaid by the member and is not covered by HIPC assistance (EBS/05/158 Revision 1, 12/15/2005).

Source: Data on net official development assistance are from the Development Assistance Committee of the Organisation for Economic Co-operation and Development, Geographical Distribution of Financial Flows to Developing Countries, Development Co-operation Report, and International Development Statistics database. Data are available online at www.oecd.org/dac/stats/idsonline. Data on food aid shipments are based on data compiled by the World Food Programme at www.wfp.org/fais/. Data on HIPC countries are from the International Development Association and International Monetary Fund "Heavily Indebted Poor Countries (HIPC) Initiative and Multilateral Debt Relief Initiative (MDRI)—Status of Implementation." Data on external debt are mainly from reports to the World Bank through its Debtor Reporting System from member countries that have received International Bank for Reconstruction and Development loans or International Development Association credits, as well as World Bank and IMF files.

Table 12.2. Status of Paris Declaration indicators

The Paris Declaration is the outcome of the 2005 Paris High-Level Forum on Aid Effectiveness, where 60 partner countries, 30 donor countries, and 30 development agencies committed to specific actions to further country ownership, harmonization, alignment, managing for development results, and mutual accountability for the use of aid. Participants agreed on 12 indicators. These indicators include good national development strategies, reliable country systems for procurement and public financial management, the development and use of results frameworks, and mutual assessment of progress. Qualitative desk reviews by the Organisation for Economic Co-operation and Development's Development Assistance Committee and the World Bank and a survey questionnaire for governments and donors are used to calculate the indicators.

PDI-1 Operational national development strategies are the extent to which a country has an operational development strategy to guide its aid coordination effort and overall development. The score is based on the World Bank's 2005 Comprehensive Development Framework Progress Report. An operational strategy calls for a coherent long-term strategy derived from it; specific targets serving a holistic, balanced, and well-sequenced development strategy; and capacity and resources for its implementation.

PDI-2a Reliable public financial management is the World Bank's annual Country Policy and Institutional Assessment rating for the quality of public financial management. Measured on a scale of 1 (worst) to 5 (best), its focus is on how much existing systems adhere to broadly accepted good practices and whether a reform program is in place to promote improved practices.

PDI-2b Reliable country procurement systems measure developing countries' procurement systems. Donors use national procurement procedures when the funds they provide for the implementation of projects and programs are managed according to the national procurement procedures as they were established in the general legislation and implemented by government. The use of national procurement procedures means that donors do not make additional, or special, requirements on governments for the procurement of works, goods, and services. (Where weaknesses in national procurement systems have been identified, donors may work with partner countries to improve the efficiency, economy, and transparency of their implementation.) The objective of this indicator is to measure and encourage improvements in developing countries' procurement systems.

PDI-3 Government budget estimates comprehensive and realistic are the percentage of aid that is accurately recorded in the national budget, thereby allowing scrutiny by parliaments.

PDI-4 Technical assistance aligned and coordinated with country programs is the percentage of technical cooperation that is freestanding and embedded and that respects ownership (partner countries exercise effective leadership over their capacity development programs), alignment (technical cooperation in support of capacity development aligns with countries' development objectives and strategies), and harmonization (when more than one donor is involved in supporting partner-led capacity development, donors coordinate their activities and contributions).

PDI-5a and *5b Aid for government sectors uses country public financial management* and *procurement systems* is the percentage of donors that use country, rather than donor, systems for managing aid disbursement.

PDI-6 Project implementation units parallel to country structures is the number of parallel project implementation units, which refers to units created outside existing country institutional structures. The survey guidance distinguishes between project implementation units and executing agencies and describes three typical features of parallel project implementation units: they are accountable to external funding agencies rather than to country implementing agencies (ministries, departments, agencies, and the like), most of the professional staff is appointed by the donor, and the personnel salaries often exceed those of civil service personnel. Interpretation of the Paris Declaration survey question on this subject was controversial in a number of countries. It is unclear whether within countries all donors applied the same criteria with the same degree of rigor or that across countries the same standards were used. In several cases the descriptive part of the survey results indicates that some donors applied a legalistic criterion of accountability to the formal executing agency, whereas the national coordinator and other donors would have preferred greater recognition of the substantive reality of accountability to the donor. Some respondents may have confused the definitional question (Is the unit "parallel"?) with the aid management question (Is the parallelism justified in terms of the developmental benefits and costs?).

PDI-7 Aid disbursements on schedule and recorded by government are the percentage of funds that are disbursed within the year they are scheduled and accurately recorded by partner authorities.

PDI-8 Bilateral aid that is untied is the percentage of aid that is untied. Tied aid is aid provided on the condition that the recipient uses it to purchase goods and services from suppliers based in the donor country.

PDI-9 Aid provided in the framework of program-based approaches is the percentage of development cooperation that is based on the principles of coordinated support for a locally owned program of development, such as a national development strategy, a sector program, a thematic program, or a program of a specific organization. Program-based approaches share the following features: leadership by the host country or organization, a single comprehensive program and budget framework, a formalized process for donor coordination and harmonization of donor procedures for reporting, budgeting, financial management, and procurement, and efforts to increase the use of local systems for program design and implementation, financial management, monitoring, and evaluation.

PDI-10a Donor missions coordinated are the percentage of missions undertaken jointly by two or more donors and missions undertaken by one donor on behalf of another (delegated cooperation).

PDI-10b Country analysis coordinated is the percentage of country analytic work that is undertaken by one or more donors jointly, undertaken by one donor on behalf of another donor (including work undertaken by one and used by another when it is co-financed and formally acknowledged in official documentation), and undertaken with substantive involvement from government.

PDI-11 Existence of a monitorable performance assessment framework measures the extent to which the country has realized its commitment to establishing performance frameworks. The indicator relies on the scorings of the 2005 Comprehensive Development Framework Progress Report and considers three criteria: the quality of development information, stakeholder access to development information, and coordinated country-level monitoring and evaluation. The assessments therefore reflect both the extent to which sound data on development outputs, outcomes, and impacts are collected, and various aspects of the way information is used, disseminated among stakeholders, and fed back into policy.

PDI-12 Reviews of mutual accountability. All three of the following aspects of mutual accountability need to be met to consider a country as having a mutual review in place: i) *Aid policy or strategy*. Developing countries are expected to have a document that sets out agreed approaches to the delivery of aid in the country, containing agreed principles, processes, and/or targets designed to improve the effectiveness of aid. This may take the form of a stand-alone policy or strategy document, or may be addressed within another document (e.g., as part of a national development strategy). Such a document should have been the subject of consultation between the government and donors. ii) *Country-level aid effectiveness targets.* Country targets for improved aid effectiveness should have been established, including within the framework of the agreed partnership commitments and indicators of progress included in the Paris Declaration. They may go beyond the Paris Declaration wherever governments and donors agree to do so. There should be targets for both governments and donors. iii) *Broad-based dialogue*. Mutual assessments should engage a broad range of government ministries and donors in dialogue. Governments and donors should also consider engaging with nonexecutive stakeholders, including parliamentarians and civil society organizations. While the focus of the criteria remains unchanged from those used in previous surveys, three questions were introduced, drawing on clearer definitions to guide a more accurate assessment of progress.

Source: Aid Effectiveness 2005–10: Progress in Implementing the Paris Declaration, OECD.

TABLE 12.3. CAPABLE STATES

Firms that believe the court system is fair, impartial, and uncorrupt are the percentage of firms that believe the court system is fair, impartial, and uncorrupted.

Corruption is the percentage of firms identifying corruption as a major constraint.

Crime, theft, and disorder are the percentage of firms identifying crime, theft, and disorder as a major constraint to current operation.

Number of procedures to enforce a contract is the number of independent actions, mandated by law or courts, that demand interaction between the parties of a contract or between them and the judge or court officer.

Time required to enforce a contract is the number of calendar days from the filing of the lawsuit in court until the final determination and, in appropriate cases, payment.

Cost to enforce a contract is court and attorney fees, where the use of attorneys is mandatory or common, or the cost of an administrative debt recovery procedure, expressed as a percentage of the debt value.

Protecting investors disclosure index measures the degree to which investors are protected through disclosure of ownership and financial information. Higher values indicate more disclosure.

Director liability index measures a plaintiff's ability to hold directors of firms liable for damages to the company. Higher values indicate greater liability.

Shareholder suits index measures shareholders' ability to sue officers and directors for misconduct. Higher values indicate greater power for shareholders to challenge transactions.

Investor protection index measures the degree to which investors are protected through disclosure of ownership and financial information regulations. Higher values indicate better protection.

Number of tax payments is the number of taxes paid by businesses, including electronic filing. The tax is counted as paid once a year even if payments are more frequent.

Time required to prepare, file, and pay taxes is the number of hours it takes to prepare, file, and pay (or withhold) three major types of taxes: the corporate income tax, the value added or sales tax, and labor taxes, including payroll taxes and social security contributions.

Total tax rate is the total amount of taxes payable by the business (except for labor taxes) after accounting for deductions and exemptions as a percentage of gross profit.

For further details on the method used for assessing the total tax payable, see the World Bank's *Doing Business reports*.

Extractive Industries Transparency Initiative (EITI) status refers to a country's implementation status for the EITI, a multistakeholder approach to increasing governance and transparency in extractive industries. It includes civil society, the private sector, and government and requires a work plan with timeline and budget to ensure sustainability, independent audit of payments and disclosure of revenues, publication of results in a publicly accessible manner, and an approach that covers all companies and government agencies. The EITI supports improved governance in resource-rich countries through the verification and full publication of company payments and government revenues from oil, gas, and mining. *Intent to implement* indicates that a country intends to implement the EITI but has not yet met the four initial requirements to join: an unequivocal public statement of its intention to implement the EITI, a commitment to work with civil society and companies on EITI implementation, a senior official appointed to lead EITI implementation, and a widely distributed, fully costed work plan with measurable targets, a timetable for implementation, and an assessment of government, private sector, and civil society capacity constraints. *Candidate* indicates that a country has met the four initial requirements to join the EITI and has begun a range of activities to strengthen revenue transparency, as documented in the country's work plan. Once a country has become an EITI candidate, it has two years to be validated as compliant. *Compliant* indicates that a country has successfully undergone validation, an independent assessment of a country's progress toward the EITI goals by the EITI International Board. Validation is based on the country's work plan, the EITI validation grid and indicator assessment tools, and company forms that detail private companies' extractive industry activities; it provides guidance for countries' future activity related to EITI compliance. Countries must undergo validation every five years or at the request of the EITI International Board.

Source: Data on investment climate constraints to firms are World Bank, Enterprise Surveys (www.enterprisesurveys.org/). Data on enforcing contracts, protecting investors, and regulation and tax administration are from the World Bank's Doing Business project (http://www.doingBusiness/). Data on corruption perceptions index are from Transparency International (www.transparency.org/policy_research/surveys_indices/cpi). Data on the EITI are from the Extractive Industries Transparency Initiative website (www.eitransparency.org).

Table 12.4. Governance and anticorruption indicators

Voice and accountability measure the extent to which a country's citizens are able to participate in selecting their government and to enjoy freedom of expression, freedom of association, and a free media.

Political stability and absence of violence measure the perceptions of the likelihood that the government will be destabilized or overthrown by unconstitutional or violent means, including domestic violence or terrorism.

Government effectiveness measures the quality of public services, the quality and degree of independence from political pressures of the civil service, the quality of policy formulation and Implementation, and the credibility of the government's commitment to such policies.

Regulatory quality measures the ability of the government to formulate and implement sound policies and regulations that permit and promote private sector development.

Rule of law measures the extent to which agents have confidence in and abide by the rules of society, in particular the quality of contract enforcement, the police, and the courts, as well as the Likelihood of crime and violence.

Control of corruption measures the extent to which public power is exercised for private gain, including petty and grand forms of corruption, as well as "capture" of the state by elites and private interests.

Expected to pay informal payment to public officials to get things done is the percentage of firms that expected to make informal payments or give gifts to public officials to "get things done" with regard to customs, taxes, licenses, regulations, services, and the like.

Expected to give gifts to obtain an operating license is the percentage of firms that expected to give gifts or an informal payment to get an operating license.

Expected to give gifts in meetings with tax officials is the percentage of firms that answered "Yes" to the question, "Was a gift or informal payment expected or requested during a meeting with tax officials?"

Expected to give gifts to secure a government contract is the percentage of firms that expected to make informal payments or give gifts to public officials to secure a government contract.

Share of firms identifying control of corruption as a major constraint measures the extent to which public power is exercised for private gain, including petty and grand forms of corruption, as well as "capture" of the state by elites and private interests.

Mean corruption perceptions index score is the country's score in Transparency International's annual corruption perceptions index, which ranks more than 150 countries in terms of perceived levels of corruption, as determined by expert assessments and opinion surveys.

Open budget index overall score is the country's score on a subset of 91 questions from the open budget survey. The questions focus on the public availability of eight key budget documents (with a particular emphasis on the executive's budget proposal) and the information they contain. The open budget index is calculated based on detailed questionnaires completed by local experts in 59 participating countries from every continent. In 2008, based on inputs received from researchers and extensive in-house reviews, the International Budget Partnership made three changes in its methodology. The first change concerns the timing of the release of the eight key budget documents assessed by the survey. The second is the inclusion of the enacted budget in calculating country scores for the index. The third is revisions to the answers of a few questions used to assess Brazil and Nigeria.

Source: Data on governance indicators are from the World Bank Institute's Worldwide Governance Indicators database, which relies on 33 sources, including surveys of enterprises and citizens, and expert polls, gathered from 30 organizations around the world. Data on corruption perceptions index scores are from Transparency International (www.transparency.org/). Data on the open budget index are from www.openbudgetindex.org.

Table 12.5. Country policy and institutional assessment ratings

The Country Policy and Institutional Assessment (CPIA) assesses the quality of a country's present policy and institutional framework. "Quality" means how conducive that framework is to fostering sustainable, poverty-reducing growth and the effective use of development assistance. The CPIA is conducted annually for all International Bank for Reconstruction and Development and International Development Association borrowers and has evolved into a set of criteria grouped into four clusters with 16 criteria that reflect a balance between ensuring that all key factors that foster pro-poor growth and poverty alleviation are captured, without overly burdening the evaluation process.

- Economic management
    - *Macroeconomic management* assesses the quality of the monetary, exchange rate, and aggregate demand policy framework.
    - *Fiscal policy* assesses the short- and medium-term sustainability of fiscal policy (taking into account monetary and exchange rate policy and the sustainability of the public debt) and its impact on growth.
    - *Debt policy* assesses whether the debt management strategy is conducive to minimize budgetary risks and ensure long-term debt sustainability.
- Structural policies
    - *Trade* assesses how the policy framework fosters trade in goods. It covers two areas: trade regime restrictiveness—which focuses on the height of tariff barriers, the extent to which nontariff barriers are used, and the transparency and predictability of the trade regime—and customs and trade facilitation—which includes the extent to which the customs service is free of corruption, relies on risk management, processes duty collections and refunds promptly, and operates transparently.

The World Bank's country policy and institutional assessment (CPIA) measures the strength of International Development Association countries' policies and institutions across 16 dimensions grouped into four clusters: economic management, structural policies, policies for social inclusion and equity, and public sector management and institutions. Scores are on a scale of 1 to 6, with 6 the highest.

The latest CPIA results show that despite difficult global economic conditions, the quality of policies and institutions in a majority of Sub-Saharan African countries remained stable or improved in 2011 (figure 1). The average CPIA score for IDA countries in the region was 3.2 in 2011, the same as in 2010. Nevertheless, for several countries the policy environment has improved and is the best in recent years. Of the 38 African countries with CPIA scores, 13 saw an improvement in the 2011 overall score by at least 0.1, twenty saw no change, and five witnessed a decline of 0.1 or more (figure 2). In short, despite a challenging global economic environment, African countries continued to pursue policies aligned with growth and poverty reduction. This pattern was observed in the aftermath of the global financial and economic crisis of 2008–09. During the global crisis, the payoffs to market-oriented, pro-poor economic reforms fell, prompting a concern that countries may backtrack on important policy gains. Yet policy makers continued with prudent policies, even in the face of contradictory policies elsewhere.

There is considerable variation in overall CPIA scores across countries, from a high of 4.0 for Cape Verde, which continues to be in the top end of the score range despite a decline in its score in both 2010 and 2011, to a low of 2.2 for Eritrea and Zimbabwe. The variation is especially marked between "fragile situations" (also referred to as fragile states) and other countries.[1] Sub-Saharan Africa has a large number of fragile states: 17 of the world's 33, by the World Bank's definition of fragile situations. The capacity of the public sector in most of these countries is exceptionally weak. Not surprisingly, the average CPIA score for these countries is much lower than that of non-fragile countries, at 2.7 and 3.5, respectively. Hampered with severe governance problems, including widespread corruption and civil conflict, Africa's resource-rich countries on average tend to lag the non-resource-rich countries: overall CPIA scores are 3.0 for resource-rich and 3.3 for non-resource-rich countries.

Nonetheless, many fragile states are making fast progress, albeit from a low base. The three countries that experienced the largest increase—of 0.2—in their overall CPIA score in 2011 were fragile states: Comoros, Cote d'Ivoire, and Zimbabwe. A pattern of larger gains for fragile states is evident over a longer time period as well. Given their weak policy and institutional capacity, fragile countries can also experience a rapid deterioration in the policy environment. By contrast, countries in the top range of scores typically show slow yet steady improvement in scores, although a few have seen policy slippages in recent years—for example, Cape Verde in 2010 and 2011, and Tanzania in 2011.

Figure 1: Overall CPIA score of African countries, 2011

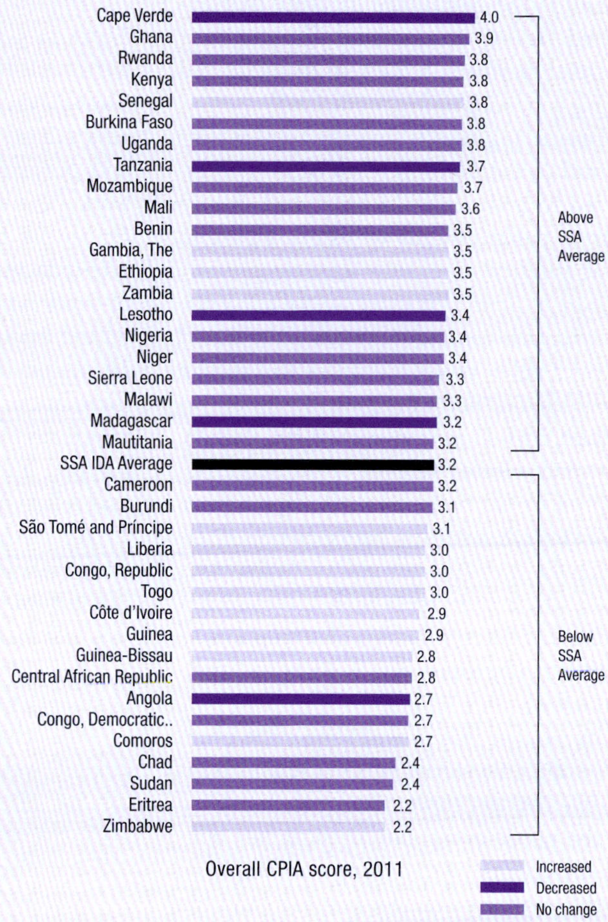

Source: CPIA Africa: *Assessing Africa's Policies and Institutions,* June 2012, Africa Region, World Bank.

Figure 2: Overall CPIA score and change in score for African countries, 2011

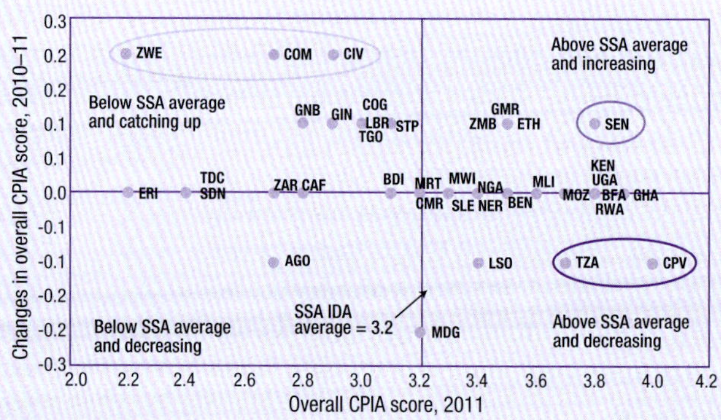

Source: CPIA Africa: *Assessing Africa's Policies and Institutions,* June 2012, Africa Region, World Bank.

There are large differences in performance across components of the CPIA, reflecting the faster pace of reform in some policy areas. Not surprisingly, in components where reforms are deeply political (or contentious) or by nature incremental, scores

(continued)

2011 CPIA Results for Africa (continued)

Figure 3: CPIA cluster scores by country group, 2011

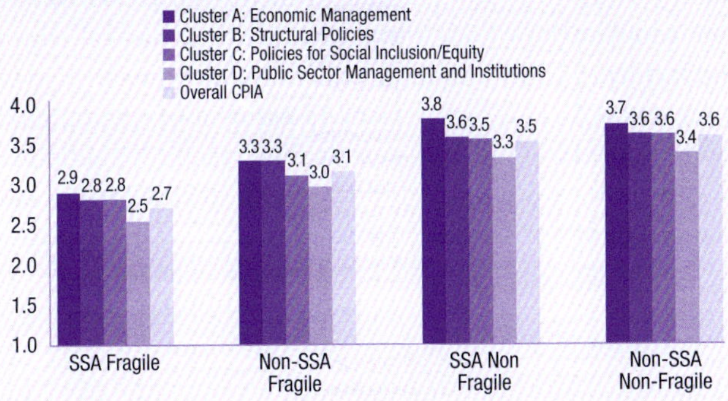

Source: CPIA Africa: *Assessing Africa's Policies and Institutions*, June 2012, Africa Region, World Bank.

improve more slowly and lag scores in other components. Performance in the economic management cluster (Cluster A), which covers monetary and exchange rate policy, fiscal policy, and debt policy and management, leads that of all other clusters. To some extent, this reflects recognition of the importance of macroeconomic stability for creating an environment conducive to private sector activity; high commodity prices have also helped. Indeed, several years of prudent macroeconomic policies meant that African countries entered the 2008–09 global crisis with policy space to counter the sharp external shock.

A close second in performance is the structural policies cluster (Cluster B)—covering trade, financial sector, and business regulatory environment—followed by the social inclusion and equity cluster (Cluster C)—covering gender equality, equity of public resource use, building human resources, social protection and labor, and environmental policies and institutions. The governance cluster (Cluster D)—which includes property rights and rule-based governance; quality of budgetary and financial management; efficiency of revenue mobilization; quality of public administration; and transparency, accountability, and corruption in the public sector—lags all other clusters.

The overall CPIA score for African countries lags that of other IDA countries: the average score for the two groups are 3.2 and 3.4, respectively. But comparison by country groups yields a fairly uneven picture. Policies and institutions in African countries, excluding fragile states, compare well with those in similar countries in other regions, with the average scores being 3.5 and 3.6, respectively. But the comparison of fragile states across regions is starkly different, with African fragile states exhibiting much weaker performance than non-African fragile countries. The performance across areas of the CPIA follows a similar pattern, further highlighting the weakness of policies and institutions in the region's fragile states.

Notes

1 The World Bank defines "fragile situations" as either: (a) IDA-eligible countries with a harmonized average CPIA rating of 3.2 or less (or no CPIA), or (b) countries with the presence of a UN and/or regional peacekeeping or peace-building mission during the past three years. IBRD (International Bank for Reconstruction and Development)-only countries are not included in the fragile situations list.

- *Financial sector* assesses the structure of the financial sector and the policies and regulations that affect it. It covers three dimensions: financial stability; the sector's efficiency, depth, and resource mobilization strength; and access to financial services.
- *Business regulatory environment* assesses the extent to which the legal, regulatory, and policy environment helps or hinders private business in investing, creating jobs, and becoming more productive. The emphasis is on direct regulation of business activity and regulation of goods and factor markets. It measures three subcomponents: regulations affecting entry, exit, and competition; regulations of ongoing business operations; and regulations of factor markets (labor and land).
- Policies for social inclusion and equity
  - *Gender equality* assesses the extent to which the country has enacted and put in place institutions and programs to enforce laws and policies that promote equal access for men and women to human capital development and to productive and economic resources, and that give men and women equal status and protection under the law.
  - *Equity of public resource use* assesses the extent to which the pattern of public expenditures and revenue collection affects the poor and is consistent with national poverty reduction priorities. The assessment of the consistency of government spending with the poverty reduction priorities takes into account the extent to which individuals, groups, or localities that are poor, vulnerable, or have unequal access

to services and opportunities are identified; a national development strategy with explicit interventions to assist those individuals, groups, and localities has been adopted; and the composition and incidence of public expenditures are tracked systematically and their results fed back into subsequent resource allocation decisions. The assessment of the revenue collection dimension takes into account the incidence of major taxes—for example, whether they are progressive or regressive—and their alignment with the poverty reduction priorities. When relevant, expenditure and revenue collection trends at the national and subnational levels should be considered. The expenditure component receives two-thirds of the weight in computing the overall rating.

- *Building human resources* assesses the national policies and public and private sector service delivery that affect access to and quality of health and nutrition services, including: population and reproductive health; education, early childhood development, and training and literacy programs; and prevention and treatment of HIV/AIDS, tuberculosis, and malaria.
- *Social protection and labor* assess government policies in the area of social protection and labor market regulation, which reduce the risk of becoming poor, assist those who are poor to better manage further risks, and ensure a minimal level of welfare to all people. Interventions include social safety net programs, pension and old age savings programs, protection of basic labor standards, regulations to reduce segmentation and inequity in labor markets, active labor market programs (such as public works or job training), and community-driven initiatives. In interpreting the guidelines, it is important to take into account the size of the economy and its level of development.
- *Policies and institutions for environmental sustainability* assess the extent to which environmental policies foster the protection and sustainable use of natural resources and the management of pollution. Assessment of environmental sustainability requires multidimensional criteria (that is, for air, water, waste, conservation management, coastal zones management, and natural resources management).

- Public sector management and institutions
  - *Property rights and rule-based governance* assess the extent to which private economic activity is facilitated by an effective legal system and rule-based governance structure in which property and contract rights are reliably respected and enforced. Three dimensions are rated separately: legal basis for secure property and contract rights; predictability, transparency, and impartiality of laws and regulations affecting economic activity, and their enforcement by the legal and judicial system; and crime and violence as an impediment to economic activity.
  - *Quality of budgetary and financial management* assesses the extent to which there is a comprehensive and credible budget, linked to policy priorities; effective financial management systems to ensure that the budget is implemented as intended in a controlled and predictable way; and timely and accurate accounting and fiscal reporting, including timely and audited public accounts and effective arrangements for follow-up.
  - *Efficiency of revenue mobilization* assesses the overall pattern of revenue mobilization—not only the tax structure as it exists on paper, but revenue from all sources as they are actually collected.
  - *Quality of public administration* assesses the extent to which civilian central government staffs (including teachers, health workers, and police)

are structured to design and implement government policy and deliver services effectively. Civilian central government staffs include the central executive together with all other ministries and administrative departments, including autonomous agencies. It excludes the armed forces, state-owned enterprises, and subnational government.

- *Transparency, accountability, and corruption in public sector* assess the extent to which the executive branch can be held accountable for its use of funds and the results of its actions by the electorate and by the legislature and judiciary, and the extent to which public employees within the executive are required to account for the use of resources, administrative decisions, and results obtained. Both levels of accountability are enhanced by transparency in decision making, public audit institutions, access to relevant and timely information, and public and media scrutiny.

Source: World Bank Group, CPIA database (www.worldbank.org/ida).

TABLE 12.6. POLITY INDICATORS

Revised combined polity score is computed by subtracting the institutionalized autocracy score from the institutionalized democracy score; the resulting unified polity scale ranges from +10 (strongly democratic) to −10 (strongly autocratic).

Institutionalized democracy is conceived as three essential, interdependent elements. First is the presence of institutions and procedures through which citizens can express effective preferences about alternative policies and leaders. Second is the existence of institutionalized constraints on the exercise of power by the executive. Third is the guarantee of civil liberties to all citizens in their daily lives and in acts of political participation. Other aspects of plural democracy, such as the rule of law, systems of checks and balances, freedom of the press, and so on are means to, or specific manifestations of, these general principles. Coded data on civil liberties are not included. This is an additive 11-point scale (0–10). The operational indicator of democracy is derived from codings of the competitiveness of political participation using some weights.

Institutionalized autocracy is a pejorative term for some very diverse kinds of political systems whose common properties are a lack of regularized political competition and concern for political freedoms. The term *autocracy* is used and defined operationally in terms of the presence of a distinctive set of political characteristics. In mature form autocracies sharply restrict or suppress competitive political participation. Their chief executives are chosen in a regularized process of selection within the political elite, and once in office they exercise power with few institutional constraints. Most modern autocracies also exercise a high degree of directiveness over social and economic activity, but this is regarded here as a function of political ideology and choice, not a defining property of autocracy. Social democracies also exercise relatively high degrees of directiveness.

Source: Data are from the Integrated Network for Societal Conflict Research (INSCR), Polity IV Project, Political Regime Characteristics and Transitions, 1800–2010 (www.systemicpeace.org/inscr/inscr.htm).

Technical notes references

CDIAC (Carbon Dioxide Information Analysis Center). n.d. Online database. [http://cdiac.ornl.gov/home.html]. Oak Ridge National Laboratory, Environment Sciences Division, Oak Ridge, Tenn.

Chen, Shaohua, and Martin Ravallion. 2011. "The Developing World Is Poorer Than We Thought, But No Less Successful in the Fight Against Poverty." *Quarterly Journal of Economics* 125 (4): 1577–1625.

FAO (Food and Agriculture Organization of the United Nations). 2010. *Global Forest Resources Assessment 2010.* Rome: Food and Agriculture Organization.

———. n.d. *AQUASTAT.* [www.fao.org/nr/water/aquastat/data/query/index.html]. Rome.

———. n.d. *FAOSTAT.* [http://faostat.fao.org].

———. n.d. Food Security Statistics database. [www.fao.org/economic/ess/food-security-statistics/]. Rome.

IDA (International Development Association) and IMF (International Monetary Fund). 2011. "Heavily Indebted Poor Countries (HIPC) Initiative and Multilateral Debt Relief Initiative (MDRI)—Status of Implementation and Proposals for the Future of the HIPC Initiative." International Development Association and International Monetary Fund, Washington, DC.

IEA (International Energy Agency). Various years. *Energy Statistics of OECD Countries.* **Paris: International Energy Agency.**

ILO (International Labour Organization). Various years. *Key Indicators of the Labor Market.* Geneva: International Labour Organization.

IMF (International Monetary Fund). 1977. *Balance of Payments Manual.* 4th ed. Washington, DC: International Monetary Fund.

———. 1993. *Balance of Payments Manual.* 5th ed. Washington, DC: International Monetary Fund.

———. Various years. *Balance of Payments Statistics Yearbook.* Parts 1 and 2. Washington, DC: International Monetary Fund.

———. Various years. *Direction of Trade Statistics Quarterly.* Washington, DC: International Monetary Fund.

———. Various years. *Government Finance Statistics Yearbook.* Washington, DC: International Monetary Fund.

———. Various years. *International Financial Statistics.* Washington, DC: International Monetary Fund.

———. Various years. *Direction of Trade Statistics Yearbook.* Washington, DC: International Monetary Fund.

———. Various years. *International Financial Statistics Yearbook.* Washington, DC: International Monetary Fund.

IRF (International Road Federation). 2011. *World Road Statistics.* Geneva: International Road Federation.

ITU (International Telecommunication Union). n.d. World Telecommunication/ICT Indicators database. Geneva: International Telecommunication Union.

OECD (Organisation for Economic Co-operation and Development). 2011. *African Economic Outlook 2011: Africa and Its Emerging Partners.* Paris: Organisation for Economic Co-operation and Development.

———. n.d. National Accounts Statistics database. Paris

———. n.d. Creditor Reporting System database. [http:\stats.oecd.org/index.aspx?DatasetCode=CRSNEW]. Paris.

———. n.d. National Accounts database. Paris.

———. Various years. *Geographical Distribution of Financial Flows to Developing Economies.* Paris: Organisation for Economic Co-operation and Development.

———. Various years. *National Accounts.* Vol. 1. Main Aggregates. Paris: Organisation for Economic Co-operation and Development.

———. Various years. *National Accounts.* Vol. 2. Detailed Tables. Paris: Organisation for Economic Co-operation and Development.

OECD (Organisation for Economic Co-operation and Development) DAC (Development Assistance Committee). Various years. *Geographical Distribution of Financial Flows to Developing Economies.* Paris: Organisation for Economic Co-operation and Development.

———. n.d. *International Development Statistics.* [www.oecd.org/dac/stats/idsonline]. Paris.

Ravallion, Martin, Shaohua Chen, and Prem Sangraula. 2009. "Dollar a Day Revisited." *World Bank Economic Review* 23 (2):163–84.

Standard & Poor's. 2000. *The S&P Emerging Market Indices: Methodology, Definitions, and Practices.* New York: Standard & Poor's.

———. 2012. *Global Stock Markets Factbook 2011.* New York: Standard & Poor's.

UNAIDS (Joint United Nations Programme on HIV/AIDS) and WHO (World Health Organization). Various years. *Global Report: UNAIDS Report on the Global AIDS Epidemic.* Geneva: Joint United Nations Programme on HIV/AIDS.

UNCTAD (United Nations Conference on Trade and Development). 1995. *Handbook of International Trade and Development.* New York and Geneva: United Nations Conference on Trade and Development.

———. 2007. *Trade and Development Report 2007: Regional Cooperation for Development.* New York and Geneva: United Nations Conference on Trade and Development.

———. n.d. UNCTADStat. Information Economy. [http://unctadstat.unctad.org]. Geneva.

UNESCO (United Nations Educational, Scientific, and Cultural Organization). 1997. *International Standard Classification of Education.* Paris: United Nations Educational, Scientific, and Cultural Organization.

UNESCO (United Nations Educational, Scientific, and Cultural Organization) Institute of Statistics. n.d. Online database. [www.uis.unesco.org]. Montreal.

UNICEF (United Nations Children's Fund). Various issues. Multiple Indicator Cluster surveys. [www.childinfo.org]. New York.

———. Various issues. *The State of the World's Children.* New York: Oxford University Press.

UNICEF (United Nations Children's Fund), WHO (World Health Organization), World Bank, and United Nations Population Division. 2010. "Levels and Trends of Child Mortality in 2010: Estimates Developed by the UN Inter-agency Group for Child Mortality Estimation." Working Paper. New York: United Nations.

UN Inter-agency Group for Child Mortality Estimation. n.d. Child Mortality Estimation Info database. [www.childmortality.org]. New York.

———. 2011. *Levels and Trends in Child Mortality: Report 2011.* New York.

United Nations Statistics Division. n.d. "International Standard Industrial Classification of All Economic Activities, Third Revision." [http://unstats.un.org/unsd/cr/registry/]. New York.

United Nations Population Division. 2009. *Trends in Total Migrant Stock: 2008 Revision.* New York: United Nations, Department of Economic and Social Affairs.

———. 2011. *World Population Prospects: The 2010 Revision.* New York: United Nations, Department of Economic and Social Affairs.

———. Various years. *World Population Prospects.* New York: United Nations, Department of Economic and Social Affairs.

United Nations Statistics Division. 2010. "Implementation of Population Census Topics in the 2010 Round." [http://unstats.un.org/unsd/demographic/sources/census/2010_phc/census_clock/TopicsPerCountry.pdf]. New York.

———. Various years. *National Accounts Statistics: Main Aggregates and Detailed Tables. Part 1 and 2.* New York: United Nations.

———. Various years. *National Income Accounts.* New York: United Nations.

———. Various years. *Energy Statistics Yearbook.* New York: United Nations.

———. Center for Systemic Peace. 2011. Polity IV Project, Political Regime Characteristics and Transitions, 1800-2010 [www.systemicpeace.org/inscr/inscr.htm]. USA

WHO (World Health Organization). n.d. *Global Atlas of the Health Workforce.* [http://apps.who.int/globalatlas/]. Geneva: World Health Organization.

———. n.d. National Health Account database. [www.who.int./nha/en/]. Geneva.

———. Various years. *World Malaria Report.* Geneva: World Health Organization.

———. Various years. *World Health Statistics.* Geneva: World Health Organization.

———. Various years. *Global Tuberculosis Control Report.* Geneva: World Health Organization.

WHO (World Health Organization), UNICEF (United Nations Children's Fund), UNFPA (United Nations Population Fund), and World Bank. 2010. *Trends in Maternal Mortality: 1990–2008: Estimates Developed by WHO, UNICEF, UNFPA and the World Bank.* Geneva: World Health Organization.

World Bank. 2000. *Trade Blocs.* New York: Oxford University Press.

———. 2011a. *Doing Business 2012.* Washington, DC: World Bank.

———. n.d. Doing Business Online. [http://doingbusiness.org]. Washington, DC.

———. n.d. Enterprise Surveys Online. [http://enterprisesurveys.org]. Washington, D,.C.

———. n.d. Private Participation in Infrastructure database. [http://ppi.worldbank.org]. Washington, DC.

———. n.d. PovcalNet. Online database. [http://iresearch.worldbank.org/PovcalNet]. Washington, DC.

———. n.d. World trade Indicators Online database. [http://worldbank.org/wti]. Washington, DC.

———. n.d. World Bank Economic Policy and Debt Online database. [http://worldbank.org/economicpolicyanddebt]. Washington, DC.

———. n.d. CPIA database [www.worldbank.org/ida]. Washington, DC.

———. Various years. *Global Development Finance: External Debt of Developing Countries.* Washington, DC: World Bank.

WTO (World Trade Organization). n.d. Regional Trade Agreements Gateway. [www.wto.org/English/tratop_e/region_e/region_e.htm]. Geneva.

———. n.d. Regional Trade Agreements Information System. Online database. [http:/rtais.wto.org/]. Geneva.

Primary data documentation

	Currency	National accounts						Balance of payments and trade		
		Base year	Reference year	System of national accounts	SNA price valuation	Alternative conversion factor	PPP survey year	Balance of Payments Manual in use	External debt	System of trade
SUB-SAHARAN AFRICA										
Angola	Angolan kwanza	1997		1968	VAP	1991-96	2005	BPM5	Actual	S
Benin	CFA franc	1985		1968	VAP	1992	2005	BPM5	Actual	S
Botswana	Botswana pula	1993/94		1993	VAB		2005	BPM5	Actual	G
Burkina Faso	CFA franc	1999		1993	VAB	1992-93	2005	BPM5	Actual	G
Burundi	Burundi franc	1980		1993	VAB		2005	BPM5	Preliminary	S
Cameroon	CFA franc	2000		1993	VAB		2005	BPM5	Actual	S
Cape Verde	Cape Verde escudo	1980		1968	VAP		2005	BPM5	Actual	G
Central African Republic	CFA franc	2000		1968	VAB		2005	BPM5	Preliminary	S
Chad	CFA franc	1995		1993	VAB		2005	BPM5	Actual	S
Comoros	Comorian franc	1990		1968	VAP		2005		Actual	S
Congo, Dem. Rep.	Congolese franc	1987		1968	VAB	1999-2001	2005	BPM4	Estimate	S
Congo, Rep.	CFA franc	1978		1968	VAP	1993	2005	BPM5	Estimate	S
Côte d'Ivoire	CFA franc	1996		1968	VAP		2005	BPM5	Estimate	S
Equatorial Guinea	CFA franc	2000		1968	VAB	1965-84	2005			G
Eritrea	Eritrean nakfa	1992		1968	VAB			BPM4	Actual	
Ethiopia	Ethiopian birr	1999/2000		1993	VAB		2005	BPM5	Actual	G
Gabon	CFA franc	1991		1993	VAP	1993	2005	BPM5	Actual	S
Gambia, The	Gambian dalasi	1987		1993	VAB		2005	BPM5	Actual	G
Ghana	New Ghanaian cedi	2006		1993	VAB	1973-87	2005	BPM5	Actual	G
Guinea	Guinean franc	1996		1993	VAB		2005	BPM5	Estimate	S
Guinea-Bissau	CFA franc	2005		1993	VAB		2005	BPM5	Estimate	G
Kenya	Kenyan shilling	2001		1993	VAB		2005	BPM5	Actual	G
Lesotho	Lesotho loti	1995		1993	VAB		2005	BPM5	Actual	G
Liberia	Liberian dollar	1992		1968	VAP		2005	BPM5	Actual	S
Madagascar	Malagasy ariary	1984		1968	VAB		2005	BPM5	Actual	S
Malawi	Malawi kwacha	1994		1993	VAB		2005	BPM5	Actual	G
Mali	CFA franc	1987		1968	VAB		2005	BPM5	Actual	S
Mauritania	Mauritanian ouguiya	2004		1993	VAB		2005	BPM4	Actual	S
Mauritius	Mauritian rupee	2006		1993	VAB		2005	BPM5	Actual	G
Mozambique	New Mozambican metical	2003		1993	VAB	1992-95	2005	BPM5	Actual	S
Namibia	Namibian dollar	2004/05		1993	VAB		2005	BPM5		G
Niger	CFA franc	1987		1993	VAP	1993	2005	BPM5	Actual	S
Nigeria	Nigerian naira	2002		1993	VAB	1971-98	2005	BPM5	Actual	G
Rwanda	Rwandan franc	1995		1993	VAP	1994	2005	BPM5	Actual	G
São Tomé and Príncipe	São Tomé and Príncipe dobra	2001		1993	VAP		2005	BPM4	Actual	S
Senegal	CFA franc	1999	1987	1993	VAB		2005	BPM5	Actual	G
Seychelles	Seychelles rupee	1986		1968	VAP			BPM5	Actual	G
Sierra Leone	Sierra Leonean leone	1990		1993	VAB		2005	BPM5	Actual	S
Somalia	Somali shilling	1985		1968	VAB	1977-90			Estimate	
South Africa	South African rand	2005		1993	VAB		2005	BPM5	Preliminary	G
South Sudan	South Sudanese Pound			2008						
Sudan	Sudanese pound	1981/82[b]	1996	1968	VAB		2005	BPM5	Actual	G
Swaziland	Swaziland lilangeni	2000		1968	VAB		2005	BPM5	Actual	G
Tanzania	Tanzanian shilling	[c]	2001	1993	VAB		2005	BPM5	Actual	G
Togo	CFA franc	1978		1968	VAP		2005	BPM5	Actual	S
Uganda	Ugandan shilling	2001/02		1968	VAB		2005	BPM5	Actual	G
Zambia	Zambian kwacha	1994		1968	VAB	1990-92	2005	BPM5	Preliminary	S
Zimbabwe	U.S. dollar	2009		1993	VAB	1991, 1998	2005	BPM4	Actual	G
NORTH AFRICA										
Algeria	Algerian dinar	1980			VAB			BPM5	Actual	S
Djibouti	Djibouti franc	1990			VAB		2005	BPM5	Actual	G
Egypt, Arab Rep.	Egyptian pound	1991/92			VAB		2005	BPM5	Actual	G
Libya	Libyan dinar	1999			VAB	1986		BPM5		G
Morocco	Moroccan dirham	1998			VAB		2005	BPM5	Actual	S
Tunisia	Tunisian dinar	1990			VAB		2005	BPM5	Actual	G

Note: For explanation of the abbreviations used in the table see notes following the table.

b. Reporting period switch from fiscal year to calendar year from 1996. Pre-1996 data converted to calendar year.

c. Original chained constant price data are rescaled.

Government finance									
Accounting concept	IMF data dissemination standard	Latest population census	Latest demographic, education or health household survey	Source of most recent income and expenditure data	Vital registration complete	Latest agricultural census	Latest industrial data	Latest trade data	Latest water withdrawal data
	G	1970	MICS, 2001; MIS, 2006/07	IHS, 2000		1964-65	2010	1991	2000
B	G	2002	DHS, 2006	CWIQ, 2003		2011-2012	2005	2006	2001
B	G	2011	MICS, 2000	ES/BS, 2003		1993	2010	2010	2000
B	G	2006	MICS, 2006	CWIQ, 2009		2010	2006	2010	2000
C	G	2008	MICS, 2005	CWIQ, 2006			2005	2010	2000
B	G	2005	MICS, 2006	PS, 2007		1984	2007	2010	2000
C	G	2010	DHS, 2005	ES/BS, 2007	Yes	2004	2009	2010	
B	G	2003	MICS, 2006	PS, 2008		1985	2006	2009	2000
	G	2009	DHS, 2004	PS, 2002/03		2011	2008	1995	2000
		2003	MICS, 2000	IHS, 2004			2009	2007	1999
C	G	1984	MICS, 2010	1-2-3, 2005/06		1990	2009	1986	2000
C	G	2007	AIS, 2009; DHS, 2005	CWIQ/PS, 2005		1985-86	2010	2005	2002
C	G	1998	MICS, 2006	IHS, 2008		2001	2010	2010	2000
		2002					2009		2000
		1984	DHS, 2002				2009	2005	2004
B	G	2007	DHS, 2005	ES/BS, 2005		2001-02	2010	2011	2002
	G	2003	DHS, 2000	CWIQ/IHS, 2005		1974-75	2010	2010	2000
C	G	2003	MICS, 2005/06	IHS, 2003		2001-02	2010	2010	2000
B	G	2010	DHS, 2008	LSMS, 2006		2011	2010	2010	2000
B	G	1996	DHS, 2005	CWIQ, 2007		2000-01	2010	2008	2000
	G	2009	MICS, 2010	CWIQ, 2002		1988	2002	2005	2000
B	G	2009	DHS, 2008/09; MIS, 2010	IHS, 2005/06		1977-79	2010	2010	2003
C	G	2006	DHS, 2009/10	ES/BS, 2002/03		2010	2010	2008	2000
B	G	2008	DHS, 2007; MIS, 2009	CWIQ, 2007			2008	1985	2000
C	G	1993	DHS, 2008/09	PS, 2010		2004	2009	2010	2000
	G	2008	DHS, 2010	LSMS, 2004/05		2006-2007	2010	2010	2000
B	G	2009	DHS, 2006; Special, 2010	IHS, 2010			2007	2010	2000
	G	2000	MICS, 2007	IHS, 2008			2010	2010	2000
C	G	2011			Yes		2010	2010	2003
	G	2007	DHS, 2003; AIS, 2009	ES/BS, 2008		2009-2010	2010	2010	2000
B	G	2001	DHS, 2006/07; HIV/MCH SPA, 2009	ES/BS, 2004		1996-97	2010	2008	2000
B	G	2001	DHS, 2006	CWIQ/PS, 2008		2005-2007	2003	2010	2000
B	G	2006	DHS, 2008	IHS, 2010		2007	2006	2010	2000
C	G	2002	DHS, 2007/08	IHS, 2011		2008	2009	2010	2000
	G	2001	DHS, 2008/09	PS, 2000/01		2011	2005	2010	1993
B	G	2002	DHS, 2005; MIS, 2008/09	PS, 2005		2011-2012	2010	2011	2002
C	G	2010		IHS, 2007	Yes	2011	2009	2008	2005
B	G	2004	DHS, 2008	IHS, 2003		1984-85	2003	2002	2000
		1987	MICS, 2006				1990	1982	2003
C	S	2001	DHS, 2003	ES/BS, 2009		2012	2010	2010	2000
		2008							
B	G	2008	MICS, 2010	ES/BS, 2009			2010	2009	2000 f
B	G	2007	MICS, 2010	ES/BS, 2010		2003	2010	2007	2000
	G	2002	DHS, 2010	ES/BS, 2007		2007-2008	2010	2011	2002
B	G	2010	MICS, 2010	CWIQ, 2006		2011-2012	2005	2010	2002
B	G	2002	DHS, 2006; MIS, 2009/10	PS, 2009		2008	2010	2010	2002
B	G	2010	DHS, 2007	IHS, 2006		1990	2010	2010	2000
C	G	2002	DHS, 2005/06	IHS, 2003		1960	2010	2010	2002
B	G	2008	MICS, 2006	IHS, 1995		2001	2009	2010	2000
	G	2009	MICS, 2006	PS, 2002			2007	2009	2000
C	S	2006	DHS, 2008	ES/BS, 2008	Yes	2010	2010	2010	2000
	G	2006	MICS, 2000			2001	2008	2004	2000
C	S	2004	MICS, 2006	ES/BS, 2007		2012	2010	2010	2000
C	S	2004	MICS, 2006	IHS, 2005/06		2004	2010	2010	2001

Primary data documentation notes

Base year is the base or pricing period used for constant price calculations in the country's national accounts. Price indexes derived from national accounts aggregates, such as the implicit deflator for gross domestic product (GDP), express the price level relative to base year prices.

Reference year is the year in which the local currency, constant price series of a country is valued. The reference year is usually the same as the base year used to report the constant price series. However, when the constant price data are chain linked, the base year is changed annually, so the data are rescaled to a specific reference year to provide a consistent time series. When the country has not rescaled following a change in base year, World Bank staff rescale the data to maintain a longer historical series. To allow for cross-country comparison and data aggregation, constant price data reported in *Africa Development Indicators* are rescaled to a common reference year (2000) and currency (U.S. dollars).

System of National Accounts identifies countries that use the 1993 System of National Accounts (1993 SNA), the terminology applied in *Africa Development Indicators* since 2001, to compile national accounts. Although more countries are adopting the 1993 SNA, many still follow the 1968 SNA, and some low-income countries use concepts from the 1953 SNA.

Rebasing national accounts: When countries rebase their national accounts, they update the weights assigned to various components to better reflect current patterns of production or uses of output. The new base year should represent normal operation of the economy—it should be a year without major shocks or distortions. Some developing countries have not rebased their national accounts for many years. Using an old base year can be misleading because implicit price and volume weights become progressively less relevant and useful. To obtain comparable series of constant price data, the World Bank rescales GDP and value added by industrial origin to a common reference year. This year's *Africa Development Indicators* continues to use 2000 as the reference year. Because rescaling changes the implicit weights used in forming regional and income group aggregates, aggregate growth rates in this year's edition are not comparable with previous editions with different base years. Rescaling may result in a discrepancy between rescaled GDP and the sum of the rescale's components. Because allocating the discrepancy would cause distortions in the growth rates, the discrepancy is left unallocated. As a result, the weighted average of the growth rates of the components generally will not equal the GDP growth rate.

SNA price valuation shows whether value added In the national accounts is reported at basic prices (VAB) or producer prices (VAP). Producer prices include taxes paid by producers and thus tend to overstate the actual value added in production. However, VAB can be higher than VAP In countries with high agricultural subsidies.

Alternative conversion factor identifies the countries and years for which a World Bank-estimated conversion factor has been used in place of the official exchange rate (line rf in the International Monetary Fund's *International Financial Statistics*).

Purchasing power parity (PPP) survey year is the latest available survey year tor the International Comparison Program's (ICP) estimates of PPP. PPP rates are calculated by simultaneously comparing the prices of similar goods and services among a large number countries. In the most recent price survey conducted by the ICP, 146 countries and territories participated, including China and India. The PPP conversion factors are from three sources: (a) For 47 high- and upper middle-income countries, conversion factors are provided by Eurostat and the Organisation for Economic Co-operation and Development (OECD), with PPP estimates for 35 European countries new price data collected since 2005. (b) The remaining 2005 ICP countries' PPP are extrapolated from the 2005 ICP benchmark results, which account for relative price changes between each economy and the United States. (c) For countries that did not participate in the 2005 ICP round, the PPP estimates are imputed using a statistical model. More information on the results of the 2005 ICP is available at www.worldbank.org/data/icp.

Balance of Payments Manual in use refers to the classification system used to compile and report data on balance of payments items. BPM4 refers to the 4th edition of the IMF's *Balance of Payments Manual* (1977), and BPM5 to the 5th edition (1993). The BPM5 redefined as capital transfers some transactions previously included in the current account, such as debt forgiveness, migrants' capital transfers, and foreign aid to acquire capital goods. Thus the current account balance now reflects more accurately net current transfer receipts in addition to transactions in goods, services (previously nonfactor services), and income (previously factor income). Many countries maintain their data collection systems according to BPM4. Where necessary, the IMF converts such reported data to conform with BPM5. The balance accounts are divided into two groups: (a) the current account, which records transactions in goods, services, income, and current transfers, and (b) the capital and financial account, which records capital transfers, acquisition or disposal of nonproduced, nonfinancial assets, and transactions in financial assets and liabilities. Discrepancies may arise in the balance of payments because there is no single source for balance of payments data and therefore no way to ensure that the data are fully consistent. Sources include customs data, monetary accounts of the banking system, external debt records, information provided by enterprises, surveys to estimate service transactions, and foreign exchange records. Differences in collection methods—such as in timing, definitions of residence and ownership, and the exchange rate used to value transactions—contribute to net errors and omissions. In addition, smuggling and other illegal or quasi-legal transactions may be unrecorded or misrecorded.

External debt shows debt reporting status for 2010 data. *Actual* indicates that data are as reported, *preliminary* that data are based on reported or collected information but include an element of staff estimation, and *estimate* that data are World Bank staff estimates.

System of trade refers to the United Nations general trade system (G) or special trade system (S). Under the general trade system, goods entering directly for domestic consumption and goods entered into customs storage are recorded as imports at arrival. Under the special trade system, goods are recorded as imports when declared for domestic consumption whether at time of entry or on withdrawal from customs storage. Exports under the general system comprise outward-moving goods: (a) national goods wholly or partly produced in the country; (b) foreign goods, neither transformed nor declared for domestic consumption in the country, that move outward from customs storage; and (c) nationalized goods that have been declared for domestic consumption and move outward without being transformed. Under the special system of trade, exports are categories (a) and (c). In some compilations, categories (b) and (c) are classified as re-exports. Direct transit trade—goods entering or leaving for transport only—is excluded from both import and export statistics.

Government finance accounting concept is the accounting basis for reporting central government financial data. For most countries, government finance data have been consolidated (C) into one set of accounts capturing all central government fiscal activities. Budgetary central government accounts (B) exclude some central government units and provide an incomplete picture. These are based on the concepts and recommendations of the second edition of the International Monetary Fund's (IMF) *Government Finance Statistics Manual 2001*. The IMF reclassified historical *Government Finance Statistics Yearbook* data to conform to the 2001 manual's format.

IMF data dissemination standard shows the countries that subscribe to the IMF's Special Data Dissemination Standard (SDDS) or General Data Dissemination System (GDDS). S refers to countries that subscribe to the SDDS and have posted data on the Dissemination Standards Bulletin Board at http://dsbb.imf.org. G refers to countries that subscribe to the GDDS. The SDDS was established for member countries that have or might seek access to international capital markets to guide them in providing their economic and financial data to the public. The GDDS helps countries disseminate comprehensive, timely, accessible, and reliable economic, financial, and socio-demographic statistics. IMF member countries elect to participate in either the SDDS or the GDDS. Both standards enhance the availability of timely and comprehensive data and therefore contribute to the pursuit of sound macroeconomic policies. The SDDS is also expected to improve the functioning of financial markets.

Latest population census shows the most recent year in which a census was conducted and in which at least preliminary results have been released. The preliminary results from the very recent censuses could be reflected in timely revisions if basic data are available, such as population by age and sex, as well as the detailed definition of counting, coverage, and completeness. Countries that hold register-based censuses produce similar census tables every 5 or 10 years.

Latest demographic, education, or health household survey indicates the household surveys used to compile the demographic, education, and health data. AIS is HIV/AIDS Indicator Survey, DHS is Demographic and Health Survey, LSMS is Living Standards Measurement Survey, MICS is Multiple Indicator Cluster Survey, MIS is Malaria Indicator Survey, and SPA is Service Provision Assessments. Detailed information for AIS, DHS, MIS, and SPA is available at www.measuredhs.com/What-We-Do/Survey-Types/DHS.cfm for MICS at www.childinfo.org.

Source of most recent Income and expenditure data shows household surveys that collect Income and expenditure data. Names and detailed information on household surveys can be found on the website of the International Household Survey Network (www.surveynetwork.org). Core Welfare Indicator Questionnaire Surveys (CWIQ), developed by the World Bank, measure changes in key social indicators for different population groups—specifically indicators of access, utilization, and satisfaction with core social and economic services. Expenditure survey/budget surveys (ES/BS) collect detailed information on household consumption as well as on general demographic, social, and economic characteristics. Integrated household surveys (IHS) collect detailed information on a wide variety of topics, including health, education, economic activities, housing, and utilities. Income surveys (IS) collect information on the income and wealth of households as well as various social and economic characteristics. Labor force surveys (LFS) collect information on employment, unemployment, hours of work, income, and wages. Living Standards Measurement Surveys (LSMS), developed by the World Bank, provide a comprehensive picture of household welfare and the factors that affect it; they typically incorporate data collection at the individual, household, and community levels. Priority surveys (PS) are a light monitoring survey, designed by the World Bank, for collecting data from a large number of households cost-effectively and quickly. 1-2-3 surveys (1-2-3) are implemented in three phases and collect socio-demographic and employment data, data on the informal sector, and information on living conditions and household consumption.

Vital registration complete identifies countries that report at least 90 percent complete registries of vital (birth and death) statistics to the United Nations Statistics Division and reported in Population and Vital Statistics Reports. Countries with complete vital statistics registries may have more accurate and more timely demographic indicators than other countries.

Latest agricultural census shows the most recent year in which an agricultural census was conducted and reported to the Food and Agriculture Organization of the United Nations.

Latest industrial data show the most recent year for which manufacturing value added data at the three-digit level of the International Standard Industrial Classification (ISIC, revision 2 or 3) are available in the United Nations Industrial Development Organization database.

Latest trade data show the most recent year for which structure of merchandise trade data from the United Nations Statistics Division's Commodity Trade (Comtrade) database are available.

Latest water withdrawal data show the most recent year for which data on freshwater withdrawals have been compiled from a variety of sources. The freshwater resources are based on estimates of runoff into rivers and recharge of groundwater. These estimates are based on different sources and refer to different years, so cross-country comparisons should be made with caution. Because the data are collected intermittently, they may hide significant variations in total renewable water resources from year to year. The data also fail to distinguish between seasonal and geographic variations in water availability within countries. Data for small countries and countries in arid and semiarid zones are less reliable than those for larger counties and countries with greater rainfall.

Map of Africa

IBRD 39767

JANUARY 2013